ACROSS THE *Divide* TO THE *Divine*

I. Murphy Lewis

Memoir:
Across the Divide to the Divine: An African Initiation

Young Adult:
Why Ostriches Don't Fly and Other Tales from the African Bush

Dissertation:
Across the Divide to the Divine with the Kalahari San's Trickster God, Mantis an Essential Component in the Mythological Structure of an Individuated Culture

Short Documentaries:
Why Ostriches Don't Fly
How do you name a song?
Music that Floats from Afar
To the Sacred Forest of the Lost Child

Disclaimer:

Where I come from and where I have traveled to, and on this planet which we Live there are still laws, rules, contracts, codes, religious dictates, absolutes, orders, sacred words, loyalties, spells, curses—whether we like it or not, whether visible or invisible—which govern, are often binding and forbid the mysteries and the secrets from being exposed.
Out of respect, I have chosen to honor some of these mandates.
So, some experiences, some aspects, some names, some places will remain hidden and/or may only be alluded to.

ACROSS THE
Divide
TO THE
Divine

AN AFRICAN INITIATION

BOOK ONE

A MYTHIC MEMOIR OF RECLAMATION

BY

I. MURPHY LEWIS

Part of a Triptych:

Book One,
Across the Divide to the Divine: An African Initiation

Book Two,
Across the Divide to the Divine: The Invisible Dane I Love

Book Three,
Across the Divide to the Divine: The Paris Twiggy Project Complete

10% of *Across the Divide to the Divine* sales will benefit the Kalahari San Bushmen, the Maasai Warriors.

Copyright © 2022 by I. Murphy Lewis

Published by IML Publications LLC
www.imlpublications.com

Distributed worldwide by Ingram Content Group
www.ingramcontent.com

Book cover design by Erin Rea
www.erinreadesigns.com

Plate images by Vetkat Regopstaan Kruiper Org (copyright Belinda Kruiper Org)
vetkat.co.za

Interior layout by Medlar Publishing Solutions Pvt Ltd, India
www.medlar.in
Interior additons: Zhaoying ZHU

All rights reserved. No part of this book may be reproduced in any manner without the written consent of the publisher except for brief excerpts in critical reviews or articles.

ISBN: 978-1-955314-22-0 (Paperback)

ISBN: 978-1-955314-23-7 (EPUB)

Library of Congress Control Number: 2022920797

IML Publications LLC
151 First Avenue
New York City, NY 10003

10% of the sales of Across the Divide to the Divine: An African Initiation will benefit the Kalahari San Bush-men-and-women, the Maasai Warriors through the Global Voice ® Foundation: www.globalvoicefoundation.com (we will add this to the back cover as well if we can find room)

DEDICATION

To my first family, the Kalahari San Bush-men and Bush-women:
For nurturing me with your life-changing trickster tale, "Why Ostriches Don't Fly." For holding my dissertation with grace.

To Mom and Dad:
wherever you are on that other side of something, thank-you for that first journey into the Kalahari, "There, by the First Fire."

To the Maasai Warriors:
For embracing me in a way I could never have imagined, for your dedication to my healing through your intricate knowledge of divination and herbs. For holding those past existences and the present as if a delicate child, a treasure in your hands, nourishing me with broths, teas and listening ears. For being the mirror, to what was held within and meant to be revealed, all in due time.

To those who have been rejected, humiliated, abandoned, betrayed, battered, or traumatized, who have experienced *prejudice or injustice, who are trapped in an internal or external prison, who are in search of a true identity, whether **gender related and/or a greater Self, whose voices are held back from the revelation of truths, and for those who are certainly at a loss for words:
May a pathway of acceptance, freedom and a course of action through soulful empathic expressions, however unorthodox they might be, through the spoken or written word as podcaster, author, blogger, instagramer, TedTalker, through the playing of an instrument, as an actor/actress, photographer, gardener, builder, designer, architect, dancer, painter, singer, or chef so that the myth that rings true, in a way everyone can embrace it, without deleterious ramifications to the planet, families, friends, or even strangers, honoring all our historical experiences, choices, realities, faiths; thoughtfully and carefully stepping into the world (as I am attempting to do here), and as Sir Laurens van der Post urges, "Hasten Slowly!"

*About Racism: "And the whiter, straighter, Christian, majority culture you are, the more mistakes you're gonna make" (Bréne Brown, *The Call to Courage*). Those of you who are from the BIPOC (black, indigenous, and people of color) community, I hope you can extend grace for the mistakes I'm making here, for this very, very human attempt of mine to reveal the prejudices I've encountered and have been a part of creating. Please note: Because BIPOC is not very personal, I will be using "people of color," "men of color," and "women of color" throughout the book.
**Throughout the book, for simplication, I will only be using he, she, him, her, we, they and them, but know that I am aware of each of you: LGBTQIA2+ and those expanded one-hundred-other-gender-identifications, honoring your process wherever and whomever you are!

Part of a Triptych:
Book One, Across the Divide to the Divine: An African Initiation (1998 to 2005)
Book Two, Across the Divide to the Divine: The Invisible Dane I Love (2005 to 2011)
Book Three, Across the Divide to the Divine: The Paris Twiggy Project Complete (2011 to Present)

"Every night, or many nights, the unconscious tells us a story, and though they often do not seem to be immediately connected, they do accompany and promote a maturing process in the personality of the dreamer."

—Marie-Louise von Franz,
The Interpretation of Fairy Tales

"The stories told to me were like arrows. […] Stories go to work on you like arrows. Stories make you live right. Stories make you replace yourself."

—Benson Lewis, a Cibecue Apache; Keith H. Basso,
Wisdom Sits in Places

"Though I was blurred with fear, I could still hear and feel the knowing. The knowing was my rudder, a shimmer of intelligent light, unerring in the midst of this destructive, terrible, and beautiful life. It is a strand of the divine, a pathway for the ancestors and teachers who love us.

—Joy Harjo,
Crazy Brave

"What matters is the division into three self-sufficient beings. We could call them the I, the Self, and the Divine."

—Roberto Calasso,
Literature and the Gods

CONTENTS

Author's Note xiv
Why Ostriches Don't Fly xvii
Prologue, Initial Initiations xix

PART I
ACROSS

1   For Which to Fly 3
2   *There, By the First Fire* 12
3   The Little Hunger 27
4   The Apparition 34
5   Sets a Seamless Course 40

FIRST JOURNEY IN

6   Rising into the Thermals 48
7   Food of Plenty 58
8   Loss of Place 62
9   First, They Give Me Stories 66
10 A Life for What? 74

FIRST INITIATION:
SECOND JOURNEY IN

11	Flights Unknown	80
12	Jewel in My Stigmata	88
13	The Water Course Way	95
14	The Naming	99
15	Watermarks and Bubbles	109
16	Beyond This, There Be Lions	115

THIRD JOURNEY IN

17	The Release	124
18	Adaptation	130
19	Of Goats and Gifts	139
20	Martialed Into Mother	147
21	Of Blood and Bones	152
22	Links in a Chain	156
23	Gagging in the Face of	163
24	Glimpse of My Personal Legend	168
25	Completions All the Way Round	176

FOURTH JOURNEY IN

26	New Twist	179
27	Transmission	182
28	Geese Decree	191

PART II
THE DIVIDE

29	Demarcation	203
30	Transporter Transported	210
31	Natives Concur	216
32	Only Skin Deep	227
33	*On Sacred Land*	232
34	Delicate Strands	252

Contents

35	Bull and Stag	.264
36	Unequivocal Declaration	.268
37	Surrender the Blood	.276
38	Universe Conspires: The Dreaming Way	.281

FIFTH JOURNEY IN

39	Coming Home to the Cows.	.285
40	In the Womb of the Dung Hut	.302
41	Endearments and Intangibles	.305
42	Africa Within	.317
43	My Private Irene	.335
44	Family Rituals.	.341
45	Testifying to the Numinous.	.344
46	Maasai in My Household	.346

SECOND INITIATION:
SIXTH JOURNEY IN

47	Rhythmic Nature of Womanhood	.351
48	Ajumble.	.357
49	Middle of My Muddle	.362
50	Prey to a Leopard	.366
51	Do Not Take a Gift of Cow Lightly.	.370
52	Wrinkled in Time.	.374
53	The Laiboni Ceremony—Wedlocked	.376
54	Forty Wild Buffalo	.383
55	Tracking Myself.	.390
56	After the Wedding, the Ladder Broke: The Second Initiation	.393
57	An Elemental State	.397
58	Morning After	.402
59	Stripped of All Accoutrements	.404
60	The Final Severing	.408
61	Even the Sawed Off Pencils	.412
62	Ruminations	.415

63	Non-Duality—The Both/And	.417
64	Wedding, Wedding, Wedding.	.420
65	Tricky Out There	.422
66	Downward Spiral	.424
67	My Aim so Poor	.427
68	What Am I Not Conveying?	.429
69	Intermission: The Queen Leaves the Board	.433
70	Colonial Encounters	.436
71	Cutting the World from the Moorings of the Feminine	.444
72	Inside the Anomie	.451
73	A Meeting of Minds—Female that is!.	.453
74	Harken Unto My Cry.	.455
75	The Gathering	.458
76	Holding the Substance	.468
77	Spate of Bad Luck.	.470
78	Wildebeests on the Loose	.473
79	Out of Captivity	.478

PART III
TO THE DIVINE

80	Parts of You, That Don't Belong to Me	.487
81	What Lies Beneath	.491
82	Walled From the "Other"	.505
83	Across What?	.510

EPILOGUE

84	The Divineness of It All	.514

Acknowledgements	.535
About the Author	.537
About the Artist	.540
Work cited.	.542

AUTHOR'S NOTE

Blessed in more ways than I can even imagine or even begin to see, of which the biggest of these gifts was in being "let in," so to speak, into the lives of several indigenous groups in Africa—the Kalahari San Bush-men-and-women and the Maasai Warriors—as both an initiate and a student of their stories, music, and rituals. Through them, I have been humbled, awakening into the privileges I've come from and didn't even know I had and continue to have, to name a few: parents who loved their children and each other for over fifty years, being white, middle class, with clean running water, higher education, and a home.

Every day, through that carbon footprint of mine—from thousands of sky miles earned in a fashion career, the drawing up of too much water, the overuse of paper, the creation of loads of plastic trash shipped out to sea in hopes of someone else disposing of it—I commit "microaggressions,"* which in turn become "macroaggessions" to the Earth, the Stone People, the Plant People, the Four-legged, the Two-legged, the Creepy Crawlers, the Finned, the Furred, the Winged Ones, and All Our Relations.** (same footnote as the one below)

AUTHOR'S NOTE

Today, as I share this intimate tale, I may commit other microaggressions as I delicately walk on the borderlands, entering the crossroads of engagement with other cultures and religious beliefs, particularly with the Kalahari San Bush-men-and-women, the Maasai Warriors, a few African American friends, and briefly with the Navajo, the Hopi, and the Zulu. Therefore, I stand in the only position possible—that of the Seventh Direction. Here, I humbly place myself, as all human beings—in the center of their own universe, (possibly) in their soul's first choice—facing out to the winds of the South, the West, the North, the East, to below of the Great Mother, to the above of Father Sun, Grandmother Moon, the Star Nations, and the Great Spirit.** (so I think this footnote would be Ibid)

So dear Two-leggeds, as you join me in this reclamation of mine, I know you will heartily extend grace for the many pages relating to these experiences and engagements, which spring forth from thousands of pages of research, field notes and personal journals.***

Of course, you are welcome to secretly slip through to the initiations with the Maasai, which are marked in the contents page as "first journey in, second, etc." Although I may encourage "the read" of this movement of soul that is happening to me, and perhaps to all of us, through the interactions with the San in There, by the First Fire (Chapter 2), with the Navajo and Hopi (Chapters 31 to 34), and with my bi-racial friends, Ike Brady (Chapter 42) and Larry (Chapter 81).

At times, I may mispronounce or misspell words, names and even, possibly, misrepresent**** people and certainly "see through a glass darkly."***** The greatest intention I have is to honor each of these encounters respectfully to all those who have taught me and have completely been "shifting the metaphors of my life."******

May Across the Divide to the Divine: An African Initiation be free from judgment, create acts of inclusion, build footbridges,*******, mend fences somewhere, to someone at some time, seven generations forward, back and beyond.

Book One – Across the Divide to the Divine

Restoring the Earth, Vetkat Regopstaan Kruiper, a Bush-man

WHY OSTRICHES DON'T FLY

A long, long time ago
when animals and people
could talk—
the trickster god, Xamsakayuba, while out on a hunt,
came upon Ostrich browning her meal—
and oh, it smelled so good!

It was the first time Xamsakayuba
had ever laid eyes on fire.
So, to steal fire from Ostrich,
he set about making a trap,
tempting her with the most irresistible fruit of all, the plum
high in the Merenda tree.

Of these, Ostrich ate heartily.

"No! No! No!" Xamsakayuba urged, "You must eat higher up,
they're much better up there."

Why Ostriches Don't Fly

Stretching, reaching, Ostrich stood on her two-toed feet
raising her wings for balance,
and as she did, she felt the fire go out of her.
Xamsakayuba had stolen the fire,
from underneath her wings.

In shock, Ostrich blinked her beady eyes,
while Xamsakayuba began his journey home.
Ostrich chased after him, but was left behind in a trail of grapplethorns
that Xamsakayuba had cleverly laid.

So Xamsakayuba took fire to his wife, Tumtumbolosa,
and to all his people.

And never again would Ostrich lift her wings to fly.
In fact, she was never quite the same;
she hung her head down low burrowing in the sand
and forever, some would say,
she has kept one egg outside her nest to remember what she is about.

—*as told and drawn for Murphy by Kua,*
a Kalahari San Bushman at DiPhuduhudu, Botswana

PROLOGUE

INITIAL INITIATIONS

> *"Women (and perhaps men, too) who do not [...]*
> *scribble the poem down when it comes bubbling up [...]*
> *are denying something at their peril. [...] will undoubtedly and*
> *inevitably engage in a variety of perversions of that creativity..."*
>
> —Patricia Reis and Susan Snow,
> *The Dreaming Way: Dreams and Art for Remembering*
> *and Recovering* (parenthesis, a Murphy addition)

Somewhere between my childhood-fairyland-of-the Kansas-woods and adulthood, much as Ostrich—I had lost what little fire was left. Bits and pieces of memory were left blank scattered across the plains, those huge fallow fields, plowed in recovery, uncultivated, unsown, brimming with potentiality, waiting for the sheer chance of seed to be planted. Yet, this emptiness within had become seared by the sun, parched, falling through the desiccated cracks of the earth, swirling particles into a Dust Bowl, buried inside that Pandora's box of mine.

Prologue

Until *The Rains Came*, until another people group, the Maasai Warriors wove their magic spell about me, and then an achingly slow reveal, into revelation, into understanding.

When the Kalahari San Bushmen's story, "Why Ostriches Don't Fly," found me and became published in my young adult book, I did not yet understand Ostrich's loss of fire to be the thematic symbol of *that* childhood experience. I only knew something was ultimately the matter with me. Something wasn't right inside. Something had been shattered. Something had forced me into a re-naming, shoved the "I" in Irene to the back of my peace-meaning-name, into a "Renie" trailing after me through junior high and high school. Until the university where I abandoned *that* name altogether, for Murphy, a determined "sea warrior." To be perfectly honest, I was secretly oozing with unhappiness, wondering if I could ever fly again, and for that matter, even run.

As a child, I yielded. I complied. I modified, until I morphed into "Murph."

One summer evening on the golf course with the family, Father asked me to set aside the writing of my book, *The Ghost of Messer's Hollow*, for business—to specialize in the art of golfing, bookkeeping, as teller, college grad, Dale Carnegie-ite. "You'll *never* make a living as an author." Though the family had once praised me as a great writer, at the tender age of nine, my precious gift—that personal inclination of mine was rejected—that which came so naturally to me, was no longer permitted.

With Father's statement, "You'll *never* make a living as an author!" With his forceful wisdom, in his knowingness of all things "men," he had granted me a way through, passing on the keys to the kingdom, to the prevailing myth—that which he believed meant an easy "survival." Perhaps he understood at the time, for I certainly did not, that with his proclamation (among other things) the dye had been cast, a spell, which twisted and distorted me into a form, which could, in time, "fit" into a societal match; as if tossing, kicking my original blueprint aside into his. Preparing me for a world where everything had a driving force of yang. But what I had a yen for—writing, which for me, was more yin—I would later learn, was not necessarily encouraged, often not monetarily honored, nor even, at times, allowed.

At one time or another we may become accustomed to these small, abrupt ejaculations—"You'll never be a…" "You're a loser!" "Your skin is not the right color!" "You're weird cuz you're gay!" "You're crazy!" "Something's wrong with you!" "This is just *our* little secret!" "I'll kill you if you ever tell!" What seems so

Prologue

entirely insignificant become the susurrations, the whisperings, the murmurings haunting us, deforming us. From Father's reaction, I learned right then and there, who I was, wasn't enough, shifting the ground underneath my feet, shattering the known reality, and so, I learned how to conform until I wasn't quite sure who I was. However, what I did know was deep down inside something was utterly wrong within…

From this "wrong" feeling, I had developed a litany, a cover story, which I told over and over to others. *Was I asking them to feel sorry for me?* No, I believe it was an attempt to get to the actuality of it, to recover from whatever "it" was. To be honest, I couldn't even define what had happened. There were no words. In fact, it wasn't so much about what *had* happened, it became, instead, what our culture and our families said about *that*. I couldn't accept I'd lost my fire and that that in turn informed who I was (or let's just say, who I thought I was and would become). And that that person I had wanted to be, I believed, could never be recovered.

So that I, too, was no longer myself, I was just a small part of an echo of the greater story which pervaded the landscape and would inform how I would proceed, climbing *their* mountain, fulfilling Father's and others' dreams for many, many decades, taking years to re-activate the "yin function" in my life and pursue that yen of mine for writing. Not grasping that way up on that platform between lives—these parents, this homeland—I had chosen to be born through and into these circumstances. According to James Hillman, this family was "my soul's own choice," yet "I do not understand this because I have forgotten" *(The Soul's Code: In Search of Character and Calling)*. Yes, in the transition between one life to another, I'd lost all memory of that decision.

Sometimes in certain cases, to forget, to accommodate is necessary—to adjust to fit into the culture at large. Acculturation. In Madeleine L'Engle's *A Wind in the Door*, scientist Mrs. Murray's words reverberate: "A life form which can't adapt, doesn't last very long." I didn't know a person *could* adapt, yet still, remain true to their Self. Instead, I had become "fashioned," so to speak. Acclimatized. Goals were set for me. Determined. Shanghaied!

At the time, my elders inform me, the solution, the key, is not inside myself, but outside. Whatever is within me is not good enough. Left with the necessity to jockey for position, even jockey for love, I turn outward toward a more masculine way of life—to being more direct, thinking logically, moving in a forward linear action of achievement. For if I can't be me, which dwelt in the more circular

Book One – Across the Divide to the Divine

Prologue

forms of yin of connectivity, of listening, of intuiting, receiving—what else is there but to search for another source, lurk around for "the ideal," endeavor to be "fixed" by those who know better, those in authority, to compensate! I had never come upon Seneca's warning in *Dialogues*, "We perish because we follow other men's (or women's) examples."

Even in the women and men around me, I don't find a path. The men are doctors, lawyers, bankers, real-estate brokers, not quite in the poetic, painterly, or challenging frame of mind as Robert Bly, Alfred Stieglitz, Edward Hopper, or Martin Luther King. The women are not quite in the Vanessa Bell or Georgia O'Keefe expression, nor as Rosa Parks in the daring fight of civil rights, nor Jane Fonda, Gloria Steinem, Simone de Beauvoir in the feminine revolution yet. Amongst our small-town neighbors there are no passionate painters, sculptors, or writers, and certainly no rebellious activists. If there are, they remain hidden. Not until my life in New York City, do powerful examples arise.

For the time being, I can't distinguish between what is mine, theirs. I am trapped inside Father's mythology of what is "right," the story he wove for himself: to be a great businessman, a banker, serving the farmers of Eastern Kansas. (And this, by the way, he does marvelously!) Father's mandate becomes one of my first initiations into the world we live in, domineered by white firstborn males (of which he is one), where the rest of us—heterosexual, lesbian, and butch women, or second, third born or effeminate men, and those of color (of which I cannot boast or speak for all, for, at the moment, I am only one of these)—become another border for the manifestation of *these* men's destinies.

While Saturn's "white" sons rule the world, I am eventually, as one of Patricia Reis' mythic *Daughters of Saturn*, rudely awakened out of the Belly of the Father to find I had already been defined by this prevailing myth. At first, in a highly unorthodox manner, in order to create definition, I will react against the system, wildly bucking up against husband, organizations, church, state, Halston, Badgley Mischka, Escada, guru. To psychoanalyst Sylvia Brinton Perera, this reaction is often a woman's dilemma where "she has only an animus-ego, not one of her own, with which to relate to the unconscious and the outer world." From this position, I will attempt to solve the problems before me, and this will give me a measure of control, as I test and unearth the inner strength.

Unable to use outright power, the "other," a person of a lesser color, race, or gender, and certainly a woman (including myself in this equation) will often engage in strategies of rebellion and resistance, or subtle forms of manipulation

Prologue

"based on *persona* adaptations [. . .] thus she (he) has almost no sense of her (his) own personal core identity" (Brinton Perera). No matter what the status of a person is—rich, poor, young, old, white, black, yellow, red, BIPOC, or LGBTQIA2+ and those one-hundred-other-gender-identifications —we live in the quiet undertow of our mother's. As Adrienne Rich explains: "I (we) live under the power of the fathers, and I (we) have access only to so much of privilege or influence as the patriarchy (or the matriarchy, in service to this hierarchy) is willing to accede to me (us), and only for so long as I (we) will pay the price of male (or of those in authority's) approval" (Parenthesis, my words).

In spite of all this, in the summer of 1998, this cowgirl self of mine was pulled into the beyond, into something greater, peregrinating all the way to Africa, to my *ultima thule*, that distant unknown and extreme region of discovery, in search of an "I." By the time this adventure began, I had already completed five safaris to the Kalahari San Bush-men-and-women in South Africa, Botswana and Namibia in search of the perfect story.

Early on I had begun to realize that no matter what was going on in my life, the perfect story of that moment, at that time, would and could see me through. I could trust this. Stories had done this for me as a child—not just in writing them or seeing them across the big screen, but also in reading myths that existed the world over. Tales figured at the forefront of my life, for I desperately needed them, carrying ten books at a time from the library.

If I couldn't work my way out of something, I'd read into a heroine or a hero's life, of those who had discovered (or at least attempted) a pathway through the challenges of their lives, out of their predicament, out of the present into a new future. Until they could, in the end, come to define the past as an "experience." These characters, I considered friends, built and continued to build hope in my heart.

After school, Mom would plop me in the front seat of her car, handing me juice through a straw, potato chips, a chocolate bar, and off we went to see the librarian Miss May, for the return of the last books I'd checked-out and for my next set of tales. The two of them must have known I needed a fable to revive me—out of what Churchill called his "Black Dog Days," which for me had become the black-hatted-man-nightmare. I discovered that each of us need stories to jolt us. A tale to turn tail from the grueling dark forces within and without, conveying us to something inordinately wonderful.

Prologue

Through books, whole worlds opened plunging me into places I'd never gone before. A simple requirement of the Bible's "Joseph and the Coat of Many Colors," "Daniel in the Lion's Den" or just piles and piles of Carnegie's free literature by my bedside—even if I didn't have the time to read them—could do the trick, could catapult me into the great unknown of an adventure, adventures, I imagined would one day be mine!

This odyssey to Africa, however, would be one for the books (or would be one of those books), which would take me further still to the Samburu, to the Maasai Warriors of Kenya, of Tanzania, in search of something or someone who might uncover what had vanished—an innocence, an instinctual knowingness, that flame within. For I was "dying" to recover the young girl's fire, to retrieve what an intuitive will tell me of a past life, where I had been kidnapped. A life, I must set right.

So badly will my soul want this recovery, I will reset a similar pattern to bring me into my adult Self. Only then could I reclaim enough of the Self so this memento of an encounter can ring forth truthfully. Yes, an extreme experience, yet to be discovered—and what a child will often go through in order to establish their specific calling in the world—would mean taking extreme measures for recovery, across the borderlines of a small-town Midwestern existence for another continent to heal one woman's story. Mine.

Though I served briefly on the staff of the Osawatomie High School Newspaper for two years, I'm not a professional journalist, so I'm not in the facts of who, what, when, where, or why. In fact, then, I was more of an editorialist, with a more emotive approach. But since I was thirteen, I've been a regular diary writer, and even in that executive career, I kept a large black notebook to verify conversations with associates, deals made with heads of states (mainly because I had lost the art of tracking). Anyone who knew me in fashion will verify, I was fiery, more apt to fight a battle than concede, so this is more emotional than maybe someone else's memoir for this story caught me in the whirlpool of its power. So, it's not simple, because I'm not. It may even appear messy. It's just complicated because I am complicated.

Even so, I will attempt to tell *that* complicated truth. In other words, this book is *my* opinion and one must realize in this interpretation, I am far from perfect, certainly human, and these experiences with a people whose lives, whose dung huts, whose businesses I have been a part of could be considered mere reflections of the light, of the shadows and undifferentiated aspects of myself, of what I saw at the time through *their* weaknesses and strengths, which in the end were probably mine, which I shall attempt to faithfully reflect back.

Just as someone else rolls out of bed to bow toward Mecca or takes an hour break in the middle of the day to practice yoga, or TedTalks up a storm of change—to become embodied, to be their authentic self, so that everything comes into divine order—eventually, I will choose to stay home. Saying "no" to all those about me, to write this book in triptych form, to face my historical truth, to reweave the past into the wholeness of a tapestry, so that this narrative in turn, may warm your heart, and I pray may positively affect you, and you, and you. For certainly, I know it has had, and is having, an indubitable effect on me.

Sitting around the fire with the Bush-men-and-women in the Kalahari Desert, and later, with the Maasai Warriors, I had this feeling within—just as I had inside those childhood books—of the narrator's power to affirm us, to help us achieve transcendence, filling me with such hope. From their influence, I had and would gain so much insight, and now, courage. I did not know when I was with the Maasai, they would find the perfect herb for the cure, weave the powerful branches of the Strangler Fig tree, breaking the curse, setting me free within, helping me create new vows, healing one story only to be re-wounded, cracking open of another. After this, it would take another ten years, until I felt quite safe, to access and rewire other memories.

However, in this book of many words, my dear reader, I cannot tell all (but will reveal more and more in Books Two and Three). What I will tell you is, of that disjointed life in New York City, a glimpse of my childhood, of the first fire with the San Bush-men-women-and-children. And of the *six journeys in*, when the Maasai Warriors took care of me, began to re-assemble the fracturing, the dismembering, giving me back my "I"—setting me on a course toward restoration both within myself and in relation to those who have been "other-ed." Yet, I did not know, in order to transcend, I would have to face the truth of where I was and am, I would have to weave back along a long trail into prior *impedimenta*, those encumbrances of other existences, and the lives of the ancestors, to come into a resolution of a sort.

This story, *Across the Divide to the Divine: An African Initiation* is an American woman's initiatory journey before, through, and after the Maasai Warriors, a story of our collective past, my past, a story of our time, a story of reclamation. A way, in which, to speak.

Life is good, Vetkat Regopstaan Kruiper, a Bush-man

PART I

Across

"This is the story you might tell and I might tell it differently, for there is a story within a story within a story and another one around that one."

—Vetkat Regopstaan Kruiper, a Bush-man, an artist

I

FOR WHICH TO FLY

*"I had a compass from Denys. To steer by, he said.
But later it came to me, that we navigated differently.
Perhaps he knew, as I did not, that the Earth was made round,
so that we could not see too far down the road."*

—Karen Blixen (Meryl Streep), *Out of Africa*

Before we navigate into that deep connection I formed with the Maasai Warriors, into that *first journey in*to Kenya, I must briefly take us, dear reader, backwards to the beginnings of those encounters with the San Bush-men-and-women, the "First People" and their stories, that first moment at the first fire, in Botswana, and how this all came about through another instrument.

Thirteen years before I ever set flight for Kenya, a harbinger of a gift arrives—as if on wings itself, tumbling from a little white box—a golden airplane with a rhinestone-spotted back. Exquisitely penned on a tiny, embossed card were the words: "Murphy, I saw *Out of Africa* and thought of you! I love you, Patri-

Part I: Across

cia." Patricia, a woman whom I had confided most everything to—my former mother-in-law, a trained psychologist, now turned penpal—is, actually, in truth, thinking of me. Her son had divorced me that Autumn, and just like that, his declaration of love had been dashed on the rocks of the sea I was now adrift upon. Nevertheless, his mother had sent me this small craft, lifting me airborne.

Since the divorce, several men had been vying for me. Number One, a real estate magnate, had given me a two-carat diamond I'd held in hand for several weeks, until I concluded with a "No." Number Two, an Italian dandy, who "hit" on me every time I entered The French Corner in downtown Phoenix to hear my favorite jazz singer, Lucy.

One night Number Two urges, "With me, you must see this movie, *Out of Africa*. It reminds me of you." I immediately responded with a "Yes"—not because of him. But because of this gift of Patricia's and a rather large curiosity that the two of them recognized in me, something, which had to do with Africa, *That* yes, sweeps me into the golden colors of Kenya, elevated inside Mozart's "Concerto for Clarinet and Orchestra in A," up and over Lake Turkana, taking wing with Denys Finch Hatton, with the pink flamingoes—moved, refreshed, hopeful.

For weeks, months, years after seeing this film, I became obsessed with Baroness Blixen's life. Patricia's wings had been a premonition of sorts, they set me reading Blixen's writings under her pen name, Isak Dinesen, as well as her magazine articles and other books of those near and dear: her husband Baron Bror Fredrik von Blixen-Finecke, her paramour Denys Finch Hatton, her rival Beryl Markham—as if anyone could rival the Baroness. Her exquisite prose, life of high style, and adventure fueled this heart of mine, motivating me. With a VHS recording of *Out of Africa* in hand, in fits, starts, rewinds, and stops, I sketched the outfits donned on Meryl Streep in her role as Baroness Blixen, preparing the groundwork, for launching a new path to Parsons School of Design and Fashion Avenue in New York City. *Even then was I, a fashionista, like the Baroness, bound for Kenya?*

To add to this hankering of mine for Africa, a few years later, in NYC, while recovering in the hospital with an appendicitis, a broken heart, amongst other things, my girlfriend Gail Segal, a poet, a filmmaker, an astrologer, gifts me Sir Laurens van der Post's *A Mantis Carol*, claiming, "you are the *one person* I know who will get it." Once again, piquing that curiosity of mine, I dive in captivated with Martha Jaeger's dreams of the Kalahari San Bushmen's trickster god, the

1: For Which to Fly

praying mantis (Xamsakayuba), and of the woman who strangely grew up with a Bushman in the heart of Manhattan. Gail's gift of van der Post becomes, as Patricia's golden airplane, wings for which to fly and will soon transport me to Botswana, but more importantly, over the course of nine years, will slowly and completely shift that purpose of mine.

A Mantis Carol spurs me into reading whatever van der Post has written. Inside *Patterns of Renewal*, I discover he understood this plight of mine, "one of the tragedies of modern man (woman) is that he (she/they/it) is (are) cut off from experiencing this immense dynamic pattern of renewal deep in himself (herself, themselves, itself)." Van der Post was claiming that this natural capacity exists within the San Bushmen's own wellspring.

His words affirm, I had been "cut off" from this knowingness. Truly identifying with the Bushmen's "All-Devourer," greedily swallowing everything in his path, as I was doing in my fashion career, as I had done in the wanting of another woman's husband. For I had lost that innate source. Instead of looking within for the answers, I was looking out to others, suffering from what Africans fear most of all, purposely calling it the "loss of soul." As a result, I found myself in bed, sick, thanking God for these pages of Sir Laurens, for the tiny praying mantis' visit within these lines, giving me the impetus to fulfill a greater longing.

Sir Laurens' *The Heart of the Hunter* fires me onward, the San Bushmen, their tales, had now interlaced with mine, granting me a sense of wellbeing and purpose, inflaming a hunger in me to learn more about their trickster god, Mantis and his odd little family of wife Rock Rabbit, daughter-in-law Porcupine, and son Rainbow. Igniting a re-discovery of that younger animistic self, that had been lost in the woods of childhood. These enchanting stories break into my glazed-over heart, filling me with such a yearning for "the great unknown."

As if on wings itself, this news from afar, these fables, from the Kalahari had impacted me. Suddenly a trajectory becomes indisputable: I want to study and collect the parables of these people, share them with children, who had never figured in my life before, except within the out-pouring of my love for someone else's husband. As well, I began to reclaim my own eleven-year-old self, "Irene," who for the last twenty-one years had been in hiding.

Hear myself declare, "I shall write my way out of fashion." Perhaps, I had never really been "in" fashion after all! (In the Ready-to-Wear Industry, with styles and shapes coming and going, it's impossible to remain "in" fashion for very long!) Eventually, I am able to write my way "out," however, *not* in the manner imagined.

Luckily, at St. John the Divine, I happen to hear Sir Laurens van der Post's speech, causing me to initiate an unprecedented correspondence of six letters each. Shortly after this talk, I typed a note: "Dear Sir Laurens, the 'Empty Basket' is the tale I love the most [...] I have a great desire to share this and other Bushmen myths with young children. I feel these stories will expand their horizons, open them to other ideas and nationalities and develop the muscles of their hearts and souls [...] just the idea of Ostrich lifting her wings to give humankind fire will be more than delightful"—Irene Murphy Lewis (19 September 1993). Though I hadn't used my first name for years, strangely to him, I write "Irene," as though I have the prophetic inclination that an integration with of that childhood is beginning.

Due to my grandfather's damaged and ancient typewriter, each letter I type is in uppercase. As though, I am shouting at Sir Laurens, trying to get his attention to this new calling of mine. Even though "the SHOUT," he doesn't seem to mind and responds back and forth over the course of three years. Each letter from him arrives as if telegrams from heaven, confirming these pursuits of mine are "meant" to be, responding, "Thank you for your letter of September 19 which only came to me in a roundabout way this morning. I am so glad that the little you heard me in the cathedral led you on the Bushmen trail to discover the wealth and riches of their stories"—Laurens van der Post (4 December 1993).

I didn't know then what a miracle this letter was. I didn't know then how important it was to "catch him," I didn't know then he was almost eighty-six, almost eighty-seven when I would finally meet him, eighty-nine when our correspondence would end, ninety when he would cross to the other side.

One of the contacts van der Post would eventually offer, the photographer David Coulson—whose photographs are featured in his book, *Lost World of the Kalahari*—will become fascinated with our correspondence, stating, "Murphy, due to his writings, his travels and speaking engagements, Laurens would have a stack of a hundred letters at a time. It was as though he knowingly pulled your letter out of the pile and was meant to specifically answer *you*."

Thomas Young's double-slit theory. Even though Sir Laurens and I were in two different realities, two different countries, the Bushmen's light from Joseph Conrad's *Heart of Darkness* was shining through from another dimensionality, linking us in a quantum mechanical way. Miraculously, from *A Mantis Carol*, an exchange forms, born from our mutual love of their tales, which alchemically forges a golden path for me, which might never have been taken.

Van der Post believes me, trusts my words. For he knew the power of the tales, knew from the exchanges he'd had with others—a story could change a life as it had changed his, as it was changing mine. In every one of these correspondences to him, this enthusiasm rings forth: "I so want to be full of soul and to be able to share this with our broken society"—Irene Murphy Lewis (2 January 1994).

At this moment, I am in denial that he is a very busy man. A man who, for the last thirty-six years of his life, had become a prolific author of eighteen books, with a BBC series, *The Lost World of the Kalahari*, as well as, two films, *Merry Christmas Mr. Lawrence* and *A Far-off Place* derived from his writings, and eventually a documentary, *Hasten Slowly*. A kind of mythical guru to many, a magical storyteller, who makes the ancient Bushmen tales come alive.

Through his book Jung and *the Story of Our Time*, he inspires me to read more C. G. Jung, to continue to explore my life psychoanalytically, giving me the deep gut longing to live a mythic life, to discover my own "dream language," and hopefully, to dream in cataclysmic, connective forms, turning me toward a deeper imagination, to listen to the still and the small—the tiny praying mantis, the Bushmen's trickster god.

In September of 1994, in London, during a business trip for Mary McFadden, van der Post unexpectedly invites me for tea. A man who is prolific, who is a friend to a prince, to a prime minister, who travels the world speaking to vast audiences, is asking me for tea! *Who wouldha thunk*?

For this moment, I have prepared, reading hundreds of pages from the Marshall family and the Harvard Research Team, who have been studying the !Kung Bushmen on the Western Edge of Botswana at /Kae/Kae. As well, from one of van der Post's suggestions, I had reached out to Paul Mills from Clarke's Bookstore in Cape Town, who shipped me, "out of print" books of Wilhelm H.I. Bleek, his sister-in-law Lucy Lloyd and his daughter Dorothea, which I heartily devoured. So, I had already begun to gather and rewrite Bushmen stories in a poetic rhythm for kids.

While in England, I had been at cocktails parties and a pheasant shoot in Oxfordshire with new acquaintances, the Cambridge crowd: a former rugby player turned developer (I had a "crush" on), a prince from some small country, and at the time, a "sixteenth" from the crown turned author, who are absolutely shocked at this correspondence with Sir Laurens. They can't even believe I'm invited to his home in Chelsea. According to them, I should be nervous, but I'm not.

On my way, in a taxi, in a journal, covered with Gustav Klimt's Kiss, I quickly pen: "Lord, history is about to be made—*my* history anyway. Help me to speak clearly and distinctly, not to please or be someone else, but to be true to my own self, to you, to Laurens. And most of all, give me wisdom and direction of what to ask, what I need to make this book successful. For our meeting to be a blessing to us both."

Being here, as I jump out of the cab and dash up the stairs, seems like the most natural thing in this new universe of mine. Even so, at first sight, I'm pinching myself into belief. Though slowly losing her memory, his wife Ingaret—former Jungian analyst and author of her memoir, *The Way Things Happen*—with crutch in hand, greets me at the top. Beside her, Sir Laurens van der Post, gallantly stands and with a sweep of his hand, invites me to join him.

With crew and cameras set up around his library, he has taken a break from Mickey Lemle's documentation of his life in *Hasten Slowly*, to sit quietly in casual conversation with little ole me. As the tea arrives, in such a compassionate, and yet, hearty voice, he inquires, "What can I do for you, my dear Irene Murphy?"

In my thoughts, I exclaim to myself: "He is very real, not a god at all, but fully human!" Yet to him, quite out of breath, I responded to his question (reiterating some of the text from my letters): "I dream of visiting the Kalahari San Bushmen, to discover more of their transformative tales with the hopes of sharing them with American children. But everywhere I turn, everyone tells me: 'There are *no* more Bushmen!' 'No one *can* take you there!' 'No one *will* take you!'"

"Perhaps, they mean, there are only thirteen 'real' hunter-gatherers left."

"Do you know how I might find them?"

"Once a friend of mine, Eva Monley, the producer of my film, *A Far-off Place*, was told 'there will be a Bushman under a tree waiting for you'—and there he was. Somehow, in the Kalahari, at the right moment, it just happens. You can trust that!"

During our discussion, every so often Sir Laurens rises, walking back to another room to Ingaret. I hear him kindly say, "I'll be with you very soon!" Even so, on and on this glorious exchange continues. He is so helpful, mentoring me forward.

1: For Which to Fly

And that was it, Sir Laurens opened a window for me, kindly offering important contacts, his friends John and Andrea Hardbattle, whose son I would later meet; film producer Eva Monley; National Geographic filmmaker Tim Liversidge; Museum Curator Alec Campbell; and photographer David Coulson. Then he generously signed a copy of *The Voice of the Thunder*, sending me on my way with all the possibilities before me.

Afterwards, with exuberance, I thanked him in writing, "For me it was a very meaningful moment to meet someone who doesn't stop at 65, the "proper" age to retire, but is so filled with life and its importance that you have taken another twenty-three years to share your insights to a world without soul" (5 October 1994). I couldn't stop writing to him and sent another letter a few months afterwards: "You are right, we are in a dark time and definitely in isolation. Oh, to belong, to feel connected as the Bushmen are to this world" (18 December 1994)!

That moment, at Chez Sir Laurens, was indeed kismet; he had given me the keys to what seemed to be an inaccessible kingdom. Through this list of contacts, I could dial up, I could fax, I could reach out. Here, they were at my fingertips. Eva Monley opened her home where the walls were filled with photos of all the famous actors and actresses she worked with, serving me smoked salmon and a whiskey with ice to the top of the glass. Any of the questions I had had about the Bushmen were answered. A journey into the Central Kalahari Desert was now possible for me, as each of them recommended Izak Barnard of Penduka Safaris, as he and his son Willem have a deep connection to these hunter-gatherers. Yes, these friends of Sir Laurens were carving a way into the Bushmen's lives, making this inkling about a book of fables from the Kalahari a possibility, and eventually, a reality. For I was convinced—from that history of mine that I was just beginning to slowly uncover—children need these.

As a child, after dinners, I'd take a drive with Dad to the bank where he worked. While he'd finish paperwork, I'd sequester myself at his secretary's desk, reading folktales, conjuring up the enchanted beings I'd met in the wilds of the Kansas outdoors and in the nightscape, planting the physical and spiritual in words, with illustrations. I designed small books and cards filled with simple poetry, prose, and images for family and friends. By the end of Second Grade, I had written and drawn two hundred short stories, proudly reading them to fellow students in the front of the class.

Part I: Across

It was as though van der Post was recalling that prolific-writer-self, lassoing with rope, drawing her back into my very being. As well, in NYC, a few months after that tea, I attended Barbara Seuling's seminar on How to Write *a Children's Book and Get it Published*, co-mingling with a group of writers to present some of the myths I'd gathered. The star of the class, an award-winning author, blusters: "Murphy, your stories are something you can stick in a binder to place on your shelf for safekeeping."

This illustrious writer completely bursts those hopes of mine, which in turn conjured a dream I'd once had, of Mother placing a brown paper bag over my head during a parent/teacher's conference at the Paola South School. *Had she feared I would blow, would speak the unmentionables?*

The truth was, as a child, I was already an empath, already a dreamer. I was walking up to family and acquaintances saying things they must have thought were "crazy." To my family members I would divulge, "I had a dream about you last night where…" Once, at four years old, I even walked up to a woman at our church, and said, "You look like a witch!" Well, she did! She was covered from head to toe in purple; even her grey hair had been rinsed with violet. As I looked up at her curiously innocent, everyone around us went silent. *What could they say?* Later, Mom had wished she'd explained, "Irene has just seen Wizard of Oz for the first time and loved Billie Burke as Glinda, the good witch." However, words couldn't form for her audacious daughter.

That's what I did. Sometimes I spoke the unspeakable, what I saw, heard, felt. Oftentimes, from the office, Father brought news, shared confidences to us at the dinner table. From this information, I must have revealed something horrible to someone—because from then on it was known, "Don't tell Murphy anything. She can't keep a secret." *So, was this why the dream of the paper sack thrown over my head?*

Yet, that is only what my subconscious wondered. However, in real life, in Fifth Grade, the teacher, Mrs. Carol Mann told Mom I was finishing the lessons early in class, then, disturbing those around me, who weren't finished. Mother suggested, "Irene loves to write. Perhaps, she could pen a book of stories while others are completing their assignments." In affirmation, Mother bought me a pale green spiral-bound notebook, where I wrote and illustrated *The Ghost of Messer's Hollow*—about the "spooky" being in the neighborhood. Not long after, Father told me I couldn't make a living with a pen—that, I must become a businesswoman. *What did they fear? Had I written something that could not be told?*

1: For Which to Fly

For here they were, ganged together—the star of the writers' group, Father, and even, Mother—placing these scribblings of mine I held so dear onto a shelf for safekeeping, paper bagging that voice of mine. *Were the Fates determining closed lips?* Yet, somehow, I had a will to speak, in the only way I knew how. Luckily for me, Ms. Seuling mentions Libraries Unlimited World Folklore Series. Within three weeks, I possess a contract for *Why Ostriches Don't Fly*, with an allotment of time to travel to the Kalahari Desert for photographs.

Just as Ms. Seuling and Libraries Unlimited, van der Post affirms this voice of mine, "It is great to know you are forging ahead under your own steam in such a little known but terribly significant dimension" (31 March 1995). Steam is right. Fire is more like it. Plans were being made, carved in stone or certainly, flights booked. The cast of characters I'd met along the way, had set things in motion.

On the 3rd of August 1995, I dash off a response to Sir Laurens: "I've the best news ever! My parents and I will be off to the Kalahari Desert […] I thank the gods for you, for the light you show to the world has illuminated my darkness. You've given me great hope and direction. In America, people have either run to secularism or fundamental ethics. And so, I was having such trouble finding a place to worship; a place to connect that is mystical. But through your writings and Jung's I am no longer afraid to leave (the formalities of worship) […] to find a path, the work I need to be about and my own myth! Hurrah! To your faithfulness, to these precious hunter-gatherers, the Bushmen—for their light as well. I am praying this letter finds you healthy and close to the completion of your book"—Murphy.

Even so, I was on my way. Perhaps it meant, I married that first husband for a mother-in-law, who would come to know me in a way I had just begun to uncover, who, just as Denys to Karen Blixen, would offer a compass for which "to steer by," for which to fly, setting me on runway in golden airplane toward a fashion career in NYC, and now, bound for South Africa, for Botswana. However, I had yet to "see too far down the road," to Kenya, for that Maasai initiation to come.

2

THERE, BY THE FIRST FIRE

> *"...fire was a divine gift stolen from the gods, that Prometheus suffered the cruelest of punishments, [...] it is light in darkness, safety against the beast and animals that prowled and threatened life in some long-forgotten prehistoric night; it is warmth against cold, it is what brought us from an age of ice, gripping the earth from pole to pole, to this privileged moment in time, cooking the food we are to eat, warming this room against the winter which that cold wind outside is bringing up so fast."*
>
> —Laurens van der Post, *Jung and the Story of Our Time*

Warmed by the new fire that was surging within me, those brave parents of mine—fascinated with the book deal from Libraries Unlimited, fascinated by my connection to van der Post, who wrote *Night of the New Moon*, now, one of their favorite books—came along on that first journey in. Departing from a

2: by the first fire

steamy North American August to a South African winter of miles and miles of bush and sand, surprisingly scorching hot on this twenty-miles-an-hour, twelve-hour-days of a two-day drive into the Kalahari Desert. In 1995, throughout Botswana, there are no tarmac roads in, so due to this strenuousness of the moving sand, our truck broke down several times.

Much to our dismay, we discover our guide Afrikaner Izak Barnard, with no fear, carries no gun, no radio. For the broken engine, we watch him cleverly carve a new fan from a sheet of metal, while telling us tall tales reassuring us of how he once had raised his hands to frighten away an elephant, and for an entire night, while trapped under his Land Rover, had delicately kept a hungry, yet playful lioness at bay with a shovel. "Yes," he announces, "the Kalahari Desert is no child's play!"

Because of Izak's wild accounts and skills, the three of us set aside our fears, trusting him, for he seems to be just the man to lead us. Even more importantly, in the 1970's, he had briefly led the safari for Prince Charles and Sir Laurens into DiPhuduhudu to film *Testament to the Bushmen*. So, we are somehow kin in our love for his writings, both of us, feeling a wash of pleasure in this acknowledgment. The good news is Izak has been traveling in and out of the Kalahari for over thirty-five years with film crews, advertising agencies, writers, van der Post's daughter Lucia, Peter O'Toole, and Lauren Hutton.

Of Sir Laurens, as well as history, Izak is a great reader and a storyteller of Bushmen tales, which opens a way into incredible conversations for me, solidifying my own research. (Later, in the spring of 1996, on my next journey into the Kalahari, at DiPhuduhudu, he and his friend, the botanist Johannes Vahrmeijer will read through my entire book, editing, and affirming.)

That first evening, as the sunset in this middle of nowhere spread its colors across the wide-open African sky, as the Gecko lizards rhythmically chirped their evening song far more elegantly than the Kansas cricket, Mother called to us. We discover her standing on the packed desert sand, pointing at a tiny spectacle of beige barely visible in her tracks: the praying mantis. To the Greeks, Mantis or mantic, meant prophet, pertaining to divination or prophesy. In Latin, *mantis religiosa* holds a more elegant descriptive name of his spiritual proclivities. To the Bushmen and the Hottentots, Mantis is the harbinger of good fortune.

"Oh, Mother, you knew not to smash him, standing up for this dear creature. Sir Laurens would like that!" As I throw my arms around her, "Remember what he had written in one of his first letters to me about the terror Gail's roommate

Book One – Across the Divide to the Divine **13**

had had of a praying mantis on his bed in the middle of New York City?" I repeat his words, "'For the mantis, who often inspires fear in those who have not met him before, because still at a deep, deep level in our primordial unconscious he brings fire which is the first spark of real awareness in human life'"—Laurens van der Post (letter of 3 September 1994).

Years before, on Waterworks Road in Paola, Kansas, I'd encountered a green Carolinian praying mantis while attempting to climb the large oak tree where my brothers built a clubhouse behind our home. But neither this childhood fascination nor van der Post's book *A Mantis Carol* equal the experience of this first encounter with this creature on the evening of my first night of my first venture into the Kalahari Desert. We regard this visitation as an open greeting, a validation of our trek. As we squat in the sand to pay our respects, I realize that the praying mantis is missing one arm. Broken, like me. As though "the voice of the infinite in the small" had now spoken to us through this creature (van der Post, *A Mantis Carol*).

As if a pronouncement of what's to come, the following morning as we rise for breakfast, as we prepare to go further in, surreally, ghost-like, a beige Brahman bull walks into our camp. While the young men load the Land Rover, Izak walks us about the campground, gently instructing "how to read the desert sand," the spoor of the animals. In the night, we had visitors, scorpions, and jackals. For me, to carry across the ocean, Izak finds treasures for my altar, a praying mantis cocoon and the shell of a Tak Tak beetle.

As we begin our drive through the Central Kalahari Game Reserve, Izak stops the truck, to observe a scarab beetle wonderously and slowly rolling a ball of dung across our path. Throughout our day we have other sightings, three antelopes, Gemsbok, run alongside our Land Rover, as a small group of ostriches throw up their tails as they cautiously and proudly prance away. In the distance, a family of cheetahs runs like the wind across the sands. Two black Korhaans do a mating dance, soar, fall, tumbling almost to the ground, then pick themselves back up again, only to soar once more.

As the sunsets, we come upon our destination, a little village called Molapo, a Kudu, an antelope with a mask-like white-painted face peers at us through the glass. As he cuts in front of the Land Rover, he sweeps his elegant curly-cued horns, as if a theatrical gesture, "Meet my friends." For instantly, we see them—San women and children running out of their grass scherms, out of their round huts, waving, dancing, and clapping with faces filled with delightful, beautiful white smiles. We wave and clap in a glorious exchange. What I had wished for, prayed for—*is happening!*

That evening, while setting up our camp in a kind distance from their village, four San elders consisting of two men and two women pay us a visit, shaking our hands. Then, gently, the eldest woman touches Mother's face and mine. Little did we know we were suffering from what Eduardo and Bonnie Duran in *Native American PostColonial Psychology* consider "acute Cartesian anxiety disorder." We had been separated from ourselves, our dream lives, our gut-knowingness. So, just this caress of the old Bushwoman's hand to the cheek, her knowing look into our eyes, strips off layers of fortification around the heart, a rare sense of finally "being home" seeps in as rainwater to parched earth.

As we grasp hands with her, the tears cascade down our faces. Van der Post would have confessed, as he once did in *A Mantis Carol*, this is "another demonstration of how a journey to new places in the physical world can encourage a journey within to places where the mind has not been before." We little thought how we were being prodded forward into a new way of seeing.

While our twenty-eight-year-old cook, Prika of the Baye people, prepares mielie meal for the Bush-woman, along with the other three chieftains, they take their places around the fire, smoking fresh tobacco, peeling, and eating the oranges we offer them. There, by the first fire, as they sit observing us, as we, them, we have a moment of exchange where our vast differences tumble into ash upon the sands of the Kalahari, into a brief blissful peace, of unification of all our commonalities.

As the evening wears on, some of the magic wears off, because what mystifies us is that everyone is eating separately—first, the Bush-men-and-women, secondly, the blacks, and now, the whites. When Father questions Izak about this, he nonchalantly replies: "This is how things are done in South Africa, in Botswana. And besides, they *like* being together."

Izak's comment spurs on a lively sociological conversation between this Afrikaner and us, (which will slowly begin the remaking of the way in which I see and will see those who are of another color, race, creed). To him, we must confess our countrymen had instigated partitions through the Jim Crow Laws, as well as slavery, and the ripping of our Original Peoples from their lands. So, we must acknowledge we're therefore no better in our treatment of people of color, that we were as much Colonialists, a part of a caste system, as they were.

Yet, we, ourselves, must admit, we have been far removed from the horrors of South Africa's Apartheid. In the Dutch African or Afrikaans language, Apartheid means "apartness," separating the whites from the Indians, "the coloureds," as well the black Africans (who were considered the lesser). However, the Nobel Peace Prize winner, Archbishop Desmond Tutu considers this differently, for to him, everyone of every color is part of *The Rainbow People of God*.

"Between 1960 and 1983," Izak reminds us of the details, "in a forced segregation, 3.5 million black Africans were moved into ten appointed tribal homelands, *bantustans*." Sadly, those who were relocated lost their South African citizenship. This remembrance crushes the spirit of Mother and me as we grab hands in solidarity. For it had happened again—whites determining the future for those of color. So, I blurt out, "It makes such sense why Mandela rebelled against Apartheid, forming the African National Congress)." For those very beliefs Nelson Mandela had been imprisoned for twenty-seven years. At this historical moment in time, however, in 1995, this well-educated man, a lawyer and the president of the ANC, Mandela, of the Xhosa community, had already been serving as the President of South Africa for one year.

Yet, even though South Africa had liberated Mandela, had elected him as their first black president and declared Apartheid "officially" over, little had changed while we were sitting by this fire in the Central Kalahari. The Truth and Reconciliation Commission, which would eventually be led by Desmond Tutu, had not begun. But these were facts and figures Mom, Dad and I could draw upon from newspaper articles, from conversations about our own experiences, from books, and later, from the internet, and yet, we were and are still separated from these frightening realities, by the color of our skin, by our middle-class existence.

So, here we are, in the Kalahari, in an "act of exclusion," as whites, sitting up on folding chairs, around an official foldout table for dinner. The San leaders have briefly eaten their "mielie meal" on the logs placed around our fire, and then, had gone off to be with their community. The black Botswanan men, who serve our camp as the wood gatherer, tent builder, the cook, the mechanic, had eaten within their own circle, again, low to the ground, perched upon those same logs. "They don't want to join us," claims Izak.

Yet, we, white Americans, Father, Mother, and I, didn't insist that the blacks should join us, forgetting that silence always affirms the practices of the elite, of the ruling order. Archbishop Tutu, a man who believes in universal suffrage for all, enlightens, "If you are neutral in situations of injustice, you have chosen the side of the oppressor. If an elephant has its foot on the tail of a mouse and you say that you are neutral, the mouse will not appreciate your neutrality." Most likely the mouse will be squashed, unless you push the elephant to the side and stand up for this little creature, as Sir Laurens, Gail and Mother had done for Mantis. However, in this instance, we didn't push, nor insist.

What I did not know, was that though the San Bush-men-and-women would later win a land battle in South Africa, they were excluded from this dismantling of apartheid. In *Representing Aboriginality*, Sarah Clelland-Stokes explains, "Although the San shared the status of Other to the European settler Self, their small numbers and low political profile distinguished them from the majority black population that was subjugated under British colonial rule and later under a settler apartheid government." Though their drawings of human figures from the rocks and caves are honorably front and center of the South African coat of arms. Even so, to Clelland-Stokes, their presence somehow "destabilises the legitimacy of the belongingness of the black people of South Africa." In ten years, I will feel this full effect of destabilization the San's presence creates, when they visit the United States at the Big Bear event, in "The Gathering" (Chapter 75).

Even so, we, as Americans, (as per usual) proudly viewed ourselves as different, perhaps, even, better. Izak didn't know that every week, in Osawatomie, our elderly cleaning lady, Dorothy Turner, who was an elegant *café au lait* gal, sat always at the lunch table with us. She was part of our family, inside that story arguing out the dailies, as we were a part of hers. Yet, in truth, Dorothy and her partner, whom my father loved dearly, still lived on "the other side of the tracks." It occurred to me, we didn't have dinners or picnics with them, nor join them at their church, nor they ours.

If we were willing to admit it, it went deeper still. We had been living on lands that had once been the Osage and the Pottawatomie Ameri-Indians, and yet in this region, in the state of Kansas, there were no signs of their existence, no recognition of them as peoples, except, perhaps, for the name of our new hometown, Osawatomie. They had been obliterated in genocide and the few that were left were moved onto the reservations. If we were willing to admit it, this is how things remain in America as well.

Later, when I would visit Izak's farm, I would see first-hand that Izak was really living a life with little separation between whites and blacks. For me, this is humbling to see how active and engaged he was. Just as ours, his family had a kind of Dorothy, too, Pritzy, who was deeply entwined in their daily lives, working in the home as both cook and cleaner. She and her family lived in a home in the back of their property. The mechanic, Jacob, and all the other farm workers had small bungalows, too. Izak and his wife Anna, even built a school, employing several teachers, where black kids came from miles around to study. I would eventually have a chance to tell stories to these children.

And dear reader, please note, as I proceed, as I write into this issue of "people of color," I am not an historical expert, nor do I know what it feels like to be someone of color or know what hellishness it is to be a black woman working five jobs to support her family. I write this through a slow thirty-year awakening, through my own engagements with a few biracial friends, two African people groups and a brief interaction with a few Zulus, a few Navajos and a family of Hopi. Please note as well, that I will make mistakes, because for over the course of more than sixty years, over the course of the writing of this book for some odd twenty years, the vernacular of descriptive names "given" to people of color continuously changes, taking many forms and many of these are harsh and rude and judgmental.

In the 1780's members of the Göttingen School of History determined POCs, people of color, as "negroid," who were originally named the "Ethiopian" during the age of Colonialism and in the African diaspora—the Transatlantic Slave Trade that took place from the 1500's to the mid-1800's—for millions upon millions of victims. These terms, according to Frantz Fanon, sadly dropped all the unique people groups into the term, the "common African," without any concern for their distinctive cultures or beliefs. More horribly, many white Africans have called black Africans, "kaffir"—just the sound of this can break one's heart.

When I was a child, in our small town, I heard the harsh and offensive n-word from time-to-time. Though I was never allowed to speak thus (and now, I can't even begin to write it without a cringe). From my grandparents, I had overheard "coloured," which they had used in their time. A South African friend, Belinda Kruiper Org, who is considered "Cape-coloured," is not offended by this description. These slang terms will morph and move, through the Négritude Movement, meaning "blackness" in French.

What will rise is "Afro-surrealism," "Creaolite," to the 1960's as "black consciousness," "black is beautiful" to 1980's as "Afro-American," "African

American," to later be simply and warmly, more inclusive as biracial and BIPOC. One of my friends from the Mauritius says, ""A l'Île Maurice d'où je viens, nous sommes un mélange." They are a blend. Her mother looks white her father "de couleur du marron comme moi." The color brown of a chestnut, like her." I'm sure these names will continue to evolve as have the terms changed for others. In his "Interlude" Tommy Orange exudes, "We are Indians and Native Americans, American Indians and Native American Indians, North American Indians, Natives, NDNs and Ind'ins, Status Indians and Non-Status Indians, First Nation Indians and Indians so Indian we either think about the fact of it every single day or we never think about it. [...] not federally recognized Indian kinds of Indians. [...] We are full-blood, half-breed, quadroon, eighths, sixteenths, thirty-seconds" (*There, There*). Sadly, once again, these terms don't define their own people groups as either unique or distinctive.

The same challenge goes for the Kalahari San Bushmen: "The names given to them (the San) by outsiders emphasized their perceived collective "otherness," rather than the distinctness of the various groups. [...] The early Dutch colonists called them Bosjesmen, from which the term Bushmen is derived. The Tswana use the Setswana term Masarwa (plural: Basarwa), which carries the negative implication of 'those who do not have cattle' (and who therefore have no value or status)." The Hottentots "called them by the Nama word Sonqua [...] from which the name San derived, meaning "those who forage," as opposed to those who herd livestock" (*Voices of the San*). Many of their distintive people groups like the name "Bushman" as it signifies "people from the bush." Others feel "San" is "least derogatory."

At an elders' meeting one Khwe, //Anikhwe replied, "Maybe we are the ones doing the right thing, because Adam and Eve were not living in a luxury house; they lived like us. These names they give us like Basarwa, they also show that we have the right to say that we were the first people" (*Voices of the San*)!

Hopefully, as the universe becomes kinder and more receptive to those who have been "other-ed"—and please note, when I use the term "other," I do not mean this derogatorily—because at different times and in different places and for different reasons anyone can be disappointingly "other-ed" and excluded.

At the time of this adventure into the Kalahari, "cross-cultural understanding" was the rage within the universities—though thirty years later, this notion won't be enough for relating. What we had forgotten is that this system of cross-cultural understanding was dominated by academics, by the rules of the then ruling white males. For at least five centuries or more, these males were "the gatekeepers" of the worldview, which I would soon discover the difficulties within this system, even as a white woman, while writing a dissertation about the stories of indigenous peoples, who had been "other-ed," and who had influenced me. In 1943, Kurt Lewin first used the terminology of "gatekeeping."

In *The Wretched of the Earth*, Frantz Fanon considers the studying of colonized people as "lactification" or "the whitening of palatable knowledge."— *Was what I was busily doing considered, "measuring others?"* I hope not. It is not my intention. Often our ever-imperialistic view, determines the Western system as "right" and that "others" are either "wrong" because "they" don't have our forms of thought or reasoning or intelligence due to shapes and sizes of the brain, as in the theory "biological determinism." Francis Galton used the term "eugenics" in 1883. Charles Darwin considered this "survival of the fittest," immediately separating the "civilized" from the "savage." A "we" versus "them" kind of reasoning. *Isn't that rather narcissistic and prejudiced?* Perhaps genes do determine some. *But aren't BIPOC often held within the systemic racism environ, just as the Bush-men-and women, whom we were amongst, who are suffering even now from minimalization?*

In Racism *without Racists: Color-blind Racism and the Persistence of Racial Inequality in America*, Sociologist Eduardo Bonilla-Silva explains that after the Civil Rights movement of the 1960's, whites, who lived apart, far away in the suburbs, had grown to believe that the ugliness of racism was over. As we sat around this first fire, maybe this was true for my parents and me; we imagined ourselves as living in a "post-racial" age and we could then stand in judgment of the Afrikaners and Apartheid. Instead, we had only been far removed and insulated from—what Robin D'Angelo would later deem in *White Fragility* as— "race-based stress." Instead, we were hung up by our reactions and emotions that swung between moments of anger, fear, guilt, confusion, misunderstanding, and now, by the fire—silence.

In *OprahDaily*, Samantha Vincenty's article, "Being 'Color Blind' Doesn't Make You Not Racist," awakened me to the reality that even though our parents had been "educating" us quite differently, there are degrees and levels of colorblindness and if we were really honest, racism still oozed within our very pores. *What were those degrees and how could they be quantified? And how could we free ourselves from these prejudices interwoven in our beings, from the very people we lived separated from?*

2: by the first fire

From my luggage, for this discussion with Izak, I pull out several books of Sir Laurens that I had been reading, and as per usual, I had been folding and underlining various pages. Both as a journalist and a novelist, van der Post had been ahead of his time, attempting to carefully write into these issues. The first of these books, *In a Province*, published in 1934, by Leonard and Virginia Woolf's Hogarth Press, is clearly against bigotry: "If the system perpetuates a colour-prejudice we can counteract it by refusing to admit a colour-prejudice in our own lives, we can live as if no colour-prejudice existed." Only the problem is, at that time, when he wrote this and in our time ninety years later, "colour-prejudice" existed and exists, which means people, who aren't white, are left out of the system we've so carefully constructed around us.

Later, in 1955, *in The Dark Eye in Africa*, Sir Laurens will further explore this subject stating the "terrible unconscious projection which modern European man (woman) thrusts upon the natural African [...] the insidious civil war raging in the innermost being of modern man (woman), which prevents the white man (woman) from ever seeing the black man (woman) as he (she, they, it) really is (are)." *How do we, therefore, see with new eyes? And then when we can see, how do we make a difference when the dividing lines are so deep?* Van der Post lived in a time of complexity with this horror, as do we—and yet, he continually spoke against it, as Izak, my parents and I were arguing into the nightmare of this truth.

Certainly, as we remain at our foldout table, certainly in the way we live as what D'Angelo describes as the separation we create through our established institutions, country clubs, films, billboards and what is then distributed to us, versus to the blacks. To D'Angelo, we "whites" are insulated within our own comforts, with "protective pillows" far removed from the people of color's everyday existence. For an example, for many years, only the elite in America have had healthcare until Obamacare, just as South Africa's healthcare, "NHI," was slowly being introduced in layers at the time of our visit.

According to D'Angelo, I wasn't just described as "fragile," or "pillowed," I was unconscious to those needs, to those cries around me, again, with no empathy. And when I had begun to hear these cries, I noticed I had and have a long way to go from being moved from this present and very stuck position.

On that first night, after the Chiefs departed, even though we were separated by color—by their scherm huts and our canvas tents, their logs, our chairs, their mielie meal and our rice, vegetables and meat—during our very "white" dinner

Part I: Across

in the center of the Kalahari, there is still magic. Four praying mantises appear on the candles, on our shoulders, tilting their heads toward the one speaking, the person moving quickly. They seem thoughtful, meditative, as though the San men and the women elders had alighted on our table, continuing their observation, asking: *Who are these people? Why have they come? What do they want from us?*

Later, to attempt desegregation, along with the young British guide, Alex, I will join the Botswanan men at the campfire, to share, to stare at the thousands of stars, of the Southern Cross and Scorpio under this expansive sky of Africa. On this journey, Alex and I particularly develop a relationship with the cook Prika, and the handyman Bayeti, a father of five, from the Matabele people, whom we grow to adore.

Throughout this African night, sage wondrously permeates. Later, through the crack in the tent, I can see the glow of the campfire as it dies down, as the breath of the wind pulses to the rhythm of my heart, flapping the canvas for the next blow. I am enchanted and have fallen in love with the Kalahari and its people.

In the morning, Dad comes running to the tent, calling, "Wake up, Murphy, come quickly! We have visitors."

From his urge, I quickly dress and topped with my black hat, leap out into this new and glorious moment to hear Izak warmly shout, "Well if it isn't Billy the Kid's girlfriend!" (Oh! He did love Western movies.) A nickname, which will stick to me for the duration of our friendship!

The San pour into our camp, the men take their place around the fire, talking, as the women and children gather in small groups under the trees. They smile, observing us. Even Izak's close friend, Ra di Tshipi, man of iron, joins us, riding up on the back of a saddled donkey. In the corner of his eye, he catches me with camera in hand and proudly poses for my book. Yet, in Ra di Tshipi's strength, he exudes everything that is gentle and humble. Even so, I learn he is suffering from tuberculosis, which is common amongst the San people. Later, on the back of our truck, he will travel to Maun for treatment paid for by Izak.

While Father suffers from a kidney stone, flat on his back on a cot in the shade, Mother, with the children, creates a made-up language, making them laugh with her own stories filled with the actions of moving rocks, leaves, bugs and stick characters. Through Izak's interpretations, I sit quietly listening to the San's fascinating tales.

One girl, who has a red scarf elegantly wrapped around her head, I name Jackie O. A young man, Mohombu, draped in a UCLA sweatshirt, introduces me to more of his culture. "One day," he announces, "I dream of being a lawyer."

Away from our camp I find the children, Jackie O. and Mohombu included, imitating their parents' healing ritual, clapping, singing, and dancing with rattles wrapped around their ankles made from the cocoon of the hairy caterpillar. My newfound girlfriend, Kesidilwe will not dance. So, I stand up, questioning, "If I dance, will you?" She runs away. But Gakebarapele chases after her, pulling Kesidilwe back. The two of them join me, following me, mocking my every move, which makes everyone laugh hysterically. The women in the distance clap along with us. With our whole beings, we sing, dance. Liberated, I toss off my hat. I don't believe I've ever had such pleasure or felt so free.

But the precious San will not be so free. In fact, I will not return to this area to see them, because soon, in 1996, they will be moved from this homeland to the Northwest, outfitted in Western clothes, Western educated, only to live in prefab homes at the edge of the Kalahari. Some say their removal was due to the pressures from the government in order to receive money from the World Bank. Others said it was due to the discovery of diamonds. Though the San will petition for their land, with Survival International and with John Hardbattle and Roy Sesana's First Peoples of the Kalahari (FPK), they will not return to live in the Central Kalahari Game Reserve. Ten years later, at "The Gathering" I will meet Roy Sesana.

On one of our early morning game drives, while Alex and I are perched on the roof of the Land Rover in search of wild animals, I tell him of van der Post's talk at St John the Divine, at 85, hands clasped with enthusiasm, his fervor for life, for truth. Amidst the whistling winds of the Kalahari, Mother pokes her head out of the sunroof, almost losing her hat, shouting to Alex, "Passion! She speaks of passion in Laurens," as she points at me, "Look who's talkin'!"

Perhaps Mother was right. This passion for story had become full-blown in me. Maybe from the fear of the past, those challenges I'd experienced, as well as this broken heart. Fire had hidden, had tucked himself underneath those wings of mine, as Fire had done to Ostrich, until Mantis had cleverly stolen Fire away, arousing her. In the Vedic text, Roberto Calasso reminds, it is written "Long before Fire aroused fear, Fire had felt terrified of itself, and of what men (and gods) would ask it to do" (*Ardor*). They were so afraid of the Fire god Agni—

rather than taking any kind of responsibility for him—his own brothers had vanished into the night.

That's how powerful Fire is, how dangerous it can be—people, even the gods, flee from it. When inflamed it arouses, when inflamed it consumes, devours, and destroys. Fire ignites sexual desire. I know. I've been consumed by it. And yet, as the herald, Mantis stole Fire from Ostrich and from me, awakening both of us to take responsibility for our own, and leading us, slowly, back to our essential selves, restoring our memories of this knowingness, restoring our natural God-given passion. For ever since, Ostrich became the fastest running bird and Murphy will eventually write lickety-split a whole lot of words!

Yes, at that first fire in the Kalahari, I begin to come into that Self of mine. I hear stories I'd never known; see things I'd never seen before—lions at the kill, tall giraffes moving across the landscape, little springbok antelopes springing up and down in the distance, unforgotten sunsets—one so amazingly moving that the Matebele Bayeti, the British Alex, and the American girl, me, in enraptured agreement, held hands across the differences of nations, of color.

At the end of this first safari into the Kalahari, when I had wept and wept over the profound connection, which I had felt in Africa, I threatened to move there. Izak warned, "Don't! It's a harsh land, just come and go whenever you please!" Then he wrapped his arm around me, as we walked, enlightening me with a tale, "After I brought an African American into the Kalahari Desert, he knelt down and kissed the sand, thanking God that his relatives—even though they had been slaves—had survived the boat across to the Americas."

I believe Izak wanted me to perceive that this man recognized Africa's wondrous beauty as well as its brutality and cruelty, with the knowledge that this African American's life in America, though wrought with a horrible history, though wrought with racism of its own, was far better. Perhaps I may not be willing to admit, nor seize, in the land of the beautiful and the free, that what many of us possess is much more than others can even imagine—at least in the possession of "things." (Though I must admit, I find the Africans I've met—with far less than we have—far more content.)

For these reasons, for the magic, and more, for the integration of something I'd been separated from, divided from—both within myself, from the blacks and the Original Peoples within my own culture—and more, I would travel to Africa many times. For I was determined, for I had not forgotten Izak's final words to me on that first trip in, "Ride the white horse of life, Murphy, before the black horse of death comes to get you!"

With his encouragement, Izak and I would venture to the Okavango Delta, trailride across the Moremi Reserve on horseback with P.J. and Barney Bestelink; white-water-raft the Zambezi River with the German family Bausch, with game drives across the Caprivi Strip, where we came upon forty elephants, lifting their trunks in a waving gesture of good night, as though Flora Dora Girls. At DiPhuduhudu, I'd film the Bushman artist, Kua, as he drew and performed a tale, I'd clap with the Bush-women as the men danced; observe a healer throwing the bones, granting me the exposure to the ancient art of shamanism, divination, as well as to their innate art of living as hunter-gatherers.

After the second trip to Botswana, I would type a letter to Sir Laurens, "I just returned […] meeting a few of the very gentlemen that you filmed in *Testament to the Bushmen*. I found them so warm and intelligent. Two of the San at DiPhuduhudu illustrated some stories…" (1 June 1996).

During that time and beyond, I will have journeyed to the Kalahari Desert a total of ten times gathering stories and music, for fear the San's culture might disappear, all traces lost. As well, I would finally have a launch date, Spring 1997, for the book, *Why Ostriches Don't Fly: And Other Tales from the African Bush*, which Sir Laurens would acknowledge, "I am so glad your book is coming out. I think you have done wonders" (4 June 1996). This note was his last correspondence to me. Thought he would not see the book in the official form, I pray it gave him hope for that world beyond which he would soon track into.

All I know is that I would recommend any opportunity in "the return" to Africa to anyone, white or black, yellow or red, rich or poor, young or old. For I felt as though I had been threaded back to something I could not describe where I was all at once home and at once full to the brim and complete. That something, which had not been inside of me up until I had touched the African soil, had come to stay. That I felt myself part of something greater as though I had been with Odysseus on a long sea voyage, having just re-found the land of my birth, the land of our Father's Father, our Mother's Mother—perhaps, the original and common land of everyone's. And just as the African American above, I had wept, kneeling reverently on hands and knees to this Thine own continent.

Through this trip to Africa, through Izak's story of this African American, through this engagement with the San, the Botswanan men at the fire, and the readings of van der Post, a slow effect was taking place in this life of mine. Bit by bit, I was being educated into the Indigenous Mind, slowly separating me, or certainly propelling me from remaining exclusively within the Western Mind I'd been inducted into. I became thankful for this, as Eduardo Duran had been to his friend and teacher, Tarrence, for saving "him from becoming possessed of Western worldviews."

The San people, as well as Sir Laurens, had affected the way I would and will continue embrace those whom we have slighted as the "other." For the Bushmen-women-and-children had accepted my otherness, somehow changing that relational vibration of mine. Returning, to strangely find I'd attracted bi-racial friendships, establishing those as some of my most predominant relations in the United States.

In New York City, in the Twentieth Century, the life as an International Sales Director for Mary McFadden had been a protective shell, and then (due to the San and their god Mantis), all those beautiful, hand-painted jackets and pleated pants began to fall away, so the bona fide me could be revealed. Once I shed this corseted shell, once this glamorous armor tumbled to the ground, the true Self, the genuine and legitimate Murphy, began to breathe. I did not think I could ever revert to that former self. For at such an innate and profound level, I was irrefutably marked, transfigured.

If it had not been for Gail's gift of Sir Laurens' book, I might have stayed forever "in" fashion, I might have stayed tangled up in an affair with a married man. The San stories were restoring me, as well, those precious moments in Africa would begin the "dislodge" from what I thought was "love," eventually opening that heart of mine to meaningful lifework. But first, I had to deal with that hunger of mine that was growing greater by the day and would require an "initiation."

3

THE LITTLE HUNGER

*"The first dance (of the Kalahari Bushmen) […] is […]
the little hunger […]. The second variation they call the dance
of the great hunger. […] the first one is of the physical […]
the child experiences the moment he is born and satisfies […]
at his mother's breast, and which from then on stays with
him for the rest of his life on earth […] the second dance is
the dance of a hunger that neither the food of the earth nor
the way of life possible upon it can satisfy."*

—Sir Laurens van der Post, *A Mantis Carol*

8:45 a.m., 77th Street and Lexington, 4, 5, 6 Subway, the never-ending commute with the rest of the worker bees, jammed up and jelly tight. The inevitable I wake up to five-days-a-week, fifty-one-weeks-a-year, for I am only allowed a mere pittance of a week's vacation. The waiting for. The anxiety. The sweat of the crowd leaning in from the platform: *Is it the express, the inside track?*

Part I: Across

No, at last, a train on the outside track arrives and the veritable stockpile into the cattle car. The rude push from behind, the shoving into. *Why do I put up with this?* Oh, that's right, I had a dream.

Squished next to the neighbor who coughs or the one who separates me from her with that perfectly folded Wall Street Journal or crumpled New York Times. If I'm really unlucky: heavy breathing with a hard-on that bumps against my ass. *(Where is the #metoo movement when I need them to register such biological acts?)* Oh, the pleasantries of living in the city, sharing space after breakfast with some six-hundred-odd people aboard ten-linked-metro cars to participate in this ratted-race to the office and back again. *Why?* I couldn't be sure, but like Frank Sinatra, I just needed, wanted, longed, hungered, "to be a part of it, New York, New York."

In Kansas City, in the liminal space of one year between the divorce and preparation for Parsons School of Design. In the evenings, I'll take sewing lessons and, in the daytime, I'll sell fashion in three different part-time jobs: Hall's on the Plaza, Lark Lynn Furs, and Effets—where I can push the limits, wearing a pink tutu, white leggings, very high stilettos, a rather large hat, hair shorn as short as Annie Lennox. With my *Effets* boss, on a buying trip to Los Angeles I'll hear the best one-line ever from a dashing Russian: "Can I fall in love with you tonight?" I chuckle at his creativity, but even so, I cannot fall in.

During Easter vacation of that same year, Mom granted me the gift of a long weekend at the Waldorf Astoria, a Broadway show, and an opportunity to interview with Graphic Design firms. That first glance only affirms a hankering that had to be satisfied. But without a permanent NYC address, no one will hire me. So, when an offer comes to be a nanny for a nine-year-old girl, Courtney, my twenty-nine-year-old self grabs that one-way ticket from Kansas to Lady Liberty for a position that lasts long enough to pave the way.

Until, finally, I had "made it." For eleven years, I'd been living in a four-story walk up, a tiny, railroad apartment on the Upper East Side at 303 East 81st Street, #4RE. The first year, I'd slept in the living room in a queen-size futon bed that folded up and acted as a couch. Jewels, a dear friend of my ex-husband's, slept in a twin in the only tiny bedroom with enough space for a narrow dresser and a row of bookshelves lining the passageway to the little bathroom (oh, so very NYC) comprised of a miniscule tub, shower, sink, and toilet, just room enough to stand at the mirror to brush the teeth. After Jewels, I had a series

3: the little hunger

of Italian roommates, the longest running—Antonella, who soothed me with delicious meals when I was suffering so from Renzo the married man.

During the last six months, while *Why Ostriches Don't Fly: And Other Tales from the African Bush* takes wing into the world, my salary soars as I step into the role of Vice President of International Sales at Halston for their re-launch. Between **that** and selling a gift of stock from Mom and Dad, I'll submit a bid for a loft in Tribeca at Church and Leonard. So, I will finally have a home of my own.

In this aggressive success as a salesperson on Fashion Avenue, where I'd been leading buyers, managers, and shoppers from across the U.S., Europe, and the Far East through showrooms and retail stores with heavy trunks of gorgeous clothes, that brokenness of mine had begun to reveal itself. One must understand as I write this, I'm now looking back almost twenty-five years, unconscious then, to what I know in the present.

I didn't know then I was empathic, and that, oftentimes, empaths are easy prey to predators. I didn't know then I had the authority to recall my own energy at anytime. I didn't know if I could just stay within the center of myself, I could bring a sense of dignity and agency, transforming through perception *any* experience. I didn't know if I kept living into what I wanted to be, my belief system, my original blueprint would eventually catch up. I didn't know then with a little more love for myself everyday, with listening to my heart more and more, I was slowly stepping out of the general inclinations into equality, overcoming what Eve Brinton calls "the power coding of the white male, first born, only son, ruling the earth." I didn't know that instead of following those in power, those in authority over me, I was quietly following the realm of the symbolic into that individuation of mine, into a truer Self. I didn't know that one step at a time, I was healing the past, so I could live in the present and hold a high regard for the wishes of my future. That I could live into the life I wanted and that this was magically happening all along the way.

In fact, at forty-years-old, I have all the "things" one seemingly wants: great friends, a successful career on Seventh Avenue, a first book published, a profound re-connection to my parents. However, I found myself shuffling the deck over and over, looking for answers, exploring the world for a more "noble" me.

For many years, I'd stay awake journaling as late as I could because I feared if I went to sleep, I'd awaken in the middle of the night to nightmares, heart leaping from adrenals drained, cortisol levels off, essentially pushing the edges,

Part I: Across

burning the candle at both ends. Of late, fantasizing about the man I cannot have, I curl up at home or on the road in a hotel to write in the latest journal. Pages and pages I'd begun at thirteen as a kind of "traffic analysis"—just as the men and women searching for clues from the German's ENIGMA transmissions during WWII—in search of me. Staying afloat, just above, just on the edge of a whirlpool of depression over something I'd been walking around for a long, long time, which, at any moment, might reach for me, drawing me down and under.

Amid this thick, persistent melancholia, about a failed marriage, among other things, I'd suffered from what the Hindus consider the causes, the effects, the imprints of a karmic ordeal. Though for work, (thank God) I can consistently rise into full performance, even so, there were and are still telltale signs.

One of these is a locked jaw. If you're really perceptive, you can see it. As though someone took a screwdriver and twisted the screw or drove a rusty nail with a blunt instrument just so, into the jowl. Ow! A contusion. A slow festering wound which leads to a disastrous death. When riding in the backseat behind the limo driver on the way to the airport for yet another work trip, I peer into his mirror. For some reason, this phenomenon, this locked jaw—of looking as though I'll never open my mouth again, ever—reveals itself! I can run, but from this revealing physicality, that "tell," I cannot hide!

Yes, the battle fatigue arises in girls, in women, and even in boys as a rigid jaw, chronic fatigue syndrome, candida albicans, eating disorders, depressions, suicidal tendencies, addictions of drugs and alcohol, obsessive compulsive disorders, PMS, fibromyalgia, fibroid tumors, prostate and breast cancer, and so on. As Patricia Reis expresses, as in the above list: "Our bodies, psyches, and souls are put on the line and register the impact and reflect the toll of our struggles." Among other things, this locked jaw gives me a glimpse of the reason for an inordinate hunger. If you're all alone and your jaw is wired shut, you cannot eat, only suck through a straw. So, a ravenousness. I was *that* hungry for love I would do just about anything. And I did, and I would, and I will.

Ultimately in this hunger, I know I am not alone. Most everyone around me seems to have a sufferance, which often remains shrouded in history or is known by the entire neighborhood, mapped on the lines of newsprint. The truth is, bit by bit, I'd been busy revealing the dross of the past, verbally, and slowly on paper. So many people have daringly shared their traumas, particularly in books and on television, I admire them for bravely making headway, setting the pace, and so I attempt to follow. Diving down into an inner journey of bodily

3: the little hunger

exploration and dreamwork, week after week, digging up the past with Freudian psychotherapist Vicki Abrams, I jimmy the lock on this jaw. I speak, I reveal, I weep. Before her, I must also reckon with the impact of my actions, those boat-like wakes of water, upon each of the lives I've touched. She remains present. She encourages.

Through Vicki, I also connect with a hands-on-healer Celia Candlin. Our first appointment is in her quaint apartment just blocks from mine. When Celia encounters what she considers, "an historical block," she recommends I meet with an intuitive, Mariah Martin, because she believes what I am emotionally suffering from—goes back, lifetimes. *How far must I go to discover it?*

At first mention, I panic, for I've been raised "Christian," told not to value "fortune tellers." Yet, even in this short session with Celia, I trust her enough to arrive at a little Greenwich Village apartment on Bank Street, where light pours in through the window, illuminating this woman, Mariah Martin, with white, cropped hair seated in the corner, shrouded in a pink shawl. Her large presence grounds the room with strength, as though a bodhisattva in *zazen*, meditation.

Accessing her mediumship, Mariah's eyes close: "I ask the divine light to guide us and protect us. I call forth the beings of light and love…" as her head tilts to the side, her arms slacken into a trance, worlds away from this Twentieth Century actuality, her narration pours forth: "I see you split in two parts, running back and forth, back and forth: as a child, shivering, hiding downstairs in the basement, then, standing on a balcony, in your whole-hearted knowingness." She breathes deeply. "It's true, the reason you came to me, for what you're suffering from is a past life." As she centered, I nervously wiggle in my chair. "In a dry country, in the desert, far away, ten lifetimes ago, you and a man, who hurt you immensely in this present life, are married, working together as shamans within the African tribe, the Pygmies."

"But" I inject, "the Pygmies aren't in the desert. They live in the jungle." *Why did I follow Celia's advice? Waste my money on this?* "Instead," I defend, "you must mean, the Bushmen?" However, in fairness to Mariah, I must confess, the Bushmen are considered "pygmy-like" in size.

"Yes," she nods, gently affirming, "the Bushmen."

"Are you aware of my children's book about the Bushmen, that I have traveled to the Kalahari Desert five times? In fact, the first time 'in' I traveled with my parents. Did Celia divulge this?"

Book One – Across the Divide to the Divine

Part I: Across

Mariah's eyes stay closed, remaining untouchably persistent, she continues: "No, but it makes sense. Your parents returned you to your first family, the Bushmen, for in fact, in this life, you need them. They have surrounded you with their love and support.

"However, ten generations ago, a tall, warrior-like tribe kidnapped you and your husband—both of you were Bushmen shamans at the time—carrying you across a whole continent, back to their homeland, in hopes you'd destroy the disease that was killing the elderly." *How did she possess this knowledge, that for centuries, people have been traveling from afar seeking these Bushmen healers?* "For these warriors" she proceeds "depended on the elders for wisdom and needed them to care for their children while they battled their enemies."

Oddly I don't think—Zulu—the people of the South, who would have been more geographically related to the Bushmen. Instead, my mind immediately jumps to the Eastern part of the Continent. "Do you mean…those who abducted us…were Maasai Warriors?"

"Yes, the Maasai."

Other than those jaunts through Dinesen's books, this legendary tribe, the Maasai, is outside my realm of study. Their long sleek bodies, their red tartan blankets nostalgically figure foremost in the minds of those who have traveled to Kenya and Tanzania.

Mariah informs that in Maasailand, my (then) husband and I had tried to find the medicine to stop the elderly from dying, but we were too far away from the familiar terrain to have access to our herbs. As if I was at fault, my then husband became furious with me, because without the cure, our lives were in danger. In the end, the Maasai killed us both. "In this life and every life after, you had played the same 'down-dog' role again and again with that former husband who became the controller, perpetrator. And you, Murphy," she urges, "must return to the Maasai to heal your relationship, only then can you re-integrate the child hovering in the basement with your higher self."

"Go back to see the Maasai?" An abnormal tenor rises in me. "I know nothing of them!" I silently ponder. One doesn't just walk up to a dung hut and knock on the door! As I march out of her office, I laugh to myself—*What does she really know about me?* Through slivers of doubt, I trumpet: "My research is with the Bushmen, not the Maasai."

Though I had been working in fashion and traveling back and forth to the Kalahari Desert during my holidays, the yearning for something more is almost

3: the little hunger

unbearable. As I walk away from Bank Street that night, bound for the Upper East Side, I try to wrap my mind around the fortuneteller's words. *Am I, as Marie-Louise von Franz reveals, an individual with a conscious attitude who must now retrace her steps to the commencement? By returning to the Maasai, could I really restore the past? Am I in fact being sent back in time to recover a piece of the puzzle? Is this quest, the intuitive has given me, a divine order from the Powers that be?*

After the safaris into Botswana, after this intuitive's revelation, the long-held goals of being a Fashion Designer are suddenly being swept aside. A new trajectory, this retracement, is forming. Even though my head is naysaying, I know in my heart Mariah is on the mark—something vaster is happening. Beyond childhood disappointments, beyond a divorce, beyond the affair with the married man, beyond the thwarting of those writing aspirations of mine, beyond those undifferentiated lifetimes—which, up until now, had been completely inexplicable and forever irreparable—are miraculously being sewn together into a pattern, into a brand-new design.

4

THE APPARITION

"Every night when we sleep we dream and a dream is a sophisticated and imaginative text full of figures and drama that we send to ourselves."

—John O'Donohue, *On Being*

When my first book finally launches with the press, Libraries Unlimited, I'll speak about those Kalahari Desert safaris to students in grade schools, junior highs, and high schools across the country, all the while I'm selling clothes for Mary McFadden. This launch seems to 'jimmy' that locked jaw into a promotion as a Vice President, where I spend four emotional "up and down" months in the $10 million re-launch of Halston in NYC. The new boss, Carmen Porcelli, is congenial, likeable, but the designer, Randolph Duke is moody, unrestrained, and hotheaded. With the pressure for Duke's success, my weight drops, hovering almost anorexically modelesque at one-hundred-and-twelve pounds.

4: The Apparition

While there, the *rumors* about Randolph Duke circulate: "cocaine-user," "manic-depressive." As well, supposedly, one night, with his brute strength, he shoves his boyfriend's body into a file cabinet. Of the truth of this actual imprint, I can attest but of the rest of these rumors I consider hearsay. Once, the rumor mongers spread, that he slung a trash basket with assorted sundries onto the head of another VP. When the basket was lifted, an unfinished soda pop and coffee trickled down her humiliated face.

All I know for sure, is when our fiery redheaded tempers go head-to-head, the argument reverberates. My boss, Carmen, runs like mad down the stairs to referee, finding Duke and me in a standoff that only happens in the Wild, Wild West. On opposite sides of my desk, our hands planted, with voices at a fevered pitch, we lean in, while underneath, hidden, Duke cannot see my knees a-rattlin'!

Thankfully, this job ends when Mark Badgley and James Mischka of Badgley Mischka throw a ring buoy across Fashion Avenue, hiring me as a change agent, asking me to fire several employees and launch the new collections of Daywear, handbags, and shoes. After two intense years, I need a vacation desperately. In fact, it had been inside this desperation when I had consulted the intuitive Mariah. But still, *to really listen? To fly into Africa without an entrée?*

That weekend, at a dinner party, seated next to my dearest friend, Jeffrey Moss, I relate this strange trance-like words of Mariah. Undaunted, he replies with his gut-intuitive bravado, "She's right. You've studied the Bushmen stories for eight years now. You said you wanted to learn the tales of others throughout the world. Here's your chance!"

At home, from the shelf, I pull Robbins' and Nooter's *African Art in American Collections*, one of the many thoughtful gifts from Ms. McFadden. As I turn the pages, I stumble upon a map with all the countries of the continent. Botswana is held in the cup of South Africa, and northeast to that—Kenya. Immediately, I drop my head into clasped hands and begin to sob uncontrollably. Just seeing the country inscribed on the page, triggers emotions, which seem bottomless. *Is it possible the past life Mariah described is true?* Unfathomable!

I phone Jeffrey informing him of my emotional response. Without missing a beat, he asks: "Whom do you know in Kenya?"

At the time, the only person I knew was the photographer David Coulson (whom I'd mentioned above as one of Sir Laurens' contacts). In fact, for four years, since Laurens' offering, I'd been faxing David for advice, research, and ideas about the Bushmen, of which he'd kindly responded. And yet, I had never met him.

"Call him tomorrow," Jeffrey encourages. "Appeal to him to arrange a visit with the Maasai."

David, a man, who travels all the time, photographing ancient paintings for Trust for African Rock Art (TARA), which will soon be captured in his book *African Rock Art*. As well, 30,000 of his digitized images will be housed in the archives of The British Museum in London. David will eventually be honored by King Charles with an MBE. Even so, he actually answers the phone. Immediately he warmly introduces me to two other well-known photographers, Carol Beckwith and Angela Fisher of *African Ceremonies*. They in turn refer me to a young Maasai, Marjana, who speaks perfect English and works for Peregrinations & Pilgrimages. Not knowing that each of the links in van der Post's chain, each of these kindnesses are important, granting me entrée into the Maasai Village, which will in turn transform the life.

Although there are difficulties in communication due to the recent bombing of the American Embassy in Nairobi, I book a round trip ticket, setting everything in motion. I pour over Tepilit ole Saitoti's *Maasai*, which had been illustrated with Beckwith's photographs. From this book, I learn that the name Maasai meant—my people. The Maasai are fierce warriors, a Nilotic Ethnic Group of semi-nomadic herders, who speak Maa of the Nilo-Saharan language family. Eight hundred and fifty thousand Maasai are scattered throughout Kenya and Tanzania. They are known for their feats of lion killing and their celebratory leap into the air, which determines both their strength and stamina.

In the midst of this preparation, an apparition emerges of an unknown Maasai Warrior. In the first dream, in a Ninja-like move, I grab his shoulders with crossed hands, cutting off his breath and choking him to death! In a second, similar reverie, I stab the painted warrior with a knife! In relief, the final dream reveals the two of us standing face-to-face shaking hands as equals. *In just this movement of soul towards Kenya, already healing the historic?*

Against the advice of parents, friends, and even the U.S. State Department, I actually head to Kenya to "mend fences" of a past life! Through this action, I am lifted out of the quotidian to face my own gnawing fears of encountering terrorists who had committed to kill Americans on sight, of not meeting the "right" Maasai, of not bringing that past into balance, and perhaps, bungling another.

4: The Apparition

From early childhood, I had learned of the shadows of the night. From those trips into Botswana, into the heart of nature, these terrors became all the more real and intensified while lying in the tent alone. Just as the Native scouts in Western movies, with ears to the floor, strangely, I could hear the shifts in the landscape, the pounding of the hooves of the zebra, gemsbok, ostrich running for their lives from the predators' pursuit. In their fight, flight, freeze, or fawn, I hoped their lack of safety would not collide with the lingering memory of my own, with a tearing through of the little canvas I temporarily called home.

It was obvious; I was not sole in these terrors. Alan Watts conjectures, even "fish swim in constant fear [...] motionless so as not to be seen, and dart into motion [...] startled into a jump by the tiniest ghost of an alarm" *(Nature, Man and Woman)*. These innate trepidations recede as I catch a flight over the Atlantic. For being airborne always gives me a sense of power, the kind experienced on a Quarter horse—a proud strength. And I can hear the words of a friend, an eventual teacher, the psychic Frank Andrews, echoing in my ears, "You're flying over the water, Murphy, to break the spell." Yes, indeed I am.

Almost twenty-four hours later, I land at the Jomo Kenyatta International Airport with no plans; no idea if anything would come together. In spite of this apprehension, as usual, the universe set a seamless course. A kind Japanese woman, whose friends reclined next to me on the plane, escorts me to the downtown Hilton.

At first, on the flight from Johannesburg, Tomoko and Keiko were skeptical of me, an American, until they discover that I am holding Ted Andrew's *Animal-Speak*, who writes, "There are many myths of a magical time and place in which there were no boundaries between humans and animals." Similar to the Original Peoples of Turtle Island, the Japanese religion of Shinto believes that spirits exist everywhere within nature, deserving our reverence and respect. When the Director Hayao Miyazaki opens the cabinet doors in the documentary, *The Mind of a Master*, he queries, "Don't know who they are, but they're here!" Only then, when these dear Japanese women know I am honoring all which surrounds us, whether hidden or seen, do they finally want to talk. Only then do they make the offering of a lift to the hotel. Thank God!

As you may notice from the above, though maybe unusual for a small-town Kansas girl, I can pick up a conversation with anyone, find things in common, cross borders between civilizations with ease. My father had taught me thus. A liberal Protestant, Dad had Black, Jewish, Catholic, and Mexican friends whom he treated as equals. Near the end of his life, we will discover, he was part of a hotline for any family that was struggling with health, financial challenges or lost their home in a fire—he and his friends would gather what was needed for recovery. By car, for these visitations, I had crossed "the other side of the tracks" with Dad to see his acquaintances, among them was his dear friend Raymond, Miami County National Bank's custodian. Raymond's daughters, Romona and Yvonne, whom we adored, became our huggable babysitters.

At four years old, I first really engaged with someone "other." Father had arranged with the organization, People to People, for young men from all over the world, who stayed in the private homes within our community and built an International Park at Miola Lake. To a youth from Hong Kong, I inquired, "So Ralph, how are things in China?" Shocked at this child's interest, he didn't correct the—at the time—distinction between Hong Kong and China. Instead, Ralph sat down on the grass, filling my mind with new imaginings. For, indeed, I had always been curious about those from "elsewhere" and beyond.

As a college student, Mother had worked in summer camps with physically challenged youth. So, some of our chums, George and Lyman, were wheelchair users. For many years, Lyman, as receptionist, answered the telephone at Father's bank. Mother's example wiped out those distinctions, teaching me etiquette, to sit alongside them, never to stand, nor lord over. To treat them as equals, not lesser. Because of Mom's openness, she encouraged me to befriend a black girl named Gracie, who was treated as an outsider, to include her in Brownies and later, Girl Scouts and Cadettes.

So, it makes sense that these dear Japanese women—as if compliments of Ralph and Gracie, and, of course, the greater "Grace," who sees over all of life— would grant me a magic carpet into a world that had just been shaken. For upon arriving at the hotel, I learn I've been deposited two blocks from the American Embassy bombing— "I must be mad to have come!" In this country, I knew of only these three Japanese women, who were now careening down the street rapidly away from me and two men, an American and a Brit (neither whom I had met). So, I reach out, dialing George and David, only to bump into their message machines! As the last rays of sunlight flooded through the clouds, I phone my parents, "I've alighted in Kenya safely or so it seems!"

Out the window, as the sun drops, as the lights are extinguished in surrounding offices, I watch as black men and women pour out of these buildings. Not one white face. I, then, presumed myself to be a reckless foreigner, certainly, of a different color—certainly in a land, where I am, for the first time, no longer the majority and now, the "other." I didn't know this was an important event for me, of feeling the outsider, that this, in turn, would inform the future, changing me, ever more so, in the way I would treat others, who are continuously "other-ed," who deserve respect. From the impact of my momentary otherness, from this "culture shock," forlorn, from the jet lag, exhausted, I fall into an immersive sleep.

5

SETS A SEAMLESS COURSE

"Upon a distant journey into unknown lands […] the gladdest moments in human life."

—Edward Rice, *Captain Sir Richard Francis Burton: The Secret Agent Who Made the Pilgrimage to Mecca, Discovered the Kama Sutra, and Brought the Arabian Nights to the West*

I awoke to the phone ringing and George Bright of Peregrinations & Pilgrimages (P&P) first words: "You actually took the risk to come. Bravo, you!" Encouraging me to be packed and ready. "A driver, Samuel, will pick you up in a green P&P Land Rover, then you'll catch a nine-seater Cessna Caravan to Samburu Intrepids Lodge for a few nights. After this safari, you will return to Nairobi for lunch with my wife, Dusty (also an American), and then you'll fly to Siana Springs. From there, (if all can be arranged) Marjana, the Chief's son, will drive you to the Maasai village in Laloshwa Highlands."

5: Sets a Seamless Course

Before walking out the door, I glance down at my lapel where Patricia's gift, the small golden sparkly plane, is safely pinned and then, a quick glimpse into the full-length mirror, as though regarding myself for the first time. After carrying a golf bag of sawed-off golf clubs, since I was three, I'd forgotten the weight had permanently lowered that right shoulder of mine, noticeably throwing it back so I walk through life left shoulder forward swinging those lanky arms in an elegant alluring way. An Aussie had once called me "coppertop" for that short shiny as a new-penny-colored-Twiggy-haircut, which has now grown long, thick, curly, auburn, yet shines as brilliantly as fire in the height of the noonday sun. Until today, I'd never realized how long waisted, how tiny, twig-legged, and vulnerable I appear.

In fact, I seem fragile, thin, white, pale and frail, even though walking around in an American-cowgirl-bravado, full of what someone once called hubris, which I have yet to grasp, is rather imperialistic. Taught to walk upright, head held high. Marching through life in what I thought was a huge masculine body. As if I could take on, endure, anything, third child, only daughter, keeping up with her brothers and "scampering off wildly over the edge of that forbidding wasteland of conventional normality. Courage…" van der Post pens. I shall need it!

For, even at the airport, there are complications. They cannot find the ticket. George sends Sami to negotiate, and I happily bump into the Japanese girls, Tomoko and Keiko again. They are off to the Masai Mara. This re-encounter makes me feel the world of Kenya, though unknown to me, is small, full of possibilities. No longer overwhelming and so "other-ing."

With ticket in hand, I join eight other passengers as we soar over the astonishingly beautiful red-dirt-terraced farms to the north. Huge white, fluffy clouds blanket all but the crown of Mt. Kenya. My head swells with Mozart's Concerto with images of Denys, Blixen's headstrong paramour. Where these two lovers once hunted, I will safari, observing animals at the kill, giraffes loping across the land until George can arrange a meeting with "the Maasai."

At the Intrepids Lodge, I, along with a British couple, Jenn and Mike, are assigned a guide for the twice-a-day game drives. The two of them are darling. I adore them, though I don't necessarily appreciate how Mike treats the blacks and the Indians, who work at the front desk. He yells at them. He demands them to serve him "just so" and "now." When this happens, I slink away from any association. For, I cannot abide. And in truth, it breaks my heart the way we treat those we have so often "other-ed." Again, I remain silent. I do not speak up for them. Even so, these employees are kind to me, befriend me, engage me in conversation when on their breaks, take walks in the garden, sit by the pool with me.

Secretly, though, I eye these newlyweds, Jenn and Mike, for I cannot wrap my head around how connected they are! Jenn thinks I am brave to travel alone. *What else? Wait for a thousand years for a mate, for a friend to come? Miss out on an adventure?* Romantically, hand in hand, they slip off to their tent after dinner. I, to my cabin alone, turning off the lights to sit on the porch, staring out over the Uaso Nyiro River to the distant half-moon overhead, bats flit and whir and I, too, am in love—with the stars and the heavens.

In the morning, I wander along the banks of the river with camera in hand, monitoring the movements of a blue heron. When I step to the side to photograph the heron, I sense, then see, a crocodile behind, tracking me. Heart pounding, I backtrack slowly. Without fear, small birds of bright blue, dragonflies, and butterflies flitter about. Everything seems alive, consciously intent.

Afterwards, on our early-morning game drives, we are swept into enchanted encounters. Two baby elephants wrap their trunks around each other, as though laughing with delight. A protective mother elephant charges our truck, lifting her trunk with a roar, then saunters off. We come upon five nervous impalas huffing and puffing, only to discover a leopard is slowly stalking them. Giraffes, in abundance, amble across the plains, as the Samburu lead their camels across the river. That day my own camel ride evokes the 1930's black and white photograph of Great Aunt Janet in Egypt. In the late afternoon sun, she is dressed properly in the traditional khakis of the time, hair tucked under her pith helmet like the one I don.

After our safari, we are driven to the Cultural Center for a glimpse at the Samburu arrayed in the most intensive pure colors. The men's black sinewy bodies are coated with burnt red ochre, as are their thin-braided locks. In contrast, the white sections of their clothes, their teeth, their eyes are electrified. They jump, chanting a haunting harmonic chorus as their song leader, *olaranyani*, sings the melody. The young girls flirt with the warriors, dancing in and out of the circle in rhythmic steps. A flautist with short, clownish red hair plays in the background. A touch of the Maasai. As I photograph them in this intense heat, snap after snap, they tease me, "You must not drain the lifeblood from us!"

"Oh, forgive me." On that note, I rewind the standing video camera, displaying their dance, which tickles them into laughter, as they point at one another with pleasure. From them, I buy two incredibly wicked dolls, replicas of the Turkana, a neighboring tribe, whom they view as ugly. And as I understand, they are in constant conflict.

In the evening, I attend the lecture of the Samburu, Lmakiya Lesarge, where I purchase his handbook, *The Samburu: A Brief Cultural Guide*, informing me about his people and their landscape. He is elegant, well spoken, and passionate about their traditions. "Our large herds of cattle, sheep, goats, camels, and many wives bring prestige." After his lecture, I meet Lmakiya for dinner, where he piques my interest with a baffling traditional tale, *nkaitini*, about Elephant who is tricked out of his honey by Rabbit. His cadence draws me into the mythological framework of the Samburu for its simplicity and its truth.

Up until my encounters with the Bushmen's trickster god, Mantis or Xamsakayaba (among other names) the African fables of wise trickster heroes—Anansi the Spider and Hare, who "sport" with one another—had been foreign to me. Except perhaps for the cartoons of Road Runner, this was not how I was educated in the West, where stealing is considered adamantly bad. To the African, whether Rabbit steals the honey or not, is not so important. Instead, for them, it is about consciousness. In other words, where one is unconscious, like the elephant ambling down the pathway without awareness of what's happening on his back, there are always losses. Here, qualities of expressions and experience abound without judgment, allowing for the depth of the culture, the development of characters. In this narration, Elephant's loss of the sweetness of honey is Rabbit's reward.

Throughout my stay, Lmakiya illustrates more fables, *nkaitini*, over meals, during hikes, and lectures. Lmakiya is proud, not in a cocky way, but assuredly as a man, conveying himself thoughtfully, with distinct, clear boundaries. Impressively he is recording the epigrams and myths of his people. Through our common interest, a quiet friendship forms.

After this first visit to Samburu, I land briefly in Nairobi for lunch with George and Dusty Bright, and several of their friends. I, who am so used to being alone, am completely astonished they found love at my age. Dusty, a former Madison Avenue Advertising genius turned African filmmaker, birthed their child, Marisella. They have given me such hope!

Part I: Across

In the afternoon, I sail over the Masai Mara in a charted Cessna to glimpse the strangely wondrous yearly "Wildebeests' March" of thousands across the grasses of the Mara and the Serengeti, as lions and cheetahs tag along, scavenging the weak animals. The endless space of the savannah is magnificent, the sheer size mesmerizing. The plane lands on the edge of the Mara. On these flights, I note: Kenya is a land of small roads. Yet, soon, in twenty years time, these roads will disappear, making way for paved highways of the China Wu Yi Company (which I will not see until 2013, *the seventh journey* in Book Three).

At Siana Springs, I feel a moment of respite from every care and concern. As if I had arrived at the end of the planet, high over the vastness of Kenya with only the need to look back, reflect, wonder in stillness—a moment completely out of touch with the known, left with the fullness of empty space. Unlike Samburu Intrepids Lodge, I take meals alone at a table prepared for me, preferring this, so I can read and write. I like the no-small-talk, no-nonsense, anonymity.

Since my arrival in Kenya, I have heard the whispers about me. Other tourists liken me to Baroness Blixen, sole, journal writer against the barren landscape, behatted with hair flowing down the back, topped in brown suede jacket, continuing to play with those New York/Paris sensibilities of Fashion she so easily embodied. Reminding me of her, at a Flea Market, my friend Jeffrey, ever the antique-buyer, had found this 1940's pith helmet, which I've adopted as a perfect foil for the khaki skirts. Underneath this chapeau, I keep cool, eyes hidden, sun-blocked, Blixen-ed. On the prop plane to Siana, even several Italian men kindly admire this on me.

Which makes me smile, for I revere Karen, for her penmanship as Isak Dinesen's *Out of Africa,* for her relationship to Africa, her soulful intimacy with her right-hand man Farah, for her respect of the Kikuyu, offering Western education to them, fighting for thevir land rights. (And later, I do not know this yet; I will grow to love the land of her birth, Denmark, and one of her countrymen, Book Two.)

In my aloneness, I have time to ponder George's description of the Sacred Forest at Laloshwa Highlands, where we will venture next "…quiet, peaceful, utter darkness at night. On foot, the Maasai will escort you everywhere with spear in hand to shield you against elephant, buffalo, lion, and leopard." Of this, I find myself intrigued, daunted.

In the sun each afternoon I bathe, read, journal, surrounded with the songs of birds, the rat-tat tatting of the woodpecker, which Andrew's Animal-Speak,

5: Sets a Seamless Course

reminds: "Listen to the rhythm inside." Everywhere the baby deer greet me with their "gentle innocence luring me away into adventure." This, I prefer, rather than rushing out the door to hop in a taxi, or boarding the subway bound for work, or taking an urgent call from buyers, Amy O'Connor, at Neiman Marcus, and Lincoln Moore, at Saks Fifth Avenue, both, whom I adore. Encouraged to go further in, I crave, "Solitude, says the moon shell. Center-down, says the Quaker saint." Anne Morrow Lindbergh ponders, "To the possession of the self is a way inward, says Plotinus. The cell of self-knowledge is the stall in which the pilgrim must be reborn, says St. Catherine of Sienna" (*Gift from the Sea*).

On safari, we come upon a lion and a lioness in a tumble of love, while nearby their cub leaps, chasing after the vultures as if a playful kitten, an ever-primal reminder of motherhood. An evening game drive is offered where we come upon eyes in the night, discovering creatures for the first time. A genet cat peers through the bush, then slips into the dark. Later, outside the tent, I soak up rays from the moon and the stars.

For five hours the next day I hike with a young Maasai and an elderly Kikuyu to observe plants, flowers. They kindly recount chronicles of their people, of the animals. As though normal, we saunter up to the gangly walkers, the giraffes. A blue dragonfly bumps into my heart, echoing great leaps forward. A praying mantis crawls across my path. Somehow, on all my trips to Africa, I stumble upon Mantis, the true guide to all travelers.

On this leisurely stroll, we visit a Maasai *enkang*, an enclosed circular area of thorn brush and dung huts. Not knowing at the time, there was an artful intention to this structure, as shown in the research of Ron Eglash's "The Fractals at the Heart of African Designs" (TedGlobal). Yes, I will soon discover, inside the Maasai's narratives, inside the forms of their rituals, divination, herbs, and living arrangements remain a protective and sacred intentionality to their circularity, their colors, the geometric shapes. Fortification against wild animals, fortification against those forces seen and unseen.

Among these warriors—a dark, noble, sleek, strong-muscled people—is a man whose head is decorated with ostrich feathers for the feat of capturing this elusively quick bird. Next to him, my guide introduces me to Kapelei, a man whose face is torn, scarred, and partially hidden underneath his lion headdress. In this brief moment, so at ease with him, I reach out to touch his wound. From this act of kindness, he reveals the happenings upon a trail with other young warriors:

Book One – Across the Divide to the Divine

Part I: Across

They'd been busy with song when they walked right into a lion at the kill with an impala in his mouth. The lion, defending his territory, had turned on Kapelei with a mighty roar and a leap, knocking the spear from his hand. Stunned and terrified, the warrior had wrestled with the lion with one hand, while the other hand set the knife free from the leather satchel strapped round his waist. With one stroke Kapelie had lodged the blade into the lion's heart earning this wild, this ultimate Maasai *chapeaux*, as well as this scar of remembrance.

Beside one of the huts, they display their traditional colorful jewelry. One piece—made of a large oval stone, formerly an earring, now hangs as a necklace trimmed with porcupine quills, I buy this for my dear friend Jeffrey. The elephant tale necklace I purchased from one woman was said to be a talisman for fertility. The other, a copper, circular grill, I find fascinating, and I want to know the meaning. "For three months after childbirth, the women wear this necklace," my guide directs, "symbolic of an eye, to protect the mother and child from evil."

"Oh, I must have that for protection! For someone is furious with me."

In the evening, at our tented camp in Siana Springs, the Maasai dance and serenade us with a tale sung in praise to their heroes, winners of the valorous prize of the lion's mane. As they move around the fire, the crowd claps, urging them onward. One elegantly long lion-head-dressed warrior, I recognize as Kapelei. He is dressed in the traditional red, with shoulders draped in crisscrossed multi-colored beads. Catching my eye, he coaxes me to join them, reaching for me with his dusty hand, pulling me into the vortex of their ancient rhythmic pulsating chant. Shuffling round the circle, enchanted, into some ancestral rite, full-heartedly, I sing and jump, for I, too, am bound skyward.

Astonishingly, I find myself weeping, weeping for the beauty of the rhythm, for Kapelei's desire to be linked—his black hand entwined with my white—for the bonding that knits together all existence into oneness. "We're all admixed." Henry Louis Gates, Jr., claims, "We've all been sleeping with each other for a long, long time. We all are Africans; the only question is whether you're a distant African or a recent African […] despite how different we look at the level of the genome we're 99.9% the same. We all come from the proverbial common ancestor, the proverbial Adam and Eve" (*Amanpour and Company*).

Perhaps because I'm a distant relative, perhaps because I sometimes believe those ancestors of mine came *Out of Africa* thousands of years ago or perhaps because of the lifetime I lived amongst them in 1787, the intimate response to their music is an unparalleled *déjà vu*. Amazingly echoing and resonating, to this, now, me, who has ventured across this entirety of the African continent, to Kenya, just because of Mariah's simple elucidation. O, thus, this *resonance* must be related to that lifetime she spoke of, never comprehending its staggering truth, and of what's to come. Not knowing this is the beginning of the reweaving of the warp and woof of my life.

A few days later, on the edge of the Masai Mara, on the edge of my hopes and dreams, what I have been waiting for, comes—in a Land Rover so significantly marked, Peregrinations & Pilgrimages.

First Journey In

6

RISING INTO THE THERMALS

※ ※ ※

"I had the feeling that I had already experienced this moment and had always known this world which was separated from me by distance in time [...] as if I knew that dark-skinned man who had been waiting for me for five thousand years."

—C. G. Jung, *Memories, Dreams, Reflections*

On the 30th of August 1998, the Chief's son Marjana, with his cousin Saifi, his friend Najuri; and our Kukiyu cook Henry Muringi, escort me along a bumpy road to Laloshwa Highlands, Kenya. Marjana speaks beautiful Queen's

6: Rising into the Thermals

English, as does Saifi. Though the two of them are Western educated, both are married to Maasai wives who live traditionally in dung huts, conversing in their native tongue Maa, and bits of Kiswahili. These first words tumble from my lips: *supa*, hello, *ashe*, thank you.

I have yet to be aware that the pretense of collecting stories will soon be thwarted and moved to the back burner of my intentions. I do not know, in meeting the Kitomini community at Laloshwa Highlands, I will shapeshift as the Kalahari Bushmen during their traditional trance dance around the fire at night, as a *therianthropic*, part human, part Mantis, part lion, part ostrich—what Mathias Guenther describes as "Crossing stations." Yes, I will transform, but not into what some Native American people groups consider as "skin-walkers," instead, into my fullness, which has been awaiting arrival on the planet.

As we grow close to our destination, Marjana elaborates, "These woods which surround my homeland are the Natada Enkidu Forest. They are classified as dryland *Afro-Montane*, one of the last remaining closed-canopy forests in Kenya." Pointing, he says, "We shall traverse across the plains of Morisodu to the edge of those trees where our village lies."

Though jostled about for another hour, the excitement builds, shifting time, so within a blink of an eye, we come to that point where before us a green panoramic expanse stretches vastly at his people's feet. "The life in Laloshwa," Marjana continues, "tends to be easy-going because we have been living this way for generations. At sunrise our wives milk their first goat, sprinkle this *kole*, east, west, then north and south praying: 'Thank you, Engai, God, for this new day. These offerings are for my Ancestors.' The milk squeezed from the goat is then boiled as a kind of Chai sprinkled with a little tea and lots of sugar. (While you're here, you'll drink plenty of this, Murphy!)

"The men and young boys take the cattle shortly, thereafter, returning with them in the evening. During ceremonies is the time for men to pray. Our cousins, the Samburu in the north (whom you've already met), live in the desert, and have much more of a struggle on the land. So, their elders gather daily to ferret out their difficulties. We, the Maasai, assemble only when disputes erupt."

When we enter Marjana's village, the children surround me, giggle, and touch my pale white skin and red nails, as though they are hardly real. Compared to their shorn heads, the women are fascinated with the length of my hair, which to me is too short at five inches below the shoulders, but to them is phenomenally long. "Have you been growing it all your life?" they want to know. "And the color? Like our young warriors, painted with the ochre stain from a crumbled rock."

With grace, Marjana introduces me to his father, Chief Ole *Wangombe*, whose name in Maa means owner of many cows—which, indeed, he has. He is handsome, quite grand in height, like his son, as well as in spirit, with sparkly eyes and a warm smile. Due to his indigenous diet of blood and milk and the lean years of drought, the Chief is lankier than Marjana, who resides in Nairobi, living a more Westernized lifestyle.

Marjana also presents his wife, Nooloisalanga and their daughter, Mwaisakeni. In his wife's trust, he leaves supplies for his people. Then, we hurl along in the truck several miles through the thick forest of the Sacred. Rough trails of bumps and slides lead us to the romantic camp, privately tucked away along the Katunga River.

"In his wisdom and thoughtfulness for our future, my father, the Chief," Marjana elaborates, "formed a contract with George Bright and his brother of Peregrinations & Pilgrimages to bring guests and monthly salaries to seven families. Together with the Bright's our community built this private campground."

Stepping into this elegant thatched-roof open-air lodge with a large burning fireplace, I find warmth for my tuckered traveler's soul. An awning-covered walkway leads to an attached kitchen. Across the meadow there is a private wood-framed tent, where I will thankfully bunk, with a grass roof, private toilet and shower. Marjana's cousin and Saifi's brother, Sarototi, and their other friends, Motoguisimile, and Lughano, greet me as they busily prepare the camp. I slip off for a hot-bucket douse and a nap before a light supper.

The first few mornings are spent hiking through the bush, coming upon glades, meadows, even wetlands. As we follow the spoor of buffalo, Marjana informs me, "We are custodians of the forest's birds, animals, and mammals: leopards, lions, buffalo, elephant, bushbuck, kudu. As well as the black and white Colobus monkeys, whom you see high up there, long tails dangling from the trees."

While on foot, I'm out of breath, partly due to fear of wild animals, and partly due to the high altitude, a mile above sea level. I remember as children, at ages nine and ten, my girlfriends, Julie and Jana Muchow and Nancy Buchman, and I were allowed to camp out amongst the stars at night. Often, we would secretly slip away. In the darkness, these girls would follow me across my known

6: Rising into the Thermals

territory, across the dam, along the borders of Ushy Gushy Canal, through the woods, along the paths, over the fence, under the highway, through the dark tunnel to the Paola Country Club for rituals of barefooted dances on the same putting greens we used for Junior Golf.

Here, however, one can smell and taste real danger. The second day, in a grassy meadow, we come upon three buffalo. They are enormous. Ferociously grunting, they spin around only to face us down. In order to protect me, Sarototi safely pushes me behind a large tree. With heart in throat, I peek, observing the happenings for I have heard tragedies connected to these fearsome beasts. With spears in hand, these four awe-inspiring Maasai stand their ground. The buffalo back up several steps then turn to scuttle away as though in fear from past failures and unpleasant memories tracking through their DNA.

Casually, Marjana, as if nothing has happened, continues the tour, directing me with his finger: "The two most numerous trees in our forest stand over there: the Cedar and Podocarpus. Of course, there are many others: the *olea capensis, olea africana, pavetta gardenifolia, zantholyum usambarensis,* and *warburgia ugandensis.*"

The sonance, the cadence of the Latin terms drifts me back to the age of nine, watching my older brother at his desk, memorizing the names of leaves, barks, flowers for his Landscape Architecture class at Kansas State. For him, I press a hot iron onto the green shapes of terra bouquets between two sheets of wax paper. This transports me to the first excursion into the Kalahari Desert with the guide, now friend, Izak, who had technically described each insect, plant, pulling a leaf, a bulb as I inhaled each fragrance, sketching, tucking them into the pages of private memoirs and onto an altar for safekeeping.

Back to the present, Marjana's voice triggers me: "On the hills, over there," he directs, "lies more of the dry conifer forest, predominantly, the *juniperus procera,* the African Pencil Tree. Our most sacred, is the oreteti, the *ficus thonningii,* the mighty Strangler Fig Tree, this, we use in many of our rituals. Women will pray in times of drought, leaving their bracelets in the crevices. Men will leave a bit of grass at the base. Observe its tenacity as it takes over the other tree, throwing its red shoots down into the earth to establish territory."

From a branch of the East African Greenheart tree, Marjana's cousin, the Chief's nephew Sarototi, prepares a toothbrush for each of us, shaving off the bark with his knife. As I scrub my teeth, the white bristles are soft and taste fresh, slightly minty. Sarototi points at plants and gestures their curative as his brother,

Saifi, further enlightens me: "My brother wants you to know our deodorant is a bundle of lelechwa; these white-bush-leaves are slipped under the armpits or wrapped around the neck (for our women admire this scent)!"

As I continue to collect feathers on the trail, bits and pieces of bone for an altar, I place a flower behind my ear. When it falls, as the gentleman that he seems, Sarototi forages, finding a supplement. *Is it here the first spark ignites, leaping up between us—a florid awakening?* He gathers flowers for the table, for my tent. Each of his quiet acts, grounds me, steers me. With a spear in hand, he walks just slightly behind, protecting me. Though his muscles are sleek and strong as the others, he is short, slight. His face is chiseled with high-cheekbones and an endearing smile.

Around the fire, however, away from the alertness he must attend to in the woods, he is loquacious. When he speaks, his hands move elegantly as his words electrically come alive. We might say, "He has the gift of the gab." His laughter is contagious, awakening the fairies in the forest, in our hearts, inviting us into the delights of his ever-active mind.

"From each family," Sarototi relates, "my uncle, the Chief, sent one boy to school to be Western educated. For this reason, my brother, Saifi, interprets this dialog in English for you, as does my cousin, Marjana. I was one of the boys who stayed home (so the cutout hole in my dangling ears)." As an example, he tugs down the circled skin from being looped over the top of his ear. "I was educated differently, in the ways of our people."

At night, I set up the altar of candles, little bronze statues, Buddha, Ganesha, Kwan Yin, Kali, Anubis, a little plaster of the Winged Victory of Samothrace (Greek Goddess, Nike), which I have carried for years on the road for fashion's sake, to solidify my movements, two weeks a month, city after city. Beside these gods and goddesses, (just as I saved those treasures from the childhood fairyland) I add the dead bugs, feathers, stones for texture, Sarototi's carved wooden toothbrush, flowers, and the broken wings of Samothrace that have tumbled to her feet, declaring her, now and forevermore, my protectress as Athena is to Athens.

In Laloshwa, I feel free of all the pathologies of the nuclear family, society, the pressures of work, the telephone, the sales numbers, the non-existent relationship; re-acquiring old skills, gaining new abilities, knowledge for life elsewhere. Having abandoned that early childhood in the woods, I have not returned to that "now" until here, here, in this magical re-awakening.

6: Rising into the Thermals

Within a few days, *or was it just within a few hours?* Something uncanny begins to unfold, subtly tipping the everyday reality: an appreciation develops between the Chief's nephew, Sarototi, and myself created without formal language—for we do not speak the same. Not love at first sight, instead, the impartation is innate, forming on a spiritual plane, more expansive than space and time, slightly telepathic, extrasensory in perception.

In *A Wind in the Door*, Madeleine L'Engle explained this as *kything*, a wordless, mind-to-mind communication, and I might add, for us, heart-to-heart, which over time becomes an endearing dance with the spirits. In spite of what others might consider our disparities of culture, of color, we build trust, composed of mutual respect and love for the omens brought to us from nature: the animals, the stars and divination—that which was greater than ourselves. Eventually, we will find other commonalities in our cultures, places where the politics and religion have slowly broken down within our structures. Where it no longer feeds our souls.

Were he and I the same? Was the ruling myth of our civilizations no longer meeting our basic psychological needs? Were we both in search of a compensatory tale? Would we make each other in our "otherness" the answer, instead of creating a new myth for ourselves individually?

Between Sarototi and I, an interpreter seems rarely necessary because the supreme presence of nature is its own language. We are united inside a wondrous concert. In this contra-distinct country, where I don't know intimacy through language, I'm not obligated to respond. Instead, their language is a rhythm that weaves in and out of the landscape, allowing me to hush.

Finally, one night, Sarototi offers his services as *laibon*, shaman. "Why am I here?" I enquire. The meanings come as if from the cosmos itself. He speaks into the plastic bottle, rolls the stones onto the mat, and then, ponders quietly, counting, as Marjana (when it is so specific, I need him) interprets: "You will be blessed on this trip. You will be given an opportunity to start your own business." Adding: "You are not very serious about a husband. Marriage is not to come for quite some time."

Slapped in the face with the truth. *How does Sarototi know what exists chaotically in my heart?* The fright I have of relationship, the fear of commitment, losing myself again in relation, losing my capacity to travel, to write, to succeed through the trueness of me. Most of all, the fear of intimacy and letting someone come close—*for wasn't that how I'd been hurt before?* Fear the bereavement

Part I: Across

of another relationship—the loss of husband, and then, of the eight-year relationship with Renzo, that unattainable married man, back in the city.

"You will meet your future husband in New York." (Actually, he's right, in reality, I do meet him in NYC four years later in 2002, but because it takes years to recover from the touch of a god or a goddess, neither of us is even considering each other then. I later re-meet him in 2011.)

"And what about the ants?" I inquire. For already, I had "accidentally" sat down in the midst of red ants three times this week, while thankfully Sarototi prudently scraped them off. I still needed to know: "Why do they keep crawling on me, biting me? Are they a sign of anger, a kind of spell from someone?"

Sarototi speaks into the plastic water bottle, shakes and rolls the stones onto the gunnysack again, "No, they come as messengers to you. You must take these words back to North America: 'Just as the ants work together, so must you and your people.'" In the midst of their crawling all over me, I'd forgotten the significance of these mythic figures, who in some traditions, are thought to be the bearers of gold from the depths. *Was this the jeweled message roaring up from down under?*

I stand, grateful for his Ancestors' comprehension of the extensive cost to personal independence to those of us living in the United States. Thankful for the Maasai gifts of insight into a society they live at such a distance from. Take heed. Observe the ants, as the Maasai say, to understand what it means to live inside an alliance of many families—sharing the land, striving for the same purpose. *How could we attempt such a thing where we honor individuality so dearly?*

"What of my confrontations with pigeons in NYC? They fly straight at my face. Descend upon me like the Holy Spirit, placing feathered messages before me."

The Chief's confidante, the elegantly tall, quiet Papa, or *Baba Budhya* smiles: "You are reconnecting with nature, listening again, Murphy."

Each night when Sarototi politely escorts me to my tent with spear in hand, we stop to stare at the expanse above. He is as captivated as me by the mysteries of the universe, the stars. *Is he Jung's five-thousand-year-old man waiting for me? Or the kidnapper of ten generations ago? Is the relationship aroused by our wonder of our "otherness," our distinctions?*

"At five years old," my mother had explained, "your first 'othering' happened."

"What?"

6: Rising into the Thermals

"Your kindergarten teacher telephoned: 'All morning long Irene stares at Urmula Varanhi, her Indian classmate.'" Mom illuminates, "So I chose to make a playdate for you, with Urmula—that's how your friendship began."

"Who could forget Urmula?" I smile. Urmula was beautiful, I reflect, as was her mother, who wore the red bindi on her forehead, dressing in the traditional Hindu saree. I loved their dark brown eyes, flowing long black hair, and their skin which was as smooth and elegant as amber.

"Her father was a psychiatrist at the Osawatomie State Hospital and a friend of your father's. To their home, they invited us to dinner where we tasted the most delicious and unusual food. They came to our house as well. In the short time they were here, you were great playmates."

"Remember her mother gave me a gift of a grey silk saree?" I was so proud of this. In honor of them, I still have it, draped over my pinky couch in my office.

Fascinating, I've been drawn to, not repelled by someone "other," just as I find myself drawn to these Maasai men, who surround and protect me, just as I find myself drawn to the "nécessite de l'ailleurs," the necessity of elsewhere to bring meaning to my soul.

These warriors of this "elsewhere," of somewhere "other than," are not just knowledgeable about herbs; they are trained as trackers, the meticulous attunement to the sounds, the cry of each bird, the signs of each animal. The crunch in the leaves, the falling of a limb from a tree means: "Beware, elephants ahead."

Sarototi and I examine each toss of his divinatory stones, each spoor on the forest's floor as though nature has something personal to say, as if God is intimately speaking through every movement. For the two of us, the signs are a fascination, a spark of delight, a trope for the day. The wind blows through the trees in a rush on the trail, and we both stop to listen. We are enthralled by this world around us.

When my two elder brothers slipped off to school, Mother longed to be solo. Often, I found her in the basement with the laundry, perhaps, hypnotized with the routine of washing, drying, ironing, with her own need for quiet. This led me, quite young, to seek solace, wandering barefoot into the backyard to hide in the coolness of the lilac bushes, to play in the sand pit, to dig holes with our guinea pigs, Laddie and Betty Boop, to peer into the window cell at our bull snake, to tease the pet toad, we named Straw—backwards for warts.

Book One – Across the Divide to the Divine   **55**

Part I: Across

When tall enough to tiptoe and reach, I dare to sneak across the wide-open field of the back-backyard of our one-acre plot, through another latched gate to the enchanted Messer's twenty "Philette Acres" of pastures, woodlands, lake, barnyard of geese, chickens, peacock, cows, and wild animals of foxes, coyotes and rabbits. An idyllic playland sequestered between the Katy Railroad Tracks, Waterworks Road, old Highway 69, the Paola Country Club (PCC), just at the beginnings of our little town. With our dog, Lassie, tagging along, racing ahead, Mother does not fear us going too far—for if she wants us, she'll ring the large silver cattle bell, suspended high on the edge of our property—and we'll come a'runnin.'

By five years old, I have already begun a natural dialog with these creatures through kythe-like telepathy, onomatopoeia, bridges are formed between the two-legged me and the four-legged, eight-legged, winged ones, and all the creatures of that Kansas earth. They respond to my laughter, comfort me when sad. Through stillness, songs, signals, instinct, these creatures open up the every day to the mystical magical world of nature.

Wandering through the woods and grasses of Kansas, even on the back of Geronimo (a horse my brother and I bought for $154), being a wise tracker is a must. Danger can often be avoided just through trained sound and sight. With the ever-changing violent Kansas weather, rattlesnakes, water moccasins, and the signs of death and birth all around me, I learn respect, caution. On these treks, I pick up feathers, later identifying them with our Encyclopedias, as the reddish orange of the robin, the hawk, the colorful pheasant, and the treasured long, elegant peacock feathers. Eventually, I clamber up trees to peer into their nests and find perfect, tiny bowls composed of mud and white cloth, containing the pale-sulfite-green eggs of a Wood Thrush, smaller than the Robin's, with a slightly pointed tiny end. Yet, I remain quiet, not touching, nor disturbing them.

Not only is a growing conversation formed with the animals, insects, birds but also an acute, expanded awareness of the phenomena of dreams, opening for me another existence outside the physical plane. To this day, these memories remain indescribable. Though I move away from these woods at twelve, for years, every Thanksgiving and Christmas, I return for an annual hike with my brothers and eventually their children.

6: Rising into the Thermals

    This art of tracking was embedded thoroughly and inextricably within me. So, it seems only natural to be drawn into the lives of some of the greatest trackers in the world, the Kalahari San Bushmen, and my newfound Maasai friend, Sarototi.

    On a walk behind the camp, Sarototi shows me his orchard of newly planted trees grown for their herbal properties, for the community near and far. We proceed along the stream, and then climb high. Looking down through the forest, I perceive the rushing stream that snakes along our campsite, a glimpse of our makeshift home. Above us, eagles fly, encircling our trail. He stops to direct my eyes to their shadows, dancing about us. And then, in a mesmeric twinkling, I'm lifted, rising, floating on the thermals with him, them. Caught in the vortex of another dimension, soaring over and above, into something more.

7

FOOD OF PLENTY

"When we leave our home and community to dwell awhile in some remote place, it happens every day that we trust a stranger, someone with whom we have no kinship bonds, no common loyalty to a community or creed, no contractual obligations."

—Alphonso Lingis, *Trust*

Across the large table from me, at mealtimes, my guide, the Chief's son, is seated in a wooden chair. Muringi prepares delicious and hearty meals for us, Motoguisimile serves, as Marjana and I share our life experiences. Further away from us, on the other side of the kitchen, on logs, gathered round the fire, the others eat.

"Why else have you come, Murphy?" Marjana curiously inquires.

"My interest is in stories. At first, I collected the Bushmen's. I'd love for the village to have a copy of *Why Ostriches Don't Fly*." Pushing the book towards him. "If your people are open, perhaps, I'd like to record your fables. But I

7: Food of Plenty

must fess up, this safari to Laloshwa was provoked by an intuitive, Mariah." As I divulge her entreatment to me "to heal a past life," Marjana listens carefully, seems taken with this premise.

The following day Marjana drives to a nearby village to find a spare part for the truck. I take the usual morning hike with Motoguisimile, Saifi, and Sarototi. The wise, elderly Baba Budhya, who is as tall and lanky as the chief, joins us. With spears in hand, the Maasai walk in front and behind me. Softly, warnings are spoken of, how to handle a possible lone elephant, a leopard in the trees. Each trek, my heart races; breath is short, nervous, alert, aware. Their favorite walk is to the waterhole to observe the buffaloes. Here, we sit, talk, eat delicacies of fruit.

When we return, we discover Marjana has not come back. At the large table, Muringi sets a solitary place for me. Needless to say, I have grown so accustomed to being a part of this little community, I object. From now on I cannot bear being solo! As his wide chef-self waddles to the kitchen, determined to ignore this request, I chase after him, "No, I can no longer eat by myself. I want to eat with you and the Maasai."

"Marjana will be angry!" He grumbles under his breath. "Besides, there is not enough food to go around!"

"Then, bring their food and mine, and we shall share. Marjana can yell at me!"

Muringi does just that and every one of us gathers around the table. At first, it is a bit uncomfortable, for some of the young men have never eaten with utensils, nor have they sat with a white guest. I encourage them to use their hands and join them in this endeavor. This act of eating collectively, sharing new flavors begins a tradition between the Maasai, the Kikuyu chef, and me.

Instead of depleting our food source, it creates leftovers. We contribute our plenty to the few Maasai grazing their cattle near our camp. By the end of my stay, we even have enough to leave behind for the community, making me ponder the actions of a man who once audaciously claimed he was God's son, blessing what little food given: "They ate and were satisfied. And they picked up twelve full baskets of the broken pieces and also of the fish. And there were five thousand men who ate the loaves" (Mark 6: 41-44).

During these abundant dishes full of new tastes, the real discussion begins. Without Marjana, Sarototi's brother, Saifi interprets. They, too, similar to Marjana, want to know why I have come.

Book One – Across the Divide to the Divine **59**

"For stories."

"We can give you stories," Baba Budhya wisely replies. "But you have come to us for something more."

And so, as I did with Marjana, I make a clean breast of it, telling them of Mariah's bidding to backtrack into a life with the Maasai, resolving our past. As I speak, there is a complete kibosh on all sounds. They, and even the forest, seem spellbound that an American-woman-shaman, a "laibon,"—they insist I call Mariah—has sent me. Stranger still, to thema nd to me, that I had been willing to follow her suggestion. Consequently, Sarototi's response is unexpected, "We do not believe in past lives."

Hmmm. A conundrum. "Look, I grew up in a Christian home—we were taught not to believe in reincarnation either. (Although, secretly, my mother and I held onto this tenant.) Yet, the intuitive's tale of this other life intrigued me. Then, every circumstance, every contact—even our mutual friends Carol Beckwith and Angela Fisher—and the subsequent dreams cut the path straight to your community."

"You say this kidnapping happened a long, long time ago?"

"Mariah claimed, 'ten generations.'"

They whisper among themselves. "It's true," Sarototi breaks the silence, "for, at that time, according to our oral history there was indeed a drought—so, no extra food. You were foreign. Had you not cured our elderly, we would have taken your life." With a smile of irony, as he bites into the beef, he replies, "we probably would have cooked and eaten you!"

Again, soundless emptiness falls down around us, for we are stunned with the strength of his declaration, placing this tall tale of mine within their historical setting. I can only respond to the sheer incredulity of their recollections by revealing what I know of the San Bushmen through textbooks of explorers' and anthropologists' documented accounts, and my meager moments with them. The Maasai become fascinated with the notion that tribesmen throughout the continent sought and still seek the Bushmen's healing wisdom as the Maasai had done in the past life of 1787.

Yet, to each of us, though uncanny, Mariah's prophetic words hold water, forming a link of intimacy, creating solidity, and a new directive. Whether they fully grasp reincarnation or not, they choose to consider my course of action, respecting this spiritual quest and commitment to mend the long forgotten. In fact, they identify with part of it, trusting this decision to pursue her proposal.

7: Food of Plenty

"You have come to the right place, Murphy," Baba Budhya begins. "The forest is sacred because a seer, Baba Lengetu, lives below the hills. People come from afar to learn, to gain insight into their lives from him. From these woods we gather the needed barks and herbs, for teas and talismans. The applications of these medicines restore the mind and the body. Due to the ancient saga of the Sacred Forest of the Lost Child, these woods are enchanted." His tale continues from years ago, when their people were plagued with a drought across the land, they fled into the forest for food, water, and protection. One morning, the children, all but one girl, returned from collecting berries. Leaving no stone unturned, everyone searched for her, to no avail.

Baba Budhya's narration haunts me. Just as that little girl, I wonder, *Didn't I lose my way, somewhere between the woods and adulthood? Doesn't their story embody the lost child in every one of us—the loss of our innocence—and if possible, the importance of recovering our raison d'etre, our reason for being?* The Maasai's pursuit of this child is as this eternal search of mine for the misplaced me in one trauma after another, in the move from one Kansas town to another—in hopes of finding that reason for being.

Among the indigenous, the sick are cured through the recitations of their cosmogonic myths, the myths of their origins, which re-weave the cellular structure, the threads of their lives. Just as I have been re-membering mine with the Bushmen in the Kalahari, with the hands-on-healer Celia, with the Freudian analyst Vicki and with the intuitive Mariah in New York City, and now, with the Maasai in Kenya. And even later, as I rewrite this for you, dear reader, word for word, moment by moment, inside the loving embrace of the Akashic's Masters Teachers and Loved Ones the cure is happening.

8

LOSS OF PLACE

"American Indians, like groups of people everywhere, maintain a complex array of symbolic relationships with their physical surrounding [...] invest them with value and significance."

—Keith H. Basso, *Wisdom Sits in Places*

6th of June 1970. On the Road from Paola, Kansas to Osawatomie, my youngest brother and I hover closely in the backseat of our father's green 1965 Ford Galaxie 500. "Can't we stay in Paola?" My brother begs, "I can live with my best friend, Todd!" "Please!" I whine, "Can't I stay at Julie and Jana's, in one of the empty rooms upstairs? Their brothers are off to college." In irritation to our questions, Dad seems furious, banking the dangerous Dead Man's Curve on Highway 7.

Both of us find it hard to stomach, to imagine not being Panthers, Paola High School's mascot, instead, as turncoats. *How could we ever live in the rival red town of the Trojans, Osawatomie High School's mascot?* And so, we hang sus-

8: Loss of Place

pended together, waiting for our father's reply. As was most often the case with Dad, his decisions were non-negotiable—a final "No" shattered us to silence, and me to tears. In his mind, the family becoming part of the community in Osawatomie is essential to the acquisition of a small bank. I wouldn't know for years and years, forty-four to be exact, that *his* "No," his driving determination; this decision was based on love, based on saving us from what had happened in our neighborhood! What we had been told to forget, what I had forgotten and would forget, which would take decades to recover (and will be told more thoroughly in Book Three).

What our father didn't reckon, nor could we, was the impact of being ripped from the land, which had become our sustenance built upon memory and experiences. That, in fact, we were entering into what Edward S. Casey termed, in *Getting Back into Place*, "place-panic." Where the removal from this location would erode the very base of our foundation, our sustenance, causing us to lose our bearings. Not knowing, I had already lost mine. "Deprived of these attachments" Basso elucidates, we "find ourselves adrift, literally dislocated, in unfamiliar surroundings we do not comprehend and care for even less."

What I didn't realize then, is that historically for centuries, the desire for more, for expansion, for religious freedom, hunger of a greater kind, had driven people from their homes. Our ancestors were part of this, forcing the First People from their lands, enslaving others. In 1642, on our father's side, John Lewis, was given a homestead in Virginia from the King of England. On Mother's side, our great grandparents, the Murphy's and the Richie's left Ireland and Scotland for reasons of hunger, as well as opportunity, meeting and marrying in Pennsylvania.

The needs of the Lewis' and the Beeson's large families had brought my great-grandfathers to the Cherokee Strip Run; World War I, had ripped two nineteen-year-olds, my future granddads, from the red earth of Oklahoma and from Beaver Valley, Pennsylvania, returning them to the continent of their forefathers—one of them served in the muddy trenches of France, the other, in the Calvary in the North. WWII had torn the moorings from Dad's craft, setting him adrift on a minesweeper in the Pacific. So, for my father and his father before him, and my mother's father and his father before him, ad infinitum, perhaps this "movement," which displaced others, was absolutely the most ordinary thing on the planet. But for me at twelve, without the compass points of Ushy Gushy Canal, Bull Creek, and Messer's Hollow, without this "world-building,"

Book One – Across the Divide to the Divine **63**

Part I: Across

this built world I had known, I would slowly discover, I felt unhinged for more reasons than one.

In the fall, in this new "home" town, we make new friends and cause disturbances with others. My brother grapples with the Trojan basketball coach, who believes he is a traitor, having been sent by the Panthers to destroy the team. Of hate mail, I receive a fair share.

It won't be until fifteen years after graduation that healing would come to this experience. At a High School reunion, a fellow classmate would confess: "From the moment, you arrived in Osawatomie, my mother incessantly repeated, 'Why can't you be like Renie?'"

"Can you forgive me for those mean letters, for the shunning of you, for the ill-treatment?"

Wow! In all honesty, up until this moment, I had no idea of the conversations between that mother and her daughter, who had created the vicious mail. I only knew of the talks with my mother and her daughter, me. Mother, who—Thank God—taught this weeping-12-year-old-rejected-self, "Love her unconditionally. No matter what, heap coals of loving kindness upon her head."

If Mother hadn't taught me thus, I could never have given my fellow classmate the benefit of the doubt, to have played softball, volleyball, run track, been in honor's class right beside this gal and her slights of me. I would never have been approachable, only defended. I would never have learned the real truth.

In the end, I was so sad her own mother wanted her to be "something other than" whom she truly was within. Bless them both. "Of course, I forgive you." *How could I not?* I knew what it was to be "something other than"—for this is what I had become from my own traumas, as well as from this adventure of moving to another town.

Through this move to Osawatomie, to our "rival" town, I will learn so many lessons about separateness, exclusivity, isolation—both in creating these and in the experience, for I didn't know the ins and outs of their friendships, nor did I have established memories with these students. Though I would become "popular," though I may have appeared as fitting "in," I was never a very good "groupy," for I didn't necessarily belong. In fact, I was an outsider, inwardly alone, secretive. I would establish one very important friendship where I would reveal all. Out of necessity, I would learn to be more of an introvert, establishing an internal practice of journaling, setting me on a course toward independence.

8: Loss of Place

On the hillside, close to our first home, at 1115 Parker Avenue, looking over John Brown Memorial Park, everyday after school, our dog Lassie would envelop me in her love, licking those tears of disappointment, as I dreamt of a different future. Maybe our parents from their deep, deep knowingness had brought us here to integrate us on the soil, where Brown, this radical abolitionist, this radical activist literally fought for what he believed—against slavery. For to find connection, my afro-haired brother and I are furthered into "otherness," he plays b-ball in the hood with the blacks, learning the perfect dribble and I run track, as well as cheerlead with those black soul sisters Alma and Pam—binding us immediately and forever to "the other."

Oddly in a few months time, seven miles from the Paola homeland, our cat, Tigerena, disappears. Our dog, Lassie dies from a shot of buckshot in the butt. Later, without telling us, Dad sells our horse Geronimo. Perhaps even our pets could not endure the deprivation of the loss of land. I didn't know it then, that each of us within our family were mourning this being *without place* what Edward S. Casey reasons are "the emotional symptoms of placelessness—homesickness, disorientation, depression, desolation."

In our move, my brother and I lost our emotionally supportive friends, teachers, and Mom's consistent grounding. For in the midst of this, Mother caught the spark of feminism, taking a job at Dad's bank. Instead, I became her confidante, the cook, the occasional cleaning lady, and sometimes the chief bottle washer, specializing in tuna casserole, lemon cake, and Murphy's fried chicken.

For me, it will take five more decades "to get back into place" as Dr. Casey describes it—but this time, that place would be an internal and external landing, far from Paola, far from John Brown Memorial Park, on land where my grandfathers' fought—France.

9

FIRST: THEY GIVE ME STORIES

⚜ ⚜ ⚜

> *"'Mister, this here country (Africa) is not man's country, it's God's country. So if anything should happen, just sit down and don't worry.' His words struck me as somehow significant [...] not man but God was in command here—in other words, not will and intention, but inscrutable design."*
>
> —C. G. Jung, *Memories Dreams Reflections*

Legends abound about the Maasai being the living remnant of the Ancient Egyptian Civilization, or the Lost Tribe of Israel. Afternoons, Marjana drives me to the village where the Kitomini Community resides, to record these creation tales from the elders. In the Kario Valley, between Ethiopia and Sudan, during a drought, a Weaver Bird appeared, weaving a nest with green grass. An expedition formed to follow the bird. They built a ladder to climb high above the wall

9: First: They Give Me Stories

where the flight of the Weaver led them to flood lands, grasses of plenty. Half the community reached the platform before the stairway broke. The ones on the top became the Maasai of Kenya and Tanzania, "The people of the way through."

One day, they invite me to the circumcision of the granddaughter of the storyteller, Baba Hasa. On our drive, Marjana and I discuss the reason for this brutal rite of initiation, and of the controversy even among the Maasai over this act. "All our teachings and rites of passage for the children is to build three important traits; bravery or courage, perseverance, and patience."

"Really? But why?"

"Murphy, if they cannot pass these tests, they cannot endure the challenges set before them to live in this harsh country."

I cannot agree, nor completely comprehend. What I gather from my studies of West Africa, amongst the Bambara and the Dogan of Mali, every human is born with two souls—one of each sex. To them, the clitoris contains the "male soul" of the woman, so, to perform a clitorodectomy confirms her sexual status, removing an ambivalent organ. The female soul within a man resides in his foreskin; so, as the circumcision is performed this determines the fullness of his manhood. As if these procedures can somehow separate us from our ambivalences, restoring our gender. Compared to the West, it makes gender identification sound so simple.

In my mind, these two acts create, in both, a loss of power. These two procedures seem more of an emasculation, a ripping away the way in which a woman and a man can relate through the fullness of their twin souls. Maybe this is why in Jungian psychology there is this anima, the feminine part of the man's personality, and animus, the masculine part of the woman's personality, which when not acknowledged and integrated can end up as a projection outside of the Self onto the "other." The men I have met who were not circumcised were more connected to my female nature, which was a great relief in our interaction. The women I know who still own their clits are much more balanced and stronger.

Thankfully, we arrive too late to observe the actual clitorodectomy held inside the manyatta, the ceremonial corral. Yet, we are just in time for the festivities held at the engang, a family's circular enclosure of small huts. Everyone is gathered in large groups: women and children are separate from the men, thrusting their necks towards one another, stepping to the same beat and chanting, building to an intensive crescendo. The Warriors' dark bodies are painted with red ochre layered by white squiggly chalk lines. The women are in primary colors

Book One – Across the Divide to the Divine **67**

of clean blues, reds and whites. *And me?* I am overcome with both the beauty and the hypnotic song.

Marjana asks the elder to grant me permission to photograph the celebration. Baba Hasa extends a warm hand asking for a fair fee. So, in Murphy fashion, three things at once: I set up the Dat Player on the hillside to collect their music, station the video camera to capture the rhythmic dancing, then, start snapping stills.

The children, intrigued, observe themselves and others on the film as I rewind the show. In contrast, the Warriors are furious at this intrusion. One painted warrior curses me in Maa. Another slaps the camera out of my hand. I catch it before it hits the earth, explaining in English that I have received consent. I had heard they were haughty, arrogant, reflecting on Blixen's writings of them as "rigid, passive, and insolent."

"The Moran," the warriors, escort me to the elder in charge who is greatly offended, calling the aggressor to his side: "This is my party for my granddaughter. This woman is my guest. If you are not pleased with my decision, it is *you* who must leave, not *her*." Respect for their elders is held high in this community. The warriors concede, dispersing. Yet, they remain, as an ever-protective presence.

That night, I discover myself in a dream, standing with friends at a bar in a New York City restaurant. My pants keep falling down. I lose a shoe.

At the breakfast table the next morning, they inform Sarototi of my confrontation with the painted warrior. He is amused. I disclose the night's humiliation of loss of shoe and pants. He laughingly replies, "Perhaps your dream is how you felt at the circumcision."

"Yes, I was obviously out of place, and certainly the outsider. But maybe there is something to letting go of 'wearing the pants,' so to speak—from being 'disguised' as a man in business, walking around in the world at large simulated as a male, to having an elder navigate the terrain—to being the creative woman I truly want to be."

"Is there a *laibon* in your family, Murphy? You seem to be a bit of a seer, yourself."

Astonished, I mutter, "I remember hearing my great grandmother was a midwife. Of course," increasing the volume with enthusiasm, "there's Mariah's claim, I was a Bushmen healer in that other life. And then, there is a standing joke in my family, we are all frustrated doctors, always looking for the cure, convinced we have the right remedy for the moment."

9: First: They Give Me Stories

This discussion causes Marjana to inform that Sarototi is not the main shaman or medicine man, due to his birth, "but the village believes in him." In Maasailand, the *laibon*, shaman or medicine man is officially recognized if he is a descendant of the male bloodline of the Sentai family. Sarototi's Sentai blood is from his mother's side, keeping him from this "official" title. He is trained in general medicinal capacities, traveling village to village with other unofficial *laibons* caring for those in need. Everyone listens to him. They know he seeks the truth, proving his wisdom over and over. According to Claude Lévi-Straus, "the mythology of the shaman does not correspond to objective reality […] The patient believes in it […] The protecting […] the evil spirits, and supernatural […] magical monsters are elements of a coherent system…" (*Anthropologie Structurals*) which will bring about his/her restoration.

When white men first encountered these practitioners, they referred to them as "witch doctors." However, now I have learned that among the indigenous throughout the world, the desire to strike a harmonious balance between nature and themselves occupies much of their existences. The practice of shamanism grew out of this necessity, and still exists both in its magical sorcery and its therapeutic capacity.

Historically, shamans or medicine men and women live on the borders of the society. They are sought out for their capacity to maintain this precarious equilibrium, and for their ability to restore the lost parts of the individual or the community through the practice of soul retrieval. *In Medicine for the Earth*, Sandra Ingerman also recounts the art of "soul-remembering"—to identify the reason a soul has presently come to the earth, re-establishing their own inner knowingness—*ah, this is what I've been longing for!*

The official laibon executes the Maasai's ceremonies of initiation, rites of practices, sacrifices. In extreme cases, he imposes curses and can ostracize a person from their kinship. He unrolls the skin of a leopard, spreads it on the ground, uttering words of praise and requests to God, to Engai, to their Ancestors into a cow's horn, a calabash or a gourd, an enkidou, full of stones, shaking this from side to side, foretelling the future, enlightening the past.

With a flick of his wrist, he tips the contents of the calabash onto the fur, studying the fallen position of the stones—their "self-organizing patterns" (Ron Eglash). These stones can also be selected and placed on different parts of the body to determine health. When the laibon counts the stones in divination, there are nine potential answers. He arranges them in fives and tens until the last few stones bear the answer to the question. From this insight, he grounds concoctions into powders from the roots and bark of trees for teas or to carry as talismans around the neck, or he throws leaves into boiling water for the patient to inhale while under a shuka, or blanket, and finally to bathe in.

Unlike the "authorized" *laibon*, Sarototi houses his stones in a large plastic dirty water bottle and sits on an old worn-out gunnysack. To me, this makes his ritual more believable. Daily, I find him mumbling quietly into the bottle to his Ancestors, to his God, *Engai*, asking for wisdom of which trail to take or to search for answers for individuals or the village. He shakes, rolls the stones onto the fabric, reading them and sharing what he believes may or may not happen to us as we begin our hike. Oftentimes, bringing us laughter and delight.

One afternoon the Maasai and I gather round the truck's radio for a special report, an email from my youngest brother in Kansas. From Nairobi, George Bright of Peregrinations & Pilgrimages shares his message with us. "Your nephew has won his first football game but has hurt his knee. The doctor says he will be well enough to play on Friday."

All of us are mystified at how peculiar this account sounds. To be far away in Africa in the arms of the Sacred Forest, and yet, to receive news that has traveled across the ocean, all the way from the middle of America as though a stone's throw.

This inspires a dialog between the warriors and me: "How ironic that the boys in America have this sport, which is to build them into winners, captains of industry." I remark, "Many of these games are filled with battering, hazing, humiliation, domination and cruelty. Though some of them are team sports, it often seems to be, every man for himself. These rituals do not seem rooted or spirited enough to reach the souls of our adolescents for the transformation into adulthood. However, in your young adults, I see depth residing."

"Our youth are shepherded and aligned with what naturally matures them," Baba Budhya depicts. "On behalf of the continuity of the tribe, every child is imbued with myths of the strength and courage of their Ancestors and guided into their future leadership roles through ceremony."

As an example, Sarototi shares: At fifteen, he lived in a cave with a group of warriors and ate from a bull and digested herbs, which made them wild with strength, building their confidence, preparing them to track lions. To encourage one another, they sing songs of others of those who had gone before, as they spread out in a long line from the bush to the plain from the brave to the weak

9: First: They Give Me Stories

in hopes to goad a lion. If the lion appears close to a warrior, he knows he is not allowed to stab him, but if the lion chases, ah! That is another thing altogether.

One morning, as a lion rose up out of the riverbed, the circle of warriors closed in. The lead warrior cried out, "It is time for bravery, but not a time to throw spears or clubs." Pressured, the lion charges each man, searching for weakness. When he discovers the weak link, he leaps at the two fearful warriors, knocking down and injuring Sarototi. With intimidating strength, which is hard to imagine, the lion tosses the two warriors over his head into an Umbrella Tree. The lion reels, leaps again, grabbing another warrior, tumbling to the earth with him, and as he does, two other warriors spear him in the back and along the spinal column. The first pierce earns the warrior, the mane, the second stab, earns the youth, a tail. The lion dies with his grasp so tight, so strong around the youngster, in order to recover him, they must peel him from the cat's embrace.

"As intelligent as we fight," Sarototi reveals, "so must we be in the ways of rehabilitation. To have the power to kill, one must also have the power to cure."

Immediately, to free the two warriors, they cut down the Umbrella Tree. Another man slayed a wildebeest and from the hairs of his tail, they sewed Sarototi's wound. In the bush, they gathered leaves, preparing herbal mixtures to pour into these gashes, binding, and stopping the blood. With their red and black *shukas*, they carry the wounded, walking in a long line toward the village. The new leader wore his prize possession, the mane—part of the kill—wrapped around his head. The second warrior held high the tail from the tip of his spear. They sang full out, about the bravery of the men who had led them, of the men lacerated, but, alive. A triumphant moment for the young Morans' initiation, as everyone in the village rose in awe of those who faced the ever-powerful lion.

Affirming the truth of this tall-tale, Sarototi lifts his *shuka* to show me the scar across his thigh from this lion. Just as a wild boar had gored Odysseus, so Sarototi has his initiation, which is believed to be a softening, feminine rite, through the loss of blood. For many generations (though, now, hugely controversial due to endangered lions), this rite has mysteriously efficiently resolved the angst of teenagers, creating a sense of brotherhood into the act of making men. Indeed, Sarototi stands now as a Junior Elder, participating in many of the tribal discussions along with the Senior Elders.

"Since my initiation fifteen years ago," Sarototi intimates as his brother translates, "we live in a new world where law forbids Maasai boys to hunt lions in preparation for manhood. Nor do we raid other people's cattle or steal their wives as we once did." He confesses wholeheartedly, "Yes, I must admit, our brutality—which kept us safe from slave traders—proceeds us. We have been forced to change. Among the young men, there is now a mass-exodus to the cities. As well, the church is slowly penetrating the walls of our beliefs, discouraging divination, discouraging the use of herbs."

On the last morning, Sarototi, Saifi, and Lughano escort me to a different waterhole, the place, I am informed, where Sarototi and Saifi's father slayed a leopard. These warriors are fierce enough to face and provoke those who prey on the lives of others—the leopard and the lion, the guardians of the underworld. The Maasai are slayers of such shadows. I do not yet know they will use this knowledge, eventually slaying mine.

As we stand on the ground of bravery, three geese fly around and over our heads, until finally they find their bearings to land. As they do, Sarototi and I catch each other's eye, smiling.

Ted Andrews claims the number three represents magic, and as well, geese, call us into those magical, mystical childhood fairy tales. Instead, in our Western Society feats of acquiring a large home, an expensive car, the maintenance of beautiful bodies with vitamins, exercise and surgery, are the measurements for our success. In Laloshwa, everything seems full of enchantment. Everything has meaning. I cannot imagine having a heritage like theirs, where bravery before a leopard, a lion, the flight of a goose, the pursuit of the ants' message are revered with sacred respect.

In these last few moments in the Natada Enkidu Forest, Motoguisimilie, Sarototi, and I measure what is most meaningful and ceremonial. From the influence of reading *Animal-Speak*, and the recollection of Messer's Hollow, we decide to display courtesy to nature, to the sentient ones through Native and Maasai reciprocity. "The truth is, we have never been out of touch. We are always connected to the Earth and it to us. Everything we do repercusses upon it, and everything within it repercusses to us" (Andrews).

To enact this connection, we climb to the high point overlooking the camp, where with laughter we dig a small hole to bury the souvenirs of this stay found along the paths of our daily walks: feathers of a goose and a midnight blue Turacao, a swath of my red hair, a black-eyed Susan, a yellow Candlebush flower, a dead Lady Bug and a green spider. From Roberta's Native satchel, I draw out the sage stick to light. With an Eagle feather in hand, we each fan ourselves with the cleansing smoke, and the world at large. A stillness, a balance wash over us.

9: First: They Give Me Stories

For the last good-byes, Marjana drives me to the village to meet the seer, the "official" *laibon*, Baba Lengetu, whom everyone has mentioned. Unlike Sarototi, he has all the famous paraphernalia of a proper shaman—not to mention his face is painted with streaks of white making him fierce, daunting. Before, when the elders demanded payment for their expertise, I pleaded, "I don't have enough money with me. So, it will take time, for I must send it via a wire transfer from the United States through George Bright." But after meeting Baba Lengetu with his spot-on knowledge about a personal matter and his piercing look into my eyes—holy cow—I extract cash at the first bank machine we come upon, sending this back via messenger!

As I depart, Sarototi offers me the golden prize: He walks me through his family entrance, *kishomi*, into the *engang*, the extended family corral to his dung hut, *enkaji*, the family home. He introduces me to his beautiful wife, Kisima, and his new baby boy, Lesainana. Within Maasai tradition, the first three months of a new baby's life are precious. For protection from "the evil eye," the child is hidden in seclusion, a threshold where only close family members are allowed.

Then, I begin to weep and weep about this, for I have crossed the sacred family portal. I am struck with the realization: he, they, have enough trust to share this hallowed life's moment with me, particularly at a time when this young Maasai is most vulnerable. Thankful for this, I shake my new friend's hand, saying *ashe*. He smiles, "*olesari*."

"Farewell, to you, too!" Smiling, I glance back, absorbing Sarototi's faith in me. Not knowing, that someday, twenty-five years later, this precious child, Lesainana, will be our correspondent, our gracious link, bridging the gap of our distance of language.

In the divination, Baba Lengetu had declared, "You will have a safe trip. Yet, you will not find gas at your first stop." By Jove, he was right! After a few wild hours of driving on fumes, we barely teeter into the second gas station ninety-five kilometers later—nothing short of a miracle.

In Nairobi, the last few hours are spent playing tourist with Marjana. We drive to Karen Blixen's romantic home, now, a museum. Finally comprehending her love of Kenya, completely, I touch down, ground, remembering her words, "Here is where I ought to be."

10

A LIFE FOR WHAT?

"Mimi ni, kwa sababu sisi ni; na tangu sisi ni, kwa hiyo mimi ni."
"I am, because we are; and since we are, therefore I am."

—John Mbiti, Kenyan Theologian

The African philosophy known as Ubuntu/botho, is so different than René Descartes, "*Cogita Ergo Sum*," "I think, therefore, I am." Hindsight, they say is always clear, although within my thinking brain I cannot be sure the days with the Maasai are even comprehensible. On the flight to JFK, as I observe the people surrounding me, a light switches on. "I am" changing from this encounter, to this philosophical "we are." For I now believe, the Maasai, and even these people on the plane, are this planetary tribe of mine. Mbiti pens, "What happens to the individual happens to the whole group, and whatever happens to the whole group, community or country happens to the individual. People, country, environment and spirituality are intricately related." In other words, we're on this journey through life together— "since we are, therefore I am!"

10: A Life for What?

Dressing for work in my NYC home, the first morning, I reach for the black Halston cashmere shrug. It's not here! Oh! No! For the fall season, I need to look just so for the first day back. Oh! No! I left it on the back of my chair in my tent. Fax Marjana.

"By now, Murphy," Marjana scrawls, "it's impossible to track. Somewhere in Laloshwa, your sweater is warmly on the back of a Maasai herder as he shepherds his cattle into the forest!"

I laugh, thinking: Sophisticated couture clothing on the runways of the warrior's landscape while I serve duty in Western activity on Seventh Avenue, pressed into the pressure of ever-increasing the sales figure of five million more for the coming year. And suddenly, the twelve-hour days are filled with just *that*.

In the evenings, when I worked for Mary McFadden, my girlfriend Brigitte and I had ridden bicycles twice around Central Park, for a 12-mile distance. Eventually, when I travel across Seventh Avenue to Badgley Mischka and move to Tribeca, in the dark, alone, along the Hudson River, I will continue biking for sanity. I eat quickly, then work until midnight, on *Africa Within* (the former title of this memoir), which I coined from van der Post's discussions in *The Dark Eye in Africa*: "You have an America, we an *Africa within* us [...] Not until we have travelled and known those great continents within [...] and know them without, shall we be ready for our next great physical adventure which I truly believe will be to the stars." Later, I will take his advice, crossing America to meet those we have wounded. But now, with the constant pull toward the corporate world of finance, I keep trying to have an inner focus of something greater than myself—that *Africa Within*.

However, in this new role of boss, there are other demands upon me. I usually wake up at three in the morning to write down those dreams of mine, scribble notes of "to do's" on a pad next to the bed, leaving voicemails for my staff on their office message machines, sleep a few more hours, then, rush off to early morning meetings. I don't depart the office until 8 or 8:30 p.m. On the way home, in the Town car Badgley Mischka provides, I'll catch up with my parents on the cellphone. If I'm not on the road for business, I do the same thing the next day over and over, a caged hamster on a Ferris wheel. Circular. Samsara. Even with my best friends, Jeffrey, Richard, and Gail—I'm too busy to see them more than once a month—*a life for what?*

Yet even though I'm hamster-like, circling, repeating, perhaps I am slowly rebuilding a life. *World-building? Wouldn't it be wonderful, if it was for something worthy, a cornerstone van der Post spoke of in The Dark Eye in Africa: "a warless nonracial world [...] (where) those races and those aspects of life which we have despised and rejected for so long"—exist, are embraced, and brought into equality?*

Before I fell in love with the Kalahari Bushmen through the writings of Sir Laurens van der Post, I had little funds to float; in fact, I was quite grounded in Manhattan. Even if I wanted to go on a vacation, it meant Mom and Dad flew me home to Kansas for the one week I had available. Five years before I became flush, before becoming a Vice President, just when I committed myself to share the Bushmen's tales with children, while attempting to write my way out of fashion, Keeble Cavaco & Duca (KC&D), a hot young public relations firm, somehow "chanced," and I would say, "synchronistically" came upon my name, through a friend of a friend of a friend, asking me to calligraph invitations for the Runway Shows of major American Fashion Designers.

In other words, for each African safari, I'm now miraculously funded, through this freelance job, because this "gig" of calligraphy gives me an additional $10,000 a year—thank God I studied this fancy writing at the University. As well as the mileage, I earn from the flights throughout the country for Trunk Shows at Neiman Marcus, Saks Fifth Avenue, and Nordstroms, setting me free on the runway with South African Airways, and the beginnings of the pursuit of who I wanted to be. Kismet!

The envelopes, along with a pen to match the Fashion Designers' theme for each runway show, are rushed to me at each job, each move upward: Mary McFadden to Halston to Badgley Mischka. A dash home from the office, a bite to eat, and then, I settle in, perfectly postured at an art desk to calligraph into the wee hours of the morning. In Zen-like pleasure, listening to Alberta Hunter's "My Handyman, he threads my needle, creams my wheat," or "The Chronicles of Narnia" on tape, I calligraph address after address of the Who's Who of Fashion, who will grace the front rows: the movie stars of the moment, Marisa Tomei, Sarah Jessica Parker; the socialite "it" girls, the Miller sisters; the likes of the popular press, Anna Wintour, Suzy Menkes, Andre Leon Talley, Bill Cunningham—just to catch a glimpse of the super models: Naomi Campbell, Linda Evangelista, and Christy Turlington as they don the latest in style.

As KC&D's calligrapher, they include me on the list of attendees. From our office on Seventh Avenue, I quickly run over to the tents in Bryant Park to gaze upon the phenomena. In a downtown loft, the finale of the Isaac Mizrahi show, Naomi slinks down the catwalk, dressed in leather cowboy chaps. When she turns, her gorgeous butt is naked, except for a butterfly tattoo. And I, along with the rest of the audience, am orgasmic with, "Ahhh." Amazing that this fancy writing on envelopes creates a priceless entrée into the world I am *really* meant to inhabit—Africa. *Who woulda thunk?*

Occasionally, for a meal after work, I attempt connection, meeting my elder-sister-friends, Jane, Connie, and Ruth. Normally, I have avoided women—for I couldn't be a part of the suffering of other women's lives. I couldn't endure what I considered to be weakness, couldn't get too close. *Was it for fear what little resolve I had might crumble?* In my fashion career, I worked mainly for and with men, whom I tended to respect more (except for the brief and exceptional moments with Joan Arkin at Leonard of Paris, and Dede Shipman and Mary at Mary McFadden).

Throughout my time in NYC, these three women, Jane, Connie and Ruth, I trusted, I needed these meals full of conversation. They grounded me, believed in me, affirmed me. Then, ever so lonely, I'd walk up Madison Avenue, and later, (when I moved south) through Soho, peering into store windows for inspiration, for ideas.

Concerned about this aloneness, my friends Gail and Paul set me up on a double date. While I'm in the bathroom, the date asks them, "How does she live?" "For fashion, she travels six months internationally, and for her holidays, for stories, she ventures to Africa." Without trying, without exploring a potential relationship, this man writes me off. Without even asking if I plan to stay in Fashion, he runs out before ever walking in. I conclude, perhaps men don't want women who aren't around and available to them on a daily basis, who are living a kind of Up in the Air life as George Clooney's character, Ryan Bingham. Every forty-eight hours, in another city, in a high-end boutiques, I had to be perfectly coiffed, organized, making presentations to the sales staff, in dressing rooms with rich clients, wined and dined by managers or store owners. When I returned to NYC, I'd hide in my apartment for forty-eight hours, recovering. On Monday morning, I'd be back in the office for two more weeks before hitting the road again. And then they added the responsibility of Europe, which had all the appearance of glamorous. Yet, it wasn't. Yes, if I was perfectly honest, there was no room for a man.

But maybe there was something more—*Were "normal" men avoiding me due to the scent of the past? Or was I avoiding them?*

Just before the return to Kenya, I have an important session with the hands-on-healer Celia. Over the last several weeks, she has questioned me about the events of my birth. "Seems there is some trauma around the beginning of your life that is affecting you with claustrophobia and possibly how you relate to men."

Turning to Mother for insight, I query, "What was my birth like?"

"Everything went fine, Murphy, no difficulties. When I was pregnant with you and your brothers, I was so happy. I went walking every day, took good care of myself, looking forward to each of your arrivals."

"Are you sure about mine?"

"Yes."

The next day, Mother mentions something briefly: "Oh, I forgot to tell you that you tried to come out of the womb with your nose up."

"Did I?" So, surprised, as she'd never mentioned this before.

"No. Not at first. No. In fact, in the middle of the birth, the young doctor panicked, believing your nose would break my pelvis. Therefore, I panicked too, thinking the cord was wrapped around your neck. And then he numbed me with an epidural. Later the doctor made plain how he tried to flip you over several times to stop your 'incorrect' movement. Eventually, you came out nose up, despite the doctor's intentions of thwarting you, for you were always bound and determined."

Yes, out there, somewhere between lives, I'd been floating in safety in the womb of the Universal, *Padmasavana* space, then, in there, safely in the womb of my mother, until this rather rude awakening!

After I explain this to Celia, she helps me to understand, "Often when there is a trauma around the birth, the mother will emotionally separate herself from the child."

"When I grow quiet," I tell her, "I sense this tremendous separation. For we have had, my mother and I, for many years, a low-riding conflict, an unspoken breach—no matter how many times we attempted to converse or weep in one another's arms—we could not seem to really mend."

"Let's take a deep breath, Murphy, and slowly, enter into that moment in the womb."

10: A Life for What?

Delving into these explorations with her is often strange. Usually, when I grow calm, a song tumbles out, leading us. This time is different. The memory springs forth: the feeling of warmth, happiness, security, and then, the reverse experience—in a dark passage, cut off from the rhythm, the pulsing, alive, reassurance of Mom—and suddenly, that aloneness! Everything frighteningly stops. I start to suffocate. Everything goes foggy. Then, the doctor grabs, yanks, turning my nose to face the side. Yet, the right leg is wedged in such a way I cannot comply and flip face up. Each time, he re-positions me; I right myself up again and again until I come out of the passage, nose upright.

From the bottommost point, I sob hysterically. Holding my hand, Celia quietly reassures me, instructing me to call all the cells of the body to move toward the pain, asking each cell to return to their original and natural state, when I loved being inside Mom.

For an imaginary rebirth, Celia suggests I choose a new doctor to deliver me. I choose Sarototi. He won't be afraid or shocked if my nose is up. Instead, *he* will welcome me; welcome me in my full strength. Slowly, I redirect my cells for a smooth entry from Mother's womb onto this planet. As if in Fairyland, outdoors, under a tree, "Little Irene" lands in Sarototi's arms. He delicately hands me to Mom, who embraces me with a kiss. The animals and birds gather round to greet this new creature. On this etheric plane, Mother and I are magically re-connected, no longer repulsed from painful memories.

A few days later, ironically, as though being reborn has prepared me, I move into the new home in Tribeca, a novel location, a wide berth, a safe dung hut—of my own. Under the Maasai's influence, "he who walks in dung has life," I drape the darkened pine wooden floors with Charolaise Cattle rugs—since I dare not spread manure.

One month later, I board a plane bound for Kenya..

First Initiation

Second Journey In

||

FLIGHTS UNKNOWN

> *"Kealakwa nkai etaena."*
> *"God is far away and close by, too!"*
>
> —Lmakiya Lesarge, *Proverbs of the Samburu*

Before my *first journey in*to Laloshwa, I'd written in my journal about an anxiety. I, who have traveled so often solo, had been more terrorized by the thought of the aloneness, the possible emptiness in the presence of the dark Sacred Forest of the Lost Child, than for the encounter of wild animals. Perhaps the fear had been a reminder of the quiet childhood in Messer's Woods—before all went awry. Strangely, there, in Laloshwa, I had immediately permitted, accepted, and even re-acquired the calmness I had known as a child.

11: Flights Unknown

In contrast, and perhaps due to the loneliness of the NYC life, I want to be with and be embraced by people who completely accept me, have no fears, are neither shocked nor afraid of my nightmares from the past, nor hold judgment, nor carry shame within their beings, with an awareness on a far grander scale. Not the fifty-minute reprieve conferred through a visit with the psychoanalyst, only to re-armor the self stepping into the subway, swept back into the chaos of the everyday life of the metropolis. Instead, I find myself breathing into relief, for in a day, those who finally hear, know, and understand, will surround me.

Before returning to Laloshwa Highlands, I once more overnight at the Samburu Intrepids Lodge to touch base with the Samburu Lmakiya. On this occasion he chooses to introduce me to his family, near *"O'loolokwe,"* the flat top mountain. While driving, of course, he shares more Samburu tales with me, always piquing my interest.

Upon arrival, his older brother, *lalashe*, greets me "Hello, it's great to see you again. I've not seen you for a long time." *Did he remember me from 1787?* How bizarre and wonderful to be "culturally" acknowledged in this way. I also meet Lmakiya's older sisters, nkanashe, and their daughters (his nieces, *nkapiyio*). Of them, I snap photographs, for they are elegantly beautiful. Later, the eldest will become the poster-woman for the 2009 newsletter and website of Global Voice Foundation, a 501c3, I will launch in 2002 to honor and benefit the Bush-men-and-women and the Maasai.

Driving back, Lmakiya informs me that during his holidays when he is free, he has continued to travel amongst his people, particularly educating the youth in conservation and documenting the wisdom of the elders. Because he believes his people have but fifty years left of their traditions (if that), he is possessed with an urgency to transcribe and disseminate these tales. Later, through George Bright of P&P, I will send cassette tapes and a new tape recorder to Lmakiya to assist and encourage his endeavors, until they will be eventually embodied in his book, *Proverbs of the Samburu*.

Immediately after this visit, I am swept off by plane to Wilson Airport, then by Land Rover to Lake Navasha and Laloshwa Highlands through the Chief's son, Marjana.

To this Maasai family I've seemingly stumbled upon, in this *second journey in*, I am drawn more than ever, to re-align, to awaken to the taste of hot, fresh goat's milk, kole, with leaves of tea and lots of sugar poured in, to hear their rhythmic chanting, their ancient stories at the fire. To catch a glimpse of the red colors of the Maasai, scattered across the plains as they lead their herds of goats, cows. To come upon a leopard at the kill, the giraffes loping over the land, to track a lion's spoor. In the evening, I want to hear the mourning dove coo, to watch the sunset while perched upon the Laloshwa Highlands.

"Yes, Murphy," Sarototi acknowledges upon my arrival, "I'm not surprised. I knew you would return right away. I rolled the stones, and what I saw is that this time you would fly on a white bird with blue wings. The others wouldn't believe me."

Marjana laughs at Sarototi, "I told him how far away you live, how intense your work is, how travel is expensive. He would not listen. Sarototi kept declaring, 'It is true! She will come soon!' And here it is, three months later, and you've come back to us."

"What airline did you fly?" inquires Sarototi.

"Last time I flew South African Airways. This time, through Paris, on Air France."

The baffled Marjana exclaims, "Isn't Air France that white bird with blue wings?" Except for Sarototi, the other Warriors are astonished.

"It's all about birds for you, Murphy," Marjana recalls, "Yesterday, remember before our drive to Laloshwa, we stopped at Crescent Island Game Park? There, we had two African Fish Eagles circling round about us."

"Yes, they lifted their beaks, threw their heads back, making a 'wheeee-ah-kleeuw-kleeuw-kluuu' at us. They even gifted us their feathers! See?" I pull out their offerings from my journal.

"Yes, today, you even encountered the Monkey-Eating Crowned Eagle."

On a log across from me, Sarototi squats, seeming to sense the bizarreness of it, too. *How can this white woman from another land be so connected to him, to his people, to their way of being?* His divination, affirming my arrival on a different airline, a white bird with blue wings, and now, these symbolic gestures of birds!

Staring into the fire, I listen to the familiar sounds of the forest: the gentleness of the Katunga River as it skips over the rocks; wind transiting through the trees; bats whirl and whip; the pearl-spotted owlet's 'oo-oo' and the echoing, chattering 'quock quock quocking' of the Colobus Monkeys filling the night with fullness, as round and about me, the Junior and Senior Elders speak softly amongst themselves of these miraculous oracles.

"Do you know why you are here?" Sarototi investigates. "Why you have come back?"

11: Flights Unknown

"I explained it before—for stories, and more truly, because of that strange urging of Mariah's." What I'm not revealing is, after a brief one-month courtship with Peter, Managing Director of our condominium association, I have fled him, arriving sober, broken-hearted. *Why do I bring in men who do not stay? Or do, and I don't want them to? The pain of this on-going pattern gnaws, grips. Is this why I travel to a foreign land in search of a mediator for the divisive energies, which often plague me?*

"Yes, of course, for stories. And yet, our dear friend," Baba Budhya nudges, "this time it has become apparent through nature's affirmations, you have returned for something *greater* than stories—to heal that past life."

Squirming uncomfortably, "Have I?" As if they read between the lines of my sparkly smile. Obviously, the armor I clutter around in is louder than I might have wished, unlike those little Badgley Mischka dresses cut smoothly on the bias that glide from showroom to party. *How do they always seem to "get" me? Grasp the vastness and complexities of my soul?*

"Murphy," Marjana turns toward me explaining Baba Budhya's meaning, "many believe Laloshwa Highlands is the last bastion of the *laibonok*, the Maasai ritual experts that hold the deep-rooted cultural secrets. Here, we do not heal someone unless an eagle has hovered over his or her head at the point of illness," affirming the poignancy of the moment. Though our drive to Laloshwa was bumpy and long, we'd had no incidents, except oddly, flights of eagles, the Tawny, the Bateleur—hovering over our heads, flying across our path—continuously!

"Really? All their flights around us had meaning?" And I cannot help but think of Ted Andrews' *Animal-Speak*. *Is this another way of the eagle speaking to us?* After this comment, I grow silent. A fervent brooding voicelessness simmers as I recollect the constant tug of war formed between the natural affinity toward creativity and the opposite way Dad steered me. Also, I feared that any love relationship I choose might bind me in the same way and I might never get back to that creative me. So, the fleeing from Peter. (Again, I avoid this bit of detail with them.) Instead, I describe the rebirth experience with Celia in November.

As though he knows I avoid an important subject, Lughano draws a quirky smile: "We know about rebirthing, Murphy. It's a common practice of ours. Sometimes it's a necessity, as you have discovered, as when a child has a traumatic birth such as yours, we take them back through that experience, ushering in a new beginning."

"What do you want us to do for you while you are here?" Sarototi picks my brain. "Do you want a child? A husband?"—A normal assumption for a struggling single woman.

"Ultimately, yes, yet something is holding me back, tugging me away from that innate knowingness, from my desires and wishes, preventing me from forming a family, for fear, if I do, I won't live out my true calling."

"This is why you have come!" From across the crackling flames, the *laibon*, Sarototi, rises, pointing, shouting at me, "Someone has stolen the flow from your life, and we can give it back to you!"

As Marjana interprets, these words ricochet off the stars, off the trees of the Sacred Forest of the Lost Child, from dimensions of time, through consciousnesses penetrating through the walls of my porous skin into the very cells themselves— "…and we can give it back to you…give it back to you…back to you…to you…you." Without me revealing much of anything, someone has heard, listened, grasped—is willing to hold my story with all of its complications.

For sure, Sarototi is correct: I'm out of step with the very heart of nature to the point that even the Eagles and the Maasai are winging "arrows" of truth through my very being, stories of transformation that Benson Lewis, a Cibecue Apache had spoken of with Keith Basso, *Wisdom Sits in Places*. Even the ancient Greek philosopher, Heraclitus, believed the most basic characteristic of the natural forces is that *everything flows*. And here, in this precious *Wrinkle in Time*, in Laloshwa Highlands, where I've been tessaracted into another dimension, what Sarototi calls forth vibrates on each level of my being: physically, mentally, emotionally, and spiritually. Yes, I can feel it in my bones.

Harkening me back to those precarious exposures where I struggled in the waters of this planet: in Mother's womb, and later, at three-years-old when I jumped off the diving board into the deep end of the swimming pool and just as I come up for air, the 225-pound-center of the Paola Panther State Championship football team lands on top of me, forcing me into the depths. I rise to the surface, choking, crying, and run to the telephone— "Mummy, can you come pick me up?" And lastly, while delightfully white water rafting with the Family Bausch on the Zambezi River, on a number seven rapid, our craft up-ends spilling everyone on top of me, pressing me breathless ever vaster into its dark bottomlessness. Afterwards, they find my life-jacketed-self floating, hauling me into the boat, where I lie face down, half-dead. The perfect metaphoric examples to the overwhelming condition I'm really in—I'm without flow. Tossed out of

11: Flights Unknown

the boat, like Jonah, spit out of the whale. Even the waters of Mother Earth—from the amniotic fluids, the pools, to the rivers—spew forth, attesting to this veracity.

Assuredly, Sarototi sets the wheels in motion, commanding the youngest man, Motoguisimile, to wander off into the woods for special herbs. Saifi throws more logs on the fire. The water rises to a solid boil in the old cast iron cauldron. The others sit round about me in silence.

When Motoguisimile returns with medicine in hand, he throws a branch of leaves into the boiling water, then, offering the rest to Sarototi, who wraps a small bundle in a section of a plastic bag. "Place this talisman into the left hand, Murphy. Spin it over your head counterclockwise five times. Touch your heart. Brush the herb away from you, returning the herb to your breast, repeating three times 'out with the bad, in with the good,' continuing this process throughout your stay." He persists, "On your left hand, lay this other herb, licking four times with your tongue. With what is left, rub the right middle finger in the herb, brushing it on the forehead, the side of the ears, and the back of the neck. Then, drink this tea before falling asleep."

How peculiar, that even before the intuitive's mandate, the astrologer Leor Warner, announced years ago: "An African tribe will initiate you, Murphy, leading you through their ceremonies and rituals." Though I'd been consulting him off and on for ten years, I did not believe Leor, nor did I remotely grasp what he had even meant. In fact, it sounded outlandish. If anything, I imagined the initiatory experience to be through the Bushmen. Instead, unbeknownst to me, the metaphysical world of restoration has blown wide-open through the nomadic, cattle-herding warriors, the Maasai.

Following Sarototi and his brother, Saifi, to my tent, where they instruct: "When we leave, undress, draping the *shuka*, the red and black Maasai blanket, over your head. From this bucket of herbs, inhale until the lungs exude warmth. Then, bathe your entire body from head to toe with this liquid. Do not rinse it off. Afterwards, you may apply lotion."

When they leave, I follow their instructions to the letter. Shivering under the blanket, I sit nude, sucking in the boiled herbal moisture with the lingering scent, of what I think is, eucalyptus. The aroma opens the chest wide, releasing me from the crushed, caved in ribs, from years of rolling my shoulders forward in shame. Stepping into the shower, I pour this liquid of love, of leaves, and of branches over hair, body, soaking in them. While bathing, I catch a glimpse of

Book One – Across the Divide to the Divine

the fingernail moon, the waxing crescent shining down on me with "...favorable aspects under which the enterprise is launched" (H. G. Baynes).

In 1925, while on the slopes of Mount Elgon, the psychoanalysts C. G. Jung and H. G. 'Peter' Baynes, writes Blake Burleson, observed how the Elgonyi would kneel, discharging spittle on their palms, unfurling their hands to the rising sun, declaring "Athista," meaning, Lord (*Jung in Africa*). "In this primitive religious act God is not the physical object, sun, or moon but rather the experience of emergence, or the moment of rising..." (Baynes). Yes, in this enterprise, something in me emerges. As if from God, the eagle's keen eyesight has illuminated what is true. In Christian mysticism, Andrews explains, this bird symbolized resurrection. *Am I being reborn from the waters of the earth into a fresh way of seeing?*

In actuality, I do not know that taking Sarototi's medicine will propel me into an otherworldly state, that the Maasai are, in fact, gently microdosing me. Though I've explored other cultures, it's not my nature to explore drugs, for I've never wanted to be controlled by anything. Each time I smoked marijuana—once in high school, once at the university—I suffered from a tremendous sore throat, deciding it wasn't worth it. And one of those times, while supposedly driving responsibly three other friends to their home from Peter Frampton's concert, I remember an awakening. Though I was the driver, recognizing that I had driven up to this point (half-way-home), unable to recall how I had miraculously arrived thus far. So shocked, and certainly from this incident—too chicken—I've never attempted any other mind-altering substance. I have never pursued this genre of experience.

Never did I go with my friend Lori to Peru for initiation in Ayahuasca or with Diane to meet the Huichol for an induction with Peyote. The drug era of hallucinogens is not mine, nor is the experimentation with LSD in the 1960's of Timothy Leary and Richard Alpert's (Ram Dass). I don't self-medicate with sleeping pills. I never took uppers, downers, or Prozac, nor did I ever try cocaine (though in the 80's, it and Extasy rampantly were devoured around me). I've more or less been on the "natch," so to speak. And honestly, I have difficulties being out of control, fear drinking too much, or even letting go into the full pleasures of an orgasm. Here, though, thick in this baptism by water, by fire without fear or trepidation—the herbs have claimed me, and whether I like it or not, the forest will have its way with me.

11: Flights Unknown

Dry myself. Draw in under the blanket. Overhead, I spin the little package of remedy five times. At the heart, release "the bad," conducting in "the good." Lick this essence of life, drink the tea, and pass out into a sweat.

In faith, I ingest these medicinals. Not knowing I've stepped inside an *orupul*, a magical Maasai healing retreat. Not knowing that for three days I'll care little for food, I'll care little for conversation. Though held in their keeping, not knowing this to be part of a silent and profound, yet solo ceremonial passage, to be the pivotal point, the demarcation of this incarnation—where all the past of being victim "to something," to someone, will slide away bit by bit.

12

JEWEL IN MY STIGMATA

† † †

"Physical symptoms [...] are like jewels in the body awaiting discovery [...] create the impetus for the patient to do the inner work, [...] carry the nucleus for the cure."

—Rose-Emily Rothenberg, *The Jewel in the Wound*

It is said, inside the gloves, in the open palms of the priests of old, lay the stigmata.

Inside this private tent, sleep, perspire, toss, turn as if seized with an epileptic fit. Heat roars up and out of the body. The hallucinogenic images stream through. Wake up sweating. Exhausted as if I have been running the whole night through. Look at the time, midnight. Have only been asleep for two hours. Roll over to write in the journal about the eternal figures of those childhood nightmares and their reappearance: At the side of the twin bed, the man in the black raincoat, black hat—*what did he do to cause a wide-opened bloodcurdling, yet silent scream?* And the other, on a dark rainy night, in terror for my life, seated

12: Jewel in My Stigmata

on a black stallion, without reins, without control, grasping onto his mane, as I am swept along an unknown path, galloping through the woods. Yes, there were nights upon nights I was pulled back into these nightmares.

Outside, as I tinkle, the fingernail moon still magically hangs in the sky as if saying, "Trust this form of initiation." I can see the white of fur, the flash of eyes of several Colobus monkeys reassuringly tangling in the trees above. An owl sends a message of "ooo ooo," calming me. Worlds away from the world I know of the Kansas woods, of the jungle of New York City, of friends, of family, I think, they won't believe this. *Will they lash out with those hurtful words?* "You're crazy!"

Fall back asleep, only to be stimulated at 2 a.m. to pen a paragraph or two. Apparitions, possible childhood happenings—from the very beginning of those existences flash through the memory system—*did some stranger crawl in bed with me?* Pass out again.

At six, the alarm quickens me, yet I feel a little dizzy, foggy, in fact, I creep back into bed. Moments later, as if sitting vigil, Saifi and Sarototi return to the tent with another bucket of hot water filled to the brim with herbs. They, too, must realize the exterior game plan has changed. Without words, I know, they know, there will be no hike today, no collection of stories. As of now, this crack I have fallen through to the other side of the earth is all about soul.

At the same time this phenomenon is happening to me, many North Americans are slipping down South to their southern brothers and sisters to experiment with Ayahuasca and Peyote, as they once experimented with LSD at the universities, and these experimentations are a forerunner to a concept, which will pick up speed. Miraculously, in twenty years time, within our culture, there will be forms of these "Consciousness Medicines"—M.D.M.A., mushrooms, Entheogens—therapeutically applied through guides to those friends, as well as war veterans, victims, who struggle with Complex Post Traumatic Stress Disorder through constant chronic trauma.

Soon, through the film, *Fantastic Fungi*, we will grow to comprehend "Gateway species," those supernatural, yet real Earth born powers, which lie beneath our feet. According to Paul Stamets, they are linked together, mapping the entire planet in a complete and complex web of "biological communities," having the capacity to heal and rewire us one microdose at a time. Recently, a confidante of mine, Terry Allard disclosed, "Mushrooms show you the corners of your soul, the dark rooms, the dark side of yourself. Quite revealing, they bust you. It's

Book One – Across the Divide to the Divine **89**

humbling, actually." Monthly, we confidently speak of similar traumas on the telephone from Paris, while she drives south from Santa Maria to Santa Barbara to give colonics to her private clients.

Looking back, I see Terry is right. The herbs were scouring the unknown corridors of my innards because the Maasai live their lives within the entirety of this web of fungi, in an "all oneness," held inside this mystical kingdom of the Sacred Forest. Even so, I am not aware of the tremendous re-wiring, re-webbing and re-integration taking place within, as sleepily, I strip down, throw the *shuka* over my head, inhale deeply, only to bathe once again.

Proceeding to fall effortlessly back to sleep, until stirred four hours later only to scribble scads and scads of words, thoughts, and on the pattern goes. The effects of Sarototi's herbs are as hives bursting forth from the skin. In this case the eruption is of the past, of being windswept from a divorce as though being driven off a cliff—soaring into oblivion. To be without a rudder. To be let down into the swirling deep. For that, I had originally penned a few lines:

> white rage
> the water was calm
> and then, wild and white.
> i felt your nudge
> and fell from the safety of our raft, into
> the raging waters.
> i wrapped my arms around my head, my only control
> and on i went, forced,
> slammed to and fro
> between rocks and the walls of the river.
> i knew then that i had lost you
> you could not save me now.
> i longed for tranquility, another kind of life
> but the white rage continued, having her way with me.

Just as the rocks and walls of the river, the Maasai's Sacred Forest is "having its way with me" as I find myself once again surrendering into these white waters. I don't know that that trust will become a part of my whole life just from these inhalations, these elixirs.

12: Jewel in My Stigmata

Through each and every moment, the Maasai medicaments loop me in and out of images of that ex, of the married man Renzo, floating by. Off and on over the course of eight years, I had tried to peel myself away from Renzo and what little he had to offer. But leaving had been far too treacherous because my own internal resources did not support me yet. Where Renzo didn't give, I was given the darkest night of the soul, introducing me to the Sumerian myth and that necessary Inanna-ian descent into the Underworld to restore relations with my dark-sister-self Ereshkigal. Through this *Descent of the Goddess*, "The inner connection is an initiation essential for most," Sylvia Brinton Perera elaborates, "without it we are not made whole." Here, once more, amidst the Maasai I make an earthbound plunge into this darkness.

Finally, late morning, I stumble out of bed to join the warriors who are quietly assembled around the fire. I barely drink a bit of broth. I cannot speak. Avoid telling them about these dreams for though I can write in the journal, I have yet to find the words to express the momentousness of this moment. All I want is silence. Though they are serene, I cannot endure any interaction, the brightness of the sun, even the movement about me. My being registers fatigue, the desire to nap. No one thinks this, peculiar. Instead, they set a blanket under the shadows of the trees where I sleep deliriously. Twist. Lie awake. Turn into an intense reverie, I drift, stepping back in time to childhood, other lives, ancestral stories remembered, heard, stored within the banks, the reservoirs of DNA.

"You're crazy!" The twelve-year-old students tease me: "You're weird!" "For that, your parents are moving you to the funny farm!" The Osawatomie State Hospital's insane asylum, high up on the hills, the gaping maw that hangs over that town, is a place I came to know. In Junior High, as if to defy their tease, I volunteer to play the guitar, singing for the disturbed and hysterical teenagers. In their swimming pool, I study for the Junior and Senior Life Saving licenses. Even so, I admitted to no one my low-grade depression, hoping and praying constantly in the face of the taunting around me, that one and the other don't meet inside a locked padded cell in bound jacket. For in silence, I was bound enough. In High School, a Paola friend was kept behind those walls, and I have a strange recollection of Father's threats (of which later he will deny) when he cannot understand my teenage misbehavior of deceitfulness—the dating of an older boyfriend, whom he doesn't approve— "If you don't behave, young lady, you will join Penny." Little did he know of the fears that enveloped me continuously! Perhaps the fear of it, held me together.

Book One – Across the Divide to the Divine

The herbs speak to me, through me, bring similies to the fore, purging the psyche, as peculiar memories formulate. In Estes Park, while playing miniature golf with friends and cousins, my five-year-old-self pees in her new jeans and hiking boots—for fear of what the elderly boy will do to me. *Will he come for me in the night?* Squish, squish, squish. *Do I think the pee will mark my territory, keep him away?* The pee gushes out with each step and will forever hold the smell. Each time I trail ride with Gib on his horse Helen—the stench lingers.

Floating out of the past into the present the squish, squish becomes the swish, swish of the stones inside Sarototi's plastic calabash as nearby he patiently shakes, counts, accessing his foresight and the insight of the Ancestors through this bizarre mediumship. He waits patiently for the remedies to continue their way with me. Beside me, he sets an Augur Buzzard feather, and I try to lift my head to acknowledge his gift. I attempt to say: "Tell Marjana, this afternoon we must…return to the village, *must*…record stories." Instead, my voice cracks. The weight of any form of consciousness causes the eyes to roll back into unconsciousness once more.

More sorrows. Tears. For three days, I drift in and out of a delirium either in bed at night or lying on a blanket in the shade. For years, I had been beating myself up, "You cannot express yourself any longer. You're not a poet, Murphy, you've lost that inspiration." Even so, I'd been recording these experiences, journal after journal: dreams, poems, motivations, sentiments, passions, and quotes from books that impacted me, from writers who said things in a way I couldn't, in ways I deemed beautiful. I had journaled, not for others, but for the grounding of me. For, I scrawl to live. I live to write. For, I love to play with words calligraphically as they dance on the page.

For these three days, I'm in the divine embryo of the forest's medicinals, in the womb of the tent, apart from the greater community of Laloshwa, apart from the greater community at large, the universe that I know. Held as a precious vessel, protected. I had been afraid I was running out of excuses—of being "wronged" of being wrong, staying inside my smallness, disconnected from source, inside the illusion of separation from everyone and everything. *Would I no longer feel a-lone? Could I simply live life on purpose? Was I becoming all-related, all-one?*

Each day, for meals, as if hazed in twilight, I briefly move to the fire to sip their foamed-goat-milk tea amongst their muted selves, then, back again to the blanket, to the cabin at night to pursue what little rest I can find. Instead, I

12: Jewel in My Stigmata

pitch and roll and wake up weeping, only to scribble some more. The tick tock of the clock, I carry, registers two a.m. A part of me no longer knows what day it is. *Where am I?* The plans: the collection of stories, the hikes, the conversations are placed on hold. The body seems determined to repossess me, to re-member me, to clear out the debris or certainly to acknowledge it, to reconstitute, reclaim the little girl, reclaim the "I."

Here, it seems, I am forced backwards into the very thing I'd been running from. Hour after hour, terrorized with nightmares, creatures of the dark, Nazis chasing after me. Meetings with those I know or don't. Some impact me so much I cannot snooze, the tide of them pulling me in and out. From these, I fill one hundred pages of a diary.

Visions, aberrations continue to pass through the mind as the prescriptive herbs are ingested, inhaled, poured over the *corps. Does Sarototi expunge the past through the vibration of the herbs, solely provoking recollections? Am I a proxy, standing for all girls, boys, women, and men stunted and held hostage from trauma and abuse? In releasing me, will it free others; help them break patterns, to leap through into freedom and their own power?*

On the third evening, we hike, for I must move. Have been running away, running so far from the past, to New York, into the coverings of couture, I had forgotten how "outdoorsy" I really am and always have been. Soak in the sounds. Bask in the last rays of the sun. Multi-colored birds alight everywhere. Water rushes by. Silently, respectfully, Saifi, Motoguisimile, Sarototi, and Lughano stroll with me to the waterhole. A family of baboon scatters. A wattle crane stretches its huge wingspan, turning to fly away from us. The gossip of the Colobus Monkeys rings out as they scamper tree to tree. As we return to the camp, as we walk down the hill, I weep silently as I see in my mind's eye people gathering, those I thought who could never understand me, are embracing me with assurance, with forgiveness, and I, in turn, am forgiving them.

In the morn, on another constitutional meander through the woods, Sarototi and I discover a huge buffalo head. Together, we know we must lift, carrying it back to camp—horn in his left hand, horn in my right. Symbolically and physically, the shape of the skull illustrates both the man's and the woman's fertility organs. *Is this a rewiring of the masculine and the feminine?* Being a Taurus (my Sun sign), I want to carry it home to that garden of mine, but Marjana informs the Customs officer might shoot me on sight (certainly fine or arrest

Book One – Across the Divide to the Divine

me). Instead, for decoration, we prop the splendid cranium against Bright's Lodge.

All the while, the seven Maasai Warriors faithfully surround me in the camp; but I don't tell them any of these images. Instead, the stigmata, as in the stigmata of the priests of old, my experiences of shame are held under gloves, *under covers*, undercover in the pages and pages of the journals I carry everywhere, as if these notes will somehow hold me on the planet, help me to face, to embody whatever the Three Fates, Ananke's daughters, Clotho, Lachesis, and Atropos have brought my way, and to whatever may come—*inshallah!*

13

THE WATER COURSE WAY

"The water endlessly flows and fills up to a certain limit, the corners it is flowing through; the water is not 'afraid' of any dangerous place, of any 'falling' and there is nothing making it lose its essence. Under all circumstances, it remains equal to its nature."

— Richard Wilhelm, Number 19, *IChing*

On Christmas Eve, the Maasai take the goat's life before me in preparation for our evening meal. Motoguisimile bends down to slurp the blood in gratification. In a bucket over the fire, they whisk, stir, preparing the bone marrow, then, offering this mixture: "Good for you. Will make you strong." I sip carefully. By the taste, I sense its vitality, restoring me from these intense days of initiation, an injection of vitamins fresh off the goat!

Sarototi leaves the campsite for the night. "He is walking to the top of the hill," Marjana informs, "to pray for wisdom in the recuperation of your flow, Murphy, as he looks south to Ol Doinyo L'Engai. This Mountain of God, in

Northern Tanzania, stands 9,711 feet, still actively alive, erupting with natrocarbonatite lava." I think this lava quite fitting for me. "After his prayers, Sarototi will hike into the village to speak with the Council of Elders, the *ilaiguanak*, on your behalf."

One person in the world (besides my parents) considers me worth praying for! No wonder I had chosen him to be the doctor to perform the rebirth for me, of that little girl's Self.

In the mystical forest, Christmas morning, childlike, in full anticipation of a festive day, I decide to drape the body in Maasai fabrics. George Bright has sent a kanga, the colorful wrap of the women, with an inscription in Swahili, "*Mungu Nisaidie*," "God help me," and I might add, "*Nipone*," "recover!" "Yes, God help me recover." At this moment, this is so true.

The warriors laugh when they see this first attempt to dress like their women. Motoguisimile helps me tie the warm tartan shuka just so. The men are shocked to see me in color for I continuously appear to them as if from an old 1940's movie—dressed in black, white, and khaki. Looking back, what is rather ironic—once again I'm adapting to my environment just as I did as a child, just as I do in the fashion industry wearing whatever the designer of the moment I'm selling. They dress me and muse me up!

In festive mode, Sarototi arrives for breakfast, clothed in sacred dress, earrings, necklaces, ankle and wrist bracelets. He is blown away at my apparel. Smiling, he says, "Does she realize today we are performing a special ceremony for her? That she is to be named?"

Translating, Marjana replies: "No! But she wants you to know, she dresses up for Christmas at home!"

In silence, we eat. Afterwards, they tell me to prepare myself for the first of two rituals. At my favorite spot, near the edge of the stream, I meditate, journal. Emblematic of transformation, butterflies amazingly flutter about. A large, green, and black one flies straight at me. According to Andrews, a creature flying overhead ignites the receiver with its potency, as the eagles had done for me. Green measures growth, healing, abundance. Black is magic, birth, protection. *Is that what I shall experience today through their ancient ceremony—transfiguration, rebirth, and revivification?*

Sarototi comes for me, and I follow as he leads me out of our campsite toward the direction of his village. At the point where a butterfly lands, he turns into the woods. No weeds, no branches scrap up against me. No bugs bite or

13: The Water Course Way

sting. Today, the Sacred Forest of the Lost Child seems reverential, aware, declaring this moment as holy. Honor the Maasai. Honor Murphy.

At the edge of the Katunga River, I shed the *shuka*, the Maasai tartan, and the colorful kanga wrapped from my neck. My jewelry and sandals are left behind. In the lithe slip of a sundress, I step forward with bare arms and legs. From stone-to-stone, hand-to-hand, he guides me to an island where he has prepared a pool of water enclosed by sand and rocks.

Sarototi faces East, the direction of the dawn, of the Eagle. And I, the West, the leopard's tracking to the death, soon, devouring the past. I rinse my face, arms, and legs with the contained water. Sarototi places a rusty red herb from the bark of a tree into my palm to scrub across the cleansed parts of the body. The herb is pungent—the scent I have grown to love—of the earth, of cattle, of Maasai. I step across the pool, then, turn to face the on-coming stream, North toward enlightened wisdom, abundance, the position of the grandmother, and the migratory Hummingbird. Bend to form a cup of water with both palms, rinsing off the herb from face, arms, legs.

Sarototi gestures for me to open a canal between the pool and the stream, and as I do, the pond is caught in the vortex of the river's current rushing South, towards the feminine, the chthonic, the subterranean, the serpent's path, shedding of my past the way they "shed their skin," (Villoldo) gushing towards the ends of the Great Mother Earth. Letting go with such force, and yet, reenergized, reconnected. Reawakening me to the natural world, calling back that whole being I was meant to be, I was born to be. And I find myself chanting a new poem:

> Yes, the river shall be in me.
> And I, in her.
> Her past, mine,
> the present, ours.
> Surging into the future
> body pulsing to the universal rhythm
> flowing, as if,
> never taken
> and yet, fully all.

Soundlessly, Sarototi walks me back into the woods. Before we enter the main trail, we squat. He reveals a small piece of torn plastic bag. Inside is another

Part I: Across

pungent herb, of which I shall never forget that aroma of healthy earth, life, potential. He motions for me to take this medicine home to daily spin it around the head clockwise four times, hurling out the bad, ushering in all that is good into my heart.

    Now, reclaimed by their archaic curative ritual, I can write a different "end" to that divorce—one *that* ex of mine will eventually approve of, "Now, this I like!" He'll say, of the "white rage" poem:

> unfolding, spinning and bending back
> until I find myself coursing
> into the likeness of things
>
> until the river, me.
> and I, her.

14

THE NAMING

"A Namer has to know who people are, and who they are meant to be. […] If someone knows who he is, really knows, then he doesn't need to hate."

—Proginoskes, Madeleine L'Engle, *A Wind in the Door*

After the ceremony we return to the fire, to our friends. The energy has somehow shifted. In the air, there is an uncanny sense that Sarototi is "the Christ" and, I, "the Church," his bride, spurring on a repartee. In front of everyone, he merrily asks, "Will you be my second wife?"

"Then you would be my second husband!" I jokingly reply.

"I would not divorce my wife!" he retorts.

"Yes, I realize that." But I push anyway. "Just because I'm divorced, doesn't mean I wanted to be or that I even agreed with it. And I certainly wouldn't expect that of you. But if I married you, you would *still* be my second husband!"

Across the Divide to the Divine Book One **99**

Part I: Across

Everyone goes quiet around the fire at this eerie throwaway line. However, what he doesn't comprehend is that I'm trying to keep him at bay. Perhaps with these few words, I can display how complicated my life is. They view me as a "poor little girl" without a husband or baby.

What others don't see is that I'm locked in a constriction of conflicts within whether I will ever be marriage material.

I air a more concrete concern: "Sarototi, need your advice. The day I was to fly to Africa, I left the faucet running in the kitchen sink while watering a plant. The water cascaded over, down into two neighbors' apartments and into the lobby. Luckily, one of them warns me before walking out the door. I worry because the neighbor on the second floor is notorious for suing people."

They talk among themselves. They are bewildered, questioning. "You live on top of someone?" Lughano asks. "How could you pour water on someone's head?" inquires Motoguisimile. Marjana expounds on the living situation in Manhattan, piled on top of one another in a configuration called a "high-rise." They listen carefully. This concept is implausible to them.

While he speaks, I reflect. Once, in London, I'd done something similar to someone else. Indeed, since a child, I've been out of sync with water. Thank God, those friends told me their insurance would take care of it. *How often has my lack of flow caused a wake of water in others' lives?*

"Sarototi, will I pay out a lot of money?"

He rattles his plastic bottled calabash, counts, then looks up: "This accident is about the lack of flow in your life, Murphy, costing you something to fix the damage. On your hand, rub the prescription I'll give you before greeting your neighbor. This remedy dissolves anger. He won't sue."

Obviously, I needed this healed within. So, I trust Sarototi again, ingesting another herbal tea of light and love—what I would learn later, though a microdose—is a megadose of change.

In the afternoon, we drive to the manyatta for another ceremony. All the women greet us in front of the *enkang*. They are wrapped beautifully with their ceremonial clothes. Sarototi's mother and grandmother embrace me, surround me, escorting me to his mother's hut. In the Maa language, *Yieyo* means mother and *Nkoko*, grandmother. Some of their names are difficult for me to pronounce, to remember. So oftentimes I call them with their title role alongside their child's more simple name, as with papa, *Baba Budhya*, naming him respectfully after his daughter. This practice of mine becomes a signature "coo"

14: The Naming

to them, *Yieyo Sarototi, Nkoko Sarototi*. My purr. In this, they are jubilantly accepting because they both equally love and dote over Sarototi.

Sarototi's wife, Kisima, his stepmother, Nooseri, and his uncle, Chief Ole Wangombe, join Marjana, Sarototi, Baba Budhya, and me. They have also included the only Maasai woman, Senga, who speaks a bit of English due to her work in the Masai Mara with tourists. She prepares hot milk, *kole*, serving me formally, treating me as a guest. The milk is warm, soothing, and comforting. As if I'm truly accepte, they, then, drink, passing around the same cup.

"Murphy, we have officially gathered today," Marjana begins, "because the tribe of Laloshwa Highlands wants to make you part of our family. And in doing so, to give you a Maasai name we have chosen "NeLaloshwa," which means, "girl of Laloshwa Highlands." To make it official, two senior elders, my father, Chief Ole Wangombe, and Baba Budhya, must be a part of blessing this new name. They shall call out NeLaloshwa three times. You must respond each time with *ayeh*, which as you know, means 'yes.'"

His father begins, "NeLaloshwa?"

"*Ayeh?*" I ask, as if to affirm.

The other Maasai rhythmically chime in: "We bless your name."

"NeLaloshwa?"

"*Ayeh?*"

"We bless your name."

"NeLaloshwa?"

"*Ayeh?*"

"We bless your name."

By the time, Baba Budhya begins his three rounds coaxing me with consecration, *ayeh*, tears roll down those cheeks of mine. *Is it because I cannot believe they accept me?* And how symbolically appropriate the name is, for to them, though forty, I featuvre as a girl—with no breasts, no husband, no child. And then, to have "girl," "Ne" intertwined with Laloshwa, in this name NeLaloshwa, is to feel at one with and included within the Kitomini Community.

While I weep, the others are whispering to one another, what I think is: "How touching this experience must be for her." Later, I learn, they were urging Baba Budhya to hurry with his benediction for they imagined the tears were due to the smoke inside the confines of the dung hut. *Did tears not figure in their society?* For a grown woman to cry, this is unheard of. Looking back, I realize in

Book One – Across the Divide to the Divine

Part I: Across

all my journeys to Kitomini, I had never seen anyone in tears, except hungry children.

Afterwards, Yieyo and Nkoko squeeze my hands, and wrap me in their arms, leading me outside where the entire village is waiting. The young, the old women, and even the little girls surround me with songs, of which one of them is so familiar: "Hakuna matata, no problem, for this moment, no worries, be happy." With the men and boys near, Sarototi smiles proudly at me.

Again, an enormous release of crying, then, I burst with joy. Cannot imagine this is happening to me. To be named is to be considered, chosen, important, seen, loved and embraced. I can feel, somehow, they have unified me, integrating me from the inside out, the outside in, from the tip of my toes to the crown. Initiating me into their circle, they attempt to teach me the art of gyrating the neck in and out to their rhythmic clapping, of which they do ever so elegantly. I, however, cannot. For this, the young women hilariously giggle. Yet, I do not mind their laughter around these incapacities for I have been enveloped in a way I've never been. As if to affirm the welcoming into the family, Nooseri, now stepmother, sister, spits into her hand, spittle, the ultimate blessing, shaking mine, rubbing me into the fibers of the inconvertible truth of this.

After the celebration, the women want to show me their treasure hidden in a storage bin. Baba Budhya's wife keeps the key tied around her neck. Unlocked, discover a corn thresher to grind what they grow. "Two years ago, when tourism was good, the Council of Parks gifted this," Marjana comments. "Now, broken. Will you help us repair it? Otherwise, a full day is required for the women to carry the kernels on their backs to Narissima to be milled."

Here is the endowment that I had asked Marjana to speak with the Council of Elders, the *ilaiguanak*, about a donation for his people, to thank them for what they have done for me. He estimates the cost at one thousand dollars, which includes the parts, and a repairman to come from Nairobi. And I, the girl of Laloshwa Highlands, am being asked to "fix" their corn machine to benefit women. What flashes through my mind is the Greek Corn Goddess, Demeter, who along with Dionysus, and her daughter, Persephone, whom I feel more akin to, formed the Eleusinian Mysteries (which we have little record of), those secret rites into the feminine, of which men and women were both initiated into.

To be welcomed into the community is novel for me. Ever since the Maasai charged me with the task of working together for the common good, I have been researching the habits of the ants. This trip to Kenya, thank God, my

14: The Naming

relationship to the ants has shifted into gentle bites on a few acupuncture points, as if a confirmation—no longer painful or all-consuming, but communal.

At dusk, on the drive back to camp, Marjana narrates, "Here, up in the hills, away from the dry valley, the cattle have the plentiful green grass of the forest's meadows. For this, as you see over there, we create a temporary *manyatta*, circular corrals with thorns. We'll stop here, as Sarototi wants you to see his cows." We amble toward their settlement. Their young cousins and brothers herd the cattle, pushing them with their bodies, with small switches, coaxing them into their protective nest for the night. "Cows are life to us, Murphy, in our folk wisdom, we say, 'Meishu lemcidashita modici e enkiteng.' He who is not stepping in cow dung is dead.'"

As part of his seeming "betrothal," Sarototi picks out eight cows for me. As we squeeze among them, petting them, we chuckle at his joke. I have a glimpse of home, here, amidst the cattle, stepping in dung, seemingly not that far from Kansas. And I laugh at myself, for my daily attempt to figuratively step in dung by walking on cow skin rugs scattered throughout my new loft, that apartment in NYC!

"With my camera I shall store a picture of each one of them." I flirtatiously bray: "Your God, Engai shall observe how well you take care of my cattle!" However, among the Maasai, the truth is: "Meeta nkiteng' olopeny," "the cow has no owner."

The young boys invite us for a cup of fresh hot milk, *kole*. We join them, drinking, watching the calves play. Lekishoni, Marjana's half brother, tells us of the night before our arrival into the Highlands: "A lion leaped over the fence attacking a cow. Motoguisimile jumped in and with no weapon in hand drove off the lion, saving the cow's life long enough for her to give birth."

Snapping a picture of this marvel, a black heifer calf, I run my palms over her smooth coat, as one of the boys feeds her. Proud to know such a courageous young man as Motoguisimile, brave as David facing Goliath. This twenty-two-year-old moran runs with me across the hillside at full speed. Perceive myself as young as he. *Without the watercourse way, did a part of me never truly grow up? Held in a state?* Yet, now, as the girl of Laloshwa Highlands, running, flowing where everything and anything is more than possible.

On the hillside, this overlook, we join the others to watch the sunset. Eating mixed nuts, drinking soda, surrounded by Maasai brethren, cattle, sense a connection to the Eastern Kansas of my hometown where one can see forever.

Book One – Across the Divide to the Divine **103**

Part I: Across

They point out "Mt. L'Engai." Oh, here, looking at this mountain, is where Sarototi beseeches God on my behalf!

As it turns dark, we make the trip back toward camp. Feet dangling through the sunroof, I brace myself next to Sarototi on top of the Land Rover. With searchlight, we spot wild animals. "The rain is pouring down upon us," Sarototi calls out to his friends below, "and we are having such fun, I do not even care." Instead, we whoop and chortle, dodging the branches of trees, spot the bouncing African springhares.

Afterwards, we dine on Christmas goat, concluding our celebration with the warriors chanting their historical bravery and winnings with lions, leaping toward the night's stars. Later, I wrap myself in shuka, warm and content inside this newly formed self, inside the little private tent.

In the wee hours of the next morning, we take our last hike. To perform a ceremony, the others wait for us as Sarototi and I hurdle across the stream, missing rocks, falling into the water. Wet, but gleeful, along the shore, light incense, bury a bit of hair, a favorite rock, and a feather we had discovered together. For I know in the spring, the Katunga River shall rise, washing these fetishes into her and once more, I'll be the quintessence of her never-ending current. We grab hands, bounding across the stream.

Again, an inexplicable joy arising, for in this present-day experience, I am re-embodying the unbounded twelve-year-old, innocently loving, in a real friendship with a boy, as I once had with my childhood friend, Tom, until I was swept away from the trauma I'd just begun to remember to another town, Osawatomie. Striding proudly back, we converge with the others; witness the cattle marching off to graze. The young boys stand shyly behind the cows, drinking their morning sustenance of fresh milk, kole, in a fashion, toasting us.

At the campfire, we pass the rest of the morning. Tease Sarototi, "Your magic potions are working—for I have fallen in love with your people, with Laloshwa, the cows, and with you!"

"Good!" Everyone laughs at his reply.

On a blanket, in the meadow, situate myself near Sarototi as he speaks into the calabash to his Ancestors. I prepare presents for his grandmother, his mother, and for him as well. Think of his mother, whose husband comes to her no longer because of his younger wife, Nooseri. I, too, sleep alone, so my comprehension is far-reaching, in fact, massive. As if to resolve the empty bed syndrome I darn

14: The Naming

and clean the long silk underwear. Though for me, they haven't taken away the loneliness, yet they do provide warmth!

As Sarototi counts stones in divination, I craft him a necklace of brightly colored string, attaching the feathers we have accumulated on our treks, pen him a farewell letter. Overhead, a family of Colobus monkeys, five adults and three babies, greet us. Throughout this stay, they have been chatting up a storm. We are both amused at the number, as he gave me eight cows—eight, the symbol of eternity, the endless knot of infinity. While in this setting ensemble, the other men tease him: "You can't even plead with her for a cup of tea in English, how can you marry her?"

After lunch, I quiz Marjana, "Why all this talk of marriage? Is your cousin really serious about his proposal of marriage?"

"No, I don't think so, NeLaloshwa. Whenever a person is under the care of a laibon, the Maasai usually joke about their togetherness—for in a way, you are intimately married in the unification of this endeavor for the cure."

"Whew! I'm relieved. Glad he is not serious, for it might be very complicated for us."

Thankfully, Sarototi remains very true, borders clear. Each night, he continues to be the perfect gentleman escorting me to the tent, never crossing the hidden lines drawn. Yet, he dances on the edge of these boundaries, on the edge of what he is attempting to set right. Surely, he knows this, has been warned by the elders. Perhaps this is why he proposes the formality of marriage, versus pushing us toward sex for sex's sake.

On the morning of our departure, I offer seven hundred Kenya shillings to each warrior for their care of me. There, Marjana and I draw Sarototi aside, presenting him with the magic potions I travel with: Sandalwood and Eucalyptus Globulus essential oils, Homeopathic Arnica, Udder cream for his "milking cows," Tea Tree antiseptic, and the Balsamic incense he loves. Marjana hands him the letter I have written—fifteen hundred shillings fall out—enough for him to buy a goat. He grins. Marjana reads him a poem that I bestowed only to my dear childhood friends Julie and Karen:

> "The best in you and the best in me,
> hailed each other, because we knew,
> that always and always since time began,
> we were to be, the best of friends."
> —Walt Whitman

Part I: Across

At this point, Sarototi is so moved, he cannot look up. Marjana continues to the second page: "This necklace I have made consists of feathers we have discovered along each path taken. Through the spirits of these birds, I pray the baby Down will keep you warm and safe at night; the Dove, that you may always have pleasure and peace in your home; the Turacao, a life full of color and laughter; and the African Fish Eagle, for illumination and strength."

As I reach out to hug him, tears pour forth from me. Returning the embrace, voice cracking, he bestows upon me the last of the medicines: "This herb is to be rubbed on your palms, NeLaloshwa before the meeting of the neighbor, the man you have conflict with and anyone else."

As we crawl into the cab of the Land Rover, I peek back as Sarototi stands, waving. He does not have a dry eye, nor do the rest of the men. As we drive away, along the bumping road through these sacred woods to Nairobi, I weep so hard, as if I might never, ever stop.

In the night, fly across Northern Africa, bound for Paris. Peering out my window, view circles of protective fires surrounding people and their livestock. While we are busy making money in Manhattan, there are indigenous groups living united in communities of sharing, dancing, and singing under the stars. *Do they dance for the rest of us? Can their feminine grace and masculine strength balance the destruction?*

So far, no—it appears imbalance is everywhere, in families, communities, and nations: unfairness, famine, prejudice— "the haves and the have-nots." Underneath the wings of this plane, lie the once colonized. "The greatest weapon that the colonial powers have used in the past against our people," Malcolm X explained, "has always been divide-and-conquer." Throughout history, in Oriental and Occidental cultures, conquerors and dictators have been masters at dismantling, unraveling the faith in the indigenous' beliefs, so they could no longer stand together. Systematically they dominated, confiscating all their riches, building upon their sacred sights, utilizing this power, then wielding it over time through systemic racism.

After Cameroon was finally "heard," Charles de Gaulle announced, "Je te comprends." "I understand you!" releasing them into freedom from Colonialism. Yet, how often this is done, once power is yielded, someone else steps in to wield power once again. So, the Cameroonians experienced another kind of trouble. Inside Jean-Marie Teno's film, *Afrique, je te plumerie*, "*Africa, I will fleece you*," titled from the French ballad, "Alouette gentille alouette, je te

14: The Naming

plumerai la tête," "Lark, nice lark, I will pluck the feathers from your head." He portraits: "Ah, my children, independence and its companion, violence. They were soon to be wrapped up in the pale of silence." Only to be beaten into another form of submission, into a new form of colonialism.

So in turn, on the African Continent, the power of Western Civilization had poisoned the now black leaders from their ways of leadership, and their followers with Neocolonialism that has brought about war torn countries, other forms of greed, genocide, and out of control child soldiers, who are taught to cut themselves off from all feeling by shooting their families, as soldiers rape women and children, as impoverished refugees dismantled and dismal pour across borders in search of relief. And always there is the eternal story of girls circumcised and dowried into young marriages with elderly men, their money absconded; others kidnapped, used for pornography, sold into prostitution or enslaved.

What if we could move from our destructive pasts of Colonialism and Neocolonialism into Postcolonialism? Postcolonial would be where there is no one in colonial power over the colonized, where those have been pushed under, "other-ed," into Gayatri's "subalterns," have voice in every segment of the society.

Our Western fast-paced culture does not seek, nor root in the ability to penetrate into the core of the problem—so perhaps why our imperialism scratches the surface with little awareness of the effects on those encountered, who are often considered "below" us. Instead, from Africa, we glean their resources, the diamonds, the coal and even the indigenous' traditional herbs are preserved in chemicals and mass marketed. With our Western medicine, we are masters at emergency, at countering infection, and yet, often we attack the disease allopathically destroying even the robust cells, leaving the body challenged to move the chemicals up and out of the body without the wisdom of how the traditional herb can be gently, homeopathically used. Yet, in *Mapping Caves*, according to Shelley R. Noble-Letort, more and more, in the West, we see hope and movement toward integrative medicine.

However, the soul corporeality the indigenous shaman conveys is the capacity to deal with the fractures in the psyche. Inside their unified tribal system, they can rewire the split with herbs from their treasured forests. Here, lies the hope. The indigene understands homeopathically, when the body is dis-eased it has its own capacity for wholeness, knows how to bring in the balance, that each of us is a portal to our personal offerings for the community, a conduit between heaven

Part I: Across

and earth, the seen and unseen. That strangely, I will soon discover, just a little herb rubbed upon the hand brings peace between brothers, sisters, neighbors.

15

WATERMARKS AND BUBBLES

"Frankly, much resentment is justified. Terrible things happen. We commit unspeakable acts of harm upon one another, sometimes knowingly, sometimes not. Hatred and rage can be strong components of resentment, and they are both associated with justification […] being justified in your hostility and anger doesn't neutralize the consequences […] They still cause harm to the one who holds them; the injured party doesn't get a pass on the damage. Resentment is an equal opportunity state: it hurts all involved."

—Linda Howe, *Healing through the Akashic Records: Using the Power of Your Sacred Wound to Discover Your Soul's Purpose*

Once more, the *laibon*, Sarototi, is right—the simple granules of his herb diffuse tension. The water cascading from my apartment to another's has caused no anger to erupt from the neighbor below, in fact, the insurance agent confirms, he has no damage in his! Whereas the friendly neighbor, who phoned from the second floor, warning me of the deluge tumbling down upon his head, has watermarks and bubbles defined upon his wall, and so does our lobby. The expense to pay the deductible is minor. A check from my insurance arrives which allows neighbor two, a new paint job and provides the building with money to finally, miraculously, improve our foyer.

From the Kenyan visit, such a transformation happens that honesty enters my relationship with Peter, the Managing Director of our building, (whom I was fleeing). We are now able to become friends and partners on behalf of our condominium association. Months later, I will introduce him to a woman who is blonde, more athletic, more fun—his type. (They're now married!)

On the sands of the Gulf of Mexico, just days after New Year's of 1999, just days of uniting with a new tribe, feted in champagne bubbles, thirty-four of Mother's relatives celebrate her seventieth and Father's seventy-fifth birthday, and their fiftieth wedding anniversary. Wrapped majestically in the colorful jewels and fabrics of the Maasai, I arrive. To equalize existing tensions, my palms are coated with Sarototi's herbs to bring in peace. For inside our family's dysfunction, is this slight competitive energy that begins on the golf course or the tennis court, persisting through every nook and cranny.

Some of the members of the blood are frustrated with my choices, while they maintain the hearth at home, expanding the family business. They view me as "the wild card!" The renegade. Continually prodigally returning in coats of many colors, having all the freedom that being the third born baby, only daughter confers! Not to mention I have the determination to surpass their expectations, creating "the tomboy" who tries to outrun, out throw, slide into home base, and out drive the others.

Unlike my siblings and cousins who have marriages with families and successful careers, I have spent the last fifteen years paying off credit cards from the slow rise out of a divorce, painstakingly building a career trajectory in an incredibly expensive city and finding a window into the subtleties and boldnesses of "me." Since twenty-two, I have been peeling off layers, trying to understand these "why's" and "what's" wrong with me, these undercurrents in the sanctioned offices of counselors and therapists in Chicago, Scottsdale, Kansas City, New York City; in and out of jobs and various careers with base salaries, a "victim" tripping over her own two feet.

15: Watermarks and Bubbles

On this holiday, with the help of Sarototi's medicinals, the celebration is smooth. Amidst much laughter and delight Mom and Dad's love life is re-told, rewoven as tribute to them. Intimate walks and talks on the beach with cousins and lots of adventures with the college and high-school-aged nieces and nephews.

In spite of the powerful Maasai resuscitation, on the return to Manhattan, I still stir at 4 a.m. with pressures from work, continuously leaving messages on the office phones of my associates, scribbling an eternal "to do" list, and journaling dreams. Upon arrival at the office, I hear the news, "Finally, Anna Wintour is coming to our new showroom." All of us fuss, prepare and doll up, ready to meet the queen of fashion. To be honest, I don't really remember this. I am so nervous I go unconscious. Years later, Jeffrey Moss must remind me. "Everyone," he divulges, "the sales staff, our public relations associate Karen Handley, and the designers rolled out the red carpet, standing at attention in the front lobby. She said not a word to anyone. She was a cold breeze. The ice princess." Briefly, she came to see the collection, speaking only with James and Mark.

Though the year begins with so much excitement—accompanying bosses, James Mischka and Mark Badgley, and the PR gal, Karen, to Munich, Germany for a fundraising Black Tie Fashion Show for the head of Escada, Wolfgang Ley, and from there, flying on to Milan and Paris to show the collection—I sense, there is something out of balance. Upon homecoming, we discover a huge deficit of $1.8 million. With scorn, our internal CFO Bob, charges, "What are you going to do about it?"

"Oh, you're looking for a fall guy, huh?" Well, I won't play that role, choosing instead to resolve the question with Amy, the buyer from Neiman Marcus, who plans a huge millennium package of gowns for late autumn, for all the special events in the country. And in the end, with that chat and another, with salesman Jeffrey Moss, with his servicing of the small boutiques across the country, we make up for our loss at the end of the year.

It had begun to occur to me that with the CFO Bob, I wasn't necessarily safe. Throughout this crisis he had made some seething comments, "With your incapacity with numbers, you'll never be a President." *How could he even know I was interested in climbing the corporate ladder?* Though I was notably ambitious, I never shared personal or business information with him, other than what I had to.

In the midst of this deficit, Bob's comment made me quite defensive. "What are you talking about?" I inquire. "When James and Mark and you want me to make ten percent more, I find the right clients, who are able to sell that much more of our goods, who will make up the difference. And it happens." To me, it was about working with those who were out in the field, in the retail stores. Always within my mind was the question—*How could I help them improve their businesses?* So, in turn improving ours.

For me, it was less about numbers and more about building relations. However, I could do numbers, as a teenager, as a bookkeeper in my father's bank, I had sat at an adding machine, and later, as a teller, counting money. So, if I had to, just as Bob, I could sit with a calculator forming all kinds of numbers through percentages. I preferred being on the telephone with the buyer or being in the dressing room with their client, helping them look "just so" for a wedding or a bar mitzvah or their engagement party.

Perhaps, after all, I am my father's daughter. For, he had once confessed to me he wasn't any good at mathematics. So, in truth, I was more like him than I thought, for I knew expansion only came through the building of relationships, through reciprocity. If we were available to our customers throughout the country, throughout the world—as Father had been to those in a four-county area, listening to them, serving them—we would continue to improve our relations, to succeed.

But more importantly, I was more feminine than I thought. I wasn't linear in my thinking. There was something in me that was more interested in the personal relationships than the abstract. The Maasai had turned me inside out, opening my heart. Unlike numbers, one couldn't necessarily quantify or measure these mysterious soft parts within, which were as powerful as the numerical (Blummer and Meyer, *The New Medicine*).

This crisis at Badgley Mischka, however, forces me to confront another layer of pain. *What meaning has my life without the bond to the Maasai? What am I doing in a large city without fortification?* I must form a supportive family.

That evening, as the intuitive Mariah and I walk through my new Tribeca condominium, bearing candles, she, in her oracular manner declares: "Standing behind you is a tall man with a long stick."

"A spear?"

"Yes."

"Is the man a Maasai? Is it Sarototi?"

"Yes, and he says: 'I love you. Therefore, my father and I are protecting your back door. We are here to be called upon.'"

To be thought of in this manner, makes me sob. That here, inside my library, where I pray, where I write, he is. I have mor support than I realized.

"You are afraid to start your own business," Mariah divines. "You don't need to be, but if you hold onto those anxieties, you won't be able to." As I sob, as the tears flow, the trepidation falls away. "As your fear dissolves, four tribesmen with antler headdresses circle you, dancing." In the old days, the Bushmen danced with antlers on their head, as did some of the Original Peoples of Turtle Island. *Have I connected with these people for both my own recuperation and to pass on their wise myths?*

As you may recall, when Sir Laurens and I first met, he claimed, "There are only thirteen real hunter-gatherers left among the Bushmen in the Kalahari."

Slowly through loss of land, the encroachment of Western societal pressures, alcoholism, accidental, and mysterious deaths, they are dissolving. As for the Maasai, a mass exodus of young men pouring into the cities for trades and education, the culture is dissolving. Many of them keep Maasai wives, returning for ceremonies on holidays and weekends. *How will they preserve their traditions?* I wonder. *Or must we trust conversions, departures, new beginnings?* Soon, in ten years time, upon *the seventh journey in*, there will be technology, cellphones, motorcycles, churches, highways, postmodern thinking infiltrating their villages and their psyches.

In many ways, the people in Africa are wiser than us. We, in the West, judge them for their lack of modernization, of "things," of education, of money. Yet, in the cities there are modern buildings, cars, good jobs. Many are extremely educated. As well, they gain profound wisdom through a connection to nature, with a communal capacity to nurture their gifts. They value bravery, perseverance and patience—a scholarship of storytelling they glorify as equally timeless and practical.

In an attempt to integrate the way the Maasai live, I join a spiritual therapy group; because in the city context of the everyday, I starve to relate, long for intimacy, reinforcement, love. In fact, not only do I fear relations, but I also haven't a clue how to build a family. At first, I proceed with caution, never wanting to subject or lower myself to or have a "need" for a compound of hurting women. The voice of the patriarchy echoes in my mind: *Why associate with frailty and weakness?*

Listening to my girlfriends' narrations of their confrontative therapeutic congregations, in comparison to the gentle circle of the Maasai, has frightened me, keeping me away from these eventualities. So, even though I attend, I hold back, rebel inside, secretly scoff. Luckily for my famished self, I cannot remain a spectator for long. I discover the nature of the group is kind, consisting of six dynamic ladies: Mary, Anna, Christina, Martha, and me, ranging from ages twenty-eight to forty-seven, with the leader, Betts Cassady at sixty-one.

Every week they each reveal their own fears, horrors, longings, hopes without judgment, with loving intent, they contribute, listen, affirm. Slowly, within eight weeks or so my razor-sharp—you better believe it—guard drops. As a part of this women's enclave, where everyone is valued, encouraged to stand firm, I permit myself to do what is necessary to thrive, to draw healthy boundaries with my family, my bosses, and my short-term boyfriend. They observe, as I change drastically and soften. According to my girlfriend and colonic therapist, Terry Allard, "Bearing witness is what heals, is what makes a difference!"

Several months in, Lori, an expert in Ohashi massage, whom I go to monthly, touches the bottoms of my feet, "This is the first time in our two years of bodywork that your whole nervous system is aligned, Murphy, and it's a continuum!"

"Can you really feel the difference?"

"Yes!"

Only one year after Sarototi's invitation to regard the industrious ants, and the Maasai, began to enfold and embrace, I have rewired. The very cells of this body are united en masse working together. For the first time, I gain hope and my ever-faithful friend, the low-grade depression, departs. Now, enveloped in a compassionate makeshift family of newfound women, wholeness and integration emerges. We become open to those around, attempt to accept the challenges before us. We are less and less victims to our circumstances, building steps upward toward becoming more and more true to ourSelves.

Similarly to the Maasai around the fire, our women's circle performs rituals to say good-bye to an old way of relating, to resentments, to grievances—lighting candles, revealing our hearts, meditating, celebrating, laughing, crying—miracles. A community of women, a gaggle of geese, the seven Maasai allow me, as I integratively allow them, into the dailies of work, aspirations, friends, and family. As from *Essays on the Intellectual Powers of Man*, Thomas Reid enlightens: "The whole of each is in every part of the other."

16

BEYOND THIS, THERE BE LIONS

"Beyond this, there be dragons."
—Berkeley Cole to Karen Blixen about Denys, *Out of Africa*

Before I ever met the Maasai, I met an Afrikaner, who shared a common attunement to the animals, the Bushmen, their music. We clicked. He shared everything with me, books he had read, photographs he had taken, Kalahari music he had recorded. After dinner with friends and family, the two of us had climbed the water tower to catch the last glimpse of a sunset across the Western Transvaal of the South African farmland he loved. It was powerful, immediate, love at first sight—and we all know how these things often go—under the covers where he showed me the stars.

The connection had unnerved me. I felt I'd met my match. This musicologist had become the dividing line between what was and could be, extricating me from

Part I: Across

a past love (that married man—Renzo). Drawn through our commonalities, our desires to gather Kalahari music and the crackling chemistry between us—*what could I do? What would I do?*

From him, I ran far away.

For three years, I had pondered his proposal to combine our work. However, each time I traveled through the Okavango Delta with another guide or with the Bausch family and onward to Kenya, I avoided him.

Finally, I gave into my longings and had traveled back through the bleak and wondrous desert of the Kalahari with this Afrikaner, whom I will dub, "The First Man" along with two other adventurous men. For I'd wanted to reconnect with the Kalahari San Bushmen: their beautiful Mongolian-like faces which ooze gentleness, and the soothing, yet haunting music that lulls up and out of the harshness of this great thirstland. That's the thing about Africa— a lion at the kill devouring a zebra, the vultures flying overhead until they take over, the hyena circling the camp—so, in your face, raw, real, hunger, thirst, brutality, life, and death. I wanted this, as well as to rediscover their trickster god Mantis: his tranquil, concentrative and cunning ways of pursuing food, to listen to the sly tales of him; to hear the "tchak, tchak, tchak" of the gecko, the mournful song of the doves, to see the hopping toads and the wispy moths that fly across our paths.

With the First and Second of these men, I finally form a strong hard-working team, recording, writing, filming, and photographing the music of the Bushmen and their symbiotic partners, the Bgalagadi, the people of the Kalahari. Normally, my *modus operandi* had been to incorporate a massive amount of activity, doing "all of the above" as a one-woman band with many hands. This trip into Africa is the first time I pursue these dreams with someone else.

But in the evenings, the energy turns sour. The man I thought I had fallen in love with ridicules me, and the two others "gang up" with him. Perhaps, the cause is the alcohol they consume around the fire. Perhaps, due to the depression, due to the observance of the daily challenges these Bushmen, these hunter-gatherers' must face—forms of colonialism, prejudices, loss of land, brackish water, tucked in isolated tented or brick confinements. As the night grows long, I contract into misery from the Bushmen's plight. But also, to have come so far from Kansas, from Fashion Avenue to re-encounter this baiting, bullying, scapegoating, suppressive mentality shaming me for being lesser, an outsider, a woman was fatiguing. The perfect reflection of the Bushmen's struggles (though

16: Beyond This, There Be Lions

theirs was a thousand-fold more debilitating in comparison to mine). Even so, underhandedly, these three men elicit my attention; forcing me to draw swords to defend what little territory I have left.

One of them warns me about the First Man: "It's impossible to win with him."

"I do not care about winning, but I shall put up a good fight." A bolt of lightning strikes a chord of admission: sleeping with the ruler, the First Man, meant I'm tangled up in a place I'd been before. *Did I imagine, in lying with him, I'd be afforded protection?* In fact, in having sex with him, I had become acutely susceptible for I was slowly growing accustomed to these abusive transactions—"*If I do this, have sex with you, will you love me, like me, want me?*" Much later, Eve Brinton will acknowledge this tendency of mine, "This willingness to please, for a pittance of recognition, is what you had become *best* at offering to others." Eventually, I will have to reckon with this.

During the remainder of the trip, I attempt to ignore them, which doesn't seem to make a difference. The treatment continues. Finally, I slip away, oftentimes to the tent, or to the Land Rover to pen thoughts, to gather strength. I wonder if I am perplexing to the First Man. For he has come to know this vivacious wild forty-one-year-old American as a woman who dances, flirts, laughs, is witty, well-read, thoughtful, pretty, dreamy, a feminine cowgirl. Yet, it must be unnerving to encounter the masculine parts of me—the writer, photographer, filmmaker, successful businesswoman, who is the independent, who doesn't appear to need him.

One evening, in avoidance, I risk a walk far away down the path to catch the sunset. As the three men see me depart, caution against: "Lions!" As if Berkeley Cole's warning, "dragons"—to Karen Blixen's announcement of her new love for Denys Finch-Hatton—could stop her. Just as Karen, I would have much rather faced dragons or lions than the barbs around the fire, the "isms" within the community of conformity, and so, I march off, determined. As the golden-globe hovers in the distance, a few sprinkles strike my nose, with the thought: Perhaps as Una in Edmund Spenser's *Fairie Queen*, I'll tame the lion!

These three resemble the hierachical order of the men in my nuclear family. The Afrikaner is the leader, the alpha male explorer, who can survive in the wild. He is fearless. Carries no gun. In his body, he signals his standing. Lions plop down opposite the fire from him as if he is their equal. In my experience, the Dutch/African's relationship with the bush sustains a vital respect. "The

Part I: Across

second" in command, yet, still a follower, is Namibian attached to the First in the way the oldest is connected to a father. They "get" one another. *The Third Man* (named after one of my favorite movies) is French/Swiss and plays the role of the younger, sensitive one, as easily as he speaks with me, he can slip to the other side, to bond with the men. Struck by the reality I have re-created my childhood, I turn to inquire within, so, *where is your mother, Murphy?*

She is not here!

Though my mother has been extremely loving and available to me as a friend, during her own childhood and mine, she was unable to defend herself (let alone me) against the testosterone barbs around the dinner table. Instead, she molded into, mirroring a tough tomboy. But it didn't and doesn't keep us from experiencing the verbal "one upmanship," which to the men comes off as a mere tease. But we both are sensitives, so, one of us, in her nucleus in the 1930's, and mine in the 60's, usually left the table in tears.

No wonder Mother had trouble being available to resolve many of my own questions. No wonder, I find myself in this recognizable vulnerable position, stepping into the fight, flight, freeze or fawn syndrome, I know so well. In running away, I risk death by lions. In defense, I risk the sword of harsh words. I did not bring along an ally to stand graciously in solidarity and truth. I do not know how to do this. I have yet to practice what I have gained from the Maasai, nor from group therapy. Instead, I must rise up in the only way I know how—which isn't worth much—to be my own sister, mother, friend. Next time, if there is a next time, I shall bring a strong female friend. Three verses one with a muzzle, always pleasing others, is not a balance.

Surviving that foray amongst the lions, however, the hard pelting rain forces a return. While they cook, I face the verity, huddling in the Land Rover to sort, paragraph by paragraph searching for reassurance. Nevertheless, someone above must know the challenge I face. For there, in front of me, on the dashboard, on top of the leader's hat, a sighting, an affirmation, a small bright green praying mantis!

That night, again, another sign, I am aroused from a sound of what I presume is a mamba snake, scraping along the edges of the tent. For measly protection, I reach for Granddad's pocketknife. Flipping on the flashlight to stare at the opening, flapping from the breeze, I see the mamba snake has magically transformed into a praying mantis, which flies and then lands on a water glass to catch bugs. This chameleon trait, I later learn is synonymous with

16: Beyond This, There Be Lions

both Mantis and the San Bushmen, who are known to anthropomorphically change into lions or small creatures. Perhaps this arrival of Mantis is actually the wise woman, who had so lovingly touched the faces of Mother and me.

In the morning, that praying mantis is floating dead in the cup. As memory, to carry home in the journal, I gently lay her down to dry. When I return from lunch, from the heat of the day, she is alive and well, seizing insects once more.

Through these encounters with Mantis, I begin to believe this female/male prankster energy had the ability to speak to, negotiate with, and navigate what author Reis considers the ever-powerful controlling energy of the patriarchy—what I had been experiencing in a very yang manner from the First, Second, and Third Man and as a businesswoman. Mantis has the ability to play bawdy games and slights of hand, engaging people in laughter and joy. He/she speaks from the indigenous mind, teaching both children and adults a way of seeing from many vantage points, transforming the world into one of possibilities, and in a very yin-like manner, linking the Bushmen comfortably, and even perhaps uncomfortably, with the many parts of themselves. "And always Mantis would have a dream" (van der Post).

After this sighting, I fall deep asleep into a dream about a home I share with a man and a woman. When I dash off to work, she unveils the house to the entire neighborhood—opens windows, screen doors, so everyone can see inside. I return daily to close everything, complaining to the landlord, we live with. He listens, informing her: "You will have to depart unless you stop exposing my property."

When I awaken, I fathom the truth—like me, the woman in the reverie wants to bare herself, even to the possibility of sexual assault—to fabricate any kind of connection than none at all. In the past, those accountable haven't necessarily sheltered me. However, this man in this dream, safeguards the home we share. Though the dangerous part of me flirts with these men, and even with the Maasai, Sarototi, the forbidden—one third of me is beginning to be the father, the protector. That's hopeful! The other third closes up the house from exposure, speaking up on her behalf.

A few days into the trip, the third male pulls me aside in his whisperingly intimate way: "When you wash yourself from inside the tent, we can see everything through the dark green mosquito net. You think, because you don't turn on a light, we can't observe you. However, *we can*! I didn't want to tell you because I've been enjoying the view. In fact, if you weren't with our leader, I would want to be with you. Whichever man you choose, I thought you should be aware."

Mortifying. Slowly the light shines on my alluring nature revealed both in dreamtime and reality. Though unconsciously, *still*, this is being acted out. Jung believed that that which is not made conscious becomes fated. He was right. From past experience, I should have known better and for this, I must take full responsibility.

Speaking of signs and oracles—on the last night, while having sex with the leader, a long, thin-legged red roon solifugae (a cross between a spider and a scorpion without a tail) crawls across us. I squeal! He flips on the torch, captures her with a cup, setting her outside the tent. The red roon reappears. The First Man repeats the same ritual, this time taking her further from our nest. Indeed, a sign, we'd been walked upon, aroused out of our arousal into the greater nature of things.

The following day, at the end of another long hot travel through the Kalahari sands, I utilize the full force of my Taurean self, ramming my head into the First's stomach, shoving him into the Land Rover, declaring: "I am Maasai. I am NeLaloshwa, girl of Laloshwa Highlands!"

He is completely floored: "What are you doing?"

"It's for all the grief you have been giving me! In fact, I've been wanting to do that this entire trip."

"Now, wouldya getta load of that," The First Man motions to the men, "Murphy gives good head!"

"It's true, I do." With all the bravado I can muster, still attempting to gain an equal hand, I set forth my last royal-college rebuttal: "Don'tcha wish ya knew how good?"

Determine. Want nothing to do with his business, to be under his tutelage, cooking or traveling under his boss-ship. Shall not give my life to him or to anyone who does not give me deference. No, if I return here again, it will only be for my own projects. I resolve to say good-bye to the entanglement with him, breaking the agreement to be subservient to the Alpha Male. I am no longer interested in being in a relationship where equality does not reside. But, what I cannot admit to myself, is that I'm bound at the ankles, due to be tripped up again and again in these inequalities and tantalizing allurements.

In the daylight, after the tears of letting this affair go, I finally grasp: To a very, very small degree, the relationship with these three men, symbolizes what

16: Beyond This, There Be Lions

I had seen amongst the Bushmen in their mistreatment from the whites—the brokenness, the unfairness, the discrimination, the humiliation continually suffered on a daily basis. Inside my being, I know Mariah was right, these Bushmen are my first family. In these brief moments with them, I have loved and lived amongst them peacefully, respectfully.

However, here, there is a separation—between the San Bushmen and us, the white Afrikaans, the white Namibian, the white Swiss, the white American—as there is a separation between the blacks and whites in America. What is happening here is awakening me to what is happening and has happened in my own country, and how I have been and am of the dominant race within this world of ours.

Before I travelled with these three men, I had read George Gilder's, *Men and Marriage*. At the time, I imagine it was due to trying to understand why I wasn't married and to grant me a grasp at how men think. However, the most disturbing information was his chapter on "Ghetto Liberation," maybe because the Bushmen had made me conscious of color, of those who have and those who don't, of those who are pushed to the outside, who are obscured. Though Gilder writes as an educated white man who lives on the "better" side of the tracks, his thoughts are compelling.

Recently, on *The Rest is Politics* podcast, Rory Steward and Alastair Campbell interview Dr. Robert Sapolsky, a neuroendocrinologist who has been studying the effects of stress amongst wild baboons in Kenya for twenty-five years. He who equates inequality with ill-health. "Every step down on the socioeconomic ladder [...] health is worse, the sheer number of diseases, the incidents of them go up, their impact goes up, life expectancy is shorter the further down you are." The horror is poverty can kill. It keeps people from accessing what they need from clothing to schooling, from housing to health care, from hunger to starvation. To Sapolsky, "It's not [just] being poor, it's feeling poor. [...] people feel poor being surrounded by plenty." Subordination is apparent to people who never receive empathy, who have little or no exercise, who are never allowed a sabbatical. "You're going to live next to a toxic dump [...] more likely to smoke, to drink in excess, the food you eat is high fat, high carb because that's chaper" ("The Illusion of 'Free Will', The Psychology Behind Donald Trump, and The Science of Stress").

Speaking of stress, my new Bushmen friends live ghettoed, in cement block housing, or tented camps. They receive hand-me-down clothes and are now

Book One – Across the Divide to the Divine

educated inside schools that don't think like them. This ghetto is a system, that whether we want to admit it or not, we, "whites" control. "A tangle of pathology" exudes Daniel Patrick Moynihan. The "epitome of our [America's] domestic problem," writes Gilder. To Gilder, broken relationships create poverty. We have a system that only provides "feminizing" jobs for the men, and welfare for the women and her children. So, in the end, the woman doesn't need the man. Gilder explains that fatherless youths, particularly young black boys, are unable to find their way, are therefore "less responsible, less able to defer gratifications, less interested in achievement, more prone to crime, lower IQ's than boys with intact fathers." These young boys enter ghetto schools with mostly female teachers to end up competing with mostly female students with better aptitude. This life is counter to the attractive "swashbuckling life" that draws them into hellraising, hanging out, freeloading.

Patricia Reis believes that within the culture's patriarchal rule, no one fully escapes the burden. One has only to turn to literature to see its full impact on the son. In Western society, this idea of the son taking over for the father is considered progress; but instead, it puts tremendous stress on the father and on the son as well, especially when these men are raised inside the ghetto. "Whatever its manifestations, individual men pay a price for living in a culture that is predicated upon father-rule" (Reis, *Daughters of Saturn*). This keeps the man working toward the American Dream: straining, distorting, creating an off-balanced relationship between fathers and their children. The patriarchal system places staggering requirements on the father, leaving the son to help carry the burden. Some men, Reis explains, are able to succeed beyond their father's capacities, while others are unable to fit within the society's expectations and find themselves alone, bereft and broken down.

Gilder suggests the only solutions are for black women to be unavailable to men unless it involves the commitment of marriage—that's easier said than done, I imagine—and for whites to create a job market which meets the deepest drives of a man—not just "the feminizing jobs" of fireman, construction worker, and policeman. "The most surprising fact about our ghetto tragedy is the way we doggedly refuse to understand it—and the way we endlessly perpetuate it" (Gilder). The community is left with the distortions of female dominance with the male on the hunt, as the outlaw.

The most "harrowing centuries of slavery and racism" is then "reduced to lowest terms of mother and child [...] the broad-shouldered heart of the black woman." To Gilder, the woman is the blacks' secret of survival, but this secret also stagnates the ghetto, and ends in the "glory of the cornered male." Gilder believes without "the submission to femininity" we lose the enduring theme of social order, leaving "the ghetto as the exemplary crisis of our society." *How do we resolve this question? Shift the social order? Create deep driven jobs to satisfy the men's strong masculine orientation? Embolden a Truth and Reconciliation Commission to rectify the imbalance and see where this might lead?*

This first family of mine—according to Mariah—the San Bushmen are not squeezed inside the ghetto, instead, for over five hundred years, they have been squashed inside the harshest land, the Kalahari Desert. Only within the last thirty years have they been moved to its edges, in Botswana, in Namibia, in South Africa, on the borderlands of the place they have learned to rely upon as hunter-gatherers. They are dying off, dwindled to 100,000 people. They are constantly inundated with barriers: the battle for and loss of land, hunting rights, due to the infiltration of "white" farmers and ranchers; they struggle with tuberculosis, hunger, the loss of spirit and therefore, the destructive powers of alcohol, the challenge of the integration of their children into "white man's" school systems, the World Bank's classifications—and therefore, the loss of their own traditions. *How do we resolve what we've done to the indigene?*

Back home, though I cheered with two black girls Alma and Pam, I realize now, I never went to their home, nor they to mine. In the 1970's I never invited them to swim at the Paola Country Club. I wouldn't dare. In fact, I never even thought of it. It was just so. Round about me, Tracy Chapman's poignant song of this actuality circles: "Across the Lines / Who would dare to go / Under the bridge / Over the tracks / That separates whites from blacks" (Across the Lines). Oh, Alma and Pam wherever you are, I hope you can grant grace for that insensitivity. (From my high school friend, Kathy Holloman, I will soon learn that Pam has already passed to the other side of the veil and Alma, under an alias, is writing successful books from her home in California.)

This journey into Botswana, Namibia, and South Africa, I have walked under the bridge, over the tracks of separation. The Bushmen's losses, I know not how to resolve. Though their tales have saved me from vacuity, I am not their savior. They are sovereign beings. Yet, each journey in, I shall attempt to be present, whenever and however I can, continuing an exchange. And even though "there be dragons" and lions, my words shall continue to pour forth about these truths, now, confidently, a Maasai, NeLaloshwa, the girl of Laloshwa Highlands.

Third Journey In

17

THE RELEASE

> "It fell to the floor, an exquisite thing, a small thing that could upset balances and knock down a line of small dominoes and then big dominoes and then gigantic dominoes, all down the years across Time. Eckels' mind whirled. It couldn't change things. Killing one butterfly couldn't be that important! Could it?"
>
> —Ray Bradbury, *A Sound of Thunder*

What will happen if I continue to step back in time into that former life? What are the deleterious effects on them, on me, on those back home? I wonder about this as I leave the Bushmen and the First, Second and Third Man behind, as I fly

17: The Release

northeast to Kenya in the attempt "to continue to heal the relationship with the Maasai."

At the airport, Marjana meets me with Muringi, the cook, his cousin, Saifi, and Joseph, from the Luo tribe, who is the mechanic, the mender of the corn thresher. The news that its working has traveled throughout the highlands. Because of my gift, women won't have to carry heavy sacks to a faraway town any longer. The people are grateful. For this, I have come for a brief celebration.

Even the long drive into Laloshwa, watching the evening sun enveloped in darkness is an adventure for me. Unlike the kinetic streets of Manhattan of jackhammers and honking taxis, we have ephemeral sightings of a leopard, two African springhares bouncing off in a kangaroo-like manner, vultures finishing the kill of a zebra, dominating the dastardly hyena.

The rain has fallen in bucket loads, so as we enter into the density of the Sacred Forest of the Lost Child, the truck slides to and fro. Just two miles from our destination, our top-heavy Land Rover frighteningly slides sideways off the path. Luckily, we are slammed against a tree, which stops our tipping over. All of us pile out of the vehicle to push—with no success. There is much discussion about whether one of us must walk dangerously through the woods for help. Marjana is convinced we will be fine. Around a tree, we tie a cable. Within minutes with the strength of the winch and a snatch block pulley (our saving grace), the truck is conveyed onto the trail. This edgy moment is part of the exhilarating romance for me, part of the reason for being here. Though the Maasai have their own boundaries, laws, and mores, the expanse is an invitation to what feels like a borderless place where we meet in relation, on this land, which has become a necessity to my soul.

Upon arrival to the camp, the warriors greet me, "Sopa, hello, NeLaloshwa, sopa!" As my ears ring with the delight of their given name.

To recover from jet lag, the huge transition from city to outback, I retire for a nine-hour rest. At the crack of dawn, in a strange moment of shapeshifting into these surroundings, I arise to sit across the fire from Sarototi, who waits wordlessly for me. *After eight transformative voyages into Africa, how can I continue this intense fashion career I've lost all heart for?* As Sarototi tenderly massages my sore shoulders with oils, I cannot help but shake off the survival shell, weep from this juxtaposition of him versus the Kalahari confrontation versus the intensity of New York City.

Midmorning, Baba Budhya, Sarototi, Motoguisimile, Saifi, and I hike to our favorite waterhole. As we pass their sacrosanct tree, the Strangler Fig, Baba Budhya remarks: "Girls who cannot have children wrap the roots around their neck or drink tea from the bark."

"I need to do the same." I nudge myself. "Not necessarily for children but for the sake of the creative nature inside. All my efforts have been in 'servitude' to others. I want to live my life on purpose, to be—juicy, fruitful, generating!"

We follow a grand old shuffling buffalo, who in his aloneness has lost his power, chased from the herd. On the other side of the pond, we rest, peel our fruit, speak of the challenges of survival, nature at its cruelest, as the bull pitches, rolls, and grunts. *Is this how to cope when we don't fit? When we can't have what we want?*

The following day, Marjana, Sarototi and Baba Sarototi listen patiently to the list of my concerns that entails, encapsulates others' demands—how I allow suppression, how I am controlled, pulled, tethered. Amongst themselves they particularly discuss the stress from the job, how it ages me, consumes me, keeps me from listening to my nephew, takes me away from the longings of the heart, to travel unfettered, meeting indigenous people, expressing through pen and paper.

"Do I raise money for these projects? Do I start a new vocation? Teach? So, I can travel in the summer?"

Once again, in interest of these queries, they esteem me, accessing the augury, shaking and rattling, counting each rock. Marjana informs, "Sarototi believes you will start your own business, do what you are meant to do, but it will take longer than you think to leave your job."

The Maasai gently query: "Are you bitter, angry about your career?"

"Considering I have just gone headstrong into 'the First Man' in the Kalahari, a kind of older protector in the desert. I declare, 'Yes!'" They chuckle kindly. "I suppose, as the youngest child and only girl, it is a means of establishing ground." *Does it harken back to that past life, the persistent power struggle with that former husband of mine in 1787?*

The Maasai ponder the similar nature of the relationship with the Afrikaner, the First Man, where I am protected and yet not safe. They do not condemn me, nor criticize, nor censor what is said. I announce: "Upon my return from the *second journey in*, I flew home again, only to visit with Mom and Dad. But

17: The Release

I'd refused to attend the neighborhood's Christmas dinner." As I try to throw light on the conflicts which may continue to arise.

Sarototi wants to give me special herbs for peace to apply when I return to Kansas. I can say anything to these warriors, and yet, I have held back what I wanted to admit, so I burst out with these words— "I'm not orgasmic!" Making a clean breast of it, "Not just in sex, but, in all of my life—a form of impotency! I feel held back, unable to let go, to enjoy, to experience the fullness of the Self. I am not sure that inside lies the capacity to pursue what I want out of life, to go full tilt!" For the first time, I think they'll be shocked. Marjana does not blink as he elucidates. Intently I regard Sarototi's face, his father's, as they digest these comments—they do not flinch. This gives me courage to go on: "I'm not sure you can grasp a woman having an orgasm. Women in our society are not circumcised."

"Yes, NeLaloshwa, we understand."

On Sarototi's mat, the stones are in a pile save one. Baba Sarototi, points at this singular pebble: "Who is this that is holding you back? Who keeps you from doing what you want?"

In the hush, I listen to what's inside, the first reaction is, my father. Toss the idea away. That is too easy—a normal reaction to blame others, particularly the parents. Must be someone else, something else! No one springs to mind. So, I dare— "My father!"—as the lingering taste of memory arises.

Again, they point to the lone stone: "Yes, your father—the way he arranged your life—even trying to have power over your life's purpose."

"I suppose you're right. Dad actively sought to steer me away from the natural inclination to be a writer, just as he tried to direct the careers of my brothers. He was not alert to the danger of this for me, nor aware it was a form of emasculation, severing me from my own innate knowingness." Oh, how I had wanted to be a wordsmith!

Again, they act without judgment towards Dad and me, instead, these are taken as a matter of course, a part of the everyday experience of being human. They acknowledge the strong men about them. They want to know Dad, asking various questions: "What is your father's age?" "Oh, if he is seventy-five, hmmm, he would have been in the same initiated age group as the Chief's father." Once more, an avid conversation ensues among the Elders about similar men.

They examine this continual reoccurrence of domination the span of this embodiment. The Tibetan Buddhists' *samsara* is the circular existence we live

Part I: Across

over and over in our many lives, what Freud defined as repetition compulsion. Until there is some force within or outside of the self that jimmies this loose, breaking the pattern. To transform this, I came to one of the most powerful warrior cultures on the planet, which has been feared for five hundred years or more. For this, it has been conjectured, due to this fierceness, they were never sold into slavery. These males comprehend the value and necessity of strength yet are wisely not governed by these traits.

Baba Sarototi then announces: "We have agreed another ceremony must be performed."

Wasting no time, they lead me down a familiar trail. We stop to stand underneath a massive Strangler Fig—their most hallowed, the most formidable tree of the forest. As it expands, it overcomes another, claims its ground. Against this same force, this entire course of being, I have been reckoning. So up until now, my identification has been with the smaller tree, overwhelmed and strangled. As if to prove, I have always had the Strangler Fig's nature within, its potential for growth, I yank the clips out of my hair revealing curls that match the color of the strangler's shoots and aerial roots. *Aren't we all meant to grow as this tree, reaching out, finding a way, overcoming each obstacle?*

They instruct me to walk into and through the V-shape where the two trees conjoin. As I bend down, crouch, step into the darkness, a guide appears in the form of a large dancing yellow-grey Swallowtail Butterfly, enlightening me with yellow for optimism, inspiration, with grey for initiation and imagination. Feeling a weight lifted, I shout: "Oh, my gosh, a Butterfly, the symbol of transmutational, dancing joy." Amongst Chaucer's trees, fairies flit about butterfly-winged, as the Celtic forests were the abode of such creatures. *Are they with me, conducting me across the threshold to form new delicate winged patterns of change?*

On the other side of the passage, the warriors stand, greet me with twinkling smiles, not amazement, just pleased as if they had known all along the Swallowtail's appearance, a guide and friend in nature. Not forced by aggressive, fearful hands or forceps, their gracious manners regress me into and through another birthing canal, onto a launching pad.

"You do not have to worry any longer, NeLaloshwa. You will prosper vigorously with tranquility. You have been released," affirms Marjana. "Our God, Engai will rid you of this feeling of being noosed."

17: The Release

Baba Budhya slips away down the path to a larger Strangler Fig to obtain parts of the aerial roots. In reverent quietude, he braids three strands together as we stroll back to our camp, to the fire where Sarototi soaks the twisted band in milk, *kole*. "For peace, *e-seriani*," he avows. He sprinkles it with a secret white herb. Around the circle, the bracelet is handed to each Senior and Junior Elder to spit their spittled blessing. "Kneel down," Sarototi instructs. Gently, he places a dry herb on each of my hands: "Lick four times, the right and the left palm. Brush it on the forehead. Spit, then rub your hands together and move it across the chest."

As I submit on bent knees, Baba Budhya ties the braided band around my wrist. "You are to wear this for four days. Remove. Subsequently, place the bracelet under your mattress upon your arrival home."

With a blessing, Sarototi anoints: "May the herbs entwine you, NeLaloshwa, separating you from the undermining power of those around you. May you leave the intertwining task to the Strangler Fig, who is naturally called to this God-given mission. Only, she is meant to grow this way. Instead, you will gain fortitude and gutsiness as your own entity, yet, at peace with Father, family, and all creatures."

18

ADAPTATION

> "...I had come to learn something of the way that sort of murder is committed. It's not done by bright and flashing steel, nor even an honest stab in the back, but by the slow and subtle poison from our true individual destinies. For it is not destiny that is fated or doomed but our evasion and betrayal of it."
>
> —Laurens van der Post, *Yet Being Something Other*

At nine years old, having set aside that heart song of mine, I scramble towards different pursuits. In my father asking me to give up self-expression, I become "a composition re-written into a new form," with only knowing how to work from the outside in. It will take me years to learn how to live from the inside out.

In High School, what I really long to do is pursue music, theatre, literature. Oh, I dabble a bit—I'm in one play, sing in the choir, scribble editorials for the newspaper, play my guitar, create a few songs. The compensative urge pushes me

18: Adaptation

to a striving struggle—every desire is set aside for the adrenalin rush to wrestle with men. To be like them, what I thought, I must be. Honestly, I've been on the run all my life, trying to keep up with those big brothers of mine. Not aware that there just might be enough love to go around for everyone and that it just might be possible to remain true to the Self, creating a healthy love for me.

The only declaration the parents can make is: "You're a better athlete than your brothers." Which is not entirely true, as my brothers become experts in a field—both playing college ball—one on the golf course, the other on the basketball court. Had Mom and Dad said, "a well-rounded athlete," they might have come closer to the truth. Because without my capacity to express myself as a writer, I don't know what to specialize in, I compete in every sport that is presented to me—bring home six or so trophies—all-league volleyball, regional softball, junior golf, and (the funniest is) most wins in roller-skating limbo. Shoot six or eight points per basketball game, play a mean game of defense. Earn five or six medals from track. Brazenly, I even try to walk onto the men's golf team—but the coach won't allow it!

For four years, at the University of Kansas in the Art and Design Department, sequestered, I rediscover myself, wearing "styled" clothes. Away from the dominion of family, in this Paradise on "the Hill" I become a dreamer again, believing in possibilities, no longer exiled from the Self. I have clear moments of absolute freedom as I had had as a child in the woods. I become involved with a non-denominational Christian organization, a wonderful mix of black Methodists and white Presbyterians, full of song, laughter, and support. Through this network, during a summer retreat in Myrtle Beach, South Carolina, I fall in love with my future husband on a double date. Though I'm dating his roommate, he has no qualms at stepping in. For our first date, with bouquet in hand, he gushes: "You are the pink lily amongst these white daisies."

Through romantic letters and phone calls, he conducts our courtship from his dorm room at Miami University of Ohio. We're rushing headlong into this relationship. At Thanksgiving, I jump in my little silver Audi, "Frodo," trekking the miles to Oxford. Here, he introduces me to his friends, particularly his best girlfriend and prayer partner, Jewels. Over tea, Jewels and I discover that we adore each other. She's a tan, spirit-filled brown-eyed, brunette, "me." She makes me feel at home and a part of his life.

This fiancé of mine to be, is a Matthew Broderick look-alike (especially in his heyday in *Ferris Bueller's Day Off*) with button brown eyes, the hair to match,

Book One – Across the Divide to the Divine   **131**

a svelte athletic body. He intelligently reads as much as I do, particularly history, loves politics and is in the International Studies Latin American program. To top it off, he loves to dance to oldies. He's teaching me the FoxTrot. Over the Christmas holidays in Kansas, during a swing dance, he asks me to marry him. By Spring, both sets of parents delightfully rendezvous to approve our match.

In an email forty-two years later my ex responds: "It was a wonderful whirlwind romance like nothing I had ever experienced, I was completely smitten with you, I could think of nothing else. [...] Classic infatuation, because even though I thought I knew you, I clearly did not. [...] I take the blame for rushing things. I could not wait to be one [...] (to) share my life with you. I was 20-years-old. I forgive myself for my ignorance about how life really is; I believe you have forgiven me too. I hope."

(Of course, I forgive him! What little we knew at twenty and twenty-one.)

At Kansas University—at the same time our lightning speed romance is happening at a distance from one another—the leaders, Dan and Sharman, are asking me if I want to join the ranks as a kind of crusader evangelist. My liberal Presbyterian heritage balks at that, instead, believing in a loving God who only judges people according to what they know, I think, *why do I need to proselytize?* Kindly, I turn them down, "No, my calling is to be a creative artist."

They do not coerce me. They respect my path.

By June, I move for the summer to Ohio to study Spanish in preparation for an adventure to Bogotá with my fiancé. This trip never happens due to our parents' fear over the bombings at the Dominican Embassy, 27th of February 1980, and so, as if a solution to those concerns, we, at the ages of 21 and 22, walk down the aisle instead.

The first few months seem idyllic. We stroll under the Oxford stars as he recounts J. R. R. Tolkien's *Fellowship of the Ring*, smoking his pipe, wrapping his arms around me. And then—six months of bickering about our future, six months of intimacy thwarted. What I have learned is that this husband's religious organization, though associated with mine, is more conservative, less forgiving, and far more structured. Marrying and moving into their standards smothers my newly found Self. Even "the dress" must change to cater to their cleaned-up and proper preppy code—longer skirts, little bows tied at the neck. Yes, I was doing an "adaptation," just as Theodosius Dobzhansky, the evolutionary biologist reiterates as necessary: "the evolutionary process whereby an organism becomes better able to live in its habitat or habitats." Yes, once again,

18: Adaptation

urgings from the community, from a husband, I'm morphing into what I think is the "proper" Murph.

And my husband, he just doesn't know what he wants to do with his life. The looming standard is to become an attorney, following his father's footsteps into his private practice. To me, this pursuit seems natural for him. In fact, I'd thought I'd wed a future attorney. But the other stress he has is from his leader who insists, serving God best means joining the ranks of "this" crusade for Christ. The battle begins because he wants to join the brigade, and in this organization, it *just* happens to be necessary for both the husband and wife to serve.

I'm not quite aware that just as my father did, my hubby is asking me to give up my heart song. What the bridegroom isn't aware of is that I have a pattern set in my memory bank, when the men start "arm-twisting," I concede. ("Not all the time Murphy! You were hardheaded at times, and you should remember it. You were a strong woman and still are." He opens up to me in 2022.)

Even so, what I long for more than anything is to be loved, liked, wanted. So quietly, the good little Christian wife, a mistress of concessions and a master of a vastly fading trade as an artist simmers and rebels within. Rejecting my gifts, I abandon myself once more. "Okay. I'll commit to two years *only*."

For these two years, we set aside our disagreement. For the summer, the nightmare is, I must raise our "donated" salaries in Paola and Osawatomie with private individuals, picking up the phone and soliciting friends and family. For me, this is absolute hell, and quite frankly, embarrassing. Of course, I fall increasingly ill. During menstruation, for three to four days, the raw pain is so great, legs so stiff, almost catatonic that I cannot relax the feet, cannot work. Without the full knowledge of the past, I try to explain the strange ache that pierces the anus to the doctors. They recommend an easy out—a hysterectomy. To Mother and I, this is an extreme intervention for something that seems much more psychological.

As an alternative, I turn to a Naturopath, who introduces me to Michio Kushi's macrobiotic diet. For the rest of our life together, we strictly eat beans, rice, vegetables, which drops our weight—mine to one-hundred-eight pounds—as well, the menses cramps drop miraculously to a normal eight hours a month.

Our evangelistic service finds us at Northwestern University in Evanston, Illinois. In our apartment, we set up a monthly soirée for the students to discuss ideas, imbibe in celebratory wine and whiskey. Along with Kim Carnes, I survive the two years inwardly singing, "I'm hanging on by a thread too many voices in my ears…" Not only that, I have such a hankering for something. I often come to my husband on bended knees weeping. With a raw neediness, I'm dependent on him. I do not entirely comprehend this: that the "me" has been pulled out from under my story, out of what makes me tick. Perhaps, as well, that woman's intuition of mine senses he is pulling away, for we are slowly unraveling at the seams. Of course we are!

While my mate's ministry steadily and methodically continues, I meet with four disciples whose outreach soars to one-hundred-sorority girls in Bible studies. As though the rebellion within towards the cause and the attempt to get to the bottom of my own depression with honesty and vulnerability to these young women, serves. I throw out the organization's notion of the Four-Points of Christianity. Instead, from the heart, from those childhood favorites, I share the beefy stories of the Old Testament and of Jesus. I open their eyes to those concerns about the judgments within the Pauline Epistles, enlightening them to the Gnostic Gospels, strengthening the archetypal feminine. Their ministry soars. A few recover from anorexia, bulimia. Suicide attempts drop.

At the end of our term, the head of our household announces, "I want to stay for another year. I think the students need us."

"If we do," speaking of suicide, "I'll die." Surely, my husband hears me. (Perhaps, he thinks I'm exaggerating as people so often think.) However, he does not listen. All of a sudden we're signed on for another year, re-raising our money, spending the summer with Mom and Dad, telephoning and visiting our "funders." Though I adore these friends and family of mine who "give"—each call, each ask, each visit is a weary weep full of tremendous strain and embarrassment.

Thankfully, upon our return, we have a new leader, Rick Blade, who is psychologically savvy and confronts my depression. "You need to do creative work."

"I know. I'm slowly dying. For I cannot do this any longer, I cannot share the gospel, I cannot proselytize." It was true. As if I had a preclusion to convert anyone, as if I would dare to meddle with anyone's beliefs. I, instead, befriended others, wanting to know: *Who are you? Where did you come from? What makes you tick?* I confess: "Even when I try a conversion, I (thankfully) discover the person God has graciously brought before me is already a Christian and just needs support, which I can and do give them…but, Rick, we're required to convert—remember?"

Acts of subtle rebellion continue. Within the organization, it's obligatory that we share the gospel so many times a month. To avoid this uncomfortable act, I begin to lie (how very unChristian of me)—making marks as if I had made conversions upon this weekly form. I get a kick out of this deceit. As well, we are also not "allowed" to earn money. However, Rick encourages it. Secretly, I take a part-time job as a Graphic Designer. Inside this rebelliousness, I successfully live through another year at Northwestern.

What I've forgotten to mention, or have I? Rick Blade called me a "narcissist"— *Had he sensed that need of mine to be center of attention, self-absorbed, popular, Homecoming Queen, cheerleader?* Little did he know this self-absorption was just a cover up for the pain I was suffering from, the lack of knowingness, for the aloneness within. Though he wasn't a "working" psychologist, he had a Masters in Psychology. Yet, as far as I knew, he had never officially practiced. But because I was uncomfortable with myself, I listened. This harsh comment cut me to the quick. In fact, it humiliated me partly because I knew on some level, he was right, partly because it meant Rick and my husband had been secretly discussing "the weakness of this wife of his"—my inability to handle any form of criticism, to crumble at first mention of those incapacities.

It was true. I was *that* fragile. For I'd always known "something was wrong with me" and this low self-esteem meant I couldn't endure the judgment of a critic. And now, this sickness, a "symptom" according to psychology's perception, which could flare up in varying degrees and could be harmful to relationships as well as to the self, had been named and acknowledged. I felt mortified. Shamed.

However, below the symptom was a cause, which both Rick and my husband knew bits and pieces of. Maybe they didn't know all the details or even how deeply I'd been wounded (I certainly did not) for I protected the story even from myself. However cruel Rick's comment had been, it was the beginning of the cure, for I did go to a sex therapist, and after the divorce, to other therapists in various forms, along the way towards recovery.

Later, I would gather, I've never been a true narcissist, because I have always been highly self-reflective. (No kidding!) As my editor and writing coach, Gay Walley will eventually say, "You're self-focused about soul. No narcissist could do such a thing." In twenty-years-time, the Maasai will have taken it to another level, understanding it in a very African way, that lack of flow is "just" an imbalance, "just" a *dis-ease*, which can easily be brought into balance and harmony.

Part I: Across

Thankfully, at the time, the sex therapist encourages me to privately lie naked in front of a mirror, legs spread, with finger and vibrator exploring the mysterious crevice, which helps me build a new relationship with the vulva. Yet, the real deal is, I compensated to maintain this marriage, setting us up as unequal. We don't ever really recover from this attempt at raising funds and ministering to others while we're inside our own unglued marriage, and that shaking out of the trees, the falling leaves of the autumnal past.

At the end of our three years of service, my husband moves us to Arizona. Nine months later, he leaves our nest for good. In a few months, he'll have an affair with another woman, an associate of his boss. I'll awaken in the middle of the night, in Eastern Kansas, to this knowingness—for I had flown home to inform my parents of the divorce. In the morning, when Mother awakens me, she finds me weeping in bed. I announce, "It's happened Mother, he slept with her, I must return today."

Because we only had one motorcycle and one car, my husband had to pick me up at the Phoenix Airport. While driving me to the apartment, I asked, "You slept with her, didn't you?"

"What do you mean?" He looks around as if someone had informed. Yet, he knew as well as I did, we no longer had common friends—so no gossiping could be linked to this intuition. "How did you know?"

"Come on. I'm in love with every inch of your body. You think I wouldn't feel it if you touched someone else?" And then I pleaded some more. "Can't we just separate for three years—I'd like to go to NYC for fashion."

But he disagreed with these terms, confessing, "I know we're not right for each other. I do not want to waste any more of your life or mine in a futile attempt to make things work. If you are honest with yourself, you would agree."

To his face, I protest. For he was entirely wrong about me, I actually did not agree.

A few months later, at Goldwater's, in the Graphic Design Department, the policeman delivered the official documents to me. I was crushed. I refused to sign, for I did not want to be party to it. Even without that signature, he was allowed the divorce. Over the next five years, I wept off and on, because I longed to be married, to be wanted, to be thought of, to be a part of something greater. I kept thinking he, whom I thought to be my best friend, would call, reconsider, even miss me, as much as I missed "us."

18: Adaptation

Not long after, my wise mother would admit, "If he hadn't divorced you, *you* would have eventually divorced *him!*" So, others, besides my ex, could see what I would not believe—that we were not well suited.

How little I knew of myself then, and yet, how necessary it was that our lives parted. In fact, he recently replied, "I did you a great favor by setting you free to do all that you have done. That would never have happened if you were married to me, even outside of the ridiculous religious world we were in." Yes, just as this comment from him, I will be able to see how our separation, as well as the Maasai herbs and the passage of years were much needed and have brought such healing to the past.

Over time, those memories, which will emerge and reemerge from time to time, will slowly be carefully woven into a pattern of understanding, until one day they'll stand separate from me as pages in a memoir. Miraculously, almost forty years after our divorce, my ex and I will engage with one another (for the third time in our divorced history) about this chapter. I will learn how he felt about the "white rage" poem: "…well written […] expressive […] But it makes me very sad to think I caused you that kind of pain. […] *not* my intent."

It will be years later, in my marriage with a Frenchman, that I will begin to understand the differences in my capacity to touch. What it can mean if one can take it in, receive it. Back then, in Evanston, in Scottsdale, I could be his close friend, his companion, his jogging partner. I could play tennis and golf with him. I could have intellectual and spiritual discussions. I could have wild sex with him. But if I'm completely honest, looking back, I see, though I didn't have the words for it, I couldn't endure certain levels of touch and I certainly didn't have the awareness of it. Perhaps one could say it was a different kind of connection with him than it is for me now. Yet, after what I'd experienced in my childhood, touch was too much. It wasn't him, it was me. People would comment to me, "When you come into a room together, you sit separately, not on the couch. Even at dinner, he doesn't throw his arms over your chair to link with you." We weren't what I sense now on such a tactile level with my French husband. While reading, I find our legs twisted around each other, feet touching under the covers, and even when we watch a movie we're connected somehow, somewhere. Publically, we might be caught holding hands, kissing, leaning in. In other words, it was far less about my ex and far more about my own incapacities. It would take twenty-five more years, the healing of the Maasai, years of therapy, a willingness to open the door to another person in a deeper way. Touch.

Part I: Across

In those moments of what seems to be a necessary separation, how difficult it is to share the deep love and respect one still feels for an ex—even though one can no longer remain as "one." I'm so glad this manuscript with the Maasai causes a reconnection between us. Waves of detonation, of healing threads that have taken place years later as though their medicine keeps working.

In the writing of this story, I will grasp I'd chosen these experiences before this lifetime, so that I could become more and more embodied on this planet, all the while incorporating my light body. And now, *"Here, am I,"* uncannily sent, pulled beyond any logical reason to this continent revealing these compensations, these contortions, these former heartaches to the Maasai, retrieving that which was once lost, buried, shamed—only to be loved, affirmed, healed, to be reborn again through the Sacred Fig, ever closer to my destiny.

19

OF GOATS AND GIFTS

"Mpagi ni Mungu."
"God is the Sustainer."

—a Maasai Kanga proverb

To rethread the story, we travel out of the forest to their manyatta, encircled homes, to prepare for the celebration of the working corn thresher. From afar, many Maasai have traveled.

To his smiling cousins, Marjana hands five thousand Kenya Shillings to purchase three fine goats. To Ted Andrews, three means creativity, birth, a mystical manifestation. His cousins return with a black one for protection, birth, and magic; a brown for grounding and new growth; and the third one is white for purity and truth, spotted with red for sex, passion, strength, as according to *Animal-Speak*. I love the happy spirits of the young men, Lalalana and Oleteti, who have purchased the goats. Photograph these two cousins, as they beamingly hold them. They will use the rest of the cash to purchase traditional beer, *ol-turmet*.

To a "five-shack" town, Endassa, another trading center, we drive ten miles away to purchase rice, *ormushele*, potatoes, *irmurungu*, salt, *enjumbu*, flour, *orgali*, packaged milk, *kole*, and tea, *ormanjani*, sadly forgetting tobacco, *orkumbau*, the favorite smoke of the men.

Returning to the village, we crawl out of the truck and are greeted graciously and happily by Yieyo Sarototi and Nkoko Sarototi. Nkoko, Sarototi's grandmother, caresses my face with her hands. Delighted about our return, she melodically jabbers on and on. Then I grasp her expression, she is proud of her family, pointing at her grandsons: Marjana, Sarototi, Saifi, and of her son the Chief, who stands next to her. In acknowledgement of this beautiful truth, of my thankfulness, I gently grab her hand and lightly touch Chief Ole Wangombe's upper arm.

Everyone gathers elatedly, they are elegantly dressed. I wrap myself in Marjana's gifts, a *shuka* and a multi-colored kanga, with the words: "*Mpagi ni Mungu*," "God is the Sustainer." From a people who are not my blood, color, nor culture to be allowed to share in their rituals, is a generous gesture. Contentment radiates from me.

Unlocking the shed, the women demonstrate the results of the money gifted to them nine months before: the smooth humming of the corn-grinding machine. A few months ago, Joseph, from the Luo tribe, had traveled from Nairobi, bringing parts to repair, educating an elder Maasai in the art of its care. We put a bag of fresh kernels in the machine. Miraculously, amidst all the noise, finely ground maize appears. The women smile and pose for pictures. Nearby, the children giggle and cheer, clowning in front of my camera.

After several hours, I take a break, retreating into the Land Rover to read and rest, for not knowing the language can also bring on much fatigue. To the open window, two young women stroll. One of them questions: "NeLaloshwa?"

"*Ayeh?*" Yes?

Then, she exposes her nubile nipples. She wants to know: "*Do you have breasts?*"

Shake head, "No," revealing my very flat Twiggy chest. This discovery amuses them. The other girl with a child wrapped around her waist inquires, though I'm not sure of the exact translation, I know she infers: *Do you love Sarototi? Have you slept with him?*

19: Of Goats and Gifts

Once again, I shake the head back and forth "No," burrowing into the book. They proceed to bend over in laughter. I grow tired of people speculating. He is *just* a friend. At present, he is the man who has chosen to participate in healing me. For that, I remain grateful to him. Period.

Returning to the celebration, observe Sarototi as he stares at me proudly, points to the crest above his home: "Just there, on the hillside, I will build a house for you."

Many of the Maasai believe I shall live with them one day. Affirming this, his mother and grandmother encircle me with hugs. Other women gather, too. One girl removes her leather belt, wrapping it around the waist, finishing off my appearance. Not knowing she is measuring; I show it to Marjana: "Can I buy this?"

"No, wait, they have gifts for you."

Nkoko, Sarototi's grandmother presents a three-circled disk necklace to protect me from "the evil eye." Sarototi announces: "She has given this to you because she loves me!" He turns to the men, suggesting: "Regard NeLaloshwa, she naturally ties her shuka and dresses just as a Maasai woman. Not like us, the men whom she spends time with."

"Yes," I say, "except with black army boots and little earrings."

They howl with laughter. For they are aware that I have not the ability to wear their earrings. In childhood, their earlobes are cut and expanded with round discs. When the men hike, they loop their long dangling earlobes up and over their ears, so they won't get tangled among the bushes and the trees.

The girls and the children curiously crowd around, attempting to increase my Maa vocabulary, which results in twisted tongue and is, oh, so funny to everyone. As if this might bring about the necessary comprehension, we cross the borders of our physicality touching one another's hands and faces as if the risen places of Braille for explanation. Placing her hand upon the ground, Sarototi's mother erects a place for me. We watch her grandchildren dancing about us, blowing bubbles and chewing the gum that Marjana and I have brought for them. Marjana's first daughter, Mwaisakeni, has grown tall, adorned in a pretty white dress, self-possessed, twirling, baring her once hidden beautiful bum.

Since I first met Sarototi's son, Lesainana, wrapped in Kisima's arms, the day I crossed a threshold of trust within our fragile relationship, he has grown. Today, Lesainana runs and plays with the others with a small spear in hand.

Book One – Across the Divide to the Divine

Part I: Across

The men and women cook and eat their meals separately. And yet, today, the men want me to photograph them as they prepare the goats: killing, skinning, sucking up the blood—what is for them a necessity. They monitor my reactions. Setting the camera aside, at the fire, I seat myself next to the Chief while they cook and stir what we call "bone broth," though thicker, from the boiling of the sinew and the dissolving of the bones. "Drink this," nourishment to strengthen the essential self.

Marjana leads me to the women. Once again, he asks Senga to guide my conversations. She has a young child wrapped on her back. The afternoon has turned chilly and misty. Warmed from many layers, I wrap the extra *shuka* around the two of them. Grateful, she leads me to Saifi's larger dung hut to eat with the women, where I devour a bowl of delicious, hearty goat stew. They watch me eat, want me to be satisfied. We attempt to share what little conversation can be minimally interpreted. The children poke their heads into the darkness of the dung hut. When I glance at them, they jump back shyly running into the harsh, contrasting light.

In the cool of the evening, for a more formal event, the men and women gather sitting separated by gender. The men, Chief Ole Wangombe and Sarototi stand up to talk, to encourage their people to care for the corn-thresher. Marjana rises to introduce me, acknowledging what NeLaloshwa has done for the women. To honor me, four women come forward with the leather belt I had wanted to buy, along with matching wrist and ankle bracelets, and a huge necklace, *enkerewa*, which is given to the bride at a marriage festival. Slowly, ritually, they tie these gifts around my arms, legs, waist, and head. *Oh, this is an anointing.* In gratitude, tears pour down my cheeks.

Wouldn't Granddad Lewis have honored this—the plant from our homeland feeding the Maasai? Though he was a butcher, in the autumn, in his old Ford pick-up, Granddad loved driving Father through the back roads, talking of this and that farmer's success, as the stalks climbed lusciously high into the sky.

Afterwards, Senga ushers me to Sarototi's dung hut, where his beautiful wife Kisima prepares tea, *ormanjani*—more fresh goat's milk, *kole*, than water, *engare*—sweetened with lots of sugar, *esukari*. The usual crowd of Baba Budhya, Chief Ole Wangombe, Nkoko, Yieyo, and Sarototi surround Kisima's tiny fire in the small dung hut. Behind her, the new baby cries for the "the little hunger" for mother's milk—not knowing that just as the Kalahari Bushmen, his "greater hunger" must be fed by something beyond himself.

19: Of Goats and Gifts

I share chocolate with their children who giggle and hide as they eat this wondrous treat. Offer fabric wraps, the latest designs in Kangas for their wives to thank them. We drink tea heartily. I stare at Sarototi's elegant wife, Kisima, for I am quite taken with her. Dressed in an exotic iridescent orange wrap, queen of her domain, she looks rich, dark. I see elements of the women of the Somalian North.

Although I do not know everything that is being said, piece together their talk of Sarototi and me. If the young girls and the *moran* are teasing me, Kisima must be aware of the rumors. Long to tell Marjana: *Please tell her not to worry. I did not come to take away her husband, or to even share him. Please tell Kisima, Sarototi's and my love is spiritual and wrapped around our relation to the animals, herbs, dreams, the winged ones. At its most magnificent, we have the same ears with which to hear nature!*

For some reason, I do not. Instead, biting my tongue, I step gingerly between the invisible drawn borderlands of our cultures. Delicately searching for our common ground. Here, there is much deliberation in the unspoken. Guided from within and from Nkoko, his grandmother, I learn that wordlessness creates relation and is infinitesimally more potent than speaking.

In spite of the attraction, the magnetism between Sarototi and me, I have chosen to revere us, maintaining distance from a sexual union, believing there could be too many ramifications for our health. On the physical plane, we are worlds apart. Sense, that to bring our universes together, two different types of fluid, is to break a taboo, wreaking havoc in our bodies, calamity amidst the tribe.

As the ritual commences, Sarototi takes two pokers, placing them in the burning coals. I fear—*Is he marking my body, as they do their own?* He removes his grandmother from the edge of their sacred bed. "NeLaloshwa." With his hand, he motions, "sit." Into the center of the hut, he pulls the skull of a buffalo, jogging the memory of the *second journey in*, our encounter with that huge head, carrying it back to the lodge—he, on one horn, and me, on the other. Perceiving the significance, perchance that moment with Sarototi was the beginning of me embracing the buffalo's spirit, which they respectfully fear because of its uncontrollable brutality. Know if I desire freedom from victimhood, of being controlled, I must essentially embody the bull's fierce strength within, to remain invincibly true. I have not known this invincibility, nor this clarity of knowingness.

Part I: Across

Sarototi shreds the olive branch, placing it in the center of the skull as Marjana discloses: "The olive branch is a symbol of peace, *e-seriani*. Whenever a Maasai offers a leaf, a branch or a seed of this plant, he has made a pact: to never make war against this person."

Cull through all the myths, recalling the Greek Goddess Pallas Athena; the female warrior who bears the gift of a grafted olive tree for peace. In the book of Hebrews, Jesus himself offered up prayers and supplications, which in Greek meant— "extending an olive branch"—immediately linking Sarototi's act to the rites of the ancient Athenians, the Middle Eastern peoples.

After that, Sarototi places the two red-hot tongs in the skull. The mixture sizzles. "Two, four, eight are lucky numbers in Maasailand." Marjana continues. "Place the *shuka* over your head." As Sarototi sprinkles white herbs for peace on the heated pokers, the smoke burns and tickles the nose, makes me cough. Immediately, he splashes fresh milk, *kole*, for peace, which smolders and is to be inhaled reverently into this being of mine. Through this inhalation, Sarototi ignites the fierceness of the buffalo, so I embody the full-blown male energy of Taurus.

With the symbolic peace of the three earthbound forces: the olive branch, the white herb, the white milk, *kole*, I reunite with the feminine of the Greek and the Maasai: the young maidens, Persephone and Budhya; the mother, Demeter and Kisima; and the wise crone, Baobo and Nkoko. Inside the magical herbal scents, the smoke of the Maasai revivifies me. The evening air is cold, I, however, sense warmth, blanketed in their loving care.

As we turn toward the campground, for a night game drive, Sarototi once again climbs with me through the skylight atop the roof of the Land Rover. *Imagine doing this in New York City on Fifth Avenue? What wild game might we see?* We bounce along as branches and thorns try to scrap us off. Into the woods, he shines a powerful beam in search of wildlife, bound and determined to capture pairs of shining eyes. Yet, we do not. Instead, we chase them away with raised voices, singing out with sheer gusto, striking upon a familiar chord, an unknown tune of words, of wants as though not a care in the world, only what resounds from our full hearts and lungs.

Around the big table, we gather. The meal is electric with shared laughter and conversation in Maa, in English, in Kiswahili. We finish our pleasure at the fire with the Maasai's serenade, of great warriors' feats. The moment is filled with electric potency as several of the men jump, touching the sky—the Maasai, the

19: Of Goats and Gifts

Luo, the Kikuyu, sense it, and so do I. Outside the borderlines of color, race, and creed, of ancient battles over policies and prizes and power, we have been united for all eternity. Though it may take years and years to express myself in the Maa language, yet, truly, what has passed between us is rare, is on the far side of the spoken.

As usual, my favorite warrior, the *laibon*, Sarototi walks me to the tent, guides me with a lantern, protects me with his ever-ready spear. We stop, as we do every evening, in the middle of the meadow to gaze at the wondrous stars, *ilakirr,* and tonight, the new moon. The beginning of all beginnings. Turn toward Sarototi: "Did you know the moon's phase is the same as my first ceremony?" Kismet.

Sarototi smiles at me with what I believe his words are, "Yes, of course." A thought races through my mind: For the Bushmen, the stars are the sacred Ancestors, *enk-akui*. I have adopted this soulful belief. Maybe Sarototi has, too.

At the tent, he raises his hand, saying politely and graciously: "Salame, NeLaloshwa, salame!"

"Yes, peace, to you, too." As I bow from the waist.

However, this time, he waits. Looks at me differently. As though he knows, as do I, that in one brief moment, one belted out song, something special has happened between us. I pause as well: *Is this the night?* Rather, I extend these little white palms to embrace his dark-as-the-night strength, and pour out, "*Ashe, ashante!* Thank you for this!"

"Lala salame." He grasps my hands, too, bowing. Throughout the night, his blessing peacefully penetrates the submerged, yet warm sleep wrapped in *shuka*, infused with bull.

In the morning, begin the new ritual of Sarototi's secret herbs tucked tightly in a green plastic bag one inch in diameter, open this, to find an herb to dip my tongue into four times. With fingers, take a pinch and drop a bit into the palms, rubbing them together, and then across my face. The grey bundle is to be taken overhead with the left hand, circling around clockwise, five times. Then, placing it on the chest, to exhale the imbalance, inhaling health.

As I drag my luggage to the fire, I want to shout, "*Don't want to leave!*" Saifi brings me eggs and ham, hot milk, kole with tea, omanjani, chai. Everyone is busy around me, packing, loading the truck. Have gathered my good-bye gifts, slipping an envelope of Kenya Shillings to each of the warriors to thank them for their kindness, for their watchfulness. For Sarototi, I have saved the usual presents of money, udder cream for his cows, incense, and essential oils. He hands me the last package: "When you have a visitation, this curative tea is to mend the relationship."

We hug, with what Mom always coined, "tears of liquid love," tumbling down my face. The innocence, elegance, care of the relationship is irresistible, causing great esteem towards one another. *Is there a marriage in the world for me, where lies both honor and freshness, love and passion?*

To the Land Rover, they escort me, where we are swept into an intense group hug. I weep, weep. Concerned, Baba Budhya looks at me with those wise eyes of recognition: *Just because of the ritual does not mean the load shall be light. We have sent you on a mission—as the fierce, yet peaceful bull.*

This call, I do not take frivolously. A bracelet around the wrist, the aerial roots of the fig tree's prevailing potentialities will accompany me to Manhattan, to be planted beneath the mattress, perhaps, transforming the patterns configured for generations in the West. Herbs are carried for peace, forgiveness.

The distance between our worlds is as vast as the Atlantic Ocean separating our Continents. Daily, live in a world where nature hardly matters anymore, where even the natural fibers, the natural colors, the changes of the season have lost their significance. In the Fashion Industry, where I toil, though defined as different divisions of ideas and seasons: fall, winter, spring, summer collections, ultimately there is little distinction, except between coats and swimsuits. People travel so much from one extreme climate to another, there is now tropical wool, a year-round fabric. Many of the textiles are "man-made" to adjust to any climate. The buyers exclaim: "That's what our clients want!" About grey, they say: "The color of the moment!"

In New York City, I have personally "lived" in and worn black for fifteen years season after season. Of course, this is done for convenience, for practicality's sake—small closets. The colors of Autumn and Spring have been tossed to the side. And gawd forbid, if I come dressed in "color," I might not be "chic" enough to pass muster among the fashionistas or to shake hands with the likes of Anna Wintour. Yet, "Here, am I", sent to Seventh Avenue once again.

20

MARTIALED INTO MOTHER

"Everyone is involved in the construction of their world…Everyone is an artist…Everyone has an imagination…"

—John O'Donohue, *On Being*

Even before meeting the Maasai, I had been feisty, determined to prove myself athletically with sawed-off golf clubs at three years old to tap dancing and acrobatics, to yoga at eleven with Mom at the Ursuline Academy in Paola, to jogging daily down the back roads of Kansas, and as a running back for a GDI—a gosh-darn-independent—women's football team at the University of Kansas. Later, this athleticism would turn into a line of defense, for I had never really felt safe in New York City. Fearing I might become the victim at the hands of another. And so I was naturally drawn to the martial arts.

Part I: Across

After the *third journey in,* during one of the brown belt tests, I have to prove the capacity to release myself from a man. My *uke*, partner, Raphael, and I plan a unique display. Though younger, he is taller and heavier than me. His figure is stalwart, so, the action of easily throwing me to the ground appears more violent than usual. He straddles me. Before he can pin down my arms, I reach up to choke him. The class gasps. This aggressive, yet, subtle action becomes the distraction I need to toss him to one side, setting me free. Now, a "stud," I pass the fourth Kyu class with a roaring applause.

What I don't realize is the resounding impact this will have upon me. Filled with the Buffalo's strength, I have distinctly become a warrior, once again, identifying with the men. Not only am I no longer a victim, but I also have the knowledge, the power to choke a man to his death, the ability to destroy a perpetrator, and in turn, become one. Whether I can actually utilize this dangerous tool or not, I fear it can be used not only for protection but also for evil.

Because of this, I step away to gather my thoughts, to find peace and calm. I no longer want this masculine body ribbed into a six-pack that I have worked so hard for. No longer want to be in competition with men, instead, I want to soften my hard thin body into feminine curves, to be female, to be myself. With friends Jeffrey and Richard, I experience a homecoming to yoga in the neighborhood with Caroline Oberst. After each session, Caroline's lilting cadence soothes, "You are not this body. You are not this mind. You are something supreme. You are something divine. You are something eternal." Of course, it will take me years to live into her words, to really believe them.

Meanwhile the ongoing reverberating reaction of taking a stance, challenging people, being more myself, lays bare the cracks, the carefully covered chaos. The more I retrieve myself, the harder it is to capitulate to the overarching culture's patriarchal trance. The Maasai ceremonies have broken the entangled cord of those paradigms that have been wrapped around and about me, paradigms that no longer serve.

Interestingly enough, after I had declined to be home at Christmas, the men in my family were angry. Only Mother draws near, maintaining a dialogue. I boldly appeal to her to meet with my spiritual psychotherapist to talk about the ways the "yang" system breaks apart the mother-daughter bond. Her immediate response to fly to New York, shocks me. Nervous about her arrival, I begin

20: Martialed Into Mother

to ingest the herbal tea Sarototi had laid in my hands with these words: "For reconciliation with anyone who might have hurt you."

Together, we rendezvous with Betts for a therapeutic session, where Mother declares, "No matter what Murphy has come here to say, no matter the past, I want to have her in my life." Across the couch, she reaches for my hand, turning toward me with tears in her eyes: "I love you. I remain committed to you. I am sorry if my own wounding kept me from protecting you and taking care of you in the way you needed me to."

With wide eyes, I look across the intimate space towards Betts. *Could this really be happening?* As though the magical reconnection between Mother and Daughter in that rebirth session with Celia, of Sarototi catching me, placing me gently in Mom's arms has finally formed into an actuality. Where all of us are held, surrounded by Nature! And now, here we are, in reality, with a witnessing woman furthering this intimacy.

Betts gently welcomes this much sought after maternal declaration and affirmation. And wow, what these acknowledgements feel like to this Little Irene—to the one who was lost between fairyland, the woods, and adulthood—is tremendous. Opens my heart wide! In reaction, I give way to tears, and spontaneously my nose pours forth with blood.

"Yes, Murphy," Betts affirms. "You've been bleeding all your life. No one noticed until now."

So often as a child I had displayed signs of trauma, bravely hiding my tears, holding my tiny borderline-anorexic body perfectly, avoiding certain foods, bleeding onto my pillow, wetting the bed well beyond the age of normalcy, with continuous kidney/bladder infections, and therefore, continually swallowing massive doses of antibiotics.

However, something in this moment has been created. Something has formed. Forged in the fires of Africa. From the art of self-defense, into the revelations of group therapy, into the softening of yoga into the feminine, I had somehow come full circle into a reconciliation of rebirth, into this divine moment, into the loving arms of my mother.

For her last morning in my home, I cook pears. "Mom, before you board the plane, I've fixed something warm for your tummy."

"No, I don't care if I ever eat again."

"I'm sorry?"

"How will I…I face your father?"

"Excuse me?"

"In flying here, in indulging...in listening...in understanding your pain, your past, I've gone against his will." This is strange for my mother to admit.

"For the first time in our fifty years of marriage, I have said, 'No'...broken the pattern."—that tacit agreement. "No longer serving every *one* of his wishes."

They've been so happily married—was there something to this? I don't ask. She doesn't clarify. But, I know, more than ever, she has made such a bold and beautiful act. "Thank you for coming all this way. Few mothers would dare."

Instead, we embrace, and I share with Mom of my meeting with Celia last night after our talk with Betts: "On the massage table, Celia unfolded, 'This is the very first time I've touched your body, Murphy, and feel no pain.' In my contemplation with her, Mom, I saw you and me, meeting as grown women, holding hands, skipping into the sunset!"

"It's true. Isn't it?"

"Yes."

As she tightens her grip, as if she'll never let me go, tears roll down my mother's face as she declares, "Oh, let's just stand here by the window and look out at that view until the car comes."

The eternally entrapped feminine Sophia and my little self, hiding in the basement, have had a loving hand extended to them—both in the witness of Betts, the singing amongst the Maasai women, the intelligence of Celia, the rebirth, and now, from the declaration of love from my mother—lifting us out of the darkness. And somehow through this action of being seen, the feminine has been recovered, restoring us into the light.

At five in the morning, ironically before us, out of the Western window, hangs the fullness of Grandmother Moon, whose nature exudes femininity, whose nature ebbs and flows, comes and goes. Wrapped in my arms, Mother weeps under Her entirety.

"Mom, thank you for standing up for me, for love."

After Mother's departure for the airport, I crawl back into bed for a little nap before work. In my dream, a man is coming to harm me. I see myself in mediation, sitting cross-legged. Overhead, a praying mantis flies into a tree. The insect's quick and decisive maneuver causes the man to stop. Mantis proceeds to place his praying hands together in supplication, then extends the olive branch of peace. Through this act, the man is rendered harmless.

Somehow, in saying good-bye to what preceded, a certain way of relating to men has passed. As though I've taken a stand and yet, I no longer have to defend myself, appearing as easily as integrating the love from the Mother into my depths, as though the child in me has said, "Won't hide in the basement from the entire neighborhood. Won't pretend any longer that everything was 'picture perfect.'"—Because, it wasn't, and, it isn't. Because we're human with frailties, with pasts often full of messiness, wounded in our way. Functioning dysfunctionally!

For the weekend, as my advocate, Mother leaves, as though carrying the white milk, *kole*, the white herb, the olive branch, peace, *e-seriani*. She flies to Kansas to mingle with our family, our neighbors in celebration. All goes well, there are no more conflicts about Murphy's choice not to come.

The following week, inform Betts, "You, Mom and I are just as the Maasai women, though they live in a chauvinistic society, they fiercely bond to one another. For the first time, among the powerful force field of stubborn men in our lives, Mother and I are a united front."

Don't even think we need to talk. Just holding hands, hearing her gentle words, "I love you," are enough. What I had come to realize is, it wasn't so much about what men did or didn't do to me. What I had desperately needed and missed was Mother's love, acceptance, reassurance, and support no matter what. Just knowing she was there without judgment.

To commemorate, I ingest the last of the white herb from Sarototi. A significant day, peace has come to *my* household. Restitution. Ever since, this conjunction with Mother, my body is so relieved, I want to sleep, sleep for a month. Two months later, at a niece's wedding, Dad, Mom and I are talking, laughing and dancing again. Becoming centered as a meditative Mantis, I am able to command respect with the right to my feelings and choices, to at least attempt to hold my own amongst the lions, tigers, and bears.

21

OF BLOOD AND BONES

"I have ransacked my oldest dreams for keys and clues..."
—Vladimir Nabokov, *Speak, Memory*

Every year, the weekends which entail "Memorial" and "Labor Day" I venture to Montecito, California to bring the fashion collection of the moment—six trunks of gorgeous clothes—to the small boutique, Whitney West.

On Sunday, while spending the day lying on Butterfly Beach, journaling, reading, pondering the present, I become fascinated with two young girls, ages two and four, playing in the ocean with their parents. The oldest is beautiful, sensual. The curves of her body are perfect. Her attractiveness strikes a thought, stirs a memory of me, photographed, as a child. After the birth of two boys, how beautiful I must have appeared to everyone around.

In the Christmas photograph, amidst three generations, I'm held in Daddy's arms. Oh, so loved. Red, soft curls cascading down that long white neck, not to mention that pretty little rounded Raphaelite body. Yet, when I emerge a girl of nine, my hair is cropped short, straight, forcing a smile, withdrawn, arms pulled in, overly thin, lanky—am struck by the twist of it all. *What other compensations was this young girl forced to make?* Because I still don't know.

So, with much on my mind, I pay a visit in the center of Santa Barbara to a new acquaintance, South-African born urologist, surgeon, Dr. Dave Cumes, who also trained as a Zulu sangoma, medicine man, learning the art of "throwing the bones." Through the craft of divination, Dave can perceive the general wellbeing of a family, a problem, or an illness. As he calls out to his Ancestors for wisdom, I strangely drop into a reverent humbleness, a willingness to tune into those on the other side of the veil for instruction. My first inquiry is about February. I have a sense an ending is looming for me—*Dad's death? The dissolution of the job?*

The response falls out of the bag, onto the grass matt, through the arrangement of the bones. "Your father's death is not imminent," Dave enlightens. "However, he is slowly dying of an incurable disease." Though I have not informed Dave, I am aware of Father's problems of minor strokes, T.I.A.'s, damage to one side of his brain—the ever-threatening dementia. So, this news is not surprising.

"The Ancestors are not worried about your work, per se. They are more interested in your calling. The sooner you pursue it, the better. They set no time limits. However, they say, your father is against this mission."

The watercourse way is my writer soul. When I published *Why Ostriches Don't Fly*, Dad wouldn't come to the book signing. Instead, he prefers our telephone conversations about business, for this, I consult with him in the daily dealings as a Vice President. To Dad: individuation equals separation equals betrayal.

Dave asks me to throw down the gauntlet. "You must reconcile with him. You need his support. In this life, he may not encourage you, yet, in his death, he could block these pursuits. Remember, Ancestors feel strongly about honoring father and mother."

Tricky. *How to esteem one's parents and still remain true to the Self?* Our eldest sibling is a master at this. I remember the argument in the living room between father and son, Dad wanting him to become a lawyer, to advise him. Instead, this brother pursues the love of his life with abandon—designing golf courses. And yet, he still manages to keep a deep bond of friendship with our father.

"The shrinking violet nature of your mother, allowed the feminine in you and in her to be trampled upon. Without her firm stance for love, compassion and gentleness—without her command over the strictly yang attributes—these qualities vanished from the household." Just as I had seen played out with the First, Second and Third Man in the Kalahari. "Leaving an imbalance. Even the feminine within your father and your brothers is run roughshod."

I beseech the Ancestors: "What about my new date, 'the Martini Man' of Madison Avenue? He wants to invest twenty-to-thirty thousand dollars in my Bushmen documentary film."

At first, the answer is positive. "Doing the film together might 'set things right' for both of you," Dave adds, "it may be even financially rewarding."

Subsequently, with each roll after that, the bones spell disaster. In one toss, we see images of me sitting on the money, my calling turned upside down with a witch inside. Evil lurks everywhere. On the spot, I lose the heart and desire for the film.

"The problem is not the project, but is he a man of integrity?" Dave beseeches.

"The Martini Man's integrity seems fine. Our approach divides us. He wants the movie to be successful, to make money. *Who doesn't?* However, I want to preserve the old traditions, to give dignity to the Kalahari people and if money comes, I want it to benefit everyone, equally, all of us."

What concerns me most is Dave's comment: "The Bushmen will turn against you, and this will in turn jinx the Martini Man."

"What I decipher in the bones is you have a full life, Murphy. Nevertheless—despite all the work you've done—this part with your father, his denial, his power to hold you back, is bigger than anything you can personally attempt. In the Old Testament, in predicaments such as this, they made sacrifices to the gods. Have you ever thought of performing an animal sacrifice? My sangoma, Philani, can help you make one."

"No, I've never thought of this." In fact, I'm not sure I like this notion of sacrifice. "But I will think about this." As he walks me to the car, I casually mention, "What you saw in the divination—Mother's bone near Father's—it's true, she's always been close to him, and yet also true, what you said, 'her back is now turned to him.' This began when she visited my therapist, Betts—supporting me, somehow betraying my father."

Abnormally, early in the morning, in dreamland, on Butterfly Beach I secretly perform an ancient animal sacrifice. Talk about a fast response from the spirit world! Holding the bird down, I plead with her for forgiveness, thanking her for the restitution of our father/daughter relationship. The white chicken, once covered with brown and black spots, when cut, turns red as blood spews forth onto the sands. Unbeknownst to me, I've cleared a pathway. For in three years time I'll live in Santa Barbara, walking weekly along this shore.

That day, I call Dave with the news of my version of a sacrifice, stepping away from a weekend in Montecito distinctly different. Listen to the gods, the goddesses, the Ancestors, for they have spoken. They have declared their disputes, their complaints against me. I have taken heed. I let go of the Martini Man and his money for this clearer passage. And the Martini Man easily lets go of me, whom he and his hunting friends consider a "silly" woman they couldn't take seriously, because she—I—wouldn't go to bed with him until he had divorced his wife, a woman whom he'd been separated from for eleven years. (A great way for him to keep other women at a distance.) Yes, that "silly" woman, me, wanted a commitment in marriage. Yes, my dear reader, more and more, even I am attempting to have a bit of discrimination!

Close your eyes, the tide can change, and your history can be washed clean forever.

22

LINKS IN A CHAIN

"The logos of the soul, psychology, implies the act of travelling the soul's labyrinth in which we can never go deep enough."

—James Hillman, *The Dream and the Underworld*

 My captivating, haunting, and enlightening dream life overtakes me, leading me, carrying me along the via regia, Roman, for the Royal Way. As if the Maasai knew, as if Baba Budhya's last concerned glance confirmed, something greater is happening, *will* be happening. Sir Laurens van der Post, the Maasai, the Bushmen, open the floodgates, reigniting the powerful magic of those childhood fairy tales.
 Once I feared the deluge, as the Little Dutch Boy holding back the dike with all his might, until the watercourse way had loosened the dam within, until part and parcel of the river's flow. Once restored, that *Waterworld* of mine shifts. As once it did, water no longer chills my body. I soak inside the bathtub. Though it's small, I slide down under the water, slinking around as if a mermaid.

22: Links in a Chain

Before Judy or Jim's massage, inside Shiatsu Rincon's Jacuzzi, in the form of a cannonball, I spin underwater, letting the current take me where it will.

For inside the integral brain, those thinking, thought-processes, the synapses had been fired-up, neuro-transmitters re-wired, re-stoked from the precision of each healing, each thoughtful act the Maasai had been performing on my behalf. This re-intelligenced "I" of me gathers, eventually spinning me out of fashion, leading me way out west, towards other pursuits. This inner intelligence will become what Whitman and Perera describe as "the Guiding Self," what the Kalahari Bushmen distinguish as the "tapping," the knowingness which springs forth from within—and I might add, becomes a centrifugal force to be reckoned with!

Early on, in being taught to look outside myself towards others, toward those who had "the solution," I came to believe they knew better, knew what was right, more than I did. Luckily, in this case, I have met the right kind of people who could set me on a path, who could help me face the wars within being fought at that very moment. Those helpers were like the Jungian dream images, becoming "the People Way." Each one leading me to Africa, each one part of the outer movement of spirit until the Maasai had healed the flow within. Once that was done all else became "the Dreaming Way," an inner movement of soul—which meant I could now move into a more "whole" version of myself. "The only road," von Franz reiterates, "which unites the outer and inner world is the road to our own wholeness, the process of individuation..." (*Individuation in Fairy Tales*).

The "outer" links in a chain—these people—re-wove the intricate threads to the "inner" dreamlife, leading me through the developmental process. The first (as you may remember) was my former mother-in-law, Patricia, whom I had confided in over tea and who had graced me with that golden rhinestone plane. Together, we had shared a respect for the Native Americans whom she had worked with during her years at the university. As well, she had come to know me in a way others had not, spurring me into a relationship with Africa (as you know, dear reader) through the film *Out of Africa*.

From 1988 on, during those weekends in the Poconos with Jeffrey and Richard, I discovered them to be friends who expected nothing other than the exchange of friendship, who listened, who shared, who talked for hours over breakfast, or a fine bottle of wine into the night. When the way wasn't clear, they reflectively shot "arrows" of truths into me, making suggestions, telling me stories, which gave me the possibility to transform through, as Benson Lewis, a Cibecue Apache spoke of.

In other words, Jeffrey was always willing to be honest, "Something's wrong, Murphy, if you're pulling up your jeans like a man after sex and jumping into a taxi as if nothing had happened." For I'd been predicated upon and therefore when I hadn't sorted that experience, if I wasn't careful, I could become a predator of sorts, even briefly obsessively stalking Renzo, as he at first had stalked me. In my lack of clarity, there were ways I seduced, pulling men in, maybe even making them feel used, and spit out.

Another link in the chain was Dr. Eileen Miles. At the time, she was an emergency doctor (now, solely a pediatrician) who shopped with me at Bergdorf Goodman, where I managed the boutique of Jean Muir on the second floor next to Chanel. Dr. Miles immediately saw the trapped body, the locked jaw, mentioning she could help me. On her off hours, she practiced "postural reconstruction" (now, termed "inductive physiotherapy") which she had learned in France from Michaël Nisand.

In our first session, Eileen had me knead my body out of a segment of white clay. As this took form, she noticed the designed legs were narrow, similar to Giacometti, whose figures, according to Scholar William Barrett, exemplified life devoid of meaning. It had become apparent to Eileen; I had no legs for which to stand upon. No feet to plant upon the ground. So, she slowly stretched, bent, and moved arms, legs, knees, elbows with care. "Eventually, Murphy, as your body expands, your rage will come rumbling up. When it does, I'll refer you to Vicki Abrams."

Dr. Miles was right. As the expansion, so, the emotions sprang forth. Just after a physical breakdown with Candida Albicans and an appendectomy, just before the fashion career took off, just before I began those safaris into Africa, I began seeing Ms. Abrams (whom I mentioned before), a short-term Freudian analyst. Normally she only saw a client for three months. For some reason, she continued another fifteen months with me. Along the way, I'd get glimpses, hints, scents, dreams, senses, and of course, the everyday confrontations with life was reflecting back to me the necessity to clear up—something.

Even so, I needed other people's eyes, noses, because my perception was cloudy, dim, nor could I completely sniff things out. "You have fallen on the grenade of the family," Vicki declared, "which has detonated in your belly." With her I had a way of crumbling into tears—"Stop that wimpy whining," she'd strongly encourage. "What's really resides behind those tears is your rage, your anger!" I was really being listened to. During this time, I miraculously had a sudden shift from the chronic candida and within my career. I moved from the suffocating cage of the Jean Muir boutique at Bergdorf Goodman to the active and traveling wholesale world of fashion, becoming the National Sales Manager for Leonard of Paris, and eventually, International Sales Manager for Mary McFadden.

Even at the end of our eighteen months, Vicki didn't give up on me. In fact, she continued to meet me for meals. I didn't realize she was continually supervising, making sure I was finding my way. When I was writing the book, *Why Ostriches Don't Fly*, she pushed me further, "Why aren't you writing about your own life, your own challenges, Murphy, instead of hiding those memories in your journals or in a book about the Bushmen?" She was so spot on.

When I divulged an intense dream to her, she in turn referred me to Celia Candlin for cellular bodywork. Celia in turn (as you may remember) recommended Mariah Martin, the intuitive, who urged me to heal a past life with the Maasai. Vicki and Celia and Mariah introduced me to Gay Walley who would help me form the pages and pages I'd been penning in those diaries, into a book, of my adventures in Africa with the Kalahari Bushmen and the Maasai. For I knew I must follow Ms. Abrams suggestions and write *Africa Within*, the first christening of this manuscript.

When I began my career as a Vice President, I met with Gay Walley twice a month—those two weeks I was in NYC—I'd walk up her four flights to hand her a chapter. First, I started writing about Renzo, the married man; about Sir Laurens van der Post; about past traumas. I'd see her between her own writings and the editing of others. When we first met, Gay had written about a woman who blew out of her marriage into a whirlwind over an old boyfriend she'd been visiting in prison, who later, when set free, was disturbingly available. She also had just launched her first book, Strings Attached, of a young motherless girl raised by an alcoholic father.

Therefore, I trusted she could grasp my own tales. She saw things geometrically, helping me create form of the pain (without forcing her own views of how to do just *that*). She brought compassion and love to the places I hadn't been able to concretize—those "things" that lurked—where I could finally give voice. She made suggestions asking the whys, asking for more where I needed to express, expand. She continued to write her own books, sharing

Part I: Across

them with me. Later, when I started school at Pacifica Graduate Institute, Gay would help me edit every paper, even sort the dissertation into chapters. She could distinguish the divisions where I couldn't. Until another associate, Shirley Glaettli, could cut and paste line by line, into its completion.

Vicki, Celia, Gay, Mariah. These women, these practitioners surrounded me, as Links in a Chain—the stronger embracing the weak. Loving me forward. These women would either lead me to the Maasai to heal a past life or hold my hand when I returned from those wild safaris. Along with the Bushmen and the Maasai, these ladies in NYC became stepping-stones on that pathway toward individuation, toward that "I."

When my nightmares came forward with such strength, I needed help. Vicki and Celia suggested a powerful Jungian analyst, Silvia Brinton Perera. She was the first person who mentioned I'd been rejected all my life. In turn, she referred me to the dream analyst Dr. Walter Odajnyk. Not knowing they were weaving me together from the outside in, until eventually I could weave myself from the inside out. Links in a chain, people holding hands revolving around the universe of little ole me, each of them, a reflection of the inner dream realm.

Because of the recommended psychoanalyst, Walter, I drop into the tight knit synchronistic circle of the Jungian lineage. Years before, as I read van der Post's *Jung and the Story of Our Time*, his writing hurled me into the mythological dream cosmos, as did the Maasai, preparing the way for this trenchant work of analysis. (Not for the faint of heart!) Inside these rigorous hours with Dr. Odajnyk, he expands for me the Father Archetype.

In contrast, my very public family stipulated a course into the business world of finance via the discipline of golf, working at the bank at an early age, weekly attendance at church, and the charm of the country club, (living in a glass house). "Brought up to show up," the life of the party, of the conversation—at which I notoriously excelled. The down-reaching attributes of my parents' private life—who when home quietly read, study, pray, and generously tithe—remained hidden from others, oftentimes even from me.

Whereas Dad was consistent, clear, integrous, direct, loyal to Mother, immeasurably loving to me with strong expectations, funding college, and the premier trip into the Kalahari; Walter—just as Izak Barnard and Sir Laurens van der Post—was infinitely supportive of the mythological work in Africa, that interest in social change, becoming a guide into a salubrious sense of Self, into the distinction of what is mine, and what is someone else's. Noting, with amazement, "Your encounters with the Kalahari San Bushmen and the Maasai Warriors were actually numinous, Murphy!"

"Numinous? Really?" I had to run home to pick up a dictionary to discover the word. No wonder I've had such trouble expressing those journeys into Africa. *For how does one tell of a spiritual experience of such divineness, where one is victim to the "external" moment versus the creator of an experience, which according to Jung causes "a peculiar alteration of consciousness?"* In other words, this numinosum had germinated beyond the will, without any manipulation on my part.

Distinctly, Walter provides a nameable container for innate qualities to thrive, the introversion into intensive studies of psychology, religion, dream symbolism, the illustration of those dreams, and the continuation of journaling. Just as the Maasai, he ushers me back into what I've always listened for and to: those instinctive rhythms, the intuitive nature, the internal directive. The travels to Africa, to Singapore, to London, to Munich, throughout Italy and France had impacted me. He announces: "You have become a Citizen of the World!"

The stabilizing influence of Walter substantiates the knowledge, skills, and radar developed, liberating this exuberant scholarship, blowing wide open that freedom to choose. With him I escort in reveries of initiatory dismemberment just as Osiris, reassembling the parts as Isis, envisioning the origins of life, discovering in my belly an inner Christ consciousness, that "I AM" quality, exploring alchemy through Edinger's *Anatomy of the Psyche: Alchemical Symbolism in Psychotherapy*. Whereas the Maasai ignited the pathway to the dreamlife, Walter grants comprehension, encouraging, "Why don't you consider further education at the C.G. Jung Institut in Zurich or Pacifica Graduate Institute in California?" That's an idea!

Now, every dream I conjure becomes a clue, a link in the chain where I can drop an anchor to ground me in the storms of life. Through the growing foundation Walter provides, I even create lasting friendships with straight, supportive, interesting, attractive men, which do not turn sour through misinterpreted sexual energies. Instead of bedding it, I learn to get the download of what those men have to offer as well as offering my gifts to them.

Walter reassures me, no longer analyzing me. Yet, similar to the nightscape's Native American man, who catches the thermals on horseback with flowing black hair and colorful scarves, Walter tutors me in the art of listening to the Bushmen's inner tapping, the "Guiding Self," to the art of depth psychology, so I may find the heart's tender artery. So that I may enter Goethe's "highest

Part I: Across

bliss on earth [...] the joys of personality," recovering what Jung considered necessary, "fidelity to the law of one's own being." Ushering me back to the hometown of myself, to comprehend that North Star of mine, Walter, through psychoanalysis—along with Eileen, Vicki, Celia, Mariah, Gay and the Maasai's initiation—set me down upon the earth, building a solid *via regia*, a royal dream path into the unconscious, I can begin to trust, follow.

23

GAGGING IN THE FACE OF

"Better to have peace than a full stomach."

—Maasai proverb

In the wee hours of the night, following the dreamscape, I dash down dark alleys. Stalked. Tracked. Men in black coats. Men with guns. The German Gestapo search for me. Out of breath, I lean tight into the brick wall. Constrain myself into silence. How to not be seen, sensed! Heart pounds, rousing me out of slumber.

In the present, I turn on the biker's light, attaching it to the forehead as if a coalminer seeing into the darkness of what's before me, to inscribe into those private memoirs. The reconnoitering of the Nazis is not the first. They have been after me for quite some time. *Is it because I am nomadic, I cannot be controlled, I do not fit inside the boundaries of societal formations?*

Along with his two sisters, Walter, my Jungian analyst, at twenty-years-old, took asylum in the U. S. from Czechoslovakia's Communism. Because of this he is fascinated with these European nightmares: "Though these figures of the tyrannical archetypal father complex, the overlord, often haunt the psyche, most American's imaginations are more culturally native."

"Perhaps, it has to do with a past life or my employers, the parent company, Escada of Germany?"

Not knowing of the landmines, I continually step over in the nightscape, the employees tease me at Badgley Mischka, when I saunter in late. Mark Badgley claims, "Even if you do arrive early, Murphy, you're not really *here* until 10." My long-term friend, Jeffrey, one of our Sales Associates, razes me, in particular, for he knows I won't leave the house unless everything compliments everything, from his Jeffrey Moss hat, right down to those Connie Bates Fahrenheit silver earrings and faux crocodile belt, and those antique gloves the two of us found last weekend in the outdoor market. "Once you ran all the way home to change those gloves," Jeffrey reminds me to this day, "because they didn't match your outfit." (Even for me, that's rather hard to imagine. However, in the way I dress, I am more of a 1940's kind of woman.)

Yet, besides the nightmares, they don't know the real reason I'm late. (I haven't divulged this to Jeffrey either.) Each time I leave the house for this daily grind, I need to vomit. Just as I open the front door, I have to rush back; hang over the toilet, gagging. Nothing comes out but a bit of spit, saliva. Slip a homeopathic remedy of Nux Vomica under the tongue. Exhausted, I lie down on the floor to recover, regroup. When it begins to occur at Badgley Mischka, when I'm running for the toilet there, I finally confess this to *mon confident* Jeffrey—and I know then, there must really be a problem.

Know this is the pressure from the powers that be, from what I cannot stomach anymore. Not knowing there is something deeper and darker bubbling up and over, yet, not quite ready to be revealed. *Feel* I have fenced everyday, maybe lifetimes, at war with people, with different belief systems. The terror of the Nazis pursuing me in the wee hours of the morning! Within the larger company, the Munich and the New York heads of state have rolled out their agenda for me to increase our sales to five million more. Other Vice Presidents might flat out lie or agree to ride out the inevitable until the dung "hits the fan." I've risen to the occasion before. However, this season, I announce: "It's not feasibly possible!"

As a businesswoman in fashion, I sniff out the trail of the trends, colors, fads, the day and night needs of our clients. Observe how much more or less they spend this year than last. With my sales staff, we plan the cut tickets of how many dresses and suits for production, making projections based on what we sense traversing between cities across the U.S.A. and as I traverse the European cities of Paris, Milan, and London. We meet with couture and ready-to-wear buyers, selling them the latest collections of shoes, handbags, daywear, bridal, and eveningwear, following their concerns, worries, dramas, deadlines. I stay present to the needs of my associates, bosses; keeping a close eye on our competitors; watching the women express themselves as they daily walk the streets of Manhattan and dress for the evening.

Know in my bones they will not buy one more forty-five-hundred-dollar suit, one more six-thousand-dollar gown. Nor will I be able to dredge up additional upper-echelon clients, or the *nouveau riche* (for they're not interested in *haute couture* anymore), nor will the retailers increase their budgets. Nor are there new high-end boutiques being launched. Nor will we even meet last year's numbers. The Escada bosses are visibly agitated and completely mystified with this belief of mine—that—*it cannot happen.* "But you must, Murphy!" they demand.

For this "lack of faith" in our future, and more, I have lost that status as the "girl of the moment." For this, I've been tossed to the side. I will not be given the promotion I asked for. In fact, even worse, a company presentation I made technically bombed, of course, it was "the computer's fault." Yet, without the photographic images flashed on the screen to support the narrative, I could not recover the theme to make any sense of it for the audience. Embarrassing!

Yes, to Badgley Mischka, I'd come in as a change agent, which is never easy to do (and very often, these jobs are precarious, because change agents rattle cages, stirring up trouble). Yes, hired to change, I've rolled in, firing staff, launching new divisions, and cleaning up operations, because there had been a leak—a staff member was selling our dresses from the New Jersey warehouse to someone just down the street from us, who was selling them to the public at rock bottom prices. As well, our President was selling dresses to Guilio, at our showroom in Milan, who was in turn selling them to a store in the Middle East, which was undermining the very businesses we had formed good relationships with. For this, I argue with Guilio and my boss.

To increase our business in New York City with Bergdorf Goodman and Saks Fifth Avenue, I cancel our relationships with personal shoppers. So, you can imagine, I was not necessarily very popular! Yes, I was in an argument of integrity, fighting, drawing swords for what I thought was right. But, as I said, these precarious jobs don't last long and mine is slowly coming to an end.

Not only due to the above, but also, due to James' review, which is not stellar— "You're messy, Murphy. You come to every meeting with piles of notebooks. You never know where things are." In opposition to my own report, which is full of facts and figures of four new divisions in four years, a bigger sales staff, and an eighty-two percent increase in sales since my arrival. Not to mention the daily weightiness of decisions, on the road for work half the time, the new email system versus the touch of the telephone—which I had so easily excelled—we no longer utilize. Not to mention my own weakness and incapacities—most likely, due to the wounds from childhood—in organizing the constant stream of paper with no secretary to help me systematize the files.

And why else am I being blackballed? I must confess, because I actually stood up to Escada's CFO Chris, overstepping my status with that flaring redheaded disposition of mine, accusing them of "milking" Badgley Mischka: "One doesn't make money from couture, one breaks even," I denounce. "One only wins through licensing. Every deal I've brought to the table has been crushed because your company is dissatisfied, wants double, wants more than the customary percentage of ten percent!" From Badgley Mischka, I haven't been authorized to say this, nor is it something I've ever discussed inside the framework of our company.

However, I protest. "I've seen this before! When I worked for McFadden, we asked for a $50,000 advance for a perfume license. It strapped the licensee so much; in the end, when the perfume was delivered to Saks Fifth Avenue for sales, the bottle resembled something you could buy at a 5 and dime store. In other words, we'd taken money upfront, so that, in the end, the designed bottle couldn't be made." I confess. "It was mortifying. That's what taking more from the licensee does. I'm not going to let that happen!" If that wasn't enough, I add: "And each time I lose a licensing deal, we have to compensate, we have to create a new division: handbags, shoes, etc."

"Murphy, I think you've said quite enough. There are things you just don't know. When we bought Badgley Mischka we poured thousands of dollars into their business, and now we expect a return on our money." Escada's CFO shrieked! "And if you push any further, I shall lose *my* temper, crawling through this wire to wring *your* neck!"

23: Gagging in the Face of

On one level the CFO is right—Escada purchased BEM for a price ten years ago—it's time we weren't a burden, it's time we brought home a profit. He doesn't know, though, that I heroically and historically bare my teeth as protector of the lesser, as I will eventually attempt for my indigenous friends. This tendency does not serve either of us.

Don't get me wrong! This life of being a representative, traveling the country, to Europe, to the Far East has been extraordinary. I do not have the strength of body or discipline to be a ballerina, nor the height or beauty to be a model, nor do I have the capacity to act, nor the figure to be an "it" girl amongst the rich men, who provide furs, jewels, limousines, and apartments (of which I wouldn't want anyway). For me, as a female, this life in fashion is the next best career! In a 747, flying business class, transporting six trunks of couture gowns, then, limo-bound for Neiman Marcus Beverly Hills, luxuriating after, in the Four Seasons on per diem. —*Who could ask for anything more?*

Well, I AM.

24

GLIMPSE OF MY PERSONAL LEGEND

"I feel, therefore, I am."
—Léopold Sédar Senghor, Senegalese poet

After that confrontation with the CFO, on Thanksgiving I find myself without the notorious "Martini Man." Instead, Mom and Dad have funded the travels through the Kalahari Desert again, with nine people jammed into a three-seater 1970 International Land Rover. In the back sit three students, the hired camera crew from a university in Johannesburg. The First Man, the musicologist, drives and the Second, the photographer, rides shotgun. One Botswanan, the cook, rides between them, the other, the organizer, is in the second row with me and my invited guest, a newfound friend, a soulful woman, Rebecca Allina, from Santa Barbara, whose first experience with the Bushmen, emotionally moved her so much, she just had to return.

24: Glimpse of My Personal Legend

Record heat. We slide through the sand driving two-hundred-and-fifty kilometers in two twelve-hour days. The first day, one truck breaks down. A crew drives overnight to pick up another vehicle—while we precariously wait on barren land wondering if they will return and if we'll survive. Brutal. Precarious. The following day, we venture to a place I have been dreaming of, /Xai /Xai, home of an ancient tribe of the San Bushmen. For over a sixty-year span of time, the Marshall family and the Harvard research team have observed and lived amongst them, and from whom, much I have studied.

Upon our arrival in the village, the musicologist searches for musicians. He finds two men, four women, and three children to join us. As we transport them to our camp, they sing. The rain pours down upon us. Normally, I care that I'm getting soaked in the back of the truck. However, this deluge feels hopeful, important, and so necessary in the desert. The Bushmen are thankful for this inordinately synchronistic sign of abundance.

In the late afternoon, we record the Bushmen's music, interviewing and photographing them in traditional clothing. Rewinding the camera, we let them watch themselves. They are mystified, tumbling over in laughter.

The First Man warns us of Mamba snakes, Puff Adders, and Leopards, which ushers in the thought of gangrene or instant death. Instead, in this heat, we are surrounded with honeybees sucking the moisture from our bodies, filling our tents, crawling up our backs, into our shorts, and sleeves—an irritatingly crazy way to produce film. Causing the staff to argue, painfully so, forming territories and clubs. I, therefore, remain especially thankful for Rebecca's support—for a place to express how we both feel. And even though we've been duly warned of wild animals, to walk, to repartee in the coolness of the evening away from the barking men, *is* heavenly. As I have never traveled with a girlfriend before, I can really see how supportive these intensive dialogs are.

In the hot sand, we travel two more days to Tsumkwe, Namibia, where the famous Bushman from the film, *The Gods Must Be Crazy*, lives. Sadly, we learn he is deathly ill with tuberculosis, which is common amongst the older Bushmen. We overnight at a campground where the generator irritatingly hums; the water runs from a pump. In this small rural town, I miss the edginess of the wilderness, the bathing in one inch of water, the roar of a lion.

In the daytime, we comb the desert for more musicians, where we come upon a woman of mixed blood—Hottentot and Bushmen—who sings *The*

Part I: Across

Hyena Song: The Last Stage of Life: "When we die, we are buried, and then, the hyena pulls us from our sandy graves, devouring our bones. Yes, this is the last stage of life. When the hyena comes for us. Yes, this is our end. Oooo oooo oo." To my marvel, she seems accepting of her fate as she howls the haunting laughter of the scavenger hyena. As I record, photograph her, chills run up and down my spine confirming its creepy verity.

Over dinner and beer, the staff fights again. Between the Senior and Junior Alpha Afrikaner males a struggle for power ensues. I figure, torn betwixt the young boys, whom I have hired and paid; and the original team, the First and Second Men, who still work with me towards the same goal to record the Bushmen's music.

Yet, with Rebecca here, sisterhood is stabilizing, I can say, "No"—not snared back into the dynamics of the First Man's shenanigans. Nightly able to reiterate boundaries and borders, even though I sleep in a single tent.

In Kenya, the healer/healee relationship with Sarototi is what holds me in the form of discipline in and around sex. Yet, *truly, madly, deeply* with the First Man, I will have no internal resolve. Only briefly, when Rebecca's friendship resides around the First Man in Botswana and Namibia am I able to say no. Alone (away from her), there is no "No" there. And certainly, he wasn't going to say no. Only a yes to what Murphy really wanted existed in the "me" of this time.

So, with the First Man, I could not say "no"—falling from my resolve, once in New York City, another time in Johannesburg. For morals, tenets had been instilled in me, sewn more like encasements, not as inner convictions. Nor did I have the power to hold to my own beliefs. Oh, yes, I did have those moments with Rebecca. And once, for three years in NYC—though my black friend, Patricia felt I'd lose my capacities for sex—kept men at bay.. Yet, the sheets had already been soiled from childhood, and so the value of myself was not there, there. It was nowhere to be found. For early on, at the whims of others, I had become a leaf in the wind, wounded and set adrift, in the incapacity to affect a "no."

Longingly, I wanted to be as Anthony Trollope's characters, Grace Crawley and Mary Thorne, who put their men off until all was approved and sanctioned by their families. Similarly, to Grace and Mary, I had been given good Christian principles which had become well established in my mind of how I wanted to live, but the ravages of my cultural experiences meant I had not a will for a

24: Glimpse of My Personal Legend

"no." Not for "The First Man," not for the married man Renzo—and eventually, maybe not even for Sarototi. Yes, indeed, *that* moral compass had reached a point of stagnation, no longer pointing to my true North. Therefore, that "No," had of yet to become non-negotiable.

When the film project is complete, Rebecca and I fly from Windhoeck to Johannesburg to Swaziland for a face-to-face with the *sangoma*, the "medicine man" Philani, who originally trained Dr. Dave Cumes.

In Manzini, in the dead of night, a rented car propels us through the dark town in search of the Bed and Breakfast. For me, to drive on the "wrong" side, shifting gears with the "wrong" hand is particularly foreign. Scarily so, our lodge is entirely gated, bars on the windows. Though late, they feed us, these two "white" women, a bit mad, who have ventured into what clearly feels as though a hostile territory, and certainly, the unknown.

Early the next day, we hurl ourselves down a dusty, bumpy road with the directions of: "turn right between the church and the outdoor market. If you get to Siteki, you've gone too far, then go back turning left this time." To passers-by, we ask for further instructions. No one knows of the shaman, nor certainly understands us. From the onslaught of a rushing stream, the road is severed in two. Annoyed and hot, we obviously cannot cross and turn back toward the main highway. The effects of weather were not included in the details that seem out of the Wild, Wild West.

Luckily, we pass a sign which points to the Zulu doctor's compound. The *sangoma* and his wife run from their house, hands waving high, happily greeting us. Philani, whose name in Zulu, means majestic, unforgettable, is tiny, topped with a leather cap, from which dangles a feather with a porcupine quill. His wife, Nothando, whose name in Zulu means Mother of Beauty, is indeed, hugely beautiful, with her head and body draped in colorful scarves.

Through the divination of the bones, Philani immediately engages the Ancestors. "You are a healer, Murphy, but through the written word only." So, it's true—what I've always known, I'm a writer! Melchizedek's affirmation flashes through: "…what you have always wanted to accomplish." Paola Coelho pens, "Everyone, when they are young, knows what their Personal Legend is" (The Alchemist). Yes, others are beginning to affirm *this* small little acorn—the "I Am"—the internal patterning within, what James Hillman defined as *The Soul's Code*. In a Jewish fable the upper lip is the imprint of an angel, the prenatal

Book One – Across the Divide to the Divine **171**

election of our beingness. And one day, this unique coding will grow individually into a grand oak tree—for me, *that* scribbling-journal-self.

"However," Philani declares, "the book you are writing right now is 'sphhh'—it is nothing!" (*I wonder what he would think now of Across the Divide?*) "Not even close to the manuscripts you will script later for the world." *Is he affirming my soul's purpose that was thwarted at the age of 9?* "However," he expostulates, "Your maternal grandmother is angry with you!" *What does he know about my grandmother, the woman whose name I bear? How can she be angry with me? Is it because I am not following my innate knowingness? Is she metaphorically in purgatory—as Henry Louis Gates, Jr. suggests—an ancestor waiting to be discovered?*

In Nana's case I don't think so. Though she is dead, she remains in good relation with her daughter, my mother, speaking to her continuously on the etheric. Though I sadly missed her funeral (which Mother always regretted not insisting), I can sense her support within. I've always felt, she, along with her sister, Great Aunt Janet, have been surrounding me with care. However, I'm being chastised for being out of order with her. Yet, Philani is challenging Rebecca as well. All seems upside down and backwards.

Afterwards, we are left in a room to discuss our present-day responsibilities versus training with him. *And if I must write, why would I train with him?* For this, when he returns, we announce, we cannot stay. His response is to seek the answer from the Ancestors: "The bones are not happy"—is his rebuttal. (*How could they be happy when we're so uncomfortable?*) "If you cannot remain, at least perform a chicken sacrifice and a *fermering*."

"A what?"

"A *fermering* is a common Zulu practice," Philani defines. "A *sangoma*, a Zulu medicine man falls into a state of possession, where his helping spirit guides him, to spiritually and surgically release the dark energies from the patient's field with a whisk of horsehair."

"We don't have time for both." Given that I had a reverie about killing a chicken and Rebecca has already made a sacrifice, we choose the *fermering*. Nothando and her son, *Bhekisisa*, whose name in Zulu means cautious, ride along to aid, informing us, "We'll join you as you drive into the hills on the border of Mozambique to this shaman's home, but first, you can take us into the town of Siteki, for our weekly supplies."

24: Glimpse of My Personal Legend

Amidst a sea of blacks in the marketplace, the two of us, wait in the car. *Are we going to lose our lives?* I ponder and panic, as a group of young, but dauntingly huge, Zulu Warriors dressed in the traditional leopard skins, prowling to protect their community, surround our vehicle. (Not realizing their just doing their job.) However, I recall all the tales I have heard, remembering Jung's warning to beware when you are being "other-ed!"

"Rebecca, I don't know who your god is but you better start praying."

"Okay!"

"Do you trust me?"

"Yes! Whatever you have to do, Murphy. This is serious!"

"To shift this energy, I'm leaving you in the car." Opening the door, I slip gingerly out, subtly locking the door behind me. Humbly smiling: "Hello, excuse me, hello, excuse me." Passing by the teenagers as if at ease, walking to the pharmacist, hollering: "Nothando! Rebecca and I want a soda. Can I buy one for you?"

"Yes, thank-you."

Waving at her son across the street, I inquire: "Bhekisisa, do you want something cold to drink?"

"Sure!"

In buying a "round" of soda for the four of us, I have shown my relatedness to the "other." The scheme works—for we are no longer other-ed, but a part of the greater whole. As I trot back to Rebecca, the Zulu warriors disperse.

A Zulu policeman walks by: "Are you girls alright?"

"Yes, officer, everything is fine!"

In the afternoon, along the borders of Mozambique, at a private home, tucked in the hills, Rebecca and I are to encounter a *fermerer*, a medicine man, who will utilize his helping spirits to clear off the unresolved. Whatever that means! On the fringes of this indeterminate world, our patience is tested. On the gravel driveway of this supposed wild animal to be evoked, we stand. We pace. We chat. We surmise. We question Nothando and Bhekisisa, who attend us, but their translations are minimal. Here, in more ways than one, no one speaks *our* language.

Five hours pass into the night with a chill in the air, yet, on the inside of the healer's home, noises of happiness, of warmth exude, as if a family celebration.

Part I: Across

Outside, we are restless, nervous, now, suspicious, and I must add—very hungry. *And scared?*

When Rebecca and I are ushered into a garage, there is a scramble around which boy will re-park our rental car. I wrestle to keep the keys, assert myself, resituating the vehicle. *Had they intended to ride off into the night while we encounter the fermerer?* After these shenanigans, they lead me into the ceremonial room, where I find Rebecca stripped naked to the waist. I look into Nothando's eyes. *What the hell is going on?* But she looks away, seemingly maintaining the secrecy of this ancient rite. Rebecca explains: "It's what they want, what the shaman insists we both must do!"

I shrug, decide to myself, "*Oh well, might as well strip down, unlike Rebecca; I'm flat-chested, nothing to show.*" Once more, we're delayed, except this time we're sitting on a cold concrete floor without shirts inside an old dusty wooden garage.

Finally, the shaman materializes, subsumed with his helping spirit, a buffalo, a roaring lion: panting, explosively grunting, sweating, heaving up and down on all fours, which in and of itself is quite frightening. Not to mention our bodies vulnerably exposed, that our brains are fatigued and totally rattled from the wait. But, perhaps, this is the point—we must let our guard down to shift our frequencies.

Strangely, the *bruja* transmits instructions from Rebecca's Scottish ancestor with a perfect brogue. With the tail of an animal swishing across her back, he pulls the imbalance from her body, then, surreally vomits into a bucket. After that, my mind drops into an abysmal oblivion. I haven't the foggiest idea what he spoke of, or what is swept from me. We pay a fee and manage to safely transport Nothando and Bhekisisa home, and our exhausted selves to the BandB.

As we leave Swaziland, Philani, the fermerer, Nothando, and Bhekisisa, we both wonder—from our prospective realities in America—*Who could explain that?*

Yet, upon my return, I discover Philani is right, I'm not ready, and what I'm writing is sphhh! Even though I have good references, several publishers turn down the Bushmen book/CD, *Music that Floats from Afar*. A year later they reject a memoir, *Africa Within*, about those first few journeys into the Maasai; and even the manuscript about *Lily Daché* written with Jeffrey Moss, filled with photographs of his vast collection of her hats from the 1920's to the 60's, is rejected.

24: Glimpse of My Personal Legend

Knowing what my personal legend is, uncovering the lid of that predestined vocation versus living into it is a completely different matter. Must breathe. Catch the clouds passing by, the stars hanging in the balance, digging ever more deeply for the treasure within, attempting to be true to the soul's purpose. *And Rebecca and I?* We are never quite sure what transpired!

25

COMPLETIONS ALL THE WAY ROUND

"What happens in an ideal situation is that the oppressed, in enacting his/her liberation, will also liberate the oppressor. Thus the act of liberation is a process that has love as the basic guiding principle."

—Bonnie and Eduardo Duran, *Native American Postcolonial Psychology*

Upon my return, in that treasured NYC condominium, over dishes, I start weeping. I don't want anything to ever come between Dad and me. As with Philani, as with Grandmother Rene, I want to hold my own, be myself, and yet remain in right relation, expanding over what seems to be our disparities, believing the best, accepting as well as freeing Father from whatever may be binding.

Telephone: "I didn't mean to kick you in your teeth by making judgments of others, by not joining the neighbors for Christmas dinner. I needed to

25: Completions All the Way Round

psychologically shift. Please forgive me. Forgive me for continually rebelling against you, against business, against everything you wanted for me!"

"I forgive you, Murphy."

"Thank you for all you've done for me—educating me in the bank and the university, supporting me, taking me to the Kalahari Desert, listening to me through the intensity of Badgley Mischka. I couldn't have run that 25-million-dollar-business without you.

"But please know, as I pursue 'the pen,' I have no intention of hurting you, nor our neighbors." There! I've said what Dr. Dave Cumes and the Ancestors beckoned! I didn't have to shout it. Yet, I've become an advocate for myself, for my own lifework.

For, I could not hold this against him, forever—his keeping me from my personal legend. Jung once wrote, "Can we, therefore, blame humanity, and all the well-meaning shepherds of the flock and worried fathers of families, if they erect protective barriers, hold-up wonder-working images, and point out the roads that wind safely past the abyss." Yes, I will no longer blame him. I will believe the best—that he meant to protect me from harm. I will attempt to honor him and those around me, for I don't want to be like the writers in DeSalvo's, *Conceived with Malice*, malignantly abusive, destroying those they wrote about.

"You have worked so hard to come to terms with your experiences," he exhumes. "I'm so happy and proud of you. Thank you for calling and for always being honest with me."

On Monday, rendezvous with Betts to say good-bye. We are one about the decision to leave the women's therapy group. "I liken you, Murphy, to my client, Terry, the gentleman you respect so much, whom I've known for ten years. Less and less is it necessary for me to see him. Now, only a few times a year at our weekend retreats."

"Yes. I was so impressed with him." At several of Bett's retreats, I remember the delight of "playing" football and wrestling with Terry, an assistant professor, another kind of brother.

"Just as Terry, you have grown up, especially in regard to the decision to speak with your father this weekend!"

A few days later, at the crack of dawn, actually, physically "feel" a phantasmagoric succubus crawl into bed spooning me. Inside this alter-reality, distinguish he is the former husband from 1787 and the man in this life I've

Book One – Across the Divide to the Divine **177**

Part I: Across

had such troubles with. Struggling to yell, hoarsely I demand, "Ggg…get…get out of my bed!" Escorting him through the door. Discover the lock has been jimmied. So, though vulnerable, I'm too exhausted to cope, falling into bed into a deep sleep, feel his weight against me again. In response, I turn to pulverize his face with my right hand—which jolts me out of this dimensional reality—for I have killed him!

Shocked by this violence. *Or is it unexpected bravery of Farrah Fawcett's Burning Bed?* Afraid of what really happened in the past: never allowed to fully explore nor express myself—so the coughing, the gagging, the choking, the pent-up rage. Want to yell at the doctor of my traumatic birth, at Dad and Mom for not protecting me, at the football player who landed on me in the pool, at the teachers from school, at my culture that doesn't protect the little one. Little Irene is angry, hurt, let down, disappointed, scared stiff, shaking, lonely, misunderstood, scorned—and now, perhaps, even dangerously rageful.

As I inhabit more of myself, writing a book late at night, accessing my voice, notice the hiding in a glass of wine, or in movies. *Is this that rage contained, held back and vengeful?* Fear leaving the job that sustains me financially yet protracts me from my truth. This time when I leave though, it won't be from that old pattern—an "act of rebellion"—instead, I shall rise up and out through my own gut knowingness.

The Maasai Warriors flash before my eyes sitting quietly, courageously during circumcision. Imagine a version of this bravery in the orthodontist's chair, in the continuation of showing myself at the office.

Walter, the analyst, assures: "Right now, you're more yang, mind and spirit. Soon, you'll be yin, body and soul, the fully orgasmic self you long to be. Go for it, Murphy, it won't hurt to let go into those orgasms. You'll be okay. Others have gone before you!"

His words, at least, bring a barrel of laughter and the thought—it may indeed be possible—liberation, *perhaps from suppression?*

Fourth Journey In

26

NEW TWIST

"Naamini! Lakini imari yanju haitoshi, nisaidie!"
"Lord I believe, help mine unbelief."

—Maasai proverb

Before the *fourth journey in* to Laloshwa Highlands, on Lamu Island, I spend a celebratory Christmas night (2000) and the following day with some of Sir Laurens' friends and mine: Carol, Angela, David, Debs, Victoria, John, Eva, Richard, Bonnie, Ethan, Sally, Willy and Katherine.

The following evening, I march off alone to the waterfront, above zillions of stars, below, barefooted along the lapping ocean, imploring the gods and goddesses: *"Why do these shoulders and neck ache? What separates me from me,*

Part I: Across

and me from You? Is it because I'm not on purpose? Am I destined to be a cosmic wanderer, the Cosmic Swan on a hundred-thousand-year journey? Please open the way. Subdue and integrate this division, so I'm harmonious, in this skin, in sync with the Universe, my heart beating to the same rhythm as the stars." Yes, I want to be as the Bushmen say, "walking with the moon and the stars again" (van der Post, *Jung and the Story of Our Time*).

Within the New York Fashion Avenue milieu to be on the same island with Prince Albert, Princess Caroline, and Prince Ernst is a coup. At the Peponi Hotel bar, a flirty doctor invites me to their royal party—amazingly to him, I couldn't have cared less. Instead, I'd rather talk with the filmmaker, Richard Gayer, about the challenges our indigenous friends face as they step into the Twenty-First Century. Or wander off to the beach, asking those questions about my intrinsic self: *What is within my heart that I must do, be?*

Strolling along Lamu Beach I ponder the same questions with Sir Laurens' friend Eva Monley, who has been so pivotal in my connection to the Bushmen. With her dog in tow, we talk up a storm. "Is it animals or people you're interested in?" "People and their stories." Yet, on some level, I can't explain. *Isn't soul work into our past lives often unexplainable?*

By the afternoon of the 27th, I take the boat across to the mainland and the brief flight to Nairobi to meet Marjana. Though late, we are both so anxious and decide to drive all the way to Laloshwa Highlands. Henry Muringi, our Kikuyu cook silently rides in the back of the Land Rover. For our favorite chicken dinner, the three of us make a brief stop in Naromi. The town of Narissima is asleep as we drive through. The Kitomini Community is at rest, too. As we turn the corner to the Bright's Camp, we have a majestic sighting of a herd of buffalo, *olorro*.

After the long trek, I sleep intensely where I fall into a strange will-o'-the-wisp of Mother waving at us, as Marjana and I rush down a Kenyan highway. Stop. Run across the road to greet her. As if acknowledging the commitment of her love, she bestows me with a bundle of red roses, blessing my passage towards "the somewhere" of great import. *To Laloshwa Highlands? Or more internal pursuits?*

In the morning, we drive up into the village to discover Kisima, Sarototi's wife playfully peeking, hiding sensually behind the entrance of their *engang*. Love watching Sarototi speak gently to her. Their boys, *inkiyuni*, Lesainana and Marpenzi, dance around me. They cannot wait for the fruit and the candies we have brought. They point at their noses, *enkume*, as they inhale the pleasures of these goodies.

Marjana introduces me to his second wife, the former wife of his brother, who was killed in a car accident. According to custom, Marjana adopted the widow and their two children. Am sad for her loss. Although, she is well taken care of, due to this customary procedure, she could never choose to marry anyone else. She is sweet, kind. I also meet Saifi's Atatei, his oldest child.

Marjana leads me to Baba Hasa, who once protected me from the angry warrior's response to my camera. He will translate for me today. Oddly this is the first time anyone else has stood in for Marjana. Baba Hasa ushers me to Sarototi's dung hut for another ritual. "Take four dots of this white herb with your tongue. Now, bathe in this mixture of white milk, *kole*, inside the *olorro*, buffalo skull. Do not wash this off—no shower tonight."

Exiting the hut, several women tease me: "NeLaloshwa enkiama Sarototi?" *Marry him?*

Before bed, on the stoop of my tent, I watch the new moon, *walapa*, disappear behind the trees. Of course, each and every one of Sarototi's ceremonies commiserates this moment of beginnings. Normally, I remain inside the continuing and wonderful process of these microdosed curatives. However, after this one, I wonder—*where is everybody?* There was no group acknowledgement. No Kisima making tea. Marjana did not interpret. No known elder. Not Chief Ole Wangombe, nor his loyal friend, Baba Budhya, nor Sarototi's father, Baba Sarototi, nor the usual women, who bless me, were there. And a man I have met once or twice deciphers. Something eerily open-ended about this…*Why am I suspicious?*

And what are these medicinals about? I have been so mesmerized, so cared for, taken by each experience, so unguarded, by the incredible alliance Sarototi and I have made, I never think to interrogate, to navigate, to negotiate the situation on my own behalf.

27

TRANSMISSION

"Once we enter other people's heads through their myths, we may find that we cannot get out again; we enter their hearts and their lives too."

—Wendy Doniger, "Other People's Myths," *The Insider/Outsider Problem in the Study of Religion: A Reader.*

This morning before we leave for Narissima, Sarototi consults the Ancestors. He announces: "On our way a message will arrive which shall slow us down."

Passing by the village, the four warriors and I look high and low for the missive. As we arrive at the crest of the Escarpment, we see three Kikuyu men striding toward us, conveying, "There is something wrong with the steering on our truck. Can you help us?"

To their dismay, all of us double over in hysterical laughter. Marjana tries to make plain our reaction as he points at Sarototi. "From this young laibon's divination," he explains, "You are our 'message.'"

27: Transmission

Primarily Western educated, Marjana, straddles between his daily life in urban Nairobi and the animistic world of his Ancestors that he dips his toe into from time to time. For this reason, he has never quite bought into his cousin Sarototi's practices. The rest of us are pleased because we believe. We watch while Marjana services the vehicle, pouring in the needed "transmission" of fluid.

With their truck replenished, we wish the Kikuyu men well, pressing on to the weekly market in Narissima to buy a goat for New Year's dinner. And I, of course, the only white person in the market, want fabrics, swaths, and swaths of Maasai colors to wrap my friends and myself in. The Narissiman Maasai surround the truck to stare at me. Laugh at my curly red *murani*, hair. Tease me about the latest fashion, the cow-skin skirt that I've acquired. For my New York fashion instincts have let go of the Karen Blixen khakis, giving way to the Bushmen inspired soft fur and brown suede skirts. Below, I'm wearing laced-up black boots, and on top, I've set aside that pith helmet (due to its colonial implications) for a more feminine wide-brimmed woven straw Helen Kaminski chapeau.

From the Indian grocer, Marjana buys us a thirst-quenching soda. Never drinking such a luxury in America, here, however, now, in this heat, the sugar hit is a treat. As I saunter past the stalls, the women fascinatingly touch my white hands, red nails. When they see the circular copper necklace, to protect the child from the evil one, they wonder: "Where is your child?"

As I press hands to heart, answering, "The child is in here."

They query Sarototi about this phenomenon as we hear in the background a preacher in Kiswahili over a bullhorn, "Jesus can save you."

At the end of our spree, sixteen Maasai pile into the Land Rover, with one live goat. In front, Sarototi shares the shotgun seat with me. In the truck, listen to the warrior, Motoguisimile, as he argues with two young women. I learn from Marjana that these girls claim they have just found "Jesus."

Motoguisimile yells: "*You* have your *own* God. *You* do not need *someone else's!*"

And I think of my want of someone else's husband. Yes, sometimes we want what others have, thinking it is better, thinking him more delicious, thinking this God the solution to all our problems. About their argument, I find myself feeling sad and then extremely angry, wanting to shout against the converters: *Why can't people leave others' beliefs alone?*

Part I: Across

Their argument causes Joseph Mbiti's words to encircle round about me. An advocate of decolonialization, a collector of over three hundred African prayers, he was offended Europeans (I'll add, Americans, here) believed because Africans stories were oral, they were therefore, savages, that their beliefs were evil, demonic and primitive. To Mbiti, African religions were worthy of respect as much as Christianity, Buddhism, Islam, as well as Judaism. In his translation of the Greek New Testament into his own language, Kamba, he saw a thousand discrepancies between the original and the westernized version, acknowledging that this faulty translation, as well as the original teachings brought to his people, did not fit the Africans' needs.

"Please tell them, Marjana: I come from this God they spoke of in the marketplace. Listen to your Maasai brother. Hold fast to what is indigenously true for you." I respond rebelliously! "Perhaps your God and mine are the same gods just different names." I had yet to learn of The Four Winds Society, *Prayer for Opening Sacred Space* (Alberto Villoldo), of the belief—"Great Spirit, you who are known by a thousand names"—of which I was already, naturally, through these African engagements, holding tenet within my heart.

At the time, I cannot grasp—*Why this rebellion is bubbling up as though molten lava in regards to these young girls' conversions? Why am I joining this Maasai man in the defense of his faith?* I will eventually learn of my own silent history from the abuse of others, which had been lost through the induction of amnesia through systemic suppression, which will inform me of why I had been afraid of those who had dominion over me. Whether it be older men or leaders of a particular faith, what I feared most was the form the proselytizing often takes—that is—of imperialistic domination. I did not want this for these girls!

It wasn't that Christianity hadn't impacted me, nor brightened my world. I had attended church devoutly for the first thirty-two years of my life, read the scriptures over and over, been fascinated with the stories in the Torah, prayed incessantly. I understood that whether one "believed" in Christ's death on the cross and his subsequent resurrection, something had mythologically moved and changed on the earth enough to recreate calendars from BC to AD, to light up humanity in a different manner, giving "value to suffering." As Mircea Eliade reveals, "transforming pain from a negative condition to an experience with a spiritual content" (*The Myth of the Eternal Return*). But even so this faith I was raised in, had often taken a turn to trample on others, to build churches upon

27: Transmission

their sacred sights, to make assurances, or to kill those in opposition, who held to other tenets.

"NeLaloshwa, we are bribed to believe." Motoguisimile declares, "The 'latest' church promises a tin roof home with a cement floor if we convert."

"In the Winter," Marjana confesses, "in their constructions, we freeze. In the Summer, we boil." Then, he reveals: "Murphy, Motoguisimile has been studying the Bible for a year while you have been away."

"Yes, I've read and read and read. I keep looking for God in the Bible. But, I cannot find Him. Here, in Laloshwa, however, Engai is everywhere," retorts Motoguisimile.

Can only think of Plotinus, who felt the gods and goddesses fell from the sky, when the Gnostics and the Christians reduced and simplified religion to a singular God. Oh, please, don't let the stars fall here! And yet, for this, I had to agree with Motoguisimile and Plotinus. Spirituality is expansive, full of possibilities, a multiplicity of stories.

This relationship of mine to God has always been beyond the walls of the church. As a child, with a full heart, I was on my knees every night with my parents praying. About everyday things, I walked through the woods talking out loud to Him, to the animals, to the birds, the trees, the flowers—so nature bound.

Later, just before she began to lose her memory, in tears, I tightly grasped Mother's hand, "Thank you, Mommy, for teaching me that God was bigger than the Bible!"

"No, Murphy, it's not true! From the very beginning you gave this God to me!"

No idea I'd influenced *her*. I just kept listening to the creatures of the earth and looking up and outward, towards the sunset, towards the sunrise, listening for something bigger than myself, to fulfill that "greater hunger" the Bushmen so readily comprehend.

Perhaps this was what both Motoguisimile and I were trying to say to these young girls—that love for God and His love, the goddess' love for us is expansive, not confined by church or creed or community, or even principled, and certainly not fundamental. Like "Grace" herself, in the greatest sense, He, and for some, She, or for others, "it" or "they" just exist.

For the original peoples of Central and South America, just as the Maasai, the gods and goddesses were everywhere. "When the conquistador Pizarro met the Inka ruler Atahualpa, Pizarro handed him the Bible, explaining, 'This is the word of God.'" Alberto Villoldo pens, "Atahualpa brought the volume to his ear, listening carefully, then threw the holy book to the ground, exclaiming, 'What kind of god is this that does not speak?'"

The memory gushes back of my evangelical husband and his five friends at Miami University of Oxford, each wanting to reach the unreached with the gospel: China, Russia, Africa, perhaps, even the Polynesian Islands, or Thailand. In trepidation of this, I had declared to my hubby: "I will follow you to Africa. But I will not proselytize, only live among them, writing, and drawing." Together, we never made it to Africa, only as far as Northwestern University's students. Of course, the irony is, "*Here, am I*"—sent, called to Africa, journaling, photographing, filming, and illustrating among them, encouraging them to hold fast to what they know, hold fast to Engai.

When we reach the Highlands, the truck is so full, it cannot carry us. Exhaustingly we climb by foot, leaving Marjana to slowly drive the distance. *Why have I chosen to endure this intense sun, these obstacles to be with the Maasai, a foreigner, in a foreign land?* Because, in truth, and for far too long, I have been a stranger separated from the self, from memory, from my own countrymen.

What strikes me is part of the reason I can no longer place myself inside the religion of Christianity has to do with the oppositional forces that religion causes within people. Wars are brought on by such, as well as greed for what others have that we want—oil, money, diamonds, minerals. Having been brought up as a Liberal Presbyterian, I feel I cannot afford to be inside one versus another, I cannot move in zeal about *my* faith, thinking it as an answer for someone else, who has been steeped in another religion and that religion gives them life amongst such challenges in the everyday.

Even our own psychological practices, according to Eduardo and Bonnie Duran enforce the now secularized Judeo-Christian myth— "our discipline has been a coconspirator in the devastation and control of those peoples who are not subsumed under a white, male, heterosexual, Christian subjectivity." *Who was I to separate the Maasai, the Bushmen, the Native Americans, or anyone for that matter, from what is their truth?* Their own faith, their own God may have the power to save them from despair. In fact, I had had enough experiences of domination to know that when one group overrides another's beliefs, there is a

27: Transmission

feeling of being swamped and overwhelmed, and usually the loss of their cultural and spiritual beliefs.

That evening, we gather with the Laloshwan Maasai at Baba Hasa's manyatta in celebration of his granddaughter's naming ceremony. Sarototi's mother, Yicyo coaxes me into the dance with the young warriors and their girlfriends, into a long rhythmic, pulsating train: "*eya yo eya yo eya yo.*" The chanting is hypnotic. The children laugh at my oddities. Assume their gossiping: "She's not a Maasai. Who is she? Why is she here?" For teasing and gawking at me, Yieyo swipes at their feet with a stick, commanding their obedience to welcome me.

On NeLaloshwa's behalf, Sarototi's mother stands straight and tall, transmitting this energy, demanding they accord me dignity whatever creed or color. *When have I ever done that for someone else?* —Once, perhaps, for Gracie, including her in Brownies; once, for Tanya "Apples" Weddemire, bringing her into the sales department at Mary McFadden; once, for Jade, to send her to Catholic school.

Even though I am forty-two years old, even though these girls are one-fourth my age, I still don't like being judged so harshly. *Who does?* Surely, at times, others have felt this from me. I hope not. Forgive me if so, if I've been insensitive to whom you are as a person, in your beliefs, in your ways! The sad thing is, within our society, there are people who frequently experience prejudice, whose very presence, whose words, and therefore their inner thoughts, get "cancelled out." Yet, they cannot help being who they are, nor who they are perceived to be, as I cannot help being who I am, nor who I am perceived to be. They might think, I think, I'm better. I'm certainly not! Nor am I lesser. Yieyo bravely stood up for me, accepted the uniqueness of eccentricity, ethnicity, color of skin, uncircumcised body, black army boots, her son's love for me.

Isn't this what I wanted for those young girls most recently converted to Christianity—a non-judgmental experience, freedom of belief, dignity, dominion within the Self? That they may grow up in a world where they are given the opportunity to live amongst others without being "other-ed" for their distinctions, for their color, for their clothes, for their religions, just because they don't think or look or believe the same.

What a boring universe that would be! We'd cease to travel "elsewhere," to touch down in other realities, miss a glance of a Cambodian Buddhist monk wrapped in a saffron robe chanting, never see the upper Dolpo people drive their yaks over the Himalayas, nor stand at the Wailing Wall in Jerusalem to observe the black-behatted Hasidic Jews draped in scarves rocking in a gorgeous vigilance of prayer to their God or a Muslim bowing in prayer upon her woven rug. I, for one, vote for these unique expressions to continue their existence. I've enjoyed these moments amongst a people so vastly distinctive from those high school friends dressed in red from head to toe, cheering for the Trojans.

In the end, I must confess, I had been judgmental of these young girls for reaching out to Christianity. I could have extended more grace to their want of redemption, to remember that that same Christ consciousness was within me, living and alive. Maybe I was holding onto their old ways when really what the youth wanted was an educational change. Maybe the Maasai's traditions were breaking down. Maybe within their patriarchal families, they weren't finding fulfillment. Maybe their culture could no longer sustain their wants and needs. So, because of this, these young women had turned outward to Christ. I did not know their discontent would soon be roaring up for even greater transformations, I did not know Nice Leng'ete was already out their, challenging the men, speaking out against clitoral circumcision.

Inside my tent, late that night, I experience such frustrations—feel the trip is too short, too important, too expensive to have zipped by so fast! One hike, one roll of stones, one ritual, a shopping expedition, a dance, and yet, *"Here, am I,"* on the precipice of a major entrée. Everything in my life seems vastly poignant, even, urgent.

The following day, Sarototi and Saifi seem to know my need. They demonstrate the plant that cures malaria, which tastes bitter, burns the tongue. About the year, we discuss how things have unfolded. For my requests, Sarototi shakes, rattles, and rolls the stones. "Can I leave the job harmoniously?"

Toss, tally: "You're not to leave your job yet."

Explaining the daily intensities, I note: "Not sure how long I can endure!"

The swish, swish of the stones in Sarototi's plastic bottle answer: "True, NeLaloshwa, the Ancestors are calling you to your lifework. It will be slow, hard. You will not have success at first."

"And my father? Is everything right with him?"

"Yes, Murphy. You shall have a blessed meeting with him upon your return."

"Thank you for this transmission." I continue. "Also, a few weeks ago, in Swaziland, my girlfriend Rebecca and I met the Zulu Sangoma, Philani, who wants us to train with him. He believes I need to make a chicken sacrifice."

27: Transmission

Shake, throw, count: "Through the Water and the Strangler Fig rituals, you've made your sacrifice. For truth, I bequeath an herb, to affirm this to the Sangoma. And by the way, you are not to throw the bones, count stones, or use curatives."

Wild! *Isn't that what the Sangoma Philani had affirmed?*

"In New York, the psychic, Frank Andrews has offered to teach the Tarot Cards and Palm Reading. Yes? Or do I rent out my apartment three months at a time, buy a truck, travel to Kenya, Tanzania, Swaziland, Botswana to study?"

Clatter, clatter, sort: "You won't return to Swaziland. However, in Kenya, you will have business and research in the future."

Far from Kitomini, for New Year's Eve, Muringi, the cook, the seven Maasai: Lalalana, Baba Budhya, Nkoyiak, Marjana, Motoguisimile, Sarototi, Saifi, and I feast on the goat we carried home. Afterwards, at our private fire, the warriors sing, jumping to their famous songs. With claps and hollers, Baba Budhya, Muringi and I goad them onto greater heights.

Throughout the entire night, I dream in long drawn out tales until the wee hours of the morning, when I awaken to the notion—due to immense shame—I'd held back from Sarototi, the dream of the man in bed who tried to molest me. *How many women are haunted with such dreams as this?* But worse, I had pounded him to death. *So did I mean to forget the tell?* That I, who love so deeply, could have such splenetic rage inside me, beating him to a bloody pulp, this is hard to fathom, the depths people will go to save themselves or for revenge. And yet, this element resides in me as well. I pray in reality I should never have such a need to do such a thing. I pray what has passed between us, I can rise and forgive and that which I am unable, I place in my hand, releasing this to Him, to Her, whomever is greater than the Self. And hopefully, the abuser, himself, this ethereal succubus, will set up restitution and live into reciprocity.

On New Year's Day before my departure, we travel to the Kitomini Community for our *olesari*, good-byes. I read a farewell letter to Sarototi and the warriors. Sarototi, in turn, presents me with a set of herbs: "With the yellow, lick with your tongue five times before work and every three days until its completion; with the green one, circle around your head clockwise four times, morning and night, at your chest, 'out with the bad, in with the good'; and with the small white bag, before you board the plane four dips with your tongue, the next day, wait a few days, then another few, until it is gone."

Part I: Across

In a cup of milk, *kole*, Sarototi stirs in a medicinal, "to ward off evil." He drinks, then spits into both of my open palms to rub the face. Once more, he drinks, spits, scattering the concoction upon my hands, and I massage this over the stomach, the legs, then drinking from the same mug. *With this action, does he claim me for himself?*

"Training in the Tarot is not necessary." Sarototi hugs me, pronouncing one of the most important missives he will ever impart: "You, NeLaloshwa, are already a Sangoma, a dream shaman, a *laibon*. However, the Zulu Philani is right, you are to liberate others through your writing."

Board the Land Rover sobbing: I've been anointed! *My lifework affirmed!* Even so, upon that return of mine, I will—with Frank Andrews—study Tarot and Palmistry (which is exciting, because the Native Americans trace these life patterns upon the hand as the manifestation of divine energy and Wind Breath). I'm so glad I do study with him, as the symbolism within the Tarot Cards adds to my capacity to decipher dreams and will eventually be a way to divinatorially participate with the Maasai because they comprehend these images that embody our collective unconscious. And whichever way Sarototi's and Philani's transmissions unfurl, it takes years and years, hours of writing, reading, studying, hours of contemplation, meditating, yoga, walking in the park, and praying to get to the "me" of me, finding the words to sing what is *my* tune, not theirs, not yours—mine.

Even so, something will have to rattle the cage and stalk me a little more—gurus and geese and changes in the office—in order for me to depart from that well-honed career.

28

GEESE DECREE

"It doesn't matter if you get old—that place will keep on stalking you like the one who shot you with the story. Maybe that person will die. Even so, that place will keep on stalking you. […] Even if we go far […] to some big city […] even if you go across the oceans."

—Nick Thompson, "Stalking with Stories," Keith Basso's *Wisdom Sits in Places*

A full passage of three years—though I don't know it at the time—will commence between the *fourth journey in* and the fifth. As though the unconscious knows I'm not quite ready to cross the ocean to reconnect with the Maasai, until the shooting of their arrow of *that* initiation stalks me, that Benson Lewis, the Cibecue Apache pronounced. Taking its full affect, until I had "I'd" myself a little more, until I had reestablished a right relationship with planet Kansas, planet New York City, planet Santa Barbara, planet United States.

Part I: Across

So, on planet New York City, the New Year begins with a return to the Badgley Mischka office to discover the promotion I had wanted—Senior Vice President—has gone to someone else, a new woman, Sashana, for double my salary. Their decision to hire her has uncomfortably placed a glass ceiling over my head, creating an unhealthy competition between us. Maybe it's uncomfortable for her as well because for many years now, she's been in daywear, and we specialize in eveningwear, where I'm already established with the buyers, the managers, and the private customers. So, I really know the business. But bless her heart, she'll struggle with the same challenges as I have had—unable to make licensing deals due to the strictures placed on Badgley Mischka through Escada and unable to increase the sales—and within one year's time (though we don't know it yet), she'll sadly lose her job.

What I don't realize is Sashana taking the position over me is a gift on a silver platter. For something is happening inside, something I cannot avoid, something I cannot escape—and the Universe is certainly declaring it. This calling, Jung deems as a "Vocation: an irrational factor that destines a man (woman) to emancipate himself (herself) from the herd and from its well-worn paths." I was separating myself. Attempting to find who "I Am." "True personality is always a vocation and puts its trust in it as in God, despite its being, as the ordinary man would say, only a personal feeling. But vocation acts like a law of God from which there is no escape." In other words, what's roaring up from the bottom of my being is innate; I have no option but to further on! Just as *Sula* declares, "I don't want to make somebody else. I want to make myself" (Toni Morrison).

So, over a long three-day weekend, to escape from the claustrophobic pressure of this glass ceiling and in search of what Sarototi had defined as, "a blessed meeting with" Father. I zip home to Osawatomie to arrange with Dad, the family attorney, and the accountant, the setting up of a future, the setting up of what will become the Global Voice Foundation, a 501c3. Although Dad's business-like banker response is—"A non-profit, means there is no profit, Murphy"—he, as well as Mom will *still* be our "blessed" first funders of $75,000.

So while I continue as a VP, I'll hire Tanya "Apples" Weddemire, a former associate from Mary McFadden, to work from my library at home to ignite GVF. However slowly Sarototi said it would take, GVF commences, in fits and starts, and fills these drudgery days of pressure with such hope, moving me ever closer to that innate calling.

192   *I. Murphy Lewis*

28: Geese Decree

Three months later, to further an escape, on a hot spring day, three friends and I drive Upstate New York for a gorgeous, peaceful meditative weekend retreat, where here, amidst the quiet, serene, gentle chanting, I still locate that miserable self of mine. In other words, even in this necessity for *elsewhere*, I cannot run away from me. Yes, wherever I go, even here, I'm stalked by that ever-faithful story, dashing out of the auditorium to "gag" into the toilet, to the nothingness of a dry heave. So spent, inside the stall, I fall to the cold cement.

Some woman "in charge" marches in; sticking her head below the door, confronting me, "get off the floor!" *Is she serious?* She actually followed me, to demand I comply. And worse, she sees me weak, vulnerable, revealing my nervousness.

"I can't move. I'm sick," I moan tragically.

So far, this weekend, everything I've done is "wrong," keep "breaking the rules," "disrespecting guidelines," "being too loud," so, I'm shushed, "wearing the wrong clothes"—a sleeveless, chiffon sheath, for which they instruct—"cover your arms and legs." For me, a fashionista, this wrapping up in a pashmina, adding black leggings is *their* solution, but not a match! No wonder I'm gagging!

From the moment of this existence, I have been trying to be "perfect," to please everyone inside America's institutions—the "perfect" Brownie, Girl Scout, Cadette, Christian, daughter, sister, student, cheerleader, athlete, homecoming queen, saleswoman, VP, wife. According to Father, my wild red curls are too siren-like, dangerous, so I pull them back into a ponytail to please him. For those Medusa-like snakes, that former husband of mine preferred to have them "wild," and "your white skin—tan." (But, in our society—not too dark, as if I could be anything but pink or burnt!)

The only place that was mine—besides, journaling in an incredible childhood walk-in closet—had been the adornment of being inside Mother's capacity to tailor every whim —"I want that fabric, that pattern, that shape!" She'd listen, buy it and sew it for me! *Was she helping me cover those shameful imperfections with color and possibilities?*

But in NYC, every bit and piece I've been selling are the designers' creations—not mine! For, in fact, I had never succeeded as a designer! Instead, ever since my arrival, I have been draped inside and selling the "latest" label: dangling in Brett Lewis and Connie Bates Fahrenheit earrings and belts; at Bergdorf Goodman, squeezed in Anne Klein, Michael Kors, Jean Muir; on Madison Avenue, decorated in Lee Anderson donning Jeffrey Moss' hats, which

Book One – Across the Divide to the Divine **193**

Part I: Across

I adore to this day; and on Fashion Avenue, swathed in the colors of Leonard of Paris, MMcF, Mary McFadden, (I kept a few of her treasures); Halston, and Badgley Mischka, in the end, I couldn't let them all go. Don't get me wrong. I was not suffering in these beautiful adornments. I loved every parcel and perk they'd clothed me in. And I wore them to the hilt!

However, just as Father, my ex, and inside the designers' imagination there was this notion of what that representation should be: the "just so" make-up, the clothes, the shoes, the jewelry and once again, "cut the hair, or pull the curls back in a bun!"—so familial, so familiar. *Isn't this need of the known what we turn to when we're perplexed?* And now, at this retreat, another religion from another country (which by the way, doesn't have all the answers sewed in a bag) is sewing me up into its encasement, cocooned, entombed, mummified until I'm out of breath, corseted, girdled.

At this moment, I hadn't the wherewithal to describe what Hillman coined "Pink Madness: Why does Aphrodite drive us crazy..." That *this* very nature, that the wild redheaded wavy female voluptuous (well, truthfully, flat-chested) self, as well as Sophia, has historically been crushed for centuries. Yes, we still live in a puritanical culture that shuts down, hides sex until it erupts into bizarre obsessions of pornography and the raping of girls, boys and women! The truth is, even in fashion, this femaleness has been anorexized in stick-starved models appearing more as boys than women. (The sleek well-rounded Naomi Campbell has been the exception.) Thankfully, this notion is rapidly changing. And, as for me, I no longer want to fit in anybody's cookie cutter image—and neither should you!

Underneath this rebellious stirring, there is another more controversial rumbling: I cannot bow to the guru. Honor, yes, but not bend low. "This morning, I watched her walk by," as I frustratingly peel off that pashmina cover-up I was commanded to wear, "and I cannot bow to the guru," I trumpet to my shocked friends, her followers, seated at the luncheon table. "It's not that I think I'm better than her. It's that, *I'm on the same footing.*"

Even so, one of us announces, "From her, I have just received shaktipat."

"Well, this just means she knows the 'short cut' to 'the Path of Illumination' and can slay you in the spirit." It might even reveal that her incarnations are resolved, and her wounds have been healed. I must acknowledge, "Of course, she has different gifts, has been trained how to meditate, to run her energies, and was crowned the leader. Maybe she knows who she is, knows she has access to the divine—is, perhaps, even enlightened, further along in her ascension—however, though I'm quite cut off, I'm still her equal!" Even though—for reasons I've yet to confess to these friends and for reasons, I don't fully understand—my un-contained, dramatic and ego-ed self still lies sprawled on the concrete from the gag. *And I call myself equal to the guru, equal to the task?*

Just because someone has been made a guru doesn't mean they're perfect. Individually we are only the sum total of those who have educated us. How can we expect more from those, that much like us, are *"suffering from defective education" (Jung)?* Our everyday leader is no better than the everyday parent—whom I just untangled myself from, through the power of the Strangler Fig. And yet, a projection is made upon our priests, our minsters, our shamans, our rabbis, our gurus, our politicians, even our parents, to maintain perfection.

What I hadn't read before I came, was *The New Yorker* article of Lis Harris, "O Guru, Guru, Guru" (November 14, 1994)—maybe because it was confiscated and burned in mass quantities—which unearthed truths, undermining the strength of the guru. Something I wouldn't wish on anybody. I will later wonder if due to the comment above— "I cannot bow to the guru"—I might have been under surveillance as Harris was, and so, followed into the bathroom in gagging mode. For the guru was and will be holding down the scandals of sexual abuses from the original leader, Swami Muktananda and several other members within her organization, amidst hidden financial misconduct, which will be exposed in another article in *Salon*, "The 'Eat, Pray, Love' Guru's Troubling Past" (Riddhi Shah), and a book, Marta Szabo's *The Guru Looked Good*. And for those who will leave discontented, there will be a website "leavingsiddhayoga."

And me? In thirteen years, memories will make sense of the gagging, how that gagging was constantly returning me to the center of the self, to the center of the wound. And even more importantly, it will reveal why I can no longer tolerate being under the helm of *anyone*. Further understanding that swapping one religion for another—whether the songs are more beautiful and the meditative position more elegant—just means one is still held in some form of *obedience*.

In the meantime, speaking of subordination, there are changes happening within our office, I've been unable to speak of. Before this weekend, our Badgley Mischka CFO Mark, had secretly whispered: "Sashana is writing you out of the budget." Of course she is, because I won't bow to her authority! He urges, "You must find another job!"

Part I: Across

These last few days, Mark's incantation—"find another job"—circle round about me. *Do I really want to work for someone else?* For I know this company—besides working for Joan Arkin at Leonard—is the sincerest Seventh Avenue can get. If I were going to continue to sell beautiful clothes, I'd rather be at Badgley Mischka. *Or would I? Isn't this "being pushed out" a gift from the Universe?*

Once again the rise of the Aphroditic nature has become so systematically shut down and covered up, that it's coming unglued, so that I can no longer put a lid on it. Know this rising rebellion, this internal shift within has nothing to do with any of "them," with this organization, or with the people at Badgley Mischka, or Escada. It's not *their* fault. It's just that, I can no longer abide authority. Soon, I will recognize I'd been so let down, so betrayed by those who had jurisdiction over me that I would be forever unable to bow to a guru or to a boss.

Yet, there are those moments when people stake a claim on us, have power over us, and we willingly give ourselves over to them. Sometimes we just can't see through the trees to our liberation, which mysteriously lies so wholeheartedly within the forest. More often than not our educators, as well as our parents, gurus, leaders, priests are not fully developed human beings. Instead, they are "personifications" of the methodical way they've been taught. In other words, they are not necessarily the way forward into the trueness of *our* being. According to Robert Morgan, "fully realized adults are artists that parent the future." *How do we become those adult artists and paint the future?*

To be honest, it's becoming apparent that neither this group nor this job, are serving my life purpose. Nor in the midst of them can I seem to resolve those past struggles. Comprehend, it all adds up to me and me alone! I once heard Ney Bailey, author of *Faith is Not a Feeling*, state: "If you fly a rotten apple to Los Angeles, it's still a rotten apple!" Rotten or not, inside me lies the way, the seed, the courage to march out of this misery, out of a life "in" fashion—which is an absolute *must*!

To shed this skin, this way of being into wholeheartedness, I slip out of the group meditation to take a walk around the lake. As I round the far corner, two geese come up over the hillside, squawking at me. They just don't stop. Instead, they protest without ceasing. Follow. Waddle along beside me. When I increase the pace, the two of them slide into the water, paddling as fast as they can to keep up, still cackling up a storm! Stalking!

28: Geese Decree

To concur, if anyone else sees what I'm hearing, I look around. There is no witness to affirm whether or not this is real or what others might consider— "just my imagination running away with me" (Norman Whitfield, Barrett Strong, The Temptations). *Yet, isn't my imagination of these stalking geese just as valid and legitimate? And since, I won't listen to the guru, have the gods and goddesses sent the only creatures I will listen to?*

Somehow this notion provides the willingness to place myself upon the grass, gather into, endeavor a meditative state. And given we're at a spiritual retreat, I can finally calm down, surrendering to the message of the Canadian Geese: "Your mind is discombobulated, out of harmony, caught in a dichotomy, echoing the sound of our voices back and forth. You're too afraid to trust. Just follow your heart. Open your arms wide. Expand your chest. Let go. Fall into the arms of the Universe, our dear sister."

On this land of the guru's, I grasp what they have to say. Even if that Self is divided in dichotomy, into the form of two geese squawking in my head, that Self can still guide me out of Father's and other people's notion of what they want me to be dressed-up as. At Badgley Mischka, what had propped me up, were those daily business conversations with dear ole Dad. With his memory loss from hundreds of T.I.A.'s into a drastic descent into dementia, he can no longer track the details, nor no longer does he have an agenda for me as a "successful businesswoman." So, I can let go of *that*—for I've been there, done *that*! And without his support, without his guiding light and those parameters to please him, it becomes necessary to leave behind the *accoutrements* of fashion, this coiffed-up life.

Yes, after so diligently increasing the numbers 82% for Badgley Mischka, somethings gotta change. In fact, eighteen months after the white *sangoma* Dr. Dave Cumes decreed, seven months after the Zulu *sangoma* Philani decreed, five months after the Maasai *laibon* Sarototi decreed, two months after the gaggle of geese decreed, I'm meant to be something "other." For I now know, that what I'm doing is not born out of my innate calling. I know, I must take the risk, falling into the Multiverse's arms.

And so, one day in May—the 8th to be exact—the CFO Mark will let me know, "You're back in the budget, Murphy. Sashana can't live without you!"

Yet, instead of Sashana's decision encouraging me to stay, I'll trust, I'll listen to those geese. Immediately, I'll stroll majestically into James' office to resign, shedding skin, flinging off the authority of Father, untangling myself

Book One – Across the Divide to the Divine

Part I: Across

from that way of life, untangling myself from the corporate business world, of culture, of the guru, and any and all hierarchical forms. I just want to work differently, outside that system, to not be tied to a desk, maybe even, work from home.

So, there! Freed, as a wild stallion, walking out of bridal and bit, walking out of that well-honed career, officially launching a non-profit, attempting to give voice when I *can* to my dear friends the Bushmen and the Maasai…and perhaps, someday, little ole me.

And so, I'll march out, away from the given and the known, towards the unknown, towards the intangible—the invisible world I'd re-discovered in Africa—towards the newfound sovereignty within.

28: Geese Decree

The Great Dance, Vetkat Regopstaan Kruiper, a Bush-man

PART II

The Divide

"If we could first know where we are, and whither we are tending, we could then better judge what to do, and how to do it. […] of putting an end to slavery agitation. […] it will not cease, until a crisis shall have been reached, and passed. […] 'A house divided against itself cannot stand.'"

—Abraham Lincoln, 1858

Part II: The Divide

> *"First, color-blindness legitimizes racism's need for an "other" in order to flourish and maintain its influence within the fabric of society. Racism and white supremacy are not aberrant, insofar as the oppressors—the status quo—exploit the "others" (the oppressed) in order to maintain their elitist control, as well as to claim that they are neutral. Close examination repudiates this false sense of neutrality. Second, meritocracy allows the empowered—the status quo—to feel "good" and have a clear conscience: many would ask why the powerful would not have a clear conscience since they maintain a majority of the wealth and power in society. The powerful maintain power and only relinquish portions of it when they have nothing to lose; furthermore, they receive platitudes and compliments when they do choose to dole out portions of their power."*

—Nicholas Daniel Hartlep, "Critical Race Theory: An Examination of its Past, Present, and Future Implications"

29

DEMARCATION

"Irreversibility is humanity, wounded by the arrow of time. The most subtle gesture for showing the gods the meaning of irreversibility, the scourge of humans, is libation: spilling a noble liquid onto the ground, losing it forever. [...] a gesture of homage [...] A way of telling the gods: Whatever we do, we are this spilt liquid."

—Roberto Calasso, *The Celestial Hunter*

For three years (as I mentioned before), I will not return to the Maasai. For I am in the departure zone, leaving the reality of victimization in the ashes, not quite ready to step onto a new platform soaring as the Phoenix. Yet I am bound for, as well as I am bound to my destiny to rebuild, to "remake the Murph." Not knowing that I'm being reformed from othering the "other." As well, I am no longer so much about what I "do," but the essence of how I do it, how I approach a thing. It isn't a wonder zone of—*What am I going to be when I grow up?* Instead, an ongoing pursuit for story, following the heart's longing to

Part II: The Divide

write, continuing the collection of their tales, while I'm here, and whenever I can return. The *laibon*, the *sangoma*, and even the geese decree, "let go, surrender into who you are, who you were meant to be." And so, I Am.

All through the hot summer of 2001, after departing from Badgley Mischka, I prepare the launch of the not-for-profit, and along with Lisa Robinson, edit the films of the Bushmen's, *Music that Floats from Afar and How do you name a Song?* By late August, we will launch the second footage to Film Festivals throughout the U.S. and Europe—without noticeable success.

On the morning of *9/11*, I am at home in conversation with the Jungian Psychoanalyst Walter Odajnyk. We have come to that—the telephone—for prophetically he has felt a wind of change, moving his private practice to Connecticut. And today of all days, I confess to him what is finally emerging—the fury at those past abuses, the fury I feel over the continued white-male-domination, as well as the fury at the over-arching culture's paradigmatic structure that seems impenetrable and unbudgeable.

Ironically and most appropriately significant, we are interrupted by a penetration with a far greater reach than the identification to the supremacy, which erupted in childhood. For a plane has crashed into the World Trade Center shifting the paradigm. Immediately, we end our session, for something loomed larger. Within the hour, the Twin Towers collapse. What remedies I have, my associate Apples and I gather, passing them onto the two sitting in the emergency vehicle outside our building.

As Apples' concern increases from our inability to reach her family, her head pounds and rightly so. In the only way I know how, we light two candles on the altar where the goddess of mercy, Kwan Yin, presides over the living room, insisting we hold hands and pray. This ordeal, this living in a kind of unnameable war zone of what may still come, we want for no one. From the collapsing of the Twin Towers, a grey ash falls half-a-block away from my condominium at Church and Leonard, just ten blocks from the epicenter as we watch Giuliani and others covered in this ash, sprint for their lives.

The priests of old, remind us, "We are but Ash." And this ash will eventually blow through the crevices of our neighborhood windows, invading our lungs, marking a border, dividing us from the pain of those who were trapped and so acutely affected in this loss and horror, and those who can only, from a distance, observe in shock and compassion. Of which, I can now deduce—just because of those Maasai Warriors—this ash has become ceremonial.

29: Demarcation

Inside my being, I have two imaginary scenarios: a hit squad of martial artists on a secret mission in search of Osama Bin Laden, who is thought to be the Mastermind; the other, to form a hand-holding-circle, surrounding, demanding of him: "This war between us has to stop. We must attempt truth and reconciliation. We must have peace." Amongst us, even those decisions are simple Band-Aids on the greater challenges existing within the political, economic, and religious realms. For we ourselves have imperially done such damage. Having just come from Fashion Avenue where I had drawn swords every day, challenging the system, challenging the way things are "done"—*Why would I want to bring more battles on this earth? Is there a third scenario?*

Even if there is no solution, our reality has changed, as we know it. A month later, I will even hear rumors that my former employers have lost half their business. God bless them! So my gut directive—of not guaranteeing five million more, nor guaranteeing them last year's dollars—becomes peculiarly apparent. And now, there are those who want others to pay, soon, sadly, choosing to massively, exponentially perpetuate the suffering of thousands of people, who do not deserve this treatment, with the bombing of Afghanistan, and eventually Baghdad.

Yet, the British papers reveal that the Maasai, part of my Kenyan family, have driven their cattle into Nairobi to give to those families who have lost their loved ones in the Twin Towers. Recurrently, I perceive their kind, loving hearts, acting beyond the call of duty. Reminding me of the transformation that's happened inside. For once in this life, I'm prepared for this, for I've set a path toward a different kind of light, to be part of the solution, no longer part of the problem.

Though I am above the watermark, in Tribeca, not Wall Street, the residue of *9/11*, what remains is haunting. For in truth, the detritus of the tumbling rubble, lies at our feet, reminiscent of our "irreversibility," as though we are just libations for the gods, poured out upon the ground to be lost forever. Yes, as Calasso reminds, "Whatever we do," we are once again vulnerable, "we are this spilt liquid."

For weeks after, those of us who live and work below the yellow-ribboned "police line do not cross" Canal Street, view the haul of smashed fire trucks, long beams of metal dragged from the ruins. The tremors, the aftershock, the Post Traumatic Stress marks us, drawing the line between what was and is forcing us into an embodiment of the unknown, into (hopefully) an internal spiritual

Book One – Across the Divide to the Divine **205**

Part II: The Divide

change, into the liturgy for the dead, "Ashes to ashes, dust to dust"—which holds little comfort for the losses, but is, in fact, an everyday actuality. Later these remains will become just soot, soot that filters into everything I own, which must be cleaned, cleared, and Hepa vacuumed several times by different organizations sent to bode well. I won't know until later, how fitting it is that I am here amongst the dust and the dirt, to be a part of those who help the dead transition.

And from this moment onward, from the Midpoint of Irene Murphy Lewis' life, I will choose a third scenario—listening to the inner voice, a movement toward individuation—what Jung described as the potentiality of "a life individually lived." Where there is the possibility of the distinction of personality, enabling a person to live to the fullest, "an act of high courage flung in the face of life." Instead of being angry at others, *9/11* will become that dividing point between how I would live, what I would live for, stand for, and put up with. Just as the line of Demarcation in ash of the Twin Towers, the Maasai have drawn a line down the middle of my personal timeline within, taking the sting out of victimhood—where the lack of, where I am victim to, where I cannot find myself within myself—is clearly separated, and from then on, the beginning of an authentic "I" edges forward.

Oh, I will still get tangled up in the sheets, wrapped up in Liz Green

Liz Greene's "chronic, repetitious suffering or restriction, which circles back again and again" (*The Astrology of Fate*), locking down into a pattern of being—for damaged goods often become the bad girls, the Dolly Harshaws (Virginia Madsen) who attract the bad boys, the Harry Madoxes (Don Johnson), and vice versa (*The Hot Spot*).

However, tangled up I might become, whether my fatedness might go away or not, whether there is a feeling of "something irrevocable" (Greene), there is now a "Me." Perhaps, even a coagulation, certainly, a Convergence where all the parts of that "Me" have begun to Merge. And SNAP! Those in the planes on that fateful day of *9/11* had made a pathway, had burned through the penetration of our history, leveling it to the ground with the crumbling of the Twin Towers. The fury dissolves, for I have bigger fish to fry. An ending of a sufferance. A, then, to a now. For in truth, in crisis, our Self RISES.

Just as the pilots, so the Maasai have switched on a light of knowingness within, and in an instant I know where to go to specialize my writing skills, to learn more about story. From henceforth, NeLaloshwa will be set apart, where my talents, gifts, personal legend which have been declared by the Sangoma Philani and confirmed by the *laibon* Saratoti, can now be pursued. For the Maasai have unlocked the padlock, opening up the fields beyond the imagination, clearing away the long-agos so that I can drop the careful "covering" of couture clothes. To undim the dimness of my Self, awakening the spirit, which has always been there, which has shown through in brief moments, more often than I can imagine, clearly lighting the path set before me.

Just as *9/11*, the experience with the Maasai is cataclysmic. It may look subtle; girl leaves career in fashion, spending the summer launching her nonprofit organization and editing her film. However, I believe it to be a Radical, internal shift. I am living more purposefully. I see and feel things I hadn't before. In that climatic scene in Upstate New York (as we've observed in the chapter before), the "I" of me can now separate the Self from the guru without worshipping her, I can listen to geese, I can walk out of that well-honed career, and strangely, in 249 Church Street, in the middle of the night, I can see and feel the unseen—people going home after their deaths in the Twin Towers. And so it will begin, these strange ways of relating, of seeing the world differently, of engaging with new friends, those geese, those shamans, past life regressors, professors, and sometimes, if I listen real carefully, I can even fathom the intricate structures of Father's dementia.

In every one of the Maasai's ceremonies, the ash from the fires is an expression of the symbol of a letting go, a death and a rebirth into something new. Continuously, Sarototi had me lick and rub this ash upon the forehead, tying some of the residue into penny-sized plastic bags to spin around the head, pushing from the heart, "out with the bad, in with the good." These ritual artifacts gifted to me, still hang from the Maasai necklaces, vibrating me into soulfulness, connecting me to all the ancestors' bones, the plant life.

Just as the Maasai, other civilizations have utilized ashes. On the mountaintops, for rain making purposes, the Chibcha priests of Columbia scatter these remains, as the Catholic monks of old placed the dead upon the ground, upon the symbol of the cross traced from this burnt residual. So, the Romans planted ashes with their crops, feeding these to their flocks, stimulating fertility and the production of milk. Even the San Bush-men-and-women believed the Milky Way subsisted of this Ash, thrown into the heavens by their trickster God, Mantis, Xamsakayaba, who had cleverly stolen fire from Ostrich. These ash extracts

Part II: The Divide

are the living essence of their offerings, sacred renunciations for the sake of spiritual enlightenment.

Renouncing vanity, sublimating the fiery power of their lust, the yogi and sadhu's faces are caked in ash, as in this present moment I am inhaling them. We, the citizens of New York, New York, are inhaling these particles of the dead into our lungs, as now the streets are littered—and for that, for this, we will never be the same. "Memento homo quod cinis es et in cinerem reverteris." "Remember, man (woman), that you are dust, and unto dust you shall return." O, we are but the fiery divine life force, the atomic residue of light in the darkness.

The last peregrination, that *fourth journey in,* for me, was a pivot point—an energetic recovery into a new frontier—and now, even New York City appears distinctive. For I've stepped onto some new wave length, *un nouvelle Matrix,* which has made me kinetically connected to others, to the Cosmos in a way I'd never been before, as though I've turned twenty-five and knew what I wanted to specialize in, to get a masters and a PhD in *that* and that I'd finally be able to catch up to my forty-two-year-old-self. (Honestly, this catching up and liking me is a new and odd experience.)

For in trauma, self-love is lost, as well as the emotional intelligence breaks down. The capacity to make healthy decisions, develop quality choices in relationships becomes obscured, values lessened, because the self does not believe itself to be worthy, to deserve good treatment, nor to demand to be treated well. If traumatized, the capacity to possess an answer or to ask for one feels impossible. So, of course, looking toward others for a solution seems entirely natural. Nor even in the everyday the ability to make a way properly (and when I write properly—I don't mean etiquette—I mean) in a manner that is healthy and right for the self. This, too, becomes quite daunting!

Yet no longer am I blown out into particles throughout the Universe from the big bang of the childhood trauma, which I have yet to uncover, for which I had yet to realize had melted into "amnesia through systemic suppression." No longer am I dismembered, nor a house divided against itself. All of a sudden through the medicinals of the Maasai something has coagulated. Crystallized. All of a sudden through the guidance and care of the Maasai, I have irreversibly passed a demarcation line. A dividing point between being taken advantage of, of being a victim, of the inability to be myself, and of having to set an egg outside the nest as Ostrich to know what I am about—I died to *that*. Now, I am rebirthed into the knowing of who I am, the knowing of what I want.

29: Demarcation

For, in spite of *9/11*, in spite of what had been happening around me at Badgley Mischka, at Escada, I'm being tugged, almost dragged along, toward something I'm not sure I can define. Jung explains, "The fact that many a man (woman) who goes his (her, their) own way ends in ruin means nothing to one who has a vocation. He (she, they, it) must obey his (her, their) own law, as if it were a *daemon* whispering to him (her, their) of new and wonderful paths." For this, I must heed, no matter the cost, no matter whether I fail or not. "Anyone with a vocation hears the voice of the inner man (woman): he (she, they, it) is (are) *called*." Pulled toward something greater than my ego into an inner knowingness. "That is why the legends say that he (she, they, it) (possess) possesses a private *daemon* who counsels him (her, their) and whose mandates he (she, they, it) must obey" (C. G. Jung).

Inklings shimmer within, the Guiding Self, that private *daemon* has been awakened, she hears something new, she steps across the threshold toward it, a transportational pathway glimmers.

30

TRANSPORTER TRANSPORTED

⚜ ⚜ ⚜

"In stepping across the threshold, a woman (and perhaps a man, too) steps out of the constructs [...] (into) a liminal space, a crack between the worlds [...] to unite oneself..."

—Patricia Reis, *Daughters of Saturn: From Father's Daughter to Creative Woman*

In the slow and agonizing aftermath of *9/11*, our city is soaked in bereavement. We have crossed across a threshold into a shift of consciousness. Spontaneous candlelit convocations of old and new friends across the planet, happen. Relatives post pictures "have you seen my...?" Within days what turns out to be the departure of 2,996 people, the loss of three buildings, the sobering of the American consciousness and the world—*they* begin to come.

30: Transporter Transported

At first, I cannot really fathom *them,* telephoning the intuitive Mariah, to confirm my senses: "Yes, Murphy, when you feel this pressure in your chest, someone *is* in your living room asking for assistance. Those who died in the Twin Towers are in a state of confusion. They're in shock. They have no idea what has occurred. Your home is their safe haven. You are called to direct them into the light. Tell them to reach up towards their relatives, towards their new lives."

Mariah's right, I hear noises at night. Of course, I do. On the south side of my apartment, I live across the street from a jazz bar, The Knitting Factory, and on the west side, on the thoroughfare of Church Street, where taxis and limos have glide into Sixth Avenue loaded with Wall Street businessmen and women. (Well, not any longer, since *9/11*). However, these sounds are different and I sense it. For I awaken around three in the morning with a pain just above my rib cage.

The first night in the living room, I stand quietly. Piercing, pleurisy-like pain stabs my breastplate. *Is it true what Mariah said?* —That there's a woman sitting on my plush white chair. Cannot *see* anybody. Cannot *even* feel her. Everyone will really think I'm absolutely bonkers now. Well, this time I won't blame them. But I certainly won't divulge this. "Hello Miss! Mariah says I can help you find your way home. Come." I usher her toward my front door. Between the elevator and this opening, is a private foyer, a place of umbrellas, a mirror with hand-painted walls. Where the hand-blown pastel-colored-Italian-glass globes dangle, I indicate, "Reach up toward these lights. Your grandmother is waiting."

A pain still stabs my heart. *Oh! She must be a bigger personage than I thought.* So, I swing the door to its full width. And whoosh! The ache in my heart disappears. Close the door, trembling. They continue. For days and days, approximately ninety days, I awaken every morning at three o'clock with the same indications. As if Hermes himself, the ever-faithful psychopomp, I guide them home.

One evening, the intuitive Mariah; her friend, Sarah; and my friends, Joy, Kevin and Emmanuel gather to pray for the *9/11* victims and for the men, who died for their cause taking others to their death, to cross easily to the other side. "Those pilots are going separately up an escalator into the light." Mariah channels. *To where?* I wonder. I have yet to grasp this, though Mariah informs, "Each person, the perpetrators, the victims served their purpose, dying for us. We can thank them for this."

Part II: The Divide

Back in Kenya, I had died in that initiation and had come to life in an altogether extraordinary manner. And therefore, I could see (well, let's just say in this instance—I had begun to *feel*) people in a similar state, in a state of transition. Because of this, because of what I had been taught in Africa, I seem to be able to help them find their way to their ancestors, across the borders, that thin veil, which exists. Their (the Maasai's, the pilot's) demarcation line, incinerated a way of being, putting a death to the past, a boundary between that which was and now, is, shining a searchlight on the dark places, revealing truths.

So, oddly, in listening to the ache in my chest, led me back into a conversation with Mariah, which led me to listen to the people, who had died in the Twin Towers Tragedy, who had been so jarred they cannot find their way across to the other side. Day after day for almost three months, one after another, they arrive in my apartment in the middle of the night—and I, magically, mystically hear them, guiding them with the tools of Sarototi, the instructions of Mariah, who have encouraged me in this endeavor. Each act, a movement towards an "I."

After thirty days of psychopomping, my nephew makes a visitation, sleeping on the couch in the living room. I forget to warn him. He awakens, too, to the strange and subtle disturbances. Observes me open the door as I release them into eternity, into what the Tibetan Buddhists reveal, *Padmasavana,* the in-between-state, floating between this reality and the next. In the morning, we speak of this. *He actually believes me!* We light sage, moving the smoke around the room to cleanse the space for others to appear. Further igniting this, we perform a makeshift circular ceremony of drumming, dancing, singing.

In this most destabilizing moment, in our current historical experience, what has created division instead opens the divine possibilities within the heart. People across the world have lit candles. Have held hands and prayed for us. Unusually, New Yorkers sit in cafes, talking with people they've never spoken to in this lifetime! As in days of old, neighbors gather on stoops and steps, interacting. As an uncanny stillness has swept over NYC from this sudden nightmare, for the first time, we are deeply aware of the essentiality of one another.

So, in this atmospheric wonder, another support group forms. A Chinese woman, Joy, a former Buddhist nun, who has been performing hands on healing for me, invites me to join her friends, other healers, Peter, Lawrence, Nako, Philip, and Thomas to restore one another within this climate. Each Monday night, we take turns placing one person in the center for all the rest of us to lay hands upon. I've never done this, ever. One girl who has studied Reiki encourages me. "Just open yourself to God, or a higher power, and let Him, Her, and the Light flow through." I can actually feel heat transpire. Through my mind's eye, I see visions, colors, sharing these insights I gain. When they heal me, I feel surrounded with love, with ritual, with new life, as though on my own continent, I must learn how to live inwardly out, instead of outwardly in according to society's mandates, to embody more fully this "I."

From another religion that thrives through ritual, this Buddhist friend, Joy, helps me formulate the rite that will revealingly explain and incorporate those numinous African experiences. And so it is, that forty-eight friends, and two nephews gather for my marriage ceremony at the still-standing condo on Church Street. The intention of the evening is to marry the two parts of myself together: Irene and Murphy. Irene, which means peace, represents the feminine, is my given name, my Nana's name, and is the one who vanished into the woods of my childhood and was found of late in "the Sacred Forest of the Lost Child." And Murphy, which stands for sea warrior, is also my given middle name, Nana's maiden name, the name my brothers called me, the name I've been using since I was nineteen, which upholds the masculine, embodying the survivor.

At the entry, in preparation for the ceremony, Apples and her dear friend Jacqueline cleanse each guest with the smoke of burning sage. The guests bring a pot of food for luck and dinner afterwards. While they sage, I bathe in a curative traditional ritual of hot water and herbs, then wrap myself in Maasai ceremonial clothes, colorful beaded necklaces, bracelets. Into the living room, Joy escorts me by elbow. Everyone is seated in anticipation. I place myself on a carved, wooden, round West African table. Seven close friends: Gay (reads for herself and Gail), Richard (reads for himself and Jeffrey), Audrey, Philip, Celia, Kevin, and Apples gather around me to represent seven directions to read words of guidance, love and care. Holding the eighth direction, my young nephew sits among them, reading the final gift of words:

> Healing - I now know its importance.
> Loving - I now know how.
> Caring - I now know why.
> Trusting - I now know completely.
> Protecting - I now know in what way.

Part II: The Divide

> An honest soul incorporates all of these.
> An honest soul you have shared with me.
> I believe in you, in every path you take.
>
> To help heal, love, care, trust, and protect that which was, is, and will be. Your soul has equipped me to protect myself and now I will give my all to protect us.
>
> Mother, Father,
> Aunt, Uncle,
> Sister, Brother
> Daughter, son,
> My Godmother,
> I love you, Murphy."
>
> —*Peter Murphy Lewis*

As tears course down my face from these special words, Joy leads me to the statue, Kwan Yin, the goddess of mercy, of compassion that stands as a sentinel in the living room. Here, I speak vows of commitment honoring the voice of each part of myself. From two candles, I light one, gifting myself two sterling silver rings: one, a panther, my totem, representing the strong exuberant Murphy; the other, a heart, the Peaceful Irene, which slide easily *ensemble* on my left hand. For now, this marriage to myself is enough.

An email flies in to commemorate the day: "Murphy, we pray like Jabez that God will bless you indeed, expand your territory…that His Hand will be with you and He will keep you from evil. You have blessed our lives so much. Even at birth you were facing up toward God and His fascinating world of people and challenges. We are one in the Spirit with you always, Mother and Dad." I'm sure Dad approved of this, yet I know how mother writes—this note is from *her*. In blessing me, the Maasai have opened up the potentiality for other blessings from parents', nephews, friends'—even in this willingness to integrate Irene to Murphy in marriage.

From the initial circumnavigations with the Kalahari Bushmen and the Maasai Warriors, I have brought back striking unnamed colors, which emanate from a palette. In the past, I have appeared quite normal and acceptable in

30: Transporter Transported

fashionable clothes. These I shed, for an ever-changing and "chosen" wardrobe of my own. *What will it look like?* I know not. Even so, I draw on these African essences, my now accessible companions whom are summoned upon waking or sleeping. So, that all things, weave together for good.

I'm not talking black magic, voodoo. Not attacking others or playing games. These cohorts liberate life through navigation, allowing the occupation of the webbing of life, to call on other dimensions. The Maasai taught me, tutored me into my real nature. No longer fighting against Father or others. In releasing the torment and the divisions, I can let go of those divergent things, so, I give Martin—whom I had ten dates with but could never kiss—to Audrey and Peter to Leslie (these relationships last to this day)! Don't have to harshly divorce these men, just pass them on to amazing women, who are meant to be with them! Have changed so much, can perceive, I don't belong to Peter or Renzo or to Martin, I can kindly let them go!

For today, I have given Irene away to Murphy and Murphy to Irene.

As if becoming myself in the middle of New York City is a must, I'm no longer on the floor from "the gagging" where I couldn't absorb the undifferentiated. Though still steeped within the cauldron of *9/11,* I'm up and functioning in a chaotic world. No longer quivering with chaos inside. Before it was the other way around!

After ninety days of playing the transporter, of ushering people across the threshold, after marrying into the manner of all things, I feel transported, which will mean I can rest in my parents' home in Kansas for a month, connecting with people I've never known before, people honoring Native American rituals of fire walks and sweat lodges.

31

NATIVES CONCUR

*"To the Winds of the South,
Great Serpent,
Wrap your coils of light around us,
Teach us to shed the past the way you shed your skin,
To walk softly on the Earth. Teach us the Beauty Way."*

—Native American Invocation, Alberto Villoldo, The Four Directions

After the challenges of *9/11*, in January 2002, for one month, I move into my parents' home in Osawatomie to rest, while they, as retirees, play golf in Florida. To heal, Mother suggests myofascial release therapy from a gifted woman, Roberta Ashton. Similar to Mom and Dad's knowingness of the importance of taking me to "my first family," to the San Bushmen-and-women in the Kalahari Desert. This suggestion of hers will lead me into a fuller integration of those roots of mine, displaying the demarcation zone between what was before the tumbling of the twin towers, and after.

31: Natives Concur

I seize this gift of Roberta, who with long, grey braided ponytail, performs miracles on my body with her warm hands and gentle heart, explaining: "My husband Clint and I have built a traditional sweat lodge and practice many of the rites of the Native peoples with a group of friends, believing ourselves to have been Lakota in another life."

So as this rootedness ignites, I'll be discovering more about the original keepers of this land, and to those who are of mixed race. In Tommy Orange's *There, There*, the half-white, half-native character Edwin Black, who is searching for his medicine man father, complains of his white mother: "I've always hated when she says, 'Native American Indian,' this weird politically correct catchall you only hear from white people who've never known a real Native person. And it reminds me of how removed I am [...] she never did a single thing to try to connect me with my dad." Edwin continues, "I use Native."

Just as Edwin's mother, I have been disconnected from his dad, disconnected to those I've always called "Native Americans." Tommy Orange's text brings me into a reconnection to "Natives" just as Robert and Clint offer me.

Just as I cannot necessarily prove I was once a Bush-woman some ten generations ago, I'm not sure how Roberta and Clint can *know* they were Lakota. Even so, they've piqued my interests. Since a child, I've always felt myself more in alignment to the Natives, than to the sensibility of cowboys and soldiers. In fact, at thirteen, my friend Karen and I—not quite "pretendian"—tied our hair in braids, dressed in skins and rode bareback on our ponies in the Osawatomie Jamboree Parade. But hidden from others, in the back woods along the Marais des Cynes, we named the land, Horses' Honor, and our favorite pond, Tadpole Territory. Perhaps this differentiation happened for me, even earlier, in Paola on those walks, talking to the creatures, those morning trailrides with Gib, where the Confederated Allied Tribe once lived, a consolidated group of the Kaskaskia, Peoria, Wea and Piankeshaw, who were originally led by Baptiste Peoria of French and Indian ethnicity.

"Wouldcha like to hear Grey Eagle channeled through one of them?" Roberta inquires.

"You betcha!"

Had the Maasai had an inkling that their initiatory practices would lead me on another mission to reconnect with the land of my birth, with the ways of its indigenous peoples? Mom's introduction to Roberta, Roberta's introduction to Grey Eagle, displays the borderlines the Maasai had expanded for me, stepping

Book One – Across the Divide to the Divine

Part II: The Divide

over and across, to engage in "the crossroads" with others. For strangely, I'd returned home many times before, yet never ever attracted people involved in such rituals as these.

To recover our ancestral karma, as well as my personal, I had become a wayfarer, traveling the world. And yet, there were, as we have seen, penetrations awakening me—dreams, relationships, as well as pages and pages I'm reading in advance from the Mythological syllabus of Pacifica Graduate Institute, which I am considering as a place to study.

At the time of my *third journey in*, American-born-of-Goan-descent Margaret Mascarenhas' *Skin* appears on the scene. Her book, *Skin* is inspired from her own return to her ancestors' homeland. The protagonist Pagan explores post-colonial issues of the differences in complexion, in the color of the eyes, which is as light as her Indian grandmother. In Goa, she discovers the strange inversion of the caste system, where the Hindu Brahmins only converted to "Portuguese" Catholicism, inter-marrying to protect their property rights until 1961. No one could imagine that their cousins, who didn't convert, lived, draped in darker skin, outsiders to this privileged world.

Even more revealing, Pagan's old ayah, the family's maidservant, Esperanca, weaves a tale of the slave trade, the long sweeping affects—in the other direction—across the Indian Ocean from East Africa to Goa, from the Sixteenth to the Nineteenth Century. Each line of Mascarenhas moves me back and forward through time, shifting my reality into other kinds of truths. And this moment on the earth in Kansas is part of that reclamation, as hers was of India.

On the first full moon, to a laughing audience, Grey Eagle in a low majestic voice channels himself with humor through the mouth of a beautiful dark-haired woman, Kathy, "I was once 'Red Eagle'—now very grey!" My astonishment increases when he remarks: "There is someone in the room (you know who you are) thank you for what you did for the lost souls who died for us in New York City. Now, you can rest. Your work is complete."

From this unseen connection, the mystifying experience from *9/11*— listening for the dead, ushering them across to the other side—has been noted. From those many ceremonies with the Maasai, from that ceremony among NYC friends of marrying those two selves together, of "Irene" and "Murphy," brings about awareness and new friends I've never had before and the capacity to receive this pronouncement of the now very "Grey" Eagle.

31: Natives Concur

Through Grey Eagle and his friends: Kathy and her husband, Rick, Roberta and Clint, another form of a baptism begins with potlucks, past life regressions, sweats, hot-coal fire walks. Just as Sharon Butala, "I began to see that traditionally Amerindians do not make a separation as we do between the mythological and the physical worlds" (*Wild Stone Heart*). Similarly, they view Nature and all its elements as the Maasai and the Bushmen, as "endowed with soul."

Through these new friendships, I am encouraged, causing me, even more, to become reconnected to this homeland of mine and more consciously this time, to its Original Peoples. So, I ramble across Kansas, stopping in the Flint Hills to ride horses at Jane Koger's Homestead Ranch. Onward at the place of my conception, in Newton, I crawl down a ravine those older brothers of mine played in, knock on the door of the house we had once lived as a family.

Discover the archives of the doctor's notes burned, the doctor dead and the hospital, where I'd been so oddly birthed, had been crushed and bulldozed into a wasteland. So, just to make things right with the doctor, meant, that evening, in my hotel room, with Kathy's assistance, I had to go quiet, to converse across the dimensions of time, to face his Higher Self and mine in a field of waving wheat. I learn from him that he was rather young and shocked at this determination of mine. The last thing he wanted was an insurance claim or a court case over the broken pelvis of a mother. From this, I draw a conclusion with this anger towards him for not trusting the need to birth myself face up. Between this doctor and I, a completion arises. Peace.

A down-reaching relationship to the great feminine being none other than herself, Mother Earth, I find, as well, through the people of North and South Americas, an honoring of Her. During the menses each month, on behalf of all women on the planet, these new friends encourage me to join them in the practice of stopping all activity, to sit by the fire or light a candle, then releasing the blood onto the earth. When I can, wherever I am, I attempt some hours of each month to honor Mother Gaia.

At the same time, as if on wings, the *Prayer for Opening Sacred Space*, (Villoldo) is offered to me through my friend, Dr. Faccio. On the earth, each morning (or as often as I can), feet hip-width apart, I spread my bare toes and bow to each of these directional force fields. Eventually, it will become a chant, a mantra that filters through the day and night dreams. The first part will evoke the Chthonic Mother, the keeper of the waterways: "Great Serpent [...] to shed the past the way you shed your skin."

Part II: The Divide

The detonation of the induction of this prayer will mean I'll dream in two's, in two minds, in two sections. Roll over from one side to the other but recognize, not to the other side as in left to right, but to the left side below the surface, into the immeasurable. Dropping into the depths of a dimension I have yet to comprehend, of what is yin, left, and yet, right-brained—what men have often historically considered as part of the mysterious unknown, undependable, confusing, unfixed, unfixable, "hysterical," and dangerous. What women fear will be misconstrued, misunderstood, mined, contaminated.

In the fall of 2002, within a year of leaving Badgley Mischka, I'll depart Manhattan for Carpinteria, California, to study at Pacifica Graduate Institute; I just do, and no longer care what anyone thinks. The first semester I'll commute once a month for three days of classes. This school becomes the perfectly honed vessel to nurture writing skills, with the potentiality to further the development of structuring a well-honed sentence (or in my case, as you know by now, dear reader, a certainly very long complex one). PGI will call me across the continent, to become more grounded, to express those encounters with the Maasai. This education is what I need, to write myself beyond fashion into an embodiment. This, too, will allow me time to integrate, forming words around this numinous experience of mine Walter had once affirmed.

More importantly this new movement of soul will transport me, over the course of five years, through the chronology of some odd fifty-thousand-pages of research of ancient myths along with divine interactions between engaging fellow students, and inspiring professors. I'll study world myths, learning of the notorious butter thief, Krishna, who, whenever he opens his mouth, the entire universe is revealed and of Raven, the Pacific Northwest First Nations' trickster, who is the creator of light and of all things.

Inside this magical kingdom in Santa Barbara County, surrounded by a bevy of hands-on healers—distinguished chiropractor Michael Luan, who encourages me to expand my mouth (and therefore my body) with a little crank with orthodontist Dr. Albert Chinappi; rebirthing expert Dr. Wendy Ann McCarty; tantric master Pamela Madison, and masseuse Genevieve Klein—I will go further and further into the original wounding.

Amongst the hills, they call "The Riviera," not far from the coast, I'll temporarily make my home in a tiny one-room apartment—claiming that here, I'm closer to Africa's cooing of the doves and wild animals, with the most pleasing one-hundred-and-eighty-degree view of the ocean. In Santa Barbara

31: Natives Concur

amidst the outcry of the mating Raccoon, the call of Falcon, and the Crow's harsh messages, I find quiet and miraculously the America within is becoming ensouled. As if forty years older than I am, I'm so fatigued from the corporate push, I'll crawl into Cheri Clampett's restorative yoga classes to rest, to actually take a breath in pillowed and blanketed poses.

Between PGI classes, for ten days at a time, I'll fly back and forth from California to Kansas to attend to Dad's fast-growing passage to the other side—and I don't mean his death, I mean into a world we have yet to understand, dementia, what becomes known as multi-infarct MID, which is caused from multiple "silent strokes" disrupting blood flow to the brain.

On one of these visits, Dad has a confusing moment just after midnight. He flies out of bed, runs around the house flipping on lights, opening the front door, as if to check time. *Is he late for work?* Mother and I jump up from a sound sleep to discover him sitting on the couch, head in hands, "I'm all tangled up in my mind." Together, we secure a snuggly bed for him. As he settles into the gentleness of our prayers, he gives mother and me "the blessing." Placing his hands on our cheeks, on our heads, announcing what he adores about us, beseeching God on our behalf. After this moment of magic, I leave them alone.

In acknowledgement to the hugeness of this blessing I've always longed for, a bucket load of tears tumbles down my face. Stand: stare out the front door, through the screen at the waning moon that hangs high in the sky larger than life. There, captured in the light is our flowering plum tree of thirty years that really, has never grown any larger in the rocky, clay soil. On this night tide, swaying in the Kansas wind, this spindly tree appears as though a deer on her hind legs, hands folded, petitioning God on Dad's behalf. "Yes," I say, to imagining into this world again. "Yes," I say, to feel as I once did as a child where everything—even the plant life, as well as the song of the birds—is alive and synchronistically engaged.

While her husband sleeps, Mother joins me weeping, wrapping her arms around me tightly. I point. She, too, perceives the tree-deer praying, and proclaims, "Oh how absolutely enchanting!"

Mom's right! Indeed, in spite of Dad's health challenge everything 'round about us is full of enchantment. More importantly everything within the vast terrain of forty years between Father and me—is put to bed—so to speak. For just days before he had faced me, grasping hands, beseeching, "Is everything alright between us?"

Part II: The Divide

"Yes, Dad, everything is forgiven, is settled."

In the early hours of the morn, on the terra firma of the forgotten Osage and the Pottawatomie men and women, more hallucinations, where just as Helen Keller determined to learn from Anne Sullivan, I'll, too, attempt their earthly sign language. Expressing with hands, fingers, pounding against legs, reverberating claps, drumbeats, with an elemental knowing that each movement has meaning, and that I have such a long way to go in the comprehension of this extraordinary capacity to exude. *Is this dreamlife inspired from the reading of the mythology of the Original Peoples of Turtle Island?*

Even so, if I learn the steps, the lessons, their languages, though born here, I realize I will never be "Native," for I am but, from a family of "settler colonialists" (Michael Lechuga, *Visions of Invasion*). In another dimension, in what appears to be another time, another man instructs me in a more elaborate storytelling method. *Are they giving me the clues of how to communicate with Dad inside his "dis-ease?"*

In accordance with these dreams, I'll return to PGI to attend four days of summer session, where a Lakota teaches our "Native American" class. For three days, in a semi-circle, our group is held spellbound with Paul Zolbrod's *Diné Bahane': The Navajo Creation Story*, their "beauty way," as they emerge from the very earth itself. Later we are held captive, as though in the Longhouses of old amongst the Native gatherings, receiving lessons of soul: "Historically," Dr. Chris shares, "the Iroquois have utilized this construction for numerous kinds of rituals; birth, death, initiation, peacemaking. Over the years, they have discovered, there is so much sorrow on the planet, they now open it almost exclusively for suffering hearts."

To learn more about the Longhouses, Dr. Chris has us read *White Roots of Peace: The Iroquois Book of Life*, where Chief Leon Shenandoah states, "The Peacemaker (a Huron) came long ago—before the Europeans came [...] at a time [...] of great conflict among the Indian Nations living here—from north of Lake Ontario and all through the Finger Lakes and the Mohawk River to the Niagara River. It was a civil war." In the 1200's, through the leader, Tadodaho, under the Great Tree of Peace, the Council Fire of the Confederacy was formed with "The People of the Longhouse," "Haudenosaunee," comprised of the Five Nations: Seneca, Cayuga, Onondaga, Oneida, and Mohawk. Deganawidah declared, "so that we [...] shall in future have only one body, one head, one heart. Five hundred years later, the Tuscarora people joined, forming the Six

31: Natives Concur

Nations. This "pax Iroquois" influenced Benjamin Franklin to similarly unite the thirteen colonies, influencing the concept of democracy.

In the conclusion of our class, Dr. Chris guides us through a grieving ceremony. Breaking off in groups of two, where we are to reveal an intimate loss. The rules are no interruptions, no touching, only a confidentiality of sharing. In this exchange, cross-legged on the grasses of Casa de Maria, the Pacific Ocean stretched before us, a kind and loving fellow student, Joan, and I privately hold space for one another as we release our bereavements, our heartaches, our tears, for a burial into the earth. Both of us walk away profoundly touched. And we'll carry this gift, so graciously given, of the Original Peoples' capacity of grieving to our family and friends across the country. Because, often, I discovered, we grieve alone. For it's true what a fellow PGI graduate Dr. Clara Oropeza, shared with me as we later discussed the edits of this chapter: "Within American culture we lack these deep rituals for loss and we long for this access."

In the chapter, "Massive Trauma and the Healing Role of Reparative Justice" clinical psychologist, victimologist, traumatologist, Yael Danieli explains that "the conspiracy of silence most often follows trauma." Once again, this grieving alone. However, this inability to find a place to express through words or "to narrate the trauma story" creates more destruction for the victim and their entire community. For, no one wants to hear!

Yet, even so, the very people who originally knew these traditions have had their rituals stripped from them (by our ancestors) and are struggling. Within Tommy Orange's fiction-reality, the Native character, Jacquie Red Feather, who is in "suicide prevention" states, "I had one community I was working with recently in South Dakota tell me they were grieved out. That was after experiencing seventeen suicides in their community in eighteen months. For how do we instill in our children the will to live? [...] there has to be an urgency, a do-whatever-at-any-cost sort of spirit behind what we do" (*There, There*).

Maybe things might change for the Natives, if we, as whites, had a place to gather, to grieve, to get at and to admit the original wounding our ancestors, *the traumatizers*, created that's been compounding generation after generation, causing the Original Peoples' internal angst and external deaths even today.

Twenty years after WWII, Yael Danieli discovered that a group of the Nazi Holocaust Survivor's claimed that no one, not even health-care specialists, were willing to hear, nor to believe the original trauma they had experienced, nor the continuation of that suffering that kept rising up to bite them in their everyday

Book One – Across the Divide to the Divine

Part II: The Divide

lives. "They, and later their children, concluded that people who had not gone through the same experiences could not understand and/or did not care." What Danieli calls the "Conspiracy of Silence" ("Massive Trauma and the Healing Role of Reparative Justice"). I would say—about those who could not listen—it was more that they could not face the horror of what happened, they could not take it in, could not digest it. It was so horrible; it could not be real.

If I only knew how to confess to the Original Peoples of Oklahoma that both of the large families of my great grandparents (on my father's side)—the Beeson's and the Lewis'—planted flags during the Cherokee Strip Land Run of 1889. *Would the world be a better place?* My family was part of the fifty thousand settlers who forced, once again, the five civilized people groups: the Cherokee, Chickasaw, Choctaw, Muskogee (Creek), and Seminole into smaller plots of land. Originally, in the 1830's, one hundred thousand of these five Original Peoples, along with some slaves, were displaced from the Southeast of the United States in an "ethnic cleansing," spurred on by the Indian Removal Act of 1830, in what has become known as the Trail of Tears. The Cherokee were particularly removed due to the discovery of gold in Georgia. This story is dramatically and honorably told in the stage performance, *Unto These Hills*, in Cherokee, North Carolina.

From this land rush of displacement, Father's great grandparents became farmers, and their children, my grandfather Gordon Gilmer Lewis, a butcher, and his wife, my grandmother Edna June Beeson-Lewis, a teacher. Their son, Dad, would be educated through the G.I. bill to become a banker and my Aunt Donna, a telephone operator.

Our family internalized these stories of the past, until a confession of my grandmother Edna June when she was close to her death at ninety: "I was born in a sod house on the red dirt of Oklahoma. My father and mother, in a covered wagon, made the Cherokee Strip Land Run." Yael Danieli claims, "What lies within genocide is the 'conspiracy of silence.'" *Were my great grandfathers, was my grandfather, was my grandmother, was my father, were my siblings, and was I, tangled up in this web of the violence of silence?* James Baldwin claimed, "People are trapped in history and history is trapped in them." *As Nana, our grandmother was growing close to the veil, towards her parents, had the ancestors' guilt arisen, so that she had then revealed the truth?*

From *Healing the Soul Wound: Counseling with American Natives and Other Native Peoples*, I follow Duran's instructions to his client, lighting a candle,

31: Natives Concur

running a bundle of sage through it, draw the smoke toward me with open hands, surrounding the body, the room, around the computer I write with, the journal I take notes in. Dribble an essential oil, "release" in the water above the candle to burn. Today, the 1st of September 2023, though I am far from the red earth of Oklahoma, inside the prayer of the Akashic Record, inside the six directions of the *Prayer for Creating Sacred Space*, I clear this energy of our ancestral abuse on behalf of the Natives and on grandmother's behalf.

From this text, I agree with Duran, the male in me is wounded because a man abused me, just as my white male ancestors and their quiet wives, who were probably abused themselves, confiscated the lands, displacing and killing the Natives. So, on and on this abuse goes. Those of the Five Civilized Tribes, who were left, continued to carry this wounded "male" within.

In Michael Butz's clinical study, "The metaphor of a vampire for working with abuse," he had discovered that this is often the experience of the oppressed and rings forth in their dreams. Metaphorically the vampire penetrates the victim's field, and he/she/they/it cannot get free from the vampire's power. The vampire is trapped inside—their head, their culture, their actions, their vagina, their anus, their myofascial—constantly informing them, whether wanted or not. Duran agrees with Butz, the victimizers, are vampires: "Sometimes that energy from the vampire sits in there creating problems for you"—and I might add, creating problems with those we interact with. In consulation with his client, Duran continues, "this spirit of incest (or rape or sexual abuse) has been chasing you for a long time. [...] the perpetrator's spirit is shot into you. Like in witchcraft [...] Perpetrators are sorcerers, you know. Someone did sorcery on them, then they became sorcerers because no one helped to heal them." Again, it builds. One abuse on top of another, informing the next abuse until we're all tangled up together and haven't a clue how to sort it, how to unravel one abuse from another.

The taking over of their land was as if "a rape," that rape has continued to do harm to the Natives. And oddly, I believe, it has come back to bite me (as we will soon discover) in a sexual way. In our white supremacy, we have dampened down the truth, have ignored the power of our acts upon the Natives. Maybe those crimes are erupting within our white race and we can't see it, so we keep abusing others. In his "Interlude," Tommy Orange blows wide open this denial, "If you were fortunate enough to be born into a family whose ancestors directly benefited from genocide and/or slavery, maybe you think the more you don't

Part II: The Divide

know, the more innocent you can stay, which is good incentive to not find out, to not look too deep, to walk carefully around the sleeping tiger" (*There, There*). And so, we, I, gingerly tip toe around the tiger before he roars and devours us.

Duran acknowledges in *Healing the Soul Wound*, "Our culture has been affected by a long history of violence *against* other cultures,"—across the planet, in the battles of World War I and II, the silence of the Jewish Holocaust, the devastation of the bombing of London and consequently the German cities (as well as other European cities in Italy and France), the atomic bombs dropped upon the Japanese cities of Nagasaki and Hiroshima, the destructive war in Vietnam, the two Desert Storms in Iraq, the war upon wars in Afghanistan and Korea, Ukraine, Gaza, the colonialism throughout the world, particularly in Africa and India, ad infinitum. And right here on our own soil we've created other atrocities: the Civil War, the stealing of the land of the Natives, the ripping Africans from their homeland to enslave them, and now, the border control and its complications and the exclusion of our neighbors, the Mexicans (and misusing them in our corporations as child labor).

Wouldn't it be wonderful if people of color were free to be themselves (not scrunched into our Western-Cartesian way of thinking or scrunched into land we don't want)? We would then be inclusive! In the prologue of There, There, Tommy Orange affirms, "We've (the Original Peoples of Turtle Island) been defined by everyone else and continue to be slandered despite easy-to-look-up-on-the-internet facts about the realities of our histories and current state as a people." *Based on these realities, what if we made restitution" to the finned, the furred, the winged ones, the creepy crawlers, the two-legged, the four-legged" (Villoldo) to the Original Peoples of this land? Wouldn't we live more graciously? Wouldn't we live in equality? Wouldn't the Earth herself transform?*

But at this time, in this moment of the story (twenty years ago), I don't know Duran's writings, nor Yael Danieli's work as a victimologist, nor Tommy Orange's award-winning book, nor have I met Deena Metzger, who will begin to train me in the art of restitution. I've only experienced one grieving ritual, and I only know of Sarototi's ceremonies, yet I don't know how to perform these, nor have they quite penetrated my life, as we will soon see.

32

ONLY SKIN DEEP

"Is it wrong for me to love my own? Is it wicked for me because my skin is red? Because I am Sioux? Because I was born where my father lived? Because I would die for my people and my country?"

—Sitting Bull

O, wise Sitting Bull, it was not wrong; it was not wicked to be red of skin.

Of her own color, Joy Harjo in *Crazy Brave* enlightens, "The skin of my figures, I colored them orange, the closest color I could find in my box of eight crayons to capture the skin tones of my mother and father."

O, wise Sitting Bull, you had the right to protect those of your own color, to defend the land you treasured that had been your peoples' for tens of thousands of years, handed down to you from your children to hold in sacred care for their futures. Of course, you fought back!

William Notman's 1885 photograph of Chief Sitting Bull, Thathanka Íyotake (his Lakota Sioux name), reveals the fierceness that typifies its meaning

Part II: The Divide

"Buffalo Bull who Sits Down," whose resistance brought about the death of Custer, as well as the death of over two hundred fifty of the Seventh Cavalry and their defeat at Little Bighorn, Custer's Last Stand (1876). On Memorial Day, 1999, finally, red granite markers honored this historic site—of what the Native's call "The Battle of Greasy Grass"—on behalf of the Lakota, Sioux, Arikara, Northern Cheyenne, and Arapaho Warriors, as well as their women and children who died there (Kathy Johnson, indigenouspeople.net).

How do we know what lies beneath the color of the skin? For often what is above, determines who we are and what choices and judgments will be made because of it. In Sitting Bull's case, the color of his skin would drive him and others to rise up in rebellion against the United States' Army. And eventually, to cause our "whiteness," the color of *our* skin, to slaughter them for their differences and drive the few that were left into reserves of our choice. Our want of what they had—exquisite land as far as the eye could see and beyond, as well as freedom from our pasts—constructed this history.

In 2023, as I rewrite into this manuscript, as I try to understand the role of my ancestors and myself in history, I feel the impact. I feel distraught. My head spins with vertigo and I weep for the annihilation of the Natives.

Yes, on thousands of hills, from poisonings, from sterilizations, from shotguns, from diseases, from starvation unfathomably, countless numbers of the Original Peoples have died on their land, on Turtle Island. Our—as in Europeans and their descendants—invasion and conquest, according to David Stannard, constitutes "the worst human holocaust the world had ever witnessed" (*American Holocaust: The Conquest of the New World*). Some estimate their deaths at 12 million; geographers at University College of London claim 55 million, others have concluded that over the course of five hundred years 100 million from 1,000 different communities have died. In *Counting the Dead: Estimating the Loss of Life in the Indigenous Holocaust, 1492-Present*, David Michael Smith piles more numbers on top of these numbers, noting that at least twelve hundred more Natives have been slaughtered since 1900. Smith distinguishes this "on-going" decimation, as an "indigenous" genocide, because the Native populations did not originally consider themselves "American." The poet, singer of the Muskogee Nation, Joy Harjo assisted in the protests against a few of these "killing(s) of Navajo street drunks for fun by some white high school students. They had been questioned and set free with no punishment" (Crazy Brave). I repeat: No Punishment.

32: Only Skin Deep

Oh, if we could but change the past and even this present, to have lived then and now, differently, with permission and in respect on their land! But I do not necessarily speak of revisionism, here. I speak of fairness, of equal representation. But I don't want to be a part of this continued decimation. I want there to be consequences. To put a stop to it. This book is my protest.

In America, based only on what I had read and had heard, but not however, from personal experience, I was "aware" of the ramifications of running the indigenous off their land, of the slavery of the Africans—the fall out of those disastrous tragedies that continue their accumulative effect to this day. And yet, due to the neighborhood I grew up in and live in now, and due to the color of my skin, I can so easily possess this knowledge and not know what to do about creating change. Nor know how this past permeates the lives of the indigenous on a daily basis. How the issue of being of another color in all the countries of the world can mean rejection, exclusion or if you're of lighter skin—complete acceptance.

In *Buddha in Redface*, in his dialog with the wise man Tarrence, the psychotherapist Duran, discloses what he observes amidst his Native clients, "so much pain and shame underneath all the trauma. [...] It's called intergenerational post-traumatic-stress disorder, and it has profound effects even across generations." It becomes woven into their very beings, curling into their bodies and systemically passed on to the next generation, until it takes everything they have to get out from under *our* control. *How can I make restitution?*

In a *Washington Post* article, Daniel R. Wildcat reveals that reparations for the Natives is far more complicated than it is for the Black Community, because "Territory is irreplaceable, [...] air, water, and biological life on which we depend is a natural relative, not a natural resource" ("Why Native Americans don't want reparations"). On Indianz.com, an article, "The Black Hills award approaching 1 billion," Tim Giago (Nanwica Kciji—Stands Up For Them) concludes, "And yet, the poorest of people in all of America refuse to accept one single penny of the award." In other words, the Sioux don't want money; they want the Black Hills in their possession—for the government to give it back to them. Period.

At this moment in time, I hadn't figured out how to be a part of reparations. Nor, other than reading and writing about it, am I still sure.

Though it's a dated response, and "the white man's way" in the back of the book of *The Dark Eye in Africa*, (1955)—published from a lecture at the C.G. Jung Institut—van der Post answers questions. He challenges European-

Americans, to "beg" the Natives "pardon and patiently beseech" them to "relearn from them the lost language of the spirit," to discover "the secret of recommunion with the rejected half of our life and of wholeness with our sacred Mother Earth, if pride of reason and excess of humanity had not turned our hearts to stone."

Of course, to "beg" someone for forgiveness sounds rather anxious and eager—even insensitive—without engaging with the person first to find out how they feel and what they want or need. Or to ask to "relearn" from the very people we hurt may be taken as an insult and what Dr. Chester M. Pierce termed, a "microaggression."

To me, even though dated, even though worded in a way we wouldn't necessarily agree with today—it was a beginning for a white man, for van der Post to care. Actually, he did travel back to Botswana to apologize to the San Bushmen for what his ancestors had done to them. His encounter with them would change his life forever. He would become a "sensitive," and as a writer, prolific. He would introduce the First People to a larger audience and as I mentioned before, wrote against the issue of Apartheid in South Africa.

As I have already declared, my first readings of van der Post's books had set a kind of example for me. I admired this return to the Bushmen as well as his rekindling of relations with the Japanese after they had imprisoned him during WWII.

Carl Gustav Jung, a friend of van der Post's, also set about reparation and to cross the borderlands of the differences between people of color and whites. In 1925, for five months, Jung went to East Africa, as recorded in Burleson's *Jung in Africa*, to rediscover a part of himself that had been denied, as well as to build relationships with several people groups. To Burleson, this journey was a "watershed" event, dividing the way in which Jung would proceed with his work of psychoanalysis and writing, forming many of his ideas there, on the continent—impacting many peoples' lives, one of them being Eduardo Duran. Just before Africa, Jung had spent a month with the Pueblo in New Mexico, where he learned from Chief Ochwiay Biano that white men only "think with their heads," whereas the Pueblo think with their hearts. Maybe to survive what we did to the Original Peoples, we as European-Americans have separated ourselves from our chests, from our bodies, from our feelings and emotions.

Jung's internal/external adventures, as well as van der Post's were influencing mine, mostly because, I did not want to have a heart of stone or to become what

32: Only Skin Deep

Suzanne Kingsbury calls, "a cinderblock man"—those who "worship the brain, running the world through power, avarice and greed." So, from this provocation of Sir Laurens, I had flown to Africa to connect to the Kalahari San, I had undergone Jungian analysis, and eventually walked out of that Seventh Avenue career which had been slowly fashioning me into a perfectly coiffed "cinderblock."

And now, I had decided to shift this balance with the indigenous in America. Though soon I would learn this is easier said than done.vv

33

ON SACRED LAND

*"He hadn't found them fit enough or good enough to want to know their names,
and believed himself too good to tell them his.
They looked at his skin and saw it was as black as theirs,
but they knew he had the heart of the white men...."*

—about Milkman Dead, Toni Morrison, *Song of Solomon*

Attracted by my interest in the original ways and the land of the Natives and to attempt reconciliation, I head for New Mexico and Arizona, where I had lived briefly for three years. For a few days, I stay with Rebecca—the girlfriend who had traveled with me to the Kalahari Desert—and her husband Tony. They holiday near the ruins west of Albuquerque at El Morro, which was known as a desert oasis with a pool of water at its base. To the Spanish Conquistadors El Morro meant headland. The Zuni people, however, embodied it with a sacred name, *A'ts'ina*, "the Place of Writings on the Rock"—messages from the Great Spirit.

So, I knew I was walking on sacred land. At the time, however, what I did not realize is that the entire Earth, Mother Earth, is sacred and that I was always walking on hallowed land whether I chose to remember it or not, whether I honored it or not. I had been walking throughout the world where blood had been spilt in battles, in sacrifice for beliefs, for color, for family. Maybe the land is not "officially" consecrated. Yet, all the bones of our ancestors are resting below our footsteps, as well as the dinosaurs, the animals, the plant life, the birds of the air, the fish of the rivers, of the lakes, of the streams and of the oceans. Sacred. *How often had I walked onto other peoples' land without respect or honor, without introducing myself, without walking with grace like Toni Morrison's character, Milkman Dead?*

On an afternoon hike, with Rebecca and Tony's friend, Charlie Mallery, a homesteader, a sensitive, an industrial artist of wooden tables, who lives nearby, leads us to this promontory point where the ancient ones, tall sandstone rocks, guard the land. To me, these monoliths are like clothed Ninja's. One is a stately Maasai woman. To others, they are the Kings, Queens, Chiefs, Buddha, and Kwan Yin. Here, within the tranquility of these stately beings, we grow calm, quiet.

While meditating, we encounter a Bull Snake. Charlie's action of kindly leaving the snake alone makes me aware I stand in the presence of an Izak, "The Old Man of the Kalahari"—a man I love deeply—who lives respectfully with nature, without disturbance. Just as Izak, Charlie knew enough to know that within the oral traditions of the land we were walking on, the creatures are cherished. The horned serpent, Awanyu, is the guardian of the waters of the earth and painted, sacredly, upon the walls of their caves. Among the Aztecs, Kukulkan, Yucatec Maya, Q'uq'umatz, Tohil and K'iche' Maya, the feathered serpent bears the name Quetzalcoatl. "There is a big snake that lives in the water. He rules over the water; he is the king [...] His name is !Xangu," says a South African Bushmen from the !Xun community in Schmidtsdrift (*Voices of the San*).

Charlie's way of being, of respect, touches me to the core. And so, all night long, I dream that a Native version of him, long hair and reddish-brown skin, is healing me. On this original property of the Ancient Ones, upon this oasis, I sense their blessings, which they have so generously bestowed.

Part II: The Divide

Not far from the Four Corners, where the four states of Colorado, Utah, New Mexico and Arizona connect, I stop to reminisce about the first Fashion Show I ever produced in 1986 for Plaza 3's merchandising class (*The Phoenix Gazette*, April 4, 1986). At that time, I was newly divorced, and so, with my girlfriend Brenda, I had driven north from Scottsdale to Window Rock, the Capital of the Navajo Nation, to help. The truth is, I arrived in the afternoon to discover the students were so well organized they didn't really need me. That evening, on the runway, fifteen Native models displayed the wares of three Navajo students—Ben Holmes, Jennifer D. Taliman, and Thomas Litson, along with a known designer, a Havasupai, James Uqualla, Jr.

In my journal I had penned: "It was fabulous, I was so proud of them. Ben, Jennifer, and Thomas looked great!" What I loved most, was that their designs were "hip" as well as a true expression of their own personalities and their culture.

Even then as a teacher, I wanted to be in "right" relationship with these brave Navajo students. For it was such a pleasure being a part of their adventure of expressing themselves through clothes. In class, daily, we had such fun, joking about "fashion jail" and "fashion hell" for those of us who were wildly dressed. My former Global Voice associate, Michael Lechuga—now one of our ally advisors and author of *Visions of Invasion: Alien Affects, Cinema and Citizenship*—recently reminded me, "even though you are aware there are complex cultural, political and spiritual barriers in relationship to indigenous people, you have always wanted to find and build kinship with them." It's true. These engagements are necessary to my soul and have always been a great gift.

As I crawl onto the Window Rock, looking out from this hole, which is perfectly and naturally formed in stone, I stand with reverence, thanking these three Navajo. For, little do they know the impact they had had upon my life; their sewn designs, their interests in class, their fashion show, their courage to be themselves, gave me the impetus to leave Arizona behind to study fashion in NYC. Without our interactions, maybe I would never have ventured to Africa or returned to America more human with a softer heart and the will to make amends.

To further align with the land of my former students, into the evening, I trailride through the National Monument, Canyon de Chelly, with another Navajo, Hok'ee, which means "high-backed wolf." For at least 5,000 years or more, on the Colorado Plateau, the Navajo Nation has lived and worked this land together. With a little bit of negotiation with the manager, I hire Hok'ee from the corral, outfitting us from a local store with sleeping bags and food. *Why couldn't I be like everyone else taking a normal daytime trailride? Was I avoiding the heat?* On this adventure, I'll certainly create it.

Even so, I'm determined to camp under the stars on Navajo land, the place called Tsegi. Along the trailride, I'm so curious, so thrilled and inspired, I ask him a thousand questions about his people, their stories, their ways. However, the further we go into the canyon, the further we go into the night, little sprinkles turn into a steady rain.

Strangely, we don't hear them—his associates, who are yelling, high up on the rim of the Canyon with truck and trailer. *Are they trying to save us from the possible deluge of rain-turned-roaring-river that can happen in this region?* Without this news from above, our only option to attempt dryness is to follow Hok'ee's suggestion of taking shelter in his Aunt and Uncle's hogan. I agree with him, not knowing there was any possibility of assistance. Nor did I have an inkling that this retreat might put us in an odd predicament.

As he breaks the lock to cross the threshold, I don't question his decision. After a long, hard night of riding on horseback, I'm tired, I'm wet, and I'm cold. I don't disrobe in front of him. Instead, I remain fully clothed sliding into my own sleeping bag—that thankfully, is the only dry thing I own. The last thing on my mind is sex. With you dear reader, I must divulge, I was not interested in tempting Hok'ee. Even so, I must candidly admit, I had not fully come into awareness of my own power of seduction, the drawing in of men (as we had seen in my engagement with the three men in Botswana). In a few years time—partly due to this story with Hok'ee and the one you'll soon learn of, with the Maasai Warrior Sarototi—this seduction game of mine will begin to unravel and slowly dissolve in Santa Barbara with the gentle guidance of the chiropractor, Michael Luan.

Yet, in this hogan, throughout the night, several times, (perhaps pulled by this undifferentiated projection born from the pasts, that discombobulation of mine) Hok'ee tries to crawl into my sleeping bag. Disturbed from sleep—something I will believe I'd experienced before—I'm irritated. I try not to be rude. But I am direct. Perhaps I'd even been rather icy towards him, rejecting him, making it uncomfortable, certainly for me, and maybe even for him! Though exhausted, I should have been honored, more kind, saying "thank you for your interest, but no." For in fact, Hok'ee's want of me was a compliment.

Maybe other white women had come to Canyon de Chelly *wanting* sex. I'd heard rumors that some European women travel to Africa for just *that*—looking for a different kind of sexual experience. Maybe Hok'ee had already had these encounters, something I wasn't necessary about, or at least what I was conscious of. Yet, because of this lack of consciousness I had created what they term in psychology, a *transference*. In *Healing the Soul Wound*, Duran writes of Jung's image of this occurence, for a true "transference to occur, there must be a hook for one to hang one's coat on." Yes, I had hung my hook right out there for Hok'ee to get hung upon.

Early in the morning, we don't discuss what has happened between us, which has now caused a tension we could cut with a knife. Instead, we silently saddle the horses. Scarily, at least for me, and certainly, precariously—which might be the perfect metaphor for this adventure—we ride out of the canyon up the slippery rocks to his associates. As they shove the horses into the trailer, in their Native tongue, I think, they are bantering about the "goings on," of our middle of the night, because I sense more strain. After this truck ride, I will never see Hok'ee again.

Innocently, as if nothing had occurred, I returned to the hotel in Chinle for breakfast. Later that night, at a party, (though I don't know this yet) Hok'ee drinks too much and circles the parking lot looking for my vehicle. Discovering the SUV, he calls from the front desk, then knocks on the door of the room. From the other side of the wall, where I am quietly studying, Hok'ee receives another "no" from me. To be honest and certainly naïve, I am totally surprised at his *want* of me.

I do not further engage, as I do not want this "disturbance." My door remains locked to him. Today, I see the border I had drawn in the sand, in this separation with the "no," which becomes one more form of rejection for him, from another white person. He is rejected for being a part of his community, for being of a different skin, with different ways. Similarly, we as white Americans have excluded the Natives. Locked our doors from their society.

In *No Name in the Street*, James Baldwin exudes, "Not everything that is faced can be changed, but nothing can be changed until it is faced." I must admit, I couldn't open that door to the other side, to what I didn't want to see, what we as whites had created. I was afraid to face him for fear of what might

33: on sacred land

come at me. And I won't face this until many, many moons later in the writing of this chapter.

Yes, at times, I can be so disassociated. Sometimes (based on that history of mine) I can forget the context of who I really am—white, middle-class, privileged—and how this self of mine projects out in confidence to other people wherever I am. I, who should know better. Even my future *belle-sœur*, French sister-in-law, will ask me, "What is it about you Americans that makes you so confident?" I could only conjecture that it is a *persona*, a kind of cowboy, cowgirl bravado—of Gary Cooper in *High Noon* or Natalie Portman in *Jane Got a Gun*—that is layered in through education and is honored. And though I had already crossed several borders: selling clothes in Milan, in Paris, in London, in Munich, in Singapore, researching stories in South Africa, Namibia, Botswana, Kenya; interacting with Blacks, Indonesians, Chinese, Italians, French, Germans, Muslims, Lebanese, Afrikaners, Jamaicans, Puerto Ricans, San Bushmen, Maasai and briefly with Navajo students, I still had so much to learn.

Whether I had had experience with other nationalities or with indigenous peoples, whether I had crossed those borders or not, to me, this scene with Hok'ee reveals the origins of that abuse of mine, which requires me, here, at this point, to finally declare it was "sexual." For, in being a victim myself, I was now drawing in someone else into this web of mine—and dangerously so—possibly creating another victim as well! But I don't know it yet. I, also, am not aware that this victimhood of mine—that original wounding—is part of *my* initiation. And I will later learn from Linda Howe, in *Healing through the Akashic Records: Using the Power of Your Sacred Wounds to Discover Your Soul's Perfection*, that the wound is in fact hallowed and holy and in turn, is the gift to others.

Again, innocently, the following morning I arrive at the arranged Navajo Sweat Lodge to discover the whole community knew about our trailride and my rejection of Hok'ee. *As I step out of the SUV, which loudly radiates the color of the sun, can they only see the color of my ivory skin, which for them may symbolize an insensitive "settler colonialist?" Had I become what Dr. Lechuga recently challenged me not to be: "a colonial trope of white folks moving through Native spaces easily?"* Gawd forbid!

Through her powerful question, a fellow graduate of PGI, Dr. Clara Oropeza pointed out the tension inside this tale, this engagement, "How do you as a white woman access knowledge from the Natives and these experiences without creating harm?" Huge unanswerable question! A true reality.

Part II: The Divide

For I had come for something that seemed so simple, for what Tony Charlo, a Flathead Salish had described as a traditional Sweat Lodge: "We sweat and talk to the spirits. We beg for our lives and the things we need. [...] We go in and talk to them. The main one is an old man who has been with us for a long time. It's great grandfather. That's what we call him" (Michael Joseph Raymond, "Native American Traditions: The Deilemna of Alcohol Use Among the Flathead Salish"). I had so longed for Charlo's connection to that grandfather!

In *Healing the Soul Wound*, Eduardo Duran had once described that there is an "Indian Way," that only a Native would understand. Perhaps this is what the elders are speaking about—from "another way of being" than mine. For immediately, the Navajo elders surround me, lecturing me, shooting me with "arrows" of truths for the mistreatment of this young man, for this transgression on their land—and rightly so. Here, were those stories that stalk, which Benson Lewis, a Cibecue Apache had mentioned to Keith Basso. And so, they sling: "Because of you, he felt the 'fool.'" "Because of you, he got drunk, desperately driving around under the influence." "He could have had an accident!" "He could have been killed." "Are you aware of the humiliation you've caused him?" *Hadn't I claimed I wanted to learn from the Natives?* Because, here, right now, were the words of wisdom coming at me, challenging me to rise up and take responsibility, to become *aware*. Wherever you are, all of you, thank you for caring, for telling me the truth!

Later, I would understand I had clearly come together with Hok'ee and even with these elders, dragging along my own cultural biases, my own "white way," and that *that* cultural bias of mine may have been just another one of Pierce's "microaggression" for him and for his people. Often, we are who we are, we bring to the table what we know, as I had in this instance. In fact, when I think back, I would never have asked a white man I didn't know to camp overnight with me, to expect he would not arrive with sexual expectations and want them fulfilled. For the white man, it would have been *implied*. So, we could also consider that I trusted this Navajo implicitly, on this overnight, both with my body and my life!

As I listen to the Navajo elders, my face flushes with embarrassment. Yet, I stand perplexed. I was caught in a dichotomy. I could be both innocent in my own mind, and yet guilty in theirs. Tongue-tied, I cannot seem to respond or even defend myself. Though not a virgin at forty-five, I thought turning him down proved my intentions were pure, and his response not to proceed past that "no" of mine was highly honorable. That together, we hadn't muddied the waters. That we hadn't mixed juices, and therefore, I hadn't brought disease as my ancestors had. But maybe, if I'm willing to admit it, I had brought another kind of *dis-ease*—that wound of mine.

I don't realize that once again, my own shadow, my own "black hole"—which is horribly incorrect and quite rude in this Woke moment, and is more rightly named, my own "white settler-colonialist hole," which is so big, I've tripped and tumbled someone into it. It seems my understanding of things the "white way" had wreaked havoc in this Navajo's life. Yet, I don't remember ever apologizing to Hok'ee or to the elders. (Though that's rather hard to believe, as I grew up super guilty, over apologizing to everyone for everything, even for things I hadn't done. Even when I played tennis and hit the ball where they had to run to get it!) So, I probably did say, "I'm sorry." *But how often does "sorry" really help?* Well, as I rewrite this, I have an urge to correctly apologize, because what I did was unconscionable. To this day, I don't know how to reach out to him. Only his first name is buried inside a journal for safekeeping. I have no contacts there and I don't know if he is dead or alive. Now, I live on the other side of the Atlantic Ocean sequestered more and more after Covid.

In Robert R. Weyeneth's article, "In the Power of Apology and the Process of Historical Reconciliation," he asks, when perpetrators apologize and there is the response of forgiveness wanted, how can it be done without their presence? For "the dead cannot forgive" Or can they? Weyeneth wonders, "What forms do historical apologies take?" —*mine, for twenty years ago and my ancestors for one-hundred-and-thirty-five years later?* In "The Three Parts of an Effective Apology," Christine Carter explains, "I'm sorry isn't enough" (*Greater Good Magazine*). If you've ever been the victim and had to force an apology from a perpetrator, you know it doesn't weigh in the balance, it doesn't make up for the fact of "the original trauma." In fact, it often falls flat, seems fake, as if you had to draw it forth from them with all your strength—and even then, it can feel not real. In "Making Peace Through Apology," Aaron Lazare believes one must make "acknowledgment of the offense; explanation; expressions of remorse, shame, and humility; and reparation."

Apologies can appear to be a closure for some, and yet, the greatest fear is that an apology means the pain must somehow end. But when you're inside the healing of the trauma—whether it's yours or has been passed down generationally—an apology can appear empty, vacuous, as though it could never make a difference. Trauma, even with a "sorry"—anyone who has been traumatized will tell you—can take a lifetime or more to heal.

Apologies can come from a podium, or in a letter, or from a court ruling along with a "moneyed fee," or face-to-face, or, in my case, paragraphs inside this book. A special day can be established on a calendar. In 1999, there was a "Reconciliation Walk," "a symbolic act," a gesture, to apologize 900 years later for the sacking of Jerusalem. However, look at the nightmare that's going on between Israel and the Palestinians right now.

A $20,000 check was given to the Japanese survivors, who experienced the Executive Order 9066, the United States government's incarceration during WWII. *But can money really soothe?* One only has to look at the documentary, *And Then They Came For Us*, to see institutionalized fear and hate that existed, exists. Robert Weyeneth questions, "What is an appropriate formula for compensation?" *How can trauma or genocide be measured?* People, especially corporations, fear apologies because it may reflect an admission of guilt and might mean compensation. Weyeneth conjectures, "There seem to be two camps when it comes to misgivings about the utility and wisdom of historical apologies. On the one hand are those who regard the practice as the slippery slope of ill-conceived revisionism." That indeed, as one draws up the past, Weyeneth explains, it opens a "Pandora's box" for other injustices.

Jessie Jackson once said, if you're going to apologize, you must be willing "to be a part of the healing process" (*Charlton Post and Courier*).

If I'd been in my "right" mind, the clearer mind I think I now have, after years of experiencing what the Natives describe as "White Man Talk"—psychotherapy, I might have reacted differently. To Duran, this "White Man Talk" is considered "soul healing." So perhaps now, through this long-term soul healing I've been doing, as well as the initiation with the Maasai, my mind has become deeply entwined with my heart. Indeed, that heart of mine will soften particularly after the finalizing of the Maasai ceremonies, after accessing the Akashic Records from 2006 onward, after living for many years in another culture, after the WOKE movement and the subsequent literature, and after the generous insights of my professorial friends Dr. Lechuga and Dr. Clara Oropeza, both of Mexican descent and indigenous roots.

Had I been in this "softened heart," I would have explained (not necessarily as an excuse) the twisted history I had come from. That within it there had been a breach of a taboo, and because of this, I suffered from prolonged, chronic trauma, which in turn created a Complex Post Traumatic Stress Disorder, which I had yet to fully understand or even had yet to name. Maybe, as I had mentioned before and something I've been exploring in 2024, that this wounding of mine had been formed from the original wounding of the violation we had done to the First Peoples of Turtle Island. The Ramifications of Those Violent Acts. For more and more we are gathering understanding of what it means to be wounded but we're just starting to unpack what happens to the body and the psyche when one is the violator, he/she/they/it, who wounds someone else.

Today, on February 13, 2024, Father's birthday, I find myself gagging over this painful historical past. Yes, I didn't just gag at the Siddha Yoga retreat in 2001, I am retching now in Paris, hitting the tiled floor on my knees, once again, grasping for Nux Vomica. But this time I must chuckle at myself, because Nux Vomica is really a temporary solution for the huge impact of Europeans upon Turtle Island. Just to research, to write about it is to find it indigestible. Even so, whether we want to admit or not, it's inside all our memories, inside our DNA. *How can it not make one retch?* Just as Wilfried Wils' associate, Lode, retches in the 2023 Netherland movie, *Will*, (directed by Tim Mielants). Based on a true story, Wils and Lode are auxiliary policemen in Antwerp during WWII, who, against their own knowingness, through the coercion of the Nazis, must betray their own countrymen—Jewish families—shoving them into trucks that cart them off to internment camps and eventually to their deaths. Confiscating their goods, their homes. Killing them. Yes, much of our past remains unresolved.

Yes, some of my past remains unresolved, un-mined, and certainly, hidden—most of it hidden from myself, and therefore, from most everyone else on the planet. As well, I had never resolved what my grandmother Edna June had revealed when I was in my late twenties—that my great-grandfathers' claims on Oklahoma territory pushed out the Natives from their homelands. These wounds gaping open is why I'd come this far for the Sweat Lodge in the first place, why I was traveling and searching the world over—to reconnect and reclaim and restore both the inner me and the outer, the way in which I relate to myself and to others, especially those who have been "other-ed." I longed and long for reconciliation.

In Japanese there is a word KY, *kuuki yomenai*, "one who cannot read the air." Sometimes not knowing the languages of the Bushmen and the Maasai had actually helped me to observe in a way I had not before. In every discourse (or so I thought), I had learned to watch, read into actions, facial expressions,

Part II: The Divide

body movements. However, I had been engaged in communication in the same language—English—with the Navajo Hok'ee, and yet, I had missed his meaning, I had missed "reading the air." Something had been clearly off. According to Meyer's *The Culture Map*, I needed the wisdom of Japanese HR executive, Kenji Takaki in order to ask: "Am I picking up messages you had not intended to pass?"

Maybe these reactions of Hok'ee's were trying to say to me that he had read between the lines my longings, my wants, just as his "high context culture" always does. Only later, he would discover the wants weren't sexual. The original want I had had was of remorse, to "beg forgiveness," as van der Post had once urged. To truly confess what my people had done to his—but I hadn't admitted this. For in fact, I was clueless about how to begin this process because I was too ashamed. I realize now that many of us have trouble doing this truth and reconciliation work because the grief and despair (and gagging) is so great for what we did to them that we fear that once we go to the reality of Tommy Orange's *There, There*, we'll break apart, break down and not ever recover. *That old White Fragility of D'Angelo's* rising up!

Not only am I presently gagging in 2024, but I have also been crying, too. Though the indesign has been done for this book, I'd postponed the launch for two years for further research about the Original Peoples and to get down dirty to the nitty gritty of these truths. I had more reading to do. More interviews. Ask two readers, Lechuga and Oropeza to "read." And, if I was going to be honest, to just sit with what I had already written. In the fall of 2023, I'd have to add two more chapters in the middle of the book, where we are right now. Then I'd have to sit again for six more months, digesting, or at least trying to.

Even though I'd come for this ritual, with Hok'ee and the elders, as well, I kept avoiding the confession of that other want of mine—to learn from them. *When I didn't respond "normally," sexually to Hok'ee, had he thought, had the elders wondered if I was like every other white person trying to stay in power or to co-opt their culture?* Of course, I cannot voice whatever is happening in Navajo land. Yet, here, I was on their land, asking about their stories, and doing a traditional ritual—*was I trying to take from them?* It makes sense, because I came from a people as Tommy Orange writes, who "took and took and took and took" (*There, There*) and are still taking. I hadn't come with this intention to take, to steal—but Charles Wallace in Madeleine L'Engles' *A Wrinkle in Time*, once said to the three otherworldly creatures, who had just arrived, "the road to hell

242   *I. Murphy Lewis*

is paved with good intentions." From the Navajos' point of view, maybe those good intentions of mine, are really just filled with the thievery of the white man, as they had been once before.

Many judge our interests in the Natives' rituals as "cultural appropriation" but what if it's just hungering for something deeper. I wanted that stone cold heart of mine to soften, to melt as it had slowly been doing overtime with the Bush-men-and-women and the Maasai. Maybe this want of mine, the "want" of white people, of "wanting more" is, in actuality, a great compliment—but then again this could be considered our avarice or greed of always taking. I wasn't the only one who hungered; I had friends and associates sweeping North and South America and the world over for answers.

In *Native American Postcolonial Psychology*, the Durans, who are both soul healers and descendants of the Original Peoples: Bonnie, a professor in social work and public health, and a Buddhist practitioner, and Eduardo, a psychoanalyst, explain this phenomenon, "All we have to do is see how much hunger there is currently in the white community for Native American traditional values. Many white people have realized that their individualistic worldview is not working and are looking elsewhere for a more community-oriented way of life that is more existentially and spiritually meaningful." The Durans were right, at least, for me, I wanted something deeper, a more alive knowingness. *Why couldn't I just disclose this?*

Counter to the Original Peoples' cultures, I grew up in a universe divided against itself. "Science," according to Levi-Strauss, "to build itself up against the old generations of mythical and mystical thought, [...] could only exist by turning its back upon the world of senses." For Bacon, Descartes and Newton "the real world was a world of mathematical properties which could only be grasped by the intellect [. . .] at odds with (of what they considered) the false testimony of the senses" (*Myth and Meaning*). I live inside these forms of Western thought, where everything stands in opposition and is split off from everything else. "Women and nature, man and woman, humans and animals, body and soul, mind and emotion, matter and spirit" (Susan Griffin, *Woman and Nature*). Dualism. Separatism. Binary forces.

Not only that, according to Dr. Lechuga in *Visions of Invasions*, as I had mentioned before, I had come from and am still a part of "the ideology of settler colonialism" where "power is communicated materially and multidimensionally in the U.S. [...] Not only that, but knowledge/power is produced to materially

Part II: The Divide

invoke subjectivity." To Lechuga, it was not just an "event" that "happened to Native peoples on the North American continent" or to the Mexicans whom we code as "aliens" and continue to control and discourage with our "Remain in Mexico" policy. Instead, it is "sustained and evolving" a *constant* conversion of their land into *our* property and they themselves into targets "using a racial marker of whiteness and language (and therefore Europeanness)" upon them. Constant. Oppression.

In recent history, "whiteness (h)as (been) the invisible norm against which other races are judged in the construction of identity, representation, decision-making, subjectivity, nationalism, knowledge production, and the law" (Moreton-Robinson). *How do we come down from this? See and value others as worthy?* Warren Montag once disputed that "Whiteness became an invisible norm through the universalization of humanness, which simultaneously erased its racial character and made it a universal" (Moreton-Robinson). This movement of "whiting" others is tragic—people lose their uniqueness, their character, their ways, "and so disappear," as Tommy Orange pens. Fanon, in *Black Skin, White Masks: The Experiences of a Black Man in a White World*—originally published in French in 1952—exclaimed, "For the black man there is only one destiny. And it is white." Today, seventy years later, there has been little movement about this truth either for the blacks or the indigenous.

In 1835, land that was others'—such as the land of the Australian aborigines—was deemed *terra nullius*, "land belonging to no-one" a declaration by the British Governor, Richard Bourke. The aborigines became victims to all the decisions of the British. This *terra nullius*—what Kate Foord determined as a *white fantasy* of "land belonging to no-one"—has been a problem the world over for indigenous peoples: for the Aborigines, the Kalahari San Bush-men-and-women, now, the Maasai Warriors in Tanzania and Kenya, the Original Peoples both in the North and South of the Americas. This concept of the "land belonging to no-one," gives us "whites," whom Lechuga names, "the settler colonialists" "the right "to walk onto their lands and stake claim as my great grandfathers did. And "the right" to block the border against Mexicans as we are doing today.

In *The Underside of Modernity*, Enrique Dussel, an Argentine/Mexican academic describes those who are on the periphery of the contrasting thought of the European-ness of Kant, Descartes and Foucault, live continuously on this "underside" of modernity. The left-out people. The outsider, from *The*

Insider/Outsider Problem in Religion: A Reader. Dussel's philosophy was against the exploitation of colonialism, imperialism, racism and sexism, which is again about exclusion. While he describes those living on the "underside," I, on the otherhand, have classified as the "other-ed," having pulled this classification from Karen McCarthy-Brown, "Writing About 'the Other.'" Lechuga uses the term, alien. Gayatri Chakrovorty Spivak, in her article, "Can the Subaltern Speak?" uses the descriptive word of "subaltern," as less than, different than, those who are "the denied humanity," whose own history remains withheld from our textbooks. To Spivak, "the subaltern has no history and cannot speak," and what's even more disconcerting is her final thought, "the subaltern as female is even more deeply in shadow…"

Malcolm X spoke out against this being lesser than. "America is a colonial power […] She has not only deprived us of the right to be a citizen, she has deprived us of the right to be a human being, the right to be recognized and respected as men and women" (Militant Labor Forum). To "colonize the mind," writes John McLeod in *Beginning PostColonialism*, is the art of the "whites," creating an inferiority complex within the colonized, in the persuasion of our values, inferring to them that our way is the only way in which to make perception of the world. How destructive.

In the film *Sami Blood*, Elle Marja, a 14-year-old reindeer herder experiences racism and intimidation both in the society and at her nomad school. To Stine Sand, "The animalization trope means portraying colonized people as animals, associated with body, not mind, and nature, not culture. The infantilization trope projects the colonized as less culturally developed, as an immature, as a child" ("Dealing with racism: Colonial history and colonization of the mind in the autoethnographic and Indigenous film *Sami Blood*"). We, as the dominant race, have lessened the indigenous just because they are different—in their thinking, their ways, their looks. In *Existential Africana: Understanding Africana Existential Thought*, Lewis Ricardo Gordon, an afro-American philosopher, conjectures: "How might the peoplehood of dehumanized people be affirmed?" WOKE is certainly inquiring into and requiring this question to be answered.

For Hok'ee, I cannot speak. Nor can I speak for the Navajo, nor someone of Sami blood, for I haven't walked two moons in their moccasins. I have no idea what it is like to be him or Elle Marja. I/we can only sit quietly and hear what they are telling me/us. Once Joy Harjo cut her body to express the angst of being an "outsider" outside of the majority's culture. For Harjo, "The mark of

Part II: The Divide

pain assured me of my own reality. The cut could speak. It had a voice that cried out when I could not make a sound in my defense" (*Crazy Brave*). Maybe the drunkenness of Hok'ee is part of that cry. Again, I cannot speak for him.

Even so, perhaps Hok'ee and I are just a reflection of something similar, something deep inside. If I had been swamped by the man, who had taken advantage of me, how much more Hok'ee had been swamped from the whites lording over him, a culture alien to his own sensibility. Hok'ee is the glaring truth of what I had yet to get a hold of. So, if I'm suffering from Complex P.T.S.D and the division of soul, *how much more is he?* And again, this reflection of this wounding of mine could really be the wounding my great-grandfathers administered to the Native through the stealing of their property, driving them further west and into reservations of what whites considered as "unwanted land," to their demise.

With that in mind, I should have been more careful, walking softly on his territory, on their sacred land, with the politeness Mother and Father had instilled—for I *was* a guest. I should have been more aware. I didn't know what I know now, that: "the separation in the psyche happened when the colonizing people overwhelmed the psyche of the Native American through the forceful imposition of a mythology that was foreign and differentiated in a totally opposing cosmology" (B. Duran, E. Duran). That Hok'ee's wound, their soul wound happened—not just through genocide or through the move to the reservations and later, to the cities as part of the Indian Restitution Act and the Indian Termination Policy. What Native Tommy Orange declared were acts to "make them (Natives) look like us (whites). Become us. And so, disappear." A kind of *droit du seigneur*, right of the Lord, *jus primæ noctis*, right of the first night with the bride—slowly diffusing the line until they are non-existent. Yes, slowly, our culture has been about control through "the overwhelm," the deluge of other ideas, of our "white Cartesian thought," as well as our religion, forced continuously upon them.

The psychiatrist and political philosopher, Frantz Fanon, who was born in the French colony of Martinique and was considered a Francophone Afro-Caribbean, once divulged: "a normal Negro child, having grown up in a normal Negro family, will become abnormal on the slightest contact of the white world." When I grow quiet, I can access this child of color whom Fanon describes, as shaking from the impact of our whiteness. Fanon's words should have told me that just this slight contact—a night on horseback—which seemed so innocent to me, could throw off the balance of Hok'ee's world and could be just one more microaggression built upon all the others.

For so long, I walked around in shame about what many might consider an "embarrassing blip" in my history. I considered it otherwise. I considered it, HUGE. It took me years to admit it, to write into it and to confess to my friends and associates Michael Lechuga and Clara Oropeza. I'm grateful for them for both hearing me and opening up my brain to pour in new thoughts and ideas and other books for research. Dr. Oropeza, professor and author of *Anaïs Nin: A Myth of Her Own*, recently extended grace, "You can't blame yourself, Murphy, this is a complex thing. You're fleshing out this contact with Hok'ee, which had caused an off-balance for him and the community. I wonder to what extent the experience between the two of you also reflects the greater historical tension of mistrust among Native communities and white people that has been happening for hundreds of years. So much has happened before us that we don't always know all the stories that drive us in our own desires, making restitution deeply complicated and layered." Yes, we consist of thousands of emotions stored in a little almond shaped amygdala inside the center of our brains.

Perhaps our encounter, my rejection of Hok'ee, had touched upon one of those layers and brought about a regression into drunkenness, maybe making him feel like a failure because he couldn't have me. "At the point of trauma, the psyche may have attempted to regress in order to escape complete annihilation" (B. Duran, E. Duran). Maybe he thought my "wanting more," meant sex, when what I really wanted was to heal our historical abuse upon his people, for connection to the Great Spirit and to be rid of whatever was ailing me, which again, was probably caused by our original violent acts against them. Again, I repeat, I just didn't know how to express this tremendous hunger of mine that was shooting out in all directions and therefore, hard to get ahold of and had become a dangerous hook for Hok'ee.

According to the Elders, to the community, I had tempted and tantalized him. Maybe they believed I had even purposely teased him. At the time, I couldn't seem to grasp this. Though I've tried not to be a colonialist, I don't understand that I naturally walk around in privilege. I stand confident, appearing as if I can claim all as mine. *Is the belief installed in this whiteness—"the world is my oyster?"* If so, then this nature of "confidence" is innate, and that it was imbedded somehow within the education. And for that, Hok'ee may even have felt I demanded him to fulfill me. No matter how I slice it, I had taken advantage of someone whom many "consider" to be lesser than me—a typical "white" failure. As well, I don't know I'm playing with fire, that my own flamboyant self is out of control, that Hok'ee is the image of an inkling of the future, of what will happen between Sarototi and me. *What was I thinking? Why did I put us both in this situation? I, who knew better—Or did I?*

Even so, my actions, that Protestant frigidity of mine and the historic, had driven Hok'ee into a drunken state. Inside the Native cultures, the indigenous, as well as within the San Bushmen's, there is a deep, deep problem with alcoholism. "The soul-wounding process has left a spiritual emptiness in the person who is an addict. In essence, the person is replacing spirit with alcohol spirit in an attempt to fill the void created by historical trauma" (Duran, *Healing the Soul Wound*). Some say this thirst for spirit, had increased when their old ways had been suppressed and had been whisked away through the colonial oppression, becoming "painfully aware the overwhelming onslaught of the conquest, which literally rapes the psyche" (B. Duran, E. Duran).

Of her father's alcoholism, Joy Harjo exclaims, "He did not like the hard edges of earth existence. He drank to soften them" (*Crazy Brave*). Rightly so, our "white" ancestors were those hard edges who had raped the indigene, the Original Peoples of their culture, of their land, of their inner knowingness.

Anyone who has #metoo-ed for being sexually raped, dominated or abused physically, mentally or emotionally can begin to grasp the Original Peoples' reality—of what it means to be emotionally torn apart, to lose soul, forever in pursuit of its retrieval. Those who have had these experiences often suicide or end up in an asylum or as drug addicts on the street. But most likely—though many of our ancestors fled Europe or other countries for many different reasons—we do not know what it means to be ripped from the land of our forefathers and foremothers without a choice, or to experience mass genocide, or what it means to lose all those sacred rituals held in keeping both on the land and within the wisdom of the elders. In *Healing the Soul Wound*, Duran enlightens, "My understanding from the teachings of Tarrence is that when the soul is wounded it goes back into the 'black world' (unconscious)." Perhaps this step into unconsciousness leads the bewildered soul to alcoholism. This lost soul part, trapped in the unconscious, must be retrieved, recovered through talk therapy, through shamanism, through reconciliation.

Originally, "the implications of alcohol," the challenge of alcoholism, the notion of it being a "spiritual problem" and its relationship to initiation had been explored through Michael Joseph Raymond's thesis, "Native American Traditions: The Deilemna of Alcohol Use Among the Flathead Salish." His research was derived from his conversations with nine of their elders. Bonnie and Eduardo Duran affirm Raymond's study, "the illness that it (alcohol) inflicts on the individual may be an initiatory one. [...] The fact that through the process of being addicted and the subsequent recovery a person undergoes extreme personal pain, injury, and sometimes actual psychological and physical dismemberment alludes to shamanic initiation." One of the Flathead Salish elders had gone through the extremity of this initiation, healing his "dis-ease" with alcohol, transforming into a spiritual guide, which in turn helped others within the community.

In *Healing the Soul Wound*, Eduardo's teacher, Tarrence names alcohol, "the medicine" that can be used for good or ill. If misused, there is always a "price to pay." For his Native clients, Tarrence suggested to Duran, the way to deal with "alcoholism" was through a "life and death ritual." This ceremony makes perfect sense in Joy Harjo's confession: "I drank to obliterate my life"—to die to it. Harjo lists the types of alcohols she tried as well as the sensations given, advising. "You must use them carefully. They open you up. If you abuse them, they can tear holes in your protective, spiritual covering" (*Crazy Brave*). I

n *Drugs, Addiction and Initiation: The Modern Search for Ritual*, Jungian analyst Luigi Zoya explores the meaning of the loss of ancient ritual in the lives of post-modern men and women and their longing to recreate this "participation mystique." Zoya believes that even if the culture eliminates initiatory practices—as in the Ghost Dance at Wounded Knee, which was "stamped out militarily"—"it cannot eliminate the fundamental archetypal demand, which ends up expressing itself in simplified surrogate forms and then deteriorates because it is unconscious." That our longing for these ancient practices is what drives Natives and whites into alcoholism and drug addictions as well as this white girl's search for initiation.

In *Of Water and the Spirit: Ritual Magic and Initiation in the Life of an African Shaman*, a Dagara from Burkina Faso, Dr. Malidoma Patrice Somé once noted that mothers cry when their boys go off to be initiated, because mothers are aware, some don't survive this passage. Inside the initiation there is a spiritual death to their childhood. In fact, the initiation is often so intense some boys physically die. Through this process, those who return are not often recognized

Part II: The Divide

and don't return to their mothers in the same manner, for they have been severed from the apron, spiritually dying to a way of being. They have been initiated into adults.

All night long inside that rainstorm, had Hok'ee and I been on verge, on the borderlands of a physical death, or death to a way of being, another kind of an initiation? And then, later, was Hok'ee's driving around drunk another transformation into a new passage for his life?

If alcoholism is an initiation, what if something was ignited between the two of us—Hok'ee and me—in coming together. Maybe we downloaded information to one another without having to have sex. Something I had once learned from my psychoanalyst Walter.) Maybe we sparked "Fire," an awakening. That it was less about rejection, or a no, or about sex, and more about the appreciation of who he really was. Perhaps what had been different is, I hadn't treated him as lesser or even "other-ed" him. I trusted him in a way I wouldn't have trusted a white man, and he, me. Nor did I ask him to fulfill me with sex. For there were more important things that brought me to his land: friends, the want to walk their territory with respect, a bear dream, the desire for connection with the Original Peoples, their tales. These wishes had caused me to fly from Santa Barbara to Albuquerque, to rent an SUV and drive across their landscape.

Yes, what if we remove the question of things being sexualized or out of "colonial tropes" of whites walking too easily on the Original Peoples' land? What if we had both been transformed, initiated? What if he'd been changed from my appreciation of his stories, of riding out into the night in the rain, of not taking advantage of him? I had come to their traditional land for their rituals. —For him, was the respect I showed a contrast to all his other interactions with whites? If this is so, I must have confused him. For isn't often sex associated with a little death? What if his ancient tales, the rain, the earth, and his respect for my "no" had changed us both? Caused us to die to something?

At the time I had not read Eduardo Duran's *Buddha in Redface*. I did not know that like Duran's ancestor, the Maasai Sarototi and I would come to believe either through an ancestor or our past life we were involved. That he and I had been a part of a group of spiritual leaders from all over the world—ethereally and physically—who had gathered together five hundred years ago to plant uranium in the Four Corners, taking revenge on the Conquistadors for their decimation of millions. If this was so, I needed to touch down on the dirt where I had been a part of poisoning others, to take responsibility for five centuries later the experimentation of the atomic bomb on Navajo land as well as, our destruction upon the Japanese.

If this was true, I had returned for multi-dimensional reasons beyond my knowingness, beyond space and time. As an example of who I really was in this dimension, in 2003, I enter and exit the Sweat Lodge over and over, because I cannot endure the heat of my own impurities, the stains of the past. Of course, the Navajo elders enjoy pointing this out to me, jesting. "Look at her, she cannot sit with the past." "Look at her, she cannot face what she has done."

Was my infection now becoming Hok'ee's? Had my impurities become a vampire bite? My rusty hook an infection to this young man's life? As in the past, a common cold decimating a whole village? For, I was and am a carrier of undifferentiated energies, unaware of the power I hold and had held as an allusive, attractive and privileged white woman. And both my personal past, as well as my ancestors had not been fully reckoned. So, I have had to come to terms with, I had/have a projection that was/is often transferred to those around me.

Once, I had mentioned that the Jungian analysis I had chosen to do with Walter was not for the faint of heart. However, I had yet to grasp that the initiation with the Maasai would be, in the end, extreme enough for me to have to process this over many, many years. And even this initiation with Hok'ee has been such a journey. Though my initiations may not have been as brutal as our violations upon them or as painful as the Natives' initiation through alcohol, to the Durans, "suffering is a sacred thing and should not be wasted." And so, I embrace the extremes of an initiate, the natural suffering that goes with it, (even this lesson from the Navajo elders).

Trusting and praying that those who have suffered because of me, will find their way through their initiation with an extension of Oropeza's "Grace." To Duran, "healing does not imply curing or getting rid of suffering. Healing has to do with being able to harmonize with all that life has to offer." To Grace and Harmony!

34

DELICATE STRANDS

"It took only one person to tear away the delicate strands of the web, spilling the rays of sun into the sand, and the fragile world would be injured."

—Leslie Marmon Silko, *Ceremony*

From the reflection of the yellow SUV, I had spilt the rays of the sun onto the sands of Canyon de Chelly, into this "fragile world," perhaps, unraveling the "delicate strands of the web" of their culture held together through stories, through time, injuring Hok'ee, injuring the Navajo Nation once again.

There just were and are ramifications from our ancestors' decision to take away the Natives power through the removal of their rituals. "The old man put his sack on his lap and began to feel around inside with both hands. He brought out a bundle of dry green stalks and a small paper bag full of blue cornmeal. [...] 'There are some things we can't cure like we used to,' he said, not since the white people came" (Marmon Silko).

34: DELICATE STRANDS

Late afternoon, after the Navajo Sweat Lodge, filled with a shame I can taste but cannot swallow, I drive down the road to the Home of the Hopi Tribal Government, the Third Mesa, to the New Oraibi (o-RYE-bee), the Village of Kykotsmovi (kee-KEUTS-mo-vee), which means "Mound of Ruined Houses." To the People of Peace. To meet with a Hopi friend of Rebecca's, Humieta, in hopes to break through the walls of those disparities my culture had infamously created, in hopes of encountering a man or woman, who might remember Willoughby F. Senior, who had lived among them in the summers for over thirty years.

As I travel closer, writings circle round about me. As a young woman, I had read Senior's book, *Smoke Upon the Winds* and had been impacted by his kind conversations and his experiences with the Old Weaver, as well as his careful protection of the Hopi's way of life—to somehow safe-keep their culture from the obliteration by white man's ways. For class, I had been reading Frank Waters', *Book of the Hopi: The First Revelation of the Hopi's Historical and Religious Worldview of Life*, written with the help of White Bear and his wife Naomi, who translated the elders' words into English. Trying to grasp the complexity of some of their ancient history, to understand their "emergence myths" which they name, "The First World," "The Second," "The Third," and "The Fourth," each movement of the layers from one consciousness, one step into being, into the next, paradises that shift into cataclysm. The Hopi believe themselves to be the first inhabitants of Turtle Island.

In "A Container of Ashes: Hopi Prophecy in History," Armin W. Geertz explains how in each of these embodiments the Hopi climbed up the axis mundi, a giant reed to begin each world anew. However, in an Anthropos article, "Book of the Hopi. The Hopi's book?" Geertz highly criticizes Waters' text because he believes many Europeans and Americans derived their misconceptions about the Hopi. To Geertz, the Hopi's prophesies are ever moving, alive, "not static," and fully human, a prophetic community with "no prophets" ("The Invention of Prophecy: Continuity and Meaning in Hopi Indian Religion"). Geertz writes of the constant barrage, the gate crashing the First and Second Mesas are exposed to, from the "hippie invasion," from the "Friends of the Hopi" organization's romantic longing to fulfill the prophesy for the return of the Hopi White Brother and their ever-insistant search for a guru. Not to mention the general tourists the community has been besieged by.

Part II: The Divide

To Humieta, I do not reveal these readings that have made me curious, nor my want of resolution with her people—for my shame balls up this want into a tangle inside my belly. Nor do I reveal the calamity I had created and left behind me at Canyon de Chelly. In fact, I'm a little tentative. For maybe the story of Hok'ee will soon circle her village as well or had already preceded my arrival. I only divulge an odd, and yet, recent dream that had brought me to her doorstep, of a bear claw with feathers. Not confessing—for fear of claiming any kind of kinship—that in the vision, they had embraced me as clan: I, who obviously carry a great big shadow wherever I roam; I, who have been taught to hold so many secrets from those I engage.

Humieta response is of a kind teacher: "The Bear Clan is of the highest level, of which I am a member and are the chiefs who lead and care for the land. My husband, Tadanda, who is no longer walking on the Earth, was of the Coyote, who just as the Wolf, and Fox Clans protect and warn." At the U.N., her husband had spent much of his life, "coyoting," as an advocate for the Hopi.

"I'm disappointed I never had the opportunity to meet him. I've heard such amazing things."

Proudly, she wraps her arm around a little boy. "This young man is my grandson, Wesala, which means, 'the long howl of the coyote'"—relating him to his grandfather, the great leader Tadanda.

About my filmmaking with the San Bushmen, her son Kaiya challenges me. "Yes, just as you, with the Bushmen, people come knocking on our doors. They want to study us. But how do we explain to them our 'Kachina' spirits, one hundred and fifty entities, of which you have no language for? We, as pueblo-dwellers, do not express ourselves like you. Instead, be our friend, Murphy."

Kaiya was right. *How could we understand them if we have not one word for any of their spirits? How could any of us define them on our terms, in our language, when their expressions were explicitly at variance to ours?* Once, to Edward T. Hall, a Sioux, who had been educated at an Ivy-League College, enlightened, "What would you think of a people who had no word for time? My people have no word for 'late' or for 'waiting,' for that matter."

At the University of Kansas, I remember my black Methodist friends—who were part of a non-denominational organization I belonged to—used to say, "Yes, we're late once again because we're running on CPT." "What?" "We're running on Colored Peoples' Time." I loved that they could joke about themselves and make us a part of their innate sense of timing. I loved that each week they taught

34: DELICATE STRANDS

us new life-giving songs full of rhythm and hope. Perhaps we expect things from people they aren't able to conjure, as I had had trouble comprehending Hok'ee's reaction. Instead, we, as white Westerners, move our histories through time with linear thinking. The Natives' nonlinear thinking grounds their tales through "space" and "place." We separate the mind, body and spirit, whereas, for the First Peoples, "the individual is a part of all creation" (B. Duran, E. Duran). Ensouled. In *Indianz.com*, Daniel Wildcat explains, "To American Indians, land is not simply a property value or a piece of real estate, [...] "It is a source of traditions and identities, ones that have emerged from centuries and millennia of relationships with landscapes and seascapes" ("Money and injustice against the first Americans.")

Without thinking what it would do to the Original People, our ancestors had separated them, just as they had done to the Africans enslaved, ripping them from the land, from their mythology, from rituals tied into their very existence, set within the strongholds of their territories. By name, they knew the serpent, who guarded the spring from which they drew their water, the mountains of glory, the waving fields of grain, the medicine plants, and Buffalo, Tatanka, whose life in multiple ways brought them through the harsh winters, whose death informed their everyday through dreams. Whether we like it or not, there just are "invisible boundaries that divide our world" (Meyer). And we keep creating, feeding the fires of those divisions without allowing the "subaltern" (Chakrovorty's term) to live peacefully.

Hall describes these lines of divisions as *The Hidden Dimension*, those physical distances, as well as the subtle cultural rules within our exchanges, that we often have trouble grasping. In *Silent Language*, Hall explained that years before, the American bureaucracy was so busy providing jobs for the whites who worked on the reservation, moving them from place to place, without caring whether they understood Native people groups or not. To Hall, it was too disturbing for the whites to recognize the "anthropological idea that the Indians were deeply and significantly different from European-Americans, for that would have threatened to upset the bureaucratic applecart." Often, we just don't want to hear—our cultures' contradistinctions are often at variance, causing great disturbances, as I had become aware of on the Navajo Reservation.

"Thank you, Kaiya, of course, I'll be your friend. Don't worry, I won't make a film." Not thinking, in the end, I'm like everyone else, *wanting something*. (Geertz words about the besiege of others upon the Hopi land should have been

Part II: The Divide

a warning to me.) For I have an agenda, too: "But if anyone recalls the man, Willoughby Senior, who stayed on your land fifty years ago, I'd love to republish this book with one of the Hopi's dedications in the front, so that the sales benefit your people."

"We will take the book to the elders and see."

The Hopi are extremely private (and rightly so, due to the past). So, I knew the chances of anyone coming forward was highly unlikely—and of course, it was many years later. And given the story of Hok'ee that may circle after my departure, maybe no one would be interested in working with me. No one ever responds. Nor did the author's family give me permission to republish. In the end, these occurrences did not matter.

Though our acquaintance is brief, what matters is, with Humieta, I trepidatiously walk along the rim of Canyon de Chelley, the land of their ancestors, peering down at the scene of my "crime." As if Humieta knew, like detectives, we must return and view this creation, this mixup of mine from another perspective. Together we do this, as if she's holding my hand, just as Joy Harjo with "the old man" of wisdom, peering into the conflicts within her own family home, "We watched the story below us as it unwound through time and space, unraveling like my mother's spools of threads when she accidentally dropped them," (*Crazy Brave*).

Women of the past wove and unraveled tapestries telling and retelling the stories of old or of the moment. According to Chief Willem Rypertd of the Naro Bushmen in Namibia, even the men "followed the thread, a spiritual link from the healer to God, which was their telephone" (*Voices of the San*). *As Humieta follows the thread back across time, is she releasing my guilt?*

"To the Navajo, I am the teacher," Humieta declares, as she points to the National Monument, "Murphy meet, Spider Rock, Grandmother Spider, in Hopi, 'Kokyangwuti' (koh-kyang-woo-tee) in Navajo, 'Na'ashjé'ii Asdzáá!' She is the greatest weaver of tales, of fate for all creatures on this earth." Generously, Humieta reckons me into consciousness, into clarity with that fate of mine or certainly the choice I have made with Hok'ee, catching me in the web of Grandmother Spider and the story of all time upon the land of her ancestors, where the serpent protects the waters, the blood holds contracts firm. Where even a rock is considered alive and the grandmother of all.

After this sacred moment of meandering on the rim together, the two of us, Humieta and I shop for groceries for their celebration, loading up the car

34: DELICATE STRANDS

with bountiful meats for vats of stew—a brief and minor gesture of mine to heal the breach. As we take the road home, I look past Humieta, catching a glimpse of two setting suns. I decide not to mention this, for if she can't view them, I might be gravely disappointed. Intellectually, I know this double apparition, which I've heard may be prophetic, is due somehow to the refraction in the passenger window of this rented yellow SUV. However, I also comprehend the larger significance of this sign. The two of us are meeting as equals, as women, as two moons of the two suns, separate and distinct cultures in a moment of harmony across universal differences. That that dream of mine about her Bear Clan miraculously brought me here for more reasons than one.

Somehow these momentary moments of meetings with Humieta, with the Hopi, with the Navajo, with a people whose land our white ancestors confiscated, obliterating theirs in genocide and ethnocide, the removal of their culture, is such a very minor crack at amends. O, God bless them! O, Mother Earth, O, Great Spirit, forgive those misdeeds, those 375 broken contracts of our people to Turtle Island's Original Peoples. Briefly, I had crossed the borderlands of this horrible history and yet, had still stumbled and blundered.

Was this more of what the Maasai wanted me to face, not just the earth of the First Peoples of Turtle Island but the rootedness of the original wound to them and my own? How mine is lodged down deep, un-mined and often unconscious. How ours is still bound in unawareness, in supremacy. How theirs is incomprehensible to us because we've never taken the time to listen, to allow their culture to breath.

What I realize is everything I did on this journey was off because I was off. I had somehow crashed and burned. In *The Call to Courage*, Brené Brown reminds us to speak up anyway, "I don't know if I'm going to nail this or not but what I'm sure as hell not going to do is stay quiet." In the past, I haven't been outspoken, but twenty years after the fact, twenty years after these interactions, twenty years after some consciousness development, the #metoo and the WOKE movement, I'm pursuing, I'm striving, right here, right now, to change the way I walk and talk on the earth, well, certainly, the way I write.

According to Micheal Lechuga, I must have changed through these experiences with Hok'ee, with the Bushmen and the Maasai, because he recently expressed, "From our history of traveling together in South Africa (2007) and Mexico (2008), what I know about you, is that you reject the colonial way of living for a way that is more deeply connected. You, therefore, are attempting to bring closer those indigenous peoples, who you work with and write about."

Book One – Across the Divide to the Divine

Part II: The Divide

From my conversations with Clara Oropeza, she also affirms, "Because healing is so important it takes a certain sensitivity, and such a sensitivity requires deep respect for self and for Natives. You have been on a journey toward developing this sensitivity to help yourself and others to heal."

However, as a white person, even though a woman, I didn't and still, really don't completely know how to be around others who have been treated as outsiders for five hundred years, because as a white, I have been an insider. And to be honest, I cannot peel off my skin to become un-white and I certainly have not figured out the impossible—how to attempt what Clifford Geertz suggests, "putting oneself into someone else's skin" (*Local Knowledge. Further Essays in Interpretive Anthropology*). Slowly, I can only shift from within, changing the way I move and speak. Most of all, I realize there are levels of consciousness and maybe here as I write, I am reaching into another. Hopefully, I will keep growing and be a part of moving a pebble toward a mountain for change.

Yet, it strikes me that I was moving through their lands with little thought except for what I wanted—a kind of white person's way. When I observe the oil companies smashing through Alaska, which has since stopped due to Biden, or smashing through the preserve of Murchison Falls in Uganda where animals and mammals, who have taken refuge, must flee, and the livelihood of farmers is being destroyed without recompense, or the constant deforestation in Central African Republic, which means the BaAka pygmies have no where to hunt or to perform their sacred ceremonies, or the loss of land of the Maasai Warriors in Tanzania due to hunters. Sadly, I must admit we aren't transforming. I'm certainly not. *How can we continue doing what we're doing without destroying all our relations on Planet Earth?* Yet, we keep doing it. With all that I know, we know, it's unconscionable.

Over the course of five years—one of our Global Voice allies with Radio Ndjoku—Max Bale of Radio France's ePOP program, has received thousands of videos of wisdom from indigenous peoples the world over expressing their feelings and concerns about the climatic changes. Recently over tea, Max replied to this, "Murphy, even though we have all the information we need, we're not stopping the way we live and our constant consumption. We're running headlong into the wall!"

I'm speaking about myself here, too! I am a part of this. You should see the trash I create daily, the amount of groundwater I draw forth. It occurred to me, the way I live here on Mother Earth is a daily microaggression to all

34: DELICATE STRANDS

the creatures that walk upon it and that microaggression feeds into the greater macroaggression.

How do we step, talk, walk differently, respectfully both on this precious earth and with each other? How do we, who have always been included, move ourselves into awareness, understanding, reciprocity, kindness to those who have lived on Dussel's "underside of modernity?" How do we embrace our disparities? When we as whites are "other-ed"—we're not really, because honestly, (at least for the moment) we're still the dominant race.

Though, we cannot entirely relate to the horror of Natives' continuous mistreatment, in such an infinitesimal way, most everyone has been an "underdog" at times, has been "taken advantage of," has been "rejected," and/or has been "groomed" to be something other than what they were meant to be. These not-so-comfortable-moments in our lives can engender compassion, graciousness. Yet, those of us who are of the dominant race, have no clue of the power of our decisions—just as I made with the Navajo Hok'ee or even my conversation with the Hopi Kaiya—which we make with such sweeping hands from our continual elitism.

Inside the template of the Western-American mind is this notion that we are victims to what others have done to us, *9/11* versus taking responsibility for what attacks we have made that have caused others to strike back. I, too, must come to terms with our ancestors monstrously powerful destruction of the Original Peoples and the indigenous the world over. As well as with my past life as a passive, observing soldier in Custer's army. Maybe with what little sensitivity I do have, at another time, I might have been the reverse from the soldier; I might have been defending the land as a Native, obliterated for being the "other." I certainly do have more past lives to uncover.

Historically, the indigenes have suffered from the diseases and the counterintuitive ways of living from infiltrations of Western Civilization. Just as David Quammen penned in *Song of the Dodo*, they, and even we, are but chopped up into islands, fragments—fragile, so easily wiped from the face of the earth into extinction—as once 5 million or more Native Americans were, from their encounter with the Spanish Conquistadors. Even as I visit Humieta (2003), my own nuclear family teeters on the brink, no great-grandchildren, (yet) in perpetuity.

To be clear, though born in the United States, I'm not qualified as a "true" Native, as one of my high school girlfriends, who is said to be one-eighth. I

Part II: The Divide

don't have the blood type, the DNA, nor am I a part of a tribe. Our family, born on the red dirt of Oklahoma, is part of this inheritance of racism, of silence, of separating ourselves, keeping out "the other." I assume because John Lewis of Monmouthshire, England was noted in Virginia in 1653, our ancestors must have been part of enslaving those who were transported from Africa. *Yet, amongst my relatives, who would dare pass on such a horror story?*

Those of us, the younger sons and daughters, who did not inherit property in Virginia, moved to the Midwest and in another extreme action, slowly pushed out the Five Civilized Peoples. Maybe some of us were "good" abolitionists fleeing from the East Coast nightmare. Though none of us were as extreme in our radicalism as John Brown, who later was hung for his. Forever though, white Americans have affected the lives of the indigene.

If I track back just seven or eight generations, I bump into a known character in the history of the United States—Meriwether Lewis. Related through an aunt, our distant ancestor, Meriwether grew up on his father's plantation in Virginia, which enslaved Africans. Because of this, Meriwether would reject his father's vocation becoming Secretary to President Thomas Jefferson, though a known slaver himself, who birthed six children through the slave Sally Hemings. I imagine, just through that relationship alone—for Col. Charles Lilburn Lewis married Lucy Jefferson, Thomas' sister—my relatives are by no means innocent. Of this, Tommy Orange challenges, "Look no further than your last name. Follow it back and you might find your line paved with gold or beset with traps"—there, right *There, There*—I have fallen into another one of ours.

As I follow the Lewis name across the West, under the influence of Jefferson, Meriwether crossed the Missouri River, mapping the territory on the Lewis and Clark Expedition way out West. Though Meriwether, through Stephen E. Ambrose, is noted for his *Undaunted Courage* and for his fairness in his treatment of the Original Peoples, Jefferson's ultimate intention was to claim the land and declare sovereignty over them. (Some say Meriwether committed suicide over his explorations being used against the Natives.)

But if I'm completely honest, I didn't do the labor that Edward Ball, author of *Slaves in the Family*, who moved to Charleston to research the truth to discover 75,000 descendants from their slaveholdings, even tracking the African Americans' lineage back to Africa. Eventually, he would personally apologize to several of the families he grew to know. Twenty-two years later, he'll go further still into this discomfort regarding one of his relatives, a Ku Klux Klan member,

34: DELICATE STRANDS

in *Life of a Klansman: A Family History in White Supremacy*. Ball declares, "The United States was founded upon racial violence." It's not wonder we're in the state were in.

In *There There*, Orange's character, Thomas Frank struggles with his drinking, pondering the differences within his body, a kind of war that is going on, he cannot decide who to identify with—his Native father or his mother's whiteness: "You're from a people who took and took and took and took. And from a people taken. You're both and neither." I can relate to his mother's side, as I'm from a family that "took and took and took and took." Though on some level, at least sexually, I was taken from. Even so, like Thomas Frank, there is a war going on inside, a battle against that whiteness that can no longer exist without some form of restitution, reciprocity.

According to Dwanna L. McKay's article "Oklahoma is—and always has been—Native Land," at one time, "up to 100 million people of more than 1,000 sovereign Indigenous nations occupied the area that would become the United States" until our white ancestors decimated them, "leaving only 250,000 standing." These are facts and numbers quantifying how brutal our ancestors had been and to write them so easily, sounds rather flippant! And I wonder: *Are my ancestors weeping now on the other side of the veil? Are they setting about reconciliation and repair? Are they shaking hands with the ancestors of the Natives on the other side?* I hope so. In this endeavor, I hope they will assist me, us.

No different than the Afrikaners to the blacks and to the Bushmen, and the Americans to the blacks, white Americans forced these Original Peoples to new homelands across nine states, over 2,000 miles, rightly known as "the Trail of Tears." Even so, those nations who survived this tragedy still have served as the Choctaw "code talkers" in WWI, as did the Navajo in WWII. To this day, graciously they aid Oklahoma economically, culturally, and socially—funding schools, highways through the monies they earn. They have so many reasons to be proud.

Once I laughed out loud to Mother, as we drove from my homeland of Kansas to her original homeland of Oklahoma, across the beautiful landscape of the Flint Hills, "Wouldn't it be wild if the Natives make so much money from their casinos that they systematically buy the land back from us and kick us off Turtle Island?" She agreed. But maybe, in the end, we conjectured, they wouldn't want the land we have destroyed.

Book One – Across the Divide to the Divine

Part II: The Divide

Yes, throughout history, North, South, East, West, there have been barbarians at the gate. White Westerners have most recently been *that*, confiscating the land and treasures of the "other," feeding on the products the slaves produced. And beyond that, continuously practicing forms of systemic racism, colonialism, within our post modern-day institutions, which is considered "white enrichment,"—profiting from injustices done to minorities whether knowingly or unknowingly. Up until now, we have been the Gatekeepers to what is right, to the beliefs they—as in the "other-ed"—are meant to have. Forgetting, what made America great was due to the reverence of the land through the prayers of the Original Peoples for tens of 1,000's of years, as well as the slaves' spiritual cadences sung as their strong backs plowed the earth through forced devotion for 340 years. *Is the problem only skin deep or land-related, rooted in?*

What I'm recognizing is, ancestrally I'm more closely rooted to the Europeans, the white Americans, in the effects we had on the indigenes. Nevertheless, the Maasai wanted me to be in tune, akin, bringing this alignment into being. As though the Maasai knew I must come to terms with this homeland of mine, the soil from whence I came forth, the land of the forefathers, foremothers and older still the land of the Natives'—ancient men and women whose wise shoulders we stand upon, who have lived and breathed on this substantial earth. No longer can I run from what has been, but must face Father, Mother, Ancestors of the truths of what we've done, they've done, I've done and continue to do to others as white capitalists.

What I love about Humieta is that, though her community has historically been set aside, often silenced, she held her own with me as an equal, because she is, who she is meant to be. And with the perfect amount of hubris she stands a proud storyteller, a proud member of the Hopi's Bear Clan.

After having spent the evening with Humieta, in my hotel room, in the wee hours of the morn, I'll awaken from a reverie as a coyote, a song dog, strangely ululating at my father. *Is this a warning, a message to walk softly as I depart from their sacred land? In Quantum Coyote Dreams Black World*, Eduardo Duran explains this yipping and yapping as outside "the nouning of reality" as "Coyotying Howling." *Am I, too, the growl of the grizzly or like Wesala, the long howling of that coyote?* Of this sacred creature, Bonnie and Eduardo Duran exude, "Thanks to the spirit of Coyote (as the Sacred Clown), who in his impeccable wisdom continues to carry us into places that are painful, tricky, funny, ridiculous and unknown. […] especially when we least expect to be taught."

34: DELICATE STRANDS

Certainly, as a human, as I drop into these immeasurable dimensions I've encountered, vast emotions have arisen (not to mention the tears and the gagging), as I drag along a bag of this life and others, layers upon layers, attempting resolution (or certainly stirring up trouble) wherever I go.

35

BULL AND STAG

*"To the Winds of the West
Mother Jaguar
Protect our medicine space
Teach us the Way of Peace. To live impeccably.
Show us the Way beyond death."*

—*Prayer for Opening Sacred Space*, Alberto Villoldo, The Four Winds Society

Living in the hills, on the borders of the wilderness, near "the Winds of the West," what is left of the outback behind this little Californian town shows up—the deer, the raccoon, the possums, the coyotes. On a rare evening, a stag with huge antlers, steps across the yard. As though a human being, he takes the stairs into the garden. Tip-toeing, I follow. Hiding behind the bushes, I observe him eating roses. Through the branch, he catches my eye. With trepidation, I stare into the face of a wise old man.

35: Bull and Stag

Particularly now that the Bushmen, the Maasai, and the Native rituals have so entered my heart and soul, whenever I get a chance, head for the outdoors to sink my toes into the grass, praying to the West. Perhaps this is why I have perched in Santa Barbara, weaving somehow the encounters with Africa and the intimacy I had had as a child tracking in nature—the cooing of the doves, the smell of burning olive wood, the honeysuckle penetrating the night air.

At ten o'clock each night, set books, pen, and paper aside, pull on my favorite grey sweater, lace up those black army boots, top those red-haired curls with a furry Kanga baseball cap to stroll along the winding dark over-hanging-tree-lined Las Alturas Road. I need to reconnect, to somehow loop back to Laloshwa Highlands, meet with Sarototi under the stars. At the overlook, peer out at the twinkling lights of the city, pondering an argument for a potential thesis, wondering if the Kitomini Village is arising early to forge into the Sacred Forest of the Lost Child with their cattle, in search of water and meadows with grasses of plenty.

Along the way, there are frog ponds. Sliding the wooden pestle across the back of the frog, a percussion instrument, I attempt communication: "Croak, croak!" The neighborhood drops into silence. Whispering to one another, "*Who is this big bull frog that is calling out to us?*" And on and on the conversation goes. Reminding me of "The Frog Prince," of the young girl who must kiss the frog for his kind return of her rubber ball. She slyly puts him off. *Who wants to kiss a slimy green thing, anyway?* After dinner, when Frog arrives with his request, her anger becomes the grabbing of his legs, flinging him into the wall. He splatters, popping out a prince. *Am I springing him forth?*

Upon my return to Santa Barbara, when I'm not in class, I study mornings, afternoons and nights and continue psychoanalysis (now in Ojai as Walter and his family have moved to California). However, I don't confess the almost seduction, the wily coyote happenings in Canyon de Chelly. So, Walter reassures me, no longer analyzing me—yet similar to the Native man, who appears in my dreams, who catches the thermals on horseback with flowing hair and colorful scarves—tutors me in the art of listening to the Guiding Self, so that I may find my heart's tender artery.

Yes, I'm even being re-educated by messenger birds. Each morning around ten or eleven o'clock, I hear the piercing cries of the hawks: Mother, Father, and Baby. Dropping my eruditions, I rush out to greet them, waving, "Hello!" They "peeer, peeer, peeeeer," a hello, taking flight down the hill toward the ocean—

Book One – Across the Divide to the Divine **265**

Part II: The Divide

not knowing their flight pattern is directing me to my future home. Keep wondering: *Are you hawks or falcons?*

A few days later, Father Hawk perches on a branch in one of the Three-Sister-Eucalyptus-Trees. Here, my art desk is perfectly located to catch a glimpse of the ocean, and now, this majestically proud creature moves, turns, and preens, displaying his characteristics, what bird watchers distinguish as the "jizz" of the bird—his yellow ochre sand and reddish color, the plumage, "the moustachial mask" (J. A. Baker, *The Peregrine*), the pristine strong shape, that "peeer, peeer, peeeeer" sound, and his habitat for hunting. Yes, he's answering those inquiries of mine. Due to a re-awakening, a re-orientation to the capacity to listen, just as my childhood self, I can apprehend (not in an auditory manner) the animals' words. So, I pull out a guidebook, searching for the likes of him, "The hardest thing of all is to see what is really there" (Baker).

"Wow!" I holler through the screen, as I raise the page: "You're a tiercel peregrine!"

And he flies off his perch, as if declaring, "Well, of course! What took you so long?"

From the past, I'm being re-educated as well. On the telephone, in a regression with the intuitive Mariah, in the furtherance of the past life with the Maasai, I discover I died with the curative for their elders tucked in my hand, victoriously, secretly remarking: "I choose to die withholding this gift, for I believe, if I don't, more may die with me, not just the elderly but also the warriors in battle, then, children, and their mothers, too. I believe, my death with this powerful plant shall keep them from conflicts with their neighbors."

Mariah continues, "From this point on, the Bushman you were married to in 1787, became furious with you. For just as you both were dying, you revealed you held the medicinal to heal. Life after lifetime, he has been dominating you. In this life, he must reckon with this and will soften."

When rising out of the trance, I have a keen awareness: this is the real reason Mariah sent me to the Maasai, to discover I had taken the medicine to my grave! As a wanna-be repairer of the breach, I had, in the past, severed myself from those convictions, the allegiance to the now, Hippocratic oath. For whether a doctor agrees with a patient or not, likes them or not, he/she serves. I had done something unconscionable, breaking the vow to cure the elders. In judgment, I stubbornly stood against their choices and did not benefit the sick. Stealing from them, what was theirs: fitness and the freedom to make their own choices. No wonder, in this life, I've had such trouble determining mine.

Strangely, here, I have been making frog sounds as if a child inside the wonder of nature, inside the magic of fairy tales where the possibilities are fathomless, where a frog can become a prince, a stag the means to carry me across the mountain on a quest. It isn't so much that I have a better relationship with the animals than someone else. I'm now alert. Just as Baba Budhya had said, "It's natural"—of the messages I had been receiving from the pigeons in NYC. Just as, in the poem, "Wild Geese" Mary Oliver asserts, I no longer must crawl on my knees to be in "right" relation.

Because I'm finally listening, "all my relations" are being clarified, re-established, re-kindled. *Or am I really hearing them?* For I'm certainly blundering along in my humanness. Not realizing I keep seducing others from the wounds of my past. Even so, through the Navajo, the Hopi, the Stag, the Frogs, the Falcon, Sarototi, I've come home to the Americas, home to a way of being in relation to all—whether seen or unseen—that which momentously and magically surrounds us.

As the tutoring progresses, I perceive the gifts the nuclear family has given me, and what they didn't. They've educated me in the art of meeting people from other cultures, other stations in life. Yet, I'm aware that "not getting" what I thought I needed, was in actuality, part of the necessity of maturity into adulthood, a reconciliation of sorts, weaving back to losses, gains, and withholdings to once again step forward, spiraling down to spiral up and into purposefulness.

One of these evening-walk-tutorials, I come up over the hill, encountering the stag once more. An eerie sight, with the moon at his back, he stands Herculean erect, commanding: *Who are you, you who respect me so?* In silence, in breathlessness, we glare at one another, equal to the force of the other. *Are you a god luring me off and away into adventure?* He bows, and in my imagination, as if Perceval, I run, leaping on his back as he leaps the gated community, we bound across the hillside to recover the Grail, to recover the yin part of that Self.

36

UNEQUIVOCAL DECLARATION

"Mambo mazuri hayataki haraka."
"Good things should not be hastened."

—Maasai Kanga proverb

While studying at PGI, every Tuesday that I'm free, I attend additional training at Deena Metzger's healers' and writers' groups. Early in the morning, I trek south from Santa Barbara to Topanga with my new girlfriend, the founder of *everyday gandhis*, Cynthia Travis, whom I have so much in common. While she creates peacemaking in Liberia, I'm scouring the Kalahari Desert and Kenya for stories. Though we are in the midst of busy schedules, Cynthia and I feel it an honor, a privilege, and good fortune to train with Deena.

For the past twenty years, the "School of Deena Metzger," much like the school of Vivienne in the days of King Arthur, has had many feminine iconic

36: Unequivocal Declaration

wisdom-keepers flock to her, creating a court of hungry vivacious followers. Throughout the late Twentieth Century, Deena has been and still is a fierce poet, author, shaman, activist. After a mastectomy, on the cover of *Trees: Essays and Pieces*, her arms are outstretched revealing her single-breasted Amazonian self. Across her breast-less and scarred space, is a painted snake tattoo, declaring, "Heal the life and the life will heal you." She's beautiful. A force to be reckoned with. To be in Topanga with her ferociousness is the same as being on the Masai Mara.

Years before (while struggling in fashion), Deena's *Writing for Your Life* had affirmed what had already become an absolute necessity for me through that declaration of "writing my way out of fashion" (even if just in a journal), permitting as well as enticing me to continue into a frontier of unlimited exploration within.

In Topanga, these artsy-hippy hills hold some of the Native threads and are sustained by Deena and her (then) partner Michael Ortiz-Hill. Over this wide expansive view, imagine myself back in Kenya, back in the Laloshwa Highlands. Here, Deena refers us to the art of divination through Stephen Karcher's *Total I Ching*, the ancient Chinese form; through the drawing Angel cards; through praying to the ancestors from the six directions; through the sharing of our nighttime dreams and personal writings; and sometimes praying over one another, depending on our needs. From her I learn the art of restitution towards the indigenous, towards the animals, the mammals, nature.

Within this setting, I have a private curative meeting with a Shona "Mundadisi," whose name means "one to make us proud." He is indeed confident and curiously and magnificently corn-rolled in the blunt cut style of an Egyptian priest, the kind of man, who does not have to demand respect. Instead, his spirit, his muscled physique, his very nature commands. Just as his strong beautiful black Zimbabwean *nganga* (Shona for shaman) hands grasp mine, which now feel fragile and pale in comparison, he twists my left wrist inquiringly, "Do you know how many beads are in your Bushmen bracelet?"

"No, but very time-consuming, for a San Bushmen to chisel an ostrich eggshell into round beads!"

"Well, an old ancestor, an elephant, is coming to you through these. He is slow in his approach, but he intends to make you strong." Affirmed by this and the touching of his healing hands, the old has been released, a departure is made from the path of playing "patsy." Mundadisi charges, "you can step into your

Book One – Across the Divide to the Divine **269**

femininity, fully engaged in the world. Sage or smoke yourself with elephant or lion dung to prepare the way. For tonight, Ms. Murphy, my ancestors meet with yours, so make note of your dreams."

"I'm not sure in California how I'll find elephant or lion dung unless I make some deal with someone at a zoo. But I do have sage. As well, I will continue to make note of all my dreams."

After the healing, Mundadisi mentions, "I want to visit the Maasai one day."

"I will let you know when my next trip is. Perhaps you and your wife can join me." *Why would I offer this? I don't even know him. Or do I? Was there already something set in motion to be resolved from a mutual past?*

Ironically, at school, this semester we are steeped in the past, in the mythological stories of Africa and the African Diaspora traditions. In this Animistic tradition, I watch, listening for signs, and symbols, for the appearance of Mundadisi's grandfather elephant.

Within a few days, in the dreaming way, this Shona shaman merges with me: Reaching for the long wooden hand-carved pipe, I partake (I, who know little about smoking) with a vast inhalation of smoke. *In the dream am I inhaling lion and elephant dung?* This inhale transports me into a walk down the dusty road of life with Mundadisi, and strangely—fifty goats. *Have the goat-toed ankle bracelets I gifted him manifested into more friends to play with?* In the wee hours of this morn, I discover the truth about me—I have left one plane for another—New York City's Fashion Avenue for Pacifica Graduate Institute, the plane of outer and inner knowledge, the strange and elusive plane of the shamanic.

Deena herself, also a practicing shaman, mentored with Amanda Foulger, who mentored with Michael Harner—so we are held in the arms of a long line of shamans. Through Deena and her associate, the courageous shaman, Valerie Wolf, Cynthia and I commence further training on Thursday mornings. Similar to Deena, Valerie's prayer life to the spirit world is tangible, real. As her magical drumming begins, the dissociation from the body, a feeling of weightlessness, a shift of perspective happens until I feel as if I'm in George MacDonald's *At the back of the North Wind* with Diamond, or as Apollo carried on a white swan to the mythical Hyperboreans, catapulted through, tumbling down narrow tunnels into the underworld, guided into unimaginable realms.

In *The Water Dancer*, "Conduction" Ta-Nehisi Coates defines, is "of the great power in even the smallest of escapes." Just as his character Hiram, I will become a conductor. In this case, instead of Hiram's power of story, the "jump" is done

36: Unequivocal Declaration

through Valerie's pounding and gentle guidance. For according to Calasso, "the drum was the lake into which the shaman sank in order to enter a world that others did not see" (*The Celestial Hunter*). Through this continuous rhythm, Cynthia and I are conducted, sinking easily into the Lower World in search of one another's spirit guides. She discovers mine as "Bat."

What's bizarre is I can hear Bat speak. *Have the Maasai so imbued me with more capacities and understanding?* The first discussion with Bat is about his many names: Belfry, Blundering, Swoopy. "Through your sonar, will my third-eye wisdom be activated?" I inquire. Wildly, in this ancient art, in this surreality, Bat himself tutors me. Each day is a new dip and turn. Often, I doubt our encounters, until dissolved into the half-conscious Alpha-Theta state, I observe Bat's outline, his slit eyes, greeting his newfound friend, Murphy.

To begin the peregrination, I hold his claw as we depart from the edge of Bull Creek's Dam near our childhood home, diving briefly into the water towards the Lower World where we come upon an earthly terrain. Across the far-flung landscapes, he directs me to lakes, to rocks, to seas introducing me to thousands and thousands of faces: all types, sizes, big, little, even, a white seal. "Hello," Bat telepathically announces, "This is my new pupil, Irene Murphy!"

On another shamanic jaunt, Bat leads me through a dark narrow passage to the Upper World, where he introduces me to my spiritual teacher for this lifetime. I imagine meeting Mother's mother as I did through Philani in Swaziland. Instead, on the edge of a waterfall, we encounter a huge furry-tusked being head-dressed with glorious feathers, standing tall, catching fish with his paws. Bat reveals, "He is a Master at shapeshifting into Bear, Eagle, Elephant (not confined nor defined by any continent)." Therefore, I name him: Big Chief Bear Eagle Elephant. In my belly, I feel him strongly. *Is this the Bull-Elephant Mundadisi predicted?*

Finally, Bat and I twirl around in a whirlpool, flying through a tiny window, home, where I pass out into a restorative state. This new internal guide, Bat, has merged me with the wind, water, and earth elements, the mythological, the legendary. With him, unencumbered by earthly parameters, I soar, gliding into an abundance of insight, pleasure, and laughter. Through him, I will become a facilitator for the rest of my life.

As a child, through Pearl Buck's books, I could fall right through that hole in the ground everyone so casually spoke of, all the way to China! Shamanism became another way for me to do just that. Linked to Bat's claw I could venture

Part II: The Divide

to Africa and back without the seventeen-hour flight to Johannesburg. I had access and means at my fingertips through my little turtle rattle, I named, Ginger. Universes were unfolded and, in this unfolding, enfolded me in their embrace.

While this mentoring from Bat, Walter, Falcon, Stag penetrates the spiritual universe; I have other things to think of. Intellectually, though steeped in the mythological stories of Africa and the African Diaspora traditions, personally, I am consumed with Mother's health in Kansas. May Day I travel home to be with her at the assisted care. There, while she falls asleep early, I slip off into one of the empty rooms a nurse offers, quietly writing PGI's required assignments. Eventually with Mom, in grandmother's wooden-framed bed, I curl up next to her peaceful self for a good night's rest.

In the mornings, I coif her hair. Of late, I've been dressing Mother as a twin. If I find something fun, a hat, a tracksuit, buy one for her in orange or green, one for me in pale yellow or brown. She loves the attention. Without Dad around, she grows her hair a bit longer, softer. No longer such a tomboy. Before her nails were clear and short, now they're pink, very long, and pointy!

At Mom's special table with the other elderly, we eat our meals, sharing stories. With her, I share in these newly formed friendships. Several times a day, we walk to see Dad across the street at the nursing home. Then, nap with her. Over and over again we watch her favorite movies *Philadelphia Story* and *Sound of Music*, laughing, singing, and weeping together. As enthusiasts, we throw wine and popcorn parties for her elderly friends. On their big screen, we transport them through the films of the 1940's as Mom and I secretly swing dance in the background to the old tunes. In her coral Juicy Couture and matching Patricia Underwood tam, Mom shines as a movie star.

Playing dress-up in costume jewelry, high heels, and Mother's Mary McFadden's and Leonard of Paris (the colorful clothes I earned while in fashion and gifted to her), we skip around her private room with her now best girlfriend, the four-year-old Georgianna, the nurse's daughter, who visits mother daily. The three of us playmates, draw, color in crayons, rip-roaringly giggle at *Mary Poppins*, *Chitty Chitty Bang Bang*, and along with Audrey in *My Fair Lady*, scream out, "Come on, Dover, move your bloomin' ass."

Amidst all this falderal, between the two of us, there is much divulging. In our own ways, Mother and I are both at turning points. Our pajama parties consist of reading, lying on Nana's bed, discussing, pondering our pasts, presents,

36: Unequivocal Declaration

and future lives. As a great reader, a great student of God's word, a great prayer warrior, she passes on her wisdom, her insights.

Lately, Mom and I have been reading Gay Walley's *the erotic fire of the unattainable*. "All women should read this!" Mom declares. "She writes the things I felt but couldn't say!" Both of us want to produce it (and so we do in 2007), in companionship with the other two books we've published: Lybeth Boyd Borie's *Poems for Peter,* and Gail Segal's *In Gravity's Pull.* The visits with the Maasai only confirm Gay's title of that erotic fire, that which cannot be owned by another or even attained, but instead, accessing one's own source within. I want this for myself, but lately, I wonder—*will I ever attain this?*

I often can't get to my personal writing. Looking back at the last few months (and really, if I'm honest, my whole life), I find I've been preoccupied with others, sacrificing for them. Not that I don't want to—help the present boyfriend Ethan with the design of his real estate flyer, read and fix Alison's bio, write one brother about how to sort out Mother's health issues, care for the students in the first year class, write a recommendation letter for Rupert's project, listen to my dear friend Rebecca as she so kindly listens to me, set up grieving ceremonies for others—but, though I love them, each of these things take time. *How do I care, love, and yet, get to my own personal legend?* A woman's constant dilemma!

In a recent dialog with Cynthia, on our last drive from Topanga Hills, I was reminded I must return to that life's work: After a jam-packed day of training with Deena and Valerie, I admit to her, "I have a headache again!" Immediately, Cynthia and I had backtracked, pondering the why of this.

"Sometimes in the middle of the writing sessions with Deena," I divulge, "I feel so smashed with a pounding headache. Have you noticed, I leave the room filled with you and those wonderful writers, taking refuge alone near the fireplace? Because every time I venture to share my memoir, *Africa Within*, Deena confrontationally strikes. Once when I read, a gal wept in the corner. 'See, Murphy!' Deena challenged, 'If you're making someone else cry, you haven't worked through your own issues. Your expressions should not deflate, instead inspire others into transformation.'

"Maybe Deena's right, before revealing, I need to digest my own story." Remembering a poster above Arthur's jazz bar on Grove Street in NYC, which challenged, "Taste your words before you spit them out!"

Part II: The Divide

Though Cynthia admitted she didn't want to lose our intimacy and our great conversations as we traveled back and forth together, she had conjectured, "Maybe you're not meant to study with her anymore."

In the past I've believed it "good" to study with others. Gain knowledge. However, in the shamanic world of Deena and her associate Valerie, I only hold acolyte status, so therefore, I am "lesser" than. Soon, though I don't know it at the time, through the original initiation and a future ceremony with the Maasai, I will mysteriously leap into equality. Perhaps through Sarototi, through Baba Budhya, I'm learning I have more than others might be willing to affirm, more than I'm willing to affirm within myself. In fact, it's dawning on me that I just might have the answers inside.

After conversing with Cynthia about this, I take a shamanic journey with Bat, inquiring about the instructions I'm receiving from Deena and Valerie. As if the key lies deep within, Bat oddly conveys a mission— "fall into your own vagina and your own belly of wealth, Murphy." He makes me laugh, as well, for me this is surprising, because (as we know) I've always looked outward toward others. Bat further reveals: "Do your work, not hers. The headaches are the override of her—informing you: 'you have enough in *that* head of yours, (and certainly that yoni) Murphy, get on with your personal legend!"

If I'm willing to listen, Bat, and even, Deena's words are urging me to go further on, to take the yin plunge, to write and rewrite the memoir of those experiences until it's so smooth people are moved beyond weeping into transformation. I know this means, I must go down deeper into those studies at PGI, to complete the dissertation for the Ph.D., for I am forever being encouraged to do more inner work, that deep dive into the vagina.

Every night we're together, Mother and I grab hands to pray. An atmosphere of potency fills her little room— "for where two or more are gathered" (Matthew 18:20). Tonight, however (after my reflection about all my friends' needs, about the training with Deena and Valerie), to God, to her, I finally verbalize: "I don't want to restrain myself anymore, to hold back my feelings for anyone, to be 'good' through words and dressing-up perfectly, to take care of others at the expense of me, to be what others want me to be. I have clutched my small body this entire life in obedience to every one of you—Dad, my brothers, even you, Mom—acting rationally and 'together,' when I was really falling apart inside.

36: Unequivocal Declaration

"If anyone misunderstands me, that's fine! No longer will I strive to be an ideal woman, venturing to please. Tired of realizing others' unrealized aspirations, from now on, I shall state my case. Be myself in the world!" Affirming these asseverations, Mother hugs me, embracing this—my unequivocal declaration.

Returning to Santa Barbara, I break away, spin myself out into my own private space into the quiet garden in search of the "real" me, "soul-remembering" what those gifts and talents are that can, for the first time ever, be realized. The complications of the "shoulda," "coulda," "woulda's" fall away, along with the headaches and the pressures to keep up with the Jones' and other shamans, to discover the tools lying buried beneath the internal wellspring. I do not return to Deena's, nor Valerie's. Instead, I will hire a shaman to help my family and I will take to my own, listening to Bat, Big Chief Bear Eagle Elephant, stepping into the Navajo's majestic Beauty Way.

37

SURRENDER THE BLOOD

"Don't be a fool! Nothing can grow until the ground is turned over and crumbled. There can be no roses and no orchard without first this that looks devastating. You must lance an ulcer to heal it. [...] and so it is with a sensual life that has no spirit in it."

—Rumi

In Santa Barbara, I choose to celebrate this birthday in thanksgiving, and yet, before I entered into thankfulness the Tarot cards direct my attention to the cruel way, I perpetually treat myself, delivering an anecdote: "Learn to say 'no' to those who distract you from your own path, balancing the powerful pull, yet natural dark and light forces with strength and clarity." How à-propos!

Cleansing the womb with the incense of Frankincense and Myrrh, I must, according to Rumi "lance an ulcer to heal it," saying good-bye to those men I wasn't allowed to say or couldn't say, "No" to. Remorse, mortification, sadness, disappointment. In that moment, I hear this resolve within, "Make time

37: Surrender the Blood

every day for the next few weeks to release each of the men you have known, Murphy— (in the Biblical sense)." I commit to thank every man for the gifts they brought: the experiences, the joys, and even the heartaches. Initiation. Baptism. Transformation. Enhancement. Enlargement. Exhilaration rises. By afternoon the load is lightened, so I can tuck into a blanket on the golden Cleopatra couch as the low-burning fire continues, while I read, underline, and make notes inside each book for school.

What is rising from this unearthing and releasing, are relationships with men who don't get tangled up in the sexual undercurrents of the old. With roses in hand, for the birthday celebration, a kind, platonic friend, Thomas, whisks me away to dinner at Stella Mar's, making me feel feminine, alive. The two of us have many commonalities; we've both left the corporate world to explore most everything spiritual. Every Friday (that we can), at Butterfly Beach, Thomas and I have united in the sacred ritual of the Taos Pueblo, observing "Father Sun" as he sets. We will eventually participate in publishing a book, *Nanju* and *Auju*, for the Achuar people in Ecuador. Among other friends, on Saturday mornings, we meditate in Alice Keck Park. Tonight, after blowing out the candles on the celebratory cake, we gather around my fire pit that feigns those numinous moments with the San Bushmen, our mutual friends in the Kalahari Desert, drinking in the stars rising over Santa Barbara as the moon lights a path across the Pacific.

After I stop traveling back and forth with Cynthia to Topanga to study with Deena and Valerie, I start to really listen to my own womb, my own story, what I am being called to. I step into silence, into my own interior from whence an intensive dream arises. The specifics of the reverie make me wonder if it is ancestral, if there is something greater going on with Father's loss of memory and Mother's inability to cope with the challenges of his disease. If so, it will need to be explored, and I will need to recover what I can, to help them before they move across to the other side.

At the same time, a friend of a friend refers me to Deborah, a former medical lab technician, turned IT master. During her career, she began to trip the light fantastic as a shaman, training with Michael Harner, Sandra Ingerman, among others. Knowing the inner chemistry of the physicality, the inner dimensions of computers, with her feet permanently landed in this world, she easily guides her clients into the regions of the Lower, Middle and Upper Worlds. She can track with clarity, in a way my fractured mind cannot. I love how she asks lots

Part II: The Divide

of questions about everything that is presently going on, first peering into those challenges through a psychological lens, then doing a shamanic journey around that.

On behalf of my family and the entire lineage, I hire her for these capacities. For I believe the dream to be a warning. We first connect via the telephone, for Deborah, at the time, resides in Lexington, Kentucky. Eventually, she will come to Santa Barbara to work around the fire.

"In West Africa when someone dreams of a dog, there is a curse. Oftentimes a dog is caught and hung in the village to ward off the jinx," I explain. "Midway between the night and the dawn, my reverie began: I am Western saddled (and this time, unlike the runaway black-stallioned-dream of my childhood, I actively hold the reins) on the back of a brown sable stallion galloping down Highway 69 towards the town of Paola, Kansas, where I grew up. Instead of continuing under the overpass of the Missouri Pacific Railroad, we ride off-road, up the hill to face the train head-on. Rising up on his hind legs, this gallant horse neighs, expanding in height, standing as grand as our adversary, breathing the same rhythmic breath. Yet, I fear this serpentined monster will run roughshod over my mount's hooves.

"Due to our presence, this 1920's coal-black pulsingly alive locomotive slows to a daunting, yet piercingly loud halt, squaring up to us as steam, smoke rises from its belly. Suddenly, out of nowhere, a yellow dog barks, turning our attention elsewhere. She nips at the heels of the steed, who turns and irritatingly rears once more. Afraid I will lose horse over dog, one hand braces the horn of the saddle, while the other raises the reins to heel the dog. However, with his teeth, the stallion snatches *Old Yeller* tossing her to the side as if a gnat."

"A daunting, yet informative dream, which makes sense given your willingness to square up to that which haunts—the Leviathan of the land," she conjectures.

"Yes, I believe the horse and I are facing the fatedness of our family story—that which has roared up and over and through our lives whether we wanted it to or not. Perhaps the dog—though irritatingly distracting me from this greater danger—is a friend, leading me away from a confrontation I'm not quite ready for."

"The horse and the dog act as psychopomps," Deborah adds, "spirits that escort into the unexplored regions of the unknown."

37: Surrender the Blood

From this information, Deborah sets our course to liberate the family spell. Soon all I hear through my headset is the vibration of the seeds, *"swish swish,"* inside her rattle. Through Deborah, her guides, and her visual descriptions we are conveyed by flying horse and dog across the Atlantic Ocean, as once wings of Eagles transported Frodo (Elijah Wood) and Samwise Gamgee (Sean Astin) over the burning fires of Mordor's Mount Doom in *The Lord of the Rings: Return of the King*. On the Continent of Africa, we slog through six inches of mud only to find ourselves, suddenly, in the Outback of Australia.

Standing before Deborah is a wild-haired grass-skirted man, with a skeletal formation painted in white upon his dark-as-the-night skin. From behind her, I peek at this frightening being—I christen, "Skeleton Man." *Hadn't I met him just weeks before?*

Nonetheless Deborah curiously (and I might add, boldly) speculates, "Why is this journey leading us here to Australia—why not Africa—where she normally travels and is trying to clear her history?" For like me, she cannot believe, given those encounters with the Maasai Warriors in Kenya, that we've been brought to this continent— "the land down under."

Immediately the Skeleton Man bellows, "I am not interested in dialoguing with her!" Pointing at me. Though I can't place the sound of the witch doctor's voice, which is as daunting as the costume, it seems vaguely familiar. "Do you not know what her family did to mine three hundred years ago?"

In a Fairy Godmother-like way, the Skeleton Man waves a magician's hand as if a wand, revealing a moving picture of my Scot/Irish male relatives dressed in white cotton shirts, pith helmets, khaki riding pants tucked in brown boots with gun in hand. Behind them, the ladies are draped in long to the ground white cotton dresses, and matching bonnets. Before them, the Skeleton Man's aboriginal family is clothed in leather loincloth, painted bodies, facing mine. *And what do mine do?* With guns, we slaughter them—leaving their blood splattered on the whites of our clothes, hands, and bodies, spilling it onto the earth—claiming their lands as our own.

The Skeleton Man flashes his hand, and another image emerges: In a dark cave, every one of my present-day cousins, and even me, are thin, withdrawn, and cold, as his family vampirically feasts upon our pale white necks.

Quickly, Deborah calls in our guides to negotiate this plight, challenging him, "Do you not think her family has suffered enough?"

Part II: The Divide

Slowly the Skeleton Man admits that the feeding of his relatives on mine for three centuries only shackles all of us—his family, mine—to the original tragedy. Deborah offers his kin and this soulful, mournful character, liberation. Slowly they each agree, beginning their procession towards the light. We observe this noble chief reluctantly, ambling toward the path of illumination. He hesitates, turns back shouting, "Tell her, it's about power!"

I will not forget *this* Skeleton Man—his fierce strength, his tremendous size, his blackness and the brilliance of the white bones upon his skin. Not knowing, I had already met him in this life, in the form of Mundadisi—the man I would soon introduce to the Maasai.

A recollection of Baba Budhya's weaving of a bracelet from the Strangler Fig to strengthen me to face these kinds of realities, these kinds of historic monstrosities. Each step, each past life regression, each shamanic journey, each analytic session allows me to relinquish and unwind the binding threads, until they will no longer overwhelmingly feed upon me. Though slogging through the mud much of my life, here is the sequential footstep in the right direction.

The griffins, the carrier birds, who according to von Franz, "carries the hero into the land at the end of the world, or beyond the sea," transport my family and me into the Upper World, to the Temple of Isis, placing us in her sacred waters. Her sisters' Sehkmet and Hathor assist. Little cupids flitter about reweaving, rewiring our bodies with love.

While we're resting, Deborah, on my behalf, rattles her way to the Maasai, questioning, "Why didn't you mention the curse, the killing of the Aborigines? You could have released her, set her free from this."

"She was not ready!" they declare.

Neither of us is surprised. Perhaps I needed these few years between those moments with the Maasai to nestle into my "I," to stand into that readiness, able to tackle the horrors the family and I have created, to make things right with the Skeleton Man, to return Mundadisi to the land of the Maasai, to our past, to lance the wounds leading into a surrender unto the blood.

38

UNIVERSE CONSPIRES: THE DREAMING WAY

"Modern man is pitiful, not because he has lost the consolation of religious practice, but because he no longer feels any relationship to, or receives any virtue from the gods. But explaining away those irrational events which our forefathers knew as divine intervention we have also lost touch with our ancestral inheritance."

—*Mythology of the Soul*, H. G. Baynes

With having acknowledged the dreaming way within me, with having initiated me through the naming and the water ceremonies, I did not know that these Warriors, who epitomize the ultimate yang for the planet have reconnected me to my ancestral inheritance, to a pulsing relationship with that which is greater than me, having given me access to the yin, that at my fingertips, a bucket, a pulley, and a deep well from which to draw—now my *Dreams:* (figure as) *A Portal to the Source* (Perera and Whitmont).

No longer alone but armed with what Jung claimed to be "undistorted and purposeful [...] images [...] (to) assist in the completion of individual development" and what P and Whit confer as the "Guiding Self [...] an expression of this life force." Again, what the Bushmen describe as that inner "tapping," what Eve Brinton defines as the LifeMind, that *my life itself has its own mind*, its own intelligence. I am learning not to go against this Self, for if I do, no one wins, "no one ever wins in that paradigm" (Brinton).

For I have begun to hear the subtleties of my own whispering self, that inner voice—what Jung called the dreamer's own forgotten language—the original "soul's code," the Melchizedek murmurings: "When you want something, all the Universe conspires in helping you achieve it" (*The Alchemist*). Now that I was complete with the mission of increasing the numbers eighty-two percent at Badgley Mischka, now that I was complete with ushering the dead from the destruction at the *9/11* site, now that Mom had really heard me, now that Dad had sadly lost all memory—I could finally listen to me, be about my *own* business.

Inklings from my long-term friend, Mindi, matched Melchizedek's matriculations—"underlying themes [...] your heart for God and your love of writing [...] muddy work boots [...] ready to walk off into the woods to explore [...] jump on your horse" not only resonated but were being lived out in the United States, in Africa.

"In fact, it would appear as though the [...] story-telling capacity of the psyche were a powerful organizing and healing factor." Confirm Perera and Whitmont, each experience, wounding, disappointment melds "into an organismic whole of overall function." With this new knowingness, dreams are no longer excessive residuals of "flotsam and jetsam" from the waking hours—instead, have meaning and importance. So that even that scary nightmare from childhood which appeared continuously of a black horse running away with me, becomes "a surge of instinct" according to Jung, and a treasured part of the whole, an animal to engage with—*Are you a friend whisking me away from danger? A guide to unlock that history?* "A steady evolving series [...] an unfolding continuum of views, and of a seeming intentionality..." (P and Whit).

What had begun as frightening images penned in diaries, now these inscapes ooze with potentiality for an ever-expanding life. For inside the individuation

38: Universe Conspires: The Dreaming Way

process, of me becoming an "I," each dream built on the next, a patterning, a leitmotif, inside the sequence, a transcendent and magnificently meaningful template was taking form. In January, written in one journal was a mental picture, number two-hundred-and-eleven, which then prepares me for April's phantasm, number two-hundred-and-twenty-seven. What Jung names the "prospective function," one dream informing, building upon another.

Correspondingly, just as Jung conferred, I'd stepped into "a little hidden door in the innermost and most secret recesses of the soul, opening into that cosmic night which was psyche long before there was any ego-consciousness, and will remain psyche no matter how far (it) [...] extends." A timelessness, borderless, boundless, *beyond my control* dreamlife, which I thought was really good given that part of me was obsessive compulsive about everything—no kidding! Within this continuum I could go forwards or as far back in time to the First Peoples "once upona time" pronouncements "when we, the Bushmen and the animals could once speak," to play in this "fountainhead" of artistry—actively involved, engaged. Slowly I was learning that none of the bedtime visions could be deemed good or bad, even when they felt "nightmarish" or what might be interpreted as the wildness of an LSD trip (though I had no idea what a real one felt like). Less and less did I fear the imagination but honored the nightscape with respect, as that wellspring intrinsic within.

The murmurings of Coelho's Melchizedek kept repeating: "when you want something, all the Universe conspires"—integration, transformation, forgiveness, truths. Though I longed to be with my new family in the Laloshwa Highlands, to share the incredible changes which had come upon me because of them. It was as though in a way, I could not go back to face the Maasai until I'd become truly linked to the Americas, from the North to the South, the Eagle to the Condor, Jaguar to the Cougar, Hummingbird to the Monarch, steeped in ten-to-twenty-thousand years of tradition. Ready to carry to the Maasai offerings of curatives, even these dreams, which have guided me thus far, friends, another healer, a Shona, Mundadisi, and his dreaming wife, but not without ramifications, scraped knees, and a bumping into the undifferentiated humanly parts of myself.

At the end of this tutoring by the Invocation itself, by these interactions with the animals, the birds, the fish, I will be able to purchase that home on land (not four stories high like that condominium had been in NYC), where

Part II: The Divide

I'll learn to work the shamanic energies barefoot in the secret garden. Only after this reunification, at home in the Americas, can I gather with the Maasai, able to honor the Great Spirit.

For I wanted to thank these Warriors, to reciprocate professionally, and seek avenues of cooperation, not knowing it had taken three years for that *fifth journey in* to bring several tribes together in sharing. Yes, the dreams, the Natives' rituals will lead me back to the Maasai, forming a bridge from us to them, to the Zimbabweans.

Fifth Journey In

39

COMING HOME TO THE COWS

"Wholeness, healing, and harmony in human life require not only self-knowledge but also knowledge of the Other; in fact, it requires not only knowledge of the Other but also relationship to it."

—Jeffrey Raff, *The Wedding of Sophia*

For three years, I had found myself on American soil. It was now 2004. The longest period I had spent in America since I'd begun the first safari into the Kalahari Desert in 1995. The four traverses into the Maasai (between 1998 and 2001) had changed me so drastically and had meant that I could finally return home—in the broadest sense of the word—home physically on the North American soil, and mentally, spiritually, at ease within the "I" of me.

The shifts that had penetrated the everyday of New York City, those explorations in group therapy, psychoanalysis, bodywork, Ninja Taijutsu, the move to study in California, had affected a rare and poignant exchange between my parents and me, bringing me into the bosom of the family in a way I'd never been before. I had also taken a giant step out of New York Fashion into Mythology, into the high plains of Shamanism with gratitude for the Maasai Warriors.

Three years have passed. It had been a time for Global Voice Foundation to launch herself into the world, and for myself to interact and relate to the "other" as in a Jamaican family, a Puerto Rican family, Chinese healers, a Navajo guide, a Hopi family, Lakotas from a past life. My accumulated interests and endeavors of pulling people into "exchange" groups to form what van der Post called "footbridges," causes me to turn to the indigenous people I've met, to reciprocate professionally through GVF, to give to the Maasai and the Bushmen. Maybe I am not so lost as before, nor so needy. In panoply, I organize, introduce, and mix these friends.

So, shortly after Christmas, 12th of January 2004, after a-year-and-a-half into my Master classes at PGI, I return to see the Maasai Warriors of Laloshwa Highlands. This time the flight was further, from California to Paris, Paris to Nairobi, and yet, still poignant and important. I land safely, to a warm hug from the Chief's son, my ever-faithful guide, Marjana. Though I'm jet lagged and fatigued, and though we're both so anxious to be with his family, yet we've decided it's necessary to visit with my friend, Lmakiya.

So, at the Samburu Intrepids Lodge, Marjana and I meet with my friend Lmakiya, to discuss the possibilities of cooperation. First, I want Marjana to know this Samburu. Both have many things in common: their two communities consider themselves, cousins; individually, they are Western educated; and they are interested in their tribal issues. For confirmation, we use a form of divination, the Chinese *IChing*, in which none of us have grown up with, to equalize the field, to engage the question: Should the three of us work together? After brief temptations, difficult beginnings, it seems a "go," for we will ultimately move into unity, "synergy."

The following morning, we have breakfast with Lmakiya to discuss future endeavors. All three of us know we need to honor "all our relations"—from

39: Coming Home to the Cows

God to our ancestors, elders, to everything that grows and lives, the earth, the animals, birds, insects. Though we are aware of the issues, the challenges that face us, we each feel called to build alliances of equal exchange that are somewhat political but not necessarily about money. "As in the Samburu proverb," Lmakiya confides, "'Better to have peace than a full stomach.'" Continuing with other concerns, "There are few years left of my people's lifestyle. Yet, I will continue to do what I can—conservation work for the benefit of the wildlife, educating the Samburu youth of our ways, and at the Intrepids Lodge, continue to lecture. In May, I will also lecture in Boston."

"That's great! If you have time, why don't you fly on from there to Santa Barbara and make a presentation at my home?"

"I'd love to."

Marjana and I speak of the possible development of a healing center at Laloshwa Highlands where healers from other lands and other ways of thinking can exchange ideas, and where those who are wounded, can recover. "We're attempting this in a few weeks with a Shona and a Ndebele from Zimbabwe, whom Murphy has invited to visit my village. Maybe someday the Samburu can participate as well." Marjana continues. "Maybe, too, you can join us (along with our *laibon*, Sarototi) in a similar event, 'The Gathering in the Name' that will bring healers together from all walks of life, from all over the world, in Big Bear, California."

Lmakiya expresses interest, "I'd like that! I could bring my *laibon* along as well." Adding in exciting news, "I'm engaged to a Samburu, Becky, whom I'd love for you to meet when you're in Nairobi, where she is now working and studying, and lives with her daughter."

"We'd love to!"

"Perhaps you could come to our wedding in August?"

"Oh, thank you! Marjana and the Kitomini Community are already in discussions about my return to Kenya that month. We just might be able to drive north to celebrate with you!"

Afterwards, Marjana drops me off at the airstrip to fly back to Nairobi, while he drives the bumpy four hours in the Land Rover. I quietly rest overnight at George, Dusty, and Marisa Bright's home. In my serene moment, I throw the *IChing* for myself about my meeting with the Kitomini Elders, Baba Budhya, and Chief Ole Wangombe. The *fourth journey in*, the Maasai and I had been discussing the miraculous work they had done for me and how we might offer

Part II: The Divide

this to other people. So, this journey in, we will explore further the notion of developing a spiritual center and my potential move to Laloshwa Highlands (at least, part-time). The IChing coins ring out: an assembly of adaptation, progress, followed by reuniting.

After my visit with the Bright's, immediately following breakfast, Marjana and I, along with our new Kikuyu cook, Thuku—I shall miss the old and wise Muringi—peregrinate to Marjana's homeland. I don't want to miss the view, however the fatigue, the residues of the jet lag has its way with me, so I doze in the front seat, waking now and then to a bump in the road or some wild animal to'ing and fro'ing that Marjana can't resist informing me of. We stop briefly in Naromi for our favorite hearty grilled chicken lunch. Due to a recent drought, on behalf of his village, we stock up with five thousand Kenya Shillings worth of food, milk, millet, sugar, tea, and tobacco. Finally landing nine hours later, at nine o'clock p.m. at Bright's private camp, where I meditate at the fire, while they prepare a soft tent for me.

Over the course of the last few months, I'd been in touch with Marjana, and he in turn with his father, Chief Ole Wangombe, about bringing a guest to them, the Zimbabwe Shona shaman Mundadisi, whom I had met at Deena and Michael's. The Maasai are thrilled, as they've been longing for more engagement in the world at large.

I'm giving up the semi-glamorous, hardwood floor, thatched-roof tent to our future Zimbabwean guests, Mundadisi and his wife, Lindiwe, whose Ndebele name means "the one that is waited for." Then, I curl up on a cot for a brief nap until dinner. By midnight, I'm back in that little bed exhausted. Still—no contact with Sarototi, who sleeps in the hills with the cattle, at the temporary manyatta.

Thought of sleeping in, yet I'm so excited to be here, crawl out of bed at six to read at the warm toasty fire until Sarototi shows. When he does, we reach for one another's hands. He pulls me up from the log, hugs me. And all the sobs that I've been holding back from these three intensive transformative years of demarcation tumble forth. I have so missed his friendship, our conversations. With a busy life, I have somehow forgotten how resounding the bond echoes in these veins, in the underground stream of our beings.

The seven Maasai Warriors, Thuku, the cook, and I assemble for breakfast. Afterwards, Marjana interprets for Sarototi and me as we discuss the visit of the Zimbabweans. Sarototi's stones affirm the arrival of a great medicine man. The

39: Coming Home to the Cows

Kitomini Community and we, at Bright's Camp, prepare for them. By afternoon, we receive news that Mundadisi and Lindiwe have landed safely in Nairobi. While they undergo blood tests at the Nairobi Hospital, we wander through the temporary manyatta to catch up with the young boys and to observe the cattle. Saifi, Sarototi's brother, has a new black and white baby calf. I slide my hands over her fresh, smooth shiny hide, which symbolizes wealth and expectancy.

All night long, a glorious rain lightly pitter, patters, and at moments, pounds upon the roof of the tent. By four, I lie wide-awake, excited as the negative ions stir within those wild horses on the Kansas prairie. On the way to the toilet, meet and greet tiny inchworms soaking up the drops. In hopes of winding down, practice Transcendental Meditation, which only seems to crank me up to continue reading the five journals I've transported. On the flight, I had completed two. The purpose of perusing these chronicles, which span the course of the last three years, is to decipher the details, entrusting an account to Sarototi, so when he speaks to the Ancestors via the stones, each event can be placed in perspective.

In the reread of those journals, in the pouring through these writings, my lack of confidence reveals itself. As the scapegoat vibration slowly wears off, it has a residue that oozes and reverberates, still affecting the everyday interactions. Therefore, I do not fully have a knowingness—I doubt me, and so, in a reflective reflection, in Laloshwa, I will sadly project this doubt onto the two men, Sarototi and Marjana, whom I've grown to love and trust, until the reverberation of this doubt resounds into the *sixth journey in* and beyond.

Not conscious of this "doubting Thomas" within, in the broad daylight, I update Sarototi on some of the happenings: "I feel intensely sad about my parents, Baba NeLaloshwa and Yieyo NeLaloshwa. They're losing their memories. What's strange, Sarototi is after fifty years of sleeping together, they separated, Mom, in my bedroom, Dad in theirs. As though she is rejecting him at the very moment, he needs her most!"

"Yes, NeLaloshwa, we understand your sadness." Marjana briefly adds, "Of course, Sarototi shall prepare a special herb for you."

"In fact," I confess, "we've since moved Dad to a nursing home and Mom to an assisted living across the street."

"NeLaloshwa, they needed to get out of that home!" Sarototi exudes. He is right, during the last few visits, I felt sick while staying there.

"After an intense dream of a family curse, I hired the shaman Deborah, working for their benefit before they cross over."

"For the welfare of your family, the American Laibon's shamanic journeys were necessary," he affirms.

Unusual for both my parents' end of life stage is in this state of dementia, a disease yet to be fully comprehended. *Are they postponing their death? Are they afraid, atoning for something from long-ago hanging in a kind of purgatorial liminal state? Or is this just part of their allegorical version of crossing over, a very slow Bardo?*

Before entering this life, these parents were my soul's first choice. However, I realize I am not *them*. Yes, I have similar traits. The gestures, the laugh, the creativity are gifts from Mother; the work ethic and the out-going personality are bounties from Dad. With their mixture of blood, I have chosen a different path, feeling more at home inside myself than ever before.

Now, among the Maasai, when listening intently, I can follow an intention. When they are thick in a conversation in Maa, sometimes I can intuitively address the exact topic, surprising myself, and them. They tease me about this. Because, I realize, I'm shifting, "listening to the air" just as the Japanese. Though to the Maasai, I don't confess the trouble I stirred up amongst the Navajo. Even so, again and again, they remain non-judgmental with each narrative that I do share. Instead, they examine: "While you're here, NeLaloshwa, what do you need from us to ease your grief?"

"I'm not sure!"

On this, we take a lunch break. Everyone discusses our future visitors. They want to hear the story of how I first met the enchanter, Mundadisi. I share with them of that private curative meeting with him—his strong black hands in comparison to my small white ones. How this charmer induced the dream encounters with the bull and stag. They, too, are caught in his enchantment.

"NeLaloshwa, you have filled us with wonder and anticipation, for he is indeed the kind of man we want to meet." Chief Ole Wangombe affirms, "We look forward to this encounter."

After lunch, I mention to Sarototi, "Oh by the way, the cleaning lady threw away the herbs you had given me. They were in the center of an African table in the living room, tied up so creatively in 'torn' plastic bags that she thought they were empty candy wrappers."

He laughs, "I'll complete the set for you, so you can return with them."

39: Coming Home to the Cows

What's really bothering me is this: "There's something I must truly confess to you—about the lifetime we've been attempting to recover, ten generations ago—unconscionably I died with the medicine in my hands, taking your elderly, along with my husband and me, to our deaths. *Can your people forgive me?*"

"After your last visit," Sarototi confirms, "the Ancestors had revealed this in the stones." With this simple phrase, he takes the sting out of our history—with always, his kind responses. No harshness of: *"How could you do such a thing?"*

What I discern from experience is that not every divinator knows the whole picture. They are each developing the story through the lens of their lineage, their training, their skills, and their own science. Each of them has specific talents, insights, and various offerings. The art of divination's intent is to gain insight from the Ancestors, from their gods or goddesses into a situation. Oftentimes their responses have more to do with how much I'm willing to reveal, how much I'm willing to let go of, or how much I'm willing to change.

Through this passage of interaction with psychics, shamans, astrologers, ministers, therapists, and divinators, as they share their gifts, I have discovered it necessary to first and foremost ground myself, attempting to listen to my own heart. As much as I have sought their wisdom, drawing on them as a source of guidance, I have attempted to never give my power over to them, never let anyone be guru. This notion is rather a nice thought, but to be completely honest, in my own hunger and "neediness," this has often been way beyond my capacity.

What I really want to know is: "From the past life, have I already given the medicine back to your people, bringing our relationship into balance?"

"Yes, NeLaloshwa, it's happened, we think this rain is part of that."

"You mean the rain is not due to Mundadisi's arrival?"

"No, it's you, NeLaloshwa," Marjana adds, "you're the one who thought to bring them all the way from Zimbabwe. Normally, for Sarototi's divination, you would have to bring six cows at twenty-four thousand Kenya Shillings. However, this is neutralized, as you are part of our family." Every time, I hear this affirmation—tears roll down my face.

After dinner, I take a leisurely walk with Sarototi and Lalalana for a social call at the temporary manyatta where the young men and a few elders are grazing the cattle. I rub the soft fur of Saifi's new black calf. On the way home, we stop to listen to the birds, follow the spoor of the lion, his pawprints, his dung.

Part II: The Divide

Tranquilly, I go to bed early to read, until a rustling in the grass. Swear, I hear Sarototi outside the tent. Quietly, I wait. He speaks. Reticently, I respond, but, again, in our own glossolalia. I do not open my tent flap. He slips off into the night.

Then, a flash comes of another shamanic journey. In November, three months ago, on the etheric winds, Deborah (on my behalf) had been transported to Sarototi and his father. As if to expose the truth, as if to check for hidden agendas, she had observed a whirling funnel of dirt stir, flipping up Sarototi's *shuka* exposing his manhood, his nakedness. *What was the message of this vision? Did this display—he has no ill intentions? Or is it a warning, disclosing his interest in sex alone?*

As I fall into a disturbed sleep, I can't help pondering: *Why did he come? Does he have an insight? Did he invite himself to my bed to reveal his hidden jewels? Did he have a message about tomorrow? Did he have a dream to convey about our work?* Our non-verbal supposed, grand, and romantic "kything" begins to pose bewilderment in his pursuit of further intimacy, and perhaps, even, poses downright problems.

In the wee hours of the morning, at the sound of the "quock quock" of the Colobus Monkeys, I awaken, shaken from a disturbance in the field and a nightmare of a woman stealing that purse of mine. In the everyday reality, I search the tent confirming all my valuables are here. Having just been assured by the search and by Sarototi's claim that I have resolved the past with his people, this hobgoblin infers something more—a not so subliminal energy at play. *Is it the Skeleton Man wanting payment for the ills my ancestors have caused?*

According to Fontana's *The Secret Language of Dreams*, symbolically, historically, the purse is the womb—that which a woman can powerfully offer as a favor, or withhold, and has value—her jewels.

In spite of the sexual tension, the constant joking of marriage, the relationship with Sarototi has sprung from a natural trusting affinity. Whichever the case may be, I question: What is now being robbed through our exchange? *What is being tampered with? Does it have to do with his silence at my tent last night? Did he leave a medicinal trick?*

From my history—of which much I am unaware of at the time—I still did not have the tools to protect myself completely, nor am I fully in awareness of this. This "me" is flirting with both the subtle and the dangerous. For so long I've been busy seeking the remedy, as well as organizing this event for the Maasai and

39: Coming Home to the Cows

the Shona, I have completely forgotten to enquire, draw necessary boundaries where leopards leap, where cats might have my tongue.

What I cannot imagine is—it's all boiling up. At the time it's as if I'm inside Louis Bromfeld's *The Rains Came* where everyone who either lives in Ranchipar or arrives in Ranchipar wants something. The Remittance man Ransome is running from the wickedness of the west (and from his own), Lady Edwina Esketh wants to possess the beautiful Indian Dr. Safti, Lord Esketh wants the best horses the Maharajah has, the Christians want to convert the sinners. In Laloshwa Highlands, Kenya, the Shona and the Ndebele want healing, confirmation, and protection from the Maasai. They need money. I want insight. The Maasai have been in survival mode from the drought. They need rice, potatoes, corn, and their water pumps repaired. The Chief wants to share their work with the world, to build a healing center, to bring more light to his district. *Is this the purse being stolen—all of us wanting something from someone else?*

Nonetheless, in this tenuous situation, it seems, there is a seam running, which has rent through the fabric of my everyday existence—a fault line—right smack through the middle of the underground coal. Something lies buried, un-mined of mine that creates these eruptions, causing others to fall into the fissure as I dance lightly above and over this divide. And perhaps I am as J.K. Rowling once was, "in search of something I could not then define." Not knowing the fracture from the male determination when I was young, will in turn determine another in the *sixth journey in*, of which is to come.

From this nightmare, I can't help but ask: *Why is the female part of me ripping me off, undermining me?* In this moment what is surfacing is the purse, my vulva has been "pinched," "fingered." If I do not become intently conscious, Jung's warning steps in: "When an inner situation is not made conscious, it appears as fate." What must be, will be.

No matter how hard I try, I cannot run from what is unconscious, from what I've been unable to access, and the dreamlife attempts to reveal. As Bailey said, a rotten apple flown to Kenya is *still* rotten. Perhaps to continue to rest in the care of Sarototi, a man who has brought me thus far is to give him dominion through divination, through the herbs. So, in the dream, the feminine (the woman who is stealing my purse) is betraying the feminine to the masculine. I'm tripping myself up. I'm not doing what I say I meant to do: listen to myself and not the guru, nor am I taking responsibility for myself. Nor am I standing as my own advocate.

Part II: The Divide

It's not Sarototi's fault. In the Shamanic Middle World of events, both of us are turning the jump rope, luring, and inviting one another where the undifferentiated parts live, reflecting one another and demanding fulfillment. Here, on the Dark Continent, the trickster's stratagem and the dead ancestor spirits, who have not been "crossed over" properly, require the life force of others for sustenance. No wonder this continent has such problems.

In the DNA, within my original third-born-only-daughter coding, Eve Brinton divines, lies submission—of which, she believes, only love for the self can break. Since I have such trouble loving me, however, I have tended towards subservience. Those natural instincts have been to notice everything about everyone else, trying to fill in the blanks for them. A very female trait, I mastered as a child. On anyone's face, I can decipher a disturbance, running like mad towards him or her to "fix" whatever trouble they might have. Historically, the feminine in me can wield control through the subtleties of manipulation, temptation, the withholding of sex, rebellion through sickness—and now, she steals my purse.

The yawning abyss of this divided self has been the undistinguished seductress desiring attention at most any cost. This division is where I remain "real," mortal, my Achilles heel, where the wound lies always open, vulnerable to the sudden attack of an arrow, the stalk of the storyteller (*Wisdom Sits in Places*). Others might trip over the scab, fall into the oozing puss. I have not lived that carefully, thoughtfully in my sexuality, subsequently, appear an abused woman willing to take on further abuse. When all along, what I fear is that a deeper connection will only bring about more of the same. Maybe due to this, I've even misused men with the way I push them away, seemingly taking relations so lightly.

Being quite virile, Sarototi cannot resist, deliberately seeking me out. *Is he the Hound of Heaven nipping at my heels? Is the Black Stallion of that childhood nightmare carrying me off into the darkness?*

In Santa Barbara, my lifestyle tends toward calm, peaceful, studiously, riding the tide. Yet here, in Africa, in this bewitching field, on the borderlands, on the edges of the unknown, I'm in the drama of another adrenalin rush with another man. Finally, grasping, all of life teeters on a delicate balance, even our hearts, our bodies, our earth, and this tribe.

Determined to step into the light of the day straight up and honest, I approach Sarototi's cousin. Not to accuse him, but to help me navigate the

39: Coming Home to the Cows

murkier, underground crack, forever restraining that which is ensepulchered: "I don't want to hurt our relations, Marjana. What is happening? Is Sarototi intending to marry me or is this just fantasy? I believe this would be detrimental for us both." I don't reveal Sarototi's appearance last night, or of the dream of my lost handbag.

"No, I don't think that's his intention," Marjana slowly ponders. "And yes, I agree, NeLaloshwa, it wouldn't be in your best interest."

After lunch, I converse with Sarototi about the household I grew up in (our White Anglo-Saxon Protestant ways), my inability to speak up, to say what I needed. Words encased with complex feelings were held down as if we hoped they might be swept away: anger, frustration, the smoldering undercurrent of lava bubbling just below the surface. There were secrets, things unspoken. I always admired the Italian and Jewish families who seemed to argue so easily, even my Catholic friends seemed more able to express themselves.

Regardless of this communication, he spins us back to our marriage, shares a dream he had of me birthing his son, a son he doesn't recognize. "I, too," respond back to him, "had a dream several years ago of a kind of 'marriage' between us but not in the way I think you imagine—that kind isn't meant to be. Ours is a spiritual friendship, related to our engagement with God, with the Ancestors."

Away from the fire, Marjana and Sarototi have a long discussion. Their talk seems harsh, particularly from Marjana towards Sarototi. I sense Marjana does not approve of Sarototi's feelings towards me. *Is the future of my womb being negotiated?*

In the afternoon, in the Land Rover, Marjana carts us to the manyatta to see the family. Yieyo Sarototi is adorable. Hugs me, talks up a storm as though I understand all. In her little hut, she fixes tea for Marjana's mother, his third wife, Jackie, Saifi's wife, Nkoko Sarototi, and me. Jackie, whose knowledge of English is better than Senga's, elegantly interprets for us. So, for the first time, surrounded by these women, I comprehend their words. An intimacy forms as they fire questions at me so fast; I can barely catch my breath. But even so, in this exchange, a peacefulness seeps in—a relief. They want to know me, as I do, them. Even the mundane, of which necklaces and bracelets to purchase as gifts for Mundadisi and his wife, is pleasurable. I shall leave these welcoming treasures on their beds upon arrival.

Privately (and unusually), Sarototi performs another ritual for me with only Baba Hasa to interpret. Lemongrass is burned in the fire, "To open your

Part II: The Divide

eyes, NeLaloshwa," he illumines. *How did he know my eyes have been bothering me? That I am attempting to open my third eye?* He places milk, *kole*, inside the buffalo's, *olorro's*, horn. "With the whiteness of this substance, wash your toes, feet, hands, face, then step over the horn, taste the herb, licking it five times from this black obsidian stone, (an exalted, prehistoric rock used as a knife before they possessed metal). This ceremony is to give you strength, courage." In Laloshwa, the wonders, the magic never ceases.

In the evening, our Zimbabwean guests, Mundadisi and Lindiwe alight just in time for us to meander high into the hills for the sunset. Here, though it's far away, one feels equal to the Mountain of L'Engai. On the way, two eagles soar over us, illuminating our path, affirming Mundadisi and Lindiwe's need for healing. With their appearance, lots of infectious enthusiasm spreads among those in our little gathering. The anticipation has been great.

In honor of our guest, Baba Budhya and the Chief light a fire the indigenous way with flint stone and grass. As it erupts, they toss in cleansing herbs for each of us. "That all the hills, and the trees from the forest participate—for they are the wood beneath our prayers," declares Chief Ole Wangombe. "Through the flames, the smoke, our prayers are lifted into the sky, closer to Engai so that every one of them is heard. When the sun drops, the pain is carried away!"

We dance around the fire, chanting a Maasai song, answering Baba Budhya with an "ayeh" of yes, as he cries out. The smoke rises, greeting, blessing our serene faces. Settled, we listen to the dreams of Lindiwe, the Ndebele, whose name means to inspire, uplift. Her words of wisdom shower down upon us: "The Zimbabweans ruined their land—don't ruin the land of your forefathers! Stay true to your traditions."

As coordinator to this big undertaking, I form a solid foundation between the Maasai, the Ndebele, the Shona, the Kikuyu cook, and myself. Yet, underneath lies the sizzling dance of courtship Sarototi attempts with the uninterested woman—me. An island of separation makes for the depth of emotions, the crux of the matter.

Dinner is full of disappointment for me. The main conversation is in English, so Sarototi misses out, and so do some of the other Maasai. Also, I feel a little uneasy around Sarototi. Mundadisi's presence, a man who treats me as an equal, shines a novel light on our relationship, providing an unexpected contrast to that former reverie of Sarototi. He's no longer the guru, no longer perfect. He's normal. In the last three years, we've both experienced great changes. The Maasai

39: Coming Home to the Cows

rituals transformed me. Not to mention leaving Badgley Mishcka, launching Global Voice Foundation, shamanism with Deborah on behalf of my ancestry, tracking dreams with Mundadisi, and pursuing school. Through these, I've risen up, grown up with a more heightened awareness.

Through the veil in the night, I see Mundadisi and Lindiwe helping everyone, those far away in Kansas, and the Maasai. In the dream, Mom has lost Dad, as he runs away in his dementia. I want to shake her shoulders to say, "Stay alert!" However, in the reverie, when the old warlock, Mundadisi, the Zimbabwean Shona, arrives to greet them, Mom and Dad are snuggled in bed together—as if he has healed their recent breach. As he is doing with my Maasai family, among the community in Kansas, Mundadisi makes a visitation, publicly discoursing, exhorting. *If he is the Skeleton Man from the past, are we making the past right?*

Another image flashes before me of the Maasai performing surgery on Lindiwe's upper arm, bloodletting. An examination. An operation. In an herbal induction, all the universes are smashed together, so that, from her springs a field of plenty, blessings—corn, vegetables, fruit.

At the fire, in the morning, I share this dream of Lindiwe's letting of blood for provisions of plenty. The Maasai are thankful. Performing this operation, they offer Mundadisi and Lindiwe roots to drink. Lindiwe is impressive, a dramatic storyteller, a dreamer, a wife, a mother of thirteen. Unlike me, she *really* knows the "I" of who she is. She dreamt that two Maasai warriors sit in the hospital at the bedside of her grandmother, who had nursed Lindiwe at her breast. In response, the Maasai guide her to the Katunga River where Mundadisi summons the Water Spirits, the Njuzu, to perform a cleansing and a blessing. It has been so exciting, these incredible inner and outer exchanges, that now, everyone is exhausted, napping in their tents.

In the late afternoon, Mundadisi and I have a private discussion. "Why does Mantis, the trickster god of the Bushmen appear to me so often?"

"Mantis is your ancestor, the Bushmen's spirit. I call her Grandmother."

"Yes, she is, he is, the great dreamer—just as Sir Laurens van der Post said, for Mantis: 'the dream would show him what to do.'" I'm grateful that she's/he's ever present to me!

As Mundadisi listens to one of my dreams about *the manuscript being inside my belly*, he seems a bit mystified. Of course, Africans *do* read. However, traditionally there have always been those gifted in "oral storytelling." "What is within my belly," I explain, "is meant to be physically embodied in the written

Part II: The Divide

word and according to the Swaziland Sangoma Philani, is my transformative gift, just as you are a healer."

For me this calling is painful, lonely, and obscure. I haven't given myself permission to immerse myself to the extent and with the same intensity as I did with my fashion career, where I was so public, so "out there." The parts of me that have been split off are only now re-integrating. So, it's easy for me to veer off the path, nor do I understand the discipline of sitting before a blank piece of paper, is as important as the actual writing.

"My intention," responds Mundadisi, "is to perform a ceremony with elephant and lion dung."

"Ahh! Yes, what you had recommended in California. Thank you!" While we speak, the ants that usually come to bite me, are now just crawling around on my water glass quenching their thirst. Hopeful!

Part of this encounter, of our togetherness, is to experience the diverse community, openly holding one another's dreams, watching the elders impart knowledge and generous advice. Perchance, the last few years' hazards I have encountered might have been smoother if underscored with the advice of the Maasai for their communal spirit unites in guidance rather than reactivity.

Early the next morning, I show up at the fire to overhear Mundadisi contributing his belief of what each man's talents are. To Marjana: "You're not fulfilled, nor are you near enough to your Ancestors. Your people must give you a ceremony to bring you home, igniting your future as Chieftain." Chief Ole Wangombe beams with gratification as he discusses the how and when of this event.

"This is true," as I throw my arms around Marjana in a hug, "the world needs you to speak up for your people, and your people need you to affirm them."

"NeLaloshwa," Marjana exclaims, "we are so surprised at Mundadisi's wisdom. He carries the same knowledge of the herbs used for ceremony."

"Yes, he is both affirming your work and a friend in your enterprise."

"Perhaps," Marjana adds, "you, NeLaloshwa, are here three-to-six months a year and we build a large compound to work with people from all over the world."

As he sets forth the ceremony, Mundadisi's eyes turn wild and red in trance: "I call on the lion spirit and the great white eagle to possess me." From the river, he culls a stone for the Chief. As though extolling the moment, a dainty yellow

39: Coming Home to the Cows

butterfly, a hairy caterpillar, a grasshopper, and a spider appear, two eagles skim the trees. Up and down Mundadisi points and declares: "Ancestors as you fly, inch, jump, and crawl, we pray to you, to God, asking for rain, not just for the Maasai, but, for all the earth."

Mundadisi is the kind of warlock whom you could imagine commanding the elements—bringing forth rain. To the Maasai, he channels: "Wear blue and white, don't use plastic, only use traditional leather. Sarototi, even your calabash must not be a plastic bottle, but a true natural gourd." Commanding, "And you, NeLaloshwa, for the next part of your ritual, you are to stay in the manyatta tomorrow night!"

At naptime, rest, re-group; scour each journal for insight, dreams. Prior to dinner, Mundadisi sets me in front of a shovel of hot coals, placing lion dung consisting of hair and bones, and a glob of dried, grassy elephant dung. As I inhale the fumes with the *shuka* overhead, he heralds: "Lion signifies the Warrior Spirit which sits courageously in your belly. The elephant represents the Grandmother Spirit who emboldens you with her unequivocal matriarchal protective and communal strength."

"Yes," I respond. "Big Chief Bear Eagle Elephant has been guiding me ever since we first met."

At the first whiff of the dung, it tickles my throat. Into the recesses of my being, I inhale, as the harsh smoke penetrates the lungs, undergoing serenity. With one hand on the chest and another one on the back of the heart, Mundadisi presses, anchoring in these soulful character qualities. Onto the coals, he throws a twig from the Strangler Fig: "To ground you to the Earth, to her nurturing spirit."

At dinner, the whole crew is quietly pensive.

Through the night, I observe the images that slide across my screen of the sometimes unkindness, the judgments experienced in America. Sleep informs the morning with a message, "Don't want to go home to *that*!" In contrast, I muse, among the Maasai Elders, there is appreciation. If I propose an offering, there is a spirit of receptivity, generosity, friendliness, participation, and reciprocity. *Do I stay?*

In the distance, I hear Mundadisi calling the Maasai. At my tent, he asks: "Are you ready my dear?"

"Yes!" I holler, as I scramble to pull on my clothes.

Part II: The Divide

First, at the fire, Mundadisi has prepared an earth ritual for everyone. As the Maasai inhale smoke from the hot coals scattered with elephant and lion dung, I join them, each taking our turn under the blankets, hacking, sometimes laughing. Generally, we are very serious. For the water ceremony, he leads us to the Katunga River to re-ignite the Njuzu, the water spirits. With large branches from the Olive Tree, he drenches us with cold water, which makes us shake and shiver, declaring: "To cleanse you!"

In the aftermath, Mundadisi returns us to the fire, where he combines earth, water and fire, steaming hot rocks with water, adding to a mixture of herbs regularly utilized by the Maasai. Placing *shukas* and towels over the group, he creates a cave of sacred enclosure, a makeshift version of the Navajo Sweat Lodge. With more laughter, lying down together, we continue coughing, clearing the energy. As if a dear friend, I end up with Sarototi in front of me, spooning him. In response, he tenderly rubs my hand. The shared experience is both a reverie and a delight. These actions make them trust Mundadisi.

Afterwards, the Maasai generate a ritual for Mundadisi, to protect him from the voodoo of the jealous "witch doctors" in Zimbabwe. Lindiwe and I are to stand and watch. "NeLaloshwa, now, you are to be the scribe of this moment!" To scribble in the details, I reach for my journal.

Mundadisi steps over a rock to stand before Chief Ole Wangombe and Sarototi, the laibon in training. Sarototi has made a fire from a sacred herb for the ritual ash, which he sets on the stone. First, the Chief and Baba Budhya kneel before the rock, licking the mixture. "This is to prove to you, Mundadisi, that *this* is not poison." He follows suit, bending, tasting. "Mundadisi, you are to step toward each of the designated rocks, then throw them one by one to the four directions: straight, right, left, behind, igniting the protective blessing." Chief Ole Wangombe instructs us to follow Mundadisi single file across the stream, shielding him: "To put these others behind you. To bless those envious and jealous of you. To guard your back."

We've just been through a Maasai's version of: "Get thee behind me, Satan!" *Can you imagine this as a requisite on Seventh Avenue? What would happen to the entire industry?* We'd be so busy burning, licking, and throwing rocks in all directions, no one would have time to steal designs or curse with harsh criticisms.

At the fire, Marjana enlightens us: "Last night, inside my dream, Sarototi professes, 'I have completed the herbal treatment of NeLaloshwa. Now, Marjana, it is your turn to move toward your own destiny. Now, you must go!' Sarototi

39: Coming Home to the Cows

keeps pushing and pushing until (in reality), I fall off my cot onto Sarototi and Kutata, who were sleeping on the tent floor."

Chuckling, gratified, we acknowledge the truth of this message for Marjana, affirming the words of Mundadisi from the day before. Everyone keeps repeating to Marjana: "Come home to your people! Prepare the way for your chiefdom!"

And I am thrilled! Even Marjana's dream professes my cure through Sarototi is over!

After lunch, we venture to the village. For their cooking, we carry jerry cans of water from the Katunga River. Along the path, as we listen to the water slosh around, popping lids, cascading over the sides and out Sarototi's door, as if pouring libations before the gods and goddesses, he laughingly declares, "For the Ancestors—they must be *very* thirsty!"

Today, Lindiwe and I call Yieyo (mother of) Sarototi's body back to health. As we lie down beside her, we open the energy field, heat rises in the body, my neck turns red hot. I petition God to release her energy up through the crown of my head and hers. Lindiwe prays, too. Within moments, astonishingly Sarototi's mother rises, chatting away. Where two or more gather in prayer!

Mundadisi and I place our hands on the inflamed knee of my friend, the storyteller, Kuroo, praying for her rapid cure. To several others, Mundadisi dispenses herbs. The Kitomini Community is thankful he is here. The reciprocity is happening, the restoration of my relationship to the Maasai for dying with the herb ten generations ago.

40

IN THE WOMB OF THE DUNG HUT

> *"Western medicine cures the body, while psychology treats the mind—
> but healing attends to the soul and the spirit."*
>
> —Alberto Villoldo, *Mending the Past*

While the others return to Bright's camp, as commanded by Mundadisi, I bed in the village for the night, staying inside Sarototi's dung hut. Kisima, her three little boys and Sarototi sleep in one bed. Alone, I nestle into a rough, hard, straw bed for a noisy night full of light drizzling rain and the next-door neighbors who toss and turn, toss and turn.

As I fall asleep, I feel the vulva open. Correctly, Mundadisi knew, this is the place to be inside the symbolic initiatory womb of the Maasai, as in the ancient Asklepieion caves on the Isle of Cos. Though chilly, I wear those faithful New York black leggings, socks, turtleneck, and a softly knit Patricia Underwood

40: In the Womb of the Dung Hut

beret with the colorful Maasai *shuka* thrown across me for warmth. Even so, I sleep wildly.

In the morning, rouse early to the familiar tinkling of the goat-bells already echoing across the plains. The rain, I continue to hear, represents mist and mud today. However, in their future, it equals green pastureland for the cattle, cornfields growing strong and tall. Kisima stirs the embers, preparing tea for the children.

Appropriately I have started my menses after Mundadisi's rituals of fire, smoke, earth, and water—the four elements stirring up feminine vitality. With the low light of the fire, quietly and quickly maneuver to dress discreetly. Using a bottle of water and cotton balls, I quickly wash my face; apply the customary Chanel red lipstick to match those Dragon red nails—for the children who always find this amusing.

When Marjana arrives, I gush: "Gosh, Sarototi has some raucous neighbors! They moved around all night!"

"What do you mean, NeLaloshwa? Are you speaking of the calves? The Maasai bring the little ones into their dung huts every night—it protects them from the lions and keeps the family warm."

Flushing beet-red with embarrassment, "Oh! Of course!" I howl. Clearly, what I just don't want to admit is the calves kept me warm through the night—not a man.

With our tea for breakfast, in solidarity, Marjana's mother and Nkoko, the grandmother of Marjana and Sarototi, Kisima and I, serenely assemble around the little fire.

For lunch, the others arrive from Bright's Lodge. Mundadisi, Lindiwe, Thuku, and I eat with the men in the bush. In the shade, I curl up on the ground to nap, recovering from those wild and hairy neighbors that kept me awake all night. I prepare gifts—inside a little tan bag designed by my friend, Roberta, for Sarototi—three coins for the IChing, a dove's feather for peace, matches to light his way into the world beyond.

For medicine from Mundadisi, a young warrior appears, with a bad swollen ankle in the appearance of an old man's gout. When I place both hands on him, the energy feels dark, dense, black. In his wizardry manner, Mundadisi touches the boy's leg, as he exorcises the pain into himself, his face grimaces. "If you hadn't come to me," he confidently proclaims, "you would never be able to walk

Part II: The Divide

again." For Mundadisi "knew almost all forms of sickness were a theft of souls" (Calasso, *The Celestial Hunter*).

In the village, we gather for a final ceremony with the Kitomini Community. Marjana reiterates Mundadisi's urging to continue to wear the traditional clothes, to avoid the use of plastic. "Stay true to Engai and open your minds to people coming from all over the world—medicine men and women, people in need, peacemakers," he announces. "And as a gift from NeLaloshwa, the water pumps are to be repaired next week."

The people venerate Mundadisi and Lindiwe with gifts of bracelets, necklaces.

The Maasai, in turn, reward Sarototi with ritual items that affirm and establish him as their official *laibon*—a goat-skin pelt to sit upon while counting stones, and a huge bull's horn for his healing practice. I bestow him with an official gourd, *kibuyu*, for his pebbles of divination, and say: "Thank you, ashe, for restoring me, for taking special care."

Through Marjana's cousin, Sarototi's brother, Saifi, a declaration is made: "NeLaloshwa, we trust you, now. You may walk the land and choose a place for your home. We thank you and gladly welcome you back, anytime."

Once again, I am moved to tears, as their words, as their "healing attends to the soul and spirit" (Villoldo)."

41

ENDEARMENTS AND INTANGIBLES

"Your soul knows the geography of your destiny [...] the map of your future, therefore you can trust this indirect, oblique side of yourself. If you do, it will take you where you need to go, but more important, it will teach you a kindness of rhythm in your journey."

—John O'Donohue, *Anan Cara (Soul Friend)*

From the healing we—the Maasai, the Kikuyu, the Shona, the Ndebele, the American—have shared and experienced, there is "a kindness of rhythm" to this journey of ours.

Late afternoon, we travel back to our camp to rest, for everyone is exhausted. By evening, for our last night, we assemble around the fire. I rub medicine on two of the men: Katata's cut on his toe and Lalalana's burnt hand. In the open-air lodge, we have a huge meal and conversation around the table. The night before, while I was in Sarototi's dung hut, the Kikuyu cook Thuku, with his multi-lingual capacities, initiated the talks, urging everyone to share what they have embodied in this togetherness of ours.

Tonight, Thuku continues, graciously interpreting for everyone, uniting us in our final moments. And so we are encouraged to speak, each of us around that table: the Maasai, the Kikuyu, the Ndebele, the Shona, the American. Mundadisi and I share our wish that Sarototi and Marjana will: "Join us, you and the Samburu for the Journey to the Heart event in September!"

A festival of gratefulness begins: The Maasai speak of what they have gained from Mundadisi and Lindiwe: "We thank you Lindiwe, for your dreams and intuition, for urging us to remain true to our traditions, to care for our land, to remain swathed in our colors." "Mundadisi, we want to acknowledge your gifts of rehabilitation, your knowledge of the herbs, the integrative ceremonies, for trusting us with your story."

To the Chief, Mundadisi replies: "My esteem goes to you for carefully bringing opportunity and support to your people through schools, light tourism, and therefore, for a future for generations and for sustainable income."

Of the first time they met me, the warriors speak: "I was curious about you." Katata surmises. "What does this American woman want from us? Now, my mind has changed." Lalalana threw in his belief: "Overtime, I have observed you, NeLaloshwa. You keep your word."

Steadily, over time, I had been—I didn't know it until this moment—proving myself. According to them, over six years, five visits to Laloshwa Highlands, a track record, the sum of all my efforts has been carefully laid down. And because of this journey with the Shona, with the Ndebele, the Maasai consider NeLaloshwa an equal partner in their greater work.

"Yes," Chief Ole Wangombe affirms: "When you say you'll send money back, you follow through. You always do what you agree to—build lasting continuity and a respectful friendship."

For these accolades and more, in front of everyone, I weep and weep. *Why do they impact me so? Is it due to all they've done for me? Or have I never received such blessings?* Though I've been loved, I've never before had a family consider, include, and embrace these spiritual offerings and talents of mine, as the Maasai have. (During the infantile stages of its development, this part of me, this extra-sensory perception must have been quite confusing for my birth family.)

41: Endearments and Intangibles

Honestly, in Africa, I've just been interested in getting and giving love, in recovering the dead and the buried as the intuitive Mariah recommended. Underlying that and due to the rejection of those innate gifts in the past, I felt so desperate, traveling afar and afield to rearrange the internal locater within myself, because the building of a family seemed utterly impossible. And here, finally, there is one.

What I don't want to admit is, suddenly, while I'm weeping from these praises, Mundadisi glances at me with eyes I'm no longer sure of. *Is he warning me as once Baba Budhya did, of what's to come?* The Maasai just protected him. They just praised him. *Is that it? Had I forgotten to praise him, to praise Lindiwe, to praise the Maasai?* I thought I had chimed in, in that British-kind-of-way, "Here, here!" —with my water glass, a toast of admiration. Amongst them, I've been so happy that they've understood one another, that they've had such a wonderful exchange.

Is Mundadisi baffled by this weeping woman who was so strong just moments ago? Maybe for a man, for a Shona, it is scary to watch a 45-year-old woman melt. Maybe in his mind a healer can't be a "crybaby." But maybe that was it— we were all seeing the feminine rise. No longer was I a hard woman in pants walking around the streets of NYC proving myself as good as any man. Instead, to these people, I had let my hair down; I'd become vulnerable, soft, nurturing, and yet strong.

Mundadisi didn't know that Mother and I had recently made an honest choice to choose love, truth, acceptance and forgiveness for one another through the psychologist Betts, that afterwards, we had melted into tears, embraced into human kindness. Mundadisi wasn't aware that since a child, Mother had always gently touched my face, honoring this expression: "Don't be ashamed of your tears, Murphy. These are tears of liquid love."

In Africa, maybe for men, the proving of themselves in circumcision— for bravery and courage and perseverance, to be "cut off" from the foreskin, the feminine, severs the capacity to even recognize this. Though that can't be completely right, because I find them compassionate, understanding. Yet, maybe amongst the Shona as the Maasai, crying just isn't allowed or even known— except in babies.

What I'd forgotten is Mundadisi had met me after that Demarcation point, after the *fourth journey in*, after I'd left that well-honed career and settled in California. He hadn't seen the division that had once been within. How I had

Part II: The Divide

been divided against myself. How I couldn't come into the right relationship with my vocation, nor even with my family. Perhaps he hadn't grasped the miracle that I was now so thankful for, the miracle the Maasai had performed on me. How these people had given me back my dignity. Though it wasn't mine, they had grounded me in the roots of their African heritage, granting me an assemblance of a cultural identity, now fostered as *Africa Within*, causing me to shed such loving tears. *Had he known this through the gathering of information from the Maasai and thought I hadn't honored them enough for this?* Maybe I was so busy crying I'd forgotten to be grateful!

Perhaps Mundadisi can project the future—what will be undermined between the Maasai and me. Of course, at this time, I have no awareness of what will be—the *sixth journey in*—where for several reasons, the foundation of this "perfect" relationship between the Maasai and me, will be rocked. It will slowly come unglued, will slowly crumble—and won't come together for many, many years.

Because of my own trauma and challenges, I had crossed this field into Africa, already sullied and searching, so no longer in the groove of American purity, no longer defined as "good." What the Maasai had done was bring me back into alignment with something incontestable within myself, something internal, indefinable, and perhaps even, filled me with what my friend Steven Lum calls, our innate "nobility." However, I did not know that "whenever something positive constellates in the unconscious" as what had happened to us in this gathering of dreamers and healers in the *fifth journey in*, "there is a danger of a stiffening of consciousness against it," von Franz had once warned. *Is this what is happening within me? —and is Mundadisi warning me?*

For the past few weeks, we've been working on the land where tribal warfare existed—for sure, between the Maasai and the Kikuyu, and where the Colonialism of the British had closed a 99-year agreement. Now, this white American girl comes in and perhaps certain sensations arise, *"What does she want from us?" "Who does she think she is?"* She, who will receive our story, write a book, and maybe even make money from its sale. *Is she co-opting our ways? As she wraps herself in the Maasai shuka, practicing African shamanism, is she, too, committing cultural appropriation?*

What Mundadisi doesn't realize is that most everything I have is shared, which is why I often don't have cash flow because I've given it all away. I want to benefit him, his wife, his huge family—everybody! Because, in point of fact,

41: Endearments and Intangibles

I want everybody to have what I have, whether they want it or not. However, Mundadisi doesn't know this about me.

Though Mundadisi doesn't need a savior, maybe has concerns about his return home, returning to Zimbabwe, a place that was once Apartheid Rhodesia, where everything is upside down, desperately twisted and controlled by *regime security*—something I may never be able to grasp. As I write this, Tony Childs' haunting voice swirls around: "What you gonna do Zimbabwe? […] You want to run in the wind […] See no more crime in your lifetime" (*Zimbabwe*). Of course. Absolutely. Liberty for all.

Part of the problem is this sickness lies in all of us—the politics and pull of money being the measure of distinction—again, the haves of the upper echelon versus the have-nots, who often, in some societies, become thought of as the "lower caste." Part of the problem is I wasn't upfront, putting the coins or the truths on the table, of the systemic racism that permeates our cultures, that infects every interaction we have. I had imagined it hadn't existed in our perfect moment of togetherness. But I've forgotten, I'm from the predominant culture. Mundadisi's encounter with me could be totally opposite of mine with him. *Is Mundadisi, through the Skeleton Man challenging me, telling me it's about the power game?*

Yes, again, it's the lion lurking, the grandfather elephant in the room lumbering around each meal within the lodge, scraping his trunk against the picnic table, sniffing up scraps, stepping on the toes of that little creature, that mouse, with his giant padded feet, with his tusk he digs into the sweet potato—revealing desires, revealing biases no one wants to speak of.

With Mundadisi, I've never revealed my concerns about those who still practice the art of Colonialism (and the possibilities that I might be one of them either actively or in my silence), nor have I spoken of this with the Maasai. To neither of them, have I discussed imperialism, which may blatantly remain inside my very Self, manifesting in forms of projection outside my very Self, unrealized by me. I've been unable to accept that many of us have been brainwashed, that I*'ve* been brainwashed with a colonialist spirit that is naturally dwelling within, epigenetically, slipping out in insensitive words or actions, oozing through my very pores as I walk around as if I owned the world. *Have I become Lederer's The Ugly American?* For in the wee hours of the morning, I'm beginning to have dreams of this, of how I've been taught to carry myself is symbolic of what our race considers our superior qualities. God forbid! Goddess, help me from these insensitivities!

From this reverie of concern, on that last night, the *fifth journey in*, Thuku's voice awakens me. "Did you hear this, Murphy?" As everyone disperses to their tent, "Before your departure, we've each agreed to sing a song tomorrow around the fire." *Did he attempt to bring cheer back into my life, when all along I fear what is uneven, unspoken will come back to bite me? Must that look on Mundadisi's face be reckoned with?*

Afterwards, by the fire, I remain, while Thuku interprets for Sarototi: "The people are worried, NeLaloshwa, that you believe the tribe has not given you enough." *Had they seen the reflection of the want on my face?* "We heard your comment about wanting a child." Make note: onto others my longings, those psychological projections—that "shit," according to Brené Brown—are seeping out, and are now being observed. I cannot hide. *Is this what Mundadisi is sensing, too?* She wants more. I can only think of Vera B. Williams' children's book, *"More More More," Said the Baby! What could I say? Will there really be a child birthed between us in this lifetime? But how? Was there really a child born between us from our past life?*

For I had once had a vision that there was such a baby. In fact, someone who has been or is without a mother that needs me, clings to me. *Is that child searching for his mother, the child that had been cut from my belly lifetimes ago? Or is there a child now?* And therefore, the people deem it necessary for him or her to be educated in the Western world, in America. *Who am I to imagine that I have the ability to raise one of their children?*

For the Maasai are not like us, where orphans exist, lost, lonely, and cut off. Even if a child loses their parents, that child is integrated into a loving world, made to feel at home, embraced. In the subconscious, maybe this is my own inner Irene longing to be loved, cared for. So much of myself has gone missing. I reach out, instead, to take care of other people, adopting, when it's really about me.

Though in the past, I've had someone else's husband, I don't need someone else's child. Instead, I reveal to Sarototi, "No, don't worry, everything is fine." Not that I'm fine, but certainly don't need to extend myself when I need to nurse the child within. "For in every adult there lurks […] an eternal child, something that is always becoming, is never completed, and calls for unceasing care, attention and education" (Jung). Oh, that I may take care of the child within, so that she doesn't ask others to take responsibility for her!

"NeLaloshwa," Sarototi affirms, "I completely trust you now. Whatever you want I shall do for you."

Right here, right now, through our friendship, I've been recognized, changing their worldview about me forever. Because I've brought Mundadisi to their homeland, they accord me additional respect, fortifying and underscoring the trust between the Maasai and me. Now, they believe what Global Voice's mission has been about and this, in turn, is affirming.

"Then I must relate a revelation I had before my arrival to Laloshwa." Crisscrossing my legs at the fire, I begin: "Sarototi, you lead me down a path to your engang, your home, filled with young cattle. (How fitting that I had slept in your hut the other night with those noisy neighbors!)" He leans in smiling as I continue: "You turn to face me, beckoning me to follow. 'Come, NeLaloshwa, come.' You step backward over the kneeling calves, continuing to guide me. Coaxing me along with your hands until we arrive on the other side of the dung hut into the light. As if through the womb into a rebirth, to a completion of the healing, reconnecting to our forefathers."

Across all divisions, across all disparities, across the divide to the divine…

"Isn't this why in Marjana's dream, you shouted, 'the work with NeLaloshwa is complete.' That, it is, in fact, Marjana's turn and no longer necessary for me?"

"Yes, NeLaloshwa." Sarototi responds. "I had a dream as well. Someone comes to me with a mark or scar on the face, someone whom I help release wounds from her back due to spears. Now, see, you brought her to me, the marked woman was Lindiwe, and I have removed the enemies' marks from her and from Mundadisi." Miraculous.

Even so, in this gathering at Laloshwa Highlands, this illness of something unnamable has seeped into all we have done—*Is it the purse stolen? Or Bromfeld's The Rains Came, where everybody who arrives in Ranchipar, in Laloshwa Highlands wants something?* Murphy wants a child. Mundadisi and Lindwe want healing. The Maasai need rice. Nature reveals the metaphor of the day, the corruption, the dis-ease, the earthquakes, floods, prejudices, which we must confront, just as the Maasai must face the Buffalo. It's boiling outside the tent and inside my very being—and I haven't divulged it.

In the morning, we rush around packing, loading our bags into the Land Rover. I give gifts to Sarototi of herbs, money, and share with him a long personal

Part II: The Divide

letter. With Saifi and Sarototi sprinkle milk, *kole*, a libation around the tent for the Ancestors. Sarototi discovers a red Turacao feather for me. I bestow him with an owl feather. Around the last fire, with these feathers we sage ourselves, apply sandalwood oil for wisdom at our temples and our third eye as the Maasai chant a lullaby blessing.

Then Marjana, Mundadisi, Lindiwe and I are swept off to the village to say *olesari*, our good-byes to all the Elders, the children, and the women, whom I reach for, hugging one another with such love. Around her neck, Nkoko—the eldest in the community—grandmother to Sarototi, Marjana and Saifi, has respectfully tied the white fabric from Swaziland gifted from my dear friend Rebecca. I snap a photo of Nkoko's kindness as she wears it proudly, linking our worlds together with such elegance, respect.

For presents, I leave Sarototi and the others, handmade suede Navajo moccasins with their symbolic geometric shapes trimmed with multi-colored beads, which I had purchased on my last visit to the Four Corners. He slips these on, uniting with the ancient woven threads. Threads of what I believe is another history, five-hundred-years ago between Sarototi, the Natives and I, which merges in Duran's book, *Buddha in Redface*—another prehistory Sarototi and I have yet to explore.

On the trek to Nairobi, as I ride shotgun for Marjana in the front, Lindiwe is behind me, as Mundadisi is caddy-corner in the backseat beside her. Bumping down the rocky road of the escarpment, we are still in the high of our togetherness—at least, I am. From an exchange that doesn't happen every day in the subways, the suburbs, the business world, or the subterrestrial places of our unconscious—this unexpected, fully contained, profound generosity naturally sprang forth between us.

Eventually, as we roll across the terrain I'll have an inkling, of those unresolved issues spilling out from my gut, feel the stiffening of these unsaid something's, of a kind of an attack on my spleen—not necessarily intentional—which slips in. For unconsciously, I've left a hole wide open in the energy field, below the ribs on the left. What I didn't know at the time is that Mundadisi is calling me further into healing, smack in the place in the spleen where I'm unclear. Stalking me with story, shooting me with that "arrow" of truth the Cibecue Apache Benson Lewis explained to Basso.

If I explore this notion of spleen, as James Hillman, would encourage, "follow the image," I would note that the spleen is often associated with bad temper,

41: Endearments and Intangibles

spite, melancholia, feelings of anger or ill-will suppressed, dark malevolence, or a grudge. *Who am I holding a grudge for?* The spleen has been known as the seat of passions and emotions. *What is stirring up inside of me? What am I holding back?* "What is the 'thing' not being said?" Brené Brown inquires. Well, I'm not saying it!

At the time, though I'm aware of the "news" of what's happening in Mundadisi's country, I cannot imagine the nightmare of living in Zimbabwe—the hunger, the unfulfilled wants, the desperation, the spleen of the country is swelling with fury. *"What you gonna do Zimbabwe?"*

In my lack of awareness and experience, these thoughts will slide into me, festering. I could not see it the same as I did Baba Budhya. I did not realize Mundadisi was a fiercer teacher, one who would challenge his student to the end. Instead, that evening, I'll write in my journal, "I knew something was very wrong between him and me." On the drive, without being specific, I even turn around, "Are you okay?" He affirms he is. But I'm not convinced. Even so, I will spend the spring season delving into past lives and shamanically clearing off this energy, to learn it is mine.

In *Patterns of Renewal*, van der Post once wrote, "We hide behind what we know. And there is an extraordinarily angry and aggressive quality in the knowledge of modern man (woman); he (she, they, it) is (are) angry with what he (she, they, it) does (do) not know; he (she, they, it) hates (hate) and rejects (reject) it. He (she, they, it) has (have) lost the sense of wonder about the unknown and he (she, they, it) treats (treat) it as an enemy." I will later learn even what we think, as well as what we speak, has the power to curse others. *What if instead, Mundadisi is the perfect mirror to my undifferentiated selves?*

I will ponder: *Is this more about me? Am I angry?* I don't think that's the way I normally am. *Or are things rumbling up between the Maasai and me, and Mundadisi feels this? Or to form intimacy do I reveal things I shouldn't? And where I need to build bridges, do I lock down instead into that familiar, familial proper "perfect" Protestantism I've been raised in?* Though my pigmentation is ivory, again, I cannot pretend to be pure, nor "good"—because I'm not. And black to me, does not figure "bad," nor dirty, nor at fault, nor always needing to carry the blame.

But later, through psychoanalysis, through past life regressions, through deeper study, I would come to recognize this as an oozing of what I would name, "my own unconsciousness" of those things I had yet to take responsibility for,

Part II: The Divide

which had been projected onto Mundadisi as perhaps, the "culprit." And even though I had assigned this upon him, it had backfired and was slowly festering within and was for me, very real. "And when you don't acknowledge your vulnerability, you work your shit on other people" (Brené Brown). Sometimes we just do project whether we mean to or not.

Even while this is all simmering on the roads of Kenya, for lunch, we stop in Narissima with Marjana's wife, Jackie, and a brief gasoline stop in Naromi. We drink a cold bottle of water to counter the dusty, but beautiful terrain. The wind whips up the dirt and these intangibles, these unspoken feelings into small tornadoes, slapping us in the face. Even so, more blessings, more rain is around the corner.

In Nairobi, at the clinic, we drop Mundadisi and Lindiwe for their final check-ups. The update is that they have bad bacterial infections in their stomach. Based on their mal-nourished diets, of course, they do. Antibiotics are given for their cure. In another vehicle, they are whisked off to the airport bound for Zimbabwe. As Marjana and I stop by Peregrinations & Pilgrimages to see everyone—particularly, Motoguisimile and Saifi, who are back to work—to thank them for another remarkable visit.

In their home for dinner, I'm thrown into the world of the haves, of the white Americans, as George and Dusty entertain fascinating guests, United Nations employees, journalists, photographers, and those from NGOs stationed along the Kenyan-Somalian borders dealing with the fallout of civil wars and unrest, impressive generous souls living on the front lines. However, in *The Silent Language*, Edward T. Hall explains, most of "our goodwill and great efforts of the nation has been wasted in its overseas programs."

I'm so preoccupied with their acts of generosity and my concerns about Mundadisi, I forget the time, missing the flight, missing the chance to arrive in London early to visit with our mutual friends Carol and Angela. In the dreamspace that night, I look out an unrecognizable window, realizing I'm on the same path with the Maasai. So, even though Mundadisi and I appear to be at odds, by my interaction with "the haves," I am reassured. I must be in alignment, I must be "right" on schedule. Yet, if he is disturbing my field, awakening me, something must really be off-kilter within.

The next evening, I'm tucked into an economy seat, sleeping the nine hours to Heathrow, where I enjoy breakfast and a nap in a chair between flights. Then, the ten-hour flight bound for Los Angeles. So tired, I sleep another four.

41: Endearments and Intangibles

Through film, *Sea Biscuit* transports me on his back across time and dimensions. Yes, I had to acknowledge, I had become similar to those people around the Bright's dinner table, taking whatever I had received and giving it away—those offerings. *But was it really helping? Was it just our guilt that reached out as saviors and wasn't really solving the problem?*

Whatever skin I've been born with, whatever skin I had chosen to be embodied in, in this lifetime, I am a "human," a very flawed humanitarian in more ways than one. Certainly, I've become an abolitionist, attempting, here, right now, to bring awareness to an issue thousands of years old. However, by the time I get home, I'm sick the entire Spring Season—attempting to clear off what is not mine, holding fast to what is!

Upon this return, Global Voice wire transfers $6,000 for Mundadisi and his wife for their precious gift of sharing their culture with us. *Why hadn't I reassured him of this? Yet, how could he have believed we would honor him?* Looking back, I'll realize, privately, he took the time to heal me, to listen to me— "the little suffering" white girl. I never once pulled him aside to say, "What do you need from me?" "What can my gifts do for you?" *Write an article about your work? Help you set up your website? Introduce him to someone who needs healing?* Instead, I had imagined providing the round-trip to Laloshwa, the healings from the Maasai, and sending the money will be enough. *Will he feel the money silences him?*

In *Critical Race Theory: an Introduction*, Richard Delgado and Jean Stefnacic admit "social scientists call the event a 'microaggression,' by which they mean one of those many sudden, stunning, or dispiriting transactions that mar the days of women and folks of color. Like water dripping on sandstone, they can be thought of as small acts of racism, consciously or unconsciously perpetrated…" What for anyone who is "white" would mean nothing, but for a person of color, everything. *Are we aware of how we come off?*

Before I left Kenya, in appreciation, I had secretly given Marjana fifty thousand Kenya Shillings—approximately one thousand dollars—for twelve cows. Six cows are for Sarototi, four for the Chief, and two for Baba Budhya. Oh, I wish, oh, I wish, in a few weeks time, I could hide in the Sacred Forest, peeking around a Strangler Fig as the Maasai herd this gift of cattle up and over the Highlands from Narissima and across the plains to the Kitomini Community. This image brings a smile to my face, tears, and an inordinate reservoir of African

Part II: The Divide

laughter as the plane lands me soundly in California, where I am bound for a new home, bound to live into a destiny I had yet to step into and trust.

Even so, amongst these shared endearments, something intangible had been conjured up between Mundadisi and me. Something that will fester, something, perhaps, that had long been festering between our communities—separating us, due to those differences. *Is it only skin deep? Or something deeper still?*

42

AFRICA WITHIN

"As marginalized people we should strive to increase our power, cohesiveness, and representation in all significant areas of society. We should do this though, because we are entitled to these things and because fundamental fairness requires this allocation of power."

—Richard Delgado, *Critical Race Theory*

These continued trips into Africa and Mundadisi's reaction towards me and mine toward him, was causing me to go deeper, go below our color differences, go into the cracks and crevices of our cultures, to the *Africa Within*—the places no one wants to go, where we're required to be fair in our allocations.

"Here, am I"—whether I like it or not, whether anyone likes it or not—a white-skinned female, who believes underneath and to the very bone of my bones, I am heart and soul at home in Africa. In fact, I believe I have had many lives on the soil of this great continent. Even so, to others who can only see skin deep, I may appear as someone rather striking and overly positive, who wields a

Part II: The Divide

certain amount of power through those looks, through that "moxie" of energy, and through money, which seems to flow through these hands "oh, so freely."

Certainly, though Mundadisi doesn't know it yet, I know how to give dollars away. Though I worked briefly in the bank of Father's, though he taught me the principles about money—more by osmosis than by words—little do I know how meagerly I comprehend dollars and cents (sense), both in the capacity to squirrel it away for a rainy day and to invest it wisely, sensibly. Around money, I was not perfect—I never have been. Mother used to tease me that I believed money grew on trees, I'd encourage, "Just write a check, Mom!" In high school, during the course of a year, when I was so angry with Dad over a boyfriend, he wouldn't allow me to see, I secretly stole $20 from his billfold from time-to-time. Surely, he knew this, he was a banker, and was aware of the money he withdrew. Later, I would confess this, for I *wanted* him to know how much I'd been hurting and so therefore, wanted to hurt him, too.

The more I had conformed to Father's pronouncements, earnings in the Fashion Industry had eventually come easily for me. Yet, in terms of the non-profit, Global Voice, in these endeavors, I had no idea where to conjure the money. Nor did I in the least comprehend how to draw it in from the depths of my calling—this will take years upon years as I unravel the core of the trauma.

What Father had known, are the tales we tell ourselves, the tales inside our heads, which often have more power than belief structures showered upon us. For years before, I had begun to weave a story, which informed me, "I'm not worthy of anything." Though I never revealed it, Dad must have sensed this and had tried to stop this notion. From the Kansas City Star, he'd cut out the latest positive statement from Norman Vincent Peale. I'd stuff it in the Science book, transporting it from class to class, repeating it over and over. Through the university I did the same with both Peale's encouragements and with verses from Psalms. With little note cards of positive thinking, with that little finger of mine, I held back the dam of depression, of lack of will, of lack of that belief in myself. No wonder I have given everything away that comes to me. Believing, I didn't and don't deserve it. And now, that tide of belief was magically turning.

Amongst the Maasai, they'd been teaching me the true value of myself and the value of being true to that. Other than cows and wives, for them the accumulation of "things," of money, doesn't matter as much as being happy together. There, I've gained the trust of those who are "other" than—and an assemblance of a bit of love for me. In spite of this, or because of what little

42: Africa Within

love I had conjured, something between Mundadisi and I had veered off-road, off-kilter. *Is it the grandfather elephant he originally sent me, circling the room, measuring the imbalances between us, which no one dares speak of?*

What I had yet to grasp was the fate of what it means to be privileged, to be born a white-middle-class-American. The Maasai, the Shona, can hardly understand this reality, let alone me. Of late, it means to step into honesty, to clear my karma, our ancestral debts in some form, to be about reciprocity, to change the way I walk in the world imperially—hopefully more humbly than I had with the Navajo and with greater reverence. Eventually, it will mean, I must bring the subject to the table, to the present, to listen.

But here we were. They were they. And I, I. "The shoe that fits one person pinches another; there is no universal recipe for living. Each of us carries his (her, they, it, their) own life-form within him (her, they, it)—an irrational form which no other can outbid" (Jung). Unable to literally walk in their shoes, I could not even begin to imagine how brutal their history had been, had become because of wars, famine, colonialism, the patriarchy and all its forms.

Today, in the United States alone, according to the FBI, there exist 33,000 "violent" street, motorcycle and prison gangs, who control neighborhoods through illegal activities of robbery, drug, gun and human trafficking, prostitution and fraud. Eighty-seven percent of those gangs are filled with men of color. I can imagine that with exterior and interior pressures, especially on the male of color, these gangs are easily fed with young men in need of direction and inclusion.

Many believe these gangs build up from what happens in the trauma of being excluded, of originally being "curfewed," of being a second-class citizen with minimal rights, lack of opportunities, low-income housing. Where one lives at a "safe" distance from those in opposition, where one is forced to live on the other side of the tracks, where a whole community of blacks, within a 35-square-block radius, can be silently massacred in Tulsa, Oklahoma on May 31, 1921. A genocide, which would not be "named" for almost 100 years. *Were there others?*

In an article from the *Journal of Pain Research*, "Could epigenetics help explain racial disparities in chronic pain?" —we are enlightened, "that the lived experience of African Americans tends to be more stressful than on non-Hispanic Whites, which can be reflected epigenetically and increases the risk that African Americans will suffer from more debilitating chronic pain" (Aroke, Joseph, Roy, Overstreet, Tollesbof, Vance, and Goodin). Stress from systemic racism,

Part II: The Divide

from genocide, passed on from generation to generation can, not only, cause separation, loneliness and poverty, among other things; it causes a continuous "ache" inside the "pain" body and the mind.

In Jungian terms, when an individual is traumatized, the psyche is split into autonomous complexes, which the ego fortifies against itself. But as overwhelming memories arise, often triggered by other wounding experiences, "the complex […] can compete with the ego for dominance of the conscious personality, causing neurotic conflict, or more serious disorders, such as Borderline Personality Disorder, Posttraumatic Stress Disorder, the dissociative disorders, or even psychosis" (Brian R. Skea, "A Jungian Perspective of the Dissociability of the Self"). "Things" that happen can trigger those who are in this situation causing them to be "offset," "off-line," and without a proper supper, or even love, support and acceptance—and the hunger for these "things"—may be unable to handle other variables that come their way.

As well, what no one ever wants to talk about, either in America or in Africa, are those who are suffering, who were left behind, who remained on what many call "the Dark Continent." —*Weren't they the ones who betrayed (more than likely, forcibly so), who sold their own kind, their own brothers and sisters, their own tribal members, and neighbors, sending them on boats across the sea on that Middle Passage, sometimes to their own burials in its depths? Are they still paying for those decisions?*

Is Mundadisi's Zimbabwe suffering from this? When the country was Rhodesia, the Shona and the Ndebele were originally under Portuguese and British rule. Not far from there, black slaves were taken from the ports of Mozambique to India, to Goa as recorded in Mascarenhas' *Skin*. *How can anyone measure the karmic debt on both sides of the Atlantic, on both sides of the Indian Ocean?*

In "My Great-grandfather, the Nigerian Slave-Trader" (*The New Yorker Magazine*, July 15, 2018), author Adaobi Tricia Nwaubani bravely goes where few are willing, confessing her unease as "African intellectuals tend to blame the West for the Slave trade, but I knew that white traders couldn't have loaded their ships without help from Africans like my grandfather." Henry Louis Gates, Jr., in the *PBS* documentary, *Wonders of the African World*, was one of the first to delve deeply into this topic. "I got in a lot of trouble for that show," he says, cheerfully. "I was the first black film-maker to talk about African involvement in the slave trade" (*The Guardian*, March 10, 2024).

Men like Adaobi's great-grandfather were the intermediaries, kidnapping adults and stealing children from their neighbors and their enemies. Through her father's admission, Adaobi was to discover, her great-grandfather, Nwaubani Ogogo Oriaku, "dealt in palm produce and human beings. [...] His business was legitimate at the time."

Adaobi's confession is starkly raw, making it hard to comprehend this kind of treachery, to sell a neighbor bound for slavery. Maybe his actions were more than betrayal. Maybe it was a form of survival. Maybe her great-grandfather was forced at gunpoint to proceed. *Who are we to judge?* Our white ancestors committed other forms of treason: transporting Africans, selling them into indentured slavery for generations, treating them as lesser, separating those who spoke the same language, separating the men from the women and children, as well as abusing them sexually, physically, emotionally and mentally. My race was a part of these forms of treachery.

About treason in this lifetime, in Book 3, I'll get to the bottom of one of my own experiences in childhood. Through that history of mine, I've learned what betrayal is, and have decided it's better to have it "done unto you" than having ignited the treason in the first place. For some odd reason, when it's "done unto you" you strangely feel guilty, setting about the reparation and healing of this, forever making sure you owe no debt to anyone. "Because of this *traison*," my French husband says, "you're free, Murphy."

However, if you are the "doer," you hate, you despise the person you betrayed, rarely is there remorse, at least publicly. Perhaps they don't want the exposure. So, it makes sense that our white ancestors rarely came clean with their crimes, nor have we shifted the balance of that power taken. For usually, there is no admittance and a life full of committing further abuses. Perhaps for the abuser at the end of their lives, they'll remember and confess or of late, hang themselves from a rope (as we can see from the results of the #metoo movement). But in my mind, being the one who wounds means, it festers inside their very soul, on the land, in the waters, where it all began. *Is it festering in Africa?* Even today, that continent has the highest rate of modern-day slavery. *And what of America, below or above the Mason-Dixon Line, is our history undoing us? If Adaobi's relations shipped their own people to Brazil and Cuba, what of mine?*

To transform their karmic debt, admirably, Adaobi's family chose to perform a ritual on the land, where they still live, where her great-grandfather, due to his greatness, was buried with a leopard and six slaves. Perhaps, it's time

Part II: The Divide

I walk Virginia and Oklahoma, to do the same. *If we dug into that red dirt of the farmland we tilled, who else would we find buried in our ancestors' graves?*

On *Amanpour and Company*, Henry Louis Gates affirms, "I don't think that guilt is heritable." Or transferable. So, I can only judge myself; I cannot judge the Africans, nor Mundadisi, nor even my own relatives, for, to be honest, I'd never even walked a mile in their shoes, nor they, mine. I'd never even seen how Mundadisi lives in Zimbabwe. Maybe like the elephant to the mouse, I'd stepped on his tail. I'm sure I've stepped on others, some of these crimes I've been accused of and others, they've let pass. "Yeah," of these, Brené Brown declares, "you're going to learn you have blind spots that you didn't even know you had!"

My black friend Ike Brady says, "No one is a villain here! That's not the point. In fact, we can't change the past, but we can 'admit' the past happened. Admitting brings us into awareness and awareness causes transformation. Then we can be an advocate, a footbridge, an ally."

Though some of us may look freer, we are all tied up in different forms of human bondage from our histories, our ancestors, our past lives, our entanglements, our traumas. If we weren't in the worst situation as slaves shackled, we were slaveholders—though for this there is no excuse. Perhaps our families were beholden to Kings and Queens, to parents, to taxes, to a certain kind of lifestyle of forms, customs, religious notions that can also break your back. Or fear of what it meant not to serve or to do what was required. By no means do these "beholden to's" weigh the same in "pain" as the person of color (except perhaps where we cannot see it, karmically or in our internal organs or on our lands for treating them so wickedly). Yet this does not release our white ancestors from this crime and the need for us to seek reciprocity through prayer and ritual as Adaobi's family has done.

Of these family histories in Africa, of Mundadisi, I have little comprehension, for I am transpontine, from the other side of the Atlantic Ocean, from the other side of the tracks, separated by borders, customs, rituals, countries, continents, culture and most probably, by dollars. At this moment, you might even say, "ahhh, that's all very white of you, Murphy!" Well, if you want it to be about color, it can so easily be about that, for it has been, for thousands of years.

In *Between the World and Me*, Coates writes (with little hope for change) to his fifteen-year-old son, about the challenges he will face within the white man's world as he walks around in a black man's body. For a black man, according to Coates, will stand out because of his skin, drawing trouble into him. Inside the ghetto, lessons abound and circle: "don't argue," "don't talk back," "live without error," "never get in the way," and at all cost, "lay low." It's either that, or be shot, or be beaten to a pulp, beholden to drug lords or incarcerated. A kind of life many people of color have been squashed into.

The sad thing is, I can only compare his ghetto life to my own "white" childhood of peculiar abuses, of the constant pressure to fit in, to "Be perfect!" Immediately, one sees these experiences as "minor," how much more extreme, how daunting and horrible it is for Coate's son, how forever and a day he may be personally erased, losing his voice, losing his identity, and must become invisible for just being born into a darker skin! All his dreams and imaginations are flushed down the toilet. *Or what of the black woman holding down five jobs to support her family? In the Review: The Critical Difference*, Barbara Johnson wrote of "a sterotype," is "an already read text." Henry Louis Gates, Jr., continues with this thought when a woman reported him for a crime he didn't commit, "They look at you, and you've already provided a narrative, a narrative that's been superimposed by the history of stereotype" (*Amanpour and Company*). So often people of color are thus-ed whether we want them to be or not!

Ta-Nehisi's book makes me think of a conversation I once had with a dear friend, whose complexion is as light as mine, about raising a son with darker skin. Early on, on an occasion, she gently, lovingly urged him: "never feel less because of the color of your skin, make this be the token of your power." Except for one black girl, he went to an all-white high school where he stood out as Homecoming King, as a leader. Though whenever he drives a fancy car, he can still be pulled over for a JDLR—because, sometimes to a white policeman, who perhaps is unwilling to admit he's jealous—it "just doesn't look right."

My girlfriend's son doesn't make a big deal about this, taking it as a matter of course, handing over his driver's license, the vehicle registration to the "authority." Yet, still to this day he has no fear—boldly taking on an entire city to federal court and winning. More power to him! May more people of color have these powerful allocations of fairness and equity!

My best friend Jeffrey's mother, Eva, was Puerto Rican. His grandmother, whose skin was black as the night sky, was a descendant of slaves from Africa and from the Tiano peoples who lived in the center of the island in the mountains. She happened to marry a blue-eyed Spaniard. So therefore, Eva's complexion was as fair as mine. In the early 1950's, unlike all her other siblings, whose pigmentation faired dark to café au lait, she was able to boldly launch herself into the white man's world, as a flight attendant and later, selling jewelry only to land herself in Florida, marrying a German Jew and then, a second "white" husband

Part II: The Divide

in New York. Some would say, "Not everyone is so lucky." Her complexion, which took her far from home, would mean, I would come to know Jeffrey, a kind of brother I had never had before.

Luck or not, even amongst those of color, within their own families, such as Eva's—where the café au lait sibling is chosen over the darker skinned sister, or the darker skinned girl is rejected for the lighter skinned bride for an arranged marriage—prejudice exists and still thrives. In Brit Bennett's *The Vanishing Half*, twin "light-skinned" sisters Stella and Desiree, are marred by their history, by their light-skinned father's lynching, by their mother's job, cleaning houses for the white rich. Mentally split from these experiences, they'll split apart into different worlds, as one twin chooses to marry a black man, the other a white wealthy man.

Even amongst ourselves, within our own families, as well as, in our communities, bigotry exists, thrives on the vine, threading through all of us, those "tentacles," penetrating in regions we don't and can't imagine. To be honest, it's even much more complex and tangled up than we want to admit, with ancestral, past life issues, sibling rivalries, normal jealousies, revenge and that desire for what someone else has.

Once, due to my relationship with his wife, when a Jamaican man and I were building a friendship, he pronounced, "Even though you're white, I realize, you're just like me. Your shit stinks, too!" Bluntly, he had spoken a simple, yet profound truth, that we are all human, performing similar and necessary acts, whether we are laced with color inside or outside, perhaps we all have *Africa Within*. Forever after, from this gentleman's acknowledgement, he and I stood on common ground. We could shake hands and see ourselves from a long and distant common ancestor. No matter where our families hail from, "there is no such thing as racial purity" (Gates, Jr., *Amanpour and Company*). In fact, there is darkness and light in all of us. When I turn around to flush the toilet, it is only then that I realize how much I really do stink, and that many of my actions towards people who are different than me, have stunk. There is darkness in my present, in my past.

Traveling to Africa educated me, changed me from the inside out, awakened me, introduced me to friends I would never have had without this. "Perhaps travel,"—as many of us have done throughout the world—Maya Angelou enlightens, "cannot permit bigotry, but by demonstrating all people cry, laugh, eat, worry and die, it can introduce the idea that if we try and understand each

42: Africa Within

other, we may even become friends." For me, like this husband of a friend, I could call a spade a spade. For I was comfortable in Africa, as I was in America, where for me, the differences of color had faded as the sun drops daily from the sky. At least, I thought so. But I still realize I'm not making a difference, and I'm still separated by an "us" and a "them." I still live in a predominantly white neighborhood. *From this position, how can I effect change?*

Such as the civil rights Freedom Rider, Congressman John Lewis, who eventually became, "the conscience of the Congress" in his relentless pursuit of justice, in his relentless pursuit of the Voting Rights Advancement Act of 2021! Lewis understood that marching on behalf of George Floyd's murder was "another very, very long step down the road toward freedom, justice for all humankind." As a young man, John Lewis marched from Selma to Montgomery on Bloody Sunday, when State Troopers almost beat him to his death. But heroically he rose again and again, demonstrating against apartheid where he was arrested outside the South African Embassy, and again, at the Sudan Embassy, for being against the genocide in Dafur. Oh, that we could all be so courageous! Oh, that one of my relatives could have been him!

Maybe in the past we were slave owners. Maybe we didn't stand up for justice, for change. However, those values within me have grown. I am who I am and now, I want others to see what I see, how I view the world—and for that, to be a part of what Henry Gates, Jr., called, "lifting the floorboards" of Western Civilization, exposing the places where racism still remains. To shake hands, to build allies, to treat people of color with respect, as equals, to shift the order of things.

Even though I'm not an activist in the way John Lewis was, more and more, I am realizing, even though I've become an introvert later in life, I can define myself as what my friend, *Cerebral Women* podcaster, Phyllis Hollis declared me, "an abolitionist." That I can declare to you, through my parents' education, through my friendships, through the Bushmen's guidance, and through the Maasai's initiation, I am less and less colorblind! But I still have such a long, long way to go. I'd like to become more and more of an ally.

We, as Americans have this notion, "that the United States is a friend of freedom, that its ideals are everywhere popular, and that any opposition is just a misunderstanding that will evaporate when people from different cultures clasp hands in a far-off village" (Daniel Immerwahr, "The Ugly American: Peeling the Onion of an Iconic Cold War Text"). Indeed, this is a lovely idea, but

Part II: The Divide

when we smash our noses up against truths, we may have trouble hearing, as in Black Lives Matter, as in Asian Lives Matter, as in Desert Storm, or what I was experiencing with Mundadisi—I must confess, it's not as easy as it sounds. *How can we step into these complexities, these truths, facing them boldly, without what D'Angelo considers "White Fragility" blocking us from change?*

To his students, Henry Louis Gates, Jr. relates, "Under the floorboards of Western Culture there are two streams that are constantly running, one is anti-black racism and the other, anti-semitism [...] both are rooted because of economic insecurity" (*Amanpour and Company*). To Gates' comment, I would also add (and I'm sure he would, too), that there are oh so many more streams of racism— against the Original People of Turtle Island, the Asians, the Puerto Ricans, the Caribbeans, the Jamaicans, the Mexicans, the Islamic, of anyone of Middle Eastern descent, of other religions, those of different sex-orientations LGBTQIA+, ad infinitum. (Forgive me for dropping each of you into categories that can rarely define you as a unique person or a unique people group.) Many "non-white," "non-caucasian," "non-heterosexual" people experience bigotry and beatings due to their differences, out of not fitting into the typical characterizations every day. Acts of Exclusion. Acts of Aggression.

Within the American system, according to Delgado and Stefnacic in *Introduction to Critical Race Theory*: "At one period, for example, society may have had little use for blacks, but much need for Mexican or Japanese agricultural workers. At another time, the Japanese, including citizens of long standing, may have been in intense disfavor and removed to war relocation camps, while society cultivated other groups of color for jobs in war industry or as cannon fodder on the front." Stereotypes, as well as images of minority groups shift from time to time; "a group of color may be depicted as happy-go-lucky, simpleminded, and content to serve white folks" (Delgado and Stefnacic). When really and truly that smile plastered on the face, can be far from true. They can actually be experiencing what Pierce termed "microaggressions," which can hurt, make a person feel let down, left out, discouraged, spinning them into dangerous acts of rebellion or crimes for sustenance that often bite them back.

In 2022, according to the YWCA, women are challenged daily, particularly due to the ramifications of the coronavirus pandemic, which has hugely affected the Latina/o/x and the Black communities. As well, inside our country's educational, healthcare, pay and housing systems they encounter structural as well as systemic inequity. The disparity and inequality are appalling—as women are paid 82 cents for every dollar paid to a man, black women earn 63 cents,

Native American women 58 cents, and Latina/o/x women earn 55 cents—compared to what white men earn.

How do we rip up these floorboards Henry Gates, Jr. speaks of, to pour in the soothing balm of healing, reconciliation, restoration? To create equality? How do we recover those whose lives have been damaged by continued ostracism and genocide for generations? How do we shift the balance?

For many years, Deadria Farmer-Paellman has been shifting the balance for the black community. She was first inspired by her great grandparents' bravery, who fled their life of slavery from St. Helen's Island, rowing a boat all the way to Georgetown, where they blended into the crowd! Then, later influenced by an archeological dig in Wall Street and from this, she determined to be "an architect to build the case for reparation." In the same courageous manner as her ancestors, she became an attorney and a researcher between the links of the slave trade and the American corporatations' interests during the 1900's. Her first case was against Aetna Insurance for insuring "live" slaves, with the slaveholder being the beneficiary. She also discovered one-third of New York Life Insurance Company's first investments were slave policies.

From these revelations and "wins," Farmer-Paellmann created a trust fund for the descendants of slavers. In 2000, motivated by her actions, Tom Hayden introduced the Aetna Bill, the slavery disclosure law, which was passed in the State of California, creating fourteen other laws, which passed around the country on the state and municipal level. The Aetna Bill gave African Americans free access to documents. Farmer-Paellman declared, "So we can find ourselves and pull ourselves back together" (*Reparations Task Force*).

Unfortunately, Michael Brown and George Floyd's deaths (as well as many others), would bring life to the BLM issue, forcing us to face what has been buried under those "floorboards" Henry Gates, Jr. has spoken of—the genocide of 10 million and the incarceration on the plantations for generations upon generations of many more—not to mention the disparities between what whites have and the dregs the rest of the people are left with. Even so, BLM has thankfully awakened me, forcing me to rewrite into the similarities and the disparities between Hok'ee, Sarototi, Mundadisi and me, and all the fears that would come along with that.

As the Black Lives Matter movement reared its head, an old friend, a football-basketball-star from Osawatomie High School, Ike Brady, whom we

Part II: The Divide

all looked up to, would reach out to me via Facebook, thanking me, letting me know that our family never defined him by color, instead, he wrote, "You treated me with respect." His reaching out caused me to contact him, to find out more about his experiences then and now. Ike reminded me that my brother had been a bridge for him, an ally, driving him to Paola to play basketball with some of their "white" stars—Steve Anthony and Paul Shoemaker. Ike said it did something for him, expanded his world, made him feel included, drove out his fears. Maybe it's as simple as that, inviting someone to play along—inclusion.

Once when Ike was twelve, in junior high, his literature teacher, Mrs. McVay, played a recording of Mark Twain's *Adventures of Huckleberry Finn*. As the derogatory n-word was read, tears rolled down his face as he stared out the window, enduring the moment. He was the lone black child in the room. Surely Mrs. McVay saw him weeping, for most teachers are aware of each of their students. However, she didn't stop the recording, to "teach" her students how powerful and vicious words can be. The disrespect to a black person, when such a word is used to define is again, Pierce's "microaggression."

After the reading was over, the teacher pulled Ike into her office to apologize. She didn't call his parents for a parent-teacher meeting. She went directly to him. Both Ike and I felt it was her own shame around her mistake—of not speaking about it amongst his fellow students when the book was read. Despite this, somehow Ike's character rose. He understood things like this are just going to happen and he must face them.

To me, this shows a triumph of spirit amidst an unsupportive environment, a small town that had yet to be impacted by Martin Luther King, Jr., or Rosa Parks, or Malcolm X. Though we were north of the Mason-Dixon line, Ike was alone, separated and unique, washed in the color of his skin, living on the other side of the tracks. He did, however, create great friendships amongst his fellow "white" students in Osawatomie that continue to this day.

One of the most shocking moments Ike had, was when some of our Osawatomie friends were visiting him in Ft. Scott, Kansas where he attended the university. They were sitting at a bar, having a beer. Suddenly, people started throwing things at them, trying to run them out of the tavern. *How many people of color have had moments such as this?*

One of the strange things Ike has encountered is the reaction some of his white friends had towards the "Black Lives Matter" movement. They argued with him, "All Lives Matter!" This notion was completely disappointing. For this statement, "All Lives Matter," attempts to step us away from the whole point of BLM, where for years black people have not mattered within the majority's cultural rule. It's as simple as that—a lack of sensitivity, an inability to give blacks their moment, their chance to be heard, to sit equal, in their own way, at the same table.

Even so, "the whiter, straighter, Christian, majority culture you are, the more mistakes you're gonna make" (Brené Brown, *The Call to Courage*). Dear blacks, indigenous, people of color and LGBTQIA2, I'm sure I'm making mistakes here, in this very, very human attempt of mine to reveal the prejudices I've encountered and didn't stand against, and therefore, the creation of many more "microaggressions" (Pierce).

In the United States, I grew up in a country that wants to remain inside the "white perfectionism," to be pure as the driven snow, thrives on teaching its children "to be good" and therefore, fears its own shadow, fears the unspeakables, fears being considered "racist." Allowing only journalists on the covers of newspapers and inside magazines and writers of books, to reveal the darkness that lies beneath. And those of "the lower caste," whom we have boxed in and silenced, are feared most of all.

But to be honest, if five hooded young men were walking down a lonely street towards me, it wouldn't matter if they were black, Hispanic, or white, I would be frightened. The truth is, people of color are the ones who really fear they won't get out alive, if they have an encounter with a policeman or are the only black man surrounded by whites. For them, it is life or death.

Yet, we've forgotten those that are "other-ed," Chakrovorty's "subaltern," or the alienated—those who have been suffering in periods of "gestation," Suzanne Kingsbury reminds, "hold the rich wisdom that needs to be brought forth." It's time we listened to the jewels, the gifts they bear.

These jewels, these interviews with my friend Ike, conjure up reactions, which I had had as a nine-year-old at the public South School in Paola, Kansas, when a group of sixth graders, three very tall, very big "mature" black girls confronted me, "After school, meet us at bus #9 and we'll take care of you!" I was afraid because I had heard they were beating up others. To be honest, I didn't know for sure what I had done. *Had I looked at them the wrong way? Had I stared at them as I had the Hindu Urmula? Had they read the signs of the abuse I had experienced, reflecting their own? Had they seen me on the other side of the tracks with my father?* And because of that, they had thought, of all people,

Part II: The Divide

I should understand them. Even so, I had let them down. I had denied them the "footbridge" van der Post spoke of, which they may have needed to survive amongst us whites.

At the time, I hadn't realized that they were more alone than I was, I, who was protected, and part of the small-town elite. And though it was a public school, it was 95% white. That in fact, our very existence threatened them. *Were they like the buffalo to the Maasai, haunted in their very DNA by the past? For, they were the ones who were vulnerable, not me.* No wonder they were defended. Here, to other whites, I might have looked as if "the victim," slipping into bus #7, dodging their threat. Nevertheless, I told no one of this, for I did not want to get these three girls in trouble. But never did I know how to deal with what had broken down between us. Perhaps they'd expected more from me, given my response to Gracie, given my heritage, given whom my father was, a man of generosity and kindness.

From having that fire stolen years ago, I've had my head buried in the sand. I've been an unconscious white person. Maybe I had believed I had the monopoly on pain. I don't. No one does. I'm so disappointed in myself. I didn't know how to listen, then! I'm willing now. Brené Brown encourages us to engage: "You know the people who are targeted by racism, homophobia, heterosexism and gender biases are not responsible for initiating these conversations and building the tables where they should be happening. That's not how this works." Yet, on the former website "PowHER Redefined" declared it another way: "We don't just want a seat at the table, we want to change how the table is formed" (nFormation for *the Firsts, the Fews, and the Onlys*). More PowHER to them!

In High School, as a sophomore, in the form of an argument, I had received a similar reaction from my "black" cheerleading associates, Alma and Pam. To be honest, I don't remember the details. More than likely I had committed a Pierce "microaggression," as I had to the three sixth graders. All I knew is that somehow, I had offended them. *Had I expected they would be fine wherever I, the white-head-cheerleader, was trying to push them?* Oh gosh, how insensitive my actions, words and ways must have been! I had absolutely no idea what they were dealing with on a daily basis. *So how could I really hear it?* And all along they wanted me to be, again, a bridge across to the other side, as my brother had been for Ike Brady, helping them dissolve the fears of the whites that surrounded them, that dominated them. I was so messed up, trapped inside my own *"White Fragility"*; (D'Angelo) I couldn't hear it!

42: Africa Within

It began to occur to me that this very white complexion of mine, whether I wanted it to or not, historically represents everything the blacks have been hurt by. Baby Suggs, who had left slavery behind, admitted that still white people came and took whatever and what little she had: "Those white things have taken all I had or dreamed of," she said, "and broke my heartstrings too. There is no bad luck in the world but whitefolks" (Toni Morrison, *Beloved*). In other words, according to Baby Suggs, I had and have become bad juju for her.

Perhaps some of us "whites" have become carriers of something that is out of order, and then we peculiarly affect those we have "other-ed"—what Michael Lechuga termed "alien affects"—whether we want to or not. For what it really comes down to is, we often fear one another, because of what has already been done and because of what we imagine might be done. I can assure you; their fear is greater than ours due to the system that we've created. However, our treatment of the BIPOC is inexcusable. Oh, God, oh, Mother Earth, as I write this, change the world as we know for the better, make an equal place for all humankind.

In the projects, in the Bronx, when I visited the family of the Puerto Rican girl, Jade, whom I was sponsoring through Catholic High School, through the organization *Student Sponsor Partnerships*, I must confess, I didn't ride the subway system that far north. I had such fear, that instead, I hired a town car to drive me. Her family had such fear about this white-middle-class girl's arrival; they kindly came down the graffiti elevator to receive me. As if their welcoming presence could protect me from whatever lurked within their hallways that constantly threatened their own survival.

Once, I brought this same Bronx Puerto Rican family together with my other friends, a Brooklyn Jamaican family, for dinner to meet my parents. It was a disaster. I had forgotten there can be a rivalry between islands, between boroughs, between races. I was clueless and insensitive. I assumed because I felt comfortable with them, they would be comfortable together. But I did not understand that we had put them in an odd situation in our white man's world. I had lumped two different bi-racial people groups into the same room without conferring with them. *Had we made them feel they must vie for what little we could offer?* I had no heart-warming words of reassurance to help remove the tension. To let them know I loved them both the same. To let them know how much both families meant to me. To let them know there was and is enough love to go around. I have come to realize that then, and now, my actions of inclusion may come off messy, clumsy. Miraculously, later, in my home, two of the young women, the Puerto Rican Jade and the Jamaican Apples would work together for Global Voice. They became great friends.

According to Brené Brown, "Yeah, you're going to make a lot of mistakes. Yeah, it's going to be uncomfortable and yeah, you're going to learn you have blind spots that you didn't even know you had." In my case, I pray this wasn't and isn't true. But I know it was and is, just from the examples of the past I have written about, the past I remember. I pray my friend, Ike from high school is right, that my family was and is different in the way we treat the "other" and that we will continue to be so and to grow into these endeavors.

As often happens, people let us down, leave us emotionally, mentally, physically. Turn on us. Turn from us. Or we turn from them. Sometimes we've been through such things together we cannot endure their face, nor they ours. It conjures up beliefs from our parents, our grandparents, and prejudices of one's religion to another, or one's color, or country against country. Sometimes we don't like one another. And many times, we don't understand each other. We don't have to. In truth, all we are is just humanly human, often just struggling to get through the night terrors, surviving the day's challenges. *How do we extend grace in the midst of these?*

More importantly, it's not just customs that make us different—the way we wear our hair or dress ourselves, or the various celebrations we have each year—there are in fact wide cultural complexities that keep us apart. Edward T. Hall said of the diplomats they "were advising, kept bumping their heads against an invisible barrier, [...] We knew that what they were up against was a completely different way of organizing life, of thinking, and of conceiving the underlying assumptions about the family and the state, the economic system, and even of man (woman) himself (herself, themselves, itself)." Hall could not really prepare them for the cultures they would encounter, because they couldn't believe they would have a problem, which is a very imperialistic attitude. "Culture hides much more than it reveals, [...] it hides most effectively from its own participants" (Hall). For him, after years of educating himself, he became convinced that it's much more important to gain an awareness of our own culture, than others.

In *The Culture Map: Breaking through the Invisible Boundaries of Global Business*, Erin Meyer further explores Hall's concept of high context communication (as in the people of Japan) versus low context (as in the people of the United States). "In the United States and other Anglo-Saxon cultures, people are trained (mostly subconsciously) to communicate as literally and explicitly as possible" (Meyer). With the thought that if you don't understand me, it's my fault. But in many cultures, as in Japan, according to Meyer, it's about "Listening to the Air." In Africa, particularly Kenya and Zimbabwe "good communication is subtle, layered, and may depend on copious subtext, with responsibility for transmission of the message shared between the one sending the message and the one receiving it." The Shona Mundadisi and I, according to his culture, both of us have a responsibility in our interactions.

In France, which fits in the in-between of high-context/low-context communication culture, Meyer explains, they use a statement, "*sous-entendu*, literally meaning 'under the heard.'" As Americans we might say, what's being communicated "under the table," though this often means to us, what is being spoken illicitly or secretly. Whereas the French would speak purposely without it being a secret; what they would mean as *deuxième degree*, the second-degree message, as in the children's tales written of Jean de La Fontaine, that meant one thing for the child and for the adults a far deeper meaning.

Maybe with Mundadisi, I had spoken the obvious, had spoken to him as though he was a child because I was too explicit, and therefore condescending and patronizing. Hall emphasizes this point, "Americans pride themselves on being outspoken and forthright." The Greeks would say we have a lack of finesse. For we as Americans, use "low-context" communication, overly stating the obvious. Maybe it was strange for Mundadisi to have me make up my own mind without consulting him or the Maasai on different issues. For we in America run our lives individually whereas the Shona, the Maasai work together as a community such as the ants and everything is discussed methodically, together, in detail before they make a decision.

When I first met Mundadisi, I had just been out of the business world for only two or three years—so those many years in business had taught me to be clear, direct—a "literal" American. I was only beginning to develop notions of metaphor and grasp mythology from the world over. *What was I now missing from what he was saying in his more subtle way? Was he not getting to the point purposely? The Chinese use the term pang qiao ce ji, beating around the bush. What was I missing from his "high-context culture" that speaks in a more subtle way? Had he struck me to awaken something within?*

Whether we want to admit it or not, I am, we are walking through a world of mass prejudices—Muslims against Christians, Christians against Muslims,

Part II: The Divide

Hindus against Muslims, Muslims against Hindus, Christians against Jews, Jews against Christians, Jews against Muslims, Muslims against Jews, Blacks against Whites, Whites against Blacks, Red against Yellow, Yellow against Red, Male against Female, Female against Male, Ecologists Against Industrialists, Industrialists against Ecologists, Heterosexual against LGBTQIA2+ or the hundreds of other gender definitions, LGBTQIA2+ against heterosexual, "Isms" against other "isms," and ad infinitum. Often, we say, "Oh! I've finally found my tribe." We like to define ourselves by color, race, creeds, religion, social class, culture, country, where we live, by our "tribe," amongst those we feel united and safe. But it is not just who we are. The truth is our commonalities are vast.

We are floating on this small planet in the sea of a giant universe, which is just a tiny, tiny part of a Multiverse. We're vulnerable, unknowing of our futures. We all have the same survival needs, similar wants and longings; to be able to eat, wash ourselves, warm ourselves, cool ourselves, relieve ourselves, dress ourselves. Safe homes. More than not, we want our children to have better than what we have. Most of us want love that is long-lasting, sustaining us in the midst of whatever we are challenged with.

We all awaken to nightmares in the middle of the night where we find ourselves in wild and wooly adventures we have yet to grasp. We all struggle with moments of rage and hatred and terror and confusion and moments when we feel out of control and at a loss. We all experience death of loved ones and our own impending death whether near or far. In times of crisis, many of us pray to someone, something greater than us.

Yet, these prejudices and these incapacities to make change fast enough are affecting our interactions with one another as well as the ecological terrain we walk upon and are dependent upon. These smear over into my Pollyanna intentions, those babe in the woods' desires to make the world a better, more peaceful place. *How do I heal this with Mundadisi? Or certainly hear what it is he is saying to me? And how do I make further recompense with the Aboriginal peoples, with the Skeleton Man?.*

43

MY PRIVATE IRENE

> "To the Winds of the North.
> Hummingbird, Grandmothers and Grandfathers, Ancient Ones
> Come and warm your hands by our fires
> Whisper to us in the wind
> We honor you, who have come before us,
> And you who will come after us, our children's children."

—*Prayer for Opening Sacred Space*, Alberto Villoldo, The Four Winds Society

From the *fifth journey in*, I return to a new home, Casa d'Irene, 19 Alameda Padre Serra, Santa Barbara. In the fireplace, a smoldering fire burns welcoming me to my new digs. My friends: Interior Designer, Kevin Hart and his then partner, healer, Dr. Emmanuel Faccio organized the red-tiled kitchen and the bedrooms, they had my walls painted surrounding me with love, care and color in a sea of oranges, reds, and mellow greens. Everywhere I turn is a miracle, the

Part II: The Divide

place where I establish the "I" of me. From New York City to Santa Barbara, swinging from the East to the West of the Self, the enantiodromia, one tendency, one way of being, to another.

When shopping Real Estate in Santa Barbara last year, I called Mother, soliciting "Would you rather see me buy the rectangular Ranch house just as yours? Or a 1920's bungalow like your mother's?"

"My mother's." Nana's—Irene's!

So, I listen to her, buying this 1940's California bungalow in memory to a dream, in memory of Nana, naming it after her, Casa d'Irene. Even the interior paint reminds me of the subtle yellow blouses she wore with skirted, hosed, pointed toe-heeled elegance. The fireplace and mantle, where I loved to stand as a child to become "toasty," is the center of the living room. Like hers, the heating roars up from the grill on the floor. So familiar and comforting, are the shapes of the small quaint cookie cutter rooms, the breakfast nook in the kitchen.

After a dinner in that nook, Emmanuel, who traveled to Peru for his shamanic studies, queries, "What are you playing with, Murphy? Voodoo? Have you encountered a brujo, or a bruja?"

"What do you mean?"

"Last night, before your arrival while sleeping in your bed, I was roused from sleep by an apparition, a pulsingly alive one-headed Tomahawk that came flying at me. I grabbed it, smashing it over and over against the wall, bloodying it into a pulp! Who is after you, Murphy?"

Thank God it was Emmanuel for I might not have known what to do. I ponder. *What's up inside me? What am I projecting outside myself that seems to have turned inward? Or is the Tomahawk, as if the "stalk" of the Cibecue Apache Benson Lewis' "arrow" of a story, a challenge to resolve a greater question within?* Maybe after seeing my tears, Mundadisi is testing my mettle: *What is Murphy made of? Has the Grandfather Elephant I sent her really made her strong?* Unlike my other visits, I am upside down and backwards, and not recovering well. An illness seems to be creeping over me.

To Emmanuel, I don't confess. I only inform him of our incredible week in Africa—all the tribesmen, women—the ceremonies. Even so, inside myself, I know someone must be incredibly angry. *Is it Mundadisi? Me? A Maasai?* Strangely I don't reveal this suspicion, as I'm unwilling to admit to Emmanuel that anything could be wrong between those magical moments in Laloshwa,

43: My Private Irene

our drive to Nairobi, and now. Next time I'll wear that Ninjutsu black suit for protection from the spirits that are not necessarily bad, just hungry!

To another associate, I collude about Mundadisi and discover something similar happened within their exchange as well—which keeps me further on my guard. "We end up talking about people instead of talking to people" (Brené Brown). And we wonder childlike: *Will she meet me after school to beat me up?* Still, there is no one who helps me bridge the gap. **Have I let down Mundadisi, as I did those three sixth grade black girls and Alma and Pam?** Maybe. Instead, the gap between Mundadisi and I grows ever wider, discovering I can easily help others but need help navigating something I have little words for. *Why am I not becoming that footbridge van der Post wrote of, so we can walk over and into these unspokens together?*

After three days of classes at PGI, I buy scented candles, old rod-iron outdoor furniture, and feathered lamps from the Remnants Thrift Shop. Then, I find myself alone in retreat, unpacking boxes of books, as well as designer clothes, shoes, handbags, jewelry from those earnings in fashion. In the in-between of Africa and California, I'm in a liminal space.

As guides within this spiritual moment, the Bushmen and Maasai are meditating near, affirming the real mission lies within, lies here in the secret garden. Drift in thought of the Maasai Marjana dressed in ceremonial clothes preparing for his future chiefdom, reconnecting to his Ancestors diving into a tunnel in the earth crawling to the other side. Wonder, too, if the gifted cows have come home to Chief Ole Wangombe, Baba Budhya, and Sarototi. To retrace those steps, I simulate Kisima's delicious concoction, over-boiling the goat's milk, adding a dash of tea, and lots of sugar. (However, it doesn't taste the same!)

On the fourth day, in the middle of the night, coming off the hills in Montecito, what might have been the high winds off the Santa Ynez Mountains, the garage and the front door blow wide open. *Didn't I lock the doors?* I always have before. Roused out of my sleep, I sense foreboding, odd witchcraft, registering as the truth. *Who has entered?* I have an inkling, it's Mundadisi. Maybe he cannot help himself. Maybe he *is* really testing me—it's no joke. The whoosh, clatter, and these hallucinations arouse me to stay alert, to re-lock the doors, to stand in the warrior position, calling forth love. To ask more questions.

Part II: The Divide

Crawling back into bed, I record the imagery of this dream just before the whoosh of the winds had slapped me in the face: On a dune, in the Sahara Desert, I reflect over our intense trip and what's ahead. "Shhh!" The First Man quiets me, pointing. "There are spiders nearby." I catch a glimpse of their large hairy selves—Tarantulas—prancing on the sands, silhouetted in the light of the moon, remembering that last night in the Kalahari Desert with the First Man, the encounter with the red roon, solifugae. *Is the blowing open of doors and dancing Tarantulas more omens, an acknowledgment to keep alert, for there are tricksters throughout the world?*

What I'm not willing to recognize, confess, are the undercurrents below the surface of what Mundadisi might feel toward me—another white person on his continent once again. *What does she want?* Healing, yes, but perhaps, *shamanic power over us? To write a book for her own glory?* For five hundred years, Mundadisi's continent of Africa has suffered from white colonialism, in various forms, from various countries, which have come and taken what they wanted from them—slaves and vast resources. *And now, perhaps, shamanic power?*

Suzanne Kingsbury reminds, "there are those who venture to other lands, other cultures practicing spiritual colonialism," which is filled with the same wanting and perhaps, more! God forbid I should take what isn't mine. *Am I co-opting their spiritual energy, their power? Is this what Mundadisi is exploring—is what she possesses hers or the Maasai's?*

Did Mundadisi sense the Australian Skeleton Man round about me, surrounding my family—wanting our blood for taking theirs? Even stranger still, was Mundadisi the Australian Skeleton Man? Are we meeting again in this life? And if so, did Mundadisi appear at Deena's, at Laloshwa Highlands to make sure our family will no longer kill others, taking their lands? In fact, though not painted with the white outline of the bones, Mundadisi resembles the Skeleton Man's black-as-the-night skin, cornrowed head, and a tremendous awe-inspiring strength.

Each step of the way, what has been happening here since the demarcation of the Maasai's herbs, is, I am getting to the Bones of the thing, of both universal truths and the truth about me. *Are my motives pure? Isn't this what Mundadisi, the tomahawk, the Maasai are asking? Will I return? Will I help them or harm them? Are my motives good or bad?* Certainly, here, now, each step of the way, as the grandfather elephant circles, these motives are being measured.

In an appointment with Chiropractor Michael Luan, he deciphers a "raper/rapee" energy is circling. "And now, you've carried it all the way home with you."

43: My Private Irene

Whose is it? Mine? Mundadisi's? the Maasai Warriors'? An American man's? On the telephone, Kathy and Rick sense this vibration as well, cleaning it off. Kathy warns, "People are feeding at your table whether you ask them to or not." *Don't I want to be the person who hosts, who invites the guests?*

Whichever way I look at it, since 2001, I had to go down, for the Platonic myth requires a growing down in four modes, writes Hillman, via "the body, the parents, place, and circumstances." Though I'm not aware of this at the time, this act, this encounter with the Maasai will mean a not very pretty, twenty-year period of going down into consciousness development. (*OMGosh if I had known this, would I have been willing to go down under?*) Aging, reconnecting with my parents in threads and truths, even the "twisted and rotten branches" of the family. Some of this looks exciting, traveling to Africa, going to school, receiving a Masters, and in a few years, a Ph.D. But in truth, it's a deep dive downward, into the unconscious—the place where Jung believes is still vastly unexplored.

Eventually I'll follow love to Denmark (Book Two), then move to Paris for marriage (Book Three). But this movement of soul will be to get the low down on who I am and who I was meant to be. Not for the faint of heart! In the end, I'll live in a place, which enlightens the Self—Copenhagen, where I'll have to relinquish the love I had longed for; I'll live in a place, which serves my soul—Divine Paris, where the "duties and customs" will call forth other requirements of consciousness. Each of these "elsewheres" I'll inhabit, Laloshwa Highlands, Copenhagen, and Paris will require me to learn *The Custom of the Country,* just as Edith Wharton's character Undine Spragg. And then of course, the requirements of my own solitary work—of shamanism and the writing of books, these "gestures" of gifts to others— "that declare your (my) full attachment to the world" (Hillman, *The Soul's Code*).

In the daylight, the worry from the flying open of the front door and the garage, from all these questions subside; peace and wellbeing, strength, and equanimity surround me in this wonderful new home with the gifts from those ancestors of mine and a novel garland of friends. Even the falcon family has found me. This morning, outside the French doors, I hear the father's piercing cry and run into the backyard. There, on the top of the neighbor's Star Pine, he sits, screaming at me, "Peeeer, peeer, peer! Hello, Murphy, I see you have landed in the place we've mapped for you!"

Then, I remember this is and always has been the falcons' pathway toward the sea. Just didn't know I'd followed their movements, choosing a home, living

Part II: The Divide

under their daily encircling, expansive flight of catching the thermals. Delighted, I wave, "Hello! I see you've found me once again," as he preens, turning side to side, displaying his "jizz" so I recognize who he is. Then he flits off to join the others.

Here, steeped in what is important to me, California blends the homelands of Kansas and Kenya, through the land, its creatures, and the studying of tales from all over the world at Pacifica Graduate Institute. Santa Barbara, itself, has united me with the energies of the Chumash Native Americans, the people of the Rainbow Bridge from this life to the ever after. *Are they still holding ceremonies in the backyard for this passage?*

Much seems to coalesce in this move. *However, I wonder how often I have encountered unwanted energies, visions of reptiles, spiders, bloody tomahawks? Are these intruders circling about, warning me of spells, incantations, the power of thoughts that can harm, when I project outside myself onto others, reflecting back the boiling up of the imbalances within?* Even though I'm human, unable to contain these wild and wooly projections, O, Hummingbird, O Grandmothers, come, warm your hands at this humble fire!

44

FAMILY RITUALS

*"To the winds of the East.
Great eagle, condor
Come to us from the place of the rising Sun.
Keep us under your wing.
Show us the mountains we only dare to dream of.
Teach us to fly wing to wing with the Great Spirit."*

—*Prayer for Opening Sacred Space*, Alberto Villoldo, The Four Winds Society

As I attempt to fly wing to wing with the Great Spirit, I board a plane bound for my hometown, Osawatomie, Kansas. Here, I visit Mother's pretty, little room at Vintage Park, an assisted care facility. She seems excited with her new life, new friends.

Down the street, in the now sold family home, Mom supervises my brothers and I as we disassemble and reassemble their fifty years together. For our own

Part II: The Divide

homes, we each pick out treasures of our parents and grandparents, stacking mounds of bounty in our chosen corner.

The youngest brother longs for granddad's homemade banjo, of which, Mom is happy for him to have. In a box, we come upon fabrics from all over the world collected from Great Aunt Janet's travels. She exclaims, "I want you, Murphy, to have these!" And to my oldest brother, "Oh! And I want you to have those cufflinks from your father." From old boxes, we pull out photos, screaming, "Look at you!" "No, way! What a hoot, look at you!"

Certain artifacts cause us to break down into tears. In particular, Mom comes across Dad's love letters of courtship. As she reads, her eyes gush forth with liquid love, "Can you believe he adored me this much?"

"Yes, Mother," I pipe up. "He loved you that much!"

For this, my brothers suggest I organize our parent's love letters in a pretty notebook for her to peruse during her stay in assisted care. I will actually do this for Mom, and she will then continue to read his letters over and over until she, too, loses her memory.

We even discover Dad's flight notebook clocking him at one-hundred-and-fifty hours—none of us knew! Once airborne, intent and focused, now he is grounded, immobile.

Several times a day we breakaway, walking to Life Care Center to visit with Dad after lunch, after dinner, to kiss him, squeeze his hand. Sometimes we read to him a poem, a paragraph from the Bible, a favorite bit from a book. Always I sing him one of his favorite songs, "Puff the Magic Dragon lived by the sea," or "Tell me why you're crying my son." Dad is only capable of sitting, staring, lying down, and sleeping. No longer interested in television, in movies, in the news, nor it appears, at times, even in us, for he cannot speak. He is about something we cannot comprehend, nor need to. Perhaps this is a slow crossing over to the other side of the veil.

On the twenty-first of February, we meet with our Reverend Leslie Murphy-King for a ritual of communion at the nursing home. In Father's private room, we hold hands, pray, sing, imbibe. He perks up. One eye is slightly open, aware. A little tear rolls down his cheek.

In the afternoon, just as Sarototi suggested, the Kansas friends, Roberta and Clint, Kathy and Rick create a good-bye ceremony for our parent's house with water and sage. At the dining room table, my oldest brother observes as Mom, and I participate. "Murphy, you and your brothers," Clint claims, "had to carry what your folks hadn't dealt with."

In the chair, in the area where Mom used to read, watching her favorite programs, the heaviness sits as if detained, held in an iron pot, simmering. One of the old pots is from the great grandparents whose settling during the Cherokee Strip Run required the removal of the Native Americans from Oklahoma. Things once forgot, now need remembrance and reciprocity. *Is this why Mundadisi in the dream had gone home to Kansas, to my parents, to help clear this? Is this what he was picking up on the ride home?*

When we sell the home of our parents, suddenly upon the return to Santa Barbara to continue this novel life, it's my life and nobody else's. Even this bungalow is different from the condominium in NYC, taking on a whole different flavor. I've gathered the four universes together, from NYC, the temporary apartment at Las Alturas, the childhood mementos, and now, the Ancestors' treasures. Mother and Grandmother's dressers, mirrors, china, chairs, tables arrive. Pillows are sewn from Great Aunt Janet's fabrics from her travels to India, China, Cambodia, Egypt, Thailand, and South America. A collection of my own fabrics from Africa, become the settee and cushions in the front bay window. Everything fits perfectly, declaring this new "I"-ness of me. Within this uniqueness, tuck me under your wings, O, Great Spirit.

45

TESTIFYING TO THE NUMINOUS

"Numinosity, however, is wholly outside conscious volition, for it transports the subject into the state of rapture, which is a state of will-less surrender."

—C. G. Jung

For the last two years, I have attended three eight-hour intensive days each month for the Masters program in Mythological Studies. Late into the night, read the required texts, ten thousand pages a year. The pressure is consistent, relentless, every three months, three papers, and oral presentations.

Honestly though, being at PGI is a sheer joy, an excellent "fit" as Walter instinctively knew, stirring up parts of the Self I never had access to. When I remark to him: "Maybe it was due to James Hillman's ambiguous, yet intellectual way he plays with words, but after reading *Healing Fiction* for school, I strangled Hillman in my nightmare, as he drove us through the Costco parking

45: Testifying to the Numinous

lot." Walter—a staunch Jungian and a bit prejudiced against the analytical psychologist, who challenges some of their very tenets—practically tumbles out of his chair with laughter.

Here, at PGI, in Walter's care and even Hillman's, I learn how to reckon with the shopping mall landscape of our culture and how to testify to the gains of those numinous, those rapturous moments among the Maasai and the Bushmen, translating the impact of those events as well as their mythology. I had waited for this change, I'd been searching for it, until it came upon me like the rushing winds of the Holy Spirit, and only then could I speak and write in tongues of angels as if never before. Words began to form.

Do the Maasai grasp how much their magic catapulted me out of the madness of what for me was Seventh Avenue into this far-reaching realm of story and culture? From them, I could finally understand the conflict within, for those pursuits in fashion took me so far adrift from that childhood self—the budding poet, the little girl pulsatingly alive in nature. The encounters with the Bushmen's stories, both through van der Post and amongst them, brought a neoteric awareness, and also a sense of home, which could no longer be subdued. What seemed irreversible was unequivocally changed.

None of those fashion colleagues guessed that this be-hatted floor-to-ceiling walking couturier maven would choose to exit the high-pressured world I had once agreed with. Not unless they caught a glimpse of my private library or knew that every holiday landed me in Africa. I walked out, not in Manola Blaniks, which I never wore, but in my black army boots, pith helmet and that soft brown mid-calf suede skirt. For I had ventured to Africa, and I wasn't coming back to *that*!

So, my original pronouncement: "I shall write my way out of fashion," I now embody. Each page in my journal, each phrase, each paper, each conclusion, each declaration written for the Masters requirements—and eventually for the Doctorate—is a testimony to the miracle of the numinousity across that great divide to another plane of existence into that "will-less surrender."

46

MAASAI IN MY HOUSEHOLD

"Ukali wa jicho washinda wembe."
"An eye is sharper than a razor."

—Maasai Kanga proverb

Four months after the *fifth journey in*, one of those guides of mine, the Samburu author from Kenya, Lmakiya Lesarge, whose eye is sharper than a razor, arrives at the Santa Barbara Airport. In his Maasai regalia, coated in many colors, he stands out, handsome, alive and electric. His graceful, kind, peaceful meditative nature creates the most beautifully contained boundaries. (So, he is very good for me!) In other words, Lmakiya, just as Walter, had become an example of the men I have chosen as my friends in Santa Barbara. For both Lmakiya and Walter could not be seduced, in other words, they were not seducible. They didn't allow me power in the game of seduction, where once I had been considered prey, and then, perhaps at times, projected this outwardly as predator.

For this reason and more, I wanted him here as a representative from Kenya. For Lmakiya had become a unique tutor—not just about his people the Samburu, not just on safari with the animals—for it was through him, through the Maasai, through the Bush-men-and-women, I had become inducted into the mysteries of the stories that lie within the history of Africa. These master storytellers were the beginning of that comprehension of the trick.

What lessons I'd gained from around the fires of the Kalahari Desert, from my own history, as well as through the writings of van der Post, Lmakiya and those professors at PGI had furthered, elucidating the why's and what's of the trickster existence and the benefits of encountering such a cunning character. How these schemes can define whom we had been before and would become after—even to the point of determining the title and main them of *Why Ostriches Don't Fly.*

Because of these talks with Lmakiya and the eventual trick I will soon experience from his cousins, I will explore other literature, and this will form the eventual treatise of my dissertation and lifework, journeying through and into the trickster's deception creating powerful transformations.

Such transformational stories exist and are shot as "arrows" urging us to be knowledgeable about our surroundings, with alertness, clarity (Benson Lewis, a Cibecue Apache). For when Elephant, carrying jars of honey on his back, is not conscious, is so road weary, Rabbit will take what is offered (even if Elephant is unwilling) exchanging Elephant's honey for mud. Such tales, according to Pelton's *The Trickster in West Africa*, were told around the fire "to put an adult mind in a child's heart and a child's eye in an adult head" developing delightful awareness in the elders and planting crystal clear wisdom in the children.

Learning, there are those who will steal your fire, who will take from you whether you want them to or not. Sometimes the tale is as Honoré de Balzac's *Ursule Mirouët's* Chapter XXI titled: "Show How Difficult It Is To Steal That Which Seems Very Easily Stolen"—filled with mesmerism and ghosts who reveal truths of the thieves. In whatever form these initiations occur, some of us recover, some of us don't. In the above tale, Ursule, who was stolen from, was lucky—everything came back to her. But her cousin, Désiré, whose father was the thief, lost both his legs, eventually losing his life.

Part II: The Divide

In Africa, (as I've mentioned before) during the transitional passages of their children, all mothers cry, relinquishing them, knowing full well, they may not return. This growing up and into, is the risk of stepping into adulthood. Especially as women, as people of color, as LGBTQIA2+, as those who are ostracized and diminished—if we are not completely shattered, destroyed, killed—we are often stripped down by life to the essence of who we are, what we are made of. What has been stolen can be utilized as a gain, breaking us down into the source within, building us up into who we really are, who we are meant to be into our personal legend. Rituals are testing grounds for everyone, for the youths' future on this planet, searing their talents and strengths into existence.

As Prometheus testifies, I will begin to grasp, fire is not just for private use. Instead, fire is a source *meant* for everyone. Even so, Ostrich believed fire was her gift, her commodity, and that *that* gift was to be carried secretly beneath her wing. The truth is, all of us have or had fire. The Vedics believed the God Agni, the God of fire was within everyone.

When she lost fire, Ostrich, like me, viewed herself as victim to a theft. Yet through this loss, Ostrich experiences her first initiation, awakening into her capacities, to what is behind and beneath her. For as she chases after Xamsakayuba, Ostrich discovers her ultimate gift, becoming the fastest bird on earth, whom she is really *meant* to be, whom she is *built* to be. What her true offerings really are. In fact, she wasn't meant to fly. She is much too heavy for that. Ostrich's true meaning is to be grounded, living on this earth into her trueness. Roberto Calasso claims, for the Vedics, when Agni—Fire himself—fell out of the mouth of Prajāpati, it "sets history in motion." When Ostrich loses her fire everything moves across the landscape, everything moves into being, everyone, throughout the world, receives fire.

In Hyde's *Trickster Makes This World*, the child's "first theft, first lie" (and I would like to say, "first initiation") sets her/him into the capacity to independently create, the beginning of the psychological individuation process apart from the parents, where the "betrayal" becomes the first realization of differentiation, a contradistinction between "us and them" inside the game of life, of free will, free choice, and destiny all in one full sweep.

In my own experience of "the trick," I, like so many others, had been jammed into an unconsciousness, an incapacity to perceive while living inside a yang driven culture. Inside this prevailing myth, I have experienced a re-wounding, furthering into a Chronic Complex Post Traumatic Stress Disorder—oftentimes

46: Maasai in My Household

feeling as though I will never recover. Inside this fight, flight, freeze or fawn syndrome, the breath grows inconsistent, intermittent from fear, takes on the opposite physical form, where the exhale becomes an inhalation, the inhale an exhalation, where the breath strangely expands in the stomach, not in the lungs. So, to attempt a calm quiet space, to hear the geese decree is often next to impossible. Although, for me, even so, the treason becomes a gift of embodiment, placing me in a container of separation from those who raised me and from the society at large, creating individuation within, escorting me into an integrative compassion for others.

The myths from Paola Library books, from the Bushmen, from the Samburu Lmakiya's narrations and from what I was now reading at PGI, granted me insight: Sometimes the characters win. Sometimes they lose. Sometimes they make "good" choices. Sometimes they don't. Sometimes, just as Ostrich, we are so shocked we cannot comprehend the reason for the trick. Sometimes it means, we forever bury our heads in the sand, where we remain "invisible" as my friend Terry claims. Sometimes it means we must leave an egg outside the nest as a reminder of what we're about. What I was soon to find out, is that these tales were enlightening me of that relationship with Mundadisi and will prepare me for the Second Initiation with Lmakiya's cousins, the Maasai. And maybe eventually, moving me softly into what Rainer Maria Rilke once suggested to, "try to love the questions themselves."

At Casa d'Irene, on Lmakiya's behalf, around Nana's mahogany table, I entertain several professors, fellow students, Cynthia, her Liberian brother Bill and his wife, my girlfriend, Lori, friends. As well as the men who are like him— Dr. Dave Cumes, Thomas, Steven Lum—whom I have formed deep connective relationships and (must cheerfully announce) whom I'm not having sex with. For through Lmakiya and Walter (as you may recall), I had learned I didn't have to have sex for the download of information, for the exchange between a man and me. Hallelujah!

Throughout the evening, Lmakiya talks of his people, of their present obstacles, of their collective history, of his collection of folktales and maxims from the Elders. Hosting him is an incredible experience, for he speaks with razor sharp precision. The gift is: Lmakiya has physically brought my African family to Casa d'Irene, as though anointing her. And I imagine, our interest, our questions have encouraged his endeavors. In the fall, to honor him, Global Voice Foundation will gift Lmakiya a computer and we will fund his attendance for a weeklong

Part II: The Divide

conference at PGI in 2004 and the Big Bear Event in 2005. Eventually, he will publish *Proverbs of the Samburu* and *Folktales of the Samburu*.

In Casa d'Irene, I wanted friends who love Africa to know Lmakiya. For it was due to our encounters, I now knew the importance of the role of the trickster in our lives. Because of him, I was on the road to knowing what my dissertation would entail. In fact, during his visit, I'm under pressure, busily writing a thesis of where this daunting task shall lead.

What I've forgotten to mention to Lmakiya are the challenges I've experienced with Mundadisi. Because I'm not sure what's really happened. *How do I peel back the layers of an onion I know little of?* A trick and the reasons for it, I have yet to grasp. In truth, Lmakiya would be the perfect person to reveal this dance with black magic, with tomahawks and tarantulas. But I don't. For, I don't know how.

On the last night, I learn that Lmakiya does not need an alarm or a wakeup call, even for our 4 a.m. departure for his plane. "Engai awakens me!" he casually replies. Inspired, I set my alarm aside, deciding if God can wake him, surely, He, even She, perhaps, can welcome me kindly into the day. But even more important than being tenderly awakened, through Lmakiya, the Maasai of my Self has come home. Soon, in just a few months, I anticipate, I'll be in Laloshwa Highlands once again for the sixth journey in, then driving north to Samburu to celebrate Lmakiya's wedding to Becky! And maybe someday, my eyes will be as sharp as his!

Second Initiation
Sixth Journey In

47

RHYTHMIC NATURE OF WOMANHOOD

*Mother Earth,
We've gathered for the healing of all your children.
The Stone People, the Plant People,
The four-legged, the two-legged, the creepy crawlers,
The finned, the furred, and the winged ones.
All our relations.*

—*Prayer for Opening Sacred Space*, Alberto Villoldo, The Four Winds Society

Part II: The Divide

On Mother Earth, at the Ladera Lane Campus, on the 5th of August 2004, we finish our last set of Masters' classes with tearful good-byes to the Ph.D. class ahead of us. My former interpreter from Paris, from the Badgley Mischka days, brings her boyfriend, a Frenchman to stay in Casa d'Irene—the third time we are all together. (What little clue I have at the time that this Frenchman will figure so grandly in my life one day!) Under the umbrella, we dine in the Secret Garden. In the morning, I will depart for Africa, as they will housesit, lie in the Ecuadorian hammock, swing in the loveseat, jump on the trampoline, inhale the aromas of wisteria and lilacs, and imbibe in fresh-squeezed orange juice and lemonade.

The following morning fly from Santa Barbara to Los Angeles for London. On the flight, watch the movie *The Prince and Me* about a Danish prince (not knowing its projecting my future into Denmark) who falls in love with an American college student, which stirs up that greatest want: to be wondrously and truly loved. Upon a napkin, I scribble, "Inside the psyche of our culture lies the myth of Prince Charming arriving to save the woman from her plight." *How does one further unite with this myth? Create a healthy union within, without projecting?*

My fiercely independent self no longer wants to wait. And yet, this film gives hopes. Even the man seated next to me on the plane today causes me to privately question, *"Is this the one?"* His looks are a cross between Gary Cooper and Gregory Peck. Alas, underlying his handsome profile and white curly hair there is a sternness. Listening, he spews forth divorce, farm failure, loss. His eyes, brows are terse, hard, unforgiving. As in the observation of Clive Owen as King Arthur: tough, cold, relentless, self-righteous, bold, unbeatable, I admit: "Still, desire to be taken" by him or Nora Robert's character in *Carolina Moon*, which I escapingly devour, as though Swiss caramelized chocolate, from cover to cover.

Longing sets up the unconscious marriage, sucking everything into it. *Am I locating a Sarototi to rescue me?* In order to fulfill this urge, how many thousands of scenarios of off-colored romances, women collapse into. In the Twenty-First Century (even as an independent woman) the prince's arrival on the scene, remains inside the heart, pulsing with abandon, I am willing to relinquish all— *Am I just an accident waiting to happen?*

We often forget that the Cinderella myth of living happily ever after with the Prince is really based on the unification of opposites and that the story itself, which has been told over and over for hundreds of years, is so very, very necessary

47: Rhythmic Nature of Womanhood

to our souls. In fact, this marriage is what brings unity and peace to a kingdom, to our interiors—the Cinderella, the Prince within, holding the darkness at bay, as I attempt to draw this near.

At the London Hilton at Heathrow, lying in the bathtub, I scrub off the flight hours. *How will I travel this sixth journey in?* Curl up into their big bed for a few hours of naptime. *Where is he? Who is the next and right one?* Not knowing that many years of internal work must be done in order to satisfy the external drive of these questions asked and those lying hidden, unasked. *Can I unmask them?* "Many people travel to Syria and Iraq and meet only hypocrites. Others go all the way to India and see just merchants buying and selling." Just as, Benson Lewis, a Cibecue Apache spoke of stories as "arrows," Rumi's poem pours in, "stalking" me with more pointed truths: "Others go to Turkestan and China and find those countries filled with sneak-thieves and cheats. We always see the qualities that are living in us." *How will I perceive Kenya this time? What kind of traveler will I be? Taking what I want, need? Tossing the rest aside? Or giving?*

Finally, at nine p.m., on the 8th of August, I land at Nairobi International to navigate the formation of a spiritual center, which may enable people the world over to imbibe, to share, to restore—an amalgamation of the Kitomini Community and Global Voice Foundation. I've come to renegotiate my standing, exploring where I play out the future as this Twenty-First-Century-Self with a basket-load of offerings. For they've invited me over and over, to live amongst them. *Will I live here three-to-six months of the year as I have fanaticized?* Envisioning this—living in the Highlands I will momentarily be transported to: *Will I really bring my furniture to greater downtown Laloshwa?*

Even though I feel profoundly respected, that I pass muster, that they set aside a parcel of Maasailand for me, I suddenly have grown uneasy. *Why is this anxiety roiling up now? What's the expectation for a life here? If I have running water and they don't, won't I be considered an imperialist and the supplier? Thousands of miles away, isn't this how I live in the United States already? And is there something more? Has the sore in the spleen, the tomahawk frightened me?* Strangely, I won't speak of this. I'll hide it. *Am I embarrassed or still too unconscious to bring it to the fore?* The unspokens of this whiteness of mine.

In this African night, Marjana, Saifi, and Motoguisimile easily greet me, making me feel so wonderfully welcome in their warm inviting embraces. As we wander through the parking lot looking for the Peregrinations & Pilgrimages Land Rover, Marjana happily informs me of his ceremony to be the next chief,

Part II: The Divide

"It's official. They dug a vast tunnel which I crawled through, forging to the other side, departing from one way of being, to another." These Warriors are masters at the capacity to create a departure, a ritualized passageway between two existences, shedding the skin of the past, shifting the vibration of the person, so that the movement into this new dimensionality is secured, holding fast.

At the hotel, I settle in for a must needed rest, stretching out the legs, however, more fears roar up: *What if I won't be able to make this center sustainable? How do I inform others of their incredible capacities as herbalist, as divinators?* John Mbiti, a Kenyan theologian reminds me that here, "In Africa, time moves backward." *So, is this fear something that is still, pulling me ever backward, back towards a past life, something unresolved—a foreboding of undifferentiated energies? Or is this just a way to live without the persistent pressure of Western time, rolling quickly into the future?*

For several weeks, I have not been able to write (even in a silent retreat)—which is strange, because I commit to paper daily—*Was I holding myself in suspension of what is to come?* Yesterday, on the plane, as I traveled over the divide, something broke open, loosened, released. I scribbled pages and pages. *Resolutions? Reconciliations?*

After an early breakfast, Marjana, his cousin, Saifi, Motoguisimile, and the Kikuyu cook, Thuka, load my bags into the already overloaded Land Rover, the time machine, which transports me back into a reclamation of the past, and forward into this *sixth journey in*. Even so, we briskly make Naromi by noon. I discover the Maasai are discouraged from their recent, very severe drought. So to encourage them, I refresh their storage units with purchases of rice, potatoes, sugar, milk, tobacco. In Narissima, we stop for our usual greeting with Marjana's wife, Jackie, eating a lovely dinner in her home. I gift her daughter a red frilly-laced dress, which turns her into a whirling dervish of happiness.

In the transportation toward Laloshwa Highlands, as I pass in and out of jet lag sleep, a reptilian dinosaur haunts me. I take this to be a warning. What I find fascinating is before every other safari to the Maasai, there were no nightmares related to them. Yet, I don't heed this invaluable signal of a stalking saurian. Whereas prior to this visit all is filled with magical support! Well, I had a few concerns—the purse dream—inside the *fifth journey in* but stuffed those away for a rainy day. *Is this that rainy day? Math, or what does this all add up to, Murphy?*

Have I tangled myself up in the sheets again? Into obligations I cannot continue to fulfill? In *The English Patient,* Kathryn (Kristin Scott Thomas) snarls at Count

Almasy (Ralph Fiennes), "An obligation? That would be unconscionable!" *Did Almasy fear this—obligation? Do people feel they owe me quid pro quo? Am I buying love?* Most of the people I have given gifts to, are those who moved me further into being an adept—and then there is a separation. *Is this where my too-much-ness overwhelms the other or is their reflection something I'm unwilling to view?* I must be more aware, thoughtful, not overtly generous. Remembering Marjana's words, "You are family, NeLaloshwa, you don't have to pay in cows." But I did, *didn't I?* After the last visit, I sent twelve cows. More forewarnings!

At Bright's Lodge, they have moved me back into that special tent with hardwood floors, tucked under the trees and heavy vines. A sour belly has roared up. *Another portent?* To relieve this, I suck on Nux Vomica, balance my energy field, rubbing essential oils on the intestinal region, plant the feet on Mother Earth, acknowledge the six directions, bidding the Ancestors to bring the land into balance after this intense drought, preparing the way for the important conversations, determine to begin this new moon with a fresh start.

In the morning, Marjana transports us to Kitomini. Sarototi's mother, Yieyo, hugs me over and over. Kisima treats me to her special tea. Rain has come as a harbinger of this visit. They are pleased. Unusually so, the men want me to practice my healing craft with some of their women. I hear their complaints. Pull Tarot Cards. Rattle. Advise. Administer.

This trip, being around Marjana, is disheartening. He doesn't explain things. *Since the healing work on me is finished, has he stopped? Is he more consumed with chiefly duties? Is he hurt I may not be able to pay him to stay the full month?* Still don't know if I can afford him. Nor have we planned out our possible trip to Samburu for Lmakiya's wedding. *Do I really want to make the long hot drive north?* Sarototi knows that after my *fifth journey in*, I have not felt well through the spring—*more forebodings, of the past rearing its head?* He urges Marjana to translate my latest dreams. And today the doctoral program feels an added burden. My father lies dying. *What am I doing alone without a husband for support?*

In the journal, I pen: "Decide to stay." *Had I thought I couldn't or wouldn't?* It's true, suddenly, something has gone askew. These safaris to Laloshwa, I have been inside a certain routine toward healing and being healed. And today, I have returned with a greater sense of this "I." Perhaps I don't know where to place this "her," of the new me.

Part II: The Divide

Bathe, wash hair. Now, freezing from a very wet head, cover it with my beret. Tuck under the covers. With a little flashlight, I continue to read Brunton's, *A Search in Secret Egypt* from the 1930's that my astrologer, Leor, suggested. Inside, Brunton describes all the splendors of Egypt—the long-hidden temples, underground chambers, shrines, and artifacts. His writings pique my interests reminiscent of a shamanic passage with Deborah of a life I had had there, where I was in training as a priestess in another incarnation. I must admit, I'm still searching, longing to go further into the mysteries.

Since my first meeting with the intuitive Mariah, I've been stepping back in time, taking responsibility for the choices of that past. Before her, I'd "toyed" with the "idea" of past-lives in my mind's eye, those *déjà vu* encounters, through conversations with Mom and friends, and dabbling in research. Once Mariah opened the Pandora's Box of possibilities, once the Maasai restored the watercourse way, those three years between the *fourth* and *fifth journey in* to Laloshwa Highlands, whenever I "sensed" a relationship with someone was "off-kilter," I'd travel to other dimensionalities utilizing the wisdom of Mariah or Deborah. And whether or not what we saw through this lens was truth or fiction—for I could not verify—I delved into the imagery as if in dream analysis with Walter, "follow(ing) the image" as Hillman encourages, visualizing how I had related to this or that person in 2000 B.C., or at any given moment, making amends for those decisions.

What I couldn't understand is that the fear of Mundadisi's attack (or what I thought was his) had taken away my trust in the Maasai, reawakening past violations both in this life and others, so that those glimmerings were now rearing their head. Urging me to heal. Yes, the shadow had arisen. I no longer felt safe.

What I don't know is something none of us can—is what's to come, just as O'Donohue, "On Being" admits: "We never know what will land on the shoreland of tomorrow."—On this dear Mother Earth.

48

AJUMBLE

"The road to hell is paved with good intentions."
—Charles Wallace, *A Wrinkle in Time,* Madeleine L'Engle

At breakfast, I feel ajumble about our plans, anxious to get on with it: the lifework, the writings, the spiritual center with the Maasai. Sarototi administers an herb, a sleeping draught to sooth these agitations as I settle into the camp.

Today, the elders discuss different ideas regarding this center. *Do they want to build? Or just allow temporary tents to be set up for our invited guests?* In the end, their desire is to keep the land true, free of further structures, utilizing Bright's Camp. Thankfully, at present, George and Thierry Bright's campground of fourteen years continues to employ seven Maasai, who protect it from marauding elephants and serve private safari guests, who drive in four times a year. At a distance, this arrangement is non-threatening, comfortable for the village, and freely accessible. So this notion of moveable tents and *A Moveable Feast* would be a nice addition.

Part II: The Divide

Last night, in the Land Rover on the drive to Laloshwa Highlands my mind raced with ideas. Today, am overwhelmed by the complications, of what lies ahead. Not even sure I want to do this project of building a Spiritual Center for healers and those who need to be healed—where people can come and go from all over the world to participate. I realize how long it has taken to complete those Bushmen projects of film, of books. *Does the tribe intend to care for everyone's individual story?* "Teach me the way Ancestors," I pray.

To shop in the market, we drive to Narissima. Today, the jet lag permeates, can hardly get up the energy to walk about. Sarototi guides me. As per usual, the people surround me, touch the brown and white pony skirt, pondering the strangeness of these braces on my teeth. Hanging out in Jackie's home, I joke with Marjana, "I'm sure after sauntering through the crowd, explaining me, Sarototi is relieved NeLaloshwa is not his second wife!" Afterwards, Marjana becomes the local taxi service as we drive twenty-one people, their food, and purchases, home. To thank him, several times we are invited into the privacy of their dung huts for tea and conversation. Again, this *sixth journey in*, is different than before, I'm in the background, not translated for, alone.

Early morning the following day, a conjured night's reverie shakes me, making me worry about this life in the Highlands. But before I go on, let me backtrack to another dream, one year ago, where I acquired a shamanic leather bag, a receptacle for tools, and like my vulva, a purse of secrets. In this present dream, what just awakened me, the husband asks his wife to get rid of an old leather vessel for something new. The wife believes her husband advocates the tossing out of her shamanic bag of tricks as an act of love. But, I feel, this is not true—*that it* could not be a loving act, to throw out something, which serves her work. *And wasn't my purse pinched in the fifth journey in?*

Another forewarning? Is Sarototi, who supposedly cares enough to honor me, wanting instead, to shut down this yin-like container of magic? But aren't they urging something new, to heal the women? In message form, the unconscious alerts: Big things at stake.

After five hours of sleep, I rise exhausted and hot from this latest news (and too many layers of blankets). *Where is a man or woman to help me navigate this?*

As a way of demonstrating that I honor their divination practice of throwing stones, I've brought *IChing, Runes and Tarot.* Sarototi loves each of these arts, for just as me, he is struck by the affinity between the everyday reality and the oracle's response, what Jung considered "synchronicity." For the entire day,

48: Ajumble

we settle down by the fire to explore, discovering that Sarototi is clearly in the midst of transformation. Burning Frankincense and Myrrh on a piece of coal, I administer the inhalation of this smoke, as the *IChing*, speaks about Sarototi: "Inexperience, in danger of throwing himself away." Well, anyway, he is a young laibon.

We speak further of the metamorphic images formed in my unconscious while we were apart: snake to cow, then, a baby, child of the cow, sitting on my lap. "NeLaloshwa," Sarototi conjectures, "the snake brings change, turmoil."

True, the metamorphosing from the adapted personae—*how can this not be tumultuous?* And yet, I believe this transmutation into cow is grounding. The annal entries of this time register a disturbance every single night. Don't know where to plant the feet. *Where am I? Or even, where am I going?* Do not share with him the other cast of characters: the puffy bird, the salamander. Notice: I do not divulge the apprehension that surrounds this sojourn, this *sixth journey in*.

How often have I done this—don't come clean with others? Rear back on the horse, turn toward the other direction. This aspect is where my split blows in. *What is to remain a protective, thoughtful boundary? What is sequestered into a simmering secret?* Given that the Maasai track people's thoughts—*do they know of these warnings?* How often I have done this, not named things as they are. It is the complex of where I come from, secrets held in keeping. So what rises from the dirt is the suppressed, the wiggling snake that is out of everyone else's control as well as mine.

"The snake," to Hillman, "is perhaps the most ancient and universal carrier of the genius spirit, the figure of a protective guardian, the 'genius' itself" (*The Soul's Code*). Maybe my own internal genie, that gut knowingness was helping me wiggle out from under whatever might entrap me, or remove me from my soul's determining. Yes, we often forget events not inevitable, "accidents" are often expressly dependent on one's own character of the soul. What the tides pull in and out of the wanting, the needs, the necessities to bring us into a conclusion. I had no idea; I was in preparation of doing just *that—at all cost bringing that trueness into fruition*.

"These last eight months away from your village has been extremely intense. My brothers, mother, and I closed our family home, our parents' collective accumulations of fifty years."

"It's okay, NeLaloshwa, to feel this loss. The good news is," Sarototi assures, "we have picked out land for you in the Highlands. We want you to stay as family."

Tears of liquid love course down my cheek. "Thank you!" I feel treasured, cared for. *Why do I not share my strong congruent base in Santa Barbara, the nurturing home of Casa d'Irene? Is my distraction the longing to be kissed as Sleeping Beauty filled with the unconscious potion?*

Sarototi's father alights to our conversation. "We like you, NeLaloshwa. Are you going to stay for good? Or are you going and never coming back?"

Only now, as this is written can I hear, can I take in—even, at this time, they were having doubts about a return. So consumed with being accepted, loved, brought within the fold of their community, I do not listen to his awareness of this inner hesitation.

Today, I pull the Tarot that represents ruin, a reflection of the negative thoughts that circled about me Tuesday and Wednesday. A ricochet of what's in portent. On the second draw: fortune, releasing me of this heavy negativity. The *IChing* reminds me that I am a traveler traveling through, just on retreat, "It's ok, not to know all."

Each day the men flock to me, (some even walk from the village). They want to have a Tarot reading for their sons, their wives. What is fascinating is that they understand the universal symbolism of the imagery of each card. Jung once wrote, *Homo Sapiens* have the same collective unconscious without regard to race or creed. So, as in dreams, here, with the Tarot-ed illustrations, we find common ground, not to mention this gives them such pleasure!

For himself, Baba (Papa) Sarototi, draws strength, which he needs for his next projection of the "hanged man." I do not investigate where he feels hung. Instead, reply, "You are to let go, surrender whatever you're struggling with, to your God, Engai!"

To me, this is positive, for the Norse god Odin, as a sacrifice of himself to himself, hung upside down from the world tree, Yggdrasil, for nine days and nights, until he gained the wisdom he needed to understand the Runes, claiming: "Then I was fertilized and became wise; I truly grew and thrived. From a word to a word I was led to a word, from a work to a work I was led to a work." For in all of us there is a need to hang ourselves upside down surging the brain with the lifeforce of blood, to die to, to throw out the whole kit and caboodle of

48: Ajumble

some old paradigm (maybe even the old leather satchel from my dream) which no longer serves, rebirthing into the fulfillment of an inner inkling.

"Yes, this is true, NeLaloshwa," Baba Sarototi affirms, "a true surrender is necessary for this moment. Ashe. Thank you."

Lalalana runs into stagnation, leading into a stately king energy sitting calmly about a rough sea. Habibi is anxious for his wife Lulani. The "waning moon" appears. "A dark passage is ahead. Pray!"

"Can you cure her?" Habibi queries.

"I'll shake my rattle, to place Lulani in an alpha-theta state (out of her thinking mind) so she can bring forth her own innate sense of knowing, the natural cure from within." We all decide I must go to her at the manyatta. On behalf of the Ancestors, I carry that "old" curative bag of sage, essential oils, Bach remedies, indigenous medicines. Women request. Men affirm. The reins have loosened. Trust.

Before bed, the goddesses Hathor and Isis assist me with all the details about Sarototi and Marjana: their cheap flights to the USA, their visit to the "Gathering in the Name" event, to Casa d'Irene, for dinners and talks at schools. I hear: "Trust the universe." I wonder if Lmakiya will join us as well.

Finally, Sarototi's sleeping draft has simmered long enough inside the body, so I drop down low. Oddly enough, he has lifted the sting of the nightmare. *And yet, what of our good intentions?*

49

MIDDLE OF MY MUDDLE

"Abandon hope, all ye who enter here."
—Dante Alighieri, *The Divine Comedy*

    After this uneasy week, at least, for a night, the unconscious world lies dormant. By afternoon, lying on a foldout hammock, reading, napping under the trees, listening to the Katunga River gushing by, I am fed with new energy for my lifework: kicking around the title for the praying mantis book, *Mantis @ Play in the Sands of the Kalahari Desert*, reflecting about *The Amduat: The Egyptian Book of the Dead*, their ancient view of the afterlife, Osiris' act of dying until sunrise, his resurrection. The shamanic trance of the Bushmen is like this; one passes out, as if a death, following the ropes to God, moving from one dimension to another for information, returning with advice which in turn recovers a patient, restores a Self, reorients, resurrects the community.

    Marjana is quiet these days. No longer the "much" needed interpreter. On former visits, I have been the center of everyone's attention: to name, to recover

49: Middle of My Muddle

the flow, to mend the girl of Laloshwa Highlands, NeLaloshwa. Their work has surely drawn to a conclusion.

In the village, as a laibon now, Sarototi figures more important after the *fifth journey in*. Even though he has risen in stature, I observe his continued kindnesses to his wife, Kisima and his boys. And back at our camp, each night, he walks me to the tent. His desire to enter rises with our approach. *Do I allow him?*

In the morning the warriors collect wood and water while I play with the Tarot. Pull the "work" card for us and we laugh for they sweat hard today. Inspired from his draw, twenty-two-year-old Nkoyiak announces to the Chief, "I desire to have a wife, yet, with a dead mother and an old father, there is no one to negotiate this for me, can you help me?"

Chief Ole Wangombe responds, "Asking me, is finding the balance, just as the card speaks."

Marjana taxis us to the manyatta. I give the children bananas, which they show their delight dancing round about us. Under the hot sun, help Habibi, Kisima, Sarototi, and his sister in the cornfield cutting stalks. Taste the delicious kernels. Do not admit to Sarototi that I secretly observe him: his body, black from the sun, young, strong, lithe, as he cuts corn, talks, laughs, speaks to his wife endearingly. His sister, who seems cold, calculated, tests me. I'm not daunted.

Acknowledging, since I've been included amongst them, being alone may not be as acute for me, yet, still, I don't fit into their groove. In fact, I will never truly be a Maasai, not by skin, hair, ways, nor language, nor have I passed through their official rites of circumcision. This reality must be discussed with Sarototi. For even in my own society, as an unusual renegade, who doesn't do it "right," I barely fit, always the "other," always a loner.

In other words, a dung hut, a Maasai name won't make the difference, and certainly marriage won't. I won't ever "belong." What I most fear here is being a second-class citizen. Girls, even married woman, are considered thus. *That* marriage certainly cannot render dissipation to this searing lonesomeness I often feel. Too restless, I might come and go one month at a time, build something different than, or similar to, and as warm as theirs. However, no matter where I perch—loneliness seeps in. For one way or another, I don't belong. Not here, not there, not anywhere. Even in fashion, I didn't belong; I didn't go to the "in" parties—always an outlier. Mostly, I must confess, I want to be loved, thought of, considered, taken care of, as I would care for another.

Book One – Across the Divide to the Divine

Part II: The Divide

Kisima and I walk back to her dung hut. With a cup of tea, she comforts my headache, which has rolled in from the heat and dehydration. I dialog with their second child, Marpenzi, whose name means "beloved." He is five and can count to ten in English and can sing his ABC's. Yieyo, Sarototi's mother, with her hands playfully sifting through the different colored beads Global Voice has gifted, discusses with me (I think) the jewelry they'll make for the men's trip to America. Sarototi returns to administer another herb to me, as Kisima stands faithfully beside him. Sweet. I love her. Perhaps, I'm in love with their love of one another. For I just love, love.

Then it's time for me to administer herbs. To draw forth the natural rejuvenating capacities inside Habibi's wife, Lulani, I rattle, riding the thermals with my guides. Jackie translates what I see. The Kitomini wives are so fascinated, the *engang* has become crowded, yet they remain respectfully silent. Inside, trapped in her lungs, is grief and loss. For from this new marriage to Habibi, she has become separated by distance from her Naromi family. What I cannot miraculously remove is the distance, nor can I integrate her into this new family.

Instead, the guide, Big Chief Bear Eagle Elephant advises simple measures to ease the grief and loss: a Bach remedy and the inhalation of eucalyptus globulus in steam form to clear her lungs, placing her head under a shuka to inhale deeply. Perhaps, due to the insight given, the women, who have now heard of her pain will step in, love her, listen to her, become her sisters, mothers, grandmothers.

Via the Land Rover, we are shepherded back to our little village to rest. In the middle of the muddle, in this little pup tent, I descend into the reading of Dante's "Inferno" for the preparation of a future class. Before I left, my mother, a positive woman, a prayer warrior, grabbed my hand and shockingly said, "All of life is a nightmare." Someone I love trusts me enough to reveal the hell beneath her feet! "It was as if sharing her terror not only did not add to, but even halted, his (my) own" (van der Post). Maybe this is why I've come to Africa, to move away from the fear humans make of their own condition, the "isms," and the groups that often gang up against others, who are different, who don't look or act like them.

Jung always encourages, keep individuating, into your own personality. Beware of being submerged within a group, lost, without your own personality or will. *And now, in the sixth journey in, will I find even here, the group can become the inferno, which threatens to keep the spirit, the soul underground? Is this what I will learn?* Codes within our "isms" our systems, our religious institutions even

49: Middle of My Muddle

within our families, hold conditions, state: "these cannot be broken." "Oh, you cannot say this or that." "Oh, you cannot believe this or that." "This is the right way." "This is the only way." We cannot hide from "isms." They exist and can control and harm.

The truth is, within, there are unwritten laws, unchangeable, invisible. We can only become aware of them as the inferno, the *calcinato*, burns off the dross, testing us, until we are shot out of the shoot of the group perception, to individuate again and again, becoming more and more our true selves. The mantis—appearing dead, floating in a cup only to reawaken again on the surface of my journal as she did on that first safari in, when Mother so astutely discovers her born anew—reminds. Do not abandon hope!

50

PREY TO A LEOPARD

"Your eye is so wise It keeps turning, turning Needing to touch Beauty. It keeps turning, Needing to find a mirror That Will caress you As I."

—Hafiz

In my attempt to be wise, to save money, I have sent Marjana back to Nairobi earlier than planned. *What was I thinking?* Not recognizing the precariousness of this decision, he leaves his half-brother, Lekishoni, in charge of translation for me. Do not know at the time, he speaks twenty words of English. *Why didn't I interview him?*

At breakfast, I learn the noisy neighbor of last night had not been a Baboon. Instead, she was an antelope, a Bushbuck, in fear for her life. (How little I know of the cries of the forest animals.) To protect myself, I had set a lamp out on the front porch—lighting a way for her vulnerable self, as she ran in and out of our camp while the best stalker of all the big cats, a male leopard, just inside our kitchen, sat waiting. *More than the reverie, is this the real metaphor of the day?*

50: Prey to a Leopard

For Hillman nudges me onward: "Follow the image!" *Am I the prey then? Innocent, defenseless, alone, representative of the vulnerable, target on my ass just as the Bushbuck? Or do I play further with the word prey, and pray to a leopard? Or pray for the bushbuck? Or pray like mad for my safety?* I must be, in other words, "game." Am I game for being gamed? Apparently, in this dimensional Africa, in this animistic landscape where the veils are dropped, not only in dreams, every one of its creatures speak, roaring up the epistle.

In an unusual consultation with the *IChing* there is an indication that the suspicions of my relationship with the Maasai is underscored with the "decline of." *In other words, do I politely decline further assistance? Or is our relationship gradually deteriorating? Our need of one another, dissolving? Diminished? The Tarot informs me the work is nearly done. Then what am I doing here? Oh right, healing a past life, building a healing center! Or am I?*

By the river, on a blanket, Sarototi and I read from a lesson book, talking in bits and pieces of Kiswahili and Maa words. He laughs at my tongue-twisted attempts at their language. Teach him English. At one point, he indicates a shared nap in my tent. Reply in Maa, "*Mayiolo.*" "I don't know."

Flirting around the edge, as honestly, I'm taken with him. Yet I don't want to acquire him as husband or intimately receive him. My longing is not obscured. His longing eats up the field. Luckily, he falls asleep. I don't. Instead, I rattle and float into the shamanic realm for answers: Inside this magical forest of the Lost Child everything is medicinal—the tree bark, the soil with their plants and flowers, the rocks with their minerals and microbes, the sky, the stars, the sun, the moon, the rain, the river, the creatures. Bat educates me: Due to their relationship with nature, *this* tribe believes *they* are complete.

When the Alpha-Theta state ends, notice both legs are covered in ants. Jump up and run lightly flinging them off. Only one bites me. The lesson: to trust, but I do not. Or perhaps they are furthering this red alert: *Move. Take care of yourself. Get out of the situation. You're playing with fire, NeLaloshwa.* A bit disappointed that the ants must continually remind, teach, I head back to my tent alone.

By early evening, Sarototi's divination stones declare, "I can trust your herbs, NeLaloshwa." This acknowledgment pleases me.

Finally, to the seven Warriors, I express the ramifications of *9/11*, the poisoning, the dust in the chest, the wheezing, the heavy metals. Twice, I paint a picture of several past life regressions with Mariah, of Deborah's soul-retrievals and the breaking of the family curse, the training with Valerie and Deena, and those interactions with Mundadisi, their newfound friend. Each time I attempt

Part II: The Divide

this conversation, the Maasai respond: "Each of these people figure as bad dreams, we'll protect you from them."

I don't comprehend their words, so I begin to explain how much these relations have meant. But the imbalance of elements in the body from *9/11*, occupies their minds. They discuss the ramifications of the lead, the uranium as representations of these energies of others around me. "No." I determinedly state. "Those who surround me in support, are not nightmares or chemicals. They are *laibons* like Sarototi." *Is it as Calasso once penned?* — "When two shamans met, it was never clear what would happen. [...] But neither could be trusted" (*The Celestial Hunter*).

Persisting, the Maasai delve into the validity of the other shamans' energies circling about me in America. I've always assumed they are comforting and supporting me up until now. *Perhaps, not?* "These laibons," they explain, "are jealous of you, NeLaloshwa." *Is this what I was experiencing with Mundadisi in the spring?* With emphasis, Sarototi declares, "They're jealous of your relationship to the dream, to the herbs, and to us."

How can this be? They are all so talented in their own right. They have a following. *What do I have that they don't?* I know in some ways, I'm a maverick. Fly off on my own. Hold my own beliefs. Don't stay underneath people long enough to be the perfect disciple. Perhaps this is disconcerting to others. I've dipped in and out of studying with many of these people—but most of them have come from harsh schools of shamanism—this doesn't often resound with me. But still, I don't tell the Maasai of our mutual friend, Mundadisi, of the flying tomahawk, of the sore in the spleen. That he is in a way, the metaphor of the "other," my opposite, the prevailing shadow within that I must dance with into the fullness of myself.

Just as we learned of the Guru's lineage above—many years later it would be revealed—that John of God and Bikram sexually abused some of their followers. *Was I being warned, not to place myself fully into other people's hands, protected from the humanness of others?* Nor had I forgotten the way Deena had challenged me, nor of one of the teachers from the Four Directions yelling at me for being late from lunch. "Something must be wrong with you," she barked, "if you go unconscious, falling asleep, and miss our meeting." I turned on her, "How can you say that when you know nothing about me? That I'm tired. That I've just finished twenty-four hours of classes in three days at Pacific Graduate Institute." *How could she know that that unconsciousness, that falling asleep was my access to something greater than myself and was even possibly restoring me?* That this was necessary for me. That looking out had been my modus operandi, and this looking in was entirely new—and holy, as well as wholly, more important.

When I had arrived at the Four Winds retreat, I was thrilled that one hundred people were there to participate. For I knew they had classes all over the world. Wow! What a different earth this will be. However, what I didn't confess to her was that the night before, in my hotel room had been horrible. I could sense all the energies of the people who had come to the event with their undifferentiated selves, with wants and needs. Many people had not done any kind of inner psychological work. This lack of personal knowledge concerned me; because where we aren't clear with these powers, we can be destructive (as I've seen from my own engagements). And besides, eerily, I had even felt a hand reach for me from under the bed. Yes, things were out of control, off-kilter!

What strikes me now, years later, is that I wasn't trusting in my own knowingness, staying in the Secret Garden growing quiet, and for that reason, I was out and about looking for something from others—co-opting—and therefore, experiencing a strong reaction. *If I'm not being completely true to me, does it appear as if I'm withholding from them? Does this cause jealousy? Rage? Frustration?* Yes, turning and turning, Hafiz reminds, in that ever and ever search for beauty.

51

DO NOT TAKE A GIFT OF COW LIGHTLY

⚔ ⚔ ⚔

"Soul-making is like any other imaginative activity. It requires crafting…"

—James Hillman

What worries me is if these other shamans are jealous of me—*what of the Maasai?* Stranger still that during the *fifth journey in*, the Chief and Baba Budhya had demonstrated to Mundadisi— "We're not playing with you. We've tasted the herbal ash that will protect you. You're even safe from us." They have never done this for me. Of course, I remind myself, he is a man (and this is a patriarchal society), a practicing shaman, yet something is wrong with this picture. Whereas the status of Mundadisi from Zimbabwe is accorded and not examined, at this very moment, mine is still being negotiated.

Around the fire, an intense conversation arises among the men, making me wary and pensive. The interpreter Lekishoni, the young twenty-year old

51: Do Not Take a Gift of Cow Lightly

half-brother of Marjana, announces: "NeLaloshwa, the cow you are to be given tomorrow from Chief Ole Wangombe is on behalf of your marriage to his nephew."

What else can they do, when I keep exclaiming: "I want a husband?!"

Without thinking, I rise from the wooden stool, before the Senior and Junior Elders, to defend myself: "What are you saying about matrimony? If this is what you speak of, know that I feel cared for, as I, for Sarototi. He is my dear friend. However, I do not believe it proper for us to marry within the customs of your society nor of mine. Besides, my father has not given permission for such an act." Noting, clearly in the back of my mind, Dad can no longer speak. *But wouldn't Sarototi already know this?*

Don't get me wrong. I love Sarototi. Love what he did for me. Love what we share together. *But do I love him enough to be married to him?* Reflect on Marjana's words during my last trip here, "Don't worry! It's not about marriage." But I'm worrying. Here, all of a sudden, I don't feel safe enough to negotiate!

"Lekishoni has misinterpreted our meaning, this is about herbs." Chief Ole Wangombe reassures me. *Oh, a slip of the tongue?* "This rite would determine you an equal to the laibon. You can then medicinally treat Sarototi." *Is this the female version of the protection ceremony they did for Mundadisi?*

In other words, this passage is a big deal. I'm not *just* a *sangoma*, a *laibon* (as Philani, the Sungoma from Swaziland, and later, Sarototi had confirmed the *fourth journey in*), but I'm also able to cure the shaman who doctored me— this is the black belt of shamanism. But *still!* I'm not really listening to Philani— he meant, "not through herbs, but through books!" *What's really happening here? Is this just a miscommunication? Or are they really talking about tying a binding knot?*

"Good. For I do not believe my father would approve." I reply firmly, as an ace in the hole from an elder's viewpoint, which they might respect. "Today," I continue, "a letter from the teacher at your school arrived for me, addressed, Mrs. NeLaloshwa Wangombe. Why is this so?"

"After our first meeting (that *first journey in*), when you walked through our manyatta," the Chief enlightens, "we sat down together, pondering: 'What name do we give her?' We all agreed, Wangombe. *You*, NeLaloshwa, have been stepping through Maasailand inside the protection of my family name, Wangombe."

Stunned. *Why are they just telling me this now? A privilege?* So I was named twice, secretly without my consent, as a Wangombe, then, secondly, in a

Book One – Across the Divide to the Divine

formal ceremony, as NeLaloshwa Wangombe. *Was Sarototi even way back then, in an assertion, staking his claim on me? Is this their conventional procedure into adulthood—the next step— marriage?*

"To have been given your name, I am honored. Ashe! Thank you! However…"

"The ceremony tomorrow," he interrupts, "is to elevate *you*, NeLaloshwa Wangombe, as Sarototi's equal, as laibon, to administer herbs to him." When the Chief speaks, it is set forth!

Before dinner, inside the private tent, I'm so honored by this black belt; I crazily trust them once again inhaling their extractions of plants through hot steam under the *shuka*, preparing me, raising me to this new level. The chest is soothed. I grow calm, completing this priming, bathing the body with the same mixture. Afterwards, I find the men still gathered, whispering around the fire. Thuka, the cook, serves me tea.

Assembled over a quiet meal, I feel relieved, endeavor to accept Chief Ole Wangombe's words. Yet, my corps trembles lightly. *Is it the new herb, or plain ole fear, or the butterfly shaking out of the cocoon forging novel frontiers?* Cannot be sure. The night before, I yelled, "Shut up!" to the Bushbuck running for her life. *Am I screaming at the vulnerable in me?* "Just be quiet!" *Had she remained silent, would the leopard have searched for other prey?* Of *The Peregrine*, Baker pens, "If I were too afraid, I am sure I should see him more often. Fear releases power." I keep insisting to myself—keep this fear at bay. But just as the falcon, just as the leopard, Sarototi keeps circling back.

I've forgotten Sarototi is just a reflection of meeting Pluto within my Seventh House, meeting Moira, or Fate through those I partner with, and in that, my own sense of powerlessness. For me with Mars under the covers, hidden in Venus means it often manifests as sexual entanglements dominated by the other. "Naturally it is not really the other who is all these things, but rather, a deity, a primeval power in life which one perceives via the other," Liz Greene reiterates. And this "terrifying other," appearing as Mundadisi, as Sarototi "forces us (me) to accept the uncivilized face of nature as a necessary ingredient of experience […] disguised as partner, lover, friend, or 'public' […] if that deep Other did not abide somewhere within" (*Astrology of Fate*). Though the psychoanalysts and the shamans will open my ears and eyes into this awareness, it will take me years (and into Book Two with *The Invisible Dane I Love*) to come to terms with this projection onto my partners.

51: Do Not Take a Gift of Cow Lightly

For me, here, Sarototi, figures as the "black man" in dream form, my opposite, the masculine animus within. As I am for him the "white woman" his opposite, the feminine anima, which lies inside his unconscious, making him believe, he is meant to marry *this*. We are the embodiment of the yin and yang. A countertransference. He is my syzygy--the sun to this moon of mine. In a way, we are right, we are meant to marry this "other"—but as I said before, "not in the way you imagine, Sarototi!" For repair. Instead, in an inner way, this is, in fact, our need, to embrace the goddess of Necessity, Ananke, just as Hillman conjectures, "a physically oppressive tie of servitude to an inescapable power." Whether we like it not, Fate— "she" who has become so unpopular, "so offensive" according to Liz Greene—draws Sarototi and me into a necessary relationship with her. In other words, we were meant to meet. *But am I meant to be outwitted into marriage?*

The deflection of these internal interrogations turns instead to business issues and what the Chief wants versus those true feelings of mine—so familiar, familial. Once again, I fawn, allowing someone to lull me into silence for just a moment, because the appearance is, they are acknowledging those talents of mine, patting that ego on the back. Nonetheless, everything in me registers as the Bushbuck last night, on high alert, panting. This time, it's not a lumbering elephant snitching food. Instead, there's a Leopard in my kitchen! And "*Here, am I,*" supposed to be crafting the soul into that writer!

Book One – Across the Divide to the Divine

52

WRINKLED IN TIME

"Trust is the most joyous kind of bond with another living being. But isn't it true that whenever we enjoy being with someone, there is a factor of risk there, and also a factor of trust, which gives our enjoyment an edge of rapture?"

—Alphonso Lingis, *Trust*

After dinner, I crawl into the dark private tent just as I used to crawl into my childhood closet for serenity, safety. Here, I ponder the longer than, larger than life, day. *Are the herbs they gave me tonight, and the cow, which the Chief is to grant me, setting me forward?* Trust. Do not question, NeLaloshwa, I reprimand, then remind myself: The bath, the ritual is to place me on par with Sarototi, to mete out medicines back and forth, in harmonious equality—the gold medal in shamanism. *But what if they are only binding me once again?*

What we don't know about healing is how much is needed per incident. On Western time, on the Midwest front, in losing my sense of identity, it was as though the forest fell down around me in every conceivable direction. *What of its impact? Have I recovered?* And then this Madeleine L'Engle's A Wrinkle in Time moment drops me into the Maasai's consciousness, their timelessness. *Am I trapped in Fairyland, never to return?*

The question is (and notice I do keep internally questioning in this *sixth journey in*): *Whom do I trust? Whose voice will I listen to? My guides? Bat? Big Chief Bear Eagle Elephant?* Forgive me for reevaluating—*but who can I count on? Is perchance the better idea: If I call on all of them, does it help? If the work is done with Deborah, Sarototi, Mundadisi, Alberto, Deena, Valerie, the Maasai, does the jealousy cancel out? Is not this a mirror image of something in me—a very large and looming Jungian projection of my own incapacity to trust myself? A mandate from childhood circles, test,* "Try the spirits, whether they are from God." (1 John 4:1)

Now that they are not clamoring to save me, and I've come on my own—all is akimbo. They have made me (and I have allowed them) to think I belong here and in actuality—I do not. *Was a kind of spiritual colonialism of wanting what they have, biting me back?*

At nine-fifteen, as these interrogations are being written in the evening pages, Sarototi strides onto the wooden veranda of this private closet. *Does he want to explain? Implore?* He stands outside. Just a green canvas and one zip separates us. I go silent. I don't answer. We may be connected, but I don't want a one nightstand, nor do I want to be his wife, certainly not owned, nor do I want to change our friendship. But whether we want it to or not, our relationship has altered from healer/healee. *Where do we go from here?*

Trust. And yet, in the West, where two people are drawn to one another, it would be two zips, maybe three (the tent, the jeans) and we're on!

53

THE LAIBONI CEREMONY—WEDLOCKED

"We often discover with Americans that they are tremendously unconscious of themselves. Sometimes they suddenly grow aware [...] and then you get these interesting stories of decent young girls eloping with Chinamen or with Blacks, because in the American that primitive layer, which with us (the European) is a bit difficult, with them is decidedly disagreeable, as it is much lower down. It is the same phenomenon as 'going black' or 'going native' in Africa."

—C. G. Jung, *The Collected Works*

Seventy-five years ago, in the mid-Twentieth Century, when Jung wrote this, some would have qualified me as, I'd "gone native." Though I won't be eloping, "*Here, am I,*" not knowing, soon, I'll certainly be wedlocked. But even so, whether they had named me or not, whether I would be married to

53: The Laiboni Ceremony—Wedlocked

Sarototi or not, I wouldn't become "native," because I would never really be "Maasai." Yet, what's more important here is, Jung is challenging my lack of awareness. Warning me, that the lack of knowing my roots, those instinctual parts of the self, my own "primitive" beginnings—Jung meant this primitive to be "psychologically," not savagely, as he had deep respect for the Africans he had met—and because of this, I would be vulnerable and easily swayed.

For over eleven hours, I've slept—miraculously by myself. However, as I become conscious of back cramps, note: I'm lying in a pool of menstrual blood.

At breakfast, announce: "I won't be going to the *manyattta* or the school today. Must sit by the fire on behalf of all the women of the world." Monthly, this shared practice of late, has become a part of the menses ritual. While seated before the cracking flames, attending to this reverent space, a bat flies in and out of the pergola. *Is it my old friend, Bat, coming to aid me?* According to Ted Andrews, the encounter of bat is symbolic of transition, the loss of one's faculties, unwary about change, holds the promise of rebirth, and the coming out of darkness into initiation. Oh, so à-propos for this moment.

During this honorarium to the feminine, I invoke the goddesses, the female ancestral line of aunts, grandmothers, mother, throwing the *IChing* about Sarototi: "inexperience (in danger of throwing himself away) changing to eighteen, repair. (Red flag!)"

In the dailies I write: "To be honest, he engages me—attracted by his personality and his body. Take great pleasure in our friendship, our shared dream life. Our spiritual connection is of a nature that I have never experienced before. When he walks me to the tent every night, he looks at me with those eyes. I love Sarototi for what he did for me, for what we share. *But do I love him enough to marry him?*"

Amid this reverie, Sarototi joins me at the warm hearth. As I listen to my divinatory practice, Sarototi, through Lekishoni's interpretations, urges me to toss the coins of the IChing for him. He is warned: "Pay attention to detail. Make no ambitious undertakings—instead, remain at a steady pace." His Tarot cards track his history as Hierophant: *Does his want of me place his role as high priest in a precarious position?* His present ushers in the winds of change. "Which way have you chosen to slice your sword?" I investigate, "For ill, or good will, and clarity?" Today, his future lies in a certain counterpoise of opposites—fire and water. "Your forecast is," I assert, "that your emotions may overwhelm you." *Is this his love of the "us" and me?*

Book One – Across the Divide to the Divine   377

Part II: The Divide

When Lekishoni departs, suddenly, surprisingly Sarototi grabs me, pulling me towards him. In this intimate nature, he has never touched me before. Of course, he hugs me when I arrive or depart. Once, he even rubbed oil on my neck and shoulders. This time, however, I resist his groping with complaints of pain. In response, he rubs my back and head, kindly caring for these menstrual cramps. It does not feel good—to be touched, uninvited and is certainly out of place.

At the time, I don't realize that being touched was challenging for me due to the past. Of my ex-husband and me, our friend Clair once said, "it's strange, you never sit next to one another with his arm draped over you. You walk in the room and choose opposite seats, not the couch." I will not understand for years that I could have sex; my body could long for that kind of touch. But intimacy, someone touching my skin on a daily basis, I will discover was hard for me. *Had I pushed my first husband away for that reason?* No wonder I would live alone for over twenty-five years between husbands. It would take me that long to heal from the sexual wound.

In the end, Sarototi cannot be satisfied. For, I won't budge, won't allow him into the dark womb-like tent. I withstand this temptation, remaining at the fire. As I draw the Tarot's "Fool" for me, I agree, I truly stand on the precipice, belonging nowhere, but with an infinite future, tied to the origins of life. *What could be more fitting than this card?*

Finally, in the mid-afternoon, the grand *laiboni* ritual transpires. Oddly, the negative has been forgot. Excited, prepared, and proud, I've ceremonially dressed in the multi-colored Maasai regalia from head-to-toe, even my sandals are decorated with their beads.

In the meadow, Chief Ole Wangombe and Baba Budhya prepare five little fires. Though the grass is dry, these remain magically in their place, unlike the ferocious flames in California, which devastatingly overtake, burning down entire forests and neighborhoods. Nearby, Baba Sarototi, Lalalana, Habibi, Nkoyiak, and Lekishoni hold the sacred space. *Where are the women? Where is the rest of the village?* They were with me when named, when thanked for the corn thresher, and when I brought Mundadisi.

Strangely, they instruct me to proceed behind Sarototi as he treads between the flames. Olivia Newton John's voice reverberates: "I'll walk through fire for you." Yes, I'd walk through the fire with him or for him. *"Here, am I"*, however, following. Not quite the position I wanted to be in. As he succeeds me, a scene

53: The Laiboni Ceremony—Wedlocked

from the movie, *Monsoon Wedding* flashes—Aditi red-roped and tethered to Hemant, as she brings up the rear—this is not a step into coequality. OMGosh! I've been united in holy wedlock! Shanghaied again!

At the end of the flames, the Chief victoriously smiles, sprinkling an herb on the hands of Sarototi and me. "Lick these twice with your tongue," he instructs, "then rub them on your foreheads."

Call it intuition, call it knowingness—*whatever*—despite their protestations to the contrary, in that usual Neptunian fogged state of mine, I've tacitly entered into a binding contract of an "arranged" marriage. The ceremony informs me that the spell of healer/healee is broken into our equality—*Did it also release the protective shield around me?* Suddenly, a sleight of hand, we are equals and yet, inside this supposed movement of soul regarded as interchangeable to their *laiboni* ceremony—arises, instead, a game of domination. Never once were my feelings considered, nor was I asked if I wanted to be married. I feel betrayed, discouraged. And I'm in the middle of that menses!

Panic! So I pop out of my body into the mind scanning the myriads of research I've done. In Africa, the Kalahari San Bushmen's daughters are warned during menarche not to be around men, nor their hunting, as though this sanguine fluid is a form of pollution. In West Africa, the blood of a "forbidden" during menses, childbirth, or defloration——is a vehicle for vitality, strength of power for the taker. (Uh, oh! We're back to the warning instructions of the Aboriginal, White-Painted Skeleton Man: "Tell her: It's about power!")

I figure—white, uncircumcised, non-traditionally initiated, American, and most certainly, off-limits—the perfect accessory of a taboo breaker. Yes, to go against what is prohibited is to gain potency. "Lions and tigers and bears, oh my!"

Historically, with either virgin, aunt, sister, niece, mother, or "other"—kings, chiefs, warriors enacted the ritual of sex to secure their place in the realm, to win the battle, to kill the marauding lion. What Laura Makarius described as "the magical violation of prohibition." *Am I kidnapped again, reenacting that former history with the Maasai inside Freud's repetition compulsion past life, present life?*

Dauntingly scary. I must be in the Middle World, a place, Villoldo enlightens, known to be full of bamboozlers, where shamans negotiate with their Ancestors hanging in a Purgatorial dimensional balance. I've become barter,

Book One – Across the Divide to the Divine **379**

fodder. Someone is very thirsty or hungry over there, across that divide. *Am I the libation for the gods?* So, once again, I must greet Mantis, the trickster.

As if Church gongs announcing our nuptials, the "ding a ling a ling" of the cattle bells calls me back into the extraordinary. After the young boys push the herd past us, I discover an Eagle feather smashed to the ground, the very essence of his illuminative spirit that punctuates this rite of passage. Of course, I reach for it. I must press the mixture of their totems: the Eagle and the Bull into the pages of my confidential memoirs that are no longer so very private and are, now, highly embarrassing, dear reader.

Proudly Chief Ole Wangombe announces, "From me, receive your cow, your ox, Pakitank." He sweeps his hand to gesture. "You deserve him, NeLaloshwa. Now, you are part of my family." *Didn't he say yesterday I already was—family? Giving me his name the first journey in?*

Lalalana leads forth their prized *Pakitank*. All eyes on me, I pet this new possession. "Wow, sweet!" *Do not look this gift cow in the mouth!* So, trying not to be impolite, I gently probe Lekishoni, "What of this cow?"

"Lovers with Sarototi." *Is this official?*

The elders, the Chief, Baba Budhya and Baba Sarototi disappear to the village leaving me with the virility of these young men. Immediately after, Sarototi grabs my wrist, points at the tent, "Sleep. Sleep." He says. As I shake his hand off, yanking my wrist away from him. For I know he means—sex! His gift to me, a colorful beaded bracelet, tumbles to the ground. "No!" I shout, as I bend down to recover the jewelry. Then, I angrily walk away. The Bush-buck stops here! *Or does she?*

As I quickly dial Marjana on the satellite phone, the eagles are circling—*surely it doesn't mean they're affirming this, does it?* "Is this...true," my voice cracks, tears burst silently, "that...Sarototi is my husband?"

"No, this ceremony is a declaration that you are a member of my family." Reiterating the familiar but questionable line. *Wasn't that established in the naming rite—NeLaloshwa Wangombe?*

And Marjana—*Is he stuck between the community, his cousin's runaway desires of elopement, his father's provision for his people, my concerns, and his responsibilities?* Though he has warned Sarototi and told me in various odd ways to resist, he remains tugged between his work with P&P, his commitment to me as a client, the expectation to return me safely to the airport versus his family's wants. He cannot risk, me, being unhappy. Nor ignore the needs of his tribe.

53: The Laiboni Ceremony—Wedlocked

"Just want to be in right relation, Marjana. Concerned, not sure this path is for me—afraid our relationship might be damaged."

"That won't happen NeLaloshwa!"

So I arrive home whole, have I just put on my Sunday best, my adaptive social skills from the Paola Country Club? Frozen. I comply. Inside the big unconscious is the too familiar, leaping over the gap and falling right into the middle of the inflammatory fires of the past.

By SAT phone, reach out to the youngest brother, middle child. Although, too chicken to tell him, I need to hear his voice. The information he provides—"Mom is not so happy at the assisted care living. She is confused, as Dad no longer knows her name. However, she's excited, for tomorrow our older brother brings his children to visit." The conversation grounds me. Yet, the truth of a marriage between a Maasai and me remains a secret.

Telephone Jeffrey, "What am I to do?"

"Are you sure about this Murphy?"

"Absolutely not."

"Whatever you do, don't tell your family. They most certainly won't understand."

Here, were the dividing lines. My own biracial friend knew how "white" my parents really were. Here, was where, I believe, white culture was pressing in on me. Here, I claimed my parents had educated us—but for their daughter to be married to a black man, to a Maasai, this was another concept entirely. *Would this bring shame upon them from the community? Upon me? Would I lose my respectability as a mythologist, an anthropologist?* Surely these thoughts were circling. Still, I knew in my heart, color would never stop me. It certainly hadn't stopped many others from biracial relations. So, I knew, I did not love Sarototi in a marriageable kind of way.

Recently I've thrown Walter over for a new psychotherapist, partly because the rules of PGI don't allow a professor to analyze a student, and partly because I've been going deep into the trauma, into the vulva through Pamela Madison's tantric sessions. (This venture makes Walter uncomfortable. It goes against his Jungian boundaries where no touch is allowed.) To the new psychotherapist, Mary Leibman—who believes the tantric work is necessary—I attempt to reach out. She does not answer, so I leave her a message, "Pray, light candles."

Part II: The Divide

That night, as per usual, Sarototi escorts me to the bedroom. Once again, I do not solicit an invitation. Later, he checks if my position has changed: "*Mayiolo.*" I don't know.

The wonder is—*where's that direct "no?"* I've done all this psychological and shamanic work, but the verity is—I can be conscious on one level and still deliver myself into what Greene describes as "chronic, repetitious suffering or restriction, which circles back again and again," re-igniting patterns of behavior brought on from earlier traumas. In shock of this reality, I internally box my ears: *Am I really healed? Cat got your tongue?* Most certainly!

Throw the Runes about my parents' thoughts as if I can conjure forth their voices. Dad issues forth protection. Mom stresses movement. "Keep about your work." About sleeping with Sarototi, the Runic Alphabet publishes: "The choice only taints the situation. Hold fast to what is right for you and has been in the past." I'm not sure these divinations help, because, historically, what I have chosen is to concede, "Yes" to the man. *Yeah, but was it right?* Surely this time, this can't be the solution.

However, Jung is right. I've grown into an "awareness," and according to him, I'd gone "native" just as Kurtz in Joseph Conrad's *Heart of Darkness*. His character, Marlow, believed Kurtz "had made that last stride, he had stepped over the edge, while I had been permitted to draw back my hesitating foot." And perhaps, years before, through the chronic moments of trauma, I'd already stepped over the edge with the broken taboo. That in that, I'd been other-ed, set apart and soiled. As well, these forays into Africa had other-ed me, further still.

54

FORTY WILD BUFFALO

"Mzizi sio jadi kupendwa ni bahati."
"To be loved is not through a love potion but through your good luck."

—Maasai Kanga

To the Maasai, this marriage is good luck.

On day fifteen of this safari, from ten to two, in the wee hours of the morn, in that private tent, I drift in and out of slumber. Have contracted a cold. Cannot catch my breath.

Later that morning, we hike to the village. At the *manyatta*, I have tea with Kisima. Sense she is a bit off. *Who isn't?* So, I finally leave for the outside world. Attempt a nap. However, under the tree, thousands of flies descend upon me. In parallel, matching these creatures metaphorically, the men, the Elders, Sarototi's father irritatingly tease me.

With Yieyo and Sarototi, I eat corn. Hug his grandmother, Nkoko. As they are quiet, I believe the women to be discouraged about not being able to express

Part II: The Divide

the happenings. *Where are my female interpreters Jackie and Senga when I need them?* Maybe these women know the truth and cannot possibly think what to say to reassure. *Are they upset, too? Do they know of my inner conflict?* Surely in this high-context culture, they see what is written upon my face, read my mannerism, are "listening in the air." Without safety in my interpreter, I, too, am speechless, and honestly, filled with shame.

Back at camp, I finally pull Thuka, the cook, and Sarototi aside. I want to shout, "Not by the hair of my chinny…" To the wolf, however, I am a fresh morsel, a pushover, as are the first and second of "The Three Little Pigs." Instead, I attempt strength, "…chin, chin!" With the flat of my hands pound on their chests— "Don't you both understand, this is a matter of heart. There is a distinction here. I love you, Sarototi, however, I'm not 'in love' with you."

Again, I assume Thuka' English is better, than Lekishoni, accurately conveying these sentiments the way Marjana always does. "Yes, of course," I continue, "it's natural to be attracted, to have a yen for someone, a yearning, particularly with each other, as we are passionate about listening to the Ancestors, to your God, Engai, to mine. Let's don't react so quickly. We must wait, think about this big decision."

Sarototi hankering to please, to placate, "Okay, I'll wait!" But I don't really believe him. "Meikooyu olelipong," the Maasai's proverb is more accurate, "you cannot advise a man who is after a woman." I hear Linda Howe's question permeate my surroundings: *"How could this possibly be happening to me?"*

The tug to consummate with Sarototi permeates every part of my being, barely clinging to my decree. That's the medicine he operates on. The heat, the burner sets in motion what he wants—me. *Be careful what you wish for, Murphy. I urge. Next time, you need to be more specific of what type of husband you want.*

A huge contrast looms between what the Maasai elders declare and assure me, versus what is irrefutably erupting beneath Sarototi and me. Outnumbered and female, I cannot reason with warriors, or with a determined suitor. Across the steps of the meadow, at the borders, at the edges of his desire, I survive another night alone.

Inside my head, Mother—who remained faithful to my father for some odd fifty years—words resound: "Remember, after midnight, it's hard to conjure up a 'no.'" "But how can sex with any man ever be bad?" *Is she cautioning me that after hours, the natural animal instincts arise?*

54: Forty Wild Buffalo

Within the folkways of many societies, in matrimony, there is *still* this dance between free choice versus arrangement. In what he has arranged, Sarototi is surging to possess me. Through free choice, I am rejecting him. *With these forces of dichotomy tugging to and fro, how long can this "mayiolo," this "I don't know," go on?*

A man has married me, and I don't want him. All signs until that ceremony have proved that I do. Yet, I don't. Though they gifted me the above Kanga to wrap myself in and magical tonics for the rite, Sarototi's love potions are not working. *Does he think this present non-interest is coyness, provocation as the Navajo Hok'ee might have thought?* The fear, the not knowing how to handle this situation is spinning me up and out of my body, away from what little grounding, what little solidity I have within this "me-ness." Definitely I've split off from this reality, somehow making me doubt the original wants and wishes.

Yucky. My body lies sticky in the blood of the menses and always with the monthlies, the truth strikes me on the head. This morning, the reality is: no one has brought water to wash in.

While I sort through the images, rolling in menstruation, at the entry point of our camp, the seven warriors have an early morning sighting of forty wild buffalo. Later, I will grasp why they protect me with spear—against marauding animals—and why, no water for a shower. Rats, I missed the spectacle. Wish they'd have come to get me, but I'm sure everyone was too busy quietly shielding the territory, so not to arouse the Buffalos' anger. A great trope for the feelings that rear up, bellowing forth from me.

At breakfast, Thuka, who loves to talk, continues his long storytelling. For some reason, at this moment, his style doesn't resonate. Agitated, I march off to the fireplace with book in hand, and later to the sun. Sarototi circles, a bit aggressively, persistent in his plea for sex. Shifting the energy of forty wild Buffalo and Sarototi entering the field, I slip off to bathe, wash clothes. *What else is a wife to do (just as my mother) but disappear to the laundry room?*

Since the ritual, every other interest has seemed to halt. No real hikes, little divination—just mine in desperation, and no more recordings of mythic tales. Just as the Warriors stand against the Buffalo, busily, subtly I defend, holding Sarototi at bay.

For the village, Sarototi being married to me is the perfect solution for him. Connubial bliss declares to the world they've officially repaired my injuries: No longer a girl, instead, initiated into womanhood. Two, he is rightfully due

Part II: The Divide

a second wife, both in his self-esteem among his people as "their" authorized divinator and, also, due to the necessity for another woman to bring in sons to attend to his vast herd of cattle—his herd is third in number to the Chief's and the Chief's son, Marjana's. Thirdly, he is a young buck, a junior Elder, just thirty-five.

For another reason: He seems to have been patiently waiting for me for six plus perchance two-hundred-and-fifty years. The whole tribe has noticed our bond for a long time and to them, this event is the most natural thing in the world. And the fifth, my little secret, his wife, Kisima, is hugely pregnant, uncomfortably, so, at this time, there must be little or no sex of much pleasure. And therefore, he stalks me, not as the Nazis in dreamscape, but, hungrily, as the high-backed wolf, Hok'ee, or that leopard on the prowl, with his "(long graceful) tail dangling down," symbolic "of sexuality and innate potential" (Andrews). Within the structures of their society (this is my sixth reason) there is nowhere else he wants to place his tail. Seventhly, his marriage to me, as did his work as my laibon, continues to protect me from the young virility of the warriors, establishing safety in their world. He has staked his claim. And eight, *do they imagine with child, I will bring more clients, more income to the community?*

This afternoon, there is a place Sarototi wants to show me. The young warriors, Thuka, and I hike with him across the Katunga River, to a plateau, a flat-planed rock formation. Here, we picnic. *Is this another attempt to win my heart, to court me?* As we meander home, his accomplishments, through the interpretation of Lekishoni and Thuka reveal his five-star self: "Sarototi, a successful trader, transports his cattle to fairs in Nairobi, negotiating good prices. He is an accomplished agriculturalist, planting corn and trees, caring for the forest, harvesting remedies for other medicine men throughout Kenya and Tanzania." He converses about his accomplishments, transporting me back to those dates with Wall Street men. "Within the Kitomini community, he is considered a worldly, well-traveled, thoughtful, educated man within the Maasai traditions. He lives without fear of his future." Though short (I add this in my mind) for a Maasai, he is handsome, elegant, with a large, winning smile, full of good humor. Even more so, as with Deborah, he is my counterpart in all things spiritual, where we dance in a field few can grasp.

Growing ever more edgy, try to reach out to therapist Mary on the SAT phone. This time, there is no answer, no answering machine. So, on the ethers, send forth another prayer to her: "Pray to all your guides on my behalf!"

At the fire, in a conversation with Sarototi and Thuka, I expound for them, "I was not, and am not prepared for this. Thought Sarototi's yearning to marry me was always a joke. I acknowledge we have a spiritual connection that is wildly unexplainable and grand. Nothing more." "Please wait, wait until you see my home in September. Observe how I live." "Want you to know, I'm not like this in America. Cannot be boxed in or trapped, go in and out of Kansas for the family and into Philadelphia quarterly for my braces." "Must see the sky, the world, travel. The mission takes me elsewhere, calls me forth."

He agrees, "Okay, I will wait to see your life in America." Appeasing me once again. "But what will make me very happy, NeLaloshwa, is if you agree to come and go from Laloshwa for the rest of your days."

How sweet. But the knot around my neck grows ever tighter. To have expressed the truth of how I live has taken all the courage I could muster. Part of me is relieved, and the rest is worried, for there are days to go. Still, feel held in custody, under siege, for I cannot just walk through this wily forest to the airport, nor is there a highway to thumb a ride. *Is this caged in feeling not just about me, but more to do with the collective feminine among the Maasai and which resides amongst the women throughout the world held in the power of men—the vibrational patterns of the past, the yin suffocating inside a very yang dominated culture? Is the masculine in me holding a gun to my head—the Leopard requiring a blood sacrifice of a Bushbuck?*

In verity, all along, I had the freedom and power to flee, to call Marjana to transport me to Nairobi. *Why didn't I think of that?* I could have pretended a conversation on the SAT phone, an emergency in Kansas! But to be honest, it never ever occurred to me. Maybe I was still a victim after all. *Was I afraid of surrendering? Afraid to admit things weren't "perfectly perfect" with my newfound family? Or was it downright fear? Fear. What will happen if I push the walls of this society down? What would the consequences be? If I revealed the chink, the flaw within the Maasai kingdom would it tumble? Or was it just years of habit, of silence?* No, that can't be totally true.

When I needed to, at Lee Anderson, I screamed at the top of my lungs at our Greek boss Nick, because I wanted to equal him, to match his scream at me; challenged Mary McFadden when she had confronted me in front of others at

Part II: The Divide

Saks Fifth Avenue; fired employees at Badgley Mischka; attacked a head of state at Escada; and drew swords with Randolph Duke at Halston. Even with my family when things weren't copacetic, I raised my fiery redheaded rising-sign-Leo temper. For some reason, at this moment, I had few words. Frozen in time. As if I was inside this story until I was meant to step out graciously. Sometimes that's just it—we do stay—even when it's not right, even we are being injured. It was as though there was a time allotted for this experience, these six journeys in, this particular one-month time-machined-exploration backward.

What I would grow to understand is there is a difference between being a victim, experiencing something beyond our control, bigger than ourselves (natural disasters, rape, living in a war-torn country, living under a dictator, crime, an accident, death of a loved one) and remaining in a victim mentality of everybody is "purposely doing this to me," where one is no longer hero or heroine. This mentality was what was shifting in me. I didn't want to live into *that* anymore. I was now re-imagining myself as even more than a heroine—because it was no longer about defeating anyone, nor about winning—it was now, only about being true.

Pass through another day with boundaries clearly cut, a line drawn through the long grasses. Speculate: *For what duration does my resolve stay intact and his cooperative agreement hold?* Without the taboo that naturally restrained us before in the roles of "healer/healee" there is nothing except this resolution that at times is dangerously murky, borderline at best. Even the Laloshwans around us have loosened this prohibition and now expect our union, wait for our consummation. The pressure is looming, the tension mounts with each new day.

Though not a virgin by any stretch of anybody's imagination or means—I feel virginal, fresh. Know, however, the act of sex will change the game. *Without a girlfriend to talk to, to navigate the nights' abyss, my natural longings, how can I endure the temptation? Where is Rebecca when I need her?*

In this place, far from the village, far from family and friends, the natural attraction for Sarototi does not serve me. The pull, the electrical charge supported by our interests of nature, sparked by divination, the constant search for the cure, listening to the Ancestors is a warm, feast waiting to be shared with delight. Oh, we so often want something we think is good for us, then find ourselves trapped unable to find our way out.

Though the moon is full, I hang on the cusp of a new moon about to tumble into his arms. Nothing saves me but "no," and that word, as I recall from teenager

54: Forty Wild Buffalo

days, is even more of a lure to men, creating a cat and mouse game. The forces of nature, what is natural, my ever trust-worthy friends till now, seem against me. Oh, Sarototi! "Oh, Jerry (Paul Henreid)!" Charlotte Vale (Bette Davis) purrs, "Don't let's ask for the moon. We have the stars" (Now, Voyager).

55

TRACKING MYSELF

"I unconsciously wanted to recreate the original trauma in order to rediscover myself."

—Rose-Emily Rothenberg, *The Jewel in the Wound*

For me, there are lots of reasons I don't want someone in my life right now: my mouth is changing, wearing braces and rubber bands just as a gawky teenager is not very attractive; my stomach suffers from irritable bowel—not knowing I could just ask the simple question—*What's eating me?* But clearly, I haven't brought myself to the bottom of the dark cavern within. As well, I have yet to embody who I am, what I want to be; nor have I learned how to thoroughly communicate, or to set up proper borders in order to make way for the development of my lifework. In other words, if I track myself correctly, I don't have a center core.

Not ready for marriage to anyone, let alone this man. There is still something not taken care of. To be honest, fear I still cannot hold my own with someone

55: Tracking Myself

else, might lose my way again as I did as a child, as I did in that union with my ex and especially with Renzo, "someone else's husband."

For me, the fashion career had been the literal and figurative cover-up of the past as well as the accommodation and the performance of the business aspects Father wanted—*that* very pristine public personae. For the first time in this life since writing those stories in childhood, these endeavors in Africa and working on my Ph.D. are my sole creation. I've been given a reprieve, a grace period, as well as the hard won potential to resurrect that personal legend, that predestined vocation, to develop the personality into its fullness, to march to my own drum, to live those aspirations of longing. And here, once more, I lose my center in the way any teenager might. *How can I reclaim my Self?*

Over the last six years, Sarototi's land has become a refuge from the crazy mixed-up world. The last place of shelter had been in the Kansas woods, the quiet side of childhood. In Sarototi, I found my match. *Simpatico*, sympathetic, in our organic approach to life, equal to one another in capacity and integrity, or so I thought this of us both.

Instead, after the *laiboni* ceremony, our days are held in suspension. We wait and wait for something to break. The dam of our desires for one another has been retained by the necessity to rehabilitate me, escorting me into adulthood, held in preservation by the mores of his society, and even mine. Now, only a single finger of the little Dutch boy sustains the pressure from the torrent of a flood that may sweep us to the sea.

And Sarototi? Does he think he can have the stars and the moon, as well? He has no idea if and when that dyke releases on a hot August night that our sweaty bodies of black and white might propel me further away from him on another kind of odyssey, a Murphy kind, that no one ever really understands. Of course, we cannot and of course, no one "gets" this changing factor in me. (For even I do not.) They might pretend to. Might even surrender to the idea of what I'm up to. But they didn't and don't know what I was and am up against.

Between them, Mom and Dad had a tacit understanding against my simmering rebellion—"don't *ever* say 'no' to Murphy!" And they didn't. For they were never quite sure what I might dive into. Sometimes these movements of soul cause exasperation even to my most stalwart friend, Jeffrey. Nights he stays up late, dialoguing with me, considering everything, in order to comprehend these choices. *And still, how does one track a person who wakes up one day to freely follow her heart without reason or logic or rationale, with calligraphy money and thousands of airline miles to use at will?*

56

AFTER THE WEDDING, THE LADDER BROKE:

"So long as his consciousness was itself trickster-like, such a confrontation could obviously not take place. It was possible only when the attainment of a new and higher level of consciousness enabled him to look back on a lower and inferior state."

—C. G. Jung, "On the Psychology of the Trickster"

By the fire, as if I could bring some "higher level of consciousness" to this, I spend the evening with Thuku as interpreter to Sarototi: "On the SAT phone, when I spoke with Marjana, he believes the cow is just a gift for me to be a part of the family—not marriage." On and on the night's conversation continues without Marjana, Baba Budhya, or the Chief to help us sort, navigate: "What of children?" "How and where do we live?" "How do other Maasai feel about this?" "I don't want to be attached to the *manyatta*, to live here all the time in

Part II: The Divide

the encasement of a wood and mud dung hut, need windows to look out at the trees, the landscape." As though the navigation of these questions distracts him from sex, empowering our separation further and further. "Can I really come and go?" "Am I allowed another lover?"

"When a husband is away with the cattle at the temporary *manyatta*," Sarototi responds, "sometimes he comes home to find a declaration of a warrior's spear outside the hut. A lover—this is possible." Softly he injects, "Yes, NeLaloshwa, you can be gone for two years at a time!"

For the moment, these answers seem to soothe, reassure. Actually, to be honest, he's discovered the psyche of Murphy, which is so different than NeLaloshwa. He has learned how to placate me, knows—like my parents—the perilousness of "no." However, none of this is really on my own terms. *Familial?* Yes, this conundrum of being the one woman with a group of powerful men. *Familiar?* Yes. Simone de Beauvoir's The Second Sex is what (I've) we've been relegated to and measured by all (my) our life! I'm the receptive yin, placing my protective yang to sleep, for I've certainly projected it onto Sarototi and onto so many other men. *Have I been drugged-roofied with his herbs, following Sarototi easily through the fire? How did I, who had the burners up for so long, not know I had become the person slowly being cooked?*

For six years, I've viewed this friendship with Sarototi as an unfathomable union, a kind of spiritual marriage. The fact that they are warriors, historically known as notorious thieves of cattle and wives, never occurred to me. Each time I traveled to Kenya, friends interjected, "Are you crazy, you go into Laloshwa Highlands to live with them by yourself?" Always believing, I have the capacity to make a choice about marriage. Of such attachments, deem myself free, which in their world, is very unfeminine, incorrect, unconsidered. While I write this, J.S. Bach's Brandenburg Concerto 6 plays incessantly, insistently, and to its rhythm, I hear the self chanting the inevitable, "We want what we want what we want!"—Whether it's good for us or not.

On the third night of our marriage, three times, Sarototi shows at my tent with an excuse: number one, the usual walk home; two, returning my journal that I had left by the fire; three, he returns with hot chocolate to warm me and candles to light up the night. At this, I burst out with laughter. For the first time in our history, I open the tent flaps to let him in, "Come in for a few minutes," patting the side of the bed, motioning for him to sit, for there are no chairs. "We need to talk about this."

56: After the Wedding, the Ladder Broke:

What whirls around in my head, is Mother repeating Mary Howitt's: "Will you walk into my parlour," said the *Spider to the Fly*, to the fly that has been buzzing around and around. And yet, though it is me inviting him, he is also the reverse, the spider, catching me, the fly, in his web.

What was I thinking? One cannot explain in our made-up language, nor negotiate with chemistry, nor negotiate with fire, as Ostrich had discovered. To force casualness to this little or no conversation, I put rubber bands on my braces, hoping this ugliness might push him further away. But the truth is, I'm tired, worn down from playing custodian. In the dark forest with seven Maasai warriors, after several weeks of being far away from friends and family, loneliness has curled around me.

Maybe, too, I'm right back where I started—the only way I know how to relate to a man is through sex. Do not register the *laiboni* ritual rendered me weak, without the protective veil, somehow making it impossible to say "no"—again, a reflection of the past. Suddenly, the barriers to keep sexuality out of the bargain are lifted. So, while the guardian of the boundary, Marjana, is away—without his voice of reason, sensibility, and responsibility to his job with P&P—Sarototi lunges at me. Unable to stop him—I succumb. *Or do I succumb because I am more tempted than I'm willing to admit? Or do I succumb, fawn, because it is safer that way than to flee through the forest?* I ponder, Trollope's title, *Can you forgive her? Or more importantly, can I forgive myself?*

With Sarototi's support, I had been here before, inside the womb of this tent, swooped inside a medicinal ritual curative, an initiation of a sort born into a slow movement of soul towards the dis-engagement of a career in fashion, into a purposefulness.

Now, I'm being tugged (what feels like backwards into the unknown, into African time) into the pull of the consummation of marriage and all its confinements. *Is this an illusion to the security I've been searching for, found, but now, not wanted—in fact, rejecting? Towards the remembrance of the past life of 1787, am I manifesting another incident to provoke me, to use as a catalyst for change? Is this too some form of an initiatory process?*

In *The Encyclopedia of Religion*, initiation "is to produce a radical modification of the religious and social status of the person to be initiated." Through this, he or she will become "another"—an "other." *Why do I keep feeling the need to "other" my Self?* Though I don't know it yet, I have had a desire to go across the

Part II: The Divide

divide to what had been "other-ed" in my culture—the black man. And what I had purposely "other-ed"—the yang, of which I had yet to integrate and accept in myself (and really won't until Book Two). Sometimes this "other," is what we long for—what isn't us. A butch needs a feminine sort of gal, as the color of white needs black, as red needs yellow. This need for the "other," the reach for something else, was part of the "beyond" for me, part of the cure.

Into this gaping maw of necessity, Sarototi tackles me more or less into his version of lovemaking, consisting of rapid insertion without kissing or touching of the breasts—pure unadulterated sex. The pressure has been building up so great around us, that in spite of his lack of tenderness, I still have a minor orgasm. Which is unusual and I might add, glorious for me. I should be happy about this miracle. However, I am not. Clearly, I feel my body has betrayed itself with this little leap towards pleasure. Without guilt, Sarototi manages his own "little death" in twos. On some level, the sex feels passionate and good in the way that it can be with anyone—or so Mother said.

I just try to free-fall—I back dive off the high diving board into the perfect surrender. This "sacrificial" letting go is so different for me. I, who travel by myself, organize safaris into Africa unafraid, letting myself be taken off into a sentimental, relational adventure with "the other" is absolutely, *unheard of.*

I'm confused because my body seems to want something entirely different! Yet, the inner me comprehends what *my* heart wants. In fact, I am the only one who does *know* when I full force, full out, feel in love; I wed, as I once did before and as I wanted to marry the married man, Renzo—when I didn't know he was married—for a second round!

No doubt, I must admit my culpability, the responsibility for the exchange between us in the way I let Sarototi walk me to the tent every night, freely confiding my frustrated affairs at home, the loneliness, and want of a good husband. We both fed the fire, which has stoked the flames into sexual abandonment.

Once upona once upona once upona time, the stairway towards change snapped, leaving many tribesmen of the Maasai behind in the Sudan. Tonight, the ladder breaks again, folding in on itself my resolve. In the privacy of the tent, we pass out into the never, never land of Nod enveloped in the darkness of the Sacred Forest of the Lost Child.

57

AN ELEMENTAL STATE

"And those who come together in the night and are entwined in rocking delight do an earnest work and gather sweetnesses, gather depth and strength for the song of some coming poet, who will rise to speak of ecstasies beyond telling."

—Rainer Maria Rilke, *Rilke on Love and Other Difficulties*

If capable of embracing the primitive in me, in him, might I have avoided this marriage taking the plunge enjoying the sex with Sarototi three or four trips ago—the guilt, shame rolling off my back—comprehending the primal passions of every man who has taken me? Every woman and man who have ever been taken? A coming poet? Me? Or a child? Or Rilke's ecstasies beyond telling into the witching hour of midnight, the time Mother said sex was good with any man? How could I have not foreseen the inevitable? That I had been holding at bay what "needed" to be fulfilled and would be fulfilled—whether I "really" wanted it or not. I had come all the way for this, to link up to my "other," to revisit and heal a history.

Part II: The Divide

At five, Sarototi arouses me for more sex. However, I have to stop him because I'm suffering from the ravages of the night before. Fall back asleep until Lekishoni arrives with a large copper pot filled with hot water for bathing. Laughingly, with my bottom on the bottom of the pot, my white legs and curly head sticking up, take an old-fashioned bath. In the cowboy way, in my dirty water, Sarototi follows.

There is no alone time to process what has just taken place, instead, we are swept into the activities of the day. *Yet, how could I not have known then that we were in the same bath together as the Red King and the White Queen of Alchemy?* That all of us were, me, the Maasai, blacks, whites, yellows, reds, rich, poor, the haves and the have-nots. We were floating in the tub of the Earth, in the Cosmos' arms, wrapped, bathed, held in our similar experiences and different ways of seeing those, winding forward into the distant future as well as transported backward time-machined to reweave our stories into a delicious fullness. *And what if, even now, far away from them as I write this, as you read this, they are healing me, healing you, setting things right?*

After breakfast we hike to the *manyatta* for a ritual. Stop for tea with Kisima. In the darkness of her little home, around her tiny fire, I cannot read her face, therefore, no idea of her sensitivities of me as the second wife, us, as kinswomen. *Can she feel my shame, feel the consummation?* (I did. While in Kansas, I bizarrely sensed my first husband with another woman in Scottsdale, Arizona!)

Even though, wrapped in the warmth of Kisima's fire, the Maasai *shuka*, and the deliciousness of her tea, I have a hard time swallowing. For everything has slid off the tracks. I've dropped into something that has engaged, absorbed me. Originally, the narrator, now, unguarded, I've tumbled down Alice's rabbit hole into the Sacred Forest, into the real-life of the Maasai. At first, tiny, vulnerable, needy, then, licking the herbs, I grew large, and luminously his equal. Now, I've shrunk once more into the silent status of his "wife."

As we tramp to the rite, Lekishoni explores, "Why aren't you carrying a camera, NeLaloshwa? You didn't use it last visit either. Do you even have it?"

Since that return with Mundadisi, I no longer carry a Canon digital, nor a film camera, nor define myself as an anthropological researcher. Even with Mundadisi, I only took the notes he required. This *sixth journey in*, I register with a different recorder now, an internal one. Instead, I figure as a mythological archaeologist digging for treasures down deep.

57: An Elemental State

"No. You're right. It's completely peculiar for me." My camera is within.

With the Senior Elders I stand just inside the trees, watching a ceremonial fight among the male and female junior elders. In a small clearing, with dancing movements, they spar with long switches from delicate willow branches, filling the air with "swoosh, swoosh, swoosh." The translation is not good, so I haven't the foggiest idea of how this peculiar game is played. I'm just here, a part of it all. Of course, the men win.

Further into the woods, a group of male elders guide me for the privilege of observing the ritualistic butchering of a cow—a first-time sighting for me. Again, I am the only woman, inside places their women have never gone before. As they prepare the meat, we slowly promenade around the fire as the Elder, Baba Budhya prays over the food. With each of his requests, we chant, acknowledging our response. In the grasses nearby the fire, reverently, quietly, I eat with Lekishoni.

Following the meal, the Senior and Junior Elders, Lekishoni, and I rhythmically, cheerfully march toward the Boma. As the excitement builds, Lalalana heralds out a line and in the traditional manner we answer singing. Upon our arrival, we circle the gathering of their young warriors jumping to their tales of victory over the lion, the buffalo, the leopard. Our festive energies, along with theirs, feeds this fiery moment of "*eya yo eya yo eya yo*." A glorious engaging sight of the men's red and black palette, encircled with the women's primary colors. Saifi's wife, Noritet and his daughter, Regina offer me a prime seat. Catch Nkoko's eye. We smile at one another as we proudly gaze upon her grandson, that new husband of mine, Sarototi, soaring into the sky.

On the trek back to Bright's Private Camp, road-fatigued, without Marjana's truck and a long day, little food, the return is full of effort. Tired, I bathe, preparing for another night with Sarototi.

In the middle of the wee hours, I jump up, startled from a series of nightmares. Not to wake Sarototi, I slide to the wood floor. Discreetly reach for a headlamp, pen, and diary to scribble. I have dreamt that Sarototi's head pops up from behind my couch at Casa d'Irene, where he has been hiding. Dressed in everyday American clothes, he appears frustrated with me. Can't seem to please him anymore because I never come home. Instead, I skate with a white man at the roller rink. About this predicament, I hear an old acquaintance's words, "Tough to love someone from another country."

Book One – Across the Divide to the Divine

Part II: The Divide

Marrying has caused me to believe I've given my life away, no longer in control, no longer in the driver's seat, as though I'm being driven off the cliff or pushed into the river all over again—only to be pleasing to him. Though for reasons not my own, I was not a virgin, yet my first husband and I didn't have sex before our marriage. Perhaps we should have. Sex might have broken the love spell, and we might never have married.

After "the forty years of wilderness" of us not speaking, my ex recently reminded, "It is not that simple, Murph. We should have been intimate on both the physical and emotional level for at least a year or so before committing to a lifetime of marriage. It was not an option given our religious views at the time, but I believe it would have been beneficial to us both in realizing how different we were and whether we were right to be lifetime mates."

How sad! Like that ex, Sarototi and I are in the "uh oh" of it all! Back peddling. The sex is dissolving the glow and wonder of our love!

After breakfast, I dispense Tarot at the fire with Sarototi, Lalalana, Lekishoni, and Baba Budhya. Sarototi pulls two cards: ruin and futility. For good reason, I believe, as there is no ground underneath our marriage. We tease him. I make him write a list of his worries and burn them in the fire. *Is he worried that he did not get the ritual power from the blood of my menses?* For, it has since passed. Nor had he broken the proverbial virginal cherry. *Has his act of marrying me backfired?*

Sarototi leaves to harvest the day's corn, to stay all night with his wife, and for the rest of the day, I attempt to decipher the cosmic wisdom of Odin through *The Book of Runes*. I cannot concentrate, nor do I feel hungry, because I'm unable to digest what just occurred. As if this marriage doesn't feel pure, nor "white" enough, I soak my toes in bleach. Something I've never done before. For something seems wrong, illegal, not in my language context, nor in theirs.

During our three years apart, the great romance of the darling girl, NeLaloshwa, under Sarototi's care, had hung suspended. And in the Zimbabwe-Maasai-Kenya adventure, everyone was so consumed with our togetherness no one recognized NeLaloshwa was/is no longer a child. That "demarcation" point, leaping from a fashion career, starting school, selling home, moving, expanding the mouth with braces, inhabiting the role of psychopomp on behalf of the lost from 9/11, training with Valerie Wolf, Deena Metzger, working shamanically with Deborah and into those past lives with Mariah and Kathy—unbeknownst to me—had radically transposed me.

57: An Elemental State

Not to mention that my countryman, George Bush, catapulted us into another war, and then, the horrible genocide in Dafur. The globe is staggeringly different, appallingly so. Bombarded everyday with CNN (if we cannot avoid watching it), the universe is moving through me, and that me is now an "I" traipsing through the second and third world steeped in shame from this marriage.

Did time stand still for the Maasai? No, I don't think so. They, too, have metamorphosed. Hit by a severe drought, losses of their own, and even touched enough, to send cows of reparation for *9/11*. We've changed. *Or have we?*

What if each of these steps along the way, are initiations? What if each of these steps along the way, are initiations? What if we changed one level more by exploring into our past lives, discovering we were the reverse, "the other" color? Maybe we would extend grace. Maybe we wouldn't have such issues with one another anymore.

And *what if there is something to this—that whites, who immigrated to America were missing something?* Set adrift from their families, their institutions, their soul selves of Europe, and maybe even separated from their ancient African selves, were in such need of connection that they transported the Black-Africans to America to bring this energy closer. However, the whites became so scared of the mysteries of these soulful, nature-bound, naturally spiritual people, whose veils between the other side—their ancestors—and this one, were so thin; the whites kept them at a distance by incarceration, slavery, rape; dividing the communities who spoke the same language and dividing the men from the women.

Even so, slowly something happened, an integration. Slowly some of the whites themselves fought the Civil War to free them. And slowly they rose up one after the other to free themselves—Rosa Parks, Martin Luther King, Jr., Malcolm X, John Lewis. And now there is another rising, in the Black Lives Matter, another step toward integration. *What if we could remove this deep divide of misunderstanding? What if we could change? What if we whites could come down off the mountain, our high places, out of D'Angelo's "White Fragility" to get down dirty to make the necessary changes?*

58

MORNING AFTER

Tanagra Statuettes are decorated with ivy leaves or tendrils assuring their wearers of the god's protection.

—4th Century B.C.E.

    Alone in the bed, at two a.m., I jolt up from a profound sleep. For the next six hours, I grow ever more gut-wrenchingly sick. I have diarrhea for two hours. From four to six, I vomit. From six to eight o'clock, dry heaves until my back and stomach hurt so badly, I can barely return to the bed. The entire camp must hear me retching as noisily as the Bushbuck calling out in fear. What I don't know is I'm oozing with shame, roaring out the guilt that's been trapped inside since childhood. *Was I, too, dancing with the death archetype, a desire to initiatorily kill off that part of me, to depart from a way of being into another?*

    Through this, I cannot help but think of the testing Richard Harris' character, Horse, goes through in the movie, *The Man Called Horse*. For his marriage, he must make a Vow to the Sun, then, as if the Hang Man, from claws driven into

58: Morning After

each side of his grand pectoral muscles—pectoralis major—he is hung. Each test he becomes more and more Native, more a part of their tribe. Until eventually, "He did not find it necessary either to apologize or to boast because he was the equal to any man on earth." This, too, seems to be happening to me—one more herb, one more initiatory challenge, one more upping the game into adulthood, into the "I." I'm just not sure I'm up for it.

Sarototi has broken through the hymen of my feminine betrayal awakening me into the rawness of that. We have consummated the marriage—making it "real"—integrating into a oneness! *Oh, my gawd!* This body, with every bit of its strength, is rejecting our act of unity. And so, I bend over and vomit once again.

Back at the village, before the calves stir, Sarototi is jarred from his slumber with these words: "NeLaloshwa needs help!" He crawls off his palette, stirs the embers setting about his divination, which divulges the remedy. Half asleep, in the dark, he stumbles down the hill to Baba Budhya's hut. "NeLaloshwa is deathly ill. Search for this particular herb." He prescribes. "She must drink this." Sending forth Baba Budhya through the woods for the medicinal, then to us at Bright's Camp, as emissary.

Though bedridden, sick, and vulnerable, I must trust, swallowing the liquid medicine that tastes "icky," yet stops the dry heaves, allowing rest. In the afternoon, Thuku soothingly administers chicken bouillon. I can barely lift my head to sip from his spoon. Unusually, I sleep straight through thirteen hours. The following day, I eat a bit of rice.

For three days, with back pain and stomachache, suffering from the result of the release, I remain so wiped out from this expulsion; I'm laced with a kind of ivy of protection, finally, an excuse from sex. Trying to integrate, and more essentially "stomach" what just happened. *Can I undertake the drive north to Lmakiya's wedding?*

On the stoop, Baba Budhya, the sentinel and guard, appears day after day as if contrite about the arranged marriage. In my mind's eye envision him shrouded in the sacrificial sackcloth and ashes awaiting NeLaloshwa's recovery.

59

STRIPPED OF ALL ACCOUTREMENTS

⚔ ⚔ ⚔

> *"To paraphrase (Edward S.) Casey: a trauma is not what happened but the way we see what happened. [...] not a pathological event but a pathologized image, [...] that has become "intolerable" as Lopez-Pedraza puts it. If we are ill because of these intolerable images, we get well because of imagination. Poesis as therapy."*
>
> —James Hillman, *Healing Fiction*

What is happening inside this transformative initiation will within three years from this time be written inside that doctoral dissertation—I must admit here—a little judgmentally. In fact, after reading the dissertation in the beginning stages, Dr. Edward S. Casey will consider being my advisor—with the advice above— "it's not what happened, Murphy, it's the way you see it that is holding you in the state you're in. The Maasai's perception and intention of

59: Stripped of All Accoutrements

your initiation into adulthood, even the marriage was and is different and not so brutal as your imagination."

I can "hear" Casey's viewpoint, but it will take many years to come into right relation with "what the Maasai did unto me," in fact, I was still inside this bruising, so shocked I still had little access to true feelings, those I had (which I had every right to), had not been reconciled. What was right for the Maasai, what they intended didn't quite compute, didn't add up for me (I couldn't even begin to wrap my arms around this)—for it went against the very Guiding Self they had restored within.

For me, based on my history, the marriage to Sarototi was as though they shot me with a stun gun, shot an arrow through the original wound—that Achilles heel of mine. I could accept Casey's notion but to imagine this forward—what felt to be a betrayal, what felt within my body as "dis-ease"—seemed as though a push through, instead of a movement into an embodied poetry.

Instead, the poetry of this act, of this "accident" will take a decade. Only then will I understand their decision for this "arranged" marriage, for this final initiation into a dream *laiboni*, rocked me to the core because it rang true, a familiar cord. Though I couldn't put my finger on it, though I had yet to remember (and won't for another ten years)—once more, a man, a group of men made a decision regarding me, without my permission, without my "yes." But this, too, though it seems "accidental" is not out of character, therefore, maybe even guardian-angel-directed and will have the power to direct my thoughts, redirect the intrinsic self's pathway.

On the third day, Baba Budhya, my steady friend, who holds the space for healing outside the tent, encourages me to sip more of the herbal medicine. I drink it and devour the porridge from Thuku. They have brought news that Marjana returned yesterday, immediately after, departing with Sarototi for Narissima. For some reason this unnerves me—I'm on the brink and Marjana is near, but not *here*, when I need him. Perhaps, he is avoiding me. Perhaps, he feels guilty. Perhaps, he doesn't know what to say. I sure don't!

After three days apart, Sarototi joins me at the fire. Later, we move to the greater fire of the sun where I lie in the hammock. He throws and counts the stones: "You are okay, NeLaloshwa, there is no sign of parasites."

Yeah, but isn't it because I bleached my toenails white and because I couldn't stomach us?

Part II: The Divide

I don't feel okay, but in the warm light, I sleep tranquilly. Nearby the cows plop, plop, plop their hooves across the river "ding a ling a ling" their bells chime. From his daughter-in-law, the mother of Mwaisakeni, Chief Ole Wangombe delivers a wedding gift, a bracelet, which has the appearance of a colorful Maasai watch. Other presents arrive affirming our marriage. Slowly sip another dose of their herbal tea as Sarototi prepares an herb to inhale under the shuka, and a subsequent bath.

For the night, Sarototi and I lie down together. However, in poor health, the sensual nature has fled, turning my back to him. For him, within his culture, two wives is a given, a gift and is sanctified. For me, I was back in the guilt of being with "someone else's husband"—this time he isn't Artemis', he is Kisima's. Even in reverie, I cannot escape our intimacy, as several messages appear: Izak, the Old Man of the Kalahari, is unable to pick me up at the airport, because it seems there is a death. *Is it an initiatory death? —mine?*

Even so, I cry from this news. Both inside the dream and in this reality, Sarototi comfortingly, from behind, wraps his arms around me as I shake and weep, crying for the death of that little child within, crying for the death of the spiritualized relationship with Sarototi, crying because my buddy, Izak, whose wisdom I need, is far away in South Africa. He cannot save me now!

In the second message, I sling back into the childhood bedroom. Everything is in reverse. The twin beds are on the opposite sides against the wall. Shrouded in light, a white, strawberry redhaired tomboy, dirty and thin stands nearby. Leaning in, holding me tight, she cries. Lying on one of the beds is a large white man with a small baby folded in his arms, and a young child sleeps astride. The room is decorated with Confederate and Yankee flags. Veiled, she slides out the door into the night.

As I pen this tale, I believe our youngest niece has died. But afterwards, the comprehension expands, through the initiatory marriage, the "me," as newborn, as dirty tomboy, as adolescent, withers, departs from the landscape, dies. For and against, the two Civil War flags represent one for the whites, one for the blacks, the dichotomous swing inside myself over Sarototi (just as I had experienced with Renzo, the married man). Inside, the incapacity to make a solid decision and make it stick resides.

With the aid of Sophia the goddess of wisdom, I attempt to summon the images through Active Imagination. I cannot. Restlessly I sleep. *How do I avoid sex with Sarototi?* For today is the ninth day of the cycle and without condoms, I

59: Stripped of All Accoutrements

fear pregnancy, the sperm drop of our boy child Sarototi has seen running across the Highlands of Laloshwa. At eight a.m., I play around with Sarototi. Laughing and giggling, crawling on top of him, I manage to avoid "real" sex. As I bathe, he wonders, "No sidai?"

Is he asking, "No sex?" Though I'm sure the language isn't correct, I reply, "Sarototi is *sidai oleng*, very good."

For breakfast, gulp down a bowl of porridge and some fruit, rush to the fire for bigger answers, stacking fifteen Tarot cards in the shape of a pyramid: A big transformation (no kidding) in communication and interactions, overcoming misunderstandings between the priestess and the fool (astonishing). *What concerns me is the princess of discs—pregnancy, creativity.* In the second row: work, science, stagnation—I give too much. Time to declare, "No!" Have the courage to step forth into that personal legend, what the original calling is. But the third discovers the undermining Self of cruelty and interference throwing me off this new path. The opposites lie together, the "both/and"—that's for sure—the black and the white, the male and the female. I've leaped into that bowl of mulligatawny soup with what is counter to, yet underneath lies the gas flame, the distillation of, forging the alchemical union of the Red King and the White Queen. It has happened. There is no turning back.

Within "the traditional marriage," the first few nights of sex have the aura of abduction. Alone, without her family, the bride has no one to turn to, to talk to. *Is this what Habibi's wife, Lulani, is suffering from? That I attempted to restore?* No longer does the taboo of the engagement withhold his longing. Held captive, the bride's wishes, wants, desires, are shoved aside in hopes of what the union will bring—consummation, progeny. Stripped of all the familiar accoutrements of bridal gown and jewels, bare, *who is she? For whom am I without these?*

Sarototi did not get the menses blood, but if the child comes—through our joint blood—the seeding, the coagulation of power. But no matter, how I slice it, whether I like it or not, whether I've vomited and gagged, I've been initiated, re-shaped. The transfiguration of this mysterious act is bubbling forth on the outskirts of comprehension. *And Sarototi?* He has fallen into the honey trap of my unconscious!

60

THE FINAL SEVERING

"I believe that what we do not digest is laid out somewhere else, into others, the political world, the dreams, the body's symptoms, becoming literal and outer (and called historical) because it is too hard for us, too opaque, to break open and to insight."

—James Hillman, *Healing Fiction*

Today in Laloshwa is a very hot day—hot outside and inside—for what is undifferentiated, undigested, and burning in me has been projected out. Sengeli, Kisima's brother, drives me to the Maasai School to assess their needs. *Where is the usual escort, interpreter, steadfast keeper of these trips, Marjana? Has he lost respect? Is he afraid to face me?*

For two years, the whole extended community of Laloshwa Highlands has been building this school. Each family group either donates wood, time, money, or workers to pour cement, build the structures. Immediately, I react to their dedication: "Global Voice commits to shipping books, providing three hundred

60: The Final Severing

dollars (approximately 25,000 Kenya Shillings) to finish the third classroom, and my parents chip in five hundred to complete the library!" They are thrilled.

Attend another ceremony, where the women attempt to define, to address my circumstances. Without a translator, we are destined only to smile, touch one another, drink tea. Exhausting. Help the women organize jewelry for Global Voice to sell back home to raise more money. *Do they see me as more capable of handling their men? Don't they realize I'm not?* Before the next visit, I need to take an intensive in Maa and Kiswahili. Sarototi and Lekishoni need to take an intensive in English, too. *But am I really coming back?*

Tonight, I pack up camp grumpily. After a long day with little interpretation and lots of disappointment, I cannot endure Thuku' slow storytelling, which seems relevant to the weight of all this. Upset. The water pumps are still not repaired. The last moments filled with business details of visas, passports, and jewelry. Behind me, the ever-lingering thought hovers: *Am I negotiating for my life, for lifetimes? Will I be able to leave?* Not sure this is even about them, but about the thematic claustrophobia of the past life of kidnap and imprisonment and withholding of the herb. *What is at stake?* Not to mention, the constant drag from Sarototi—once my way-shower, now, the reverse is true, a monkey on my back—wanting more.

Marjana's return to the village finds Sarototi has enacted the rites of "marriage" with his client and that client, me, is sick, silent, tongue-tied. *Does he fear a report to his bosses that I've been taken advantage of? Is he afraid of a confrontation? The potentiality of a complaint?* At the moment, he's more present to his two wives.

Never did I report this enactment to P&P. Never told a soul who might divulge. The other friends in Kenya, I keep the truth from. It takes a long time to admit these happenings to anyone other than Jeffrey and a therapist, because as usual I shamefully doubt and blame myself.

Not knowing: "Each decision leaves a loser and builds shadow," Hillman clarifies. So "the defeated party becomes the injured…" (*Kinds of Power*). Festers. No wonder I sleep restless all night long. Everything irritates. Tired of the nightmares, tired of the cold air seeping under the huge covers. After five days, the residue lingers—out of breath from the sore back, the dry heaves. As if nothing has happened, I'm up, shower, finish packing, then, presenting envelopes of monies to everyone.

Part II: The Divide

Sarototi, the Chief, and Baba Budhya busily weave a bracelet. In ceremonial water, they spit spittle, scrubbing it with an herb. Pray. Baba Budhya ties it around my small white wrist, rolling it to the upper arm. Once in a similar manner they freed me from a powerful father, from the family, *now, are they binding me?* At the Katunga River, I undergo a final meditation while Marjana finishes loading the Land Rover.

At the *manyatta*, in a gathered circle, the Elders are hand sewing traditional sandals. On the grass the children seat themselves about me. Ladna, Saifi's girl hangs on my neck. Lemagron, Marjana's child follows suit. Lesainana and Marpenzi (Sarototi's boys) dance around me. Sarototi's father, Baba Sarototi, sweeps his hands spanning the landscape, his declaration echoing forth: "This is your home, NeLaloshwa."

Confused and loved, ever in a sway of the pendulum, the back and forth between one notion and another, a division between the nuclear family and my independence. I answer back, "Yes." I acquiesce. But, really, within moments, I'm out of breath, and in my imagination, I'm running far from here.

"Where's your husband?" Thuku teases. "Building your home?"

Offended, I reply stiffly, "No! You knew I did not want to marry." And I mutter to myself. "And most of all, I did not want to *consummate*!" He, just as the others, did nothing to honor my wishes, nor protect me. Nevertheless, regretfully, I did not stand defiantly by myself. I was much too afraid.

I say, *olesaris*, good-bye to everyone—*is this a final severing?* The Chief, Baba Budhya, Baba Sarototi, and several other Elders form a good luck tunnel with their *shukas* as passageway for Marjana, Sarototi, and me. Just as I stepped into the vehicle, Kisima, Sarototi's wife, timidly saunters up to me, slipping an unexpected token, a necklace overhead. At first I feel uneasy. *Is this a bluff too? Is she really truly happy about my union with her husband?* On the other hand, she knows the drill here, is well aware of the games at foot.

On our way to Nairobi, Marjana reveals, Kisima's present is composed of ancient olive seeds, heralding peace. I'm reminded of his former words: "Whenever a Maasai offers a leaf, a branch or a seed of this plant, he has made a pact: to never make war against this person."

Tears pour down my cheeks. Later, inside these beads, I ferret out the women's strength of invocation, the magic of protection shielding me from their male Elders. In six weeks, when removed and incinerated in Australia,

60: The Final Severing

wildebeests shall march upon me. For now, I only know their gentle intention. *Another ivy of protection?*

61

EVEN THE SAWED-OFF PENCILS

※ ※ ※

"to avoid decisions at all cost [...] by this I mean holding oneself and others in suspension in order to hold onto power."

—James Hillman, *Kinds of Power*

As we commence our drive to the Lesarge marriage of my Samburu friends, Lmakiya and Becky, Sarototi suggests we stop in the village of Narissima to visit another *laibon*, the woman, Hakima. As the forest is at a distance, Sarototi has had a long-term relationship with her, collecting and supplying herbs. While Marjana ventures off for business and a visit with his wife Jackie, Sarototi brings along Thuku, to interpret. We wait, pace outside her home, yet, in the end—worth the "wait" in gold.

Inside her dung hut, the eighty-year-old medicine woman, Hakima, reads sawed-off pencils, akin to the reading of tea leaves, floating in water, held in the

61: Even the Sawed-Off Pencils

crest of a wooden Maasai stool. Sarototi poses a series of three questions: Is our marriage official? Will NeLaloshwa have my child? Is she a *laibon*?

Each time he asks this medium, she spits on the pencils, requests for me to do the same, and follows with the dashing of the pencils into the water. The first query takes time, as if she cannot find a response. She prays, spits, and drops. Prays, spits and drops. Sarototi is anxious, fidgets about on his wooden stool. Finally, she concludes: "The marriage will be annulled in one year if you lie *with* her." Thuku falters, the interpretation seems unclear, unsure: "Or did she mean: 'The marriage will be annulled in one year if you lie *to* her?'"

Whichever way the wind blows the matrimonial vows shall reach annulment, for in my mind he has done both—lying *with* me and lying *to* me! I feel greatly soothed. However, Sarototi is disappointed and grows ever more nervous about the second inquiry of whether I'll have his child or not, which takes her as long or longer to respond. For the Maasai, "olapa oibor inkera," "children are the bright moon." Of this, she finally enlightens with a smile, for she is pleased, seeing many, many children around me.

While relief washes over me, Thuku and Sarototi are rather confused, "What do you mean, Hakima? For NeLaloshwa has birthed no child."

"Oh, this is what I do for work," I laughingly decode, "share stories with children, and I have lots of nieces, nephews, cousins, and young friends. Though I'm not a mother, the Secret Garden surrounding Casa d'Irene is a playground with swing, hammock, large colorful bouncing balls, white Christmas lights, and colorful Spanish fountains of running water."

During the final request— "is NeLaloshwa a *laibon*?"—Sarototi is visibly apprehensive. This priestess spews her saliva onto the pencils, as I spit, too. In three seconds, Hakima reacts, bellowing, "Laibon, laibon, laibon," as she points at my third eye. Though the marriage has lost its power, the ceremony to designate me as his equal, as a *laibon*, as a shaman, has been recognized through an official medicine woman whom Sarototi respects.

"Worry" is streaked across his face. The solution, the liberation of my own power, this acknowledgment comes through another woman! No longer to be held captive by another. He cannot really possess me. She has broken through the fear and the stricture around our marriage. Hallelujah! No wonder her Swahili name, Hakima—for I cannot pronounce her Maa name—means wise, intelligent one, for she is, indeed, that. As I depart, she hands me this strange

Book One – Across the Divide to the Divine   413

Part II: The Divide

burnt red root in the shape of ginger. "Upon your return to America, you are to boil this, then drink the tea for one month." *Another ivy of protection?*

What Sarototi didn't comprehend, nor did I, is that our bonding flung us apart, shooting something right through the middle of our oneness. Therefore, I can reclaim the original marriage (that took place amidst my Manhattan friends) of the peaceful Irene and the sea warrior, Murphy, melding together a powerful force field of a knowing Self—*that* "I," the Maasai had given back to me.

For the trip to Samburu, I only have to bide time as my own charge dictates, justified to do whatever I need to do to hold my own, to elegantly exit, climbing on board the horse of my choice, that golden rhinestone plane of Patricia's—riding the zephyrs.

Who knew? Even the sawed-off pencils!

62

RUMINATIONS

"The more one can hesitate, call in counsels for consultations, hold policy roundtables and read determination papers from experts, the more important seems to be both the decision and one's own position…"

—James Hillman, *Kinds of Power*

On our way to Samburu, we stop in Nairobi. Marjana has booked a nice hotel. Sarototi, as my "husband," wants to join me in this bourgeois place. I want to stay alone. He is upset. Doesn't understand my decision, the hesitation. Taking back some form of power, I try to clarify, "Just need a night by myself. Long to sleep." Quietly inform Marjana, "I need the space." What he doesn't understand is that Hakima has awakened something inside, affirmed my own feelings about us. Maybe the beads from his wife brings another kind of affirmation.

However, through the night, I worry I haven't saved Sarototi's face, that I have embarrassed him. *In not speaking up—that I do not want this marriage—do I hold the power?* I don't want to. Just not ready to be public about a marriage,

Part II: The Divide

which is more an assignation, than about genuine participation. A new bride and oh so miserable! *Did Habibi's wife, Lulani, feel the same? Did the Elders force her hand into marriage?*

Hungry, I wander downstairs to the pool for dinner. In the twilight, the children play in the water with parents nearby. Most of all, I need to speak with a friend, someone who actually knows me. It's all so complicated. Yet, I don't call anyone.

For tonight, I have escaped him. However, a nagging conversation hovers. Our marriage for Sarototi makes so much sense, satisfies him. For me, I spent the last nine nights superstitious I'd get pregnant and have the child he's dreamt of. Yet, more importantly I've ruined something, my reputation as mythologist, anthropologist is scarred, for crossing a border not meant to be crossed, I've broken a taboo, creating havoc in our lives. That his trick has dislodged something deep within me, I cannot quite fathom.

Unnerved. Shamed and in turmoil. It's not Sarototi's fault, just not what I wanted. *Who embodies the power now?*

63

NON-DUALITY—THE BOTH/AND

> *"When a primary word is spoken the speaker enters the word and takes his stand in it."*
>
> —Martin Buber, *I and Thou*

Inside my brain, I ponder—*after my initiation, am I primary? Can I therefore take a stand?* I ponder the discussions at Pacifica Graduate Institute; breaking away from the concept of what Jung called the "either/or," the thinking of duality and logic into a more expanded thought of non-duality, Jung's "glorious both/and." Letting go of the triviality of "it's either true, or it's not," to embrace the paralogical world of quantum physics, of paradox into the depths of Niels Bohr's "great truths"—for in this situation, I certainly hold the "dichotomy" and am therefore unable to stand my ground.

Part II: The Divide

On the second day of our drive toward Samburu, we lunch at a lovely restaurant. Though other whites stare at us, I don't mind that it's peculiar—a white woman with two Maasai. However, I'm uncomfortable about the marriage. I carry the conversation graciously, socially, yet I don't express my true feelings—*I love Sarototi…but…I don't want to be married to him.*

That night we stop at the Eco lodge near Thomson's Falls on the Ewasa Narok River, near the town of Nyahururu. To our room, the Kikuyu hostess escorts Sarototi and me. As she prepares the fire, she speaks in English: "He's your husband, isn't he?" *How can she tell?*

"Yes," I confess. *If she can read from our body language that we are married, can she read the duress smeared across the face as well?* Don't get me wrong. Though I was wrapped in Maasai colors, I wasn't pretending to be other than I am; I wasn't pretending to be black. What was wild though, over the years people of color were attracted to me. After the divorce, after I shaved my hair as short as Annie Lennox, whenever I went dancing, black men—not white—"hit" on me. I have black friends in NYC that love me as deeply as I love them. Once a black girlfriend told me, "You'd be the perfect black man's wife." I wasn't attempting this. And yet, here I am, a black man's wife, but certainly the furthest "thing" from perfect!

"Maasai men are good to their wives." She continues, "He will take care of you." *Is she trying to reassure me?* As if to sing, "Hakuna Matata, don't worry, be happy."

In this hotel room, I hold him at bay. This putting off of Sarototi from sex is the fear of having a child at forty-seven-years-old, at being tied to him, at the conflict that child will experience between a nomadic and a white privileged life. No lie. Actually, an even greater fear is rejection and misunderstanding from friends and family—*what will they think?* The total destruction and loss of everything: home, money, sentenced to the actuality of living in a dirt-floor dung hut, waiting on a husband I don't love, flies on face, dirty clothes, dirty water. *What if the water pump quits working? What if the corngrinder stops grinding? Will I have to carry water? Or carry corn for a full day? How can a supposed couture princess of Seventh Avenue undergo these?*

An award-winning French anthropologist and filmmaker, Jacqueline Roumèguere-Eberhardt, who created the concept of Totemic Geography of Africa, gave up her life in France, divorcing her French husband and moving for the rest of her life to the Masai Mara with her Maasai—her second husband—

63: Non-Duality—The Both/And

where originally, she and her first husband had done their research and raised their family. Talk about the romance draining right out of me. *Is it my destiny to disappear into Kenya?*

Between the unseen and the seen, I have always been dancing on W. Somerset Maughan's *The Razor's Edge,* the magical tight wire. However, this time there is no boogie in my step. *Wonder if the challenge with the Visas for Marjana and Sarototi has to do with me? If I really am a laibon, does the power of those thoughts control their incapacity to obtain one?* God forbid!

Book One – Across the Divide to the Divine

64

WEDDING, WEDDING, WEDDING

"Usicheze na ulimwengu ukikuelemea utajuta."
"Don't play tricks with the world, you will regret when it falls on you."

—Maasai Kanga

Just as *The Sorcerer's Apprentice*, have I conjured up more than I bargained for? For on this scorching 28th August 2004, somehow it seems we have missed Lmakiya and Becky's conjugal bliss. Metaphorically this is where I believe Sarototi and I stand—a consistent underlying unrest concerning this strange liaison. We cannot attend their happy union because we aren't. Certainly, I'm not. The new Kanga that covers my shoulders from the sun, shouts at me the above words. *And I can't help wondering have all the shenanigans I've been playing with, created this?*

64: Wedding, Wedding, Wedding

With a fine toothcomb, we scour the countryside for Lmakiya's family *manyatta*. Marjana calls his cell to only arrive at voicemail, asks myriads of Samburu on the road, circles the home of Becky. No sign of life there. We eat lunch. Standing by for news, I drag a stick through the sand, as if I can conjure it forth. This heat, this exploring, is a reflection of the despair inside, of trying to acquire the solution. *Can we unbridle the riddle?*

After what feels as if days upon days of lingering on these brutally hot, dusty roads of the Samburu desert-bush landscape, we make no headway. One of these searing days is spent in the small market town of Maralal, where they are busy filming *The White Masai*. Derived from the memoir of Corinne Hoffman, a Swiss-German woman who broke up with her boyfriend, Marco, selling her possessions for the love of her life, the Samburu, Lketinga. In impassioned pursuit, she marries him, birthing his child. Later, from their internal difficulties, she flees the country with little girl in tow.

About their marriage, Sarototi wonders: "Isn't this what we are doing?" *Yes. But she pursued this man for the purpose of oneness. I came to you for restoration of an ancient history.*

Early this morning, I dream of a return to our home at 110 Rohrer Heights. However, someone else lives there (which is true). Due to many locks, I cannot enter. A man hears me. I hide below the steps. Strangely, this abode now lies right in the center of the dry creek bed.

Truly, I feel locked outside of what I cannot have—an intimate marriage I long for. And my desire to return home, lands me smack in the middle of a precarious wash (certainly of an unresolved past of emotions and my parents' dementia)—no longer a nest to run for safety.

65

TRICKY OUT THERE

"Essence is emptiness Everything else, accidental. Emptiness Brings peace To loving. Everything else, disease. In this world of trickery Emptiness is what your soul wants."

—Rumi

With no luck of winning admission to the wedding, we decide our next plan is to engage with the Samburu *laibon*. Well, a great thought, but this too takes time—for in Maa language, without markers on the road, it's "a stones throw," "as the crow flies," "off-road," amongst a few mishmash of dwellings.

When we arrive, three men on tin paint cans are seated near the old *laibon* who irritatingly points at me, "You're late," as he tumbles from his stool in judgment.

"What?" By this declaration, we are a bit surprised. Maybe Lmakiya informed him of our arrival, or perchance inside the *laibon*'s divination he registered our visitation. Nevertheless, he's extremely drunk, so are the other gentlemen. Surely, he can't know what he's saying.

65: Tricky Out There

To the *laibon*, Marjana reveals our dilemma. Not much is understood, nor does access to the divine seem possible. We're so discouraged (and a little insulted for his drunkenness)—this just adds up to the sum total of the day. We depart.

At the truck, my hunch is he'll hurl a hex at us for waiting around the entire day, without payment. In this miserable heat, whatever the Ancestors revealed to him might have been something he hated to expose, driving him to drink, resenting the fact of sticking around for another white woman who wants to flee her exotic husband. He certainly becomes the perfect mirror of our insult to him of postponement. How ironic! The friend I love, Lmakiya, whose wedding I have attempted to attend, who led us to this *laibon*, whom I learned so much about being bamboozled—now, "Here, am I," on his ancestors' land and once more caught inside the sticky web of the trickster.

Yes, it's a bit tricky out there.

With my intuitive hit, Sarototi agrees. We step back through the gate to give the shaman a gift of money and tobacco. We change our tune: "Thank you for your patience, for the care you took with your divination." Naturally, we reverently bow to them. "We apologize to you and the Elders for our inconsiderate lateness."

As we walk out of the thorn-bush corral, a flock of peaceful doves fly off, preceding us. Sarototi and I smile at one another, knowing, we have honored the Ancestors and beat the hex.

66

DOWNWARD SPIRAL

⚜ ⚜ ⚜

"Two contrary tendencies are at work: the desire on one hand to get out of the earlier condition and on the other hand not to forget it."

—C. G. Jung, "On the Psychology of the Trickster"

Just because I don't have twenty American dollars in cash for an entry fee, we cannot pay our way into an exclusive safari lodge. Instead, we must drive into Isiola, a little town full of Somalian refugees. Though a very real part of traveling Africa, I often miss these desperate scenes for I'm usually deep in the bush country.

As we fill the Land Rover with gas, a starving crowd surrounds the vehicle for handouts. Marjana warns me not to make matters worse. Nonetheless, I cannot resist giving them our bundle of bananas. Pass them to one man thinking he'll disperse the bunch. Instead, he grabs, tucks, and dashes away.

Further into this discombobulated town, we dock at the (then) run-down Bomer Hotel where we are given what seems to be, flea-infested mattresses lying flat on the cement-floored bedrooms. Though it's the worst of our lodgings ever, what I care about is a quick shower, the removal of this dirt, these days of disappointment, missing a friend's celebration, the strange encounter with the drunken laibon. Of course, Sarototi wants to wash, too, but what he *really* longs for is me, is sex. He is so busy craving me; he cannot see there is something wrong, that our love isn't mutual.

With as much muster, might, wit, and slyness, I manage to keep him from my body before dinner and after. Relieved. Through our interpreter, Marjana, I cannot seem to say to him something so simple and true— "I don't want to have your child." *Afraid I'll hurt him?*

Once I likened the intimacy between Sarototi and I as pure as the connection between *Dances with Wolves* (Kevin Costner) and Wind in His Hair (Rodney A. Grant). "*Sunkamanitu tanka ob waci*, Dances with Wolves, I am Wind in His Hair. Do you see that I am your friend? Can you see that you will always be my friend?"

Up until now, for me, this manifesto represented the union we possessed, beyond color, beyond culture, even beyond gender. I believe this is why the marriage greatly depresses me—delivering our relationship from the sacred to the mundane to the profane, and more discouragingly to the everyday. Not grasping that this is where anything that matters happens on this lusty dusty earth. Yet, I want to crawl out of my body up into the sacred! In the confusion of this, in being out of sync with the divine, the two of us can no longer "hear" one another in our private language. *Have I left my body as of old?*

With Marjana, we dine. Wonder if my face reveals the absolute desolation. At so many tables, so many times in my life, in this state, I have shown up. Don't ever want to do this again. In an attempt to release the original template from this existence, Sarototi safely restored me, and yet that safety, shockingly, has been removed. He is now an unsafe home.

No one knows the on-going insinuation of Sarototi and me has turned into unrest and pure unadulterated unhappiness. For him, unsatisfiable. He's beside himself. He's upended. Not on his turf. In and out of mine. In a hall of mirrors, in hotels. He's never been in this position before. He's not throwing divination. He's being *Burnt by the Sun* of Nikita Mikhalkov, of the Russian Revolution, by our own want of change, our own initiatory evolution.

In our bed, so close to the concrete, the cold seeps in, the darkness penetrates, noises from the street press in upon me. Still manage to hold him off another day.

Part II: The Divide

But I've grown weary and defensive. His prophesy of our child drives him closer to me, driving me further away. My reserves rise up to shun, from the dread of having a child schizophrenically split between two worlds—the Nomadic and the Western. For a child, bouncing back and forth between Santa Barbara and Laloshwa Highlands seems unfair and frankly ridiculous. *What becomes of this innocent baby? How can he resolve this daunting quest unknown to the likes of me?*

In the wee hours, several drunken men and women climb the stairs next to our room, stepping into theirs. But later new sounds splatter throughout the halls to what I think is—after the rape—a woman mourning over and over the Bedouin cry: "la la la la la la la la." The ululation echoes, bounces down the narrow lanes, circles into our window. I cannot escape this haunting chant, reverberating women's powerlessness. Hers. Mine. Ours. At one point, I rise to help her. *But how can I?* I can barely help myself. And honestly, don't know where I'd start, too terrorized to stride down the hall into the darkness. *What holds me inside this dreadful impotent archetype—my sleeping Mars hiding undercover? Fate? Where is that bucolic Maasai promise when the sun goes down the pain is swept away?*

67

MY AIM SO POOR

> *"Take away my aim which*
> *Is so poor because it is*
> *Human and give me the aim*
> *Of a star, which never errs."*

—a Bushman, Laurens van der Post's *Heart of the Hunter*

After her nightmarish cries, Sarototi turns toward me. "No, please," I plead, "just need one more hour of sleep." Again, he doesn't know what I've said, just my actions of irritation. With the sexuality thrown in, absent is our amplitude for kything. Together, we've lost our way. So, I rest. Re-align. Regroup. Pray. After that, we have okay sex. Surprisingly, I have a minor orgasm. But between the "la la la la la," and us, I feel raw, unable to digest the orgasmic response. My aim so poor!

For breakfast, in the same dive of a restaurant, Sarototi and I soberly eat until Marjana shows. I—who can talk about anything—can't speak of this present misery. Dancingly polite on the surface, I no longer comprehend what side this big brother translator, now, my cousin, is on—*what's safe terrain?* Beating around the bush. I've become a stranger in this strange land. On my soil, in my terms, at least in business, I've learned to shoot straight up. (Yet, here, I carry a lie, I cannot carry much longer.)

And Sarototi? He has become clingy, wimpy. I do not like this "new" him. In the last four hours to Nairobi still riding shotgun to Marjana's left, with Sarototi in the rear, I avoid the capacity for truth, dozing most of the way, and when I don't, feign.

At a busy Nairobi hotel, declare to Marjana, "I must be alone once again."

Too tired to hang out with Sarototi, I have a solitary lunch on the terrace. Swim. In the pool, there are a hundred children—black, white, yellow. Sarototi would have been fine here. Yet, in this present role, I have no common language with him, no way to speak. The waiter would have to translate. Can't sip a cocktail to foist this impractical untenable situation into a sophisticated luncheon by poolside.

In the evening, Marjana phones, "NeLaloshwa, can Sarototi have dinner with you and stay the night?"

"No!"

Not long after, for four hours until midnight, pass out into an unfathomable slumber, followed by a call to Deborah for grounding, to step outside the shame of this charade.

68

WHAT AM I NOT CONVEYING?

"However unwise it may be at this stage in their development for white and black to marry, we should always remember that those who do so are perhaps doing something of far-reaching historical value by demonstrating that, at the deepest levels in human nature in the dimension of love, there can never be such a thing as colour prejudice [...] the humble individuals, black and white, who have contracted a union in obedience to an urge of life in them, are perhaps unwittingly serving a cause both of history and life."

—Laurens van der Post (*The Dark Eye in Africa*)

Into the wee hours of August 30, Deborah and I talk and talk. She is positive about our wedding based on her remembrance of the love and reverence I have for Sarototi. Just as the Kitomini Community, she is caught up in the idealism of the story, in what this marriage of opposites might mean. Everyone is banking on this initiated union as though it resolves the original initiatory quest that brought me here; that it has the potential to remedy what ails the entire world; that it brings access to a long-sought root, the secret to the Twenty-First Century. Even in *The Dark Eye in Africa*, Sir Laurens believes our marriage has "far-reaching historical value." I just can't see it yet.

Part II: The Divide

Instead of being a remedy, a solution, I feel traumatized, undermined, railroaded into the consummation of how our relationship is to be defined, as if this is the only way for these elements to be united. *What have I not told her? What am I not conveying? Am I so subsumed with shame cannot even go near the material enough to unravel the nightmare?* And I haven't even revealed the dream of the slithering snake, who turns into a cow, who births a baby blond girl, who sits on my lap! This experience has become such a much vaster chronicle than a vision or transcontinental phone call of expensive minutes can contain.

Shamanically, we rattle together for several hours in search of the hidden, in hopes it might comfort me. From this moment, into my arms, I safely gather "the child within." "Thank you, 'little Irene', for carrying this burden for me, for serving me so well. I release you from the weight of this responsibility moving forward into a loving relationship with a husband who brings my sexuality into wholeness, expansive health, and full-out womanhood!" But quietly to myself, I beseech: "Sarototi, Deborah may intend you as the husband. Sorry! My prayer is not for you but for a husband that is a match, that both he and I would want one another equally."

In the morning, Marjana and Sarototi escort me to the Wilson Airport. With them, I discuss the rough night. Marjana says, "NeLaloshwa, Sarototi had a bad night, too." We talk of obtaining a green card for Sarototi so he can come and go to America. (Still, in conversation, maintain this notion of marriage with him because, if I don't, believe I might be held in this nightmare, never able to leave. Don't feel safe enough to be honest. I don't tend to be mealy-mouthed, but rather than deal, I get anthropological, running from my feelings.) *How can I explain to them the wedding felt "done" to me—not knowing it's reminiscent of the historical experience of being captured by the Maasai as a Bushmen shaman—and maybe something else?*

"Nothing really matters," Sarototi discouragingly replies. "Because we can't even communicate right now."

Relieved, yet nervously, I laugh, "Too true!" And so, begins a short dialog of our problem of being a married couple unable to express ourselves. To them, I share the discussion with Deborah, of my embarrassment around matrimony in general, of being "viewed" with a husband. This situation is not a simple black/white issue, yet "It's making my 'sex' public, especially, wedlocked to a Maasai Warrior—for isn't it just emboldened in people's imagination of their sexual prowess—ever multiplying the shame in me."

68: What Am I Not Conveying?

Marjana and Sarototi howl with laughter and with a little pride. "We understand your struggle, NeLaloshwa."

But they don't! What I can't seem to explain is, except for that young marriage of mine, all my other relationships were held in the shroud of secrecy and clandestine. "Never have I been willing to be visible with a love life." Before that first marriage, I had a clandestine relationship with a high school boyfriend because Dad did not like him, and of course, the long torrid affair with Renzo, a married man. "For me to be 'public,' is to feel exposed sexually, to be naked before others."

Can't even say to them: "Look! We've made a mistake." Normally intrepid, and certainly not a wimp, I usually speak up. Yet, it's this feeling of betrayal, on top of another betrayal (also shrouded in the past) that holds me back, making me unclear, powerless, frozen. In truth, I can't show my real cards. Our marriage has annihilated me.

"On the telephone, I've tried to tell a brother, a niece, and Mother about this wedding," I unfold. "However, I never have disclosed this to any family member." *Inside the vibration of my body is there the fear of being jailed in America for mixed-sexual relations, for a mixed-race marriage?* For I was born into a country with this law of anti-miscegenation until 1967!

Marjana asks: "Are you with child, NeLaloshwa?"

Maybe he thinks this odd, the emotions of a pregnant woman? I don't share with him, I kept Sarototi away during possible conception, that I've never had an abortion, that I don't even know if I can get pregnant. Instead, I shrug my shoulders because I really don't know. Inside, however, I feel frantic. I don't know I'm about ready to burst into fight or flight—burst into what is so natural for me, PTSD. Outwardly, I've shut down and lifted myself out of reality. This dialogue is a chess game of moveable pieces. I don't even know if I'm bound in the laws of Kenya by this marriage.

Through Marjana, Sarototi sweetly proclaims his love. "He thinks you two can learn one anothers' language in two weeks."

"No," Sarototi slips in, "In six months."

"I have explained to Sarototi that it takes twelve years to learn English in school. And just like the Kanga you're wrapped in says, 'Mapenzi hayana macho ya kuona,'" Marjana adds in a bit of humor to our intense conversation, "Love is blind." *No kidding!*

"Yeah, but we'll be a hundred years old, Nkoko's age!" Sarototi pouts.

Book One – Across the Divide to the Divine

Part II: The Divide

"Well, the challenge of communication is before us!"

69

INTERMISSION: THE QUEEN LEAVES THE BOARD

"Usisafirie nyota ya mwenzio."
"Don't set sail using someone else's star."

—Maasai Kanga proverb

Thankfully, I set sail, heading out on a mission to observe a potential prototype for the spiritual center in Laloshwa. *But is it for someone else's star?* Fly in a four-seater Cessna to Tanzania, to the Serengeti National Park's Idyllwild Camp, an idyllic exquisite campground run by an Italian couple, Judita and Pietro. They have obtained a concession, developing a partnership with the Maasai caring for the animals and the land.

So exhausted, I take a quick nap, curling up in a lounge chair of this elegant wooden tent, with an Italian marbled bathroom. Swept up in an incredible wind, a woodpecker rat-a-tat-tat reminds me to trust my own rhythms, to not tie myself to someone else's mission.

At four take a civilized tea, then press forward for a long hike with the Maasai guide Mposi, along with Pietro, and another Italian, Alessio. Discover from Mposi, that he has a bad back. I grill, "Really? Who is the pain in your back?" Wondering if the partnership between the Maasai and the Italians is, in fact, really as "equal" as they claim.

Across the Divide to the Divine Book One   **433**

Part II: The Divide

On top of a rocky point, we drink sundowners. Mount Kilimanjaro hovers in the distance. Pietro's daughter, Lulabella, accompanies us. She is three, barefoot, intrepid, brave and full of angelic red curly locks, reminding me of Beryl Markham as a child. As we load up in the Land Rover, a bat circles four times, teasing the dogs. *Is this ye ole shamanic friend, Bat, jogging my memory to seek him for help?*

Yet, I don't go inward. I don't shake the rattle to peer into this moment. I don't query Bat.

At the tent, I slip on something lovely for their formal Italian dinner, joining Pietro, his wife, Judita, Alessio, and another Italian couple. Serving us pasta, the Maasai men are dressed in white, down to the gloves—a flashback to the colonial lifestyle of Karen Blixen—concerns me. Afterwards, by the fire, in this elegant lodge, we "whites" converse, banter, dance a bit. Again, I meet with this separateness. I'm disturbed. Even so, I have been partnered off with Alessio, who sips tea when everyone departs for the night. A full moon taunts us with temptation. He wants to make out. I undertake a kiss, yet the recent "marriage" hovers about me just as Bat as a kind of warning. And my hands push his heart away.

Had Alessio caught me a few weeks before, I might have been tempted to imbibe. Normally, he'd be just my cup of tea. The rejection has him send for a Maasai to walk me to the tent. In silhouette from the moon, two giraffes are grazing near by as buffalo approach. Yet, somehow this make believe Western civilization these Italians have created separates me from this, as though there is a screen of protection from the brutality of nature, of what could be at stake. Just the Maasai ahead with spear in hand holds the truth.

How could I've explained to Alessio—I'm tangled up in someone else's star? That I've "gone native?" That I'm in a world where "Emotion is Black." No longer in the Western thought patterns where "Reason is Greek" (Léopold Sédar Senghor, Senegalese poet).

In the early morning, the Idyllwild employees whisk me away from breakfast for a game drive to the Ngorongoro Crater, and an instructional stroll along the rim. Flirtations abound with this hot-bodied yoga instructor, Alessio. Thoughts flash from him to pressing matters, my book, *Notes from Afar*, the "Journey of the Heart" Event, to how much passion and compassion I have for the Bushmen, to my predicament with Sarototi. Unlike the young Maasai girls, I'm an older woman with a will of her own, means, degrees upon degrees of education. I can afford to run away from their culture, which is not mine. *What of those girls, due to religious beliefs, are forced into circumcision, are sold by their brothers and fathers to older men they don't love, but they, in fact, fear?*

After the hike, I attempt to ease Mposi's back pain with the heat of essential oils. Poking him with more interrogations about his life. Several other Maasai gather. One proclaims, "She is a laibon." The others agree. *How do they know this, do I look like one? Do they know in their hearts or is there a Maasai hotline of that initiation?*

After lunch enter Judita's shop filled with magical Maasai creations. Buy a beautiful suede top with matching skirt, perfect foil for the Bushmen trance dances around the fire.

Tonight, an American family: Ronald, Lynnette, Laura, and Trevor participate in our formal dinner and waltzing at the fire. Struck with the thought—*Have I become a colonialist, too? Or just being white, I am whether I want to be or not?*

In the end, Alessio slobbers me with a big kiss (not that he isn't desirable)! This sally is not part of my research. I flee for the tent in shame. *For aren't I, a married woman?*

70

COLONIAL ENCOUNTERS

"...to be a person again, to rescue one's real personal self from the fiery jaws of collectivism, which devours all selfhood."

—Martin Buber, *I and Thou*

In preparation for the upcoming meeting with the Maasai of Laloshwa, I relook at Sarototi's *IChing* for this month, what he is posed with: he requires patience. Searching for a Tarot card for Sarototi, about us, and *The Devil* tumbles out. To battle against requires the strength of his will. To submit may be the death of the ego. When I unsheathe the Tarot for me, they warn that this visionary spirit may be foolhardy, unwise, that part of my heart, which is pure, may be deceived. Finally, I draw for me, the *Hierophant*—the sacred mysteries teacher of the social moral order. When broaching the concept of a set of principles, I panic—more *"thou shalt not's?"* The rebellious spirit inside of me wants not to conform—to be a part of collectivism. *For this, can I ever really "serve" as a laibon for a community? Is this what I run from—the pressure of the standard of marriage, of culture—of their requirements? For hadn't I been burned inside of mine? How could I trust myself inside any form, any foundation, or any social moral order?*

At Wilson Airport, Marjana and Sarototi greet me, driving me to the Bright's home where I will overnight until the return flight to America. In their garden, as I pen the day's happenings, kites are dreamily flying overhead. Chief Ole Wangombe and Baba Budhya have traveled from Laloshwa to Nairobi for conversation about the spiritual center. On the patio for tea, Sarototi, Marjana, and I gather around the table with them. They want to hear the news. The Chief inquires, "Is it possible, NeLaloshwa, that we could create a similar working relationship as Idyllwild Camp?"

For me, it always drops down to the basic elements. Share my concerns—I fear an imbalance—whites with marble showers and running water, the Maasai carrying theirs. "I love the strides that Pietro and Judita have made in this direction. The community they have created. The protection of the wildlife. They are incredibly generous, forming a nonprofit. But still there is a residue of the haves and have-nots." *How do we do this together, without falling under the long shadow of five hundred years of colonialism that is still very much in our vibration? From the 1960's, the National Liberation movement into Neocolonialism still hovers. Could we all perform a ritual upon the land? Is that enough time to lift a template ten times that long? To shift the paradigm to Postcolonial movements of soul?*

"Don't worry, NeLaloshwa. We've definitely decided, we don't want to build any buildings," the Chief simplifies. "Instead, each time someone visits, we'll set up temporary tents."

Under my breath I sigh deeply with relief, for this would mean I wouldn't have to raise funds for the center, responding, "This would certainly create equality?"

"Yes!"

Being a white foundation, benefitting blacks—still sets us apart, looks as though we're trying to save them. Though in truth, it would be African healers "saving" whomever we would bring. *But how would I gather those who would want a similar experience?* The depth of this inquiry is equal to the depth of other ways of thinking—a philosophical punching point. Cripples me from doing anything. *Is the spiritual center a kind of penance for me? To provide income for the Maasai, "saving" blacks? Or saving "whites" through indigenous medicines? Is this what Mariah had meant—set right a past-life—leading to the healing of others?* I've hit a stalemate that I don't know will last for years and years.

Chief Ole Wangombe has carried herbs of peace for me to bathe in and chalk to paint on my face for each shamanic journey. They are always so generous, so kind. We express our good-byes, *olesaries*, our well wishes, bathed with my tears.

In the morning, I rise for breakfast with George, Dusty and Marisella. (To these white American friends, I have yet to confess the story of this Maasai

Part II: The Divide

marriage, as though I'm in another dung hut, another home, where it's not safe to reveal a secret.)

Afterwards, I crawl back into bed to rest, journal, ponder—fall asleep. On the crest of departure from Africa, in the last pursuit of the *IChing*, I solicit: *Are we really married?* Already crossed, well underway, in progress, the *prima materia*. Set things right, gather your strength to surmount difficulties, birth pains, sprouting, but do not leave the dwelling. Something about the fact of leaving, I'm still dogged by the: *are we, or aren't we?* I want the Tarot to clarify Sarototi's Visa issue, it announces disappointment, dominion, tower.

In the afternoon, Sarototi and Motoguisimile stop by for tea and a chat. Sarototi motions for me to go upstairs to the bedroom. Act as if I don't understand, reach across for his hand to squeeze and smile. Clearly, inside the fibers of this being of mine, in a familiar domain, I can hold to this resolve.

Around the table, the three of us play with the Tarot together. Interrupting us, the white woman, Dusty, my host, wants me to go for a walk in the neighborhood while Angie, the Kikuyu maid, sets the table. Dusty informs me, "Marjana can't pick them up right now. Usher Sarototi and Motoguisimile into the garden on a blanket—for George is due home for lunch any minute!"

Later I will look back and realize, in all fairness to Dusty—though they were employees of her husband—they were my friends, not hers.

As I think of these now ostracized friends of mine—this "supposed" husband of mine and his friend—who have been thrown from the table to a blanket, I am crushed. Separation. Segregation. Yet, I remain silent. Again, as Desmond Tutu once revealed, the elephant is standing on the mouse's tail and I'm not shoving him to the side. I do not raise my voice in confrontation with Dusty. I don't even whisper. *If I, who believe what I do—professing to love the "other"—am not shouting from the rooftops, who will?* Instead, I run desperately into the kitchen, to speak with Angie, the black Kikuyu, who has befriended me, who surely will understand, "How shall I handle this exclusion—it seems so rude?"

By this, Angie is totally undaunted and non-judgmental, "Look, I have a whole loaf of homemade bread. Spread peanut butter sandwiches for them and I'll make a large pot of their favorite Maasai tea." Together, we bustle about, chatting about these disparities of culture, of the continued separation of blacks from whites in the Twenty-First Century, as we prepare an abundance for them.

Apologetically, I offer these goodies on a tray. Away from the house, I curl up on the blanket with them. Thankfully, these two Maasai grasp the situation and remain sovereign within. In fact, Motoguisimile replies nonchalantly, "NeLaloshwa, do not worry! This is just how it is!"

Around the black/white issue, of dominance and servitude, inside of me, arises a roaring conflict. What I see among the American, Italian, and British friends in Kenya is the treatment of the "other" as lesser, or certainly as an excluded outsider. But, in actuality, I am no better. Certainly, wherever I go, I see inclusion as a rarity. To be perfectly honest, I'm prejudiced toward others who form prejudices outside their comfort zone, outside their groups, and for me, colonialism is just a form of Collectivism! I don't want to be the judge, but I'm concerned. But the truth is, I said nothing! *Was I afraid to declare myself different?* Even so, I was silent to a Colonialist—therefore, I am one!

After living so intimately with the Maasai in the country, to see these white friends diminish my dear Sarototi is painful. (*Of course, how can Dusty know how much he means to me—if I don't tell her?* —But that shouldn't make a difference!) If I live among the Maasai in a home built with my specifications: with windows, wood floors, kitchen, running water, I, too, will be separated and set apart. *How do I compensate for the imbalance?* Inside this internal conflict, restless, I just want to be home—where, in fact, I must admit, I live just like *that*—as one of the "haves." So, I don't have a solution. Because when one "has," one grows accustomed to having, so one doesn't want to give it up. In fact, there is this gnawing fear of someday being without.

Just before the *fourth journey in,* at a dinner party in my apartment at 249 Church Street, my friend Larry, sheds further light on what he faces on a daily, trying to hail a taxi even as a light-skinned black man. No can do! And not only that, on the nights he drives his BMW home from work, the policemen pull him over to check the vehicle registry for ownership, a JDLR, because, again, it "Just Doesn't Look Right."

Horrified, I turn to my Jamaican friend, Apples, "You've never told me of such outrageous behavior. Is it true, you can't get a taxi?"

"Yes, Murphy, this is just a commonplace occurrence."

Later that evening, I wrapped my arms around Apples in a giant hug. Yet I could not comprehend that prejudice still exists. I had forgotten that seven years before, I had to fight with the heads of state for Apples to join me in the sales office at Mary McFadden. Thankfully, I had a convincing story—for all the buyers, the managers, and the salespeople throughout the country, who had visited our showroom or telephoned for help, knew Apples by name, loved her

Part II: The Divide

as our receptionist, missed her when she was out of the office having her baby. But even today, twenty years later, around the world these abusive prejudices, because #hateisavirus permeates, often resulting in someone being attacked, someone's death, or in the horrors of mass genocide.

I *attempt* to live without prejudice. My godchildren and their dear parents are Jamaican. In actuality, their mother, Apples, was "allowed" to join the sales force at Mary McFadden, selling couture clothes alongside me. Later, I trust her so much that she launches Global Voice from my home, while I am at Badgley Mischka. In the Bronx projects, in a tenement building with the young Puerto Rican girl, Jade, I spend Sunday afternoons in her apartment. While her grandmother cooks the chicken I bought, along with her famous yellow rice and green pea dish, *Arroz con Gandules*, Jade and I study, until we indulge in brunch with the all-female family, whom I grow to adore. Once, through a wise woman, they even induct me into their religion of Santeria. They have become a part of my everyday life, changed me, impacted me. From each of these families, one child had spoken at the GVF launch.

Casa d'Irene is a completely different ship. When my Latino friends, Miguel and Alfonso, work on projects around the home, I "get down and dirty" in the garden with them. Along with me, they laugh at those wild dreams, those conversations of mine with the snails and the hummingbirds. Organically, they help me value the land. Under the orange umbrella, on the balcony, we drink tea, coffee, and lemonade devouring "Murphy's Monster Cookies." With Nacho and his sons, we kiss one another in greeting. As Nacho rewires the house, or drops by to fix the ailing fountain, we talk of our failed relationships, our lonesomeness. We encourage: "You'll find the right mate!"

With Irene, while she, and her associates quickly clean the house, her son Elvis hangs out, helping me with a mass mailing for Global Voice. He then watches a movie curled up on the couch. When her husband, Antonio, picks up Elvis, I run out to hug him. We exchange. For an upgrade, when Judy passes on her used washing machine to me, I pass on my used one, to Irene. During the move, when I don't have room for the futon with a frame, Elvis is so proud to receive it. When I crack open a coconut, I drink the water, they eat the cream. They give me tips and advice. These wonderful people are part of this community of mine. Their smiling faces bring me joy. They reorient what is out of alignment, increasing the vitality, the Feng Shui of this existence at Casa d'Irene.

70: Colonial Encounters

Yet, isn't it still a question of haves and have-nots or have littles—and oftentimes, comes down to the color of our skin? Though certainly lonelier and more isolated, I still live in what many "might" consider the better neighborhood. I still "have" things they "might not" dare or even care to dream of.

After the stroll with Dusty along the back roads of Nairobi, I plop myself on the lawn with Motoguisimile and Sarototi, until she calls me for lunch with George. But immediately after, I, again, join my Maasai friends, until their departure. In the evening, for our last supper, I dine alone with the Bright family. Their daughter Marisella elegantly entertains us on the piano. Over our meal, learn from George that Sarototi and Marjana did not receive their Visas. Bizarre, how the tide has turned. *As if in the want to flee, have I closed the door for their entry into my world?* At nine p.m., George whisks me off to the airport for the flight home.

On this airplane bound for London, I just "happen" to sit next to Bob, a Pentecostal missionary from Texas. He has been busily proselytizing his faith to the Maasai in Tanzania: "Well, ma'am we don't mind their med'cines. But we're tryin' to rid the witch doctors of div-in-a-tion—" he rebuttals, "—de-mo-nic, ya know?"

"Hmmm, well, Bob, that's the very object of my studies," which seems to shock him. "If you take away the *laibon's* capacity to read into the stones, which for him or her is an ancient mathematical wisdom—how can he/she know what ails his or her patient? For as long as he or she can remember, that's been his or her access across the veil to that knowing Ancestor, to their god, Engai! And maybe, their Engai is the same God as ours, just clothed in a different name."

Ironically, in spite of these strong comments of mine, Bob still hands me his business card. But, again, he is a part of separating the Maasai from what he and others are afraid of, of what is strange, hard to decode, to measure. And perhaps just as Descartes—setting aside the "nightmare" of any form of "chaos" that cannot be controlled or understood—into "I think, therefore, I am." And then somehow we've added in that they must follow our way, not theirs.

Twenty years later, since this conversation with Bob, the way my Indigenous friends are being treated is changing. People are listening. A recent youtube video of "Decolonising Cultural Spaces: The Living Cultures Project" illuminates the joint meetings with the Maasai Warriors, Pitt Rivers Museum at the University of Oxford in partnership with MAA Museum of Archaeology and Anthropology at the University of Cambridge through InsightShare. Pitt Rivers Director Dr.

Book One – Across the Divide to the Divine **441**

Part II: The Divide

Laura Van Broekhoven explains, "If you truly want to decolonial science and decolonial academia, it means you are taking each others' knowledge systems seriously." It means trusting their divination, of how they speak to their God, what herbs they use for medicine, to determine which artifacts are sacred and still carry messages. To the museum staff, the Maasai representative Samuel Nangiria affirmed, "You're not just holding the artifacts. You are holding a very horrible history that our people have been through, a secret of what happened." All of a sudden it has fantastically become necessary to decolonize our museums, our homes. Another Maasai, Amos Leuka added, "The museums are committed to a partnership and the Maasai leadership is also. As long as they respect our aspirations and our existence as a community, as a people and that they will not see, maybe, that one is more superior than the other." Yes, somewhere out there in the beyond we're all equal, we're all one!

On the plane, I don't eat dinner, sleeping six intensive hours. Upon arrival, I run to the Hilton at Heathrow for breakfast, hot salt bath, and a quick snooze. Catch an earlier flight to Los Angeles. Inside the Tarot, on my little flight table, I adjust, balance, and meditate. Should I pursue a trip around the world with National Geographic? Great gain. Fortune. More importantly, wonder if there is a baby or not? The laibon, Hakima thinks otherwise! Only God and the Goddess know! Assume He/She will help me through the nine-month junket. By all calculations, an immaculate conception, which due to Mother Mary's, He/She would truly comprehend!

As though a young twelve-year old, reconnecting with my childhood boyfriend Tom—I loved Sarototi. He brought me back into a healthy relationship with that past of mine. He was my companion and friend in the mysteries of divination, in the shared love of nature. He listened and believed my story. His family became a haven for me from a world that had gone awry, from a world that had stopped listening to the forests, to nature trapped below our cement sidewalks and highways.

But to be wed! Well, whether I wanted to be married or not, I was, I am, and because of this shocking reality, I've not only fled most of those Western societal beliefs, I've now run away leaving behind *that* Maasai *shuka*, out of tribalism, out of collectivism, crossing a life-changing initiatory threshold, hopefully into further authenticity.

In a way, this trip home shall be cataclysmic with a renovated, determined Self, a bit cool but clearly with some kind of goal—a calling! *In this fleeing, will I*

70: Colonial Encounters

create "the Butterfly Effect" for other women? Will the running away from this little ole marriage toward the rush of finishing the Doctorate in Philosophy, help lots and lots of women flee from clitorodectomies, flee from arranged marriages to men they don't want?

The impact of the Maasai's initiation is great enough that it will send me along the trail of further healing and shamanic training with Deborah. I will begin to practice the energy exchange with Eve Brinton, open the Akashic Records with Marygrace O'Hearn, I will take to the warmth of Water Release Therapy with Diane Feingold, brain release with Lynn Maass, tantric with Pamela Madison, Transcendental Meditation with Signe Wilson, hands-on-healing with Steven Lum, bodywork with Michael Luan and Eric Watts, massage with Genevieve Klein, rebirthing and EFT with Wendy Ann McCarty and osteopathy with Dr. Timothy Schultz.

Slowly, through their healing hands, through the Mother energy of Santa Barbara, I will begin to call forth the power within—recovering bits through myths from continent to continent, weaving me back together until in the quiet of the library, in the fine-tuning of the dissertation, at the crackling fire amidst Tarot, *IChing* coins, and Runes, the "I" will be "I'd," and the Greater Self will begin her ascent. From here, I will be able to teach, dismantling structures, paradigms that no longer serve. Just as Richard, in *Bleak House* urges in his death, "I will begin the world." "—and with one parting sob began the world. Not this world, oh, not this. The world that sets this right" (Charles Dickens)!

Oh, please, set things right. So, I'll pray for it, believe in it and make it happen—the Decolonization of Everything.

71

CUTTING THE WORLD FROM THE MOORINGS OF THE FEMININE

"In chaos theory, the butterfly effect is the sensitive dependence on initial conditions in which a small change in one state of a deterministic nonlinear system can result in large differences in a later state."

—G. Boeing, "Visual Analysis of Nonlinear Dynamical Systems: Chaos, Fractals, Self-similarity and the Limits of Prediction," *Systems*

While at Laloshwa, among the Maasai, in their myths, psyches, and conditioning, I observe how the masculine continues to dominate the feminine in marriage, in leadership, and in the act of clitoridectomy. The female's clitoris—the apparatus which vibrates, melting her, nourishing her soul, stimulating her to fine pleasures, informing her—is removed. Some say, to access the woman's real heart is through her vulva. *What if this is also what attunes her to her knowingness? What if in cutting the clit, just as rape, her ability to stand as equal to all and her inner power are dismantled? And in cutting her clit, in raping her, we cut the world from the moorings of the feminine?*

As babies, the cutting of the cords from our mother, from one life to another, is a shock. However, this separation is necessary. Yet, in Africa, the cutting of the clit as a kind of circumcision of the clitoris, between what was and what will be is an emasculation and what the West does metaphorically—this emasculation—in the form of a psychic circumcision to the woman psychologically and emotionally. To recover from this, we must, as Paulo Freire encourages, to keep perceiving it as "freedom from" and in quest for human completion *(The Pedagogy of the Oppressed). Can we reweave, realign, and reawaken in some new form?*

Is Deborah's suggestion of late— "You're an awakener for the Maasai for their relationship to the feminine."—*a reweaving for them, into some new form? How can this be?* I thought these brave powerful warriors were changing me, and yet, according to Deborah I am igniting something in them. *So, are they looking toward me as Sarototi has been—for an answer?* Overwhelming me with this responsibility. *But what if this reconnection to the feminine is what the whole world needs most—not just the Maasai?*

In Flight of Objectivity: Essays on Cartesianism & Culture, Susan Bordo explores the *Meditations* of Descartes. "The Cartesian 'masculinization of thought,' […] is one intellectual 'moment' of an acute historical flight from the feminine, from the memory of union with the maternal world, and a rejection of all values associated with it." Descartes' decision to split off from what he feared, from his nightmare changed the course of history. His objective theory poured forth from his imagination and set in motion a split, a cleavage, a divide, a circumcision from the dark, the feminine, the intuition.

Western Civilization is still reeling from this "'super-masculinized' model in which detachment, clarity, and transcendence of the body are all key requirements" (Bordo). It was a liftoff, a removal from any attachment to the raw female and what Francis Bacon called a "masculine birth of time," where the elements of intuition, empathy, and the associative "feminine," "were rigorously exorcised from science and philosophy" (Bordo). We, as woman were "exorcised," as were anybody in association with nature—blacks, indigenous, anyone of any color, or anyone with other sexual proclivities or gender than white heterosexual males. We became objects, subjects.

In shutting down his nightmare, Descartes cuts out the heart, splitting off from the body and from a healthy connection to the feminine. Villoldo explains that with this twisting of facts, the feminine became demonized, and with that, spirituality fell by the wayside. "We live in a world devoid of the sacred. We end up believing that matter [. . .] is what's important" (*Mending the Past*).

Part II: The Divide

But *matter* isn't equal to spirit, Villoldo reminds, and comes from the Latin root *mater*, meaning "mother." To Villoldo, the sacred feminine has become warped, and in this process, we consider *"things"* as maternal, as though the ownership of these "things"—cars, houses, boats, buildings—will somehow care for us.

Instead, in Western Society, we have lost the care of the woman. Even Laloshwa Highlands, not everyone is kind like Sarototi is to Kisima. I notice that his own father is viciously mean to his second wife, downgrading her into nothingness. Although to be honest, she's Maasai through and through, tough, and seems unmoved by his rebuffs.

Reactively, inside me, a rebellion brews. These actions of men are not right in America, nor in Africa, nor anywhere. On earth, the whole system is out of balance and has been for some odd six thousand years. Women own one percent of the earth's wealth. According to the Gender Gap Report of 2022, it will take 151 years to close the economic gender gaps. (We have yet to know how the LGBTQIA+ will affect change, nor do we know how the #metoo movement, will roll out both in its honesty of splendor, and its accusative horror, truths/secrets no one has wanted to admit for years.)

The Maasai, and maybe American men, too, have yet to hear the tale of Sir Gromer's challenge to King Arthur, "discover what women want!" Through Arthur's long search and Sir Gawain's relationship, he gathers the truth from ugly Dame Ragnelle, "Women want their sovereignty." In marriage, Sir Gawain will listen, offering her a choice—to be beautiful in the day or beautiful at night. Just from this freedom of choice, the "ugly" spell is broken!

Inside the *laiboni* ritual, in the "spell," it felt as though I lost this autonomy. For this, the relationship with the Maasai, with Sarototi, may never be quite the same. For Sarototi's trick to gain consummation broke the endearment of rapture for one another, tricking me out of an old paradigm, into a new way of being. After this, it will take me years to meet a man I'm interested in, with a "shared" capacity of equality.

Deborah's belief that the Maasai men long for this new yin strength they encountered in me, mystifies. Coming to the Warriors as a child, made them tender toward me, as well, they were attracted to that American female bravado. And yet, when they have a chance to marry me, "she," the feminine becomes bound and gagged into their present paradigm, just as the Gnostics

446 *I. Murphy Lewis*

71: cutting the world from the moorings of the feminine

believe we have imprisoned the female representative, Sophia, separating God from his chosen partner—the very partner who is to ignite his self-actualization.

In that great need, that great vulnerability of mine, I actually relocate myself under the strictures of chauvinism. In a personal projection, I hand over my being, giving up clarity and awareness, allowing them to be "the saviors," trusting them. I allow them to go unconscious in their responsibility to treat me as an equal, as had the examples of my mother, my grandmother and my great grandmother before me. As women, caught in their reactions, in reverence for the men, we did not dare to call them to task.

What had happened in America is that we, as women—in becoming feminists, in demanding our right to vote, to receive equal pay—had somehow continued to place ourselves in subjugation to the white men through this "ask." As well, we hadn't helped the "other." In *Against White Feminism: Notes on Disruption*, the civil rights attorney Rafia Zakaria believes, for these reasons and more, the white feminist movement needs to be dismantled. Audre Lorde in *Sisters Outsiders*, believes white women shunned their anger, with what my grandmother Rene used to say, a "shush," with an oppressive "tone it down," when the white women called their feelings hysterical. In Zakaria's essay, she explains how white women haven't been inclusive to the ideas and issues of women of color, setting themselves up as "saviors" with foreign aid and the notion of women's "empowerment." When all along, the term "empowerment" hailed from India in a more fully expanded way.

I would have to agree with Zakaria, because, fifty years after this "second wave" of the feminist movement and twenty-five years after my own corporate associations, the power structure of the white ruling man still exists and has a stronghold. And I must confess, most of the women in my family have been in subservience to the white men in our lives. In the end, Zakaria calls on women of color to create communities of solidarity like Audre Lord suggests, that aren't about competition but accommodating all the ways of being and thinking—so that all knowledge is honored and accepted and brought to the table—equally. As well, Zakaria calls on the women of color to make Kimberlé Williams Crenshaw's "war on narrative" to reshape the stories, in a recalibration of feminism— "putting the fangs back" (Jenny Bhatt, "'Against White Feminism' Is an Urgent Call to Action for Solidarity and Justice"). To make "whiteness" visible (for it has clearly infected us all)!

Book One – Across the Divide to the Divine **447**

Part II: The Divide

In Ursula K. Le Guin's blog, "A Band of Brothers, A Stream of Sisters," understands that there is something already more organic within the engagements of women. "As for female solidarity, without it human society, I think, would not exist. But it remains all but invisible to men, history, and God. Female solidarity might better be called fluidity—a stream or river rather than a structure [...] the fellowship of women on their own terms, it tends to be casual, unformulated, unhierarchical; to be ad hoc rather than fixed, flexible rather than rigid, and more collaborative than competitive." This stream of ours gives me hope.

Le Guin explains that men are more competitive, hierarchical, often expressed in a one-upmanship. "They exclude, first, women; then, men of a different age, or kind, or caste, or nation, or level of achievement, etc.—exclusions that reinforce the solidarity and power of the excluders."

Once at PGI, my professor David Miller proclaimed, "What you're studying with the Bushmen is passé, Murphy. Western Civilization has gone on from there and has developed and evolved."

I was horrified, challenging him with: "What are you talking about? We're not superior here. We weave back to go forward." I inhale a big breath. "The Kalahari San Bush-men-and-women have an intelligence that is equal to and just as important as ours—it's just different. They know how to track, how to survive in the world—and have lived thousands of years longer than any of us have. They don't need buildings or need to define themselves as a civilization; they live in lean-to's without deleteriously harming their environment. Unlike us, they are ecologically sound. They do not take more than what is necessary from a plant, then replant it in the ground for next year. They hunt the wounded animal, the ones that don't have a chance to survive. They know how to heal themselves and others. They know how to climb the ropes to God for answers. We have so much to learn from them. They have wisdom, you and I can't imagine. They have the ability to see right through us to who we really are. I believe we need to acknowledge them for inside their ancient myths lies wisdom. They are our culture's roots. Though they are little people, we stand on the shoulders of these giants."

Dr. Miller must have heard me, because a fellow student said the next year he spoke differently about our Bush-men-and-women friends. *But what about those academicians who are busily teaching other students in this "Western" white mentality?*

71: cutting the world from the moorings of the feminine

In *Seeing Race Again: Countering Colorblindness Across the Disciplines*, there are those, such as Kimberlé Williams Crenshaw, Luke Charles Harris, Daniel Martinez HoSang, and George Lipsitz, who dare to challenge scholarship, the social life, the politics and laws ingrained within our system. Their question becomes: *How do we break up the old ways to collaborate cross-institutionally?* In the chapter, "They (Color) Blinded Me with Science: Counteracting Coloniality of Knowledge in Hegemonic Psychology," Glenn Adams and Phia S. Salter write that "White American society provides a variety of cultural-psychological tools that make it easier to deny or avoid information about the extent of racism. [...] Even if people set aside their identity-defensive biases and seek or weigh evidence in objective fashion, they can still fail to recognize racism where it exists—and oppose policies to address it—if the only knowledge tools at their disposal are ones that promote ignorance of racism" (*Seeing Race Again*).

According to Deepa Purushothaman in *The First, the Few, the Only: How Women of Color Can Redefine Power in Corporate America*: "The current rules and structures within corporations are antiquated and reflect a white, male leadership structure. They are set up to protect companies and cover up issues instead of creating transparency." It made me reflect on the choices of Bernie Madoff, of his Ponzi scheme, or the tricks of Enron's "fake holdings and off-the-book accounting practices," or the Farm Crisis in the 1980's, which changed the face of rural America, of which, my own father's bank got caught in, almost losing his shirt and many of his farming friends lost everything. Or of the Housing bubble and subprime mortgage crisis in 2008 (for which I barely got out in time). Without caring for the ramifications of what they were doing with Other People's Money, they "cooked the books." Again, it hasn't changed. "The only thing that is changing, is us" (Suzanne Kingsbury).

Deepa interviewed five hundred women of color within major corporations, whom she believes are the future brokers of power. Through these interviews, she discovered that these women felt the same as she had——"exhausted, confused, and drained of my power"—as a partner in the accounting firm, Deloitte. Just as Deepa, I, too, was on the edge, could barely eat; I had grown thin; I was gagging; I was so stressed I couldn't hear the precious words of my nephew; awakening in the middle of the night leaving messages for my staff. That was twenty years ago—*Why isn't it changing?*

"If we are going to heal the game of power," Deepa believes, "it's time to take apart the delusions we have been taught about capitalism and the underpinnings

Book One – Across the Divide to the Divine **449**

holding it up, such as meritocracy, scarcity, and competition." As women of color, they must "question everything," Deepa challenges.

I hope they find the power to do this. I pray to God that these women of color can rise together, changing the systemic racism within feminism, within the corporate world through the professional developments of DEI, of diversity, equity, and inclusion! I pray they find a way. I didn't. I didn't question enough, those power structures of the men around me, within Escada, Halston, and the Maasai Warriors.

What I don't know is that someone will be questioning the system of the Maasai, that their structure will be coming unglued. While I'd been pushing away from Badgley Mischka, away from the guru, and slowly separating myself from the marriage to Sarototi, a young eight-year-old Maasai girl, Nice Leng'ete, runs away from her ceremonial circumcision. Instead of making it a scandal, her grandfather will note her courage, affirming her. She eventually will become the force of a movement against the cutting of the clitoris that will motivate the Kenyan government to declare an edict against this act in 2011—keeping 10,000 girls' clitorises intact (and now, maybe even more). *Is she "The Butterfly Effect" on me, on the #metoo movement?*

Perhaps through Kisima's necklace, through Nice Leng'ete's bravery, the Maasai women are truly the ones affecting this feminine transformation of mine. Deepa, too, who had gained such insights from the corporate world is now busily affecting it from the outside in through her writings and podcasts. These women of color are magically flipping our universe upside down, tricking us forward into a new way of being. Hallelujah!

72

INSIDE THE ANOMIE

"An insidious nomadism endemic of modern time in which the individual, afflicted with disorientation and anomie, drifts within the indifferent spaces of housing developments and shopping centers and superhighways."

—Edward S. Casey, *Getting Back into Place*

In fairy tales, sorting is a feminine quality, a task Aphrodite requires of Psyche to categorize every seed into heaps upon heaps. Here, at home in Santa Barbara, I separate "the wheat from the chaff," the olive seeds of Sarototi's wife, Kisima, the essence of peace, appear in dream form, as I attempt to sort what just happened through the *laiboni* ritual.

Telephone Mother. We have an excellent chat. Two times a day, she walks across the street to see her husband, my father. She can only withstand five minutes for he no longer reflects her needs. She sounds so lonely and yet hopeful, forcing herself to believe with those rose-colored glasses she wears, praying for Dad's continued improvement.

When, in actuality, in one year, he has become a blob, a two-hundred-pound vegetable lying there, transported by pulley into a wheelchair, then rolled into the dining room where he cannot even lift a spoon to his mouth. Requires the care of feeding from round the clock nurses who adore him. He sleeps through the day. When someone enters his room, he cracks open his right eye to peer out. For a man who golfed daily, keeping his figure trim, immaculate at one-hundred-fifty-five-pounds until the age of eighty, this is not promising, and for some, strangely bizarre—many of his friends cannot face him.

Into the mundane of the everyday, I drag myself out the door, in the California way—driving quickly about—running to the cleaners, stopping for a manicure, shopping for groceries within this *anomie* of toing and froing. In the car, I parcel thoughts: *What of those days in Africa? How do these two realities relate? How can I integrate what just happened to me?*

Adjusting to the time zone, I quietly curl up on the couch to nap through eight hours of movies: *Bend it Like Beckham, The Way We Were, Batman Returns*. Later, in a shamanic state, I query Dad: "Why the diapers? Why the round the clock care?"

He reveals: "I never got the opportunity to be a baby. My mommy wanted me to grow up too fast!" *Is this Dad in his feminine receptive state, lying there in his blobby-ness?* The person that we know, and love has discarded his elegant suits for cotton sweats—yet, he still needs to be loved, cared for, babied—he, who was so magnanimous, commanding, powerful and successful.

For some reason this recent image of him pauses me to ponder: *Perhaps I don't want a man in this life?* Traveling as a bride with Sarototi, I never found space to write or read. I felt "pawed." In Northern Kenya at the Bomer Hotel, as the young woman ululated: "la la la la, " I thought my sanity might fracture as the gifted necklace from Kisima did in a dream, tumbling to the ground, "and all the king's horses and all the king's men couldn't put Humpty Dumpty together again." *Who could put me back together again? Was she a reflection of the past—what I didn't want to see?*

Shattered—the city life, my parents' memories, and that friendship with Sarototi, me—*dismembered, unrecoverable?* Yet, in this fairy tale we call life, inside this anomie of the fast pace California driving life, amazingly grounded, piece-by-piece the "I" is coming together again.

73

A MEETING OF MINDS— FEMALE THAT IS!

"She looked back with melancholy derision on her old conception of life, as a kind of well-lit and well-policed suburb to dark places one need never know about. Here, they were, […] in her own bosom, and henceforth she would always have to traverse them to reach the beings she loved best."

—Mrs. Anna Sommers Leath, Edith Wharton, *The Reef*

As I attempt to traverse the dark regions of memories, the "well-policed suburb" of my Westernized soul, I reach out to the psychotherapist Mary.

"The Maasai did not give you the option to wed," Mary agrees, "they thrust it upon you similarly to your treatment by men in the developmental years. Once again, your own knowingness for silence protected you, submitting to their ceremony for self-preservation." She reiterates: "As a child, stepping into a 'protective hush' served you and those around. Yes, of course, my dear, you sense this to be 'the same ole story,' however, this time, believe it or not, you've spiraled up." Smiling. "You are different, more on the planet, more secure, and in a conscious awareness."

"So being voiceless—instead of being considered 'bad'—actually serves me again and again."

"Yes. What they knew about you, Murphy," she insisted, "what they set about to repair, gave them an understanding that this act of marriage, especially based on your history, would feel to you as though an assault."

"Indeed, Mary, I think they were too busy being the ultimate magicians, conjuring my growth into womanhood—marriage, a possible baby—through union with Sarototi. They did not re-register the original injury." I muse. "Certainly, they treat women dualistically, warmly, and yet dominate them. In a way, they went unconscious themselves, fell into my shadow (or should I say, that Sarototi fell into my honey trap). For me, it's a sudden thunderclap, a reckoning. For them, it's as though they don't have a clue about the weather."

Though Mary was often at Deena Metzger's Daré's, where we opened to spirit or healed someone in need, I find it strange I don't reveal to Mary the past life of the Australian Skeleton Man. Nor do I tell her of the wound in the spleen—the "arrows" of an awakening from Mundadisi I had been working on for many months. *Do I feel she won't understand this Cibecue Apache, Benson Lewis' notion of stories as arrows? Or is it that at the time of our discussion I had not yet formed the words for these experiences?* For much of this writing of mine is in hindsight, through journaling, through the wisdom of the Akasha.

Though we do discuss Lmakiya, the Samburu Warrior—the Maasai cousin. How different he is. So opposite of Sarototi, he didn't fall into the black hole of seduction—what really is that "white" hole of mine, into the Spider's web of my making. He didn't play into the patterning from the historic. "Yes, Mary, just as my psychoanalyst Walter, Lmakiya becomes an example. Look at me! Now my new relationships with Dr. Dave Cumes, Steven Lum, and Thomas are based on friendship—no shenanigans.

"In spite of the maneuver of the Maasai, I long to travel more this year. I may miss one set of classes per semester. Worth it, if it means touching the land of all the mythological places I've been studying!"

"Oh Murphy, since you've completed your Masters, you can do your doctoral classes easily as though hands tied behind your back. You've been so generous to others. It's your turn to do what you want."

"Mary, I just want to admit—though this marriage to Sarototi has caused our relationship to sever, has caused such uncomfortability—it's also true, that I miss him, greatly! I had a connection to Sarototi that was out of this world."

74

HARKEN UNTO MY CRY

Give ear to my words O Lord
Consider my meditation
Harken unto the voice of my cry
My King and My God
For unto Thee will I pray
My voice wilt thou hear in the morning
O Lord in the morning
Will I direct my prayer unto Thee
and will look up.

—Psalm 5

When I was unhappily inside the throes of the Christian ministry, this prayerful song was sung at most every event. Of late, inside my Secret Garden this haunting tune naturally rises up and out of me, as if some great need harkens me to bended knees, returning me to the fireplace where I must strum this tune from the guitar. For some reason (perhaps it's a confession of vulnerability and a longing to be heard), it always makes me weep. Historians believe King David of Israel, wrote as many as seventy-three of the Psalms. I like to think this is one of David's for I've always related to him in the sense that he is so humanely "human."

Stepping away from the garden to sing, to pray, means, I leave the fruit rats and the Blue Jays to their hey day, with all the delicious treats of oranges,

Part II: The Divide

lemons, avocadoes, and bird seed. And of course, without me, the falcon and the crow can continue their three-day battle over eggs.

Since my challenges with Mundadisi and Sarototi, I've done so much searching of late, through healing hands and exploring past lives. What's wild is, more often than not, I have been a man. No wonder I have such trouble being female here. Today, in the shamanic field, in a life as a Native warrior, an owl drops into my hand, the stone Thomas had most recently, in reality, given me. It's as though his gift grounds another life, making it real. *Is it the same rock I'd had then, a talisman buried inside a leather pocket?* There, in that life, I had had such successes; I made others jealous of me.

In the midst of my explorations, there is one I seem to choose to confide in of late—and that is the shaman Deborah. In our soothing telephone conversation, I discover, from her shamanic journey on my behalf, "an adult woman" is moving into the left side. It seems, in another life, the training I had done in Egypt, I only completed the masculine portion, and now, the Egyptian Goddess Hathor integrates the feminine. It makes sense, as there is a more "adult," more whole me functioning in the world.

"In utero-form, you have begun to stand between men and women." Yes, I have no interest in taking sides—not very feminist of me, I know. She further enlightens, "The Maasai know this, believing you to be their bridge into the Twenty-First Century, due to the value you place on the tribe, on their understanding of their land, their plants." I have loved them deeply, and yes, of course, I believe in their capacities because of what they've done for me.

Deborah implies, "Africa is healing the middle world."

"Yes, they need to," I concur. "They have played too many games, always busy 'feeding the hungry ancestors.'"

"On your property, six Maasai and two Bushmen wait for you to integrate this feminine." Once again, as in Africa, as in New York City, there are tribal people encircling me, people who care.

"Deborah, I must confess, yesterday I did a shamanic journey around my relationship with Mundadisi. It seems he was the Skeleton Man of Australia. For every time I peered at Mundadisi, their faces, their bodies were interchangeable. No wonder I've had to sort this over and over—my family originally slaughtered his!"

While these things happen on the ethers round about me, I'm gagging again. This time due to the retainer in my mouth, which expands as I turn a

74: Harken Unto My Cry

crank. For me, it feels as though each expanse brings the terror of memory. The psychotherapist Mary, the chiropractor Michael Luan, and several others want me to stop this process. The orthodontist is casual, "I'm pleased with our results, Murphy. At least, wear it when you can—especially at night."

Yet, I imagine something deeper is going on. The challenge with Mundadisi, this marriage to Sarototi has gutted me, humiliating me, throwing me out of balance. And where I am, takes me to my knees (not necessarily looking up, O, Lord), head dangling over the toilet. Well, it must have taken me down, as I'm not writing, as they all encouraged. In Maasailand, I've been busily trying to create a cultural healing center. I'm way off course. *Is this Psalm, asking God for help, re-orienting me back to my personal legend?*

Whichever way my cry harkens, whether looking up or down in humility, I will step out once more to participate with others in "The Gathering" at Big Bear.

75

THE GATHERING

*To the winds of the West
Mother Jaguar,
Protect our medicine space.
Teach us the way of peace, to live impeccably
Show us the way beyond death.*

—Native American Invocation (Villoldo)

At Big Bear, the "Journey to the Heart" event, the (phenomenal) "Gathering in The Name" of shamans, of people of different color, of different faiths from all over the world—where the holding of hands, meeting as equals, singing, sharing dreams, listening, honoring the elemental spirits and the Ancestors—commences with a Bang. Discovering, in arriving late, I have missed the first meeting, an intimate assembly of thirty shamans. The news travels fast—that everyone magically receives from the hand of the Kalahari Bushman, Vetkat—a kind of: "and the holy spirit descended upon them" moment.

By this news, a little part of me is disappointed, as though something important has been missed, for the larger sessions are filled with over three hundred people longing for recovery, and to a sensitive, this feels encumbering. Every hour is designated to different medicine men or women displaying their gifts and capacities. I have no time to attend any meetings, either I end up

75: The Gathering

studying on my upper bunk or diving into those relationships needing repair, where conflicts rise to the surface.

The first conflict is to draw an accord between two couples, those dear friends from Kansas, Roberta and Clint, Kathy and Rick, whose community cared for me after *9/11*. As emissary, I run back and forth between the two couples, attempting to be the repairer of the breach.

Maybe my mother's lesson of "heaping loving coals" upon others still applies. To be clear—and what I'm seeing even at this "loving" event—we all walk on landmines of one another's history of wars, prejudices, jealousies, and curses. *Will this ever stop?* I'm not so sure. "Here, am I," at a healers' retreat, with healers from all over the earth and those who have come to be healed, and here we are inside the same challenges that happen out there, in the everyday!

The second disharmony is with divorced South African friends who must face one another. The biggest challenge is for the former wife to come to terms with her former husband, now, with another woman, busily walking about, filming this event. For this, there is not much I can do except be all ears and full of compassion for her.

With so many Original People of Turtle Island surrounding this moment, their adage circles— "Don't judge a man until you've walked two moons in his moccasins." And our adage— "Don't judge a book by its cover"—becomes relevant. For, to be honest, I'd never ever walked a mile in these couple's shoes.

Ironically, I also try to resolve a misunderstanding between the founders of this occasion, Kim Langbecker and Rupert Isaacson, and the Kalahari Bushmen of South Africa. While the Bushmen from Botswana, the activists are front line and center promoting their land battle with DeBeers and Botswana, these Bushmen from South Africa, I discover, are hidden behind the kitchen, under a large tree, smoking cigarettes.

"They brought my husband, Vetkat, the artist and shaman, along with his cousin, Isak Kruiper, the wisdom-keeper, and me, all the way from South Africa to participate as healers—not activists—and yet somehow we've been forgotten, deleted from the calendar," conjectures Cape-colored Belinda, the co-author of *Kalahari Rainsong*. "But, why?" she ponders, as she drains the life out of her cigarette.

Belinda's right. On the schedule, I discover a mistake has taken place. No official time has been made for the people of the South, who have suffered with their own land issues and have come in peace with curatives.

Part II: The Divide

"Our organization, Global Voice, wants your group to share. We participated, providing a movie camera to film your journey here, to the Four Corners, and to the U.N. Let me see what I can do." I start to step away, then turn back, "Oh, by the way, Belinda, did I mention, my friend Deborah says there are two Bushmen in my garden, maybe they are Vetkat and Isak!" She smiles, shaking her head in agreement.

With as much honesty and as much clarity as I can bring to and fro I go between my friends, as though Ann Eliot amidst the Musgrove family in *Persuasion*, "How was she to set all these matters right? She could do little more than listen patiently, soften every grievance and excuse each to the other; give them hints of the forbearance necessary between such near neighbors and make these hints broadest" (Jane Austen). There is something to this living in non-judgment, to living in inquiry. For I learn that Kim and Rupert didn't think the Bushmen from South Africa wanted to direct a session. They listen with open hearts, placing Vetkat and Isak inside the schedule.

What I had feared would be the fourth challenge of a third encounter with Mundadisi, however, reveals itself much more quiet, otherworldly.

"How are you my dear?"

"Fine, and you?"

As we embrace one another, there is no confession of any form—we don't seem to need one. To him, I don't reveal the flying tomahawk, the sore spleen, and the months of recovery through past life regressions and shamanic journeys, for I fear "the tell" will only expose those vulnerabilities, which he probably knew anyway, nor do I question his integrity, which I now thoroughly believe in. We never grow close again, nor do I ever see him again (at least, not yet).

What I note in this greeting is, there is no longer a strangeness between us. No longer do I feel the pain in the spleen. Perhaps Mundadisi's healing was similar to those stories shot like "arrows" (Basso). Once the arrow has done its work, it can be removed, cuts cleaned, and the breach that caused separation can be healed, the past lives recovered, forgiven, until the sting is finally gone.

Maybe I was complete and didn't need Mundadisi anymore. I just hadn't discovered that yet. Maybe he had no more to offer me, for between the *fifth journey in* with him, the sixth journey in, and this event at Big Bear, I had had the final initiation as a dream shaman. I had even stepped away from the training with our mutual friends Deena and Valerie. I had had another transformation.

75: The Gathering

Even so, I had yet to cross over into the postmenopausal zone of maturity as a crone.

Most of all, as with the guru in Upstate NY, I had not been interested in making a guru of Mundadisi, nor did he require that with me or anyone, nor did I long to be a guru myself. Of course, I was aware, that in every field, shamans, priests, doctors, lawyers, brokers, there are charlatans. But I never for a minute believed him to be one. Years later, Kim Langbecker would say, "He's always had absolute integrity!"—Which confirms for me that he was only challenging me further, testing my mettle for a purpose.

Maybe I had ventured all the way to Africa to recover the black man within—the one that whites are prejudiced against, the one that is wounded because of our actions. Maybe that movement to Kenya had forced me to heal "the Sarototi" and "the Mundadisi" inside myself, inside of those cultural misbeliefs! I had yet to know that a future journey to follow love, to live in Denmark (Book Two) would force me to heal the white male within.

In the midst of this, there is something else that is obscured from all the medicine men and women about me—on my body, a rash in the shape of a perfectly formed triangle—the point beginning at the navel, spreading across the fallopian tubes, to the edges of the hip and pelvic bones, expanding to the upper thighs. A marked woman. Have concluded it is the red bark tea prescribed by the Maasai *laibon*, Hakima. The root has pierced me systemically deeper than an antibiotic, into the very heart of the matter. Laughingly I must admit the irony, for of course, she gives me something reconciling the wounds of the past, hidden in the lower chakras, the feminine, and perhaps even cures me from her fellow tribesman Sarototi.

If the Maasai shaman Sarototi had been here, would he be pawing at me as when we studied the language, or at the fire praying, honoring my menses? Even so, he loved me. He wanted to give the ultimate gift of himself in marriage. My incapacity to speak decimated him more than if I had spoken. I feel this on the ethers intensely. And I fear this distancing has in turn detonated our friendship! I don't know that in the *seventh journey in*, nine years later, we will recover this (Book Three).

As I observe the craving amongst those who have shown themselves this weekend, I recall Deborah's words about me healing the feminine in the Warriors. Like her, now, I cannot help but believe, that everyone at this conference and these dark warriors, Sarototi and Mundadisi, are in search of the mysteries of the lost feminine in the black hole, the great yawn of the universe, the vulva—for some kind of realignment. Perhaps, this is my longing as well. *Is this the Universal Hunger, the greater hunger that the Bushmen know so profoundly—that van der Post once wrote of? Could we embrace the feminine and one day the Chinese symbol of the yin and the yang encircling us in balance and harmony?*

So vast was Sarototi's own hunger, he could not hear me say, our love is different than the typical marriage and is formed and remains in the spiritual dimension. Know I love him dearly and am in love with many aspects of him. Even had a crush, entertaining a fantasy of having sex with him. Though for five trips, I avoided sex like the plague. It was ever a constant worry, and I lived in constant vigilance to avoid such an encounter. But never did I want to marry, to cross-cultures, to hurt the relationship with the tribe, the destruction of which I feel so strongly now.

Thankfully, today, there is freedom from a "Sarototic" moment. Relieved. Glad he is not here. Being a wife of a Maasai Warrior was a public struggle for me and strangely shaming—for it clearly displayed to the world that I was in a sexual relationship, as I had once mentioned to him. *For what do people think of warriors?* Great in bed! Except for the first husband, I remained hidden in most all my relationships—for sex to me, had become "the forbidden," the taboo to be broken. As well, I'd witnessed the othering of Sarototi, set out on a blanket away from my own white friends' table. Just imagine, as a black, as a Kenyan, as a warrior, without English, what he would experience in America. Perhaps I did not have the courage or the strength to be married to a man, who would continuously experience such alienation.

However, smack in the middle of "The Gathering," my menses arrives. I want to shout out: "I'm not pregnant!" Truly, due to this, I feel acknowledged by God, as though he has harkened unto the voice of my cry, even though I'm not being transpossessed like everyone else inside these ceremonies. *Anyway, is that transpossession what is wanted, needed, necessary? Am I too closed, cold to be cracked open?* "No," my guide Bat encourages, "the initiation with the Maasai was enough!" I feel separate, as well, much of the rituals seem dramatized. It reminds me of the charismatic movement among the Catholics and Protestants in the middle of America during the late 70's. People claimed they spoke in tongues. My minister did. My mother did. My father didn't. I never did. *Am I once again only to be the observer, the writer, the chronicler, the quiet counselor?*

75: The Gathering

On the last day, early in the morning, wander to the fire. Discover people are singing quietly around the circle, yet Vetkat, Belinda, and Isak Kruiper have not arrived for their "finally" arranged ritual of resolution I fought so hard for. I search for their cabin and tap on the door. Belinda arises dreamily from her cot: "I've had a nightmare that prevents us from participating: 'On the way, we wreck our truck. At church, the police arrive. The Bushmen keep leaving to smoke. So, I join them. Then the fire passes.'" Disappointingly she adds, "Besides, everyone is already there, singing. So, we feel the session is complete."

The whole weekend these southern Bushmen likened "The Gathering" to belonging to a church with rules, with police circling, keeping everyone in line. One group's protocol: "If you come to our session, women must wear a long skirt and wear long sleeves." Another tribe demands, "You must walk only this direction around the campfire." No wonder I didn't attend each meeting. I'd be back in Upstate NY with the entrapments of a guru.

"Now, everyone has surrounded an already ignited fire." Belinda inquires, "How can the Bushmen find their way there when it feels blocked, canned, planned, unnatural, structured with the do's and don'ts of the church?"

From their South African friends, Vanessa of British descent, and Afrikaner, Charlene, I learn that all the people had anxiously come to the circle two hours before the Bushmen were scheduled. *Anticipating another anointing? How much more can a healer give?* Because the Bushmen's cabin was not far from the blaze, they felt the vibration of that energy, heard their songs.

Searching desperately in the crowd for Deena Metzger, who serves on the Council of the Grandmothers, I ask, "Please listen to their dream." As we walk to their cabin, I finally dump the load: "For the last two days, I have been back and forth between The Gathering's leaders and the Bushmen of Transvaal National Park, who have felt unwanted, as well as uninteresting due to their lack of political activism like their "cousins" from the Central Kalahari Bushmen. Deena, they feel all of us do not grasp their quiet souls of intention."

This Grandmother, Deena, sits by their bedside, listens to their vision, comprehends the importance of their presence for us, and in turn, marches to the fire, commanding: "Clear away from the center. Make way for the Bushmen."

Partly from exhaustion, partly for the way these little people have been misunderstood for five centuries, I weep. Their kind, open friends Charlene and Vanessa embrace me warmly. Then, I forge to the fire to speak. In tears, falling on my knees in supplication before the Grandmothers: the Maori Pauline Tangiora,

Part II: The Divide

the Mi'kmaq Donna Augustine, the Dine Bia, The Mayan Flordemayo, the Hopi Connie, the Zulu Virginia, and Deena.

"This is not necessary. Rise." Demands this large, luminous-eyed, cornrowed-Virginia, the wife of Credo Mutwa, the illustrious author and Sanusi, the highest order of Zulu sangomas. "Share your story with us."

And so, I cry out to the greater audience, "I want you to know the First People of Africa as I do, for they have gently, steadfastly changed my life through their music, their stories, their trance dance and their quiet ways. How strange that we have brought them all the way from South Africa and yet, still they are not embraced, nor listened to—in fact, except in cases where they're needed for healing, they're avoided, marginalized as the "other," as they have been treated by whites and blacks for five hundred years."

I leave, the now thoughtful guests, to escort the Bushmen: "We have made a place for you," I make plain, "in front of the embers." Quietly, Belinda and Isak step into the center near the bonfire. Cross-legged, beside her, I plop myself down. "Belinda," I query, "are you open to reveal your dream to them?"

"Yes!"

After she shares, everyone relaxes into laughter. Someone in the crowd shouts, "Yes, it is true, at times it has felt like a church to us, too."

Belinda smiles. "Each morning when the Bushmen arise, as if a Bible, they read the sands of the Kalahari and the crackling embers." She elucidates, "Here, we shoot the shit, share the images of the dreamscape, watch the coals change from yellow to red, reflecting the stars above, opening for us the path for the day."

Finally, Vetkat arrives. For me, his presence is necessary. He is the one who stayed away from the South African land battle that his half-brother, Dawid, led for ten years. While they fought, struggled against the government, the whites, other settlers, and amongst themselves, Vetkat, as in the shamans of old, remained in the desert, on the red sands of the Kalahari to meditate, pray, illustrate, and just as their trickster god, harken: "'And always Mantis would have a dream' they told me in the desert. 'And the dream would show him what to do'" (van der Post).

In his youth, lightning struck Vetkat, and though he lost his right lung, he lived. To the Bushmen, as well as in many other indigenous cultures, to survive this trauma is a sure sign of his shamanic capacity. He is the real deal. Vetkat shifts energy through his artwork, trance dances in his drawings, prays for the

75: The Gathering

universe. Scattered throughout his illustrations, are females nourishing the land from their huge breasts. "I believe, the men are tired," he explains, "in the future, the answer lies in the women."

Out of the darkness, a woman cries out, "Can you tell us a creation story?"

The crowd shuffles closer to the flames, nearer to them. What tumbles from the mouth of our mutual Afrikaner friend, Susan, is the tale of "Tumtumbolosa," who is so pregnant she bursts forth all the creatures of the earth from A to Z, making the group howl. The tension dissolves. Vetkat senses this, strums his guitar singing a lilting tune lifting me to my feet, stepping into the rhythm. The Zulu-part-Bushmen shaman, Virginia, joins me, as I strip-off leggings, socks, jacket, and boots, squishing my toes into the dirt. In a trance-like state, I almost fall into the fire. Virginia catches me. Soon, this motley crew from across the world has risen to dance and chant. In tribute, Rupert calls off the names of the South African Bushmen who have fallen in the battle for the land claim. Yes, wait a moment, and the tide rushes in serving humanity with the magical, mystical unification.

After all the excitement, Vetkat and Belinda embrace me: "You must come to visit us in the red dunes of the Kalahari!" Belinda charges.

"You can count on it!" (In fact, I will venture there in six months in Chapter 81.)

On the walk to the cabin catch a glimpse of a tinsel silver star amidst the rocks. Ah! A Starwoman from the heavens has landed! I reach for it, remembering the Bushmen tale of the cattleman so captivated that he grabs the Starwoman's ankle as she climbs the ladder to her homeland in the sky. Captured, she exclaims if we marry, you must "never look into this basket without my permission!" He, of course, promises. Years go by, until one day, he searches inside, "and began to laugh." Upon the return from daily chores, she knew he had looked within.

"You silly, silly woman. The basket is empty."

Everything that dwelt inside—all the love, the prayers, the wishes, the secret hopes and even more, the mysteries that had been held for him in keeping—he could not grasp. Sadly, she departs for the heavens, never to return (van der Post, *Patterns of Renewal*).

Starwoman reminds, sometimes the gap is so big—between Kathy and Rick and Roberta and Clint; between the South African woman and her ex-husband; between blacks and whites, men and women and between those gaps we had formed and had yet to be reckoned with—there is no bridge large enough

Part II: The Divide

to build across. I remember I once wrote to Sir Laurens, "May all those who read your books and hear you speak, see the stars in her basket" (2 January 1994). And build that "footbridge" he had encouraged.

Even so, from this shared experience at Big Bear, is there a new integration happening? Not necessarily a forced "bused" integration from one village to another, as in the desegregation of America, from a black school to a white that one my dear friends, experienced (with such grace). Luckily, she was not so affected from this change. For in that all-black school, she had been so advanced as a student the teacher had assigned her to the library where she read every book, she could get her hands on. So, by the time she reached the white school, she was already smarter than the majority, competing for Valedictorian.

Yes, similar to this physical busing, have we been bused on the etheric and transported to this gathering to learn to live amongst one another spiritually with a willingness to grasp and embrace our "otherness," our subtleties and the disparities of our skin that comes from "elsewhere?" Isn't this what Global Voice had tried to do with the Shona, the Ndebele and the Maasai? I can only hope for lack of prejudice, for understanding, for the embracing of us all.

What I love is—for the first time, I didn't strain, attempting to "fix it" with the Shona Mundadisi—to force an ironing out of our incapacity to conform to one another through explanation. Instead, I had gone inward, inquired, drummed, rattled, and even imagined into our past lives. Imaginarily, this is good, because according to Hillman: "Mystics recommend contemplating a dilemma rather than trying to fix it" (*The Soul's Code*). Here, at this retreat, I had been working out everyone elses' problems, but I had not completely *mined* mine—mine with Sarototi, or even mine with Mundadisi. *Had we agreed to disagree? Respected our disparities? Had we chosen not to box one another into and inside those cultural beliefs?*

If I follow Sarototi and Mundadisi as an image, as Hillman recommends, they are both perfectly my opposite—black, strong, ferocious, family men, fathers, husbands, southern, and of a distinct people group. Maybe with Sarototi, about our marriage, I had already questioned and delved and pushed until "the fix" had taken the mystery right out of our exchange. With Mundadisi, whether good or bad, all would now be shrouded in mystery of inner transformation.

In the morning, I'll drive home, missing the last ceremony, feigning a need to study. I'll begin a ponder over something else, a possible link—*Why had my father feared me being a writer? Was this why, when I told Mundadisi of this gift,*

75: The Gathering

he, too, had appeared to misunderstand? But was it not that? Perhaps he, just as my father, was afraid of the pen. Mundadisi, who was a prophetic *nganga*, who could foresee into the future, maybe he just *knew*. And *here, am I*, writing about him. God forbid I should hurt anyone.

As she scampers up that ladder towards the heavens, what the Starwoman's "hurt" husband didn't understand and I had yet to, is that each of us has within our own essence what Gay Walley termed *the erotic fire of the unattainable*—the hidden sensual well-spring feeding us, that delivers us from convention, from fitting into the group, leading us into the nomadic. And if we are faithful to forge our own path into the unknown, the indefinable, this, in turn, has the power to feed everyone around us—but only if they are willing to set aside all prejudices, to accept and trust our own personal legend.

To the Bushmen, every one of the sparkly planets in the heavens is an Ancestor; to the indigenous, the Star Nations; to the Greeks, constellations of stories—Starwomen bearing bushels full of gifts, creating unity, harmony, regeneration—and arrows of stories shot to awaken and transform. At Big Bear, each of us congregated with expectations from others. *But do any of us behold the riches within our own Self, our own basket full of mysteries and offerings, within our own medicine space, that which we can dive into and bring forth for others?*

76

HOLDING THE SUBSTANCE

> *"My feet for me restore.*
> *My legs for me restore.*
> *My body for me restore.*
> *My mind for me restore.*
> *My voice for me restore.*
> *This very day your spell is now removed for me.*
> *Away from me you take it.*
> *Far off it is gone.*
> *Happily I will recover."*

—Chantway Prayer of the Navajo, Paul Zolbrod, *Diné Bahané*

At Casa d'Irene, in the misty hours of the morning, the dream informs, an integration has happened from "The Gathering" of tribal people: of the Kalahari Bushmen, the Maasai Warriors, the Shona, the Hopi, the Pygmy. Ritually, inside the enclosure of a sweat lodge, inside a circle, I am dressed in artifacts from each of them. The shamans Valerie Wolf and Deena Metzger cleanse me with the smoke from burning sage. I feel hot, cramped. As though I serve them and they me, shifting our energetic paradigms, reminiscent of the Navajo chant—for we are recovering one another.

From this "Gathering," the Bushmen have become ever more integrated in my psyche. Before, when I traveled to Botswana, South Africa, Namibia, though they shared their music and stories with me, I never made friends with the Bushmen, instead, I felt separated and at a distance through the translations of the white Afrikaners. At present, the Cape-colored wife of Vetkat, Belinda, has brought me near, enfolding me in.

Wake up cognizant from another dream, that Virginia, half Bushmen, half Zulu, carries the liquid essence of the Bushmen in a vessel. She and I are part of those who value the Kalahari people's way of life. By the afternoon, the news is—the southern Bushmen have changed their minds—they are in harmony with the leaders of the expedition, are back on the road to meet the Native Americans in the Four Corners, and onto the United Nations platform to speak on behalf of their people.

The Bushmen's lives, like ours, are fragile, tender. In liquid form, we can spill, dry up, over-turn, bubble-over. Their existence on Planet Earth, though vulnerable, is valuable, precious material, a life-giving substance. Some say they are the oldest living peoples on the earth. For thousands of years, they have lived and survived simply as themselves, as nomadic hunter-gatherers, throughout some of the grandest changes on the planet, never deleterious to the land. Uninterested in building castles and the tallest building in the world—instead, they told stories, tracked the energies of their community and climbed ropes to God.

If we could listen, could they help us shift our way of living on the land, to live more ecologically? Can we allow them their spot, their place on this wild adventure we call life? For how important each of us is to the stability of this earth. "You could not remove a single grain of sand from its place," Johann Gottlieb Fichte illustrates, "without thereby [...] changing something throughout all parts of the immeasurable whole" (*The Vocation of Man*).

Can we trust them on their own path? Just like we have offerings, so do they. *Can we let them be in their own path, with their own offerings inside the immeasurable whole?*

77

SPATE OF BAD LUCK

"For self knowledge [...] is not a one-sided intellectual pastime but a journey through the four continents [...] exposed to all the dangers of land, sea, air, and fire."

—C. G. Jung, The Collected Works

While the Bushmen travel the U.S., I fly to Osawatomie on the 16th of September 2004, to see my mother at the assisted care. To her new friends, I lecture about the Maasai Warriors, display pictures, jewelry, maps, videos. They listen captivated, happy to leave their lives for a moment, to embark on other lands, ideas.

On this visit, each day there is more business to take care of. My brother, mother and I visit Dr. Jeff. He runs tests and affirms mother is losing her memory. He administers the same drug Dad ingests, Namenda, (which never seemed to help him) and he adds in, an anti-depressant. With everything she has been through, loss of home, the loss of communication with her husband—of course, she's depressed! He announces to her, "You can no longer drive."

She is smashed. We both cry. She is so angry with Dr. Jeff; she raises her fist right up to his chin, longing to slug him. As we step out of the office, "I have an upset stomach." She implores, "Can you hold me?"

"My tummy hurts, too." And in a love grip, we hug so tight. For relief, we stroll around the football field talking, sorting, weeping some more. I treat her to dinner at the Chinese restaurant. She bravely resolves not to ingest these pills.

The following day, at the United Presbyterian, the three of us meet with Rev. Leslie Murphy King to discuss Dad's funeral. Because my brother and I travel so much, we plan ahead, mapping out a visitation and a glorious funeral for our father who has been so public. In our discussion, all three of us cannot contain our sadness. I leave the Maasai and Bushmen material with Leslie so she can look it over. From this material, her kids, at the church, are fascinated that the Maasai have built their own school. For this, they adopt them, sending gifts of educational books.

On the Eighteenth, I travel to NYC to stay with friends Jeffrey and Richard, for several days. Then, I take the train to Phillie to see my godchildren and the orthodontist. I no longer have to wear the expansion plate, just the rubber bands and braces. So, no more gagging! Such a great metaphor for the moment, I'm complete for now. By the Twenty-first I'm on the train to D.C. to the Mayflower Hotel, where I unpack, repack, prepare for a month-long adventure.

At National Geographic, meet with author Louis Sarno, the main person Global Voice funds for his work in the Central African Republic. He is still recording the music and living among the BaAaka Pygmies. Then, I join the eighty people and author, Wade Davis, and wartime photographer, Chris Rainier, who will guide us around the Southern Hemisphere, where I will finally touch down on the mythological lands of my studies.

For mythologically, spiritually, mentally, emotionally, and physically, I have had to touch down and through all the four corners of the world both within and without, reaching out to them, bravely facing, and extending into all the areas of my life. Halfway through this venture, in Cambodia, at the foot of the Golden Buddha, I feel called to set down my camera. Not long after, what I had been feeling, this deep down pull inward, Rainier affirmed, "You become more Buddhist everyday."

On this round the world trip, passing through Customs in Sydney, on the 15th of October, they spy the Maasai necklace of olive seeds. Years of learning from bad experiences the government of Australia does not allow onto their precious isle, certain plants that grow rapidly, such as eucalyptus and olive trees. They confiscate and incinerate the protective gift from Sarototi's wife, Kisima.

Part II: The Divide

I wonder at the time if this relinquishing of the gifted necklace is part of a payment to the land and to the painted white Skeleton Man, who had informed me of the mass murder my relatives committed. *Is this once more, about power, and the letting go of the kind that wounds others?*

However, upon my return, within weeks, a bombardment of several assaults: someone robs Casa d'Irene stealing the computer, the video camera, a 35mm—$10,000 worth of equipment, my scuba gear; a new beau I think I love falls for another gal; an old beau takes me to small claims court for $5000; a neighbor forms an obsessive attachment, barraging me with scary letters and emails, which I must respond via an attorney declaring a boundary.

I, who have been so protected, fortified, and transformed by the Maasai—thought I would be forever different—feel discouraged. I have forgotten that I live within this human experience and just like everyone else have good and bad luck! But this, I know, is *something more.*

78

WILDEBEESTS ON THE LOOSE

"The so-called civilized man has forgotten the trickster. He remembers him only figuratively and metaphorically, when, irritated by his own ineptitude, he speaks of fate playing tricks on him or of things beings bewitched. He never suspects that his own hidden and apparently harmless shadow has qualities whose dangerousness exceeds his wildest dreams."

—C. G. Jung, "On the Psychology of the Trickster Figure"

After a series of hard knocks, I wanted to perceive these "incidents" those dangerous shadows through the spiritual eyes of an intuitive: "The Maasai have sent a herd of a thousand wildebeests at you!" Mariah exclaims.

On the 1st of November 2004, this news from her exceeds my wildest musings, sending me into consultation with the *sangoma*, Dr. Dave Cumes: "Most people, Murphy," he sympathized, "consider the happenings about them as just 'a string of bad luck,' whereas you consult the Ancestors, knowing full well the loss of the olive seed necklace is a foreboding."

On my behalf, Dave speaks into the bag of bones to gain enlightenment into the onslaught of circumstances of heartbreak, attorneys, and losses. He shakes these ancient artifacts of symbols. As the bones tumble out of the sack, scattering across the animal skin, they form a pattern. "The tokolosh, the witch bone," Dave interprets, "is on your back, Murphy. You are being attacked. The bones affirm; they have sent a herd of wildebeests. If you're not careful, they may trample you. Did you leave anything with the Maasai?"

"Three things."

"Do you have three things of theirs?"

"Yes, two of these were gifts."

"Your spiritual bone indicates that you are vulnerable, exposed, naked to their affronts. Because of this, you are unsafe and cannot return to Africa for six months, until you grow up!"

"Grow up? What do you mean? I'm forty-seven years old."

"I mean spiritually, Murphy, with your own daily practice to strengthen you, to clarify the life, to clean your energy field, to take responsibility for your own shadow. Without this, the Maasai (or anyone) can track and play with you."

Ahhh! That mettle of mine is being tested again. *Sarototi? Chief Wangombe? Who are you, Murphy, NeLaloshwa? Are you who you say you are? Where's your true personality, your own knowingness? What projections are out there of mine that are requiring me to pull them back in?*

At home, I carefully attend to Dave's instructions. Praying to my Grandmother as I crawl into a bath sprinkled with his prescriptive South African remedies, I recall his words, "These herbs annul the arrangement between you and Sarototi." I ponder the past, the milk baths of Sarototi, stepping over the Buffalo skull in his engang for purification: *Did they prepare me for him? Were his herbs: "Love Potion No. 9?"* Trustingly, I had ingested them, never inquiring: *What is this for? Why am I taking this and this?*

Loosening the Maasai's captive power with Dave's herbs, like the curative rituals of old, I prayerfully soak in the medicinal waters, knowing it to be another demarcation into a rebirth, a re-beginning. Pull the plug, forever releasing their vibratory energies down the drain. For a third and final time, I repeat the given prayer, rinsing the last dregs of the elements, turning my back on the tub, to that binding contract.

To complete the ritual, I light a fire in the living room. Into the flames, I toss a green and red-beaded leather upper-arm bracelet from Sarototi. As it lands, the bestowed present is transformed into a snake, writhing and slithering across the burning wood. At the aliveness of this inanimate object, my whole body shivers, remembering Belinda Kruiper's words: "the embers inform the Bushmen." Yes, and so does this bracelet.

Standing back, I fling the second item, Sarototi's photograph framed in pewter. The impact breaks the glass, out pops his portrait. Behind him, mysteriously appears, a forgotten photo of my uncle and his "second" wife, which is also instantly consumed in the blaze. The frame, the pictures metamorph into the shape of a Wildebeest skull with horns. *Are my Ancestors, too, being transformed? Is this ritual unfettering me, as well as others, from the bondage of both patriarchal families?* This transposition frightens me. Maybe destroying the pic is too much. Some people groups do not pose for photographers for fear their soul might be captured.

Urgently telephoning Dave, I divulge the happenings in the fire, the flashback of Sarototi's rituals performed inside the Buffalo: "Oh my gawd! Is Casa d'Irene going to burn down?" As I emphasize, "Please, Dave. Can you stay on the phone with me? I need you to maintain the sacred space as I complete Psyche's three tasks!"

Into the heart of the flame, I cast the red-and-black-squared Maasai *shuka*, bestowed on me as a gift, utilized in most every ceremonial moment. Instantly, the shawl molds itself into a black solid mound. As though speaking, "back up," the flame bursts out at me. "Ahhh! Dave! It's alchemical: The blanket has magically become a mountain."

"Now, do you understand how formidable they are?" He bellows over the phone. "Most of the shamans, throughout Africa, play in white *and* black magic." *Isn't this the problem with their continent—what Deborah and I had once surmised? And maybe, the problem upon the entire Earth?* —we're all playing with different forms of necromancy.

What I don't know and won't learn for another nine years is that while the fire is burning wildly in Casa d'Irene, in the nighttime, in Laloshwa Highlands, a hyena circles their Maasai Village. Until dawn they must keep the fires burning to protect their cattle, the goats and their families. *Whose talking magic here? Did my reaction, my fear match the wildebeest to the hyena?* Yes, sometimes out of fear,

Across the Divide to the Divine Book One **475**

out of revenge, we do things to one another. Thankfully, I will learn, no one was hurt and Sarototi will graciously forgive me!

Yes, there is black magic out there. But where I live, in Western Civilization there is white magic being played out all the time in the form of systemic racism.

In the Guardian article, "Why I'm no longer talking to white people about race," Reni Eddo-Lodge explains, "Structural racism is dozens, or hundreds, or thousands of people with the same biases joining together to make up one organisation, and acting accordingly. Structural racism is an impenetrably white workplace culture set by those people, where anyone who falls outside the culture must conform or face failure." We ostracize those who don't work like us. We have often hurt others, speak ill of them, take from them. We have often lived and worked proudly without noticing the "other," those whom our society eliminates, erases, committing continuous "microaggressions" (Pierce).

Every day, through that carbon footprint of mine—from thousands of sky miles earned in a fashion career, the drawing up of too much ground water, the overuse of paper, the creation of loads of plastic trash shipped out to sea in hopes of someone else disposing of it—I commit what those "microaggressions," Pierce first spoke of. "Subtle acts of exclusion" (Jana and Baran), and not so subtle, in turn become "macroaggessions" to the Earth, "the Stone People, the Plant People, the Four-legged, the Two-legged, the Creepy Crawlers, the Finned, the Furred, the Winged Ones, and All Our Relations" (Villoldo).

Of the resources drawn from the Earth, Americans use twenty-five percent, and yet we are only five percent of the population. The Sierra Club's Dave Tilford explains, "A child born in the United States will create thirteen times as much ecological damage over the course of his or her lifetime than a child born in Brazil." And here we are yelling about the trees that are being knocked down in the Brazilian Forest. One American uses the same as thirty-five people in India and fifty-three Chinese. If one dares to peer into National Geographic's annual Greendex, Moss and Sheer write, "brace yourself if you are a typical American: You might not like what you find out about yourself" ("Use It and Lose it: The Outsize Effect of U.S. Consumption").

The truth is, Americans don't like to use public transport, preferring a private car or an SUV. In fact, only one in three Americans walk or ride their bikes to work. One reason I didn't like living in California was that the public transportation was unreliable and slow, and therefore, I found myself driving the great expansive distances using massive amounts of gasoline. When I was in

78: Wildebeests on the Loose

Copenhagen, it seemed as if everyone rode their bike, including me. I discovered that forty-nine percent of the Danes ride their bikes to work or school. Daily, they measured the total average kilometers as 1.44 million. I continue biking in Paris. *How can we change the way we live and care for All Our Relations?*

At times, we have madly "Madoff" with Other People's Money. We have more than likely kept others in the strictures of our ideals. The religion, of which much of our Western Civilization has been founded, has taken over the sacred sights, the sacred lands—the power centers of the indigenous—even to the point of killing their medicine men and women. *How do we make restitution? How do we restore?*

Perhaps we have all stood on that platform above and have chosen to be on this planet at this time in history, to live out these choices, for growth, to work out our pasts, our karmic obligations, to evolve, to bring as much integrity as we can into the balance. Even so, I will continuously have to draw back more parts of my Self, to reclaim, to walk softly.

79

OUT OF CAPTIVITY

"Ubaya hauna kwao mola nisitiri na njama zao."
"There is no special place for wickedness;
Oh Lord, save me from their evil plots."

—Maasai Kanga proverb

From this face to face with hostile forces, on 1st of December, I call on further support. Throughout my living room sage smoke billows bringing the everyday into balance, surrounding me, as well as Deborah, who is finally here to help. In the background, the fire roars and crackles. As rosemary creates clarity, the consistent rattling shakes us out of our thinking minds, into the Alpha-Theta state, transporting us into the realm of spirit where Deborah stumbles upon me in the darkness of the Middle World of Africa: On the floor of a dung hut, I lie, tossed to the side, hands tied behind my back. Encircled, the Maasai Elders discuss: "What should be done with *her*?"

While they are distracted, while they contemplate the business of NeLaloshwa, Deborah slips me out of the *engang*, freeing me from these entanglements conveying me on the back of an Eagle to the Upper World into (the ultimate female) Mother Mary's blue and pink crystal palace, where I shall be restored. "We have recovered another part of you!" Deborah proclaims.

Is this the soul part from the life forgotten, ten generations ago, kidnapped, tied, dragged across the sands of the Kalahari, across the continent to Kenya, held captive? I, who withheld the herb for the cure. Or maybe this "me" is "the feminine"—that which baffles all men, particularly warriors, that which is incomprehensible even for women, residing in men and women alike.

In *The Wedding of Sophia: The Divine Feminine in Psychoidal Alchemy*, Jeffrey Raff claims, the now fallen Sophia was originally the very forge from which God emerged, serving as both his mirror and celestial companion. To create God's wholeness, Raff believes, we must reunite the devalued feminine, her wisdom, to Him.

Strangely, though born of the Mother, we (all of us, men and women alike) in most every society on the planet, tie up, hold captive our internal Sophias. As Hillman suggests in his "Pink Madness" presentation about Aphrodite, our internal feminine within, is locked in the underground, trapped in stone under the grates of NYC and cities throughout the world. *Isn't this what we all yen for, are yearning for, to set free our yin function within, our sensuality?*

Though she is "human" just as everybody else, what I love about working with Deborah is that, like the Maasai, she never holds any judgment towards me or others, or even to the dark beings we might encounter throughout our shamanic acts. "To discover our soul's perfection (it is often) through imperfect teachers" (Linda Howe). So, the colorful Swahili Kanga I had bought might be described as, "what was done unto me," as wickedness. This marriage, however, with Sarototi, another "human" teacher, was not the case. Instead, it is a gift to learn more about myself. What is more important for me, in fact, is to go further into the knowledge and acceptance of my Self through this experience.

"Thank you! Deborah, Dave thinks I need to grow up, so these things don't continue to happen. Though I've trained with the Maasai, Valerie, and Deena, I want to learn more, to be able to do for myself and others what you have done for me today. Can you take me further into the mysteries, so I do, 'grow up?'"

"You must first read Sandra Ingerman's *Soul Retrieval*. When you finish that, we will explore this idea."

After completing three papers for classes, voraciously read *en total* Ingerman's book, where I discover, when a person experiences a trauma whether emotional, mental or physical, part of the soul kindly departs in order to survive the ordeal. The goal of the shaman is to recover these parts reuniting them within the individual. In other words, Ingerman confirms the past life regression work I had been doing with others, where we retrieved ancient segments of me. In *Medicine for the Earth*, Ingerman illustrates, our spirit is divine, and therefore, can never be harmed, living on and on, long after our death. Our soul's essence arrives on earth to develop, to evolve; when parts-of-the-self are "harmed" these can be retrieved.

Clearly the experience with Sarototi is not so much about what happened, but rather gives me the impetus to further myself, to self-actualize, self-realize. But even so, the parts of me that held trauma, left behind in captivity, must be lovingly recovered without judgment and re-integrated as well. I will need years to stop hibernating, avoiding others, holding onto resentment, and to emotionally embrace my histories.

In my mind, the marriage with Sarototi comes in the form of a "trick," perhaps even, like the Starwoman, an abduction of a sort. However, for the Maasai there is an intention to affect a cure from the past, to initiate, to unite me in wholeness with Sarototi, to make a woman of me. It certainly forces me back into resolving an old pattern. And for Sarototi—love! *And God's purpose? And me?*

According to philosopher, Edward S. Casey, *Getting Back Into Place*, first, with the Self, is necessary. This will take a long, long time (and is explored further in Book Two). As the awareness of my shadow aspects develop, the magical tricks will die down—there will be less and less left for the Maasai, or anyone else to attach themselves to. And if there is a trick, my stillness and *that* "growing up," Dave had recommended, I'll discover that projection of mine. The "stunt" of Sarototi's is where the testing, where the truth of myself arises, asking of me: *What level is your Self at, Murphy?* Just as my father, Deena, and even my former husband, placed me on trial: *Will you follow your own heart, your own drumbeat or ours?*

For, I cannot be responsibly awake and a victim at the same time. In other words, the Maasai weren't "doing it unto me" or at me. On a Higher Self level, I allowed this scrutiny on my behalf. I'd been part of a prank, and understand, now, I, too, am a trickster. On the back of that black courser of those repetitive childhood dreams, on the back of the greatest hoodwinker of them all, Mantis himself—whether without voice or not—I broke out of the traditional borders of the nuclear family, of the fashion career, of a marriage with Sarototi. I used this powerful animal, this transport, this swift horse—"we domesticated," Suzanne Kingsbury implies, "and that we ride on top of" to escape, to get out from under *this, these, them*—so that I could make a declaration of independence, so I could be who I am. Less and less will I need to stir things up, for I will take full responsibility for these issues, my own black hole, which is not fair to say. Instead, my hole has been terribly "whitened." Slowly heeding the official call that beckons within.

As a patient, under Sarototi, they accorded me protection from the sexual interests of others, distinguishing me as someone in process. With them, steeped in the daily progression of the newness, as they upped the bar, guiding me ever more tenderly toward maturity. The healing held the context. Never dawning on me to investigate my status, their doings, the unconscious—of what lies beneath. With the wonder of the forest, the growth, the support, their prayers, and the trust, our friendship remained in the arena of marvel.

With consummation, everything changed.

But ultimately, I must confess, *their* scheme is *my* cure. Through the herbs, through the act of marriage with Sarototi, within six years, six visits I leap from "being stuck" in childhood, to twenty-five; knowing what I want to be when I grow up—the future Dr. I. Murphy Lewis—into the forty-six-year-old "I," straight into womanhood, straight into the present, in *real* time. Whatever happened in bygone days of the being in the "victim mentality" is lifted. No longer that flat-chested girl. Because of them, "*Here, am I*", as the beads of Kisima, transformatively landing on the planet as though for the first time.

From Hades abduction, the Greek goddess, Persephone, is transformed into womanhood, into someone who makes a difference, moving from the underworld to the earth continuously. Through Persephone and her mother, Demeter, the Eleusinian mysteries of feminine initiation rites for men and women spring forth. In the aftermath, a painting on an urn depicts Persephone elegantly coiffed, in peace luxuriating on the bed with Hades who holds a bowl of offerings. *Is this the longing of men? Of women? Of relating?* That once he/she/they/it meet(s) "the partner of his/her/they/it imaginings," he/she/theyit believe(s) a redemption will happen, moving rapidly, breaking the cherry of that innocence. Ignited, claimed, the partners are united in oneness for the task at hand.

Jung declared this union, the *conjunctio*, the marriage of the King and Queen, the marriage of opposites, bathing in the royal fountain of alchemy. Raff and the Gnostics believed the uniting of the yin/feminine, Sophia (Wisdom), and the yang/masculine, God, is a necessity, both for us and for God's and Sophia's self-actualization. Through this mystical alchemical exchange, through this fulfillment, this unification, the kingdom always rests in peace. Whether I wanted this union or not, in spite of Sarototi—the climax is a transformative achievement—we're both made over by the gods, the goddesses, by God and Sophia. I pray we both have this experience of union inside ourselves.

What becomes of this cataclysmic rupture in me, in Sarototi? Can it bring forth, ignite as Deborah said, the yin aspects in me, in Sarototi, in the Maasai? The story is far larger than him, them and even, me. *Is it for something unnamable, indefinable, the both/and, for the boundless? For I and Thou?* Certainly to attempt an explanation, to expect comprehension, is to drop into and blow open the plethora of Pandora. In his article, "Reductionism," A. R. Peacocke warns, "those who wish to explain explanations stand at the edge of Pandora's box." Indeed! But the deal is, we are, I am, standing outside and inside the box, delving down into where all these emotions, where these encounters exist and more.

Even so, the internal, as well as the external safari will continue, through the years, one inquiry will continue to drive me forward: *Where did the trick come from?* Or as Linda Howe, asks it, *"How could this possibly have happened to me?"* I will continue to explore other lifetimes and the past of this one, questioning: *What have I done unto others? What have I done to receive such a divine awakening within?*

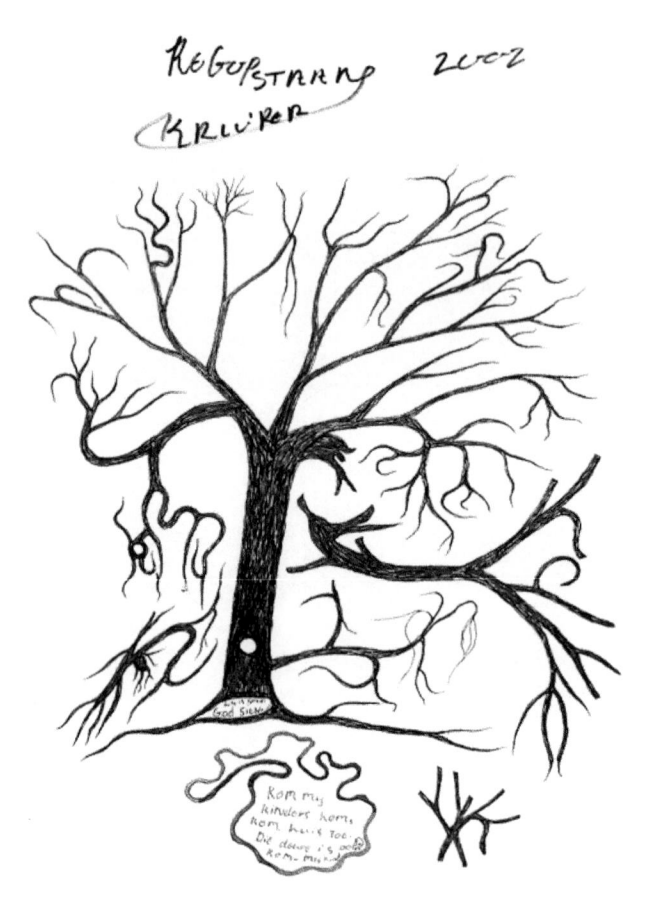

The Tree of Life, Vetkat Regopstaan Kruiper, a Bush-man

PART III

To the Divine

"The Bushmen's letters are in their bodies. They (the letters) speak, [...] a man is altogether still, when he feels that his body is tapping (inside). The Bushmen perceive people coming by means of it. [...] He feels a tapping (at) his ribs; he says to the children: 'The springbok seem to be coming, for I feel the black hair (on the sides of the springbok) [...] For I feel the springbok sensation."

—Han=kass'o, a Bushman, Wilhelm H. I. Bleek, *Bushmen Folklore*

Part III: To the Divine

> *"Ours is the spiral house we build to keep us from life's continuous outpouring from an otherwise unchecked flow into the unknown. Since what is unknown has power over us, we should otherwise be as vulnerable as the snail would be if his shell grew long and straight. The familiarity of life's experiences curls round and protects us, creating those mysterious mountain views of half-concealed windings which keep us bright with speculation and anticipation."*
>
> —Jill Purce, *The Mystic Spiral*

80

PARTS OF YOU, THAT DON'T BELONG TO ME

*"They say, that the Star shall give them the Star's heart,
that they may not hunger."*

—/Han=kass'o, a Bushman, Wilhelm H. I. Bleek, Bushmen Folklore

For a full month in January of 2005, I systematically follow Ingerman's instructions on behalf of my own recovery. Daily I rattle to surface the energies of former lovers invited and uninvited, of friends, of family, placing what is theirs into stones, retrieving that which is mine. Comprehending, as Jung has pointed out, the establishment of the ego—its very existence of health—is due to this process of differentiation and its capacity. Yes, way back when, when my life was shattered into pieces, I lost the ability to separate what was mine, theirs.

For this continued establishment of my "I," each morning, I crawl out of bed. Lie down on the floor. Place my feet on my Chi machine, which methodically (ironically) mermaid-like swishes the feet to and fro. Through the earbuds of my IPod, I listen as the drumming drops me into that liminal space, the in-between. With utter abandon, I release a grade school boyfriend, Tom, remembering the same notes we wrote back and forth to one another. "I love you. Do you love? Tell me." Bestowing the parts of him that I have been clutching, especially the little girl's hope of our forever togetherness, blowing these into a pale blue crystal, wishing him well.

Next, I release my sparring partner, the martial arts teacher, Shidoshi Anton, that I have been quietly in love with. He, too, like many men of the past, betrayed me. For several days, I have wanted to vomit releasing the pain, the disappointment, the poison. Recall the formal event as he swirls me as Cinderella, around in a blue silk embroidered tea-length bias cut Badgley Mischka dress, sweeping me off my feet. Only to learn later (as we talk on the edge of his bed, just before diving in) he still loves another. In fact, he had broken our pact: of him leaving her, me leaving Renzo. I had faithfully kept to the agreement. But he did not. In that moment, in reality, without a word, I slip out, fleeing like mad from his apartment as if the Hound of Heaven was nipping at my Badgley Mischka beaded high heels.

Inside this altered state, I will discover a past life where Anton and I had been Samurai brothers. In a battle of confrontation over his betrayal, he shockingly slashes my left shoulder. The gift of this cut, is now, to this day, *that* shoulder, that which gives me insight, rears up in defense, informs when a man isn't right for me, walks forward as a shield of protection, setting me on a run, down the streets of Manhattan. This shoulder's knowingness is the blessing of the original betrayal.

Into the future, Bat projects Anton as an old grey man, dressed in the official Ninja black uniform, wrapped with a red silk belt displaying his distinction. A ceremony is taking place. The sour stomach, the bitterness towards him flares up. I always felt he teased me with possibilities, withholding love, torturing me. Acidic burning, releases. This completes the competitive Artemis-Apollo, brother-sister relationship. I pour all the parts of him back into the white rock, the philosopher's stone from a dream, which perfectly fits in my hand. Thankfully, I bow and walk away, mailing this stone to him.

When the drumming stops, the bitterness is gone, as Barry White affirmatively croons: "Cause I found what the world is searching for. Here, right

80: Parts of You, That Don't Belong to Me

here my dear, I don't have to look no more." Through Barry's words, "right here," right now, I'm finding a love for myself that's inside of me—not just in relationship to someone else—forgiveness for others, for us. I'm attempting to create a loving partner within, liberating the sensual me. Through this stone, I mail his energy back.

In the ethers, I encounter Sarototi. Picture him in a fresh light, standing in the meadow amidst the grasses of Laloshwa, caressing them, as if in this touch, he'll be able to hear and sense me. Only now, it is I who can feel him in disillusionment, appearing a failure to the community after having pursued this white-redheaded-rejecting woman. Compassion emanates through me toward him. *Has my black hole, that white hole of mine that trips me up continuously, burned him up, too?* "Sarototi are we not where we started? —Me, forced, dragged across the desert lifetimes ago, dying, withholding the herb, the cure, able to save you, your elderly (though I didn't and I don't now). I confess: Betrothed to someone I don't want. To you, into this agate, I relinquish what is not mine and pluck back what does not belong to you. Tossing this into the Pacific."

How often have I been walking in a sea of my archaic lives, dangerously, recklessly, rebelliously damaging, affecting the lives of others? What's imbalanced in me, that brought me to their lands? What do I reflect to them, they to me? What is their need for me, mine for them—'the haves and the have-nots' of both of us?

"You didn't fail me, Sarototi! Thanks to you, and to others around me, I am well. I have hovered over "my illnesses," "my wounding," grasped onto this as *Desperate Housewives* to their husbands. Sickness gave me order in the midst of chaos, gave me the attention required. This "ill" self, too, I draw to a conclusion. Setting things right with you, Sarototi, inspiring me to rattle and bring about forgiveness in the relationship to Chief Ole Wangombe."

The Chief and I release one another from our obligations. I bless him. Thanking him for trusting me, making me a part of his family, offering his nephew in marriage, allowing me to emblematically "wear" his name as a banner of protection, honor.

Each day, rectify relations to the degree that I can. And where I cannot forgive, I place that person in my hand as an offering to the greater powers that be. While I locate the union inside of me, the outside Self mirrors this pursuit, re-reading the assignment for Walter's Egyptian course, *The Amduat*, which again takes me on the night sea voyage, through each hour into the murky

Part III: To the Divine

waters of the underworld, following it down. Carried on a barque, on a barge for this mythological, psychological, and now, hourly spiritual journey of the soul. As if the Tibetan bardo, I must forge through encountering different beings, to force the shift.

As I set forth, I sense support, surrounding me, led by those who have gone before—Apollo, Hermes, Mariah, Walter, Mary, Gay, Valerie, Deena, Deborah, the saints, Jung, Celia, my parents, Sarototi, Baba Budhya, Mundadisi—into the dark night of the soul only to rise again. Oh! Give me the heart of the star!!

81

WHAT LIES BENEATH

*Father Sun, Grandmother Moon, the Star Nations.
Great Spirit, you who are known by a thousand names
And you, who are the Unnamable One.
Thank you for bringing us together
And allowing us to sing the Song of Life.*

—*Opening Prayer for Sacred Space*, Alberto Villoldo, The Four Winds Society

On the 15th of February 2005, two months earlier than Dr. Dave Cumes had suggested, I confidently step onto the African continent. I've taken the Bush-man, Vetkat and his wife, Belinda's original invitation *seriously*, with an intention to continue on to Kenya for a visit with the Maasai. For I'm addicted, in sufferance of that nostalgia of what the French call "le mal d'Afrique." As if I need Africa, my First Family, as the backdrop, the reflection that I'm on course. There is, too, a longing to exonerate that which is not mine and that which is,

Part III: To the Divine

setting the notions of my dissertation in motion, and to draw a conclusion to my relationship with Sarototi. For the divination and herbs of Dave, the shamanism of Deborah, and the books of Ingerman have fortified me.

We begin our trip in Cape Town, where I meet the author Belinda Kruiper and her friend, tour-guide, driver, Vanessa of African Essence, whom I had also met at "The Gathering." Vanessa is forthright, feminine, lithe, yet hearty, fixing a flat tire or cooling a boiling radiator with laughter and gusto. Her ease with the Bushmen, with nature, with Mantis, and with me causes us to become fast friends.

In Vanessa's Land Rover, we meander north, stopping along the way to view paintings of the ancient Bushmen until we reach the boiling sands of the Kalahari Desert, where we pull ourselves under what little shade there is, the favorite tree on Vetkat's deceased grandfather's land. Their more permanent home—a hand-painted Volkswagen van attached to a rectangular-cement-block house courtesy of the South African government—lies on the edge of the Gemsbok National Park. Now that park has been named the Kgalagadi Transfrontier, the territory signed over in a ninety-nine year lease, which only allows the Bushmen to live along its borders (like both these properties above), to lightly hunt inside, and occasionally camp—so much for land battles, rights and privileges.

Far from the block community, on this red dune, is the illustrator Vetkat Kruiper and Belinda's second abode, a little grass shack, lean-to. Joining us is another creative soul, Sillikat, a cousin to Vetkat and also part of the well-known Khomani clan, who are widely photographed and filmed for commercials, books, and magazines. Sillikat's name perfectly describes him as he emboldens our festive brigade into wild storytelling (which the San are celebrated for) around the campfire morning and night. Along with Vetkat, Sillikat invents art out of the everyday elements of the Bush, carving wood, embossing images across the surface of ostrich eggs, and from the sinew of the antelopes, stringing ostrich-beaded necklaces, bracelets for wrists and ankles, which they sell to tourists.

While they're industrious, I read to them the beginnings of my dissertation. For, I've come for their blessings, their feedback, to affirm the direction the thesis is taking, because I don't want to take their stories in vain. In fact, I want to honor them. Through Belinda's translations, the back and forth of engagement, the Bushmen respond kindly. They are receptive, thoughtful, making me feel affirmed.

81: What Lies Beneath

This time, I've come for the wisdom of Vetkat, who has had more than his fair share of Jesus' meditative forty days and forty nights in the desert. After Belinda's translation, Vetkat encourages me, and yet, distinguishes: "This is the story you might tell, and I might tell it differently, for there is a story within a story within a story and another one around that one."

Then, pointing above his head, "a separate tale is forming there." I glance up, discovering a praying mantis camouflaged to match the grasses of their hut, is hanging upside down with a Bumble Bee trapped between his praying hands. "Shhh," Vetkat whispers, "watch what happens next." Strangely, Mantis doesn't eat Bee, but releases her, only to delightfully lick the tasty pollen extracted from Bee's body, which has been smeared upon his prayerful hands. How wise is Mantis, who does not destroy the gift bearer.

In the beginning of time, according to the Bushmen in "Mantis Comes to Life," Mantis was carried across the watery world on the back of Bee until he landed, birthing forth from a lotus (van der Post)—and I might add, as if Buddha himself. Symbiotic relations—what figures between Mantis and Bee, what configures between Sarototi and me, and now, Vetkat and me—just as the Bushmen in the Kalahari have lived symbiotically with the Bkaligadi peoples, and their affines, the lions, and eventually, even with some of the Afrikaner farmers.

Multiple stories. Vetkat is right. "There is a story within a story within a story and another one around that one." Even in my own lifetime, I have had multiple stories going, multiple experiences, which feel almost as though other lifetimes. All around us there are other things happening—the Boxing Day Tsunami and the Earthquake in the Indian Ocean and its effects are reverberating—the instant death of a quarter of a million people. Even in Scotland, the eight-hundred-year old feudal fees originally paid to the Church and to the Lairds are being abolished.

For me, among these South African Bushmen, some distillation occurs in contrast to my engagement with the Botswanan and the Namibian Bushmen. Although I felt comfortable amongst them, here, an intimacy formulates. It might be due to my interpreter. In the North, my "white" Afrikaner friends, Izak and the musicologist "The First Man" engaged in all of those encounters. This time, Belinda, the beloved Cape-coloured wife of Vetkat paves the way as never before. As though, through her, I have a direct line to God. However, it may also be because I have been transformed through the magical herbs of the Sacred

Forest. From this, my heart has been broken open, broadening. I see differently. I am different. And maybe, too, I've soberly grown-up a bit.

For this reason, shame-faced, I admit to Vetkat, the "trick" of the Maasai, the matrimony with Sarototi. The Bushmen listen intently. They are very concerned. As they push the coals into an aliveness, in search of answers, much discussion bounces about. One of their solutions is tea. Belinda boils water. Vetkat loves lots of sugar in his. This seems to satisfy us all, even though the question itself is left unanswered, dangling.

Then—much as the ritual-chicken-sacrifice-dream on Butterfly Beach after my first meeting with the South African sangoma Dr. Dave Cumes—the miraculous arrives in reverie that night while lying on the sands of the Kalahari Desert. On wings, I take flight through the ethers to Kenya to annul the marriage. As though they are anticipating me, I bump into Chief Ole Wangombe and Baba Sarototi, floating on the clouds, as if Buddha himself. Determined to remain in power, the Chief huffily declares: "We've already annulled *that* marriage of yours!"

"That's why I've come." But I wanted to shout: "Dave and I have already annulled it!" But I don't. *Hadn't this been what the laibon Hakima had predicted—if you lie with her, if you lie to her—the marriage will be cancelled within one year?* When I wake up, I'm just relieved everyone is in agreement.

In the morning, at the fire with the Bushmen, I disclose this odd, yet succinct closure. They are pleased. The magic of walking barefoot on the red dunes, laying bare the story to the Bushmen, the shamanic journey with Deborah, the bones of Dave, his herbs, the bath, *that* dramatic fire of burning their gifts has miraculously resolved the dilemma through the etheric.

Maybe all the childhood memories had not returned, maybe I wasn't done with my Ph.D., maybe the story between Sarototi and his brethren is not completely resolved, however, I had retrieved my "I," I had begun to separate myself from others, from convention, to healthily strengthen the boundaries, to take back what was mine and to give back to others what was theirs. "For their liberation, they (the oppressed) must perceive the reality of oppression not as a closed world from which there is no exit," Paolo Freire urges, "but as a limiting situation which they can transform." For sure, I am in the midst of transforming some of my own confinements. Perhaps as I change mine, my bi-racial friends, my Bushmen and Maasai friends can liberate themselves out of whatever their challenges are. For we are a bridge for one another.

81: What Lies Beneath

In reality, I had intended, after this safari with the Belinda and Vetkat, to take a real flight to Kenya to visit the Maasai. At the last minute, after the dream of the annulment, I cancel this part of the passage through a letter I pen in the shade, under Vetkat's family tree, to Marjana, Sarototi, and Saifi. I let them know I cannot return at this time, putting our plans for the healing center indefinitely on hold. For me, all is settled—naturally or should I say, in the way things are in Africa—through animism.

What I have yet to grasp, is through the writing of this cancellation letter, I must have let the Chief down, disappointing him. For the first time in this lifetime, I had not kept my word to the Maasai. In the *sixth journey in*, the Chief had graciously offered me his name, offered his nephew's hand in marriage, offered land for a home, and offered a working partnership for a spiritual center.

The return to Kenya, the "official" annulment of this marriage will be years to come—nine, in fact (Book 3). This reconnection with Sarototi will be completely liberating for us both. To give the reader, a futuristic flash of this event, I write. In 2013, in Nairobi, in the first meeting with Sarototi, Motoguisimile, Marjana, Baba Budhya, and my French husband, we will exchange dreams and speak of the night of the hyena's attempt to attack their village. After our discussion, Sarototi will grab my elbows, declaring, "I've missed you so much. You are one of the best friends I've ever had in my life." When I return to his community, we will both discover we'd written letters to one another to heal our breech. As his young cousins translate for us, Baba Budhya will sit in front bearing witness, as I weep and weep with tears of liquid joy. But the Chief, however, injured from a motorcycle ride, will not meet with me in Nairobi, nor at Lalowsha Highlands.

Another time very long time will pass, eleven years, until I will come into a resolution of sorts on behalf of the Samburu and the Maasai, Global Voice will choose two Wisdomkeepers. The spiritual center is still in question. Maybe Mundadisi knew this, was inquiring in his glance across the table on our last night, wondering if the promises I've made will really come true.

However, while I'm visiting the Bushmen in South Africa, on the streets of NYC, in broad daylight, my friend Larry has an accident, while driving his BMW, currying himself and his female associate to the office. Immediately, for the wreck he has "supposedly caused," he is handcuffed and is taken to the Upper West Side precinct, which he noted at the time, was filled with only handcuffed blacks. A warning to him! For Larry's "crime," he must face the Chief of Police,

Part III: To the Divine

sitting high up like a judge on a podium, who sneers as if envious, "Oh, this is the one with the blonde in the BMW."

When Larry complains, "the handcuffs are too tight," they squeeze them tighter, throwing him into a jail cell, where he will have a flashback to a similar experience in high school:

In 1971, on their way to a classical music competition, in mutual consent, Larry made out with a blonde in the back of the bus. Their teacher saw this, exhorting him, "Our society isn't ready for this." And so, in order to embed that thought, this same instructor expelled Larry, an all-round athlete, from any participation in sports for one year, and punished him with five "licks" from a wooden paddle. At an earlier time, Larry might not have been so lucky. He might have been hung. In *Songs of Solomon* (1977), Toni Morrison wrote, "A young Negro boy had been found stomped to death in Sunflower County, Mississippi. [...] his murderers had boasted freely [...] The boy had whistled at some white woman, refused to deny he had slept with others..."

Some states had imprisoned people for mixed race relations. Some states had fined people for this disobedience. In 1957, Hannah Arendt wrote that the free choice of a spouse is "an elementary human right," removing this right is worse than racial segregation in public schools. In 1967, in Loving v. Virginia, the U.S. Supreme Court determined the laws of anti-miscegenation, against mixed-race sexual relations, against mixed-race marriages, became unconstitutional. This law could no longer affect Larry just for a kiss.

Recently, after speaking with him, I felt to some degree, he was never quite the same from these horrific displays of power. In "Critical Race Theory: An Examination of its Past, Present, and Future Implications" Nicholas Daniel Hartlep agrees that "certain stories act and serve to silence and distort certain enclaves of people and cultures (typically people of color), while simultaneously building-up and legitimizing others', typically the majority—status quo (which retains or gains even more power through these transactions)."

Yes, the Police Chief, the Teacher acted as judges to what they considered to be the outrageous acts of Larry, and this in turn built the legitimacy of their own claims of superiority. The tightened handcuffs, the five "licks" did not aid Larry in going forward into the world or "in making him a better man." Instead, acts of this sort, weaken the fibers of the soul, remove the wind out of one's sails, sober, create Complex Post Traumatic Stress Disorder from chronic trauma, as well as mistrust, among other things. In fact, one of the things Larry mentioned,

81: What Lies Beneath

"When schools integrated us with whites, I experienced victimization. I don't suppose I'll ever know how much this affected me. I'm sure our pasts define us, how we move into the future." Larry is an example of the treatment black men, of indigenous men and women, of people of a different color or religion, are familiar with inside everyday America.

In the Twenty-First Century, in the United States, twenty of the fifty States do not allow Critical Race Theory, because they do not recognize racism. That "the caste system" still exists, according to Isabel Wilkerson, and is part of the fabric of our everyday society. That there is a patriarchal system that triumphs, that is averse to conflict, that thrives on institutional racism, that continuously feeds their power.

In *Caste: The Origins of Our Discontents*, Pulitzer Prize Winner, Wilkerson believes Nazi Germany, India and the United States are examples of three different caste systems. How discouraging. "Tentacles of caste," Wilkerson explains, reach down and across and around, surrounding us, infecting the waters. This collective behavior becomes complex and gnarly because everyone has drunk the "Kool-Aid" in service to this system. And that the "anxious efforts" of the predominant race is to continually remain superior; all the while the lower castes serve the upper narcissists in the reactionary, strange and very real "survival mechanisms" of the Stockholm Syndrome, of believing the best of their captors, their abusive abusers. "Race, in the United States, is the visible agent of the unseen force of caste. Caste is the bones, race the skin" (Wilkerson). Yes, we simply cast people into castes just for being born with a different skin color and then we leave them there without any concern or interest.

For just indulging in a wondrous kiss with a blonde, for simply having a car accident on the Upper West Side of Manhattan, my friend Larry had his bum swatted, was cast out of sports for one year and finally, was tossed into a jail cell, with the intent of emasculation. After he told me these stories, I dreamt he was in a boat ahead of me out there on the waters of life and I was floating above (like so many whites do—above the real problems below, what lies beneath). Strangely I was using a shovel, not a paddle, to draw myself toward him. When I looked down for a moment, preoccupied with my life, I missed the whale of a fish that swallowed Larry and his boat right in front of me. I just happened to glimpse the end of the tail.

The revelation of this dream is to admit that even though I have known Larry since 1998, we have only briefly—once, at the turn of the century, twenty-

Part III: To the Divine

four years later, and now—had a conversation about what it means to be black in America. That's embarrassing, that's me being preoccupied with my life, unaware of what's really going on out there in the everyday moments of the lives of people of color, I, who should know better, who should have been opening up these conversations with my friends years ago, who could have been using that shovel in my dream, to clear away the dirt, to get to the bottom of things.

Obviously, I couldn't at the time prevent my friend from the onslaught of the policeman, the judge or his teacher. Yet, every time I look down, every time I'm me-centered I miss what's happening. My black friend, many bi-racial peoples and other genders who are considered the "other," have often been made the enemy or certainly whom we have projected all our fears upon. They are being swallowed by the overwhelm of the white whale, the Moby Dick, the Middle Passage, the systems that whites have put in place, that only serves a few, that is based on a meritocracy of our measurements we won't allow them to live up to or notice if they do. And I weep and I weep.

"Color-blindness and meritocratic rhetoric serve two primary functions: first, they allow whites to feel consciously irresponsible for the hardships people of color face and encounter daily and, secondly, they also maintain whites' power and strongholds within society" (Hartlep). As a white, middle-class American, I'm part of the feeding into this, maybe all of us are, whether we want to admit it or not. "The beliefs created by the majority—the haves—oppress minority groups—the have-nots and have-too-littles" (Hartlep). Larry's maltreatments are at the root of what the society at large isn't ready to embrace, nor admit—that biases have existed and been held into form for five hundred years or more. That we're not often willing to listen to what he/she/they/it believes (believe), nor how he/she/they/it wants (want) to live and act, because we're often not willing to give it up and give into equalization and liberation for all.

In a wild rainy drive across South Africa to the Western Transvaal, on the 2nd of March, Vanessa and I are unusually at odds with our Bushmen friends, Sillikat and Vetkat. "Stop!" Belinda exclaims. "They want you to pull over."

Quite dismayed at a possible loss of time and maybe even a little confused at the necessity, I blurt: "But we're due for dinner at Izak and Anna Barnard's!"

"Yes, Murphy, we know," acknowledges Belinda. "However, whenever the rains fall, the Bushmen stop everything to sleep, listening for the dream messages that sprinkle down upon them from above."

Needless to say, even though I repeat over and over in my head Niki Daly's title, *Not so fast Songololo*, we don't do as they wish. While they rest in la la land, in the backseat, we go hurriedly along. Reminding, the words of the gifted Maasai Kanga I'm wrapped in, "Haruka, Haruka, Haina Baraka," "rush, rush, doesn't lead to bounty." Hoping our stubbornness does not harm us; Vanessa and I grab hands, quietly praying for protection from the giant transport trucks rattling by us on these narrow two-lane highways.

On my lap, lies the book *Voices of the San*—where they're finally expressing themselves, just as Vetkat and Sillikat are about the rain—but we're not listening, I'm not listening. Just as I haven't been listening to my American friend, Larry. Here, in this manuscript, the San unite collectively against van der Post, stating that he "fabricated most of his mythologizing literature for the purpose of his own interest in psychology and symbolism" (le Roux and White). It is sad that they see his acts as a kind of "cultural" or "spiritual appropriation." To me, I would say, the San can beam with pride that their stories have had and continue to have an impact across the world. Certainly, they have changed my life.

I believe van der Post actually intended, as did C. G. Jung, to find a solution to the ever-growing problem of "meaninglessness" found among postmodern men and women, and in turn to help us learn to treat the indigene, as well as our indigenous self within—*better*. What a glorious affirmation of the incredibleness of what many concur are the First Peoples on this planet.

To me, Sir Laurens' constant discussion and writings about the Bushmen is a compliment. The Jung and the van der Post search for answers and hope were never meant to harm or misuse the power of the images that had struck them in their engagements with several African people groups. Through the San's myths, van der Post somehow thought that humankind could get in touch with its ancient soul, as well as honor his Bushmen friends. In fact, he had a kind of nostalgia for their hunter-gatherer lives.

As I read through *Voices of the San*, I see within the San's narrative the same yearning for another time, of the time before when they could live freely their nomadic life, which van der Post spoke so highly of. Of a time when animals and people could talk. And I find myself yearning for this very life, the San express. Perhaps even in Voices of the San, they re-mystify themselves and create longing once again.

As Vanessa drives toward Izak's home, in my mind's eye, nostalgic memories appear: I can hear the creative songs of the DiPhuduhudu Bushmen, who had sung to us upon each of our arrivals, "Izak is coming...flash, flash, flash, flash"—dancing, hands clapping and flicking in demonstration, in imitation of the tourists with cameras aflashing. And of the mysterious satellite zooming over their heads, which fascinated them so, "Apollo, Apollo..." When I returned with the book, *Why Ostriches Don't Fly,* which they had influenced, they loved a glimpse of their photographed selves, laughing at the drawing of Tumtumbolosa who is pregnant with the whole world. Yes, those Bushmen, whom I had traveled to for my second, third, fifth and sixth safaris into Botswana, are dying. *Had I been a part of bringing about their death?* Within ten years, all but one, the young thumb piano player, will be dead. *How can one not be in longing for another time?*

For the Bushmen had only lived two hours from the political seat of Gaborone, and were known for their beautiful, sensual women, who were most likely raped by the men from the city, contracting AIDs, and in turn, infecting their own people. A small fragile community of kind generous people—the old storyteller, the White Bushmen Kora Kora Due; the wise hunter Rasekamo; and the young Kua, who drew stories for me—are gone. Just like that. No wonder I had said, "Urgent!" And now, I count myself lucky to be with these two sleeping treasures, Sillikat and Vetkat, in the back of the Land Rover.

Thankfully we arrive safely and enjoy a meal with the Barnards. After each safari, I have walked Anna's farm amidst the cows, the sheep, the garden, playing with the children and engaging with the caretakers—the black families who live on the land and study at her school. Here, I have felt at home, comfortable, loved, for Anna is a warm, generous woman, nourishing our souls.

However, that night, tucked in the little twin, in the usual bedroom, a nightmare follows behind the storm. From the other side, a bizarre two-legged, distorted-faced Kat slips through the door. Within moments, as if he deciphers my fortitude, Kat draws his sword. In response, with my blade, I slice through the air at him, and from the strength of this gesture, the bed mythically becomes a knight's charger galloping, sliding across the room, silently, yet dramatically slamming against the wall of Izak's, then back to its original corner. From this bold move, the Kat dissolves and everything grows calm. Again, the door from the beyond cracks open. A tiny "mythic" girl tiptoes across the room and into the bed she crawls, snuggling up to me. And whether I want her to or not, her body physically merges with mine, sending a tingling sensation throughout, as I fall further and deeper into the reverie.

81: What Lies Beneath

In the morning when I arise, join Vetkat and Sillikat in the garden. And there, on the outside of an ostrich egg, Vetkat has carved the deformed face of the Kat I fought in the night. I don't say a word, remaining poker-faced, yet I comprehend, just like the Maasai, just like Mundadisi, Vetkat is onto me. He sees through my want of stories, for affirmation of the dissertation's direction. He knows and generously gave me what I wanted, which was more of me. The nightscape had been his testing ground, to observe the material I'm made of.

And the reward? After the trickster Kat's appearance, another aspect of little Irene was infused. Through Vetkat, through Mundadisi, through the Maasai, I'm beginning to understand the importance of having my mettle tested. The prank serves me, helping me to locate, to evaluate where "I" stand, where others stand. The Maasai, Mundadisi and Vetkat are the perfect reflections of my shadow material, of what's unresolved in myself. As though they are summoning me to make amends from the interior, to take responsibility for me, for my actions, for my beliefs.

In *Playing in the Dark*, Toni Morrison puts forth the argument that race figures as a metaphor within American literature – even amongst the writers Poe, Hawthorne, Melville and finally with Hemingway. When I peer into this book of hers, I think perhaps I am, too, playing, dancing, sword-fighting inside this darkness, that I keep looking to the "other" to land myself, ground myself into the greater Self. That these characters that feature in the dreamfield and as men outside in reality—Vetkat, Mundadisi, Sarototi, Hok'ee—are necessary for my existence.

Needless to say, I buy the carved Kat of an ostrich egg. As a reminder, I set Vetkat's magic on the writing desk at home acknowledging the "games of power" and the importance of any "trick," which might come my way. William J. Hynes reminds me of the wildness of this trickster: "What prevails is toppled, what is bottom becomes top, what is outside turns inside, what is inside turns outside, and on and on in an unending concatenation of contingency" ("Inclusive Conclusions," *Mythical Tricksters*). And just as I complete this edit, seventeen years after Vetkat designed this "Kat," I bump the vase that held the egg and in slow, slow, very slow motion, I watch as it tumbles to the ground, shattering. Once again, the trickster topples an "ism" I had constructed, which I had held fast to, into pieces.

On his behalf, four days later, I speak of Vetkat at the gallery in Johannesburg where his artwork is briefly displayed, participating in the launch of Belinda's

Part III: To the Divine

joint book, *The Kalahari Rainsong*, with Elana Bregin. Later, with the help of other friends, Global Voice contributes six months of vegetables for Vetkat and Belinda, while they edit Vetkat's book of his art, *Mooi Loop* in their desert shack—*that* miraculous place of my annulment.

Inside the dreamscape I perceive the denouement, a way to obtain answers by wrapping myself inside a leather bag and beads, rocking onto my back with bent knees. *Are these my sackcloth and ashes?* As never before, discover within this reverie, I can decipher the bones for divination. I know what to do. My guides affirm, Vanessa has this ampleness, too.

From the gallery, the five of us, Vetkat, Sillikat, Belinda, Vanessa and I, continue our trek to Pretoria for our first encounter with Sanusi Credo Mutwa and our second meeting with his wife Virginia, one of the grandmothers at the "The Gathering" in California. In spite of how things lie between the Maasai and me—what I considered at the time as to be one of my historical "failures,"—I continue in these Global Voice endeavors, bringing together indigenous peoples.

In Vanessa's Land Rover, we tread slowly across Credo's eerie landscape. Here, scattered throughout the terrain, standing larger than life, are his ominous metallic sculptures—an amalgamation between Samurai and Zulu Warriors—as though to ward off evil, from those who seem so horribly to hate and fear him. Along the grapevine the rumor is, one of the President's former wives is one of these.

Among the indigenous, another hearsay flits about, in crisis, shortly before her death, Credo had supposedly received a telephone call from Princess Diana in need: "they're trying to kill me!" Legally, I've learned, this connection has been denied. With us, he never mentions this story. For Credo is secretive, mysterious. No one knows for sure where he lives. We are the lucky ones to finally greet him, to enter his land, as we carry the card of our mutual friends Sara and Rose, and the memory of Virginia's gracious insistence at Big Bear.

Our first evening with Credo is one of exchange of gifts and the mythological stories of old. Credo is a master at tales, particularly those of the Bantu people, having reconstructed these in his controversial book, *Indaba, My Children*, so that whites might understand the mind of the blacks, "who had no mighty scrolls on which to write […] no pyramids on which to carve the history of each and every crowned thief and tyrant who ruled […] of every battle lost and won." Instead, every tale was transposed orally, and for this he swore, "Under oath never to alter, add or subtract any word" becoming one of "the Guardians of the Umlando or Tribal History. And I, Vusamazulu the Outcast, am proud to be one of these."

Today, tucked in my copy of Mutwa's book is a colorful photographic memory of Vetkat, Credo, Virginia and Belinda, arms wrapped around one another. With GVF's assistance and our mutual girlfriend Sara's driving, they will be brought together again to share. Captured with a snapshot one more time before Vetkat's death.

Thrilled, to be near Credo, I remain at his feet, bathing in every word. He, like me, is an outlier. And so with him, as he seems to be with me, I'm at home. My favorite, "Behold the Comet" is of the woman Noliyanda, neither spirit nor human, who is "more barren than the sands of the Ka-Lahari." In her rage, she coaxes her maker and lover, the god Lumukanda, to usher in his immortal daughters to this world, those who have no respect for her. Noliyanda wants nothing more than to rid them of their lives. She kills one and takes the hand of another. For this, Noliyanda remains childless, dragged into the hut of the humans, only to be considered an "It" and "never She." I'm so lucky Deborah dragged me out of the Maasai's dung hut, though childless, I am now an "I," not an "It."

For the Mutwa's, the Bushmen bear presents as well of painted ostrich eggs, beaded necklaces. Credo offers an ancient artifact to Vetkat: "This has been held in keeping by the Zulu Sanusi's for five hundred years—of which your people bestowed. Now, the time comes to return this to you." To Belinda, he offers the cure for AIDS: "Plant this herb. Though I know, not much grows in the Kalahari. Still, water this, to bring renewal to your people, for my son has lived nine more years due to this."

Indigenous to the indigene is their capacity to reciprocate and so we attempt the same. Vanessa and I take Virginia shopping, to stock up her refrigerator and freezer. On the last day, Virginia offers Vanessa a bowl from Soweto, to me, a hand-painted sienna teapot: "Fill these with water, and know whenever you need us, we are there." On brown Kraft paper, Credo presents each of us one of his black ink paintings. To me, he bestows two Zulu lovers floating in a black canoe, beneath lies a hungry crocodile. "Beware," he conjectures, "of what lies beneath, that which can devour what love bestows."

At his knowingness, I grin, because once my former Italian roommate Antonella said of Renzo, the married man I fell for, "he has the smile of a crocodile, satisfied." From firsthand knowledge, I know this of him, of Sarototi,

Part III: To the Divine

of my first husband, and even of myself that what's on the surface, and then, those intentions and past experiences, which we hide "under the table" equally from ourselves as well as others, can roar up to bite us. Yes, we may shake hands with the right, Astrologer Liz Greene determined, but the real work goes on below, between us, with the shake of the left—in those places that test our mettle.

82

WALLED FROM THE "OTHER"

※ ※ ※

"In the United States, however, the air seemed thin and void of substance or influence. It was not, here, a sensuous medium—the felt matrix of our breath and the breath of the other animals and plants and soils—but was merely the absence, and indeed was constantly referred to in everyday discourse as mere empty space."

—David Abram, *The Spell of the Sensuous*

A few days before departing for America from Africa, the 12th of March 2005, in a reverie, in a Volkswagen, I discover myself taxiing down the road bound for the North Grade School where I attended kindergarten, first, second, and third grades. Before me is a brick wall, this little green convertible bug proceeds to jump. However, hung up on the embankment, we teeter. Horns blaring, the traffic jams up behind the divisive fortification of the VW, the brick wall and me.

In the morning, the Bush-man Vetkat deconstructs this dream, which has completely bewildered me, "In America, this is what your life resembles. I know. I have been there. Between your people and their dead loved ones, exists a brick wall." He expounds, "Perchance, flying home is rushing head long into an

Book One – Across the Divide to the Divine 505

Part III: To the Divine

incompatible orientation. Can you take a slow boat across the Atlantic, digesting this trip, preparing for what lies ahead?"

"That's a wonderful idea. Maybe I'll do that next time." I reply anxiously. "For now, I must hope for the best. I need to take this flight to get back for classes." Once again, I'm not stopping to listen to the rain, nor the dream. How very hurried, "haruka, haruka," and, very American of me!

Vetkat is right. In the United States, I live walled up from "the others," separated from the unseen, the hereafter, and the infinite—not to mention, the separation we often create from one another and from those of other countries, those of color. The Ancestors, the people of color, these "others" remain at a great and grave distance. Between the Star Nations, those Ancestors, as well as those bi-racial peoples and us, we've created a cloud covering of smog that even sailors have difficulty seeing their way through without mechanisms. *Is this as Henry Louis Gates, Jr. explains, some of us, who are further away from those African roots have withdrawn our connection, making our Ancient Ones unreachable and our relationship to the "other" untenable?*

In Africa, with the veils down, one can easily, tactually reach the other side. As the Bushmen say, "Climbing the ropes to God," repairing the broken strings, accessing their relationship with death, insights for the community, into the divineness of it all (Keeney, *Ropes to God*). For some brave healers, it can be a dangerous mission of which they are aware, they might never return. Here, in this altered state one meets the "Guardians of the Threshold," who can demand a fee, who can be benevolent or malevolent (Campbell, *The Hero with a Thousand Faces*).

In the West, to access the Great Boundlessness, I need more than just an eight hundred number to dial, more than Herbie, *The Love Bug*, more than an education out of my colorblindness to leap over this barricade of sorts. We have forgotten what Edwin Muir once wrote: "I have been taught by dreams and fantasies. Learned from the friendly and the darker phantoms. And got great knowledge and courtesy from the dead" (*The Collected Poems*).

Upon my return to America, in order to jump over that bulwark, the dream of the brick wall, I keep searching for ways to reach Father in his dementia, to meet him in the great "in between." In this pursuit, I come across Dr. Elmer Green's *The Ozawkie: Book of the Dead, Alzheimer's isn't what you think it is!* Green's belief formed from his interactions with his wife—trapped so to speak, between our world and the afterlife—held in an Alzheimer's state for her last seven years. Green realizes that people with certain types of thinking brains don't develop an astral sense quickly, falling asleep in a subconscious state, stuck, unable to slide into the light. So, he began this exploration on behalf of his wife through each of the Forty-Nine Days of the *Bardö Thödol, The Tibetan Book of the Dead*. Just as the Buddhists hold this transitional space for the dead, he sat with his wife, easing her exploration in the realms of consciousness into transfiguration, into unity with the divine, between her death and re-birth—the intermediate existence.

From Green's notion, decide I shall attempt to assist Father in his Multi-infarct dementia (MID) state. Through each day for a month, I drop into the shamanic realm to guide him through his encounters with the green monster of envy, of jealousy, the hungry and the angry gods—to transition him from his "partway there" state into what the Tibetans call "the Light of the Soul." At one point of this junket, I encounter Grandmother Lewis, Father's mother, Edna June, whom we call "Nana." She honors me with a "Thank you," declaring to me, "for the work you've done with my son has enabled me to restore the relationship with *my* father." Yes, patterns transfer from father to daughter, then mother to son, then father to daughter again, looping male, female, male, female, not just in linear terms of female-to-female or male-to-male.

From the ethereal realm, Nana asks me to assist her as well. For fourteen years, she claims, she's been stuck in the third day of the Bardo. How purgatorial awful for her! For several days, I rattle on her behalf. As if, in a Plutonian way, I am "faced with the task of redeeming or carrying something for the larger collective" as Liz Greene expresses, which is "the expiation of ancestral sin, and must become a bridge over which something ancient and undifferentiated and outcast may walk to find a welcome in consciousness." At the threshold between the worlds, I listen, honoring their pathways.

It occurred to me that maybe we could do this for all those ancestors of the black slaves drawn across the Atlantic to their demise and those ancestors of the Original People of Turtle Island who lost their lives on the Trail of Tears. We could sit with them on both sides of the Atlantic, on the walk across America, listening to their stories, their songs, their pain. And just maybe to some of those who experienced these ancient nightmares, we could bring peace to them on the other side, which might heal "seven generations forward and back." I will begin this prayer work.

Part III: To the Divine

By day thirty, for Dad, I feel this specific task is complete enough, for now, believing that all the internal work I have been doing and will continue to do, is making and will make both his and Nana's way smooth, and I pray that this too will affect those seven generations.

At the time, it wasn't so much I would or could no longer work on Father, Nana, or for the Bushmen or for the Maasai through Global Voice, it was time to be about something greater, living into the development of personality, into the predestined vocation, turning within, to that quiet, though often, small, inner voice and the stillness of the praying mantis. This personal pursuit of writing in the diary or creatively, Anaïs Nin felt that "if it is deep enough, becomes universal, mythical, symbolic" (*The Diary of Anaïs Nine Volume Three, 1939-44*). Jung believed individuation—not individualism—is well worth the work, which ignites both of us, and the universe.

Over the telephone, I inform Deborah of this internal soulful work on my behalf, as well as Father's. I question his hanging on in this state of what most believe is "nothingness."

"Your dad, though stuck in a dementia state, continues to live because he wants to watch you unfold. He confirms your work with your grandmother, his mother." Wow! While he waits, watching, in a kind of "no zone," in limbo, aware of his daughter's transfiguration.

What of those whose bodies were flung into the Atlantic, who died walking across America in tears? Maybe from these horrors, they're watching us; calling on each one of us to shift the way we interact, engage with one another. Maybe they're demanding we live as equals, treating one another with respect. I'm willing to listen. May these relations continue to educate me.

For several years, Deborah will train me as a shaman. In the summer of 2007, through her guidance, I will begin with the first client. In May of 2009, Father will transition to the other side, I pray, this takes place, easily and effortlessly for him, sliding quickly through the bardo, what Chogyam Trungpa's title, *The Tibetan Book of the Dead: The Great Liberation Through Hearing In The Bardo*—of liberation he expresses so well. I pray that from that work with him, others who have been other-ed find peace as they transition to the next life. And that somehow, someday soon, in America and throughout the world, those walls we've constructed—where we've been held psychically, emotionally by the patriarchal notions of the past, which have separated and severed us from the feminine, from the "other-ed," from the other side of something—come

82: Walled From the "Other"

tumbling down. I pray that "the other-ed" finds love within, believes in himself, herself, in a way they never have before. Orna Guralnik of *Couples Therapy*, the docu-series, claims even in therapy, couples are listening to one another in a way they never have. I pray it's true, that these movements of #metoo, in Black Lives Matters, in #StopAAIPHate have moved us and will continue to.

83

ACROSS WHAT?

⚔ ⚔ ⚔

"What was below? What was above? [...] He who oversees this [world] from the highest heavens, only He knows, or perhaps not even He."

—Roberto Calasso, *Ardor*

For so many years, I've been going across, across to Africa, across to the "other," across to be "other-ed," across into the unexplainable, into another reality—*and why?* "Only He knows, or perhaps not even He." Maybe the goddess doesn't know either. Within this "superreality"—what André Breton explained in 1924 as, "those two apparently contradictory states of dream and reality,"—I have secretly lived, most of my life, in order to survive.

In this superreality of mine, a married man wants to have dinner with a woman. "No," she says as she peers down at the sculpture he is carving. "Your heart must be as thick as that stone if you are willing to have an illicit affair on your wife!" "In the dream state," analyst Pia Skogemann suggests, "when one remembers a real voice, listen, for this is a significant message." *Perhaps this is a sign of my internal resolve with Renzo, with Sarototi?* I don't want to share a husband. I don't want to lie in the sheets where honor does not exist—even as the second wife.

Today, I take the beautiful drive across the meandering and hilly Highway 150 from Santa Barbara to Ojai to rendezvous with the psychologist, Mary, who gushes, "I've been so moved by your decision to give back the parts belonging to others, drawing back the parts that are yours, and of your most recent journey with the Bushmen. But it's sad, even as a medicine man, knowing your wounding as he did, Sarototi still got caught in the web of the very patterns you've been tangled up in for many years."

"Yes," I concur with Mary, "They'd given me back my "I," but I still didn't have the framework in which to graciously hold the marriage the community had given me. And to be honest—as I release the last vestiges of anger at the men in this life: the Chief, Sarototi, Renzo—I'm tired of explaining, writing letters, sending stones and parts, making everyone else's universe right, even in assisting Dad and Nana in the Bardo. Somehow, instead of living the life I'm meant to, I still seem to live a life of servitude towards others."

"It is the story of our time, the challenge of the woman, keeping something for herself, finding her lifework—and actually living it out is something else entirely."

"Ahhh! As Starwoman, in the Kalahari Bushmen story, all the things in her basket she had stored." I ponder. As in Gay's *the erotic fire of the unattainable*— those gifts within that often aren't meant for anyone else but us until they are meant to be offerings.

"To be perfectly honest, Mary, I cannot seem to forgive myself for having sex with Sarototi." In a way it's no different than how I felt loving another woman's husband, Renzo. I'm caught in the narrative of Trollope's—*Can You Forgive Her?* Alice Vavasor is in love with her cousin George, who isn't good for her, who uses her, whom everyone warns her against. *Doesn't that mean the work is still about recovering my "Self" with a capital "S?"*

"Here's a crazy thought—what if that notion is real 'of being true to my Self' and is so important it repairs the family and others automatically whether I "Bardo" them through the forty-nine days or not—each reparation we make, as the Native Americans say, affecting 'seven generations forward and back.' No?"

Maybe, what I had done in that life to the Maasai—holding back the medicine—was as much for me as it was for them, so there is no need to blame

Part III: To the Divine

myself. In revelation, in truths, in love, in transformation, in transcendence, I was meant to be transported Across *that* experience to the Other Side of something eating me, testing me in measures just as the world was reflecting back what was out of order outside and within.

It has become apparent; I came from a world opposite of Sarototi and Mundadisi. Even in those therapeutic moments, I'd been "Western" educated. Through Eduardo and Bonnie Duran, I grasp that the "therapy" relationship is client-based (or I would say, client-centered), the therapist gives "up power [...] thus allowing the client to become empowered." Here, now, in Ojai, I was the center of this hour with Mary, being empowered by her. However, "within the shamanic field there is evidence that the power and the healing symbolism is carried by the shaman" (*Native American PostColonial Psychology*).

Within my initiation, Sarototi and Mundadisi held the power. Their rituals "engulfed" me inside those herbs, the breathing of the lion and the elephant dung, inside the womb of Sarototi's hut, inside the sanctity of marriage, activating the spleen, activating my relationship with Big Chief Bear Eagle Elephant, testing my capacities with tomahawks and the winds off the Santa Ynez Mountains.

Once a shaman explained to Eduardo Duran that the difference between a psychologist and a shaman, is that a therapist walks the client to the cliff's edge and leaves him/her/they/it there, whereas the shaman pushes the patient, jumping off the cliff with him/her/they/it. It helped explain what Mundadisi and Sarototi were doing with me. They were getting messy in my mess; they were going all the way—not as gurus, but as guides. Challenging me to the bitter end, into the sweetness. Making a shaman of me, bringing about my wholeness into that "I."

In the evening, I re-watch *The Hours*, finding myself emotionally rocked by Virginia Woolf's (Nicole Kidman) final letter to her husband, her coolness, her intelligence, and yet, her complete vulnerability. Thinking of the abuse she experienced from most every male figure in her childhood household, of those who have lived within dysfunctional families of some form or another, or who have suffered abuses in other situations whether physically, sexually, verbally, emotionally, or mentally. Of the many lives we then live: one foot in our livelihood, another in our futures of writing of books, journals, paintings, dance, song, the imaginal in an attempt to face that past, and the other foot, sipping a glorious cup of tea while having a conversation with women the likes of Mary, Vicki and Betts who just love and accept us no matter what.

Which is true? And what of Africa—because of its relation to the other side—does this make it more real? Yes? No? I cannot be sure. But I know this; I am no longer willing to live inside the label of what Freud believed to be "wish fulfillments"— which was so destructive for Virginia Woolf and others. For all the above, what I have encountered, both in and out of this world is my super-duper superreality, whether anyone else thinks the sexual abuse is true or alleged. For me, no longer is it "just my imagination running away with me" (The Temptations)—it's as real as the squawking geese's decree, and has been important enough to explore in my journals, in therapy, in bodywork.

"The Vedic seers were masters at raising the stakes, taking them beyond reach," Calasso so skillfully explains, "(into) complete uncertainty." Jumping off that cliff into the unknown! *What have I gone Across? Across what? The divide within myself? The divide within the world? To shake hands with the "other-ed?" Across my fears to the other side for answers? Or into far more complex questions? Into what—uncertainty, the mysteries?* Perhaps. For even, "the poets inquiring into their hearts," Calasso conjectures, "is a 'rope stretched across.'" As the Bushmen shaman climbs the ropes to God, so go I, stretching across the abyss, to embrace the unknown, to my opposite, to express feelings, to express concerns, to share experiences, to discover answers, raising the stakes. As the geese remind, the role of an initiate is to let go of whatever is being withheld, of whatever is holding you back from your ultimate you, jumping in, taking a complete and total risk, falling into surrender, embracing the new.

Still, I don't have all the answers. But what I do know is, I was indeed an initiate, metaphorically leaping off that cliff with guide in hand, and will eternally be, an ever-shifting, ever-re-constructing initiate.e.

Epilogue

84

THE DIVINENESS OF IT ALL

> "Beyond all possibility of doubt, you would say, 'Here at last is what I was made for.' [...] the secret signature of each soul, the incommunicable and unappeasable want. [...] While we are, this is.
> If we lose this, we lose all."
>
> —C.S. Lewis, *The Problem of Pain*

Botswana, Namibia, South Africa, Kenya, Tanzania, Swaziland—these places, where augurs for thousands of years have been listening to the hereafter and the above through their skills of divination—I learn the art of inquiry. Not necessarily to doubt "the Self," but to ruminate: *What is it that I want? Where am I going? What is off-kilter, out of balance?* To theorize. To live in query. Predict.

84: The Divineness of It All

To regain an authentic identity—the secret signature—as much as is thoroughly possible, so I can say as C.S. Lewis, "Here at last is what I was made for."

These divinations are often reflections of what has been, what is, as well as the forewarnings of what is to come. The bones, stones, *IChing*, runes, astrology, Tarot may divine your destiny. Or perhaps the cards of life are just simply dealt and one must will the Self forward in spite of it all. For we cannot control either of these: as when the first spouse asked me to follow him into the ministry, and later left, or when Renzo lies to me about his wife's existence or Sarototi lies with me and to me, as well, or when they light the fire for the marriage of his intention. How often I have slept in that bed of shame. Whether a trick or not—the real case is—one of them wanted a divorce, one of them wanted an affair, the other wanted a marriage.

What I had come to realize is, as a child, from trauma, I had been stuck in the dreamworld, a place unbudgeable, a place I thought where I could never be awakened. That my entire universe had fallen in and through to the other side of Neverland and was the only reality I could control, the only place I could create the perfect mechanism of defense against the unexplainable.

As if I could find a way to be "kissed" into the Snow White of a re-awakening, I'd flown with intent to South Africa, where the Bushmen shot me with a barbed arrow of "*Why Ostriches Don't Fly*," a story, which I could not peel from my mind, which permanently became lodged in the psyche festering, until I could grasp it, until it became a part of me into realization, until I could find that "inner equilibrium," until I could hit the target, hit the bulls-eye for myself. And the kiss, if one could call it *that*, came from an East African Maasai Sarototi through herbs, initiation, and the rapid insertions of marital union, which turned into an internal personal power, furthering me onward, for "The aim of the mystical peregrination," according to Jung, "is to understand all parts of the world, to achieve the greatest possible extension of consciousness."

Yet when we're not conscious, relationships become what the Aboriginal Skeleton Man divined: "about power." It often comes down to *that*! However, it wasn't necessarily about other people's power over me (well, it could be about that, as well), but ultimately, I believe, the issue often lies within. Certainly, for me, there is no doubt I gave authority to others over myself, because, as Dr. Eileen Miles had determined from that Giacometti sculpture—that lies somewhere crumbled in a delicate white box—I didn't have a "leg to stand on." Possessing only what Clarisa Pinkola Estes describes as "injured instincts." In other words, the wounding had injured me, had cut me off from the capacity to access that clear instinctual knowingness.

This loss of instincts—what the Bushmen, the Maasai, the Zulu, the Shona displayed to me inside the bones, the stones, as well as within the shamanic realms—had been "the stolen flow," the loss of the "I" in the beginning of "Irene." These forfeitures gave me over to Father's dictates as a businesswoman, to the Ex as divorcée, to the married man Renzo as fodder, to the fashion designers as mannequin, as muse, and in the end, even to the very shaman himself, as wife. Eventually, I will not remain in any of those titles, in any of those forms of definitions, for any of *them*.

From trauma, I had been held in a "defined" archetype, held inside cultural beliefs and education, beyond the reach of my personal legend, and for this reason, I had been archetypally determined to shift, so determined, I flew across the world and fell into the lap of a Maasai *laibon*, Sarototi.

Sarototi had loved me more than I loved him. Still his love meant, I had finally encountered a love, which was not unrequited, instead, present, persistent, wanting. Yet, I, however, did not want this. I could have been anywhere in the world, unhappily married (and according to the first husband—even in Evanston and Scottsdale—we were unhappy). This time, it just happened to be in Laloshwa Highlands, Kenya, with a dear friend, a man who had waited for me for six years, who gave me the antidote from functionality to authenticity. For something that was much bigger than him or me, he had to marry me, so we could incubate in the closed vessel of the wedding to create the alchemical "gold," which in the end will be the making of me, and I will later learn, will be the making of him!

At the time, I'd like to have thought that the issue with me was the transformative initiations of childhood: the challenging birth, the trauma, and the imperatives of Father, and if the intuitive Mariah could be believed, the kidnapping by the Maasai from that Bushmen homeland in 1787. By the time I had reached the Maasai in this lifetime, I had been in, let's say, recovery of those first initiatory experiences through psychotherapy, bodywork. Of 1787, I had yet to grasp what that would entail to restore, not knowing that recovering an "I" would mean a greater trick of the eventual marriage to Sarototi and the uncovering of that, would begin to dislodge, would bring to the fore the rumblings of a more profound initiation, which was deeper, carefully, and protectively hidden in the resources of memory, which were not meant to be disturbed until a strong

Self could be formed in Denmark through a love for the Dane, commencing in Book Two.

What I didn't know—as I drew the Maasai tale to what I thought was the best conclusion I could make (on the ethers and by letter)—it would take me many more years to resolve. Stories shot as arrows, are such as that, they take time to churn and tumble as we on Planet Earth spin at breakneck speed round and around the Sun. What I don't know is that in cancelling a part of the trip to the Maasai in March of 2005, is that I won't return—not until things incubate in the magic number of nine, not until nine years after my marriage to Sarototi. To make the annulment official on the earth plane, I will boldly return with my "new" second husband, to annul it properly, according to their traditions. But that's a tale of a different kind (formulating in Book Three).

Yet, over the course of those nine years, there is an innate gradualness to the development of forgiveness for us both (and others), until I can come face to face with Sarototi once more. And when I do face him, it will take another six or so years to make sense of that resolution—a total decade and a half (for which, dear Reader, you will come to an understanding in the continuation of *Across the Divide to the Divine: The Twiggy Project Complete*).

What I hadn't realized at the time was that the last initiation, the *laiboni* ceremony, *that* marriage, had been a divine gift, another turning point. The Maasai had given me the "I" back, and with that new "injury" of the consummation I hadn't entirely wanted, I had been thrown back unto that Self, back into the movement of pursuing the soul's coding, as Dr. Dave Cumes had declared, "to grow up," to step further into the "I'ing" I had been missing for so long. To live into a different mentality, away from victimhood to owning all that had "happened to me" and loving it, as though Fate were divinely tricking me forward!

For inside the Maasai Warriors' divine rituals, I personally leapt out of Western history into Eliade's *The Myth of the Eternal Return*, crucified into a momentous change, "indissolubly connected with the Cosmos and the cosmic rhythms." In entering into the Kalahari Bush-men-and-women legends, in entering into the Maasai traditions, I have stepped out of the historic, the profane, the quotidian, into the sanctified. Just as a child through the books at the Paola Library, I have fallen into this secret tacit, magically re-entering the realm of "once upona once upona once upona time," what Eliade declares as "the Great Time, the sacred time." Where the wise men and women of old imbue their

Part III: To the Divine

children, fortifying them with courage into their futures with tales from the past, with the animals, the fish, the insects, the birds, and the plants as guides.

Since that lost childhood, I have been in search of this. I have re-discovered this "once upona time" for myself, as a place, as Lucy Hawkins divines, where "The shared experience of going there through storytelling will hold us together as we travel. The story will see us through" (TedTalk "Science and Storytelling"). Yes, wherever, however, in what matter we travel, "the story will see us through" *anything*—even through #metoo, Black Lives Matter, #StopAAIPHate, Covid19, the Ukrainian War and the war in Gaza. I pray for those who are in the thick of it and for those who have lost their lives and their loved ones.

The Bushmen, the Maasai have fortified me with the yarns of old, with these stepping-stones. Each step, a step toward becoming a fuller Self. Building blocks. The Mesopotamian Goddess Inanna spirals down under to face her dark sister, Ereshkigal, only to rise again. As the *Tao Te Ching* cycles, "Going on means going far, Going far means returning." Even Goethe, expresses this symbolic *uroborus*, "For what the centre brings / Must obviously be, / That which remains to the end, / And was there from eternity." Yeats, too, confides, "How many times man lives and dies between his two eternities."

In *Mystic Spiral*, Jill Purce spins us into the past of, "...that haunting scent: situations recur with almost boring familiarity until we have mastered them in the light of the previous time round..." The meditative conscious breath echoes the rhythmic cosmogonies of old. A whirlpool sucks us to the bottom, turning us upside down, only to spew us out, only to pull us ever and ever into its vortex. For "the goal of psychic development is the Self. There is no linear evolution; there is only circumambulation of the Self." Jung unwinds, "Uniform development exists at most, only at the beginning; later, everything points towards the center."

The Sufis, the Mevlana Dervishes of Rumi, swirl and orbit, revolving in resolution as their brethren Muslims circle Mecca, their axis *mundi* connecting heaven and earth, and even (if we're not willing to admit it) the hellish hell of things below we'd sooner forget than dare to remember. And on it goes, as Hillman suggests, "The circular states of repetitiveness, turning and turning in the gyres of our own conditions [...] our very essence and that the soul's circular motion cannot be distinguished from blind fate." Forcing us forever and ever into the bottom of the abyss, and then, into the magnificence of ascension again and again. We go down to go up. Up to go down.

84: The Divineness of It All

And you? How will you go up from your down? How will you find the way "Across and Into and Through Your Divided Self" (www.imurphylewis.com)? As I continue to attempt to do. Will you be like my friend Linda, aware that her suicidal self wants to leap from the balcony, and instead, takes that self to do the laundry in the basement? If you can't buy that round trip ticket to Africa for a "kiss," how can you, dear reader, do the same? Hike in the woods with close friends. Sneak out into the night with Jana, Julie and Nancy, marching across the dam of Messer's Lake, trek under the Old Kansas City Road, through the muddy tunnel to run barefoot on the greens of the Paola Country Club. Take a bus to the park, to a museum, to a basketball game to wonder at the likes of Kareem Abdul-Jabbar, as I once did as a child with my brother and his friends.

Like Adaobi's family perform a ritual on the land of your forefathers and foremothers. Visit a shrine: Komo no Okusu, the magnificent camphor tree in Japan. Or build a shrine to the invisible, lighting a candle, filling it with magical feathers and stones. Trailride along the Marais des Cygnes on horseback, on Geronimo, with your girlfriend Karen as she rides her little Shetland pony, Coco, as we name the secret park: "Horses' Honor," and the hidden pond we love, "Tadpole Territory," honoring and establishing each place's character in the world. Notice the unseen. Hear the wind. Run in the rain. "Feed the birds tuppence a bag." Feed and welcome the ants with a whole bowl of rice. When not poisonous, let the web of the spider remain in the corner of your room. Take care of someone's cat. Walk their dog. Buy groceries for your neighbor in need. Cook a casserole for someone who has lost their mother.

Join Gregg: In a Washington Post article, with painted face and feathered headdress, performance artist Gregg Deal, of the Pyramid Lake Paiute community, holds a poster, declaring, "My spirit animal is white guilt." Within the Original Peoples' communities, an energy is building—to give voice, to speak the truth, and according to the activist Susan Harjo of the Cheyenne and Hodulugee Muscogee: "The American Indian civil rights movement is really just getting started" (Wildcat). Paul Seesequasis, who is a member of the Plains Cree First Nations, published *Blanket Toss Under Midnight Sun* from the archives of photos from the 1920's to the 1970's. Despite the hard times of relocation and residential schools, he wanted to affirm the strength of the indigenous. To him this resilience is why there is a "resurgence of languages and culture of so many great artists, writers and filmmakers that we see today."

Part III: To the Divine

Again, in the *Washington Post*, Rachel Hatzipanagos article "Native Americans call for reparations from 'land-grab' universities," a demand for those universities to make amends where they've built upon their tribal lands. 150 years ago, eleven Native People Groups sold their land for a fraction of the value to the University of Minnesota. Yet, as they confront this, *how can they quantify the loss?* They've not come to a figure. In 2021, in response, the University of Wisconsin flew the Ho-Chunk Nations flag and the University of California offered free tuition to Natives. A descendant of the Bois Forte Band of Chippewa, as Garagiola stated, "…tens of millions of dollars at their disposal, but they are not looking at any ways they can improve living situations for Indigenous peoples today […] their existence as institutions, as schools of learning, are only there today because of everything that was taken" (*Washington Post, July 9, 2023*). *What if we join the Natives?* Speak. Write. Contest.

Surrender into that willess-ness and yet, will yourself against fate!

The question is, what is your Africa? It could be a fountain in the center of the block of your tenement housing. A treehouse. The beach. A closet. The fire escape. Under the table. Behind the couch.

Shoot hoops until nothing distracts you from an elegant shot. Under the defender's awareness, under, around, in and out of your legs, practice dribbling until you can be the trickstar/trickster, sliding it right past him/her/they/it. As Ecuadorian, Veronica Carerra swim, bike, and run *140 Miles of Life: A Remarkable Journey to Self-Acceptance and Love.* Learn a new dance step, finding a swing partner, as I did in my friend Jim, under the sparkling lights of the Brooklyn Bridge at Pier 1. Eat a hot dog, ride the Circle Line or the Ferry across the Hudson for fresh air. Buy a spiral-bound notepad or rainbow-colored pencils and begin again. Whip up the perfect chocolate soufflé to share with newfound friends.

Try *Stalking Wild Psoas: Embodying Your Core Intelligence* with Liz Koch and actually believe yourself into self-actualization. Take a journey to a past. Through Claudia Raikin's, *Messages of the Womb: Babies Talk Through Guided Meditation, Expanding Our Hearts and Minds*, return to the place of conception, the odd birth through *DreamBirth®* exercises. Or dive into Mahdi's novel *Khaak* to re-see a terrorist act on 144 children and their teachers in Peshawar in 2014. Submit an ePop video to Max Bale's program with Radio France making a statement about how you picture climate change in your neighborhood epop.network. Teach film, build a school—Patrimoines-Heritage—to your fellow countrymen just as filmmaker Jean-Marie Teno in Cameroon. Launch a biracial gallery for painters and sculptors as TanyaWeddemire.com. Embolden others across the world to make film with Smartphones as Nick Lunch's InsightShare.com. Track Forest Elephants just as Andrea Turkalo. Or be a Louis Sarno, living amongst the BaAka pygmies in Central African Republic for thirty years, recording their music for all to hear on Radio France's Radio Ndjoku.

Boldly return to the scene of the trauma, the rape, the kidnapping—with a guide through MDMA like the movie *Trip of Compassion* or attempt EMDR or EFT. Visit a gravesite, honoring an ancestor. Take your son or daughter to an art therapist, exploring with him/her/they/it through the fracturing of their mind or yours. Or do as I did when I was employed with Bergdorf Goodman, call the 1-800-help-line, utilizing the twenty hours of free counseling allowed within the insurance plan, or call a suicide hotline 1-800-273-TALK. If you're having mental and emotional challenges or are living with someone who is bipolar or has a narcissistic disorder—God Bless You—call the National Alliance on Mental Illness 1-800-950-NAMI. Are you an alcoholic, a drug addict? Attend Alcoholic's Anonymous. Living with one? Attend Al-Teen or Al-anon.

If you're experiencing domestic violence and are having trouble breaking this cycle—I'm so sorry—call the National Domestic Violence Hotline, 1-800-799-7233, or National Child Abuse: 1-800-422-4453. If you've been raped, call RAINN's, 1-800-656-HOPE. Unlike the 1960's, there is now an "International Rape Crisis Hotline" online page for everyone the world over. Risk the telephoning of a neighbor, a friend. Seek advice. And only when it's safe for you—with an escort or an advocate or separated by the bars of a prison have a pivotal conversation with your abuser. You'll discover more remains within, than what was lost in that experience. Sometimes just to confess it, to get to the bottom of it, *is* everything. Send an honest letter. If sending is too dangerous for you—in other words, if he knows that you remember, he may harm you—so write it, tear it up and burn it.

If you can't find someone to "divine," seek a psychic, a therapist, or have a conversation with a minister, an aunt, your mother, your father, a grandparent, your elder or younger siblings, or the wise woman in your neighborhood. Or find your ayah, the family's maidservant, let her brush your hair again and tell you the tale that's been held in secret as Margaret Mascarenhas' protagonist Pagan Miranda Flores discovers in *Skin*. Or get your hair washed and cut, letting it all go. Ground yourself after an intense day, soaking in a bath with Epsom

Salts or shower with a handful. Maybe you don't have that much water. In the Kalahari Desert, they would allow me two inches of water in a twenty-four-inch round plastic tub. I'd turn my head upside down to wash those curls of mine, then step in, squat and scrub. Because, sometimes just coming clean changes the way you view the situation. And as my grandmother said, "Everyone is beautiful with clean hair and make-up." So, paint your lips and underline your sparkling eyes for emphasis.

Peacefully march for what you believe in and just as John Lewis urged: "When you see something that is not right, not just, not fair, you have a moral obligation to say something." Even if you haven't before, say it, for there's no time like the present. Drum it! Pound it from the rooftops! "March for Stolen Lives and Looted Dreams!" For the cause you believe in, form a manifestation, like the French do every Saturday. As John Lewis urged: "Get in trouble, good trouble, necessary trouble." "Find a way to get in the way." On behalf of what Dr. Martin Luther King termed "the beloved community," create a world without poverty, racism or war by looking within and drawing out all those biases—for a transformation. Brené Brown states, "It's not a question of whether you have a bias or not. It's what biases do you have, and how many, and how bad and how deep." Attempt to get to the bottom of them. Release them. Be an ally for the "other." For, according to Maya Angelou, "prejudice is a burden that confuses the past, threatens the future and renders the present inaccessible"—especially affecting those of color.

In his books *The Souls of Black Folk* and *Darkwater*, W. E. B. Du Bois explores the issue of blacks as "suffering" from assimilation and from exclusion, but also constantly being considered "the problem." It makes me think of the comments of the Republicans recently blaming the failings of the Silicon Valley Bank because of WOKE versus the deregulation of banks in 2018 (Jamelle Bouie's "The Boy Who Cried 'Woke'"). *How can we step out of the blame game? Out of taking sides?*

In *Ain't I a Woman: Black Women and Feminism*, bell hooks, challenges the feminist movement and the middle and upper class white women who formed it. Stating that the black woman was left behind to be demoralized, emasculated in low-paying jobs. Sexism, racism placed these women in the lowest class of all. While the white woman was "virginal," women of color were considered whores to be raped, taken advantage of, and disrespected. Since this book was released

84: The Divineness of It All

in 1981, much ground has shifted for the black woman, but still much needs to change. Ain't I a Woman intersects with race and gender, tackling the marginalization of these women of color. *Can white women join forces with the black women? Why not?* In *Who's Afraid of Gender?* Judith Butler states that together, all women, all minorities must form an axis of resistance, refusing to collapse to authoritarian regimes, to "gather the targeted movements more effectively than we are targeted." Let's be inclusive. In *The Guardian*, in a review of Butler's book, Finn McKay affirms this notion: "People who may not be friends, who disagree, need to work together, because they're all in line for the same persecution, sooner or later – [...] all those minoritised."

"Unerase your ancestors, to establish their identity. Know where you come from" (Gates, Jr.) Recognize them. Honor them. *Watch Finding Your Roots* (PBS) to uncover the truth for identity's sake! Take a DNA ancestry test. With Isaacson, Henry Louis Gates, Jr. confesses, "I don't think you can embrace a universal cultural identity without having a particular culture on which to stand" (*Amanpour and Company*). Awareness about our history grounds us as Gates affirms, "I have a metaphor, which is that I think your ancestors are in purgatory waiting to be discovered and when we find them you know we unlock the doors…" —like I did with Nana in the Bardo.

Maybe you have crosses to bear and feel backed into a corner and haven't a clue how to get out. Maybe you're a neurotic *Carrie Pilby*, where reading law briefs in the middle of the night is almost more than you can handle. Just as Carrie, make a list of your favorite things you love to do and do them one step at a time. Snap a photo of each happening. Create a memory. Nap, listening into the metaphor of your day, of your dreams. *What are they? What makes you tick? What makes you cackle with delight?*

Yes, there are many ways: Read a free book from the library every week. All of a sudden, you've read 52 books in one year and been changed by them. Write a poem, a song. Learn the piano. Play an instrument until your heart sings again. Take your knees to the floor, bowing before something greater than yourself—even if it's just a dream. As Totoro, Mei and Sazuki, lift your arms up and down, reverently coaxing forth the seeds you have planted within the earth (*My Neighbor Totoro*).

You may be asking: *How do you write or paint it when you can't? When you're told you shouldn't? When it's unspoken in your culture?* Be bold like the women in Iran! A*nd pray for their safety! How do you write or act around it? Upside down,*

Book One – Across the Divide to the Divine 523

Part III: To the Divine

inside, and through it? Metaphorically? Does one become as sly as tricky as the Count of Monte Cristo after his imprisonment? Or like the Chinese, holding white paper in silence, in solidarity? Or quiet sleuths such as Walter Hartright and Marian Halcombe in Wilkie Collins' The Women in White? In Sister Outsider, Audre Lorde touts, "Next time, ask: What's the worst that will happen? Then push yourself a little further than you dare. Once you start to speak, people will yell at you. They will interrupt you, put you down and suggest it's personal. And the world won't end."

Look, I understand the fear. For years I have hidden in some odd one-hundred-and-sixty journals, twenty-eight thousand pages worth, even making a little mark throughout so the trauma remained undisclosed, for the revealing of it seemed too dangerous. Write it for yourself until it turns from revenge into a blessing, inside Linda Howe's "Pathway Prayer," as I do every day, inside the Akashic records! Dare, as Audre Lorde dares. If she can, if I can, if others can, maybe you can recover your voice, too. Join us.

Buy glorious colors and hand paint on your walls, on a newspaper, or on an old white bed sheet spread across the floor. Sketch with pens as Vetkat did or burn an image on an Ostrich egg. Snap a meaningful photograph posting it on Facebook as my cousin Murphy Strick does or post it on Instagram or TikTok. Live as Paul Gauguin in Tahiti, colorfully painting into the questions: *D'où venons-nous ? Que sommes-nous ? Où allons-nous ? Where Do We Come From? What Are We? Where Are We Going? (Noa Noa: The Tahitian Journal).* Until you make the C.S. Lewis declaration, "Here at last is what I was made for!"

In Haiku, just as Cherry, let your *Words Bubble Up Like Soda Pop* (Kyohei Ishiguro, 2021). Chalk on the sidewalk, or as the mysterious Samo (Jean-Michel Baptiste) scrawling epiphanic epigrams on abandoned buildings or watch Sara Driver's film *Boom for Real* about his friends and art. Or like Alexis Adler photograph the artist you live with, honoring him/her/they/it until it becomes an exhibition and a book: *Basquiat Before Basquiat: East 12th Street, 1979-1980,* currated by Nora Burnett Abrams.

With Camille Paglia, *Break, Blow, Burn* a new poem and join the other "43 of the World's Best" Poets. As only Hayao Miyazaki does, animate a tale *My Neighbor Totoro* where the will outweighs fate, where children and even adult hearts soar to the sky in a cat bus. For according to Jung, "creative life always stands outside convention" and to me, it thrills the soul.

Hunker down in Woolf's *A Room of One's Own*, where you can *Write For Your Life*, as Deena Metzger challenges, daily in a journal, in a notepad of morning pages through Julia Cameron's *The Artist's Way*, with Gay Walley as a coach or Gateless Train with Suzanne Kingsbury, teaching others to write in a Gateless-ly. As many of us can—type—on an old typewriter from Grandad or so easily onto our computers, or on a blog. Pen and mail that letter signed or anonymous. Or scribble it and never send it, burning it into ash that blows it into being. Declare truths. An *Africa Within* could be that simple or complex.

"One must always remember," Sir Laurens van der Post once encouraged, "that we write not alone and in loneliness but as part of a great company who cannot help it nor avoid it and must at all costs serve the living word" (letter to me, 3rd November 1994). So, join in Crenshaw's "war on narrative" with the active, transformative and "living word!"

If you don't write, stay in awareness, "Wakefulness is the pivotal point of the Vedic world," Calasso reminds. Attempt solitude. Slink into a gentle yoga pose. Sink your bare toes into the grasses or the sands of time. Light a candle. Go still. Scribble, brush, sketch, or dance in front of the mirror naked with the music blaring loud awakening your soul. Sit by the fire during your menses with all the women of the world, or with a men's group, pound on the drums. Attempt group therapy. You might be surprised how much everyone is like you and how everyone is uniquely different. Join a group where you're the "other," for the first time, an outsider to find out what that feels like. "Without community there is no liberation" (A. Lorde).

My nephew Peter Murphy Lewis became an LPN, just to understand what it means to be a caretaker to the elderly and started a thoughtful podcast. Or like my friend Richard Gorman, gently cross the dying to the other side as a doula. Or doula a baby into its incarnation as Claudia Raikin, author of *Messages from the Womb*. Or fight authoritarians, create a radical film like Daniel Roher's Navalny of the poisoning of the Russian opposition leader Andrei Navalny and make a difference.

Contact an "other": Twenty years after my experience with the Maasai, after Mundadisi gave me that look, some very important movements would arise: #metoo, #StopAAIPHate, "Black Lives Matter" affecting one another, making these issues more apparent and disturbing for many, forcing us to get down dirty and talk. It causes me to saunter over to the Jardin du Luxembourg to take tea with my French-born Cambodian yoga-prayer partner, Rotana, to discuss how

Part III: To the Divine

she is continuously "other-ed"—even in liberated France. "I had the feeling I wasn't always so respected. Now I speak up for myself." During Covid, my Chinese friend, Mei and I did an exchange, sharing our spiritual talents with one another. Her gifts lie in Reiki and the sound bowls, which was quite heavenly. When I was working on her, I had to mention, "How are you in this moment of ostracism in New York City?" "We're scared to go out, particularly my mother, who is elderly." It's no longer safe to be an Asian in America.

Get involved in other people's lives—not as a savior, but as a friend, an ally. Admit, as I did to the Maasai, to the Bushmen: "I want to know you and in turn, to uncover more of my true Self." Be about a reclamation. "Can we do it together?" To reclaim ourselves! Over the years, I have watched the San Bush-men-and-women of the Kalahari lose their lands to government, ranchers, diamond merchants, national parks. I've befriended Belinda Kruiper Org married to a Bush-man, who keeps in touch via Whatsapp. Through the Vetkat Art Foundation, she'll soon be blogging. Support wisn.org to help San with the challenge of alcoholism. One Maasai and one Samburu friend are my Wisdomkeepers for Global Voice—they tell me what is happening on the ground. As most indigenous peoples, the Maasai are once again threatened with loss of land. For over thirty years, in Tanzania, the Maasai have been fighting to maintain their lands as pastoralists. They are once again being relocated for a third time and now, in 2022, 167,000 Maasai are losing their land to elite tourism and trophy hunting. Sign the Avaaz.org petition. Write a letter. Fund "Girls Who Code" summer immersion program where girls learn the necessary computing skills. Provide learning opportunities for the BaAka. Help Global Voice broadcast the BaAka music (recorded by Louis Sarno for over 30 years) and cultural issues through Radio France's Radio Ndjoku.

Give someone hope. We are so often colorblind to the system that "keeps them in their place," that has the power to overturn their lives and mow down their houses to put up projects that are a nightmare to live in. I once tried to aid Jade and her Puerto Rican family to "get out" of the projects in the Bronx. We searched for government loans, some kind of assistance—just for one very female family—a grandmother, a mother and two daughters. We met with resistance. *But if each of us helped one student study, if each of us adopted someone to go to school, if each of us became an ally, what would the world be like?* Good education makes a difference. It helped that we encouraged Jade through Catholic High School, through Student Sponsor Partners, through studying together on

84: The Divineness of It All

Sundays. She was able to go onto the university, find an incredible husband, build a family. And now the entire family has moved out of the Bronx, living in sunny Florida. *But without that good education, where would Jade be today?*

Dive in! The water is warm, speak, engage! I once gave a lecture in Paris at the American Business School in the Psychology Department, sharing with the students that I'd gone to the Maasai Warriors because I thought I was once a Bush-women in 1787. A young black man raised his hand; "You mean to tell me you think you were once a woman of color?" "Yes." That yes, changed the lecture to a dialog. It was no longer a white girl lecturing to black, Asian, bi-racial students. It was someone who identified with them on some level or certainly thought she was one of them at one time or another. It was a radical notion. When I also raised doubts about the Christianity that had been poured into my head as a child, it brought other students forward—Islamics, Jewish, Catholics. They stood in line afterwards saying, "I'm struggling with my faith, too. My parents are mad at me because I don't believe as they do. I want a different life than what they have." It brought about human connection. It leveled the field. I wasn't someone who had all the answers because I don't.

In fact, any hubris that I once had has been deflated. In the dream I had last night of floating inside a balloon high in the sky, only to tumble to the waters below. There, I assisted others just like me to find land. A white elderly woman verbally abused the black man that was with us. I shouted, "We won't have that here—prejudices." I almost boxed her ears, placing my hands intensely on the sides of her head, as if to emphasize, "now hear this!" Yes, we won't tolerate that anymore. Hate is indeed a virus. Judgment of others and how they live and are when we can't understand them, when we've never walked a mile in their shoes, when we've never lived in the ghetto or on the reservation or felt what Pierce termed a "microaggression," or just walked down the street to the judgment and jeers and fears of others. *What do we know?*

The United States, the academic Edward Saïd explains, has been formed out of various histories that continue to live in conflict, as well as in contradiction with one another. These numerous histories—all these pasts of different people groups—are demanding to be heard. They deserve to be acknowledged so that they too can offer their contributions, "so that communities of color, the poor, and all other/marginalized groups may view themselves differently" (B. Duran, E. Duran). Just listening to the Bushmen stories, just writing them down, brought about affirmation for them. That I cared, wanted to understand how they thought, wanted to share them with American children. Sometimes just a little bit of listening is enough. It affirms those who have been "other-ed," acknowledges them.

"People of indigenous descent must struggle to recapture our own mode of representation and go beyond Eurocentric stereotypes to invest a postcolonial identity imagining ourselves richly" (B. Duran, E. Duran). Let's imagine with them—that just being true to themselves, to their heritage, to their culture, is rich enough. And what if we decolonialize everything. For what I have learned is there is a group of people who do not want to be colonialists in any form, respecting everyone's differences—I would like to be a part of that. For we are a part of a grand prism, of many different rays of light, of color—as Tutu said, *The Rainbow People of God*—yet all drawing from the same source. The French poet, essayist and philosopher, Paul Valéry once penned: "Le vent se lève !... il faut tenter de vivre !" "The wind is rising!...we must attempt to live!"—And I'd say—together, decolonialize!

Over the course of the last four months, I have been reading and researching everything and anything that will educate me into a further knowingness of my whiteness and colorblindness. As well, I have interviewed most of my black friends to learn about their past and present challenges, which has brought about another seventy-five pages. As you can see, the Black Lives Matter and the issues of the Natives have greatly influenced the direction this book has recently taken. A book that has taken years and years, which has gone through so many different levels of writing, *Africa Within*, the dissertation of *Across the Divide*, and now, this. I hadn't intended for it to morph so much. Strangely, as I wrote these last pages scattered throughout, I wept over and over. When I read it to a friend, I wept. When I read it out loud to myself, I wept. When I spoke of it, I wept.

"Developing a sociological imagination means one should be able to think beyond the temple of one's familiar to examine the social world in new and unfamiliar ways" (Aileen Moreton-Robinson, "Toward a New Research Agenda? Foucault, Whiteness, and Indigenous Sovereignty" *Seeing Race Again*). Literally, I've been bumping my head, particularly the temples, as though I need to wake up, to shift, to change the way I see, the way I treat others. Temple, Templar, a place of worship, temporalis (meaning "time," in Latin), where I'm beginning to reveal my age through the grey hairs, where four skull bones fuse: the frontal, parietal, temporal, and sphenoid.

Maybe I am integrating the Four Corners of the Natives, the four directions, the four corners of the world inside myself into awareness. In reality, we cannot help ourselves; we're inundated with the news from everywhere, everyday about everyone. We know what's happening more than ever. With mass migration we're being pressed together, connected whether we want to be or not. Syrians, Afghanis, Ukrainians, in need, have been pouring into the borders of the European Union, into the United States, and elsewhere.

How do we shift the way we envision others? To set aside biases, give others a chance? To allow others the freedom of choice as sovereign beings with wills of their own, who have rights to their lands, to their lifestyle of choice? Yet, often, stuck in our whiteness of rightness, we have become the judges, the jury, the ones who know and declare what the "rules" are. We stand to correct the Larry's of the world high above in our perch with handcuffs and "licks."

Recently, (while I'm bumping my head) several of my "white" girlfriends have had concussions. How fitting! *Are we in shock?* Perhaps, these men of color, these women of color are really shaking us up, having an impact on us. For, it's inevitable, we must change. Maybe it's a reclamation of our soul sisters, our soul brothers, our soul selves.

This last month I've been waking up in a kind of panic, heart pounding, cortisol levels up. On the back of the head, the atlas, and the occipital bone, which protects the brain, have been thrown out of balance. Part of it is, the Masseur-kinésithérapeute (physiotherapist) Sarah Doillard is rééducation périnéale (perineal and pelvic rehabilitation) the tense ligaments and muscles on the edges and the inside and above my vulva. Massaging the places I am dissociated from, where I have pain, reawakening memory. From this, when I leave her office, I feel as if my whole vagina will fall out. I feel off-kilter, a bit dizzy, headachy, maybe even a little upset in the stomach. I'm reorienting, reclaiming parts of the Self. Part of it is, I believe, I have to wake up, switch the way I walk so boldly, so confidently upon the territories of this earth, even as I ride my bike throughout the city, hopefully more aware, more observant.

Yesterday, in Paris, as I zipped along from the 6th arrondisement to the 10th in search of a new apartment, I met women of different colors. Several were walking in the bike lane, graciously apologized with huge smiles on their faces as I shouted, "Ce n'est pas grave !" We chatted as I flew by. Some veiled women were hailing a taxi between two buses, leaning out into the lane, "Excusez moi, Madame !" "Je vous en prie !" I holler!

Upon my return to the neighborhood, near the Sorbonne, there were a vast number of various kinds of students outside talking, taking a smoking break, laughing. A group of girls walked behind me near the crosswalk, I tried to catch their eye, to smile because they were adorable. Amongst these friends, an Islamic girl's hijab got caught in my bicycle wheel as I started to proceed through the green light. "Madame ! Madame !" They hollered at me. "Vous arrêtez ! S'il vous plait !" Just in time, they caught me before a crisis transpired. Luckily, I did not drag her along behind me. In a panic, I reached for her arm, "Est-ce que ça va ?" As she untangles her scarf, "Oui !" "Et ton écharpe va bien ?" Everyone laughed at my funny accent, at me, this woman overdressed and hiding under her hat, who noticed them, who stopped. *Aren't there simple acts of involvement, of noticing others, smiling, of being gracious, inclusive, kind?* Maybe this is just a beginning.

Maybe as a white woman the metaphor is, I'm no longer dragging the women of color behind me, nor dragging them down. They're here, present, making a difference, more than I ever could. Rightly so, and we're watching and cheering them on!

Madame Jahally, the woman, who does the pressing for my husband's shirts, is an immigrant to France just as I am. She is Islamic from Mauritius. She's lived here for thirty-five years. Thank God her English is better than my French. While she irons, I do the odd jobs of folding, of sewing buttons or torn pillows, hanging, and putting things away—exercises just to be near her. Over the last twelve years, we've built a friendship, over tea and sharing our dreams—some of them are so wild we must pull down Jung's symbol books and Ted Andrew's *Animal-Speak* from the library to gain comprehension. We've grown close. We now eat lunch together each week. We hug. We encourage. We weep together. Laugh. Pray for one another. Believe the best. We are advocates for each other.

It reminds me of the old sewing circles where women held the space for one another—that "gaggle of geese." Madame Jahally holds a kind of wisdom I don't have. She has a seeing eye. Knows when something is out of alignment in my home, in her family, in her children. She's trusted me with them. Her son and daughter have been my personal clients. Through the shaking of the rattle, I've traveled back through their lineage, attempting to resolve things in the present. When they're lying there in the alpha-theta state, they see things I would never

84: The Divineness of It All

see. Her daughter and I are convinced we've known each other lifetimes ago in India. The connection between us goes so deep, I wouldn't doubt it.

Through our conversations, Madame Jahally and I have been crossing the borders and boundaries of the caste system, the societal, the religious, as well as race, and color biases. We've learned to trust one another's thoughts, dreams, insights. Maybe Madame Jahally and I have been doing what Audre Lorde and Rafia Zakaria recommended—acknowledging one another's gifts, allowing one another to be heard—equally. *Could we become what Ursula K. Le Guin considers "a stream of sisters?"*—what she believes already exists.

Maybe that was it. I wanted us, every one of us, to be related and for my newfound friends to be included. I was weeping with and for the Bush-men-and-women, for the Maasai, for the First Americans, for the blacks, for my Asian friends, for Madame Jahally, for the "other-ed." For all the ways we've pushed them aside and down under. In Kenya, that last night of the *fifth journey in*, when I was weeping in front of the Maasai, the Kikuyu, the Ndebele, and the Shona Mundadisi, I could finally imagine what it would be like for all of us to come together, to share our disparities that weren't so vastly different after all and could in fact, bring about a recognition of our commonalities. I felt a part of something finally happening, a reclamation of those parts within ourselves that had been abandoned. I had met real "live" people whose lives required us to change into allies, to build a bridge for and not against. That I had found a unity within my soul, within my spirit, once I embraced these beautiful, tall, black human beings. Dare to embrace!

Through creating "Ardor," passion, great enthusiasm, Calasso maintains, is "that constant production of heat, in the mind and in the liturgical act, which will encompass the whole rite and defend it from the outside." To keep ceremonial Africa close, I make tea with burnt goat's milk, drinking in its essence. I perform rituals, lighting the fire and literally burning the manuscript in each incarnation until I can say the truth (hopefully) without a sting to myself, or anyone else (as Deena once encouraged). I keep rising into. Through fire, I attempt a liturgy of respect, reverence, consulting Christian, Buddhist, Hindu, Islamic texts, European fairy tales and indigenous myths and prayers.

Once, when I didn't have a fireplace, outside my apartment, I burnt letters of release in a clay pot, not knowing I would call forth a hundred crows. With their incessant cawing, this "murder of crows" terrifyingly filled the Three Sister Eucalyptus Trees awakening a neighbor from a nap: "What are you up to,

Part III: To the Divine

Murphy?" For "all ceremonial acts take place in an atmosphere of latent terror," Calasso elucidates, "as if handling something highly dangerous, something that has to be got rid of." In other words, it must be surrendered into the divine! For we all know within, in the bottom of our hearts: "A narrow vision is divisive, a broad vision expansive. But a divine vision is all-inclusive" (Swami Tejomayananda). Inclusive to all—no matter creed or race!

Yes, this peregrination to the Maasai, into their divinatory practices, ignited a fire that called forth nature, that couldn't be stopped, that went out of control, crossing into divineness. As I began to stir it up, inflaming the energy field, attending to the wildness within, playing with fire, I burned a hole in Mother's carpet, burned a hole in the rental carpet of a client's, burned a hole through the entire floor of Casa d'Irene. To stop this smoldering, I even had to call on firefighters, who declared: "*You*, young lady, are lucky—someone else would have burned down the whole neighborhood." (I wouldn't recommend it!)

Those releases of mine, I don't just burn. From the borders of Butterfly Beach, where I performed that dreamfelt-chicken-sacrifice, I cut cords, letting go into the Pacific those attachments I no longer need, pieces I have taken on, that, to be honest, don't fit because, in actuality, they aren't mine. Into stones, I give back what is theirs, separating at the ocean, the ones like Mundadisi, I'm not sure I'll ever be in touch with again, launching them into the waters of change. And those whom I still want to have in my life—to this second group—I send a stone with a note along with this poem (below), which had surged forth from this magically divine process of re-accessing that original guiding Self within, re-connecting into the divineness of it all:

> parts
>> i sort
>
> parts of my self stolen by others
>
>> parts of my self that disappeared
> in trauma;
>
>>> drowning in the white waters of the zambezi,
>>> wandering sad, lonely in the streets of new york,
>>> crying in the shower, nubile

84: The Divineness of It All

and yet, tainted,
bound and gagged in africa.
    parts of my self attached to men
with hunger and longing,
to women for a sip at the well.
    these parts
i call back,
    i embrace them:
the memories, the dreams, the tall tales, the tears.

    parts of others i have held onto
    i return to the rightful owners.
    i blow these parts into rocks
    throwing them into the ocean
    wrap them in packages
    mail them across the world.

i write,
    "parts of you,
    that don't belong to me."
    i retrieve
    parts of me
that don't belong to you."

i search the world
    as isis
    for brother parts,
    for lover parts.
    piece by piece
    until i find
    my purpose,
the natural order
of things.

—i. murphy lewisv

Part III: To the Divine

ACKNOWLEDGEMENTS

To JPPD, for teaching me the intricate and delicate language of love à Paris!

I would also like to thank all those who walked through the many levels and manifestations of Across the Divide to the Divine from its beginnings, especially Gay Walley. When in 1997, I climbed up her stairs several times a month, as she twirled her magic wand on those first chapters of Africa Within until its inception as a dissertation and this book. To Sharon Leeds for those long telephone conversations, feedback and many reads. To Suzanne Kingsbury for her Gateless Training that somehow miraculously transformed me into "trusting" my own inner voice as editor. To Christine Downing, who originally pulled the thesis of my dissertation out of the dustbin, adding just a few lines to "save it," serving as the advisor into its completion. It's come a long way baby! You're all the best!

And my most treasured friends who supported me over the years of building home both inside and outside, those brothers and sisters of likemind: Carol Beckwith, Angela Fisher, David Coulson, Eva Monley (somewhere in the heavens), Jeffrey Moss & Richard Gorman, Emmanuel Faccio, Tom Kollar & Jo Castagna, Kevin Hart, Sharon & Larry, Alicia & Danny Bythewood and family, Tanya "Apples" Weddemire, Karen Alleyne, Jade Sawyer and family, Cynthia Travis & family, Ike Brady, Phyllis Hollis, Linda Cassens-Stoian, Terry

Acknowledgements

Allard, Rebecca Allina, Jade Sawyer & family, Mei Leung, Rotana Tiv, Kata Van Doesselaar, Kim Langbecker, Emma Wooding, Jeannette Grace Sanford.

To those childhood friends who made magic with me: Karen Frazier, Julie and Jana Muchow, Nancy Buchman, Sherry Ventura, Alma Hinton, Pam Williams, Gracie Hoyle, Karen Frazier.

To Jane McNabb, who is no longer with us; to Connie Bates, who has drifted into another dimension; and to Ruth Davis for those nights of sushi and red wine and supportive conversation. I needed you as elder sister friends to reflect your experiences of living in Manhattan.

To those healers: Deborah, Deena Metzger, Valerie Wolf, Kathryn Alice, Eve Brinton, Dr. Albert Chinappi, Michael Cindrich, Michael Luan, Vicki Abrams, Celia Candlin, Mariah Martin, Betts Cassady, Mary Leibman, Walter Odajnyk (somewhere on the other side), Pamela Madison, Marie Odile Fessenmeyer, Eric Watts, Timothy Schultz, Isis Medina, Sarah Douillard, Marygrace O'Hearn, Eve Brinton, Mei Leung, Pia Skogemann.

To Gail Segal for "being the light at the end of the tunnel," for her knowingness, for the gift of Mantis Carol.

To Renzo. To my ex-husband. To Lmakiya Lesarge. To Sarototi. To Hok'ee. To Mundadisi. For loving me enough to jump off that cliff into those very deep waters.

To Patricia, for being a mother like none other.

To Sir Laurens van der Post (in the great beyond) for those letters of hope, for the graciousness of sharing your friends.

To Vetkat (watching over us) and Belinda and Sillikat for listening!

To Midnight, Geronimo, Helen, Laura, Kitty, Speedy for initiating me into horsemanship and saving me!

To Izak and Gib, wherever you are. I thank you from the bottom of my heart for teaching me that all life is sacred from praying mantises, plants, TakTak beetles, snakes, scorpions, dogs, horses. And for reminding me to ride the white horse of life until the black one takes me away! —Billy the Kid's girlfriend.

ABOUT THE AUTHOR

Born in Newton, Kansas, Dr. I. Murphy Lewis is a publisher, author, psychoanalytic Akashic shaman, and lecturer. She received her Masters (2005) and Doctorate (2007) of Philosophy in Mythology from the Pacifica Graduate Institute, Carpinteria, CA, with an emphasis in Depth Psychology and Culture; an Associates Degree in Fashion (1988) from Parsons School of Design in New York City; and a Bachelor of Fine Arts (1980) from the University of Kansas.

Dr. Lewis is author of the young adult book and director of the short documentary film, *Why Ostriches Don't Fly and Other Tales from the African Bush* (1997, 1998), as featured on WABC News (2002). She is the director and producer of three short documentaries, *Why Ostriches Don't Fly (1998)*, *Music that Floats from Afar* (2001), *How do you Name a Song?* (2003), and *The Sacred Forest of the Lost Child* (2007). She has given over forty speaking engagements to grade schools, junior and senior high schools; lecturing for National Geographic Journey of Man Trip (2008); The Sunflower Story Arts Festival, Mount Kisco, along with Diane Wolkstein (2009); African Art Exhibit at Northwest Missouri State University Department of Art and Horace Mann Laboratory School where she was broadcasted across

About the Author

the state of Missouri to the grade schools (2011); and for the American Business School's Psychology Department, Paris, France (2013).

In 2002, in honor of the Kalahari San Bushmen and the Maasai Warriors and to benefit indigenous peoples, Dr. Lewis became the Founding Director of Global Voice® Foundation, a fiscal sponsorship of Legacy Global Foundation, a 501c3 non-profit organization. GVF has provided water pumps, corn-threshers, education, food, medicine, and clothing. In 2018, GVF began working with Radio France's Radio Ndjoku in the Central African Republic to provide two jobs for the BaAka Peoples, giving voice to their everyday challenges, as well as to their music, which was recorded by Louis Sarno over the course of thirty years. In 2020, Dr. Lewis served as a juror in Radio France's ePop contest held to give voice to indigenous youth and elders dealing with the consequences of environmental and climate change. She created IML Publications, L.L.C. to produce art books, poetry and film by various female and indigenous artists. Her first publications include: the republication of Lysbeth Boyd Borie's 1928 *Poems for Peter* (in conjunction with Shank Painter) from the original copper plates; Gail Segal's poetry, *In Gravity's Pull* (2002); and Gay Walley's *The Erotic Fire of the Unattainable: Aphorisms on Art, Love and the Vicissitudes of Life* (2007), which resold to Skyhorse Publishing (2015), and was successfully launched in 2016 as a film *The Unattainable Story* as Mostra, the São Paulo International Film Festival where it was acquired by Europa Films for Brazilian distribution and by Random Media at Cinequest in 2017 (IML Publications is an Associate Producer); and has become a new film *Erotic Fire of the Unattainable* (2020) by Frank Vitale, written by Gay Walley. In 2021, IML Publications ambitiously launched *Venus as She Ages* a 6 novel collection by Jacqueline Gay Walley, which includes the republication of *Strings Attached*, as well as the her new books: *To Any Lengths*, *Prison Sex*, *The Bed You Lie In*, *Write she said*, and *Magnetism*. In 2023, IML Publications released Claudia Rosenhouse Raiken's *Messages from the Womb: Babies Talk Through Guided Meditation Expanding Our Hearts and Minds* and Mahdi's, *Khaak*.

Dr. Lewis has had a high-profile career in the fashion industry, as Vice President, Director of Sales for Badgley Mischka (1998-2001) and Halston (1997), and was formerly employed as International Director of Sales for Mary McFadden (1993-1996) and a Sales Manager for the Jean Muir Boutique at Bergdorf Goodman (1988-1991).

About the Author

Since 1995, Dr. Lewis has been researching the stories and recording the music of the San Bushmen of the Kalahari Desert in Botswana, Namibia, and South Africa (10 safaris in). From 1998 to 2004, during six journeys into Laloshwa Highlands, Kenya, Lewis participated in the shamanic initiation rites of the Maasai Warriors, returning in 2013 for a seventh journey in.

Through all her speeches, writings, illustrations, and unique lifestyle, Dr. Lewis opens our eyes to the magical trickster god, Mantis, and the transformative world of shamanism. When Lewis isn't traipsing through the Kalahari, she is immersed in a private practice of psychoanalytic shamanism with adults in the safety and love of the Akashic Records, editing others' books, and managing to faithfully write in her lifelong journal of fifty-two years, now 28,000 pages.

In 2006, 2009-2011, Dr. Lewis lived in Copenhagen, Denmark researching, writing, and working with private clients. During this same time period, she trained psychoanalytically at the C. G. Jung Institut, Küsnacht. Switzerland.

For the past thirteen years, she has been residing in Paris, France with her husband, Jean-Pierre Pranlas-Descours, author, architect, urban planner, and professor.

ABOUT THE ARTIST

Vetkat Regopstaan Kruiper Org

About the Artist

Born in 1969, Twee Rivieren, Kgalagadi Transfrontier Park National Park—died in 2007, on the farm Blinkwater where he lived, just outside the Park.

Vetkat Kruiper Regopstaan Boesman was a member of the Khomani San tribe who lived in the now Kgalagadi Transfrontier Park. His father was a healer and crafter in his community, and clearly had a huge impact on Vetkat's knowledge and understanding of San culture and customs. He is one of very few San artists who sustained the 'lost' (according to some) tradition of San rock art, but with ink on paper as medium. The animality, spirituality and symbolism in Vetkat's works has been the topic of several academic studies (see below).

Vetkat's works are in private collections at the Natal Museum Services, the McGregor Museum at Kimberley and the University of Pretoria. From 2002 to 2005 his art was displayed at the United Nations (UN) as part of an exhibition of indigenous art, while his 2004 tour of the United States of America culminated in his addressing the UN.

Shortly before his death in 2007, Vetkat was invited by the Department of Built Environment at the University of Pretoria to do a solo exhibition on the UP campus. All the works on exhibit were purchased by the University, and constitutes the largest assemblage of the artist's works in a single collection.

WORKS CITED AND CONSULTED

Throughout these years, in this search of mine, I've been humbled by what little I know and how much I will continue to learn, and yet, I've been steered by the wisdom and research from those of different fields of interests, different cultures and peoples, whose shoulders we stand on—in their honor:

Abram, David. *The Spell of the Sensuous.* New York: Vintage, 1997.

Abrams, Nora Burnett. *Basquiat Before Basquiat: East 12th Street, 1979-1980.* Photographs by Alexis Adler. MCA Denver, 2016.

Abt, Theodor, and Erik Hornung. *Knowledge for the Afterlife: The Egyptian Amduat—A Quest for Immortality.* Living Human Heritage Publications, 2003.

Adams, Glenn, and Phia S. Salter, "They (Color) Blinded Me with Science: Counteracting Coloniality of Knowledge in Hegemonic Psychology" *Seeing Race Again: Countering Colorblindness Across the Disciplines.* Univ. California P, 2019.

Afrique, je te plumerie, "Africa, I will fleece you." Film by Jean-Marie Teno. 1992.

Works Cited and ConsulteD

Ambrose, Stephen E. *Undaunted Courage: Meriwether Lewis, Thomas Jefferson, and the Opening of the American West.* Simon & Schuster, 1997.Andrea Turkalo: Return to Dzanga. Film by 96Elephants.org. Wildlife Conservation Society. https://www.youtube.com/watch?v=4YYe_NeA618

Andrews, Ted. *Animal-Speak: The Spiritual and Magical Powers of Creatures Great and Small.* St. Paul, Minnesota: Llewellyn, 1998.

_____. *Animal-Wise: The Spirit Language and Signs of Nature.* Jackson, Tennessee: Dragonhawk, 1999.

Angelou, Maya. *I Know Why the Caged Bird Sings.* Bantum Books and Random House, 1970.

_____. *Wouldn't Take Nothing for My Journey Now.* Bantam, 1994.

Armstrong, Karen. *The Spiral Staircase: My Climb out of Darkness.* New York: Alfred A. Knopf, 2004.

Aroke, Edwin N., and Paule V Joseph, Abhrarup Roy2 Demario S Overstreet, Trygve O Tollefsbol, David E Vance, and Burel R Goodin3 "Could epigenetics help explain racial disparities in chronic pain?" *Journal of Pain Research.* February 18, 2019. https://www.ncbi.nlm.nih.gov/pmc/articles/PMC6388771/

Ascham, Ulf. *Baron Blixen: The Man whom women loved.* Nairobi (private edition), 1986.

Baldwin, James. *No Name in the Street.* London: Michael Joseph, 1972.

Ball, Edward. *Life of a Klansman: A Family History in White Supremacy.* Farrar, Straus & Giroux, 2020.

_____. *Slaves in the Family.* Farrar, Straus & Giroux, 1998.

Bannister, Anthony. *The Bushmen.* Cape Town, South Africa: Struik, 1984.

Barnard, Alan. *Kalahari Bushmen: Threatened Cultures.* New York: Thomson Learning, 1993.

Bass, Ellen, and Laura Davis. *The Courage to Heal: A Guide for Women Survivors of Child Sexual Abuse.* New York: HarperCollins, 1994.

_____, and Louise Thornton, Eds. *I Never Told Anyone: Writings by Women Survivors of Child Sexual Abuse.* New York: HarperCollins, 1991.

Basso, Keith H. *Wisdom Sits in Places: Landscape and Language Among the Western Apache.* Albuquerque: U of New Mexico P, 1996.

Baynes, H. G. *Mythology of the Soul: A Research into the Unconscious from Schizophrenic Dreams and Drawings.* London: Baillière, Tindall and Cox, 1940.

Beckwith, Carol, and Angela Fisher. *African Ceremonies.* Abrams, 2002.

Benally, Herbert John. "Diné Bo'óhoo'aah Bindii'a': Navajo Philosophy of Learning." *Dine Be'iina': A Journal of Navajo Life* 1.1 (Spring 1987): 133-48.

Bennett, Brit. *The Vanishing Half,* Hachette, 2021

Bennun, Neil. *The Broken String: The Last Words of an Extinct People.* London: Viking, 2004.

Biesele, Megan. *Women Like Meat: The Folklore and Foraging Ideology of the Kalahari Ju/'hoan.* Bloomington, Indiana: Witwatersrand UP, 1993.

Bhatt, Jenny. "'Against White Feminism' Is an Urgent Call to Action for Solidarity and Justice." *NPR* about Rafia Zakaria's *Against White Feminists: Notes on Disruption.* April 17, 2021

Bleek, D. F. *A Bushmen Dictionary* (Vol. 41). New Haven: American Oriental Series, 1956.

Bleek, D. F., and A. M. Duggan-Cronin. *The Bushman Tribes of Southern Africa.*

Cape Town, South Africa: Cape Times, Ltd., 1942.

Bleek, W. H. I., and L. C. Lloyd. *Bushmen Folklore*. London: George Allen & Co., Ltd., 1911.

Bleek, W. H. I. *Hottentot Fables and Tales*. London: Trubner, 1864.

_____. *The Mantis and His Friends, Bushmen Folklore, Collected by the late W. H. I. Bleek and the late Lucy C. Lloyd Ed. D. F. Bleek Illustrated with many reproductions of Bushmen drawings*. Cape Town, South Africa: T. Maskew Miller, 1923.

_____. *Reynard the Fox in South Africa; or Hottentot Fables and Tales*. London: Trubner, 1864.

Bloom, Harold. Preface. *Alone with the Alone: Creative Imagination in the Sufism of Ibn Arabi*. By Henry Corbin. Princeton: Princeton UP, 1969. ix-xx.

Blumer, Ronald H. and Muffie Meyer. *The New Medicine*. Middlemarch Films, 2006.

Boeing, Geoff (2016). "Visual Analysis of Nonlinear Dynamical Systems: Chaos, Fractals, Self-Similarity and the Limits of Prediction". *Systems*, 4(4), 37-54, 13 November 2016 Department of City and Regional Planning, University of California, Berkeley.

Bond, D. Stephenson. *Living Myth: Personal Meaning as a Way of Life*. Boston: Shambhala, 1973.

Bonilla-Silva, Eduardo. *Racism without Racists: Color-blind Racism and the Persistence of Racial Inequality in America*. Rowman & Littlefield, 2009.

Boom for Real: The Late Teenage Years of Jean-Michel Basquiat. Film by Sara Driver. 2017.

Bordo, Susan. *The Flight to Objectivity: Essays on Cartesianism and Culture*. Albany: State U of New York P, 1987.

Bouie, Jamelle. "The Boy Who Cried 'Woke.'" *New York Time Opinion*, 14 March 2023.

Bradbury, Ray. *A Sound of Thunder and Other Stories*. William Morrow Books, 2005.

Brandon, Sidney, M.D. "Recovered memories of childhood sexual abuse: Implications for clinical practice." *British Journal of Psychiatry* (April 1998): 296-307.

Bregin, Elana and Belinda Kruiper. *Kalahari Rainsong*. UP KwaZulu-Natal, 2004.

Brink, André. *Praying Mantis*. London: Secker & Warburg, 2005.

Brody, Hugh. *The Other Side of Eden: Hunters, Farmers, and the Shaping of the World*. New York: Farrar, Straus, and Giroux, 2000.

———. "Life as a Hunter-Gatherer." BBC World Service. 16 Feb. 2001. http://www.bbc.co.uk/worldservice/people/highlights/010216_brody.shtml

Brown, Brené. *The Call to Courage*. Film by Sandra Restrepo. Netflix.com, 2019.

Bruner, Jerome S. "The 'remembered' self." *The remembering self: Construction and accuracy in the self-narrative*. Eds. U. Neisser & R. Fivush. New York: Cambridge UP, 1994. 41- 54.

Buber, Martin. *I and Thou*. Free Press, Old Tappan, NJ, 1996.

Burdick, Eugene and William J. Lederer. *The Ugly American*. W.W. Norton & Co, 2019.

Burkert, Walter. "Sacrifice, Hunting, and Funerary Rituals," part I. *Homo Nekans: The Anthropology of Ancient Greek Sacrificial Ritual and Myth*, Trans Peter Big. Berkeley: U of California P, 1983.

Burleson, Blake W. *Jung in Africa*. Bloomsbury Academic, 2005

Butala, Sharon. Wild Stone Heart. Phyllis Bruce Books Perennial, 2001.

Butler, Judith. Who's Afraid of Gender? Farrar, Straus & Giroux, 2024.

Calasso, Roberto. Ardor. Farrar Straus & Giroux, 2014.

_____. The Celestial Hunter. Farrar Straus & Giroux, 2020.

_____. Literature and the Gods. Random House, 2001.

Cameron. Julia. The Artist's Way. Tarcher, 1992.

Campbell, Alastair and Rory Stewart. The Rest is Politics Podcast. "The Illusion of 'Free Will', The Psychology Behind Donald Trump, and The Science of Stress." With Robert Sakolsky. February 13, 2024.

Campbell, Joseph. The Hero with a Thousand Faces. Princeton: Princeton UP, 1973.

_____. Myths to Live By. New York: Penguin, 1972.

Carrie Pilby. Film by Susan Johnson with Gabriel Byrne and Bel Powley, 2016.

Carter, Christine. "The Three Parts of an Effective Apology." Greater Good Magazine, November 12, 2015.

Casey, E. S. Getting Back into Place: Towards a Renewed Understanding of the Place-World, Indiana UP, 1993

____. "Toward a Phenomenology of Imagination," J. British Society Phenomenology 5 (1974): 10.

Castaneda, Carlos. The Fire from Within. New York: Simon and Schuster, 1984.

_____. Journey to Ixtlan: The Lessons of Don Juan. New York: Simon and Schuster, 1972.

Works Cited and ConsulteD

———. *The Second Ring of Power.* New York: Simon and Schuster, 1977.

———. *A Separate Reality: Further Conversations with Don Juan.* New York: Simon and Schuster, 1971.

———. *The Teachings of Don Juan: A Yaqui Way of Knowledge.* New York: Simon and Schuster, 1968.

———. *Tales of Power.* New York: Simon and Schuster, 1974.

Chesler, Phyllis. *Women and Madness.* New York: Avon Books, 1972.

Clelland-Stokes, Sarah. *Representing Aboriginality: A post-colonial analysis of the key trends of representing aboriginality in South African, Australian/New Zealand Films.* Intervention Press, 2007.

Coates, Ta-Nehisi. *Between the World and Me,* Spiegel & Grau, 2015.

Coelho, Paola Coelho *The Alchemist,* HarperCollins, 2002

Collins, Wilkie. *The Woman in White.* Penquin, 2003.

Conrad, Joseph. *Heart of Darkness.* CreateSpace, 2014.

Corbin, Henry. *Alone with the Alone: Creative Imagination in the Sufism of Ibn Arabi.* Princeton: Princeton UP, 1969.

———. "Mundus Imaginalis, or the Imaginary and the Imaginal." *Spring: An Annual of Archetypal Psychology and Jungian Thought.* New York: Spring, 1972. 1-19.

———. "Towards a Chart of the Imaginal..." *Temenos.* 1 (1981): 24-36.

Coulson, David, and Alec Campbell *African Rock Art.* New York: Abrams, 2001.

de Mille, Richard. *Castaneda's Journey: The Power and the Allegory.* Bloomington:

Capra P, 1976.

Cumes, David M. *Africa in My Bones: A surgeon's odyssey into the spirit world of African healing*. Spearhead, 2004.

_____. *Inner Passages, Outer Journeys: Wilderness, Healing, and the Discovery of Self*. Llewellyn Publications, 1998.

_____. *The Spirit of Healing: Venture Into the Wilderness to Rediscover the Healing Force*. Llewellyn Publications, 1999.

D'Angelo, Robin. *White Fragility. Why It's So Hard for White People to Talk About Racism*. Beacon Press, 2018.

Daly, Niki. *Not so fast Songololo*. Frances Lincoln Children's Books, 2001.

Danieli, Yael. *International Handbook of Multigenerational Legacies of Trauma*. New York: Plenum, 1998.

_____. "Chapter 2: Massive Trauma and the Healing Role of Reparative Justice: an Update." *Reparations for Victims of Genocide, War Crimes and Crimes Against Humanity*. Editors: M. G. Goetz and C. F. Ferstman and Alan Stephens. Pages 41-78, 2009

"Decolonising Cultural Spaces: The Living Cultures Project" https://www.youtube.com/watch?v=3midDMjvlLo

Delgado, Richard and Jean Stefancic. *Critical Race Theory: an Introduction*. NYU Press, 2017.

DeSalvo, Louise. *Conceived with Malice*. Dutton, 1994.

_____. *Virginia Woolf: The Impact of Childhood Sexual Abuse on Her Life and Work*. Ballantine Books, 1990.

_____. *Writing as a Way of Healing: How Telling Our Stories Transforms Our*

Works Cited and ConsulteD

Lives. Boston: Beacon, 2000.

Diagnostic and Statistical Manual of Mental Disorders DSM-IV. Arlington: American Psychiatric Association, 1994.

Dickens, Charles. *Bleak House*. Unabridged 1853. Independent Pubisher, 2012.

Dinesen, Isak. *Anecdotes of Destiny: Five Stories about Fates*. Vintage, 1974.

_____. *The Angelic Avengers*. Penquin, 1986.

_____. *Ehrengard: A Pastoral Romance*. Vintage, 1975.

_____. *The Last Tales: A Collection of Twelve New Tales of Compelling Beauty and Enchantment*. Random House, 1957.

_____. *Letters from Africa, 1914-1931*. London: Weidenfeld & Nicolson, 1981.

_____. *On Modern Marriage: And Other Observations*. St. Martin's Press, 1986.

_____. *Seven Gothic Tales*. With an Introduction by Dorothy Canfield. Random House, 1934.

DeSalvo, Louise. *Virginia Woolf: The Impact of Childhood Sexual Abuse on Her Life and Work*. Boston: Beacon, 1989.

Dobe, M. "Social Control Among the Lambas." *Bantu Studies* 2 (1923): 41.

Dobzhansky, Theodosius. https://slife.org/adaptation/

Doniger, Wendy. "Other People's Myths." *The Insider/Outsider Problem in the Study of Religion: A Reader*. Ed. Russell T. McCutcheon. New York: Cassell, 1999.

_____. *The Implied Spider: Politics and Theology in Myth*. New York: Columbia UP, 1998.

Doty, William G. Mythography: The Study of Myths and Rituals. Tuscaloosa: U of Alabama P, 2000.

Doty, William G., and William J. Hynes. "Historical Overview of Theoretical Issues: The Problem of the Trickster." Mythical Trickster Figures: Contours, Contests, and Criticisms Ed. William J. Hynes and William G. Doty. Tuscaloosa: U of Alabama P, 1993. 13-32.

Douglas, Mary. Purity and Danger. London: Routledge and Kegan Paul, 1966.

Downing, Christine. The Goddess: Mythological Representations of the Feminine. New York: Crossroad, 1984.

_____. *The Long Journey Home: Re-visioning the Myth of Demeter and Persephone for Our Time.* Boston: Shambhala, 1994.

_____. *The Luxury of Afterwards: The Christine Downing Lectures at San Diego State University, (1995-2004).* New York: iUniverse, Inc, 2004.

Du Bois, W.E.B. Darkwater: Voices from Within the Veil. Harcourt, Brace and Howe, 1920.

_____. *The Souls of Black Folk.* Dover Publications, 2016.

Dumas, Alexandre. The Count of Monte Cristo. Penquin Classics, 2003.

Duran, Bonnie and Eduardo. Native American PostColonial Psychology. Suny, 1995.

Duran, Eduardo. Buddha in Redface. iUniverse, 2003

Duran, Eduardo. Healing the Soul Wound: Counseling with American Indians and other Native Peoples. Teachers College Press, 2006.

Duran, Eduardo. Healing the Soul Wound: Trauma-Informed Counseling for Indigenous Communities. Teachers College Press, 2019.

Works Cited and ConsulteD

_____. *(aka Teoshapye Ta Woapeya Wicsasa). Quantum Coyote Dreams The Black World: Buddha in Redface Saga Continues.* Xlibris, 2019.

Durkheim, Emile. "La prohibition de l'inceste et ses origines." *L'Année Sociologique* 1 (1897): 47, 50.

Edinger, Edward F. *The Creation of Consciousness: Jung's Myth for Modern Man.* Toronto: Inner City, 1984.

Eddo-Lodge, Reni. *Why I'm No Longer Talking to White People About Race.* Bloomsbury Publishing, 2018.

_____. "Why I'm no longer talking to white people about race." *The Guardian*, 30 May 2017. https://www.theguardian.com/world/2017/may/30/why-im-no-longer-talking-to-white-people-about-race

Eliade, Mircea. *Myth and Reality.* New York: Harper Colophon, 1975.

_____. *The Myth of the Eternal Return: Cosmos and History.* Princeton: Princeton UP, 1971.

_____. "A New Humanism." *The Insider/Outsider Problem in the Study of Religion: A Reader.* Ed. Russell T. McCutcheon. New York: Cassell, 1999. 95-107

_____. *Rites and Symbols of Initiation: The Mysteries of Birth and Rebirth.* Putnam, CT: Spring, 1994.

_____. *Shamanism: Archaic Techniques of Ecstasy.* Trans. W. R. Trask. New York: Viking Penguin, 1989.

Ellenberger, Henri F. *The Discovery of the Unconscious: The History and Evolution of Dynamic Psychiatry.* Jackson, Michigan: Basic Books, 1970.

Evans-Pritchard, Edward E. *Zande Trickster.* Oxford: Clarendon P, 1967.

Fanon, Frantz. *Black Skin, White Masks: The Experiences of a Black Man in a*

Works Cited and ConsulteD

White World. Translation Charles L. Markmann. Grove Press, 1967.

_____. *The Wretched of the Earth*. Translated in English by Constance Farrington. Grove Press, 1963.

A Far Off Place. Dir. Mikael Salomon. Perf. Reese Witherspoon, Ethan Randall, Jack Thompson, and Maximilian Schell. Walt Disney Pictures, 2004.

Farmer-Paellmann, Deadria. Reparations Task Force, Witness Testimony with host, Mary Frances Barry, California Department of Justice, February 23, 2022. https://www.youtube.com/watch?v=wo8dTcuo5mg

Feld, Steven. *Sound and Sentiment: Birds, Weeping, Poetics, and Song in Kaluli Expression*. Philadelphia: U of Pennsylvania P, 1990.

Fisilio, Marsilio. *The Book of Life*. Trans. Charles Boer. Woodstock, Connecticut: Spring, 1980.

Fivush, Robin. "Constructing Narrative, Emotion, and Self in Parent-Child Conversations About the Past." *The remembering self: Construction and accuracy in the self-narrative*. Eds. U. Neisser and R. Fivush. New York: Cambridge UP, 1994. 136-57.

Foord, Kate. "Frontier theory: Displacement and disavowal in the writing of white nations." In: Moreton-Robinson A (ed.) *Whitening Race: Essays in Social and Cultural Criticism*, Canberra: Aboriginal Studies Press, 2005, pp. 133–147.

Fourie, Coral *Living Legends of a Dying Culture* Hartbeespoort, South Africa: Ekogilde, 1994.

_____, and Edouard J. Maunick. *Splinters from the Fire*. Pretoria, South Africa: Protea Book House, 2000.

Frazer, J. G. *Totemism and Exogamy*. London: 1910.

Fraser, Sylvia. *My Father's House: A Memoir of Incest and Healing*. New York:

Works Cited and ConsulteD

Perennial Library, 1987.

Freeman, M. *Rewriting the Self: History, Memory, Narrative.* New York: Routledge, 1993.

Freire, Paolo. *The Pedagogy of the Oppressed.* Penquin, 2017

Freud, Sigmund. *The Interpretation of Dreams.* New York: Modern Library, 1994

_____. *Totem and Taboo.* New York: W. W. Norton, 1989.

Gaetz, Lara. *Persephone Speaks: Tales from the Three Worlds.* Carpinteria, California: Pacifica Graduate Institute, 2004.

Gagan, Jeannette M. *Journeying: Where Shamanism and Psychology Meet.* Santa Fe: Rio Chama, 1998.

Gates, Jr., Henry Louis. "Finding Your Roots," PBS, 2012- present.

Gauguin, Paul. *Noa Noa: The Tahitian Journal.* Dover Publications, 1985.

Geertz, Armin W. "A Container of Ashes: Hopi Prophecy in History." *European Review of Native American Studies.* Volume 3, 1989.

_____. *Book of the Hopi. The Hopi's Book.* Anthropos, 1983.

_____. "The Invention of Prophecy: Continuity and Meaning in Hopi Indian Religion. U of California P, 1994.

Geertz, Clifford. *Local Knowledge: Further Essays in Interpretive Anthropology.* Basic Books, 1983.

Giago, Tim. (Nanwica Kciji—Stands Up For Them). "The Black Hills award approaching 1 billion dollars." Indianz.com, March 22, 2022. https://indianz.com/News/2022/03/22/tim-giago-sioux-nation-refuses-payout-for-stolen-land/

Giegerich, Wolfgang. "Is the Soul Deep?" Spring 64 (1998): 1-32.

_____. "The Opposition of 'Individual' and 'Collective' Psychology's Basic Fault: Reflections on Today's Magnum Opus of the Soul." Harvest: Journal for Jungian Studies 42.2 (1996): 7-27.

_____. The Soul's Logical Life. Frankfurt: Peter Lang, 2001.

_____, David L. Miller, and Greg Mogenson. Dialectics and Analytical Psychology: The El Capitan Canyon Seminar. New Orleans: Spring Journal, 2005.

Giffard, Ingaret. The Way Things Happen. William Morrow & Co., 1989.

Gilder, George. Men and Marriage. Pelican, 1986.

The Gods Must Be Crazy. Dir. Jamie Uys. Perf. Marius Weyers, Sandra Prinsloo, and N!XAU. C.A.T. Films, 1980.

The Gods Must Be Crazy II. Dir. Jamie Uys. Perf. N!XAU, Lena Farugia, and Hans Strydom. Columbia Pictures, 1988.

Goldberg, Natalie. Writing Down the Bones: Freeing the Writer Within. Boston: Shambhala, 1986.

Goldstein, Eleanor, and Kevin Farmer. True Stories of False Memories. Boca Raton: Social Issues Resources, 1993.

Gordon, Lewis Ricardo. Existential Africana: Understanding Africana Existential Thought, Routledge, 2000.

Gordon, Robert J. Picturing Bushmen: The Denver African Expedition of 1925. Athens: Ohio UP, 1997.

The Great Dance: A Hunter's Story. Dir. Craig and Damon Foster. Perf. Karoha Langwane, Xlhoase Xlhokhne, and !Nqate Xqamxebe. Aardvark, Earthrise, Liquid Pictures, and Off the Fence, 2000.

Works Cited and ConsulteD

Green, Dr. Elmer. *The Ozawkie: Book of the Dead, Alzheimer's isn't what you think it is!* 2001.

Greene, Liz. *The Astrology of Fate.* Weiser Books, 1984.

Griffin, Susan. *Woman and Nature: The Roaring Inside Her.* San Francisco: Sierra Club Books, 1999.

Guenther, Mathias. *The Nharo Bushmen of Botswana: Tradition and Change.* Hamburg: Helmut Buske Verlag, 1986.

_____. *Tricksters & Trancers.* Bloomington: Indiana UP, 1999.

Gunning, Margaret. "Sylvia Fraser." *January Magazine.* 15 Feb 2007. http://www.januarymagazine.com/profiles/sfraser.html

Haien, Jeannette. *The All of It: A Novel.* New York: HarperCollins, 1988.

Hall, Edward T. *The Hidden Dimension.* Anchor, 1990.

_____. *The Silent Language.* World of Books, 1973.

Hampl, Patricia. *I Could Tell You Stories: Sojourns in the Land of Memory.* New York: W. W. Norton, 1999.

Hannah, Barbara. *Encounters with the Soul: Active Imagination as Developed by C. G. Jung.* Wilmette: Chiron, 2001.

Harner, Michael. *The Way of the Shaman.* San Francisco: Harper & Row, 1990.

Harrell, Mary. "Journey to Imagination: A Woman's Lessons about Life and Love." Diss. Pacifica Graduate Institute, 2003.

Harris, Lis. "O Guru, Guru, Guru," *The New Yorker,* November 14, 1994.

Hartlep, Nicholas Daniel. "Critical Race Theory: An Examination of its Past, Present and Future Implications. JCT's Annual Bergamo Conference on Curriculum Theory and Classroom Practice, 2022.

Hasten Slowly: The Journey of Laurens van der Post. Film by Mickey Lemle. NYC: Lemle Productions, 1997.

Hatzipanagos, Rachel. "Native Americans call for reparations from 'land-grab' universities." Washington Post, July 9, 2023. https://www.washingtonpost.com/nation/2023/07/09/native-indigenous-reparations-colleges-land/

Hawkins, Lucy. TedTalk "Science and Storytelling." 2015. https://www.youtube.com/watch?v=E7K-qlQVpgE&t=2s

Hayden, Robert. "Middle Passage." Collected Poems Liveright Publishing, 1985. https://www.poetryfoundation.org/poems/43076/middle-passage

Helfman, Elizabeth S. The Bushmen and Their Stories, Drawings by Richard Cuffari. New York: Seabury, 1971.

Henriksen, Aage. Isak Dinesen/Karen Blixen: The Work and the Life. Translated by William Mishler. Introduction by Poul Houe. St Martin's Press, 1988.

Herbie: The Love Bug. Film by Robert Stevenson with Dean Jones, Michelle Lee, 1969.

Hillman, James. The Dream and the Underworld. New York: Harper, 1979.

_____. Healing Fiction. Woodstock, Connecticut: Spring, 1983.

_____. Kinds of Power: A Guide to Its Intelligent Uses. Crown, 1997

_____. "Pink Madness or Why Does Aphrodite Drive Men Crazy with Pornography." Spring 57 (1995): 39-71.

_____. Re-Visioning Psychology. New York: Harper, 1975.

Works Cited and ConsulteD

_____. *The Soul's Code: In Search of Character and Calling.* New York: Random, 1996.

_____. *The Thought of the Heart and the Soul of the World.* Putnam: Spring, 2004.

Hillman, Laurence. *Planets in Play: How to Reimagine Your Life Through the Language of Astrology.* Tarcher, 2007.

Holy Bible. New American Standard. Philadelphia: A.J. Holman Company, 1975.

Hollis, James. *Tracking the Gods: The Place of Myth in Modern Life.* Toronto: Inner City, 1995.

Hollis, Phyllis. *Cerebral Women, Podcast, 2016 to Present.* https://cerebralwomen.com/

Hollman, Jeremy, Ed. *Customs and Beliefs of the /Xam Bushmen.* Cape Town: U of Wittersrand P, 2004.

Hooks, Bell. *Ain't I a Woman.* Routledge, 2014.

The Hot Spot. Film by Dennis Hopper with Jennifer Connelly, Don Johnson, Virginia Madsen. 1990.

The Hours. Film by Stephen Daldry with Nicole Kidman, Julianne Moore, Meryl Streep. 2002.

How Do You Name a Song? Dir. I. Murphy Lewis. IML Publications, 2002.

Howe, Linda. *Healing through the Akashic Records: Using the Power of Your Sacred Wound to Discover Your Soul's Purpose.* Sounds True, 2016.

_____. *The Pathway Prayer Process.* September 11, 2001. https://lindahowe.com/wp-content/uploads/2015/05/Pathway-Prayer-Process.pdf

Hugo, Richard. "Writing Off the Subject." *The Triggering Town: Lectures and Essays*

Works Cited and ConsulteD

on Poetry and Writing. New York: W. W. Norton, 1992. 15 May 2007.

Hyde, Lewis. *Trickster Makes This World: Mischief, Myth and Art*. New York: Farrar, Straus, and Giroux, 1998.

Hynes, William J. "Inconclusive Conclusions: Tricksters—Metaplayers and Revealers." *Mythical Trickster Figures: Contours, Contests, and Criticisms* Ed. William J. Hynes and William G. Doty. Tuscaloosa: U of Alabama P, 1993. 202-17.

_____. "Mapping the Characteristics of Mythic Tricksters: A Heuristic Guide." *Mythical Trickster Figures: Contours, Contests, and Criticisms* Eds. William J. Hynes and William G. Doty. Tuscaloosa: U of Alabama P, 1993. 33-45.

_____, and William G. Doty, Eds. *Mythical Trickster Figures: Contours, Contests, and Criticisms*. Tuscaloosa: U of Alabama P, 1993.

Immerwahr, Daniel. "The Ugly American: Peeling the Onion of an Iconic Cold War Text," *Journal of American-East Asian Relations* 26 (2019) 7-20

https://faculty.wcas.northwestern.edu/daniel-immerwahr/UglyAmerican.pdf

Ingerman, Sandra. *Shamanic Journeying: A Beginner's Guide*. Boulder: Sounds True, 2004.

_____. *Soul Retrieval: Mending the Fragmented Self*. San Francisco: HarperCollins, 1991.

Isaacson, Rupert. *The Healing Land: The Bushmen and the Kalahari Desert*. New York: Grove, 2001.

Isaacson, Walter and Henry Louis Gates, Jr., "We are 99.9% the Same." *Amanpour and Company*, January 16, 2020.

Jacobi, Jolande. *Complex/Archetype/Symbol: In the Psychology of C. G. Jung*. Trans. Ralph Manheim. Bollingen Series 57, New York: Princeton UP, 1974.

Works Cited and ConsulteD

_____. *The Psychology of C. G. Jung: An Introduction with Illustrations by Jolan Jacobi*. Trans. K.W. Bash. Foreword C. G. Jung. New Haven: Yale UP, 1943.

Jana, Tiffany and Michael Baran. *Subtle Acts of Exclusion: How to Understand, Identify, and Stop Microaggressions*. Berrett-Koehler, 2020.

Johnson, Peter, and Anthony Bannister and Alf Wannenburgh. *The Bushmen*. Cape Town, South Africa: Struik, 1979.

Johnson, R. Townley. *Major Rock Paintings of Southern Africa: Facsimile Reproductions*. Cape Town, South Africa: David Philip, 1979.

Jones, Cathrine Ann. *The Way of Story: The Craft and Soul of Writing*, Ojai: Prasana, 2004.

The Journey of Man. Host, Dr. Spencer Wells. Warner Home Video, 2003.

Jung, Carl Gustav. *The Collected Works of C. G. Jung*. Ed. Sir H. Read, M. Fordham, G. Adler, and W. McGuire. Trans. R. F. C. Hull (except vol. 2). Bollingen Series 20. New York, Princeton, and London: Princeton UP, 1953-76.

_____. *The Essential Jung*. Ed. A. Storr. Princeton: Princeton UP, 1983.

_____. *Memories, Dreams, Reflections* Recorded and ed. by Aniela Jaffe. Trans. Richard and Clara Winston. New York: Vintage, 1989.

_____. *Letters*. Selected and edited by G. Adler in collaboration with A. Jaffe. Bollingen Series 45. Vol. 1. Princeton and London: Princeton UP, 1973.

_____. "On the Psychology of the Trickster Figure." *The Trickster: A Study in American Indian Mythology*. With commentaries C. G. Jung and Karl Kerenyi. New York: Bell, 1956. 195-211.

_____. "The Philosophical Tree." *Alchemical Studies*. Trans. R. F. C. Hull. *The Collected Works of C. G. Jung*. Vol. 13. Princeton: Princeton UP, 1982. 251-350.

_____ *Psychology and Religion: Based on the Terry Lectures Delivered at Yale University.* New Haven: Yale UP, 1938.

_____. "Psychology of the Transference." *The Practice of Psychotherapy*. Trans. R. F. C. Hull. *The Collected Works of C. G. Jung*. Vol. 16. Princeton: Princeton UP, 1982. 163-326.

Kalahari Bushmen Healers. Profiles of Healing. Edited by Bradford Keeney. Philadelphia: Ringing Rocks P, 1999.

A Kalahari Family Part 1: A Far Country, Part 2: End of the Road, Part 3: The Real Water, Part 4: Standing Tall, Part 5: Death by Myth. Dir. John Marshall, Documentary Educational Resources, 2002.

Karcher, Stephen. *Total IChing: Myths for Change*. Piatkus, 2009.

Katz, Richard. *Boiling Energy*. Cambridge, Massachusetts: Harvard UP, 1982.

_____. Megan Biesele, and Verna St. Denis. *Healing Makes Our Hearts Happy*. Rochester, Vermont: Inner Traditions, 1997.

Keeney, Bradford. *Bushmen Shaman: Awakening the Spirit through Ecstatic Dance*. Rochester: Destiny Books, 2005.

_____. *Ropes to God: Experiencing the Bushman Spiritual Universe*. Philadelphia: Ringing Rocks P, 2003.

Keeneys, The. *Climbing the Rope to God: Mystical Testimony and Teaching*. Hilary Keeney Publisher, 2017.

Kluckhohn, C. "Navaho Witchcraft." *Papers of the Peabody Museum of Harvard* 22.2 (1944): 58.

Koch, Liz. *Stalking Wild Psoas: Embodying Your Core Intelligence*. North Atlantic Books, 2019.

Works Cited and ConsulteD

Kory, Deb. "Eduardo Duran on Psychotherapy with Native Americans." https://www.psychotherapy.net/interview/native-american-psychotherapy

Krippner, Stanley, and David Feinstein. *The Mythic Path: Discovering the Guiding Stories of Your Past—Creating a Vision for Your Future.* New York: G. P. Putnam's Sons, 1997.

Kruiper, Vetkat Regopstaan Boesman. *Mooi Loop, "Walk with God."* Text by Belinda and Vetkat Regopstaan Kruiper, Designed by Gareth Myklebust, English translation, Mary Lange, Arrowsa, 2011.

L'Engle, Madeleine. *A Wrinkle in Time.* SquareFish, 2012.

Larson, Stephen. *The Mythic Imagination: Your Quest for Meaning through Personal Mythology.* New York: Bantam, 1990.

Lasson, Frans and Clara Svenson. *The Life and Destiny of Isak Dineson.* U of Chicago P, 1976.

Lauck, Joanne Elizabeth. *The Voice of the Infinite in the Small: Revisioning the Insect-Human Connection.* Mill Spring, NC: Swan Raven & Co, 1998.

Lazare, Aaron. "Making Peace Through Apology." *Greater Good Magazine*, September 1, 2004.

Lechuga, Michael. *Vision of Invastion: Alien Affects, Cionema, and Citizenship in Settler Colonies.* Jackson: UP Mississippi, 2023.

Lee, R. B., *The !Kung San: Men, Women, and Work in a Foraging Society.* Cambridge: Cambridge UP, 1979.

Lee, Richard B., and Irven DeVore, eds. *Kalahari Hunter-Gatherers: Studies of the !Kung San and Their Neighbors.* Cambridge, Massachusetts and London: Harvard UP, 1976.

Le Guin, Ursula K. "A Band of Brothers, A Stream of Sisters." https://www.

ursulakleguin.com/blog/7-a-band-of-brothers-a-stream-of-sisters

Lerner, Gerda. *The Creation of Patriarchy.* New York: Oxford UP, 1986.

Le Roux, Willemien, and Alison White, Eds. and compilers. *Voices of the San.* Cape Town, South Africa: Kwela, 2004.

Lesarge, Tom Lmakiya. *The Samburu: A Brief Cultural Guide.* Samburu: Samburu National Park, 2001.

_____. *Proverbs of the Samburu.* Aura Books, 2018.

_____. *Folktales of the Samburu.* Aura Books, 2022.

The Letters Between Sir Laurens van der Post and I. Murphy Lewis, Oxford University Archives, 1993 to 1996.

Levi-Strauss, Claude. *Myth and Meaning: Five Talks for Radio by Claude Levi-Strauss.* Toronto: U of Toronto P, 1978.

_____. *The Savage Mind.* Chicago: U of Chicago P, 1968.

_____. *Structural Anthropology.* New York: Basic Books, 1963.

_____. *Totemism.* Trans. Rodney Needham. Boston: Beacon, 1972.

Levy-Bruhl, Lucien. *How Natives Think.* Trans. L. A. Clare [from *Les Fonctions mentales dans les societes inferieures*]. London: George Allen and Unwin, 1926.

Lewis, C.S. *The Problem of Pain.* William Collins, 2012.

Lewis, I. Murphy. *Across and Into and Through the Divided Self.* Unpublished Manuscript. www.imurphylewis.com

Across the Divide to the Divine: With the Kalahari San's Trickster God, Mantis an Essential Component in the Mythological Structure of an Individuated Culture.

Works Cited and ConsulteD

Pacifica Graduate Institute. Dissertation, March 2007.

_____. *Africa Within: An American Woman's Healing Journey with the Maasai Warriors*. Unpublished manuscript, November 2001.

_____. *Holy Tricksters*. Pacifica Graduate Institute, Asian Religious Traditions, Winter 2003.

_____. *The Mantis @ Play*. Unpublished manuscript, 2002.

_____. *The Private Memoirs of I. Murphy Lewis*. Unpublished Journals, 1971- 2024, Vols. 1- 183.

_____. *Why Ostriches Don't Fly and Other Tales from the African Bush*. Englewood, Colorado: Libraries Unlimited, 1997.

_____. Larry Sanders and Paula Sharp. *Orpheus, Shamanism and Retrieval of Soul*. Pacifica Graduate Institute, Winter 2003, History of Depth Psychology.

Lewis, John. *Good Trouble*. Film by Dawn Porter, Magnolia Films, 2020.

Lewis-Williams, J. David. *The Mind in the Cave: Consciousness and the Origins of Art*. London: Thames & Hudson, 2002.

_____, and D. G. Pearce. *San Spirituality: Roots, Expressions and Social Consequences*. Cape Town: Double Storey Books, 2004.

_____, and M. Biesele. "Eland Hunting Rituals Among Northern and Southern San Groups: Striking Similarities." *Africa* 48.2: 201-45.

Liebenberg, Louis. *The Art of Tracking: The Origin of Science*. Claremon, South Africa: David Philip Publishers Ltd, 1990.

Lingus, Alphonso. *Trust*. Univ of Minnesota Press, 2004

Lorde, Audre. *Sister Outsider: Essays and Speeches*, Crossing Press, 2007.

_____. *When I Dare to be Powerful*. Penquin UK, 2020.

_____. *Your Silence Will Not Protect You*. Silver Press, 2017.

Lost World of the Kalahari. 7-part Documentary Series: *The Nature of Exploration Today: Sir Laurens van der Post; Vanishing People; First Encounter; The Spirit of the Slippery Hills; Life in the Thirst Land; The Great Eland; Rain Song*. BBC, 1956.

Lovell, Mary. *Straight on Till Morning: The Biography of Beryl Markham*. St. Martin's Press, 1988.

Luke, Helen M. *Dark Wood to White Rose: Journey and Transformation in Dante's Divine Comedy*. New York: Parabola, 2003.

Macewan, Grace. "Sitting Bull." *The Canadian Encyclopedia*. December 5, 2007. Updated by Zach Parrott and Michelle Filice, Feburary 21, 2017. https://www.thecanadianencyclopedia.ca/en/article/sitting-bull#

Makarius, Laura. "The Crime of Manabozo." *American Anthropologist* 75 (1973): 663-75.

_____. "The Magic of Transgression." *Anthropos* 69 (1974): 537-52.

_____."The Myth of the Trickster: The Necessary Breaker of Taboos." *Mythical Trickster Figures: Contours, Contests, and Criticisms*. Ed. William J. Hynes and William G. Doty. Tuscaloosa: U of Alabama P, 1993. 66-86.

_____. "Ritual Clowns and Symbolical Behaviour." *Diogenes* 18.69 (1970): 44-73.

Malcolm, Janet. "A House of One's Own." *The New Yorker*, 5 June 1995. 58-79.

Malinowski, B. "Myth in Primitive Psychology." *Magic, Science and Religion*. New York: Waveland P, 1955. 72-124.

_____. *The Sexual Life of Savages in North Western Melanesia: An Ethnographic Account of Courtship, Marriage and Family Life Among the Natives of the Trobriand*

Works Cited and ConsulteD

Islands, British New Guinea. Whitefish, Montana: Kessinger, 1929.

Markham, Beryl. *West with the Night.* Penquin, 1988.

Markowitz, Arthur. *The Rebirth of the Ostrich: And Other Stories of the Kalahari Bushmen Told in Their Manner.* Mafeking: Mafeking Mail, 1971.

_____. *With Uplifted Tongue: Stories, Myths and Fables of the South African Bushmen Told in Their Manner.* South Africa: Central News Agency Limited, 1956.

Marmon Silko, Leslie. *Ceremony.* Penguin, 2020.

_____. *Storyteller.* Arcade Publisher, 1989.

Marshall, L. *Nyae Nyae !Kung: Beliefs and Rites.* Cambridge, Massachusetts: Harvard UP, 1999.

Mascarenhas, Margaret. *Skin.* Golden Heart Emporium Books, 2011.

Maslow, Abraham H. "A Theory of Human Motivation." *Psychological Review* 50 (1943): 370-96.

Mbiti, John S. *African Religions and Philosophy.* Doubleday, 1970.

McCarthy-Brown, Karen. *Mama Lola: A Vodoo Priestess in Brooklyn.* Berkeley: U of California P, 2001.

_____. "Writing About 'the Other.'" *The Insider/Outsider Problem in the Study of Religion: A Reader.* Ed. Russell T. McCutcheon. New York: Cassell, 1999.

McCutcheon, Russell T. Ed. *Insider/Outsider Problem in the Study of Religion: A Reader.* London: Cassell, 1999.

McDermott, Gerald. *Anansi the Spider: A Tale from the Ashanti.* New York: Henry Holt, 1972.

McKay, Dwanna L. "Oklahoma is—and always has been—Native Land," The Conversation, July 16, 2020. https://theconversation.com/oklahoma-is-and-always-has-been-native-land-142546

McKay, Finn. "Who's Afraid of Gender? by Judith Butler review - the gender theorist goes mainstream." The Guardian, March 13, 2024.

Meriwether. Nelson Heath. The Meriwethers and Their Connections. Baltimore: Gateway Press, 1991.

Merry Christmas, Mr. Lawrence. Dir. by Nagaisa Ôshima. Starring David Bowie and Tom Conti. 1983.

Metzger, Deena. Entering the Ghost River: Mediations on the Theory and Practice of Healing. Hand to Hand, 2002.

_____. Tree: Essays and Pieces. North Atlantic Books, 1997.

_____. Writing for Your Life. San Francisco: Harper, 1992.

Meyer, Erin. The Culture Map: Breaking through the Invisible Boundaries of Global Business. PublicAffairs, 2014.

Miller, Alice. For Your Own Good: Hidden Cruelty in Child-Rearing and the Roots of Violence. New York: Farrar, Straus and Giroux, 1983.

_____. Pictures of a Childhood Sixty-Six Watercolors and an Essay. New York: Farrar, Straus and Giroux, 1986.

_____. Prisoners of Childhood: The Drama of the Gifted Child and the Search for the True Self. New York: HarperCollins, 1987.

_____. Thou Shalt Not Be Aware: Society's Betrayal of the Child. New York: Farrar, Straus and Giroux, 1984.

Momaday, N. Scott. "Native American Attitudes to the Environment." Seeing With *a Native Eye: Essays on Native American Religion*. Ed. W. Capps. New York: Harper and Row, 1974. 79-85.

Moynihan, Daniel Patrick. *The Moynihan Report: The Negro Family, the Case for National Action*. 1965. https://www.blackpast.org/african-american-history/moynihan-report-1965/

Moore, Thomas. *Care of the Soul: A Guide for Cultivating Depth and Sacredness in Everyday Life*. New York: HarperCollins, 1992.

_____. *Rituals of the Imagination*. Dallas: Pegasus Foundation. 1983.

Moreton-Robinson, Aileen. "Toward a New Research Agenda? Foucault, Whiteness, and Indigenous Sovereignty," *Seeing Race Again: Colorblindness across the Disciplines*. Kimberlé Williams Crenshaw. Luke Charles Harris, Daniel Martinez HoSang, George Lipsitz. Univ. California Press, 2019.

Moreton-Robinson, Aileen (ed.) *Whitening Race: Essays in Social and Cultural Criticism*, Canberra: Aboriginal Studies Press, 2005,

Morrison, Toni. *Beloved*. Vintage Classics, 2007.

_____. *Playing in the Dark*. Harvard University Press, 1992.

_____. *Song of Solomon*, Alfred A. Knopf, 1977.

Moss, Doug, and Roddy Sheer. "EarthTalk®." *E-The Environmental Magazine*. www.emagazine.com

_____. "Use it and Lose It: The Outsize Effect of U.S. Consumption on the Environment. September 14, 2012. https://www.scientificamerican.com/article/american-consumption-habits

Muir, Edwin. *The Collected Poems 1921-1951*, The Grove Press, 1953.

Murdock, Maureen. *Unreliable Truth: On Memoir and Memory*. New York: Seal,

Works Cited and ConsulteD

2003.

Music That Floats from Afar. Dir. I. Murphy Lewis. IML Publications, 2001.

Mutwa, Vusamazulu Credo. *Indaba My Children: African Folk Tales.* Johannesburg: Blue Crane, 1964.

_____. *Isilwane the Animal: Tales and Fables of Africa.* Cape Town: Struik, 1996.

_____. *Songs of the Stars: The Lore of a Zulu Shaman.* Barrytown: Station Hill Openings, 1996.

My Neighbor Totoro. Film by Hayao Miyazaki. Studio Ghibli, 2009.

National Geographic. Greendex. www.nationalgeographic.com/greendex

Navalny. Documentary Film by Daniel Roher with Alexeï Navalny, Cottage M., 2022.

Neimark, Jill. "The diva of disclosure, memory researcher Elizabeth Loftus." *Psychology Today.* January, 1996. 21 Feb. 2007. http://faculty.washington.edu/elotfus/Articles/psytoday.html

Neisser, Ulric, and Robyn Fivush. Eds. *The Remembering Self: Construction and Accuracy in the Self-Narrative.* New York: Cambridge UP, 1994.

The New Shorter Oxford English Dictionary. Ed. Lesley Brown. Oxford: Clarendon P, 1993.

Nin, Anais. *The House of Incest.* Athens, Ohio: Swallow, 1958.

_____. *The Diary of Anaïs Nin Volume 3*, Harcourt Brace, NYC, 1967.

_____. *A Woman Speaks*, Swallow Press, Chicago, 1975.

Noble-Letort, Shelley R. *Mapping Caves: Human-Earth Expressions on Integrative*

Works Cited and ConsulteD

Health and Our Environment. Cambridge Scholars Publishing, 2021

Noel, Daniel C. *The Soul of Shamanism: Western Fantasies, Imaginal Realities.* New York: Continuum, 1999.

Nwaubani, Adaobi Tricia. "My Great-grandfather, the Nigerian Slave-Trader" *The New Yorker Magazine,* July 15, 2018.

O'Donohue, John. *Anam Cara: A Book of Celtic Wisdom.* Harper Perennial. 1998

_____. Onbeing.org. March 2, 2015. https://www.youtube.com/watch?v=rZYWIW1Kjio

Ole Saitoti, Tepilit, and Carol Beckwith. *Maasai.* Abrams, 1990.

Oropeza, Clara. *Anaïs Nin: A Myth of Her Own.* Routledge, 2019.

Orpen, J. M. "A Glimpse into the Mythology of the Maluti Bushmen." *Cape Monthly Magazine* 9.49 (1874): 1-13.

Ortiz-Hill, Michael. "Gathering in the Names." *Spring Journal,* 2002. 26.

Otto, Walter F. *Dionysus.* Trans. Robert B. Palmer. Bloomington and London: Indiana UP, 1965.

Paglia, Camille. *Break, Blow, Burn: 43 of the World's Best Poems.* Vintage, 2006.

Pelton, Robert D. *The Trickster in West Africa: A Study of Mythic Irony and Sacred Delight.* Berkeley: U of California P, 1980.

_____. "West African Tricksters: Web of Purpose, Dance of Delight." *Mythical Trickster Figures: Contours, Contests, and Criticisms.* Ed. William J. Hynes and William G. Doty. Tuscaloosa: The U of Alabama P, 1993. 122-40.

Perera, Sylvia Brinton. *Descent of the Goddess: A Way of Initiation for Women.* New York: Inner City Books, 1981.

Pierce, Chester M. https://en.wikipedia.org/wiki/Chester_Middlebrook_Pierce

Plog, Fred, and Daniel G. Bates, with Joan Ross Accocella Dobe Kung Bushmen. New York: Alfred A. Knopf, 1980.

Poole, Robert. "Heartbreak on the Serengeti." National Geographic, February 2006, 1-23.

Portney, Charles. "Intergenerational Transmission of Trauma: An Introduction for the Clinician." Psychiatric Times 22.4 (2003): 1-4. 1 Feb. 2007. http://www.psychiatrictimes.com/p030438.html

The Prince and Me. Film by Martha Coolidge. With Julia Stiles, Luke Mably. 2004.

Propp, V. Morphology of the Folktale. Austin: U of Texas P, 1968.

Purce, Jill. The Mystic Spiral: Journey of the Soul. Avon Books, 1974.

Purushothaman, Deepa. The First, the Few, the Only: How Women of Color Can Redefine Power in Corporate America. Harper Business, 2022.

_____. https://www.n2formation.com/

Quammen, David. The Song of the Dodo: Island Biogeography in an Age of Extinction. Simon and Schuster, 1996.

Radin, Paul. "The Culture of the Winnebago: As Described by Themselves." Supplement to International Journal of American Linguistics 15.1 (1949): 12-46.

_____. The Trickster: A Study in American Indian Mythology. With commentaries by C. G. Jung and Karl Kerenyi. New York: Bell, 1956.

Raff, Jeffrey. The Wedding of Sophia: The Divine Feminine in Psychoidal Alchemy. Nicolas-Hays, 2003.

Raphael, Max. Prehistoric Cave Paintings. Bollingen Series 4. New York: Pantheon,

Works Cited and ConsulteD

1945.

Raymond, Michael Joseph. "Native American Traditions: The Deilemna of Alcohol Use Among the Flathead Salish." ScholarWorks at the University of Montana, 1983

Reichard, Gladys. *An Analysis of Coeur d'Alene Indian Myths*. Philadelphia: American Folklore Society, 1947.

Reichel-Dolmatoff, G. *Beyond the Milky Way: Hallucinatory Imagery of the Tukano Indians*. Los Angeles: UCLA Latin America Center, 1978.

_____. *Navajo Religion*. Princeton: Princeton UP, 1950.

Reis, Patricia. *Daughters of Saturn: From Father's Daughter to Creative Woman*. New York: Continuum, 1997.

_____. *Through the Goddess: A Woman's Way of Healing*. New York: Continuum, 1995.

_____ and Susan Snow. *The Dreaming Way: Dreams and Art for Remembering and Recovering*. Wilmette: Chiron, 2000.

The Republic of Plato. Second Edition. Translated with notes, an interpretavie essay and a new introduction by Allan Bloom. Perseus Basic Books, 1968.

Reynard the Fox. Illustrated by Alain Vaes. Atlanta: Turner, 1994.

Rice, Edward. *Captain Sir Richard Francis Burton: The Secret Agent Who Made the Pilgrimage to Mecca, Discovered the Kama Sutra, and Brought the Arabian Nights to the West*, HarperCollins, 1991.

Rich, Adrienne. *Of Woman Born*. New York: W.W. Norton, 1975.

Ricketts, Mac Linscott. "The Shaman and the Trickster." *Mythical Trickster Figures: Contours, Contexts, and Criticisms*. Eds. William J. Hynes and William G. Doty. Tuscaloosa: U of Alabama P, 1993. 87-105.

Rothenberg, Rose-Emily. *The Jewel in the Wound: How The Body Expresses the Needs of the Psyche and Offers a Path to Transformation.* Wilmette, Illinois: Chiron, 2001.

Ryan, Mike. *The Secret Life: An Autobiography.* New York: Random, 1996.

The Sacred Forest of the Lost Child. Dir. I. Murphy Lewis. IML Publications, 2007.

Sami Blood. Film, Director, Amanda Kernell, 2016.

Sand, Stine. "Dealing with racism: Colonial history and colonization of the mind in the autoethnographic and Indigenous film Sami Blood." *Journal of International and Intercultural Communication,* Volume 16, 2023, Issue 3, 29 Mar 2022 https://www.tandfonline.com/doi/full/10.1080/17513057.2022.2052156

McLeod, J. "From 'commonwealth' to 'postcolonial.'" *Beginning postcolonialism* (pp. 6–36). J. McLeod (Ed.), Manchester University Press.

https://icmotrospaises.files.wordpress.com/2016/07/john_mcleod_beginning_postcolonialism_beginningbookzz-org.pdf

Schapera, I. *The Khoisan Peoples of South Africa: Bushmen and Hottentots.* London: Routledge and Kegan Paul, 1930.

Schlemmer, Phyllis V., and Palden Jenkins, compilers. *The Only Planet of Choice: Essential Briefings from Deep Space.* Bath: Gateway, 1993.

Seesequasis, Paul. *Blanket Toss Under Midnight Sun.* Knopf Canada, 2019.

Senior, Willoughby F. *Smoke Upon the Winds.* Sage Books, 1961

Shah, Riddhi. "The 'Eat, Pray, Love' Guru's Troubling Past" Salon.com, August 14, 2010. https://www.salon.com/2010/08/14/eat_pray_love_guru_sex_scandals/

Shamanism. http://en.wikipedia.org/wiki/Shaman.

Siddha Yogis Tell the Truth. https://leavingsiddhayoga.net

Works Cited and ConsulteD

Skea, Brian R. "A Jungian Perspective of the Dissociability of the Self." *Reflections on Psychology, Culture and Life: The Jung Page.* June 6, 2020 https://jungpage.org/learn/articles/analytical-psychology/802-a-jungian-perspective-on-the-dissociability-of-the-self

Skinner, Alanson B. "Observations on the Ethnology of the Sauk Indians." Milwaukee: *Bulletin of the Public Museum of the City* 5 (1923): 1-57.

Sierra Club. "Sustainable Consumption." www.sierraclub.org/sustainable_consumption

Slattery, Dennis Patrick. *The Wounded Body: Remembering the Markings of Flesh.* Albany: SUNY P, 2000.

Smith, David Michael. *Counting the Dead: Estimating the Loss of Life in the Indigenous Holocaust, 1492-Present.* 12th Native American Symposium, 2017. Southeastern Oklahoma State University, 2018.

Snyder, Gary. *The Practice of the Wild: Essays.* Washington, DC: Shoemaker & Hoard, 1990.

Solomon, Zahara, M Kotler, and M Mikulincer. "Combat-related posttraumatic stress disorder among second-generation Holocaust survivors: Preliminary findings." *American Journal of Psychiatry* 145 (1988): 865-68.

Somé, Malidoma Patrice. *The Healing Wisdom of Africa: Finding Life Purpose Through Nature, Ritual, and Community.* New York: Putnam, 1997.

_____. "Indigenous Technology: Cultivating Ritual in Our Everyday Lives," Santa Barbara Filmworks Event, Winter 2006.

_____. *Of Water and The Spirit: Ritual, Magic and Initiation.* New York: Arkana/Penguin, 1994.

_____. *Ritual: Power, Healing, and Community.* New York: Arkana/Penguin, 1997.

Spretnak, Charlene. Lost Goddesses of Early Greece: A Collection of Pre-Hellenic Myths. Boston: Beacon, 1984.

Stannard, David E. American Holocaust: The Conquest of the New World. New York: Oxford University P, 1992.

Swami Tejomayananda. https://www.facebook.com/watch/?v=628633238413925

Szabo. Marta. The Guru Looked Good: an Impious Memoir. Tinker Street Press, 2009.

Testament to the Bushmen. Film by Paul Bellinger, Jane Taylor and Laurens van der Post. South Africa, 1987.

Thomas, Elizabeth Marshall. The Harmless People: The Gikwe Bushmen. New York: Vintage Books, 1958.

Tolkien, J.R.R. The Lord of the Rings: Fellowship of the Ring. Houghton Mifflin, 1963.

Trollop, Anthony. Can You Forgive Her? Penquin, 1974.

Trungpa, Chogyam. The Tibetan Book of the Dead: The Great Liberation Through Hearing In The Bardo with Translation and Commentary by Francesca Fremantle. Shambhala, 2000.

Trzebinski, Errol. Silence will Speak: A Study of the Life of Denys Finch Hatton and His Relationship with Karen Blixen. U of Chicago P, 1977.

Tutu, Desmond. The Rainbow People of God: The Making of a Peaceful Revolution. The Crown Publishing Group, 1996.

Twain, Mark. Adventures of Huckleberry Finn. Bloomsbury UK, 2016.

Up in the Air. Film by Walter Kim. George Clooney and Vera Farmiga. 2009.

Works Cited and ConsulteD

Valéry, Paul. "The Graveyard by the Sea." Translation by C. Day Lewis. https://allpoetry.com/The-Graveyard-By-The-Sea

Valiente-Noailles, Carlos. *The Kua: Life and Soul of the Central Kalahari Bushmen.* Rotterdam, Netherlands: A. A. Balkema, 1993.

van der Post, Laurens. *The Dark Eye in Africa.* Hogarth Press 1992.

_____. *A Far off Place.* Penguin, 1993.

_____. *The Heart of the Hunter.* Hartmondsworth, Middlesex, England: Hogarth, 1961.

_____. *In a Province.* Penquin, 1984.

_____. *Jung and the Story of Our Time.* Knoff Doubleday, 1976.

_____. *The Lost World of the Kalahari.* Photographs by David Coulson. William Morrow & Co, 1988.

_____. *A Mantis Carol.* Washington, DC, and Covelo, California: Island, 1983.

_____. *The Night of the New Moon.* Chatto & Windus, 1985.

_____. *Patterns of Renewal.* Wallingford, Pennsylvania: Pendle Hill, 1962.

_____. *A Story Like the Wind.* The Hogarth Press, 1972.

_____. *Yet Being Someone Other.* Penquin, 1984.

_____, and Jean-Marc Pottiez. *A Walk With a White Bushman: Laurens van der Post in Conversation With Jean-Marc Pottiez.* New York: William and Morrow, 1987.

van Gennep, Arnold. *The Rites of Passage.* Chicago: Chicago UP, 1966.

Vaughan-Lee, Llewellyn. *Sufism: The Transformation of the Heart.* Inverness: The Golden Sufi Center, 1995.

Villoldo, Alberto. *Mending the Past and Healing the Future with Soul Retrieval.* Carlsbad: Hay House, 2005.

_____. *Prayer for Opening Sacred Space.* The Four Winds Society. https://thefourwinds.com/prayer-for-opening-sacred-space/

_____. *Shaman, Healer, Sage: How to Heal Yourself and Others with the Energy Medicine of the Americas.* New York: Harmony, 2000.

Vincenty, Samantha. "Being 'Color Blind' Doesn't Make You Not Racist," *OprahDaily,* June 12, 2020. https://www.oprahdaily.com/life/relationships-love/a32824297/color-blind-myth-racism/

Vogler, Christopher. *The Writer's Journey: Mythic Structure for Writers.* Studio City, California: Michael Wiese, 1998.

von Franz, Marie-Louise. *Alchemy: An Introduction to the Symbolism and the Psychology.* Boston: Shambhala, 1990.

_____. *Individuation in Fairy Tales.* Boston: Shambhala, 1990.

_____. *On Dreams and Death: A Jungian Interpretation.* Chicago: Open Court, 1998.

_____. *Projection and Re-Collection in Jungian Psychology: Reflections of the Soul.* LaSalle: Open Court 1980.

_____. *Shadow and Evil in Fairy Tales.* Boston: Shambhala, 1995.

Vusamazulu Credo Mutwa: Zulu High Sanusi. *Profiles of Healing,* Edited by Bradford Keeney. Ringing Rocks Press, 2001.

Walley, Gay. *the erotic fire of the unattainable: aphrorisms on love, art and the vicissitudes of life.* IML Publications, New York, 2007

Wallis, Robert J. *Shamans/Neo-Shamans: Contested Ecstasies, Alternative Archaeologies, and Contemporary Pagans.* Oxford: Routledge, 2003.

Weinberg, Paul. *Once We Were Hunters: A Journey with Africa's Indigenous People.* Cape Town, South Africa: David Philip, 2000.

Weishaus, Joel. *The Soul of Shamanism: A Conversation with Daniel C. Noel.* 1999. 13 Feb. 2007. http://www.cddc.vt.edu/host/weishaus/intv/noel.html

Weyeneth, Robert R. "In the Power of Apology and the Process of Historical Reconciliation." Scholar Commons, Department of History, Univ. of S. Carolina, Summer 2001. https://scholarcommons.sc.edu/cgi/viewcontent.cgi?article=1199&context=hist_facpub

Wheeler, Sara. *Too Close to the Sun: The Audacious Life and Times of Denys Finch Hatton, The Adventure Immortalized in Out of Africa.* Random House, 2006.

Why Ostriches Don't Fly. Dir. I. Murphy Lewis. IML Publications, 2003.

Wildcat, Daniel R. *Money and injustice against the first Americans* Indianz.com, June 11, 2014 https://indianz.com/News/2014/014000.asp?print=1

_____. "Why Native Americans don't want reparations."*Washington Post*, June 10, 2014. https://www.washingtonpost.com/posteverything/wp/2014/06/10/why-native-americans-dont-want-reparations/

Wilhelm, Richard. *The IChing or Book of Changes.* Translation Cary F. Baynes. Foreword C.G. Jung. New York: Pantheon Books, 1952.

Wilkerson, Isabel. *Caste: The Origins of Our Discontents.* Random House, 2020.

Williams Crenshaw, Kimberlé, Luke Charles Harris, Daniel Martinez HoSang, and George Lipsitz. *Seeing Race Again: Countering Colorblindness Across the Disciplines.* Univ. California Press, 2019.

Williams, Vera B. *"More More More," Said the Baby.* Greenwillow Books, 1990.

Wilcox, A. R., *The Rock Art of South Africa.* Foreword Professor J. Desmond Clark. Johannesburg, South Africa: Thomas Nelson and Sons, 1963.

Winnicott, D. W. *The Child, the Family, and the Outside World.* New York: Addison-Wesley, 1987.

_____. "The use of an object." *International Journal of Psychoanalysis* 50 (1969): 700, 716.

Witherspoon, Gary. "Language and Art in the Navajo Universe." *Creating the World Through Language.* Ann Arbor: U of Michigan, 1977. 13-46.

Woolf, Virginia. *A Room of One's Own.* Foreword by Mary Gordon. San Diego: Harcourt Brace, 1981.

_____. *A Sketch of the Past.* London: Hogarth P, 1939

Words Bubble Up Like Soda Pop. Film by Kyohei Ishiguro, Sublimation, 2021.

Zakaria, Rafia. *Against White Feminism: Notes on Disruption.* W.W. Norton, 2021.

Zolbrod, Paul G. *Diné bahané: The Navajo Creation Story.* U of New Mexico P, 1984.

Zoya, Luigi. *Drugs, Addiction and Initiation: The Modern Search for Ritual*

Boston: Sigo Press, 1989.

GLOBALVOICE
foundation

Global Voice's logo is inspired from the ancient drawings of the Kalahari San Bushmen scattered across Southern Africa upon the rocks, walls and caves. And from their wise prophecy: "When the Little People of the Kalahari dance, then shall the Little People around the world dance, too." 10 percent of Khaak's sales will benefit other authors, igniting this dance throughout the globe.
www.globalvoicefoundation.com

IML
PUBLICATIONS

Since IML's humble erratic beginnings, the graphic symbol of the Mantis mascot has reverently danced across our newsletters, our logo, the watermarks of the website, the original interiors of our books, and now throughout this book. The hunter, the trickster god, the praying mantis is known to shoot arrows of truths through the magical stories of the Kalahari Bush-men-and-women. For as long as they can remember, Mantis has been auspiciously inspiring the mythological myths of these First People, the hunter-gatherers who nomadically walk the earth whenever they can, as our nomad authors write their way through life on the borders of civilization.